GATEWAYS

to Algebra and Geometry

AN INTEGRATED APPROACH

GATEWAYS

to Algebra and Geometry

AN INTEGRATED APPROACH

John Benson
Evanston Township High School
Evanston, Illinois

Sara Dodge
Evanston Township High School
Evanston, Illinois

Walter Dodge
New Trier High School
Winnetka, Illinois

Charles Hamberg
Illinois Mathematics and Science Academy
Aurora, Illinois

George Milauskas
Illinois Mathematics and Science Academy
Aurora, Illinois

Richard Rukin
Evanston Township High School
Evanston, Illinois

ML *McDougal, Littell & Company*
Evanston, Illinois
New York   Dallas   Columbia, SC

WARNING: No part of this book may be reproduced or transmitted in any form or by any means, electronic or mechanical, including photocopying, recording, or by any information storage and retrieval system without permission in writing from the Publisher.

ISBN 0–8123–7645–5

2 3 4 5 6 7 8 9 10 – RM – 98 97 96 95

A Special Thank You

A special thank you to the teachers, students, and administrators who helped review and field test **Gateways to Algebra and Geometry**. Their suggestions, comments, and criticisms were invaluable.

Reviewers and Field Test Teachers

Patricia K. Amoroso
Madison High School
Vienna, VA

Dr. Joel L. Arougheti
High School of Art and Design
New York, NY

Larry E. Deis
El Molino High School
Forestville, CA

Dr. Shirley Frye
Numerics, Inc.
Scottsdale, AZ

Madelaine S. Gallin
New York City Board of Education
New York, NY

Elizabeth B. Gilmore
North View Junior High
Brooklyn Park, MN

Dr. Zelda Gold
Los Angeles Unified School
    District
Woodland Hills, CA

Fern Hartman
Wilmette Junior High School
Wilmette, IL

Peg Keller
Roehm Middle School
Berea, OH

Sandy Mackay
Southern Regional Middle School
Manahawkin, NJ

Dr. Stephen E. Moresh
Seward Park High School
New York, NY

Sally J. Nelson
Garrett Junior High School
Boulder City, NV

Dr. Gail Lowe Parrino
Conejo Valley Unified School
    District
Thousand Oaks, CA

Sabina Raab
South Lakes High School
Reston, VA

Glenda Sadler
Columbine High School
Littleton, CO

Guy Sanders
Prospect High School
Saratoga, CA

Sandra M. Schoff
Anchorage School District
Anchorage, AK

Barb Simak
McClure Junior High School
Western Springs, IL

Maureen Sowinski
Roehm Middle School
Berea, OH

Richard L. Stroud
Central Kitsap Junior High
Silverdale, WA

Fred Symonds
Sehome High School
Bellingham, WA

Edward E. Wachtel
Orange High School
Pepper Pike, OH

Mary Wagner
Girard College
Philadelphia, PA

Mary Williams
Elk Grove High School
Elk Grove Village, IL

Multicultural Advisory Committee

Carlos Cumpian
Movimento Artistico Chicano
Chicago, IL

Sandra Mehojah (Kaw/Cherokee)
Office of Indian Education
Omaha Public Schools
Omaha, NE

Alice Kawazoe
Oakland Unified School District
Oakland, CA

Alexs D. Pate
University of Minnesota
Minneapolis, MN

CONTENTS

Investigations

CHAPTER 3:   Measurement and Estimation   92

Investigations

CHAPTER 4: Ratio and Proportion 148

Investigations

Investigations

CHAPTER 7: Exploring Geometry   316

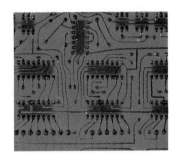

Investigations

CHAPTER 8: The Language of Algebra   368

CHAPTER 9:   Real Numbers   426

Investigations

CHAPTER 10:   Topics of Number Theory   484

Investigations

CHAPTER 11:   Solving Problems with Algebra   542

Investigations

Letter to the Student

Welcome to *Gateways to Algebra and Geometry: An Integrated Approach*. This book is called *Gateways* because it is an entrance into the world of algebra and geometry. We will build on what you know and will help you learn enough mathematics so you will be well prepared to study algebra and geometry.

Expect to learn something new each day. Some days you may feel confused, but that is OK. Sometimes it is necessary to work on an idea over a period of several days before you understand it. Then it is necessary to keep using the idea to become comfortable with it. All of this takes time. The text and problems are written in a way that requires you to work with important ideas over a period of many weeks.

We have written *Gateways* for you. We expect you to be able to read it and learn from it. You can also use it as a reference and as a source for problems.

Let us explain how the book is organized.

- **Text:** In most sections, new material will be introduced by using a few problems and an explanation that relates to these problems. Often there will be pictures and examples as well. Sample problems will appear before the problem sets. You might find it helpful to model your solutions after the examples and sample problems.

- **Problem Sets:** The Problem Sets are divided into four parts.
  1. The **Think and Discuss** problems will often be done orally in class with your teacher. These questions should help clarify the text you will have just read, and they may raise interesting questions.

2. The **Problems and Applications** will give you a chance to use the new mathematical material in a variety of situations. These problems will provide practice and will help you connect the new ideas to previously learned material. These problems will also help you to connect mathematical ideas with other subjects, such as business, science and geography.

3. The **Spiral Learning** problems will provide additional practice with material from previous sections, and will also prepare you for what you will learn later.

4. The **Investigation** at the end of each section will provide you with open-ended questions to explore and discuss with others. (Your teacher may also choose to work with you on some of the long-term unit investigations available in a softcover book entitled *Gateways to Mathematical Investigations.*)

In addition to learning specific facts and techniques, you will learn to *think mathematically.* You will learn how to approach a problem that you don't know how to do, and you will learn to think critically about problems you have solved.

You will continually be asking yourself questions like these: Should I use my calculator? Is there another way to look at this problem? Should I estimate? Is my answer reasonable? Is there a pattern here? Is there more than one correct answer? Do I need more information? And so on.

You will encounter many interesting and challenging problems in this book.

ENJOY!

John Benson   Charles L Hamberg

Sara H. Dodge   George Milauskas

Walter Dodge   Richard Rukin

Patterns

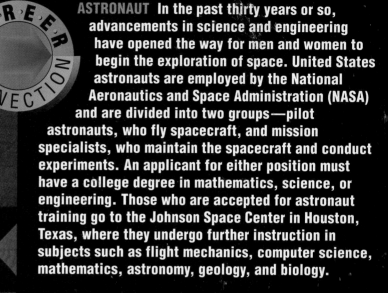

ASTRONAUT In the past thirty years or so, advancements in science and engineering have opened the way for men and women to begin the exploration of space. United States astronauts are employed by the National Aeronautics and Space Administration (NASA) and are divided into two groups—pilot astronauts, who fly spacecraft, and mission specialists, who maintain the spacecraft and conduct experiments. An applicant for either position must have a college degree in mathematics, science, or engineering. Those who are accepted for astronaut training go to the Johnson Space Center in Houston, Texas, where they undergo further instruction in subjects such as flight mechanics, computer science, mathematics, astronomy, geology, and biology.

INVESTIGATION

Escape Velocity When you throw a ball upward the height it reaches depends on how hard you throw it. If the ball leaves your hand at a speed of 20 feet per second, it will go up only about $6\frac{1}{4}$ feet before it begins to come down. If it is thrown at a speed of 40 feet per second, however, it will reach a height of 25 feet.

At what speed would a ball have to travel to escape the pull of the earth's gravity entirely? Scientists call this speed the earth's *escape velocity*, and this is the speed at which spacecraft must travel to reach outer space. Find out what the earth's escape velocity is, and compare this speed with the speeds of sound and light.

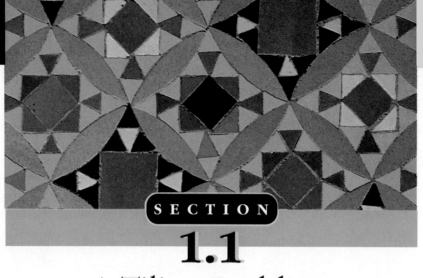

A Tiling Problem

If the following pattern is continued, how many tiles will be in the tenth figure?

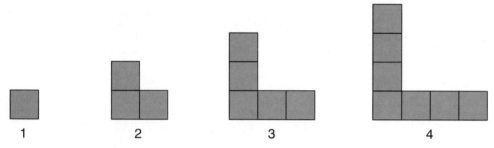

1   2   3   4

This problem can be solved in several ways.

Method 1: We can draw the next six figures, then count the tiles in the last one.

Method 2: We can list the number of tiles in each figure in a table, then look for a pattern.

Figure	1	2	3	4
Number of tiles	1	3	5	7

2   2   2

We see that the number of tiles increases by two each time. Let's continue this pattern.

Figure	5	6	7	8	9	10
Number of tiles	9	11	13	15	17	19

2   2   2   2   2   2

Method 3: We can analyze what happens. Two tiles are added to make each new figure—one tile to the top and another to the right side. To make the tenth figure, two tiles must be added six times to the seven tiles of the fourth figure. So there will be 7 + (2 × 6) = 7 + 12, or 19, tiles in the tenth figure.

Method 4: We can rearrange the tiles to make it easier to see the pattern.

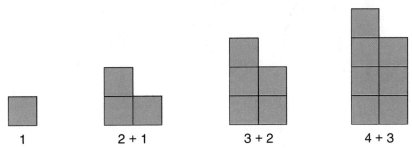

| 1 | 2 + 1 | 3 + 2 | 4 + 3 |

Therefore, there will be 10 + 9, or 19, tiles in the tenth figure.

Method 5: We can add tiles to make complete squares.

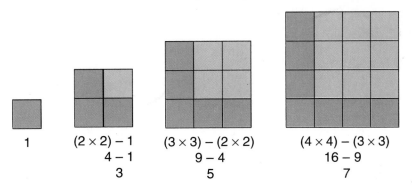

1	(2 × 2) − 1	(3 × 3) − (2 × 2)	(4 × 4) − (3 × 3)
	4 − 1	9 − 4	16 − 9
	3	5	7

Therefore, the tenth square will contain (10 × 10) − (9 × 9) = 100 − 81, or 19, red tiles.

Can you think of other ways to solve this problem? You may want to try some of your ideas on the problems that follow.

Think and Discuss

1 How many tiles will be in the eighth figure of this pattern? How do you know?

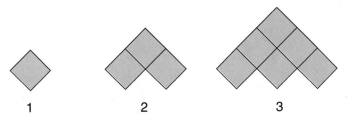

| 1 | 2 | 3 |

2 Add parentheses and symbols (+, −, ×, ÷) to make a true statement from 7 5 3 = 36.

3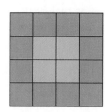

   a Draw the next three figures of the pattern shown.
   b Describe a rule that can be used to find the number of red tiles in each figure.
   c Describe a rule that can be used to find the number of blue tiles in each figure.

4 Use the pattern

$$1 = \frac{1 \times 2}{2} = 1$$

$$1 + 2 = \frac{2 \times 3}{2} = 3$$

$$1 + 2 + 3 = \frac{3 \times 4}{2} = 6$$

$$1 + 2 + 3 + 4 = \frac{4 \times 5}{2} = 10$$

to find the value of $1 + 2 + 3 + \ldots + 77 + 78 + 79 + 80$.

5 Find the sum of the numbers on the tiles in the tenth figure of this pattern.

  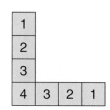 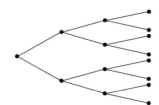

Problems and Applications

---

6 Draw the next "tree" in this pattern.

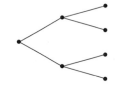

7 **Communicating** Add each pair of fractions. Describe any pattern you see.

   a $\frac{1}{2} + \frac{1}{4}$ **b** $\frac{3}{4} + \frac{1}{8}$ **c** $\frac{7}{8} + \frac{1}{16}$ **d** $\frac{15}{16} + \frac{1}{32}$ **e** $\frac{31}{32} + \frac{1}{64}$

8 Explain how to make the next figure of this pattern.

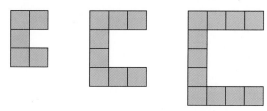

9 How many tiles will be in the sixth figure of this pattern?

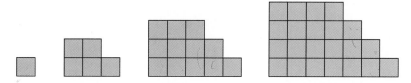

10 **Spreadsheets** In the table, 2 is in box A1, 3 is in box B2, and 7 is in box B4.
  a Copy and complete the table.
  b Find the value of
    A1 + B2 + C3 + B4 + A5 + B6 + C7, where A1 means the number in box A1, B2 means the number in box B2, and so forth.

	A	B	C
1	2	1	2
2	4	3	12
3	6	5	30
4	8	7	
5			
6			
7			

11

a Draw the next four figures of the pattern shown.
b Copy and complete the table.

Number of red tiles	3	3	9	9				
Number of blue tiles	2	8	8	14				

12 Describe the pattern shown. How many tiles will be in the eighth figure of this pattern?

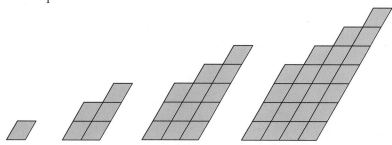

13 a Make a strip of paper a foot long and an inch wide. Experiment with folding it in half repeatedly. Then copy and complete the chart.

b When you unfold the strip, some of the folds are "valleys" and some are "peaks." Describe the pattern of valleys and peaks.

Folds in Half	Numbers of Layers	Approximate Length of Each Layer
0	1	12″
1	2	6″
2	___	___
3	___	___
4	___	___

14 Copy the figure shown, then draw the next triangle in the pattern.

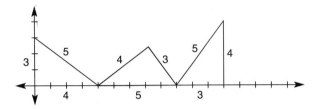

15 Spreadsheets This table contains seven boxes, A1 through A7. The value in each box depends on the computations performed on INPUT.

a Find the value in each box if INPUT is 12.

b Find the value in each box if INPUT is 0.

	A	
1	←	INPUT
2	←	INPUT + 2
3	←	3 × INPUT
4	←	INPUT ÷ 6
5	←	INPUT × INPUT
6	←	12 + 3 × INPUT
7	←	INPUT + INPUT × 5

16 David bought 12 first-class postage stamps and 15 postcard stamps. Explain how he would determine the cost of the stamps.

17 Which of these figures do you think are right angles? Check by using the corner of a sheet of paper.

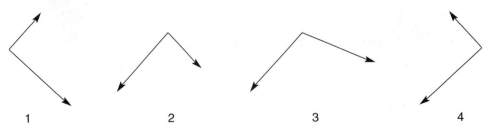

1   2   3   4

18 The numbers 1, 2, 3, 4, 5, 6, 7, 8, and 9 are on nine tiles. If a tile is selected at random, what are the chances that the tile has an even number on it?

19 Malik and Marinda sold 27 baskets of fruit to make money for the math club. Each basket was sold for $8.25.

    a How much money did they take in?

    b How much profit did they earn for the club if each basket cost $5.50 to make?

20 **Communicating**   Describe the following pattern. (The three dots mean "and so forth.")

$$Z, X, V, T, R, P, \ \ldots$$

Investigation

Tessellation Look up the meaning of the word *tessellation*. What is a tessellation? Draw an example of a tessellation, and report on some ways in which tessellations are used in everyday life.

Rice servings wrapped in banana leaves cook on a grill in Thailand—a perfect solution to biodegradable packaging.

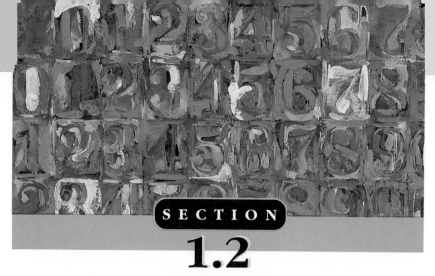

1.2
Number and Letter Patterns

Pat Tern claimed that he was an ace at recognizing patterns. One day, his friend Betty Kann challenged Pat to find the next three numbers in the pattern 2, 3, 5, and to explain the pattern.

   After thinking for a while, Pat came up with five different possibilities. (You may want to try to find several possibilities before you look at Pat's.) Here is how he explained his thinking:

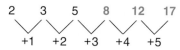

The differences between consecutive numbers increase by 1.

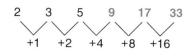

The differences between consecutive numbers double.

2   3   5   7   11   13

The numbers are consecutive prime numbers.

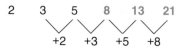

Each number, after the first two, is the sum of the two preceding numbers.

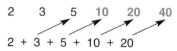

Each number, after the first two, is the sum of all the preceding numbers.

   Then Betty challenged Pat to find the next three letters in the pattern T, F, S. Here is what Pat came up with.

T F S E T T

The initial letters of *two, four, six, eight, ten, twelve*

T F S S M T

The initial letters of *Thursday, Friday, Saturday, Sunday, Monday, Tuesday*

T F S T F S

Letters repeating in blocks of three

   In these cases, all of Pat's responses were valid, because each was based on a logical explanation. Can you find other valid ways of continuing the patterns?

Patterns play an important role in mathematics. As you continue your studies, keep an eye out for patterns. See if you can come up with logical explanations for the patterns and use the explanations to make predictions about how the patterns might continue.

Think and Discuss

In problems 1 and 2, find the next four items in each pattern.

1 0, 1, 3, 6, 10, 15

2 T, F, S, N, E, T

3 Study the figures, then copy and complete the table.

Number of rays	1	2	3	4	5
Number of angles	0	1	3		

4 If I have 12 elephants, 15 zebras, 18 spiders, 23 camels, 4 dogs, and a centipede, what fraction of these animals have exactly 4 legs?

5 Study the pattern shown. What numbers do you think go in the blanks?

$3 - 0 = 3$
$3 - 1 = 2$
$3 - 2 = 1$
$3 - 3 = 0$
$3 - 4 = \underline{}$
$3 - 5 = \underline{}$

In problems 6–8, find the next three items in each pattern.

6 $\frac{2}{5}, \frac{4}{10}, \frac{6}{15}, \frac{8}{20}$

7 JK, LJ, RN, GF

8 I, III, V, VII

Problems and Applications

Communicating In problems 9–11, draw the next figure in each pattern.
Then describe the pattern.

9

10

11
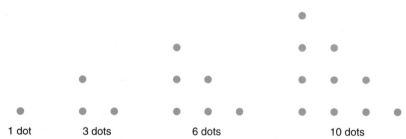

In problems 12 and 13, find the next four items in each pattern.

12 16, 14, 12, 10, 8, 6

13 2, 3, 5, 9, 17, 33

14 How many dots will be in the fifth figure of this pattern? The sixth
figure? The seventh figure? The eighth figure?

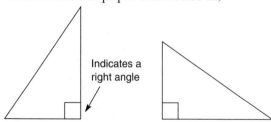

1 dot   3 dots   6 dots   10 dots

15 Draw the next two figures in the pattern. (Hint: Cut a right triangle
from a sheet of paper and rotate it.)

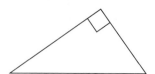

Indicates a
right angle

16 Line segments are named by their endpoints. This diagram, for example, shows three segments—$\overline{XY}$, $\overline{YZ}$, and $\overline{XZ}$.

How many segments are in each of the following diagrams?

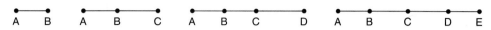

In problems 17–19, subtract the sum of each pair of numbers from their product.

17 $(5, 8)$ **18** $(9, 10)$ **19** $(1.5, 8)$

20 Spreadsheets Copy the chart. Use the formulas shown to fill in the rest of column B.

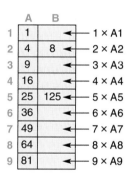

21 Draw the next three figures in the pattern.

 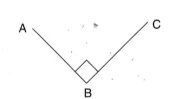

22 Find the next number in the pattern.

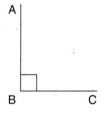 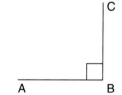

2   6   14

23 a Describe a pattern that can be used to find the number of right angles in the diagram.
b Use this pattern to find the number of right angles.

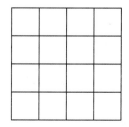

24 Study the pattern, then copy and complete the table.

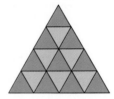

Number of green tiles	1	3	6	10			
Number of blue tiles	0	1	3	6			

25 **Spreadsheets**
  a Find the values that go in boxes B1, B2, B3, B4, B5, B6, and B7.
  b Calculate the value
  $(B1 + B3 + B5 + B7) \times (B2 + B4 + B6)$.

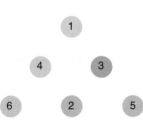

	A	B	
1	3	◄	5 × A1
2	6	◄	10 × A2
3	9	◄	15 × A3
4	12	◄	20 × A4
5	15	◄	25 × A5
6	18	◄	30 × A6
7	21	◄	35 × A7

26 Six numbered bottle caps are arranged in a triangle. The sum of the three corner numbers, 1 + 6 + 5, is three more than the sum of the remaining numbers. How can you rearrange the bottle caps so that the sum of the corner numbers is

  a One more than the sum of the remaining numbers?
  b Five more than the sum of the remaining numbers?
  c Six more than the sum of the remaining numbers?

27 Figure out the pattern used to generate the numbers in the chart. Then copy the chart and fill in the empty boxes.

1	2	3	4	5	6
3	5	8	12		
5	10	18			
7	17				
9	26				
11					
13					
15					

28 a Add 13.5 to 17.4. Multiply the sum by 7.6. What is the result?
b Add 13.5 to the product of 17.4 and 7.6. What is the result?
c Subtract your answer to part **b** from your answer to part **a**, and divide the difference by 13.5. What is the result?

29 The Samuel Davis Junior High School soccer team won three, lost two, and tied two games during the 1991 season.
a What fraction of the games did the team win?
b What fraction of the games did the team win or tie?

30 Consumer Math   A plumber's charge of $90 for a service call includes the cost of the first hour of work. For each additional hour or part of an hour, the charge is $45. What is the total charge for two service calls, one lasting 3 hours 15 minutes and the other lasting $4\frac{1}{2}$ hours?

31 Make five copies of this diagram and try to arrange the five pieces into a five-by-five square. If you succeed, draw a picture of the arrangement. If the pieces cannot form a square, explain why not.

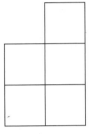

32 When planning a field trip to the Museum of Lapidary Art, Mr. Boynton decided that he needed to take at least 1 adult for every 10 children. If 74 children signed up for the trip, how many adults did Mr. Boynton need?

33 Sports   Samantha ended the baseball season with 6 home runs, 4 triples, 11 doubles, and 35 singles.
a How many hits did she have?
b How many total bases did she have?

Investigation

Patterns on a Telephone Examine the dial or buttons on a telephone to see how letters of the alphabet are matched with numbers. Which numbers have no corresponding letters? Which letters of the alphabet do not appear on the telephone? Find out why some letters are missing and why some numbers are not assigned letters.

1.3
Practical Patterns

A FAMILY TREE

In the preceding section, one of Pat Tern's patterns was 2, 3, 5, 8, 13, 21. Let's take a look at a connection this pattern has with the real world. We will use the symbol ♂ to represent a male bee and the symbol ♀ to represent a female bee. A male bee develops from an unfertilized egg, but a female bee develops from a fertilized egg. Therefore, a male bee has only a mother, whereas a female bee has both a mother and a father.

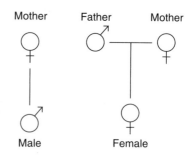

Example 1
Here are parts of the family trees of Mr. and Mrs. Bee.

How many great-grandparents do the Bees have?

Solution

Let's continue the family trees.

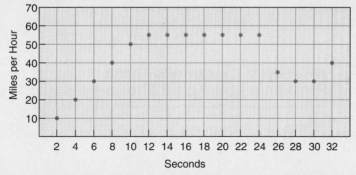

Great-grandparents

Grandparents

Parents

Mr. and Mrs. Bee

Mr. Bee has three great-grandparents, and Mrs. Bee has five. They have a total of eight great-grandparents.

OTHER APPLIED PATTERNS

Sometimes it is difficult to make predictions from a pattern unless you know what real-world situation it represents.

Example 2

What are the next four numbers in the pattern 10, 20, 30, 40, 50?

Solution

It is likely that you would predict the next four numbers to be 60, 70, 80, and 90, since the pattern seems to involve repeated additions of 10. But what if the numbers represented the numbers marking the yardage lines on a football field? In that case, the next four numbers would be 40, 30, 20, and 10. The numbers might also represent the speeds of a car as it accelerates from a standstill and travels along a highway, as shown in the following graph.

In this case, the next four numbers are 55, 55, 55, and 55. Can you think of any other real-world situations that the pattern 10, 20, 30, 40, 50, might represent? How might the pattern continue in these situations?

Think and Discuss

1 Refer to the family trees of Mr. and Mrs. Bee in Example 1. What is the total number of the Bees' great-great-grandparents?

2 The answers to the 20 questions on a multiple-choice test were BACCEDBABCDBADEBADDC. Pat Tern guessed at the answers, using the pattern ABCDEEDCBAABCDEEDCBA. If each answer was worth 5 points, what was Pat's score?

3 Is the statement *true* or *false?*
a $3 + 5 \times 2 = 5 + 3 \times 2$ **b** $3 + 5 \times 2 = 2 \times 5 + 3$ **c** $3 + 5 \times 2 = 5 \times 2 + 3$

4 **Science** The Celsius and Fahrenheit scales are two scales used to measure temperature. The chart shows some correspondences between the scales.

Celsius	Fahrenheit
0	32
20	68
40	104
60	140
80	176
100	212

a If the temperature is 50 degrees Celsius, about how many degrees Fahrenheit is it?

b What Fahrenheit temperature corresponds to 30 degrees Celsius? To 75 degrees Celsius?

5 A cable TV company was charging customers $48 to view an Old Goats on the Prowl concert. Rocky Rolle decided that he could watch the concert if he invited some friends over to share the cost. He sat down and made the following chart:

Number of viewers	1	2	3	4	5
Cost per viewer	$48.00	$24.00	$16.00	$12.00	$9.60

Copy the chart and continue it for six, seven, and eight viewers. If Rocky invites six friends, what will his share of the cost be?

Problems and Applications

6 How many circles will be in the twentieth figure of this pattern? Explain the pattern.

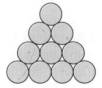

7 The chart shows amounts charged by Pam the Painter for painting rooms. What will Pam charge for painting a kitchen, a bathroom, a living room, and

Room	Cost
Kitchen	$100
Bathroom	75
Living room	200
Bedroom	125

   a One bedroom?
   b Two bedrooms?
   c Three bedrooms?

8 Spreadsheets
   a Find the values that will be in boxes A3–A6 if A1 is 2 and A2 is 3.
   b Predict the values of A7 and A8.
   c What formulas could be written in the blanks to generate these two values?

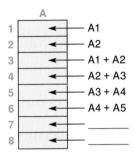

In problems 9 and 10, draw the next figure in each pattern.

9

10

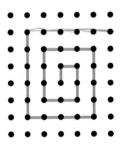

11 Nine segments of a pattern are shown. Each of the two shortest segments is one unit long. How many units long will the twentieth segment be?

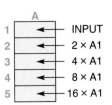

12 Spreadsheets
   a Determine the value that will be generated in each box if INPUT is 3.
   b Find A1 × A2 × A3 × A4 × A5.

In problems 13 and 14, draw the next figure in each pattern.

13

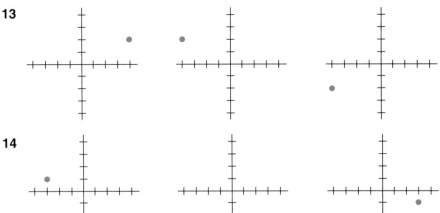

14

In problems 15–18, find the next four letters or numbers in each pattern. Then explain the pattern.

15 2, 4, 8, 16

16 a, b, b, a

17 128, 111, 96, 83

18 T, T, F, S, E

19 Communicating   Describe a situation that this graph might represent.

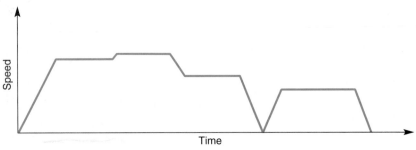

20 Consumer Math   A state has a sales tax of 5% on purchased goods. (That is, a purchaser must pay a tax of $0.05 on each dollar of the purchase.)

   a On what purchase amounts would you pay $0.01 in tax? $0.02 in tax? $0.03 in tax? $0.04 in tax? $0.05 in tax?

   b Explain how you can use the answers to part **a** to determine the tax on any purchase.

   c Use your method to compute the tax on purchases of $2.35, $38.59, and $426.87.

21

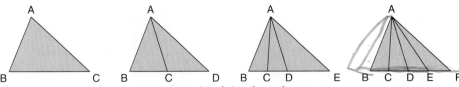

   a How many triangles are in each of the four figures?

   b How many triangles will be in the fifth figure? The sixth figure?

22 Write a paragraph explaining the pattern of the green and yellow tiles.

  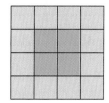 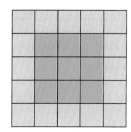

23 In a deep tunnel beneath the city of Rome, the following symbols were discovered on a wall:

(II, III) → VI   (X, III) → XXX   (VII, X) → LXX

The fourth set of symbols was incomplete: (IV, IV) → .
What might have been to the right of the arrow?

In problems 24–26, find the next three items in each pattern.

24 (1, 5), (2, 9), (3, 13), (4, 17), (5, 21)

25 (1, 1), (2, 4), (3, 9), (4, 16), (5, 25)

26 1, 2, 6, 24, 120, 720

27 The chart indicates that

6 # 4 = 12
4 # 4 = 4
3 # 8 = 24
8 # 6 = 24
7 # 3 = 21

#	3	4	6	7	8
3					24
4		4			
6		12			
7	21				
8			24		

a Copy the chart, filling in the missing numbers.
b Explain how you determined your answers.

In problems 28 and 29, copy the problem and fill in the blank.

28 ___ × 7 = 224

29 217 + ___ = 560

30 Arnold and Amy were arguing about Adrian's age. Arnold said that she was 18; Amy said that she was 19. Adrian had lived for 18 years and 11 months. Who was right? Defend your answer.

31 The diagram shows a square with its two diagonals. How many right angles appear to be in the diagram?

In problems 32–34, rewrite each fraction as an equivalent fraction with a denominator of 100.

32 $\frac{2}{5}$

33 $\frac{8}{5}$

34 $\frac{5}{5}$

35 In how many different ways can a red chip, a blue chip, and a white chip be stacked?

36 On the number line shown, what numbers are represented by points A, B, C, and D?

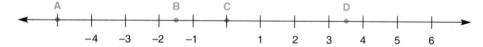

37 Consumer Math   The Dry Gulp Water Company charges a customer $5.00 for service each month, plus $1.60 for the first 1000 gallons of water used and $0.002 for each additional gallon. One month Thurston Drinker used 3460 gallons of water. How much was he charged?

38 A typical half-hour TV show has 8 commercials. If each commercial is 30 seconds long, what fraction of the show is commercials?

39 Car Maintenance   Before driving to Alaska, Biff went to a garage to have antifreeze put in his car's radiator. The mechanic said that Biff would need a mixture of $\frac{1}{3}$ water and $\frac{2}{3}$ antifreeze. The radiator held 2 gallons. How much antifreeze did Biff need?

Investigation

Technology Study the arrangement of the numbers on the buttons of a Touch-Tone telephone. Then study the arrangement of the numbers on the keys of a calculator. Find out why the arrangements are different.

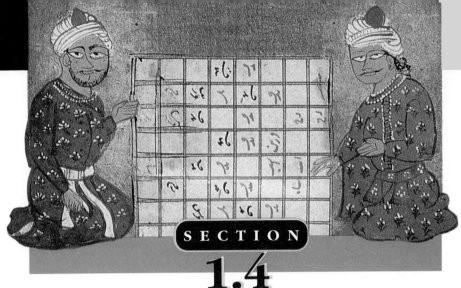

1.4
Probability

WHAT IS PROBABILITY?

Lois and Lana were playing cards when Lois suddenly said, "Oh, I just remembered! The movie *Superguy* is on TV now. Let's quit playing and watch it."

Lana was not really interested in watching the movie but replied, "I'll tell you what. I'll pick a card at random from the deck. If it's a face card, I'll watch the movie with you."

What was the probability that Lana would watch the movie?

In a regular deck of 52 cards, 12 of the cards (4 jacks, 4 queens, and 4 kings) are face cards. Thus, Lana's chances of watching the movie were 12 out of 52. The probability was $\frac{12}{52}$ or $\frac{3}{13}$.

The **probability** of an event is the fraction of possible outcomes that are favorable to that event ("winners"). In other words, it is the *ratio* of the number of winners to the number of possibilities.

$$\text{Probability} = \frac{\text{number of winners}}{\text{number of possibilities}}$$

APPLYING PROBABILITY

Example 1

If a housefly lands on one of the tiles of this floor, what is the probability that it will land on a blue one?

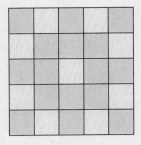

Solution

There are 25 tiles, and 16 of them are blue. The probability that the fly will land on a blue tile is therefore $\frac{16}{25}$.

Example 2

The diagram shows the games of badminton that were played at a picnic. Each arrow represents a game and points toward the loser—for example, Sue defeated Bill. "Snap" Schott wandered by during the day and took a photo of one of the games. What is the probability that the photo shows a game that Juan won?

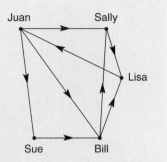

Solution

Eight games were played, and Juan won three. So the probability that the photo shows Juan winning is $\frac{3}{8}$.

Sample Problem

Problem

A bag containing five slips of paper—numbered 2, 5, 6, 8, and 9—is used for a game. A player draws two slips and wins if the sum of the two numbers is even. Is the player more likely to win or to lose?

Solution

When there aren't too many possible outcomes, we can simply list them and count the possibilities and the winners. To be sure that none are missed, however, we must list them in an orderly way.

This table shows the possible results of drawing two slips in the game described. There are 10 possibilities, and 4 of them (the ones checked) have even sums. The probability that the sum will be even is therefore $\frac{4}{10}$, or $\frac{2}{5}$. Since this probability is less than $\frac{1}{2}$, there is less chance of getting an even sum than of not getting one. The player is more likely to lose.

Numbers	Sum
2, 5	7
2, 6	8 ✓
2, 8	10 ✓
2, 9	11
5, 6	11
5, 8	13
5, 9	14 ✓
6, 8	14 ✓
6, 9	15
8, 9	17

Think and Discuss

1 When a coin is tossed, what is the probability that it will land heads up?

2 What is the probability of rolling an even number with a standard six-sided die?

3 Is the following statement true *always, sometimes,* or *never?* Explain your answer.

The probability of an event is less than or equal to 1.

4 Robin Baskin went to an ice-cream parlor and ordered a cone with one scoop of vanilla ice cream, one scoop of chocolate, and one scoop of papaya ripple. In how many ways can the three scoops be arranged on the cone?

5 What is a ratio?

6 A mosquito lands on one of the squares in the diagram shown. What is the probability that it lands on a square containing
a An even number?
b A multiple of 3?
c A multiple of 5?
d A multiple of both 3 and 5?
e A multiple of 3 or 5?

1	2	3	4
5	6	7	8
9	10	11	12
13	14	15	

7 What might the following letters represent?

A, B, B, E, D, C, A, A, C, D, E, A, B, B, E

Problems and Applications

8 a If a card is drawn at random from a standard 52-card deck, what is the probability that it will be a heart?
b If the chosen card is a heart, what is the probability that it will be a jack?

9 Copy the following statement, filling in the missing numbers.

$$\frac{4}{7} = \frac{16}{} = \frac{20}{35} = \frac{}{21} = \frac{140}{} = \frac{}{140}$$

10 The table represents the possible results of rolling two dice. The numbers at the top represent the possible results for one of the dice, and the numbers at the left represent the possible results for the other.
a Copy the table, filling in the possible sums of the numbers on the dice.
b When two dice are rolled, what is the probability that the sum will be a multiple of 2? Of 3? Of 4? Of 5? Of 6?
c What is the probability that the sum will be a multiple of 2 or 3 or 4 or 5 or 6?

+	1	2	3	4	5	6
1						
2						
3						
4						
5						
6						

11 If a card is drawn from a standard deck, what is the probability that it will be a face card or an ace?

12 Four boys (Felix, Paul, Alfredo, and Rolf) and one girl (Melissa) want to be on the school debate team. If the debate coach chooses two of them at random, what is the probability that
a Felix will be on the team?
b Melissa and Alfredo will be on the team?
c Two boys will be chosen for the team?

13 This diagram shows how some people feel about one another. For example, Sally likes John, but John does not like Sally. Richard doesn't like anyone but is liked by Sally and Chuck.
a If one of these people is chosen at random, what is the probability that he or she likes none of the others? Likes all of the others?
b If two of them are chosen at random, what is the probability that they like each other? That only one likes the other?

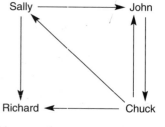

14 Four pieces of paper are used to cover four baseball cards. The cards are worth $0.10, $0.15, $0.20, and $5.00. Cal Lector is allowed to remove two of the pieces of paper and keep the cards beneath them.
a Find the probability that Cal will get the $5.00 card.
b Why might a baseball card be worth $5.00?

15 Copy the diagram, filling in the empty circles with appropriate values.

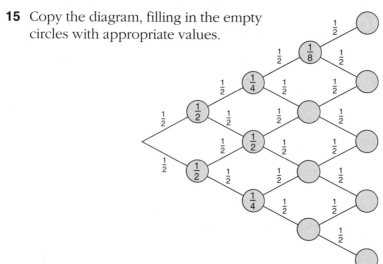

16 **Communicating**   Describe what you might do to find out what fraction of the people in your community are under the age of 21.

17 **Technology**   Many calculators use arrays like the one shown to display numbers. By lighting up different parts of the array (lettered A–G in the diagram), a calculator can display any of the ten digits. Suppose that you enter a random digit. What is the probability that
a Part E will be lit?
b Part D will be lit?
c Parts C and D will both be lit?

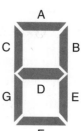

18 Gus the Guesser wrote the following answers for a true-false quiz:

F, T, T, F, T, F, T, F, F, F, T, F, T, F, F, F, T, F, T, F

Describe a process Gus might have used to make his guesses.

19 This large cube is cut into 27 smaller cubes. Suppose that you paint the outside of the large cube blue, then put all the small cubes into a bag. If you pick one of the small cubes at random, what is the probability that it will have

  a No blue sides?   **b** Exactly one blue side?
  c Exactly two blue sides?   **d** Exactly three blue sides?
  e Exactly four blue sides?

20 a Figure out the pattern used to generate the values in the table. Then copy and complete the table.
  b Find the probability that a number selected randomly from the boxes in the table will be a multiple of 3.

#	3	7	11
2	8	16	24
5	11	19	
8		22	30

◄ LOOKING BACK **Spiral Learning** LOOKING AHEAD ►

21 A hibernating bear sleeps for one fourth of a year. For how many months of the year is the bear not hibernating?

22

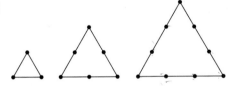

  a Find the number of line segments in each of the three figures.
  b How many segments will be in the fourth and fifth figures of the pattern?

23 Mr. Boynton is planning a school field trip. Each of the available buses holds at most 36 people, and there will be 74 students and 8 adults on the trip. How many buses should Mr. Boynton order?

24 Communicating   Describe a pattern that can be used to find the number of right angles in the diagram. Then determine the number of right angles.

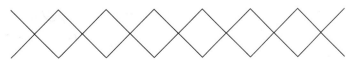

25 Arrange $\frac{1}{3}$, 0.3, and 33% in order, from least to greatest value.

26 Spreadsheets   In the table, the rule for generating the number in each box is shown.

a Copy the table, putting the number 1 in box A1 and replacing the rules with the numbers that they will generate.

b Repeat the process, this time putting the number 0 in box A1.

	A	B
1		A1 + A2
2	2 × A1	A2 + A3
3	2 × A2	A3 + A4
4	2 × A3	A4 + A5
5	2 × A4	A5 + A6
6	2 × A5	A6 + A7
7	2 × A6	A7 + A1

27 Study the way in which the following pairs of numbers generate new numbers. What are the values of INPUT and OUTPUT?

$$(3, 2) \rightarrow 6 \qquad (5, 8) \rightarrow 40 \qquad (7, 2) \rightarrow 14$$
$$(5, 7) \rightarrow \text{OUTPUT} \qquad (5, \text{INPUT}) \rightarrow 30$$

28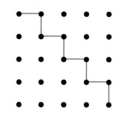

a How many dots will be connected by segments in the seventh diagram of this pattern?

b In the seventh diagram, how many more dots will be below the segments than above them?

Investigation

Leap Year   What is a leap year? How can you determine whether a given year is a leap year? If you pick one of the years 1800 to 1899 at random, what is the probability that the year was a leap year?

"You've accounted for leap year, of course?"

1.5
Tables and Spreadsheets

THE COST OF POSTAGE STAMPS

In January 1992, postage for first-class mail was $0.29 for the first ounce and $0.23 for each additional ounce or fraction of an ounce. Calculating the correct postage for every letter, however, is cumbersome. It is much easier to use a **table**, or chart. Here are the first eight columns of such a table.

Single-Piece Letter Rates								
Weight, up to but not exceeding (ounces)	1	2	3	4	5	6	7	8
Cost (dollars)	0.29	0.52	0.75	0.98	1.21	1.44	1.67	1.90

Example 1
Refer to the table of postal rates.
a Calculate the next three columns of the table.
b Neelam paid $1.67 to mail a $6\frac{1}{4}$-ounce letter. Why did she pay the 7-ounce rate rather than the 6-ounce rate?
c What would it cost to mail a $5\frac{1}{2}$-ounce letter?

Solution

a

9	10	11
2.13	2.36	2.59

b Any letter that weighs more than 6 ounces but no more than 7 ounces is charged at the 7-ounce rate.

c $1.44

So many tables are used in business, science, and mathematics that people in these fields usually find it easiest to use computer programs to create and store the tables and to manipulate the data in them. One sort of table-making program is called a **spreadsheet.** A spreadsheet was used to make the following table, which shows the meal expenses of four people on a one-day trip.

	A	B	C	D	E
1		Andy	Jenny	Diane	George
2					
3	Lunch	$4.29	$3.85	$5.59	$4.33
4	Dinner	$6.75	$6.24	$7.49	$6.85
5	Breakfast	$3.48	$3.95	$2.45	$4.76
6					
7	Total	$14.52	$14.04	$15.53	$15.94

The spreadsheet uses letters to name the columns of a table and numbers to name the rows. Each of the "boxes" in the table is known as a **cell** and is identified by its column letter and row number. In this case, column A and row 1 are used for headings, and rows 2 and 6 are used for spacing. The other cells contain the expense data—for example, cell D5 contains the amount paid by Diane for breakfast.

A spreadsheet can do calculations automatically. In making this table, for example, we "hid" the formula B3 + B4 + B5 in cell B7, so the spreadsheet calculated the sum of the numbers in cells B3, B4, and B5 and displayed the sum in cell B7. If we changed the entry in cell B3 from $4.29 to $4.39, the spreadsheet would automatically change the sum from $14.52 to $14.62. This automatic recalculation makes a spreadsheet a powerful tool for anyone who needs to make and modify tables.

Example 2
Refer to the table of meal expenses.
a What formula is probably hidden in cell C7?
b What cell contains the sum E3 + E4 + E5?

Solution
a Cell C7 contains the sum of the values in cells C3, C4, and C5, so the hidden formula is probably C3 + C4 + C5.
b Cell E7

Spreadsheets can also be used to create patterns of numbers, as the following sample problem shows.

Sample Problem

Problem

This table was created with a spreadsheet. Column A contains the whole numbers 1–9, and column B contains a number pattern. How might the spreadsheet have been used to generate the pattern?

	A	B
1	1	3
2	2	6
3	3	9
4	4	12
5	5	15
6	6	18
7	7	21
8	8	24
9	9	27

Solution

There are several possibilities. One way of generating the pattern is to multiply each term in column A by 3. Another way is to enter a 3 in cell B1 and generate each of the other numbers in column B by adding 3 to the number above.

Method 1

	A	B
B1 = 3 × A1	1	→ 3
B2 = 3 × A2	2	→ 6
B3 = 3 × A3	3	→ 9
B4 = 3 × A4	4	→ 12

Method 2

	B
B1 = 3	3 ↓
B2 = B1 + 3	6 ↓
B3 = B2 + 3	9 ↓
B4 = B3 + 3	12

In either case, the spreadsheet can copy the pattern after we define the first step. To use Method 1, for instance, we could enter the formula 3 × A1 in cell B1, then copy the formula to the other cells in column B. The program automatically adjusts the formula to 3 × A2, 3 × A3, and so forth, in the other cells.

Think and Discuss

1 This is part of a spreadsheet display.
  a Name the cells shown in yellow.
  b If column A were continued, what number might be in cell A7? In cell A8? In cell A24?
  c The formula A1 + 3 is hidden in cell A2. What formula might be hidden in cell A3? In cell A4? In cell A5?

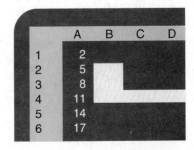

2 **Consumer Math** Mr. Goodpliers, a mechanic, charges $75.00 for towing and $49.50 for each hour he works on a car. Make a table that shows the total cost of towing plus 1 hour to 6 hours of work, in 1-hour increments.

3 a Find the area of a square with a side length of 13.
 b Find the side length of a square with an area of 49.

4 a Bill decides to hide $25.00 in his mattress each week. How much will he have put in the mattress after one month? Two months? Three months?
 b Make a table that shows how much money will be in the mattress at the end of each month for two years. Assume that every third month has five weeks.

5 In this spreadsheet display, rows 2–6 show the formulas hidden in the cells. Copy the table, replacing the formulas with the numbers they will generate.

	A	B	C	D
1	1	12	3	2
2	A1 + 1	B1 + 3	A1 + C1	D1 × 2
3	A2 + 1	B2 + 3	A2 + C2	D2 × 2
4	A3 + 1	B3 + 3	A3 + C3	D3 × 2
5	A4 + 1	B4 + 3	A4 + C4	D4 × 2
6	A5 + 1	B5 + 3	A5 + C5	D5 × 2

Problems and Applications

In problems 6 and 7, use the table of postal rates on the first page of this section.

6 What would it cost to mail a letter that weighs $3\frac{1}{2}$ ounces?

7 What would it cost to mail a letter that weighs $7\frac{3}{4}$ ounces?

In problems 8–10, find the value generated by adding the second number to three times the first number.

8 $(5, 7)$ **9** $(11, 2)$ **10** $\left(\frac{1}{2}, 5\right)$

11 At Amalgamated Acme, Inc., workers are paid $0.28 per mile when they use their own car for business travel. Make a table showing the amounts paid to workers for trips of 10 miles to 200 miles, in increments of 10 miles.

12 **Spreadsheets** A spreadsheet is used to create a table. In cell A1 is the number 4. Hidden in cell A2 is the formula A1 + 6. When this formula is copied to cell A3, it automatically changes into A2 + 6.
 a What numbers will appear in cells A2 and A3?
 b If you copy the formula in cell A3 to cell A4, what formula will be hidden in cell A4? What number will appear in cell A4?
 c What formula do you think would be hidden in cell B4 if the formula in cell A4 were copied to it? What number would appear in cell B4?

13 Perform the following calculations.

a 3×3 **b** $3 \times 3 \times 3$ **c** $3 \times 3 \times 3 \times 3$

d $3 \times 3 \times 3 \times 3 \times 3$ **e** $3 \times 3 \times 3 \times 3 \times 3 \times 3$

14 The area of square 1 is 128 square centimeters. Each of the other squares is formed by connecting the midpoints of the sides of the next larger square.

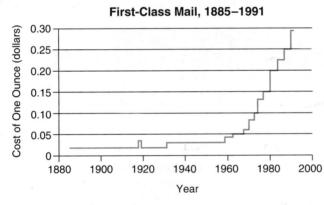

a Suppose the pattern of squares continues. Copy and complete the following table.

Square	1	2	3	4	5	6	7	8	9	10	11
Area (cm²)	128										

b What will the area of square 25 be? How do you know?

c If you knew the area of square 49, how could you find the area of square 50?

15 History This graph shows the history of U.S. postal rates.

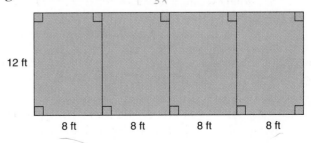

First-Class Mail, 1885–1991

a When was the increase in postal rates the most rapid?

b When did the cost of sending a letter decrease?

c What do you think it will cost to mail a letter in the year 2000? How did you determine this cost?

16 Make a table listing the side lengths, perimeters, and areas of squares with whole-number side lengths from 1 to 9.

17 Find the total length of the fencing used to enclose the four pens shown.

12 ft

8 ft   8 ft   8 ft   8 ft

18 Find the number of squares in each diagram. (Hint: There are more than four squares in the second diagram.)

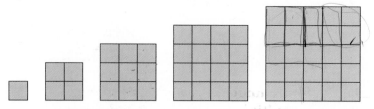

19 Spreadsheets A spreadsheet was used to create this table, which contains some of the number patterns discussed in Section 1.2. If the numbers in rows 1 and 2 were entered without hidden formulas, what hidden formulas might have been used to generate the numbers in rows 3–6?

	A	B	C	D
1	1	2	2	2
2	2	3	3	3
3	3	5	5	5
4	4	8	8	10
5	5	12	13	20
6	6	17	21	40

20

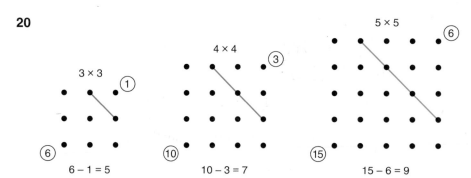

In the 10 × 10 figure of this pattern, how many more dots will there be below the line than above the line? How many dots will the line connect?

◀ LOOKING BACK **Spiral Learning** LOOKING AHEAD ▶

---

21 A beanbag thrown at Mr. Happy Face is equally likely to land in any of the squares. You win a yo-yo if it lands in an eye, a stuffed toy if it lands in the nose, an ice-cream cone if it lands in the mouth, and a radio if it lands in the blue square. Suppose that you are going to throw one beanbag.

a What is the probability that you will win a yo-yo? A stuffed toy? An ice-cream cone? A radio?

b What is the probability that you will win no prize?

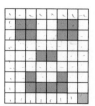

22 Perform the following calculations.

    a $3 + 5 \times 2$ **b** $5 \times 2 + 3$ **c** $3 + 2 \times 5$ **d** $2 \times 5 + 3$

23 a Find the area of the square.
   b Find the volume of the cube.

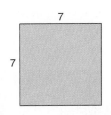
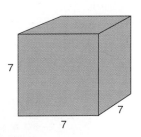

In problems 24–26, write the first number as many times as the second number indicates. Then multiply together the numbers you have written. For example, (3, 4) → 3 × 3 × 3 × 3 = 81.

24 (2, 5)   **25** (5, 2)   **26** $\left(\frac{1}{2}, 5\right)$

27 Draw the next diagram in the following pattern.

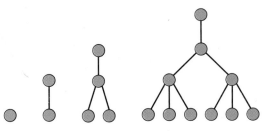

28 Wanda bought a box of Plenty Good candy. She found 7 black, 9 white, and 12 pink pieces in the box.
   a If she chooses a piece at random, what is the probability that it will be a pink piece?
   b How many more pink pieces would have to be in the box for the probability of selecting a pink piece to be $\frac{1}{2}$?

29 **Communicating**   These two-digit numbers are "cozy":

        13, 20, 24, 35, 43, 46, 53, 57, 64, 66, 76, 77, 88, 89, 97

These two-digit numbers are not cozy:

        14, 19, 27, 28, 30, 36, 39, 41, 49, 50, 59, 62, 72, 81, 90

   a Which of the following numbers do you think are cozy?

        11, 12, 29, 33, 39, 42, 45, 85, 92

   b Explain what makes a two-digit number cozy.

Investigation

Spreadsheets   Find an adult—a family member, a neighbor, a friend, a teacher—who uses a spreadsheet at work. Interview that person to find out what he or she uses the spreadsheet for. Be prepared to report your findings to your classmates.

Communicating Mathematics

DESCRIBING A RECTANGLE

In class one day, a teacher asked Stu Dent the question, "What is a rectangle?"

Stu replied, "It's got four lines, and they touch, and the lines across from each other are the same size."

The teacher then drew this figure on the board and said, "So this is a rectangle."

"No," Stu responded, "because the lines should meet at the ends."

Then the teacher drew another figure, saying, "OK, so this is a rectangle."

"No," said Stu again, "because the lines don't meet at right angles."

After thinking about these examples and sketching some others, Stu came up with the following description of a rectangle: "A rectangle is a four-sided figure made up of segments meeting at their endpoints to form exactly four right angles." Then he went to the board and drew these figures:

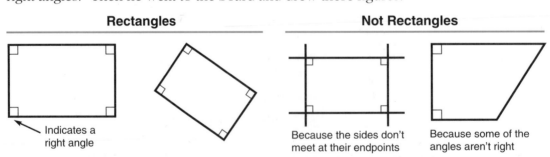

Rectangles	Not Rectangles

Indicates a right angle

Because the sides don't meet at their endpoints

Because some of the angles aren't right

Stu's final description was more complete and more specific than his original one, and he accompanied it with examples and nonexamples. Do you think that it was therefore a better description? Can you think of other good ways to explain what a rectangle is?

EXPLAINING THE ROUNDING PROCESS

You will often be asked to explain things to other people. When you give explanations, try to make them clear and complete. You will often find that explaining an idea helps you to understand it better yourself.

Example
Explain how to round a number to the nearest tenth.

Solution
We might explain the process by giving two rules and some examples:

1. If the hundredths digit is less than 5, round down.
2. If the hundredths digit is 5 or more, round up.

For example,

3.7606 is rounded up to 3.8 because the hundredths digit is 6.
2.151 is rounded up to 2.2 because the hundredths digit is 5.
3.9187 is rounded down to 3.9 because the hundredths digit is 1.

Actually, textbooks differ on what to do in a case like 9.25, where the value is exactly halfway between 9.2 and 9.3. Some say to round up, some say to round down, and some give different rules for different cases. In this book, we will generally round such numbers up.

Sample Problem

Problem

In your mathematics studies you will frequently be dealing with *equations, inequalities,* and *expressions.* Study the following examples, then explain what equations, inequalities, and expressions are.

Equations	Inequalities	Expressions
$14 - 5 = 9$	$4x + 7 \leq 11$	$3 + \dfrac{4 - 1}{6 \times 2}$
$6 + 5 = 15 - 4$	$2 \neq 3 + 1$	$x + y - 2$
$P = 2\ell + 2w$	$L_1 + L_2 > H$	$\sqrt{3} - 6 \div 3$
$A = \frac{1}{2}bh$	$3 + 5 \geq 7$	$\sqrt[3]{6 \times 36}$
$3 - 1 = 2$	$9x < 5$	$2 + 3 \times 5$

Solution

One thing you may notice is that only the equations contain equal signs. The inequalities, on the other hand, contain symbols that you may recognize as signs of inequality, such as $\leq$ ("is less than or equal to"), $\neq$ ("is not equal to"), and $>$ ("is greater than"). The expressions seem to be sets of numbers and letters joined by such operation signs as $+$, $-$, $\times$, and $\div$.

You will learn more about equations, inequalities, and expressions in later sections of this book, but these examples should make it clear that

1. An equation states that the values before and after the equal sign are equal.

2. An inequality states that the values before and after the inequality sign are either not equal or only sometimes equal.

3. An expression is made up of quantities and the operations that are to be performed on them.

Think and Discuss

1 Explain how to find the center of a rectangle.

2 Is the statement true *always, sometimes,* or *never?* How do you know?
   a The product of two positive numbers is greater than either number.
   b The product of two even numbers is an even number.
   c The sum of two odd numbers is an odd number.
   d The sum of two positive numbers is greater than either number.
   e The sum of two numbers is smaller than their product.

3 **Spreadsheets** In a certain spreadsheet display, the number 4 is in cell A1 and the formula 2 × A1 + 5 is hidden in cell A2.
   a What number will appear in cell A2?
   b If this formula is copied to cells A3, A4, and A5, what will the formulas in those cells be? What numbers will appear in those cells?

4 The fractions $\frac{15}{20}$, $\frac{3}{4}$, and $\frac{75}{100}$ are three ways of expressing the same number. Which of these forms do you think is simplest? Why?

Problems and Applications

5 Round the number 56.2281 to the nearest hundredth.

6 Write a mathematical expression representing the value of three quarters and five dimes.

7 Sung Hi's little brother added $\frac{2}{3}$ and $\frac{3}{2}$ in this way:

$$\frac{2}{3} + \frac{3}{2} = \frac{2+3}{3+2} = \frac{5}{5} = 1$$

How could Sung Hi convince his brother that 1 is not the correct answer?

8 Explain how to find the center
of a circle.

9 **Science**
   a At what temperature does water freeze?
   b At what temperature does water boil?

10 Explain why you can't divide 12 by 0.

11 **a** Find the area of the square.
    b Find the volume of the cube.

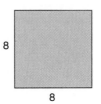

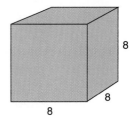

12 Explain why $\frac{3}{6}$ is equal to $\frac{1}{2}$. Write as many different explanations as you can.

13 Enter 8 $\sqrt{\ }$ on a scientific calculator. Write down the number that
appears in the display. Then clear the display and multiply this
number by itself. What do you notice?

14 Refer to the table of postal rates in Section 1.5.
   a Why, do you think, is the charge for the first ounce greater than the
charge for other ounces?
   b Construct a table for the rates of $0.35 for the first ounce and $0.25
for each additional ounce.
   c What is the cheapest way to send a 4-ounce letter and a 3-ounce
letter to the same address? Why?

15 In the following examples, what rule is applied to the pairs of
numbers to generate the results?

$$(2, 5) \rightarrow 9 \qquad (3, 5) \rightarrow 11$$
$$(4, 5) \rightarrow 13 \qquad (4, 6) \rightarrow 14$$

16 Explain how to find the area of a square.

17 Explain how to find the volume of a cube.

**In problems 18–21, describe how you could use a spreadsheet to
generate each number pattern.**

18 1, 2, 3, 4, 5, 6, 7

19 5, 7, 9, 11, 13, 15, 17

20 0.02, 0.04, 0.08, 0.16, 0.32, 0.64, 1.28

21 1, 2, 6, 24, 120, 720, 5040

22 A two-digit number is cozy if the two digits are the same or if they differ by less than 3. For example, 43, 68, and 88 are cozy numbers, but 52 and 90 are noncozy numbers.

    a Classify 46, 47, 86, and 34 as cozy or noncozy.

    b List the cozy numbers that contain at least one 5.

    c List the cozy numbers that contain a 0.

    d List the noncozy numbers that contain a 0.

    e What is the probability that a two-digit number is cozy?

    f How might you define three-digit cozy numbers?

23 **Science**   Refer to the thermometer diagram.

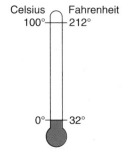

    a The *range* of a set of data is the difference between the largest number and the smallest number. The range of the Celsius scale on the thermometer is 100 – 0, or 100. What is the range of the Fahrenheit scale?

    b What fraction of the Celsius range is 1 degree?

    c Since the range of the Fahrenheit scale is greater, a degree Fahrenheit represents a smaller change in temperature than a degree Celsius. What fraction of a Celsius degree is a Fahrenheit degree?

    d How could you use your answer to part **c** to instruct a spreadsheet to list whole-number Celsius temperatures from 0 to 100 degrees along with the corresponding Fahrenheit temperatures?

24 **Spreadsheets**   Suppose you put 4 in cell A1 and 3 in cell B1 of a spreadsheet display. Then you put the formula $A$1 + B1 in cell B2.

    a The number 7 will appear in cell B2. Why? Did the dollar signs have any effect?

    b When the formula in cell B2 is copied to cell B3, the formula in B3 is $A$1 + B2. What effect do the dollar signs seem to have?

    c If the formula in cell B3 is copied to cell B4, what formula do you think will be hidden in cell B4? Why? What number will appear in cell B4?

◄ LOOKING BACK **Spiral Learning** LOOKING AHEAD ►

25 Write 5 + 5 + 5 + 5 + 5 + 5 + 5 + 5 as a multiplication problem.

26 Copy this diagram, filling in the missing numbers.

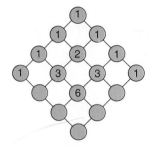

27 **a** Add 18 to 37. Multiply the sum by 24. What is the result?
   b Add 18 to the product of 37 and 24. What is the result?
   c Subtract your answer to part **b** from your answer to part **a,** then divide the difference by 18. What is the result?

28 Find the value of each expression.

   a $8 + 10 \div 2$ **b** $10 \div 2 + 8$ **c** $8 + \dfrac{10}{2}$ **d** $\dfrac{10}{2} + 8$

29 In the figure, the length of the side of square 1 is 1 cm.
   a Copy and complete the following table.

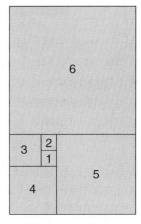

Square	1	2	3	4	5	6
Side length	1 cm					
Perimeter	4 cm					
Area	1 cm²					

   b If the pattern continues, what will the side length of the tenth square be? The perimeter? The area?

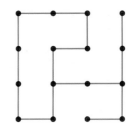

30 In a contest, Lucky Linda won a $100 gift certificate from a local department store. She decided to buy as many pairs of socks as she could. Each pair of socks cost $7. How many pairs could she buy?

31 If one of the segments connecting two dots is removed at random, what is the probability that the remaining figure will have more than one piece (be a *disconnected graph*)?

Investigation

Geometry Draw some figures that are made up of line segments. Then look up the meaning of the word *polygon*. Which of the figures you drew are polygons? If any of them are not polygons, why aren't they?

   Now find out what a convex polygon is. Draw an example of a polygon that is not convex. Is it possible to draw a nonconvex quadrilateral? A nonconvex triangle?

Summary

CONCEPTS AND PROCEDURES

After studying this chapter, you should be able to

- Recognize a pattern of geometric figures (1.1)
- Extend patterns of numbers and letters (1.2)
- Apply numerical patterns to real-world situations (1.3)
- Understand the meaning of probability (1.4)
- Calculate probabilities (1.4)
- Use mathematical tables (1.5)
- Understand how a spreadsheet can be used to create tables and patterns of numbers (1.5)
- Communicate mathematical ideas in words (1.6)

VOCABULARY

cell (1.5)
probability (1.4)
spreadsheet (1.5)
table (1.5)

Review

1 Find the value of each expression.
   a 42.5 + 3.71   **b** 42.5 × 3.71
   c 42.5 − 3.71   **d** 42.5 ÷ 3.71

2 How many tiles will be in the eighth figure of this pattern?

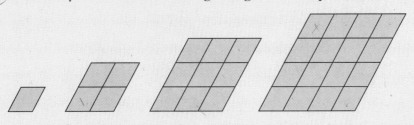

3 Jamie and Adenaky are in charge of their school's fall dance. They plan on spending $50 for rental of the school gym, $200 for custodial service, and $1500 for a disc jockey. What should they charge for each ticket if they estimate that
   a 100 people will attend the dance?   **b** 200 people will attend?
   c 300 people will attend?   **d** 400 people will attend?

4 Sales tax in the town of Ripov is 11%. Part of a tax table for the town is shown. Copy the table, filling in the missing amounts.

Amount	Tax
$0.78–$0.86	$0.09
0.87– 0.95	0.10
_____	0.11
_____	0.12
_____	0.13
_____	0.14
_____	0.15
_____	0.16
_____	0.17
_____	0.18
_____	0.19
_____	0.20

5 What is a pattern?

6 What is a spreadsheet?

7 List some reasons why it is important for you to be able to explain mathematical ideas in words.

In problems 8–11, find the value of each expression.

8 $\dfrac{8}{7} \times \dfrac{1}{2}$ 9 $\dfrac{9}{8} \times \dfrac{2}{3}$ 10 $\dfrac{10}{9} \times \dfrac{3}{4}$ 11 $\dfrac{11}{10} \times \dfrac{4}{5}$

12 Draw the next two figures of the pattern shown. Explain the pattern.

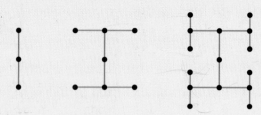

13 Is the statement *true* or *false*?

a $1\frac{3}{8} = 1 + \frac{3}{8}$ **b** $1\frac{3}{8} = 1.375$ **c** $1\frac{3}{8} = \frac{4}{8}$

d $1\frac{3}{8} = \frac{11}{8}$ **e** $1\frac{3}{8} = 0.375$ **f** $1\frac{3}{8} = 1 \times \frac{3}{8}$

14 Miss Brooks is going to randomly pick two students from a group of five—Bill, Mary, Bob, Gary, and Ellen—to be hall monitors. What is the probability that she will choose
a Two boys? **b** Two girls? **c** One boy and one girl?

15 Using a spreadsheet, Miriam entered numbers in cells A1 and B1 and hidden formulas in other cells as shown. Copy the table, replacing the formulas with the numbers that they will generate.

	A	B	C	D
1	1	1	A1 + B1	B1 + C1
2	A1 + B1	A2 + B1	A2 + B2	C1 + D1
3	A1 + A2	A3 + B2	B3 + C2	C3 + D2
4	A2 + A3	A4 + B3	B4 + C3	C4 + D3
5	A3 + A4	A5 + B4	B5 + C4	C5 + D4

16 Study the way in which these number pairs generate new numbers. Then find the values of INPUT and OUTPUT.

$(1, 2) \rightarrow 5$ $(3, 2) \rightarrow 11$ $(3, 4) \rightarrow 13$

$(5, 1) \rightarrow 16$ $(5, 2) \rightarrow 17$ $(6, 2) \rightarrow 20$

$\left(\frac{1}{3}, 1\right) \rightarrow 2$ $(6, 3) \rightarrow$ OUTPUT $($INPUT$, 5) \rightarrow 26$

17 A card is randomly drawn from a standard deck. What is the probability that the card is
a A heart? **b** A king? **c** The king of hearts? **d** A king or a heart?

18 Look at the following examples. Then explain what a quadrilateral is.

Quadrilaterals	**Not Quadrilaterals**
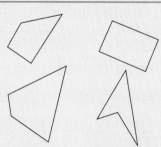	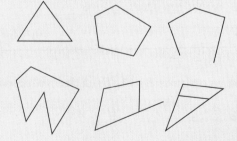

19 The Williams family used a spreadsheet to make this table. It shows what they spent to attend a baseball game between the Long Island Metrics and the Quebec Exponents.

	A	B	C	D
		Lamont	Latoya	Latisha
1		Lamont	Latoya	Latisha
2	Tickets	$10.00	$10.00	$8.00
3	Soda	$4.50	$3.00	$6.00
4	Hot dogs	$2.75	$2.75	$5.50
5	Peanuts	$2.00	$0.00	$1.00

a How much money did Lamont spend?

b How much did tickets for the three people cost?

c How much did Latoya and Latisha spend on food?

In problems 20–22, find the next three items in the pattern.

20 $\frac{1}{2}, \frac{2}{3}, \frac{3}{4}, \frac{4}{5}, \frac{5}{6},$

21 A, B, a, b, C, D, c

22

 , , ,

23 Copy and complete the chart for the rectangles shown.

Length	Width	Perimeter	Area
6	6		
9	4		
3			36
	2	40	
	1		36

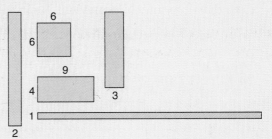

In problems 24 and 25, find as many ways as possible to continue the pattern.

24 $\frac{1}{2}, \frac{1}{3}, \frac{1}{5}, \ldots$

25 A, E, F, . . .

26 Explain the process by which each of these diagrams was generated from the preceding one.

Test

In problems 1 and 2, find the next three items in each pattern.

1 $1, 2, 3\frac{1}{2}, 5\frac{1}{2}, 8, 11, \ldots$

2 J, F, M, A, M, J, . . .

3 A box contains 3 red marbles, 4 white marbles, and 11 black marbles.
   a What fraction of the marbles are white?
   b If you pick a marble from the box without looking, what is the probability that it will be white?

4 How many squares will be in the eighth figure of this pattern? Explain the pattern.

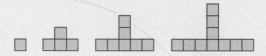

5 Zeke has $15 in his piggy bank. If he drops a quarter into the bank each day, how much money will be in the bank in two weeks?

6 How many three-digit numbers contain all three of the digits 4, 5, and 6?

7 Copy this table, replacing each formula with the appropriate value.

	A	B	C
1	4	A1 × 2	B1 × 3
2	A1 + 3	A2 × 2	B2 × 3
3	A2 + 3	A3 × 2	B3 × 3
4	A3 + 3	A4 × 2	B4 × 3

8 If you toss two coins, what is the probability that one will land heads up and the other will land tails up?

9 Explain what a square is.

10 This spreadsheet display shows the monthly salaries of three people.
   a What formula could you hide in cell B5 so that the spreadsheet would add up the salaries?
   b What formula could you hide in cell B6 so that the spreadsheet would calculate the difference between the largest salary and the smallest salary?

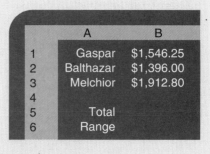

	A	B
1	Gaspar	$1,546.25
2	Balthazar	$1,396.00
3	Melchior	$1,912.80
4		
5		Total
6		Range

11 The first number in a pattern is 80, and each number in the pattern is half the preceding number. Write the first eight numbers of the pattern.

1 A jeweler charges $1 to open a link of a chain and $2 to weld it back together. What is the least that could be charged to join the pieces below into a circular chain?

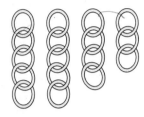

2 How many different triangles are in this figure? What method can you use to make sure that you count them all and do not count any twice?

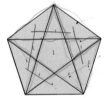

3 You have 3 bags. One contains blue marbles, one contains green marbles, and one contains both green and blue marbles. Each bag is labeled incorrectly. How could you relabel each bag correctly by looking at just one marble from one bag?

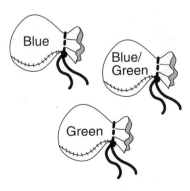

4 Twelve different shapes can be made by joining 5 squares along their sides. Three of the shapes are shown here. How many of the others can you discover? (Shapes that can be made to look the same by flipping or turning them do not count as different.)

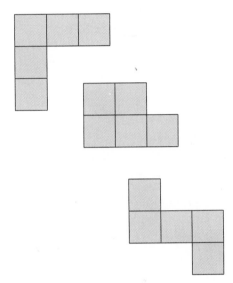

5 The figure shows five 1-by-1 squares constructed with toothpicks.

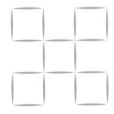

a. How can you move two toothpicks to make six 1-by-1 squares?

b. How can you move three toothpicks to make seven 1-by-1 squares?

Formulas
and
Percent

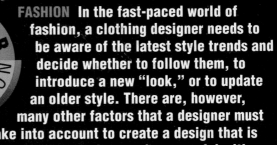

FASHION In the fast-paced world of fashion, a clothing designer needs to be aware of the latest style trends and decide whether to follow them, to introduce a new "look," or to update an older style. There are, however, many other factors that a designer must take into account to create a design that is economical to produce and successful with consumers. Among these are the amount and type of fabric required for the garment, the costs of manufacturing it, its suitability for the regions in which it will be marketed, and its intended selling price. A knowledge of mathematics helps the designer ensure that the price will be low enough to attract buyers while still providing the manufacturer with a decent profit.

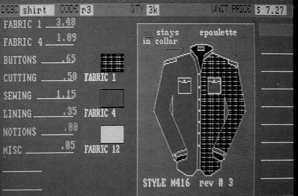

INVESTIGATION

Selling Prices How do the terms *overhead, wholesale price, retail price,* and *markup* apply to the fashion industry? When you buy an article of clothing, how much of the money that you pay reflects the cost of designing and manufacturing the clothing? How much goes for advertising costs and the manufacturer's and merchant's profits?

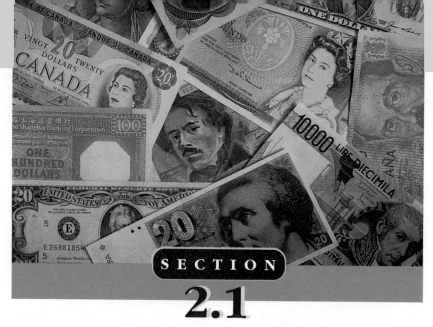

SECTION

2.1
Operations on Numbers

WHICH OPERATION COMES FIRST?

Esther and her little brother Arthur had just been paid for some odd jobs.
"How much money do we have?" asked Arthur.

"Let's see," Esther said, "we have two one-dollar bills and three five-dollar
bills. That's seventeen dollars in all." She wrote 2 + 3 × 5 = 17 on a sheet of
paper.

Arthur was puzzled. "I see that we have seventeen dollars," he said, "but
two plus three is five, and when you multiply that by five you get twenty-
five. So 2 + 3 × 5 should equal 25, not 17."

Who was right—is 2 + 3 × 5 equal to 17, or is it equal to 25?

As a rule, multiplication and division come before addition and
subtraction:

$$2 + 3 \times 5$$
$$= 2 + \ \ 15$$
$$= 17$$

Therefore, Esther was right.

One of the things you will be learning this year is how to use a scientific
calculator. To use a calculator to find 2 + 3 × 5, enter [AC] 2 [+] 3 [×] 5 [=].
(Before entering a new calculation, you should usually press the "all clear"
key as shown here. From now on, this step will not be shown in the
calculations in this book.) The display should show ⬛⬛⬛ 17.. If your
calculator gives a result different from 17, it is not a scientific calculator.

Example 1
Evaluate (find the value of) each expression.
a   30 − 12 ÷ 3   b 4 × 8 + 6 ÷ 2

---

a We divide first, then subtract.

$$30 - 12 \div 3$$
$$= 30 - \quad 4$$
$$= 26$$

b We multiply and divide, then add.

$$4 \times 8 + 6 \div 2$$
$$= \quad 32 \quad + \quad 3$$
$$= 35$$

What about cases in which we need to add or subtract *before* we multiply or divide? In such cases we can use parentheses as **grouping symbols** around the operation that is to be done first:

$$(2 + 3) \times 5$$
$$= \quad 5 \quad \times 5$$
$$= 25$$

On a calculator, you can enter $\boxed{(}\ 2\ \boxed{+}\ 3\ \boxed{)}\ \boxed{\times}\ 5\ \boxed{=}$, and the display will show 25.

Example 2

Evaluate $\dfrac{14 \div 2 - 1}{9 + 7 \times 3}$.

Solution

A fraction bar is a kind of **vinculum,** which is a grouping symbol, so we evaluate the numerator and the denominator as separate groups.

Method 1

$$\frac{14 \div 2 - 1}{9 + 7 \times 3}$$

In numerator, divide first
In denominator, multiply first

$$= \frac{7 - 1}{9 + 21}$$

Add and subtract

$$= \frac{6}{30}$$

Divide numerator and denominator
by 6 to reduce to lowest terms

$$= \frac{1}{5}$$

Method 2 To solve this problem with a calculator, we use parentheses to group the numerator and the denominator. We enter

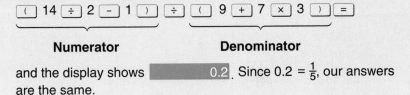

$\boxed{(}\ 14\ \boxed{\div}\ 2\ \boxed{-}\ 1\ \boxed{)}\ \boxed{\div}\ \boxed{(}\ 9\ \boxed{+}\ 7\ \boxed{\times}\ 3\ \boxed{)}\ \boxed{=}$

Numerator   **Denominator**

and the display shows 0.2 . Since $0.2 = \frac{1}{5}$, our answers are the same.

In general, then, we do mathematical operations in the following order:

1. Operations enclosed by grouping symbols (parentheses, brackets, or vinculums)
2. Multiplication and division from left to right
3. Addition and subtraction from left to right

To indicate addition and subtraction, the familiar + and − symbols are almost always used. There are, however, a number of ways of symbolizing multiplication and division.

Ways to Show Multiplication		Ways to Show Division	
Symbol	**Example**	**Symbol**	**Example**
×	3 × 5	÷	12 ÷ 4
*	3*5	/	12/4
·	3 · 5	—	$\frac{12}{4}$
No symbol	3(5) or (3)(5)		

Example 3

Tekkie entered PRINT 14/2*(12−9) on his computer. What value did the computer print?

Solution   14/2*(12−9)

First work inside the parentheses   = 14/2*3

Then divide   = 7*3

Then multiply   = 21

Sample Problems

Problem 1   One way to determine the perimeter of a rectangle is to use the formula

Perimeter = 2(length) + 2(width)

What is the perimeter of the rectangle shown?

7

12

Solution   Remember, there is usually more than one way of solving a problem correctly.

Method 1   Perimeter = 2(length) + 2(width)

                      = 2(12) + 2(7)

                      = 24 + 14

                      = 38

Method 2   The perimeter is the sum of the lengths of the sides, so it is 12 + 7 + 12 + 7, or 38.

Method 3   Halfway around the rectangle is 12 + 7, or 19. So the entire perimeter is 2(19), or 38.

Problem 2 A formula for changing a temperature from degrees Fahrenheit (°F) to degrees Celsius (°C) is

$$C = \tfrac{5}{9}(F - 32)$$

What is the Celsius equivalent of 212°F?

Solution Since we are given 212°F, we substitute 212 for F in the formula.

$$C = \tfrac{5}{9}(F - 32) = \tfrac{5}{9}(212 - 32)$$
$$= \tfrac{5}{9}(180)$$
$$= \frac{900}{9}$$
$$= 100$$

So 212°F is equivalent to 100°C. Do you know what is special about this particular temperature?

Think and Discuss

1 Why do we need rules to tell us the order in which operations should be performed?

In problems 2–5, explain the mistakes that were made in the calculations.

2 $4 + 12 \div 7 - 6 = 16 \div 1 = 16$

3 $23 - 7 + 6 = 23 - 13 = 10$

4 $\dfrac{4 + 3}{4} = 1 + 3 = 4$

5 $5 + 3(12 - 7) = 8(5) = 40$

6 Science What is the normal temperature of the human body in degrees Celsius?

7 Is the statement *true* or *false?* Explain your answer.

a $(13 + 7) \div 8 = \dfrac{13 + 7}{8}$

b $15*10/4 = (15*10)/4$

8 Philbert Chesnutt bought 6 pounds of almonds at \$2.75 per pound and 4 pounds of macadamia nuts at \$9.55 per pound.
a Write a mathematical expression for the total price of the nuts.
b Find the total price.

Problems and Applications

9 Evaluate each expression.
a $10 + 3 \cdot 5 + 4$
b $(10 + 3) \cdot 5 + 4$
c $10 + 3 \cdot (5 + 4)$
d $(10 + 3) \cdot (5 + 4)$

10 Indicate whether the statement is *true* or *false*.

a $2\frac{3}{8} = 2 + \frac{3}{8}$

b $2 \cdot \frac{3}{8} = 2 + \frac{3}{8}$

c $2\frac{3}{8} = 2.375$

d $2 \cdot \frac{3}{8} = 2.375$

11 Evaluate each expression.

a $\frac{3+5}{14+2}$

b $3 + \frac{5}{14} + 2$

c $\frac{3+5}{14} + 2$

12 Consumer Math A plumber charges $52.00 for a service call and $27.50 per hour for labor. How much does a 3-hour service call cost?

In problems 13–18, evaluate each expression.

13 $3 \cdot 4 \div 2$

14 $3 \div 2 \cdot 4$

15 $16 - 15/5*4 - 4$

16 $\frac{3+5}{2+10}$

17 $\frac{18-6}{3+9}$

18 $3\frac{1}{2} + 2\frac{1}{2}$

19 Communicating Describe a real-life situation that can be represented by the mathematical expresion $6 + 2 \cdot 5$.

20 What is the Celsius equivalent of 77°F?

In problems 21–24, evaluate each expression.

21 $4 + (3+9) \div 6$

22 $(15 - 7/10)/2$

23 $\frac{24 - 12 \times 2}{13 - 4 \div 2}$

24 $\frac{24-12}{13-4} \times \frac{12 \times 2}{4 \div 2}$

In problems 25–27, find the perimeter of each rectangle.

25
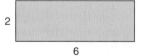
2

6

26
3.1

3.1

27
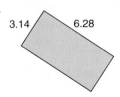
3.14   6.28

28 Copy the pattern, filling in the missing numbers.

$2 + 3 \cdot 1 = 5$
$2 + 3 \cdot 2 = 8$
$2 + 3 \cdot 3 = \underline{\hspace{1cm}}$
$2 + 3 \cdot 4 = \underline{\hspace{1cm}}$
$2 + 3 \cdot 5 = \underline{\hspace{1cm}}$
$2 + 3 \cdot 6 = \underline{\hspace{1cm}}$

In problems 29 and 30, find the perimeter of each figure.

29
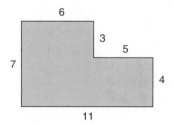
6

3

5

7

4

11

30
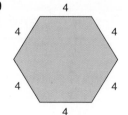
4

4

4

4

4

4

31 Evaluate $\frac{3}{5} + \frac{4}{3} \cdot \frac{7}{20}$. Write your answer both as a simplified fraction and as a decimal approximation.

32 Draw and label the next three figures in this pattern.

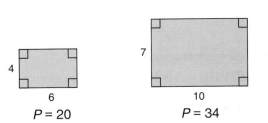

$P = 20$ $P = 34$ $P = 48$

33 Spreadsheets   This display shows some students' scores on three Latin tests.

	A	B	C	D	E
1		Test 1	Test 2	Test 3	Average
2	Tom	84	75	67	
3	Serena	94	98	84	
4	Jamie	86	74	62	
5	Ivan	93	78	85	
6	Mary	87	64	75	
7					

a What is each student's average score for the tests?
b What formulas could be put in cells E2, E3, E4, E5, and E6 to have the spreadsheet calculate each student's average?
c What is the average of all the scores?
d What formula could be put in cell E7 so that the spreadsheet would calculate this average?

34 Contrary Mary wants to put a fence around her flower garden. How many feet of fencing does she need?

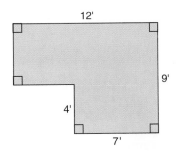

35 Consumer Math   A 5-foot-wide gate costs $15.00. A fence post costs $7.95. A 50-foot roll of wire fencing costs $75.00. How much did it cost to enclose this orchard?

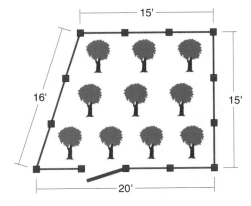

36 Consumer Math   Donald and Wendy went into King Castle Burgers and bought three cheeseburgers at $1.50 each, two orders of fries at $1.12 each, a shake at $1.85, and a soft drink at $0.89. There was a 6% sales tax.
  a What was the total cost of the items?
  b How much tax was charged?
  c What was the total cost, with tax included?

◄ LOOKING BACK   **Spiral Learning**   LOOKING AHEAD ►

---

37 a Multiply $7 \cdot 7 \cdot 7 \cdot 7 \cdot 7$.
  b Multiply six 7's (that is, $7 \cdot 7 \cdot 7 \cdot 7 \cdot 7 \cdot 7$).
  c Multiply seven 6's.
  d Multiply eight 3's.

In problems 38–41, indicate whether the statement is *true* or *false*.

38 $\frac{2}{3} = \frac{4}{6}$ **39** $\frac{9}{11} = \frac{19}{21}$ **40** $\frac{5}{8} = \frac{30}{48}$ **41** $\frac{3}{4} = \frac{75}{100}$

42 What number should go in each □, in each △, and in each ○?
  a $□ + □ = 81$ **b** $△ \cdot △ = 81$ **c** $○ \cdot ○ \cdot ○ \cdot ○ = 81$

43 Is the following statement true *always, sometimes,* or *never?*

  The product of two multiples of 3 is a multiple of 9.

44 A bag contains four chips, numbered 3, 5, 7, and 8. Three chips are drawn at random. What is the probability that
  a The sum of the numbers on the three chips is even?
  b The product of the numbers on the chips is even?

45 Most scientific calculators have a key labeled $\boxed{x^y}$, $\boxed{y^x}$, or $\boxed{\wedge}$. Use this key to evaluate each of the following.
  a $7 \boxed{x^y} 2 \boxed{=}$ **b** $5 \boxed{x^y} 3 \boxed{=}$ **c** $3 \boxed{x^y} 4 \boxed{=}$

46 If $x = 2$, $y = 3$, and $z = 4$, what is the value of each expression?
  a $x + yz$ **b** $x \cdot y \cdot z$ **c** $(x + y) \cdot z$

47 Communicating   Look up the meaning of *pi* (π). Explain what π is.

Investigation

Mental Math   A rule of thumb for estimating the Celsius equivalent of a temperature expressed in degrees Fahrenheit is to subtract 30 from the Fahrenheit reading, then halve the result. This gives less accurate results than the formula in Sample Problem 2, but it provides a reasonable estimate and can be done in your head. Use this method to estimate the Celsius equivalents of 40°F, 100°F, and 212°F. Then write a rule of thumb for estimating the Fahrenheit equivalents of Celsius readings.

SECTION 2.2

Powers and Roots

EXPONENTS

M. Ultiply wanted to use his calculator to multiply

$$5 \cdot 5 \cdot 5 \cdot 5 \cdot 5 \cdot 5 \cdot 5 \cdot 5 \cdot 5$$

He had just begun when his friend X. Ponent asked him what he was doing. "I'm multiplying nine fives," he replied. "Don't interrupt me, or I'll lose track."

Mr. Ponent pulled out his calculator. In a moment he said, "I have it! It's 1,953,125."

"How did you do that so fast?" exclaimed Mr. Ultiply. "I'm still multiplying."

"I just calculated five to the ninth power," said Mr. Ponent.

To indicate repeated multiplication of a number, we can use a special notation. Multiplication of nine 5's, for example, can be written 5^9, which is read "five to the ninth **power.**" In this notation, the 5 is called the **base** and the 9 is called an **exponent.**

Notation	Read	Meaning
3^5	Three to the fifth power	$3 \cdot 3 \cdot 3 \cdot 3 \cdot 3$
7^2	Seven to the second power *or* Seven squared	$7 \cdot 7$
8^3	Eight to the third power *or* Eight cubed	$8 \cdot 8 \cdot 8$
$\left(\frac{1}{5}\right)^4$	One fifth to the fourth power	$\left(\frac{1}{5}\right)\left(\frac{1}{5}\right)\left(\frac{1}{5}\right)\left(\frac{1}{5}\right)$

Example 1
Evaluate 3.7^4.

Solution
Scientific calculators have a power key, usually labeled ⌷x^y⌷, ⌷y^x⌷, or ⌷ ∧ ⌷. We enter
3.7 ⌷x^y⌷ 4 ⌷ = ⌷, and the display shows 187.4161 . Therefore, 3.7^4 = 187.4161.

R O O T S

Sometimes, instead of finding a power of a base, we need to find the base that corresponds to a given power. For instance, what number raised to the third power is 1000? In this case, the answer is 10, since 10^3 = 10 · 10 · 10 = 1000. We call 10 the third **root,** or the cube root, of 1000 and write $\sqrt[3]{1000}$ = 10.

Similarly, since 5^2 = 25, we can say that 5 is the second root, or the **square root,** of 25 and write $\sqrt[2]{25}$ = 5. And since 2^8 = 256, we can say that 2 is the eighth root of 256 and write $\sqrt[8]{256}$ = 2.

In the notation $\sqrt[8]{256}$, the 8 is called a **root index** and the 256 is called a **radicand.** Because mathematicians work with square roots a lot, they usually omit the root index 2 when they write square roots. Thus, $\sqrt{81}$ means "the square root of 81." (Can you figure out what the value of $\sqrt{81}$ is?)

Example 2
Evaluate $\sqrt{552.7201}$.

Solution
Scientific calculators have a square-root key, labeled ⌷$\sqrt{}$⌷ or ⌷$\sqrt{x}$⌷. We enter 552.7201 ⌷$\sqrt{}$⌷, and the display shows 23.51 . Therefore, $\sqrt{552.7201}$ = 23.51.

It is fairly easy to find exact values of roots such as $\sqrt{25}$ and $\sqrt{81}$. Most of the time, though, we have to be satisfied with approximations.

Example 3
Evaluate $\sqrt{70}$.

Solution
If we enter 70 ⌷$\sqrt{}$⌷ on a calculator, the display may show 8.366600265 . But 8.366600265 is not the exact value of the square root, since if we calculate 8.366600265^2, we get an answer of 69.99999999, not 70. The calculator could not show all the decimal places of the root, so it showed as many as its display would hold. Usually we round such numbers to a convenient number of decimal places. We might round $\sqrt{70}$ to the nearest hundredth or thousandth, writing $\sqrt{70}$ ≈ 8.37 or $\sqrt{70}$ ≈ 8.367. (The symbol ≈ means "is approximately equal to.")

ORDER OF OPERATIONS

In the preceding section, you saw the order in which some mathematical operations should be performed. Now we can add two new operations.

Order of Operations
1. Do operations enclosed by grouping symbols (parentheses, brackets, or vinculums).
2. Evaluate powers and roots.
3. Multiply and divide from left to right.
4. Add and subtract from left to right.

Example 4

Evaluate $2 + 7 \cdot 5^3 - \dfrac{6}{\sqrt{9}}$.

Solution

$$2 + 7 \cdot 5^3 - \frac{6}{\sqrt{9}}$$

Evaluate the power and the root $\quad = 2 + 7 \cdot 125 - \dfrac{6}{3}$

Multiply and divide $\quad = 2 + 875 - 2$

Add and subtract $\quad = 875$

Sample Problems

Problem 1

Evaluate $\sqrt{16 + 9}$.

Solution

Like a fraction bar, the bar above $16 + 9$ is a vinculum. Therefore, we add first.

$$\sqrt{16 + 9} = \sqrt{25} = 5$$

Try solving this problem with a calculator. (Be careful, it's tricky!) Did you get 5 as your answer?

Problem 2

Is the statement $(3 + 5)^2 = 3^2 + 5^2$ *true* or *false*?

Solution

Let's evaluate each side of the equation.

Left Side	**Right Side**
$(3 + 5)^2$	$3^2 + 5^2$
$= 8^2$	$= 9 + 25$
$= 64$	$= 34$

Since 64 is not equal to 34, the statement is false; $(3 + 5)^2 \neq 3^2 + 5^2$.

Think and Discuss

1 a Why might raising a number to the second power be called squaring?
b Why might raising a number to the third power be called cubing?

2 Evaluate each expression.
a $1 + 2 \cdot 3^4$ **b** $(2 + 3)^4$ **c** $2^4 + 3^4$

3 Is the statement *true* or *false?*
a $3^2 > 3$ **b** $1.5^2 > 1.5$ **c** $1^2 > 1$ **d** $0.8^2 > 0.8$

4 Evaluate each expression.
a 2.6^4 **b** $2 \cdot 6^4$ **c** $(2 \cdot 6)^4$

5 Is the statement true *always, sometimes,* or *never?* Explain your answer.
a The square of a number is greater than the number.
b The square root of a number is less than the number.

6 Evaluate each expression.
a $\sqrt{6^2 - 5 \cdot 4}$ **b** $\sqrt{5^2 + 12^2}$ **c** $\sqrt{17^2 - 8^2}$

7 Science If we use v to stand for the speed of sound in feet per second and t to stand for the temperature in degrees Celsius, we can find the speed of sound at sea level with the formula

$$v = \frac{1087 \cdot \sqrt{273 + t}}{16.52}$$

What is the speed of sound when the temperature is 25°C?

Problems and Applications

8 Evaluate each expression.
a 3.5^2 **b** $(3.5)^2$ **c** $(3 \cdot 5)^2$ **d** $3 \cdot 5^2$

9 What number should go in each $\square$, in each $\triangle$, and in each $\bigcirc$?
a $\square \cdot \square \cdot \square \cdot \square = 256$ **b** $\triangle \cdot \triangle = 11.26$ **c** $\bigcirc \cdot \bigcirc \cdot \bigcirc = 125$

10 Write and evaluate a root with radicand 81 and root index 4.

In problems 11–14, evaluate each expression to the nearest thousandth.

11 $\sqrt{5}$ **12** $\sqrt{5.001}$

13 $\sqrt{857}$ **14** $\sqrt{8^2 + 10^2}$

15 The area of a square is the second
power of its side length.
a Find the area of each square.
b Find the total area of the figure.

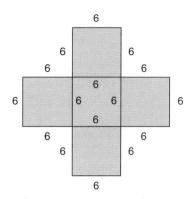

16 Evaluate each expression.
a $\left(\frac{1}{2}\right)^2 + \left(\frac{1}{2}\right)^2$
b $\frac{3}{8} + \left(\frac{1}{2}\right)^3$

17 Indicate whether the statement is *true* or *false*.
a $3^5 = (1 + 2)^5$
b $3^5 = 1^5 + 2^5$
c $3^5 = 1^5 + 1^5 + 1^5$
d $3^5 = (1 + 1 + 1)^5$

18 What exponents go in the boxes?
a $(2 \cdot 2 \cdot 2 \cdot 2) \cdot (2 \cdot 2 \cdot 2 \cdot 2 \cdot 2 \cdot 2) = 2^\square$
b $2^4 \cdot 2^6 = 2^\square$

19 Each edge of the open box has a length of 8 inches.
Find the total area of the box's sides and bottom.

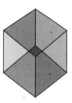

20 If $\pi \approx 3.1416$, $r \approx 6.75$, and $d \approx 13.5$, what is the value of
a πd?
b $2\pi r$?
c πr^2?

**In problems 21 and 22, indicate whether the statement is *true* or
false.**

21 $3.75 \times 10^5 = 375,000$

22 $412.35 = 4.12 \times 10^2$

23 Spreadsheets
a What values go in cells B7, B8, and B9 of
this spreadsheet display?
b In spreadsheets the symbol ^ is used to
indicate a power—for example, 5^3 means
5^3. Use the base 3 and cell names from
column A to write formulas that will
generate the correct values in B7, B8, and B9.
c Now write formulas for the values in B7,
B8, and B9, using names only of cells in
column B.

	A	B
1	Exponent	Power of 3
2	1	3
3	2	9
4	3	27
5	4	81
6	5	243
7	6	
8	7	
9	8	

In problems 24–26, evaluate each expression.

24 $3 + 5 \cdot 8^3 \div \sqrt{16} + \dfrac{10}{\sqrt{25}}$

25 $5^3 \cdot 5^4 - 5^7$

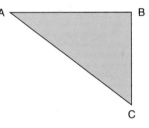

26 $\sqrt{4 + 5 \cdot 8^3 + 5 \cdot 5^3} + 1$

27 Wanda went from A to B to C. Willie went directly from A to C. Who went the shorter distance? Explain.

28 Indicate whether the statement is *true* or *false*.
a $5^2 + 5^2 + 5^2 = 3 \cdot 5^2$
b $\sqrt{9} + \sqrt{9} + \sqrt{9} = 3 \cdot \sqrt{9}$
c $7^5 + 7^5 + 7^5 = 3 \cdot 7^5$
d $\sqrt{7} + \sqrt{7} + \sqrt{7} = 3 \cdot \sqrt{7}$

29 The dots in the diagram are 1.8 units apart.
a Find the area of rectangle ABCD.
b Find the area of triangle ABC.

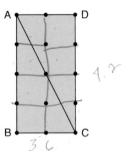

30 **Communicating** Enter the given number on a calculator. Then press the $\boxed{\sqrt{}}$ key repeatedly. What do you notice about the numbers displayed?
a 2
b 0.25

In problems 31–34, indicate whether the statement is *true* or *false*.

31 $\sqrt{4 + 5} = \sqrt{4} + \sqrt{5}$

32 $(3 + 4)^2 = 3^2 + 4^2$

33 $5 \cdot (3 + 4) = 5 \cdot 3 + 5 \cdot 4$

34 $\sqrt{5^2 - 4^2} = 5 - 4$

35 Evaluate $\sqrt{\sqrt{2} + \sqrt{3} + \sqrt{5}}$ to the nearest thousandth.

◀ LOOKING BACK **Spiral Learning** LOOKING AHEAD ▶

36 **a** Change $\frac{3}{4}$ to an equivalent fraction with denominator 100.
b Change $\frac{18}{25}$ to an equivalent fraction with denominator 100.
c Which is greater, $\frac{3}{4}$ or $\frac{18}{25}$?

37 Insert parentheses to make each statement true.
a $3 + 5 \cdot 6 + 7 = 68$
b $3 + 5 \cdot 6 + 7 = 55$
c $3 + 5 \cdot 6 + 7 = 104$

38 If $b = 5$ and $b = 6$, what is the value of
   a $b \cdot b$?   **b** $\frac{1}{2}bb$?

39 Indicate whether the statement
is *true* or *false*.
   a These two figures have the same
      perimeter.
   b These two figures have the same
      area.

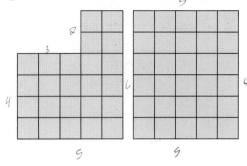

40 What is the Celsius equivalent of 90°F?

41 Carya had 5 pounds of pecans and 16 pounds of mixed nuts. By weight,
50 percent of the mixed nuts was pecans. How many pounds of pecans
did Carya have in all?

42 What is the perimeter of this rectangle?

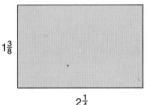

$1\frac{3}{8}$

$2\frac{1}{4}$

In problems 43–45, rewrite the fraction as a decimal.

43 $\frac{3}{5}$ **44** $\frac{7}{4}$ **45** $\frac{13}{3}$

46 Consumer Math   Susie sold seventeen seashells by the seashore for
seven dollars and seven cents each. There was also a 6.6% sales tax.
How much money did Susie take in?

47 You are given a sheet of paper measuring $8\frac{1}{2}$ inches by 11 inches
(a standard sheet of typing paper). Can you cut a 1 inch by 12 inch
rectangle from the sheet?

Investigation

Algebra   If $x = 5$, what is the value of the expression $4x^2$? Does the
expression mean $4 \cdot x^2$, or does it mean $(4x)^2$? That is, should you square
just the value of x or square the value $4x$? Or doesn't it matter? See if you can
come up with a rule for evaluating expressions like this.

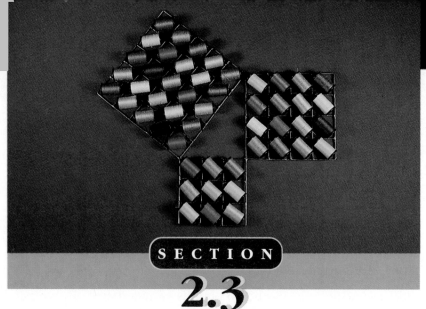

AREA AND CIRCUMFERENCE FORMULAS

You may already be familiar with formulas that can be used to find the areas and the perimeters of various shapes. Here are some frequently used ones.

**Area of a Rectangle
or Parallelogram**

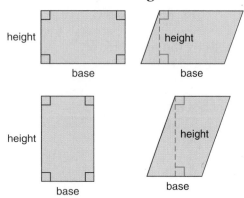

Area = base · height

Area of a Triangle

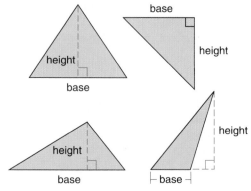

Area = $\frac{1}{2}$ · base · height

**Circumference (Perimeter)
of a Circle**

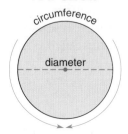

Circumference = π · diameter

Area of a Circle

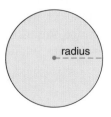

Area = π · (radius)^2

Example 1

Find the area of the parallelogram.

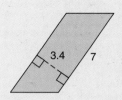

Solution

Area = base · height

= 7 · 3.4

= 23.8

Example 2

Find the area and the circumference of the circle.

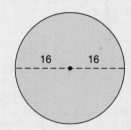

Solution

The letter π represents a number that we can only approximate. In this case, we will use the approximation 3.1416 and round the answers to hundredths.

Area = π · (radius)^2 Circumference = π · diameter

= π · 16^2 = π · 32

= π · 256   ≈ 3.1416 · 32

≈ 3.1416 · 256   ≈ 100.53

≈ 804.25

You can find other important formulas in a table in the back of this book.

THE PYTHAGOREAN THEOREM

For many people, one of the most important ideas of geometry is the **_Pythagorean Theorem._** It expresses a relationship among the sides of a right triangle—a triangle in which one of the angles is a right (90°) angle.

In a right triangle, the longest side (the side opposite the right angle) is called the **_hypotenuse._** The other sides (the sides that meet to form the right angle) are the triangle's **_legs._**

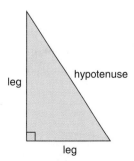

The Pythagorean Theorem states that in any right triangle,

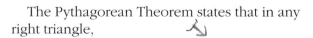

$$(\text{Leg}_1)^2 + (\text{leg}_2)^2 = (\text{hypotenuse})^2$$

Example 3

In this right triangle, the length of one leg is 7 and the length of the hypotenuse is 25. What is the length of the other leg?

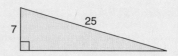

Solution

$$(\text{Leg}_1)^2 + (\text{leg}_2)^2 = (\text{hypotenuse})^2$$
$$(\text{Leg}_1)^2 + 7^2 = 25^2$$
$$(\text{Leg}_1)^2 + 49 = 625$$

Now, since $(\text{leg}_1)^2$ plus 49 is 625, $(\text{leg}_1)^2$ must be 49 less than 625. Thus, $(\text{leg}_1)^2 = 625 - 49 = 576$. But $24^2 = 576$, so the length of the leg is 24.

Sample Problems

Problem 1

The formula for the area of a trapezoid is

$$\text{Area} = \tfrac{1}{2} \cdot (\text{base}_1 + \text{base}_2) \cdot \text{height}$$

Use this formula to find the area of the trapezoid shown.

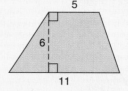

Solution

In this trapezoid, the lengths of the bases are 5 and 11, and the height is 6.

$$\text{Area} = \tfrac{1}{2} \cdot (\text{base}_1 + \text{base}_2) \cdot \text{height} = \tfrac{1}{2} \cdot (5 + 11) \cdot 6$$
$$= \tfrac{1}{2} \cdot 16 \cdot 6$$
$$= 48$$

Problem 2

A football field is 360 feet long and 160 feet wide. How far is it from one corner of the field to the opposite corner?

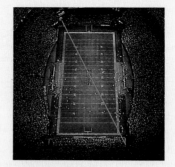

Solution

The distance we are trying to find is the length of the hypotenuse of a right triangle with legs of 360 feet and 160 feet. We can use the Pythagorean Theorem.

$$(\text{Leg}_1)^2 + (\text{leg}_2)^2 = (\text{hypotenuse})^2$$
$$360^2 + 160^2 = (\text{hypotenuse})^2$$
$$155{,}200 = (\text{hypotenuse})^2$$

Since the length of the hypotenuse squared is 155,200, the length of the hypotenuse must be $\sqrt{155{,}200}$. We can enter 155,200 $\boxed{\sqrt{}}$ on a calculator to find that the distance is approximately 394 feet.

Think and Discuss

1 a What is the perimeter of the square?
   b What is the area of the square?
   c Explain why the answers to parts **a** and **b** are different.

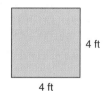
4 ft

4 ft

2 Find the circumference and the area of each circle.

a 5

b 12

c 7

d 4.5

3 Find the area of each figure.

a 4   7

Rectangle

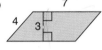
b 7   4   3

Parallelogram

c 8   16   12

Trapezoid

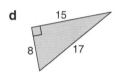
d 15   8   17

Triangle

4 Consumer Math Penny Pinscher is purchasing pepperoni pizzas for her pals. A pizza 10 inches in diameter costs $7.95, and a pizza 14 inches in diameter costs $15.45. Should Penny purchase two 10-inch pizzas or one 14-inch pizza?

5 Is the statement true *always, sometimes,* or *never?*
   a Two rectangles with equal perimeters have equal areas.
   b The hypotenuse of a right triangle is the longest side of the triangle.

Problems and Applications

6 Find the area of each square, then copy and complete the table.

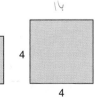
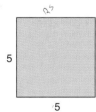

1   2   3   4   5

Dimensions of Square	Area
1 by 1	_____
2 by 2	_____
3 by 3	_____
4 by 4	_____
5 by 5	_____

In problems 7–9, what value should replace the ☐?

7 $\square^2 + 8^2 = 10^2$ **8** $\square^2 + 5^2 = 13^2$ **9** $\square^2 + 2^2 = 4^2$

10 Find the area of the rectangle.

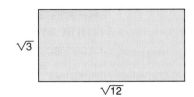

In problems 11–13, find the area of the triangle.

11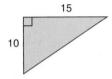

12

13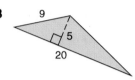

14 Indicate whether the statement is *true* or *false*.
  a $\sqrt{33}$ = 5.744562647   **b** $\sqrt{631.5169}$ = 25.13
  c $\sqrt{2.315}$ = 1.521512405

15 Find the lengths labeled *a*, *b*, *c*, *d*, and *e*. Round to the nearest hundredth if necessary.

16 Find the area of each figure.

  a 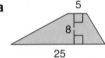   **b**   **c** 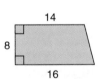   **d**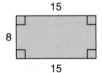

17 Find the lengths labeled *x* and *y*.

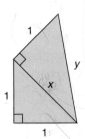

18 Find the length of the hypotenuse of the right triangle.

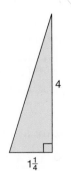

19 a Write two expressions for the area of rectangle ABCD.
b Calculate the area of rectangle ABCD.

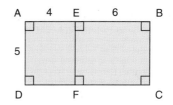

20 Sports How far is it from first base to third base in a straight line?

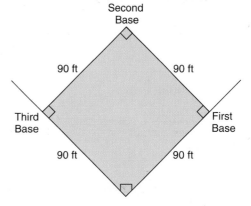

21 a Write an expression that stands for the exact area of the shaded region.
b Find the area of the shaded region to the nearest thousandth.

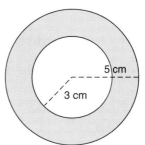

22 The dots in the diagram are evenly spaced. Wally walked straight from A to B, then straight from B to C. How far did he walk?

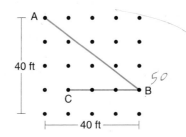

23 a How long is segment AD?
b What is the perimeter of rectangle ABCD?

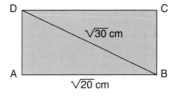

24 If a dart is thrown so that it lands inside the square, what is the probability that it will land inside the circle?

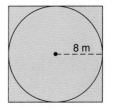

25 Find the value of $x + y - z$.

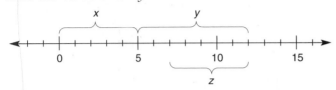

26 Copy the pattern, filling in the missing numbers.

15% of 150 is 22.5.
15% of 300 is _____ .
15% of 450 is _____ .
15% of 600 is _____ .
15% of 750 is _____ .

In problems 27 and 28, write each number as a common fraction.

27 0.7

28 2.5

In problems 29–31, evaluate each expression.

29 $5^3 + \sqrt{36}$

30 $\dfrac{3 + 5(4 + \sqrt{9}\,)}{2 \cdot 5^2 - 12}$

31 $3^2 + 4^2 - 2(3)(4)\left(\dfrac{1}{2}\right)$

32 a Rewrite $\frac{4}{5}$ as a decimal.

b Rewrite 0.35 as a fraction.

33 Consumer Math A rectangular pen measuring 20 feet by 32 feet, with an 8-foot-wide gate, is to be built. The fencing costs $4 per foot, and the material for the gate costs $8 per foot. What will it cost to build the pen?

In problems 34–36, rewrite the fraction as an equivalent fraction having a denominator of 100.

34 $\frac{3}{5}$

35 $\frac{5}{2}$

36 $\frac{35}{500}$

37 Consumer Math Edsel bought a car for $18,500 and paid a sales tax of 15%.
a How much sales tax did Edsel pay?
b What was the total cost of his car?

Investigation

Volume Look up the formula for the volume of a sphere. Use the formula to find the volume of a marble with a radius of 1 centimeter. If the marble's radius were twice as great, how many times greater would its volume be?

Percent

WHAT IS A PERCENT?

According to *The Harper's Index Book,* 22% of the potatoes grown in the
United States end up as french fries. What does this statement mean? As you
probably know, the symbol % stands for **percent.** The word *percent* means
"in each 100." So out of every 100 bushels of potatoes grown in the United
States, 22 are prepared as french fries. Other ways of writing 22% are $\frac{22}{100}$
and 0.22.

Example 1

Rewrite each fraction as a percent.

a $\frac{8}{5}$

b $\frac{3}{20}$

Solution

a Since 20 × 5 = 100, we can change
$\frac{8}{5}$ to hundredths by multiplying both
the numerator and the denominator
by 20.

$$\frac{8}{5} = \frac{8 \times 20}{5 \times 20} = \frac{160}{100}$$

Therefore, $\frac{8}{5}$ = 160%.

b Let's use a calculator to divide 3 by 20.
We enter 3 ÷ 20 = , and the
display shows 0.15.
Since 0.15 means "15 hundredths,"
$\frac{3}{20}$ = 15%.

Example 2

Rewrite 24.36% as a fraction and as a decimal.

Solution

$$24.36\% = \frac{24.36}{100} = \frac{2436}{10,000} = \frac{2436 \div 4}{10,000 \div 4} = \frac{609}{2500}$$

Since 24.36% = $\frac{2436}{10,000}$, the decimal form is 0.2436.

Example 3
What percent of 80 is 20?

Solution
When we divide 20 by 80, we get a result of $\frac{1}{4}$, or 0.25. Since $0.25 = \frac{25}{100}$, 20 is 25% of 80.

Some percents are encountered so frequently that it is useful to memorize their fractional and decimal equivalents.

Percent	Fraction	Decimal
1%	$\frac{1}{100}$	0.01
5%	$\frac{1}{20}$	0.05
10%	$\frac{1}{10}$	0.1
20%	$\frac{1}{5}$	0.2
25%	$\frac{1}{4}$	0.25
$33\frac{1}{3}\%$	$\frac{1}{3}$	$0.\overline{3}$
50%	$\frac{1}{2}$	0.5

Percent	Fraction	Decimal
60%	$\frac{3}{5}$	0.6
$66\frac{2}{3}\%$	$\frac{2}{3}$	$0.\overline{6}$
75%	$\frac{3}{4}$	0.75
80%	$\frac{4}{5}$	0.8
100%	$\frac{1}{1}$	1.0
150%	$\frac{3}{2}$ or $1\frac{1}{2}$	1.5
200%	$\frac{2}{1}$	2.0

PERCENT PROBLEMS

A good deal of the information people encounter—interest rates, election results, forecasts of rain, and so forth—is presented in the form of percentages.
Being able to understand these percentages is a necessary skill in everyday life.

Example 4
After having dinner at a restaurant, the members of the Future Accountants of America are given a bill of $350. They vote to leave a 15% tip. How can they calculate how much to leave?

Solution
Method 1 They can write 15% as a fraction.

$$15\% \text{ of } 350 = \frac{15}{100} \cdot 350 = \frac{5250}{100} = \frac{105}{2}$$

Method 2 They can write 15% in decimal form.

$$15\% \text{ of } 350 = 0.15(350) = 52.5$$

Method 3 They can calculate mentally. They know that 10% of 350 is 35. Half of this amount (5% of 350) is $17\frac{1}{2}$. So 15% of 350 is $35 + 17\frac{1}{2}$, or $52\frac{1}{2}$.

The three methods give the same answer in different forms. The tip should be $52.50.

Example 5

While shopping for designer jeans, Calvin found some on sale for 20% off the regular price of $75. How much did the jeans cost?

Solution

The price was reduced by 20% of $75—that is, by 0.2(75), or 15, dollars. The sale price was therefore 75 − 15, or 60, dollars.

Can you think of any other ways of calculating the price of the pants?

Sample Problems

Problem 1
A pizza was divided into eight slices. Gina got one of the slices. What percent of the pizza did she get?

Solution
There are several ways of solving this problem. Here are two.

Method 1 Since Gina got one eighth of the pizza and $\frac{1}{8} = 0.125 = \frac{12.5}{100}$, she got 12.5%.

Method 2 Two slices are one fourth of the pizza, and we know that $\frac{1}{4}$ is 25%. One slice is exactly half as much, or $12\frac{1}{2}$%.

Problem 2
The label on a bottle of vitamin supplements says that each pill contains 27 milligrams of iron, which is 150% of the recommended daily allowance (RDA). What is the RDA of iron?

Solution
We know that 150% = 1.5. Since 27 milligrams of iron is 1.5 times the RDA, the RDA is 27 ÷ 1.5, or 18, milligrams.

Problem 3
Ira invests $300 at 7% interest, compounded annually.
a How much will the investment be worth at the end of a year?
b At the end of the first year, the interest rate is increased to 8%. How much will the investment be worth at the end of the second year?

Solution
a Ira starts with $300. During the first year he earns 0.07(300), or 21, dollars in interest. So the investment will be worth 300 + 21, or 321, dollars.

There is, however, another way of thinking about this problem: Originally, $300 is the whole (100%) of Ira's investment; at year's end 7% more will be added, so the investment will be worth 107% of its original value. Since 107% = 1.07, we can calculate the answer directly by multiplying 1.07(300).

b At the end of the first year the investment will be worth $321, so at the end of the second year it will be worth 1.08(321) dollars, or $346.68.

Think and Discuss

1 Find each value mentally.
   a What is 50% of 90?
   b What is 25% of 800?
   c What is 46.98% of 100?
   d What is 100% of 9.4356?
   e What percent of 120 is 30?
   f What is $33\frac{1}{3}$% of 6?
   g What number is 75 ten percent of?

2 Coach Roche said, "All my players give 110 percent effort every game." What does her statement mean?

3 Is the statement *true* or *false?*
   a 3% of 6% is 18%.
   b 4% + 8% = 12%
   c 100% of 3 is equal to 3% of 100.

4 **Consumer Math** Dr. Drivegood's Car Clinic is having a sale—10% off on brake jobs, 15% off on lube jobs, 20% off on oil changes, 25% off on wheel alignments, and 50% off on car washes. The sign outside the shop reads 120% OFF ON AUTO SERVICES!!! Is the sign accurate? Explain.

5 The Chasm marked down its line of sweaters by 40%. A week later there was a storewide sale in which the prices of all merchandise were reduced by 20%.
   a If a sweater's original price was $70, what was its price during the storewide sale?
   b By what percent were the original prices of the sweaters reduced during the sale?

Problems and Applications

In problems 6–9, indicate what percent of the figure is shaded.

6
7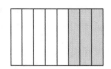
8
9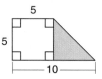

10 Rewrite each fraction as a percent.
   a $\frac{2}{5}$
   b $\frac{5}{2}$
   c $\frac{9}{5}$
   d $\frac{5}{9}$

11 List $\frac{2}{3}$, 66%, and 0.6 in order, from least to greatest value.

12 **Communicating**
   a Copy the pattern, filling in the missing numbers.
   b Explain the pattern.

   10% of   450 is 45.
   20% of   900 is 180.
   40% of 1800 is _____ .
   80% of 3600 is _____ .
   160% of 7200 is _____ .

In problems 13–15, rewrite each percent as a fraction and as a decimal.

13 15.3% **14** 2.5% **15** 60%

16 At the Café Très Coûteux, a 20% service charge is added to every bill. Find the service charge for each of the following bills.
  a $100 **b** $150 **c** $200
  d $250 **e** $300 **f** $350

17 Sue bought a pair of shoes for $34.95 and was charged 6.5% sales tax. Which of the following expressions represents her total bill? Explain your answer.
  a $34.95 + 0.065 \times 3495$ **b** $3495(0.065)$
  c $(34.95 + 0.065) \times 34.95$ **d** $34.95(1 + 0.065)$

18 What percent of the area of the square is inside the circle?

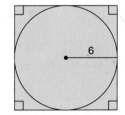

6

19 At Bali High School, the student government raises money for its activities by selling magazine subscriptions. If the students receive 18% of the total sales, how much money will they raise by selling $4380 worth of subscriptions?

20 **Finance** A certain investment pays 9% interest, compounded annually. If you invest $860, how much will your investment be worth
  a After one year? **b** After two years?

21 **Nutrition** Use the information on the label to determine the recommended daily allowance of protein.

NUTRITION INFORMATION PER SERVING
SERVING SIZE.....................10¾ OZ. (305 g)
SERVINGS PER CONTAINER.........................1
CALORIES..200
PROTEIN (GRAMS)....................................13
CARBOHYDRATE (GRAMS)...........................20
FAT (GRAMS)..7
SODIUM....................................1150 mg/serving
PERCENTAGE OF U.S. RECOMMENDED DAILY ALLOWANCES (U.S. RDA)
PROTEIN.............25 RIBOFLAVIN.........10
VITAMIN A.........25 NIACIN...................20
VITAMIN C.......... *   CALCIUM................2
THIAMINE............8 IRON.....................10
*CONTAINS LESS THAN 2% OF THE U.S. RDA OF THIS NUTRIENT.

22 **Spreadsheets** The spreadsheet printout shows scores of the six members of a bowling team. Column D is for the averages of the bowlers' scores.
  a Copy the table, filling in column D.
  b What formulas could be used to generate the numbers in column D?

	A	B	C	D
1	120	125	113	
2	146	135	110	
3	151	137	145	
4	129	142	162	
5	144	183	151	
6	137	146	166	

23 Bob, Carol, and Ted work at Alice's Restaurant. Each was hired at a salary of $350 a week. After having his pay cut by 20%, Bob later got a 20% raise. After receiving a 20% raise, Carol later had her pay cut by 20%. Ted's pay has stayed the same. How much does each person make now?

24 Suppose that the base of this rectangle were increased by 10% and the height were decreased by 10%.

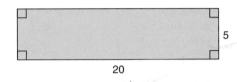

a By what percent would the perimeter change?

b By what percent would the area change?

25 **Environmental Science**   Window insulation can save 12% or more in home heating costs.

a If heating a home with uninsulated windows costs $1265 a year, how much money might be saved by insulating the windows?

b Are the windows in your home insulated? If not, how might you determine the amount of money your family could save by insulating them?

◀ LOOKING BACK **Spiral Learning** LOOKING AHEAD ▶

---

26 Evaluate $19 + 9.5^2 \div 15 + 6^3$.

27 **a** Find lengths x and y (the lengths of segments AB and CD).

b Find the ratio of x to y—that is, the fraction $\frac{x}{y}$.

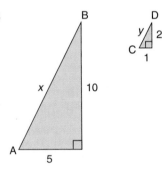

28 Evaluate each expression.

a $(3 + 5)^2$ **b** $3^2 + 5^2$

29 **Spreadsheets**   This diagram shows a spreadsheet display, along with the formulas that were entered in cells D2, D3, and D4. What formulas should be entered in cells D5 and D6? What numbers will appear in those cells?

	A	B	C	D	
1	Value I	Value II	Value III	Average	
2	5	7	12	8	+(A2+B2+C2)/3
3	9	15	21	15	+(A3+B3+C3)/3
4	13	15	26	18	+(A4+B4+C4)/3
5	7	11	29		
6	14	38	76		

30 Is the statement $24/3*5 = 24/(3*5)$ *true* or *false?*

31 Study the pattern shown. Then copy the pattern, filling in the missing numbers.

$$10^3 = 1000$$
$$10^2 = 100$$
$$10^1 = 10$$
$$10^0 = 1$$
$$10^{-1} = \underline{}$$
$$10^{-2} = \underline{}$$

32 In rectangle ABCD,
 a What is the length of diagonal $\overline{AC}$?
 b What is the length of diagonal $\overline{BD}$?

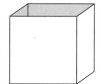

33 Evaluate each expression.

 a $\dfrac{\sqrt{16}}{\sqrt{9}}$ **b** $\sqrt{\dfrac{16}{9}}$ **c** $\sqrt{16 + 9}$ **d** $\sqrt{16} + \sqrt{9}$

34 The diagram shows a box without a top. Each of its sides is a square, and the sum of the areas of the five sides is 480.2 cm². What are the dimensions of the box?

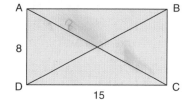

Investigation

Decimals Perhaps you have noticed that when you rewrite fractions as decimals, some of the decimals terminate and some repeat groups of digits forever. For example, the decimal forms of $\frac{1}{2}$, $\frac{3}{16}$, and $\frac{7}{25}$ terminate, but those of $\frac{1}{3}$, $\frac{5}{6}$, and $\frac{11}{15}$ do not. Using a calculator to explore these and other fractions, try to develop a rule that can be used to determine which sort of decimal form a fraction has.

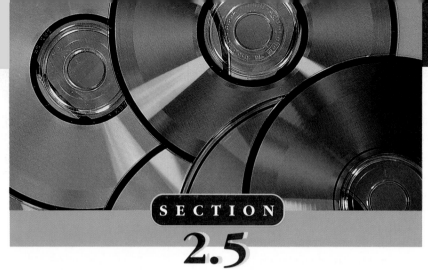

More About Spreadsheets

Bea Sharp owns a music store at which records, tapes, and compact discs are priced from $3.00 to $16.00, in $1.00 increments. One day Bea was planning a storewide sale and needed to determine how much to reduce her prices. So she sat down at her computer and used a spreadsheet to make a table showing what the price reductions and sale prices would be if she offered a 10% discount. Notice, for example, that for a $6.00 item, the 10% discount would amount to $0.60, so the sale price would be $5.40.

10	Percent	Discount
Reg. Price	Reduction	Sale Price
$3.00	$0.30	$2.70
$4.00	$0.40	$3.60
$5.00	$0.50	$4.50
$6.00	$0.60	$5.40
$7.00	$0.70	$6.30
$8.00	$0.80	$7.20
$9.00	$0.90	$8.10
$10.00	$1.00	$9.00
$11.00	$1.10	$9.90
$12.00	$1.20	$10.80
$13.00	$1.30	$11.70
$14.00	$1.40	$12.60
$15.00	$1.50	$13.50
$16.00	$1.60	$14.40

Then Bea decided to see what the sale prices would be if she offered a 15% discount. All she had to do was change the 10 in the table's title to 15. The computer instantly recalculated and printed out a table for the new discount. As she continued, simply by changing this one number each time, she was able to examine the effect of a variety of discount percentages on the prices of her merchandise. Bea was taking advantage of one of the most useful characteristics of spreadsheets—by immediately showing the results of changes you make, they let you quickly experiment with a variety of possibilities.

15	Percent	Discount
Reg. Price	Reduction	Sale Price
$3.00	$0.45	$2.55
$4.00	$0.60	$3.40
$5.00	$0.75	$4.25
$6.00	$0.90	$5.10
$7.00	$1.05	$5.95
$8.00	$1.20	$6.80
$9.00	$1.35	$7.65
$10.00	$1.50	$8.50
$11.00	$1.65	$9.35
$12.00	$1.80	$10.20
$13.00	$1.95	$11.05
$14.00	$2.10	$11.90
$15.00	$2.25	$12.75
$16.00	$2.40	$13.60

Let's explore the process Bea used to create her spreadsheet. She started by entering the headings and the value of her lowest regular price ($3) as shown. To make each entry, she moved the spreadsheet's "highlight" box to the appropriate cell, typed the entry, and pressed the ENTER key on the computer keyboard. Entering the 10 in a cell by itself allowed her to use it as a value in the spreadsheet's calculations as well as part of the title of the table.

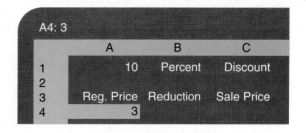

Then Bea entered formulas in cells B4 and C4 to calculate the price reduction and the sale price for a $3 item. She began each formula with a plus sign, which tells the spreadsheet that the entry is a formula rather than a numerical value or a heading. (In some spreadsheets, an equal sign is used for this purpose.) Here are the formulas she used:

In Cell B4

$$+A4*\$A\$1/100$$

Formula symbol | Times | Value in cell A4 | Value in cell A1 | Divided by

In Cell C4

$$+A4-B4$$

Formula symbol | Value in cell A4 | Minus | Value in cell B4

The formula in cell B4 instructs the spreadsheet to take the value in A4 and multiply it by the value in A1 divided by 100. (The division by 100 is needed because the value in cell A1 is a percent.) In this formula, the dollar signs tell the spreadsheet that the reference to cell A1 should not be changed when the formula is copied. The formula in cell C4 instructs the spreadsheet to subtract the value in B4 from the value in A4.

When Bea entered each formula, the value it generated automatically appeared in its cell, as shown. The formula itself is "hidden," but it (or the contents of any other cell) can be seen by simply highlighting the appropriate cell. When a cell is highlighted, whatever was entered in it appears at the top of the display.

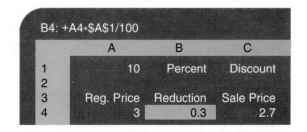

Next, Bea entered the formula +A4+1 in cell A5. By creating a formula that added 1 to the value in the cell above, she would be able to complete column A without typing all the prices. Once the pattern was established, the spreadsheet could do the work, as you will see.

A5: +A4+1

	A	B	C
1	10	Percent	Discount
2			
3	Reg. Price	Reduction	Sale Price
4	3	0.3	2.7
5	4		

Then Bea used the copy feature of the spreadsheet to copy the formulas in cells B4 and C4 to cells B5 and C5. Notice that the formula +A4–B4 changed to +A5–B5 when it was copied. As it copies a formula, the spreadsheet automatically changes the cell names so that they correspond to the formula's new position unless you tell it not to by using dollar signs in the formula.

C5: +A5–B5

	A	B	C
1	10	Percent	Discount
2			
3	Reg. Price	Reduction	Sale Price
4	3	0.3	2.7
5	4	0.4	3.6

Bea was now ready to copy the entries in row 5 to rows 6–17. After doing so, she had a list of all her regular prices in column A, along with the corresponding reductions and sale prices in columns B and C. Notice that once again the cell names were updated in the formulas, except for the reference to A1, which the dollar signs indicated should not be changed.

B17: +A17*$A$1/100

	A	B	C
1	10	Percent	Discount
2			
3	Reg. Price	Reduction	Sale Price
4	3	0.3	2.7
5	4	0.4	3.6
6	5	0.5	4.5
7	6	0.6	5.4
8	7	0.7	6.3
9	8	0.8	7.2
10	9	0.9	8.1
11	10	1	9
12	11	1.1	9.9
13	12	1.2	10.8
14	13	1.3	11.7
15	14	1.4	12.6
16	15	1.5	13.5
17	16	1.6	14.4

Bea's final step was to use the spreadsheet's format function to make it display the table entries in dollars-and-cents form. She then had the table shown at the beginning of this section and was able to experiment with various discounts. Although some commands and symbols differ from spreadsheet to spreadsheet, you can use almost any spreadsheet to do jobs like Bea's. Learn to use one and you will find that you can do amazing things.

Think and Discuss

1 Copy and complete the table.

A	B	A ÷ B	Percent
15	20	0.75	75%
3	15	0.2	20%
130		0.65	
	25	0.16	
	12		150%
6		0.2	

2 In this spreadsheet display, Lotus entered 2, 4, 8, and +A1+B1+C1 in row 1.

a If she uses the copy feature to copy row 1 to rows 2–4, what numbers will appear in row 3?

b If she then changes B3 to 11 and A1 to 6, what number will appear in cell D3?

c If she then changes A3 to +A1, what number will appear in D3?

d If she then changes A1 to 17, which values in the table will change, and what will they become?

D1: +A1+B1+C1

	A	B	C	D
1	2	4	8	14
2				
3				
4				

3 Using a spreadsheet, follow these steps:

1. Enter any positive value (like 5 or 36 or 7000) in cell A1.
2. Enter +(A1+3/A1)/2 in cell A2.
3. Copy the formula in cell A2 to cells A3 through A30.

What do you notice about the values in column A?

4 This table deals with right triangles. Using a spreadsheet, copy the entries shown, continue columns A and B to row 50, and fill in cells C2–C50 and D2–D50. (The copy feature will help you fill in the columns.)

	A	B	C	D
1	Leg 1	Leg 2	Hypotenuse	Area
2	3	4		
3	4	6		
4	5	8		
5	6	10		
6	7	12		
7	8	14		
8	9	16		
9	10	18		
10	11	20		
11	12	22		
12	13	24		
13	14	26		

Problems and Applications

5 If Wanda uses the copy feature of her spreadsheet to copy row 1 to rows 2–7, what value will appear in cell C6?

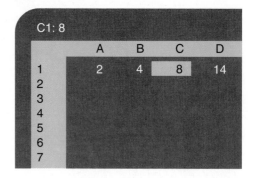

6 a What is 25% of 76?
b What percent of 46 is 23?
c What percent of 70 is 8.792?

In problems 7 and 8, indicate whether the statement is *true* or *false*.

7 The distance from A to C is the same as the distance from B to D.

8 Length PQ + length PR = length QR

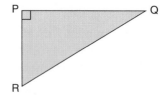

9 Spreadsheets Using a spreadsheet, follow these steps:

  1. Enter 1 in cell A1 and 2 in cell B1.
  2. Enter +A1+3*B1 in cell C1.
  3. Enter +2*A1 in cell A2 and +3*B1 in cell B2.
  4. Copy the formula in cell C1 to cell C2.
  5. Use the copy feature to continue the table through row 6.

What number appears in cell C6?

10 How many diagonals can be drawn from one vertex of this ten-sided figure? (Two of the diagonals are shown.)

11 **Consumer Math** Instruct a spreadsheet to display numbers in dollars-and-cents format. Then follow these steps:

    1. In column A, list prices from $3 to $21, in $2 increments.
    2. In column B, list what the prices would be with a 20% discount.
    3. In column C, list what the prices would be with a 25% discount.

In problems 12 and 13, indicate whether the statement is true *always, sometimes,* or *never.*

12 The product of two odd numbers is even.

13 The product of an even number and an odd number is even.

14 What percent of the perimeter of square ABCD is the perimeter of square EFGH?

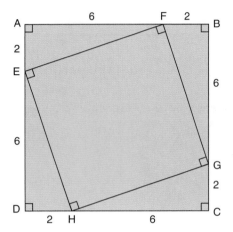

15 During the first two weeks of the baseball season, the Missouri Cardinals won 5 out of 8 games, and the Maryland Ordinals won 6 games and lost 4.
    a What fraction of their games did the Cardinals win?
    b What fraction of their games did the Ordinals win?
    c Which team won a greater fraction of their games?

16 **Spreadsheets** Use a spreadsheet to make a table like this one, showing the circumference and the area of a circle with a radius of 1. (Use formulas to generate the values in cells B3 and C3.)
    a Describe the steps you followed to make the table.
    b Use the spreadsheet to calculate the circumferences and the areas of circles with radii of 15 centimeters, 19 inches, and 25 feet.

	A	B	C
1	Radius	Circumference	Area
2			
3	1	6.283185	3.141592
4			
5			
6			

17 **Communicating** Mick asked Keith, "How far is it from Los Angeles to San Francisco by car?" Keith replied, "About nine hours." Do you think Keith answered Mick's question? Why or why not?

18 Use a spreadsheet to make a table like the one shown. (Notice the formula that was used in column B.) Then extend the table to row 20. What number appears in cell B20?

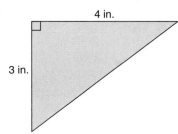

B6: −A6+12

	A	B
1	1	11
2	2	10
3	3	9
4	4	8
5	5	7
6	6	6

◄ LOOKING BACK **Spiral Learning** LOOKING AHEAD ►

In problems 19–22, find the perimeter or circumference of the figure.

19
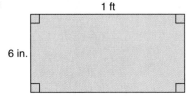
1 ft
6 in.

20
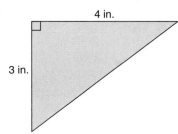
4 in.
3 in.

21
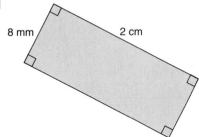
8 mm
2 cm

22
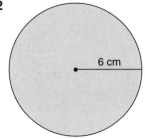
6 cm

23 List $\sqrt{4+9}$, $\sqrt{4}+\sqrt{9}$, and $\sqrt{\frac{13}{2}}$ in order, from least to greatest value.

24 Find the area of the trapezoid.

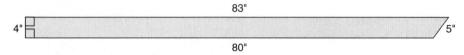

83"
4"
80"
5"

In problems 25 and 26, indicate whether the statement is true *always*, *sometimes*, or *never*. Explain your answer.

25 A square is a rectangle.

26 A rectangle is a square.

27 What percent of a rectangle's angles are right angles?

28 a What fractional part of the area of the larger circle is the area of the smaller circle?

b What fractional part of the circumference of the larger circle is the circumference of the smaller circle?

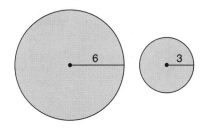

29 Spreadsheets Pete wants to make a table of equivalent lengths.

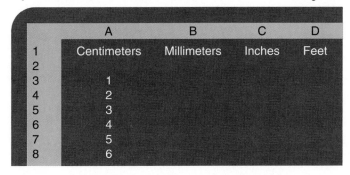

	A	B	C	D
1	Centimeters	Millimeters	Inches	Feet
2				
3	1			
4	2			
5	3			
6	4			
7	5			
8	6			

a There are 10 millimeters in a centimeter. What formula could Pete enter in cell B3 and copy to the rest of column B so that the spreadsheet would calculate appropriate values in that column?

b There are 2.54 centimeters in an inch. What formula could he enter in cell C3 and copy to the rest of column C so that the spreadsheet would calculate appropriate values in that column?

c What formula could he enter in cell D3 and copy to the rest of column D so that the spreadsheet would calculate appropriate values in that column?

Investigation

Sports Look in the sports section of a newspaper to find a table showing the standings of the teams in a professional league. If you were using a spreadsheet to generate the table, which numbers would you have to enter as values? Which could you use formulas to calculate?

Summary

CONCEPTS AND PROCEDURES

After studying this chapter, you should be able to

- Recognize the need for a conventional order of operations (2.1)
- Recognize the symbols used to indicate multiplication and division (2.1)
- Use a calculator to evaluate powers (2.2)
- Use a calculator to evaluate roots (2.2)
- Perform mathematical operations in the conventional order (2.2)
- Use formulas to calculate the areas and perimeters of some geometric figures (2.3)
- Use the Pythagorean Theorem to calculate lengths of sides of right triangles (2.3)
- Interpret percentages (2.4)
- Solve problems involving percentages (2.4)
- Use a spreadsheet to construct tables (2.5)

VOCABULARY

base (2.2)

exponent (2.2)

grouping symbol (2.1)

hypotenuse (2.3)

leg (2.3)

percent (2.4)

power (2.2)

Pythagorean Theorem (2.3)

radicand (2.2)

root (2.2)

root index (2.2)

square root (2.2)

vinculum (2.1)

In problems 25–28, insert parentheses to make each statement true.

25 $4 + 4 \cdot 4 + 4 \cdot 4 = 256$

26 $2 + 3 \cdot 4 \div 5 = 4$

27 $8 - 3 \cdot 4 + 5 = 45$

28 $2 \div 4 + 6 - 8 \cdot 10 + 20 = 5$

29 **a** Find the area of the circle.
  b Find the circumference of the circle.
  c Find the ratio of the area of the circle to the circumference of the circle (that is, divide the area by the circumference).

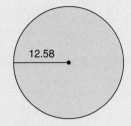
12.58

30 A building contractor is penalized 1% of construction charges for each day he or she is late in completing a project. If a contractor charges $3,260,000 to construct a building, how much will the contractor receive if the building is finished 6 days late?

31 Explain the rule by which the pairs of numbers generate new numbers.

$(10, 379) \rightarrow 37.9$ $(50, 48) \rightarrow 24$
$(100, 97.3) \rightarrow 97.3$ $(25, 40) \rightarrow 10$

32 If a dart lands on this target, what is the probability that it will land in the shaded area?

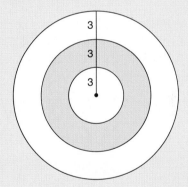
3
3
3

33 Using a spreadsheet, follow these steps:

  1. Enter 100 in cell A1.
  2. Enter + (A1+2/A1)/2 in cell A2.
  3. Copy the formula in cell A2 to cells A3–A20.

  What do you notice about the values in column A?

34 Pippin entered the numbers 1, 3, and 6 in cells A1, B1, and C1 of a spreadsheet table. He entered +A1+B1+C1 in cell D1, then entered +A1+1 in cell A2, +B1+2 in cell B2, and +C1+3 in cell C3. After copying D1 to D2, he copied row 2 to rows 3 and 4. What values appeared in the final table?

Test

1 Tommy bought a compact disc for $12.65, a set of portable headphones for $8.95, and a magazine for $2.50. If he paid a sales tax of 7%, what was the total cost of the items?

2 The hypotenuse of this right triangle is 17 units long, and one leg is 15 units long.
a How long is the other leg?
b What is the area of the triangle?

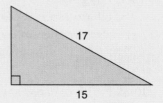

In problems 3–8, evaluate each expression.

3 $2(12 - 5) \div 5$

4 $\frac{3}{8} + \frac{4 + 11}{2^4}$

5 $3 + 3*6/9$

6 $\sqrt{14 + 15(16)}$

7 $38 - 7 \times 4 + 19$

8 $\frac{5.9 + 10 \cdot 7.3}{18 \div 2 + 6}$

9 Describe how you might use a spreadsheet to make the table shown, which lists the areas and perimeters of various sizes of squares.

	A	B	C
1	Side Length	Area	Perimeter
2	1	1	4
3	2	4	8
4	3	9	12
5	4	16	16
6	5	25	20
7	6	36	24
8	7	49	28
9	8	64	32

10 At the Art Attack store, a $12.00 box of colored pencils is on sale for $9.99. By what percentage has the price of the pencils been reduced?

11 Write and evaluate a root with a root index of 3 and a radicand of 10,648.

In problems 12 and 13, find the area of each figure.

12

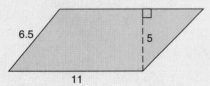

13

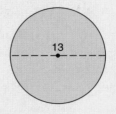

14 If you select two of the values 20, 20%, $\frac{1}{5}$, and $\frac{100}{20}$ at random, what is the probability that the values will be equal?

Each picture below represents a well-known phrase. For example, the picture in box 1A stands for "Fool on the Hill" and box 2A stands for "Stepladder." Figure out the other phrases and try making up some of your own.

1 **2** **3**

A
FOOL
HILL
LADDER
T M
A U
H S
W T

B
BODY
E E EEE EEE
E E E E
E E EE E
E E EE EE
E E E E
E E E E
EEE E E EEE
SEARCH

AND

C
LOOK
CROSSING
KOOL
S
T
E
P
[mountain illustration]

D
PLOT
DKI
E
N M
A P
R O I
R R E
E

E
MORNING
MCE
MCE
MCE
i i i i i

F
[steps] Heaven
< = >
INVENTMEST

3 Measurement and Estimation

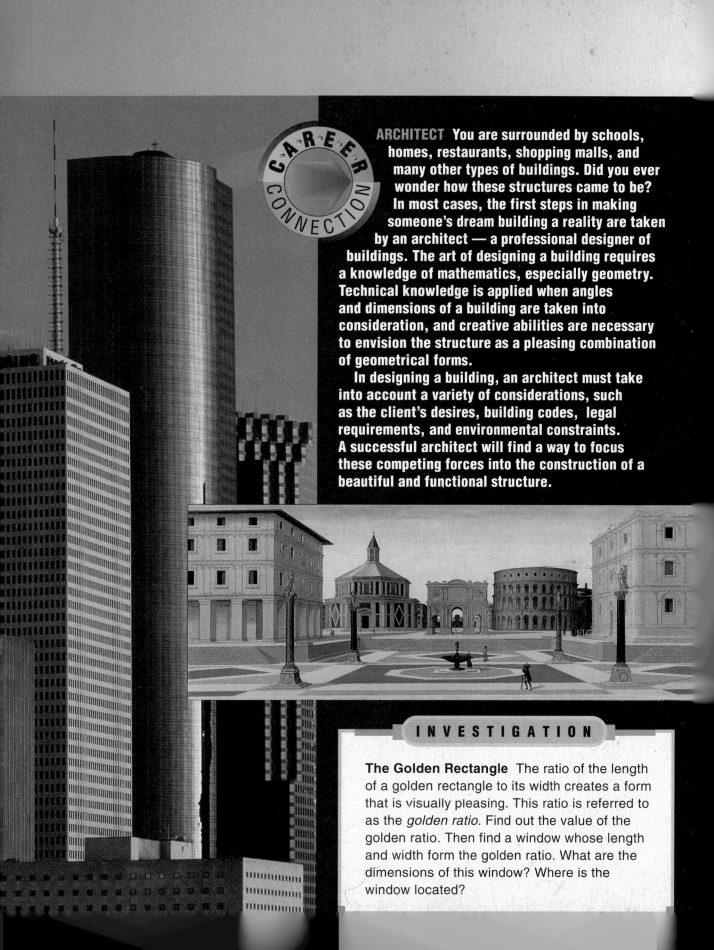

ARCHITECT You are surrounded by schools, homes, restaurants, shopping malls, and many other types of buildings. Did you ever wonder how these structures came to be? In most cases, the first steps in making someone's dream building a reality are taken by an architect — a professional designer of buildings. The art of designing a building requires a knowledge of mathematics, especially geometry. Technical knowledge is applied when angles and dimensions of a building are taken into consideration, and creative abilities are necessary to envision the structure as a pleasing combination of geometrical forms.

In designing a building, an architect must take into account a variety of considerations, such as the client's desires, building codes, legal requirements, and environmental constraints. A successful architect will find a way to focus these competing forces into the construction of a beautiful and functional structure.

INVESTIGATION

The Golden Rectangle The ratio of the length of a golden rectangle to its width creates a form that is visually pleasing. This ratio is referred to as the *golden ratio.* Find out the value of the golden ratio. Then find a window whose length and width form the golden ratio. What are the dimensions of this window? Where is the window located?

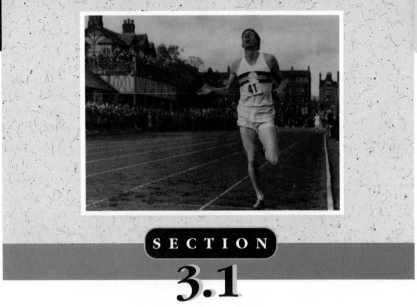

3.1

Linear Measurement

LINEAR UNITS

In 1954, the British track star Roger Bannister became the first person to run a mile in less than four minutes. Exactly how far is a mile?

A mile is a unit of **linear** measurement—a measure of length or distance. Other examples of linear units are inches, centimeters, meters, yards, kilometers, and microns. There are two basic systems of measurement, the English system and the metric system. The charts show some of the linear units in each system and the units' relationship to each other.

English System	Metric System
12 inches = 1 foot	10 millimeters = 1 centimeter
3 feet = 1 yard	100 centimeters = 1 meter
1760 yards = 1 mile	1000 meters = 1 kilometer
5280 feet = 1 mile	

Did you notice that the metric system is based on powers of ten? Many people think this makes it easier to use than the English system.

Example 1

Measure the butterfly's wingspan
a Using an English-system ruler
b Using a metric ruler

Solution

a Using an English-system ruler, we find that the butterfly's wingspan is about $2\frac{3}{8}$ inches.
b Using a metric ruler, we find that the butterfly's wingspan is about 6.1 centimeters, or about 61 millimeters.

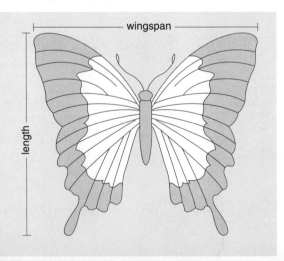

length
wingspan

A **polygon** is a closed figure made up of line segments that intersect at their endpoints. Each point of intersection is a **vertex** of the polygon. (The plural of *vertex* is *vertices*.)

Polygons are usually classified by their number of **sides** (segments).

Number of Sides	Name of Polygon
3	Triangle
4	Quadrilateral
5	Pentagon
6	Hexagon
7	Heptagon
8	Octagon
9	Nonagon
10	Decagon

Example 2
a Identify the type of polygon.
b Explain how to find the perimeter of the polygon.

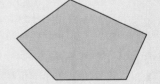

Solution
a The polygon is a pentagon because it has five sides.
b The perimeter of a polygon is the distance around it. So, to find the perimeter of this pentagon, we would measure the length of each side, then find the sum of all the lengths.

A segment that connects two vertices of a polygon, but is not a side of the polygon, is called a **diagonal.**

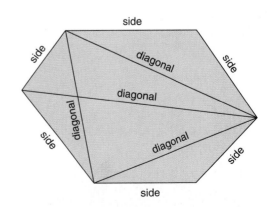

How do the two diagonals of any rectangle compare? Try measuring the diagonals of each of these three rectangles.

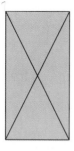 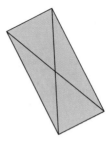 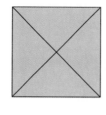

In each case, the two diagonals appear to be the same length. Segments that have the same length are called ***congruent***. Do you think the diagonals of all rectangles are congruent?

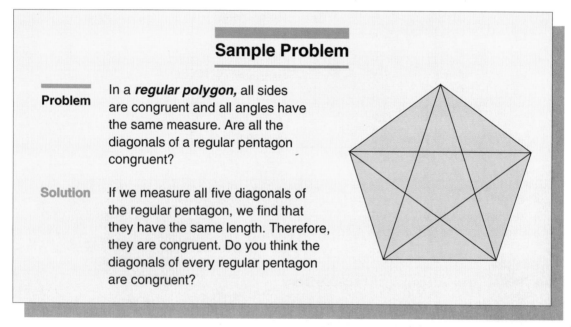

Sample Problem

Problem   In a ***regular polygon,*** all sides are congruent and all angles have the same measure. Are all the diagonals of a regular pentagon congruent?

Solution   If we measure all five diagonals of the regular pentagon, we find that they have the same length. Therefore, they are congruent. Do you think the diagonals of every regular pentagon are congruent?

Think and Discuss

1 How long is the segment?

2 Explain the difference between the perimeter of a polygon and the area of a polygon.

3 The fence posts of a fence are 6 feet apart. The fence is 138 feet long. How many fence posts are there?

In problems 4–9, is the statement true *always, sometimes,* or *never?*

4 A percent of a number is less than the number.

5 A rectangle is a parallelogram.

6 A parallelogram is a rectangle.

7 Every fraction can be written in standard form.

8 A rectangle is a quadrilateral.

9 A square is a rectangle.

10 A calculator may express a number as  which means 2×10^9.
  a Write 2 E 9 in standard form.
  b Use your calculator to multiply $456{,}789 \times 456{,}789$. Express the result in standard form.

Problems and Applications

11 Measure the length of the butterfly in Example 1
  a Using an English-system ruler
  b Using a metric ruler

12 How long is the segment?

13 Is the statement *true* or *false?*
  a The diagonals of a rectangle are congruent.
  b The diagonals of a regular hexagon are congruent.
  c All radii of a circle are congruent.
  d The diagonals of a regular octagon are congruent.

14 Copy and complete the table so that it shows the number of diagonals belonging to a polygon with the given number of sides.

Sides	3	4	5	6	7	8	9	10	11	12
Diagonals										

In problems 15–18, determine which distance is longer.

15 20 inches or 2 feet

16 1 mile or 2000 yards

17 15 millimeters or 1 centimeter

18 2150 meters or 2 kilometers

19 Find the value of $x^y + y^x$.

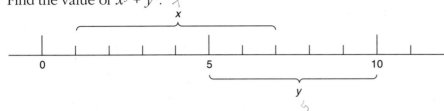

In problems 20–22, draw each polygon.

20 A 3-inch-by-5-inch rectangle

21 A triangle with sides of 4 inches, 5 inches, and 6 inches

22 A regular hexagon with sides of 3 centimeters

23 In football, a team has four downs to gain 10 yards for a first down. The Cats gained $3\frac{1}{2}$ yards on first down, 18 feet on second down, and 2 feet on third down. Did they gain enough yards for a first down? Explain your answer.

24 Cindy Centipede wiggled for 8 centimeters, walked for 35 millimeters, and waddled for 6.3 centimeters. How far did she go?

25 What is the probability that two words chosen from the set {*inch, pound, meter, liter*} both name
  a Measures of length?   **b** Metric units of measure?
  c English units of measure?   **d** Measures of volume?

26 How many centimeters are in 1 inch?

27 The horizontal distance between any two dots is three units, and the vertical distance is four units.
  a Find the perimeter of the figure.
  b Find the area of the enclosed region.

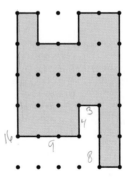

In problems 28–31, determine which measurement is longer.

28 50% of 1 yard or 125% of 1 foot   **29** 200% of 1 centimeter or 10% of 1 meter

30 400 yards or 25% of 1 mile   **31** 1 meter or 1 yard

32 **Communicating** An octagon is an eight-sided polygon, an octopus has eight arms, but October is the tenth month. Explain why this is so.

33 There are two types of socket wrenches—English and metric—for tightening bolts. Juan has a 1.4-centimeter bolt to tighten, but he has only English wrenches in sizes $\frac{7}{16}$, $\frac{1}{2}$, $\frac{9}{16}$, $\frac{5}{8}$, and $\frac{11}{16}$ inch. Which size wrench would work best?

34 Thelma and Louise wanted to find the area and the perimeter of a square tile. Thelma measured each side at 4 inches. She concluded that both the area and the perimeter were 16. Louise found the tile to be $\frac{1}{3}$ foot on each side but said that the area was less than the perimeter. Who was correct?

35 a Find the distance from A to B.

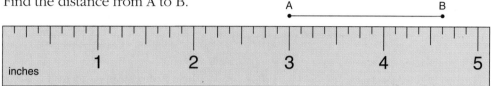

b If each $\frac{1}{4}$ inch on a blueprint represents 12 inches, what length is represented by a $3\frac{3}{4}$-inch segment?

◀ LOOKING BACK **Spiral Learning** LOOKING AHEAD ▶

---

36 Evaluate each expression. Use your calculator if you wish.
  a 4^3 **b** 4^6 **c** 4^9 **d** 4^{12} **e** 4^{15} **f** 4^{18}
  g 10^1 **h** 10^3 **i** 10^5 **j** 10^7 **k** 10^9 **l** 10^{11}

37 Multiply 3.14159265 by each power of ten.
  a 10   **b** 100   **c** 1000
  d $\frac{1}{10}$ **e** $\frac{1}{100}$ **f** $\frac{1}{1000}$

38 Evaluate each expression.
  a $\sqrt{9} + \sqrt{16}$ **b** $\sqrt{9 + 16}$
  c $3\sqrt{7} + 9$ **d** $\sqrt{4 \times 9 - 27}$

39 Use a scientific calculator to perform the following operations. What do you notice about the results?
  a 4 $\boxed{x^y}$ 1 $\boxed{=}$ **b** 4 $\boxed{x^y}$ 0 $\boxed{=}$
  c 4 $\boxed{x^y}$ 1 $\boxed{+/-}$ $\boxed{=}$ **d** 4 $\boxed{x^y}$ 2 $\boxed{+/-}$ $\boxed{=}$

40 Consumer Math A mail-order firm charges 5% of the price of an order for shipping and adds 6.5% sales tax (the shipping charge is not taxed). A spreadsheet was used to make this form for the mail-order firm.

	A	B
1	Order	276.84
2	Ship	
3	Tax	
4	Total	

  a What would be the total bill, including shipping and sales tax, for an order of $276.84?
  b Write an expression to calculate the total bill of an order of any size.
  c Use the cell names to express the formulas that should be placed in cells B2, B3, and B4 to give the correct answer.
  d If the value in B1 is changed to $475.50, what is the total bill?
  e If the shipping charge is raised to 7% and the order is $245.78, what is the total bill?

41 Which is greater, 2^6 or 6^2? How much greater?

42 Is the statement *true* or *false?*
    a $729 + 358 \cdot 254$ is less than $(729 + 358) \cdot 254$.
    b $277(589 + 816)$ is greater than $277 \cdot 589 + 277 \cdot 816$.

43 **a** What percentage of the length of $\overline{AC}$ is x?
    b What percentage of the length of $\overline{BC}$ is x?

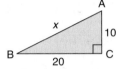

44 Harlee David's son can drive 172 miles on 5 gallons of gasoline. How much gasoline must he have to drive 130 miles?

45 **Geography**
    a How far is it from Tampa to Miami?
    b What is the greatest distance between any two points in Florida?

46 Copy each equation, filling in the blank to make a true statement.
    a $259.38 = (2.5938)(\underline{})$ **b** $81.36 = (8.136)(\underline{})$ **c** $0.0529 = (5.29)(\underline{})$

47 **Spreadsheet**   Using a spreadsheet, follow these steps:
    1. Enter the number 2 in cell A1.
    2. Enter +A1+3 in cell A2.
    3. Copy this formula to the cells below.

    a What adjustments did the spreadsheet make in your formula?
    b Use a spreadsheet to generate the pattern 1, 2, 4, 8, 16, 32, 64, …

Investigation

The English System   Write a report on the origin of the terms *inch, foot,* and *yard*. In your report, include how and when these terms were derived.

Scientific Notation

SCIENTIFIC NOTATION AND LARGE NUMBERS

The speed of light is about 300,000,000 meters per second. At that rate, light can travel around the world about seven times in one second!

We can write 300,000,000 as 3×10^8. This form of the number, called **scientific notation,** saves space and can simplify certain calculations. A number is expressed in scientific notation when it is expressed as the product of a power of 10 and a number that is greater than or equal to 1 and less than 10.

Example 1
Of 0.42×10^9, 4.2×10^8, and 42×10^7, which is written in scientific notation?

Solution
Since 4.2×10^8 is the only expression in which the multiplier is between 1 and 10, it is the only one correctly expressed in scientific notation.

Example 2
Convert 3.87×10^5 to standard form.

Solution
We move the decimal point five places to the right to multiply by 10^5.
$$3.87 \times 10^5 = 3.87 \times 100,000 = 387,000$$

Example 3
Convert 2345.6789 to scientific notation.

Solution
We move the decimal point three places to the left so that only one digit is to the left of the decimal point, and multiply by 1000, or 10^3.
$$2345.6789 = 2.3456789 \times 1000 = 2.3456789 \times 10^3$$

Your calculator probably has a key labeled $\boxed{EE}$, $\boxed{EXP}$, or $\boxed{EEX}$. This key is used to enter numbers in scientific notation.

Example 4

Evaluate $(4.267 \times 10^6)(6.34 \times 10^{11})$.

Solution

If we enter 4.267 $\boxed{EE}$ 6 $\boxed{\times}$ 6.34 $\boxed{EE}$ 11 $\boxed{=}$, the display shows $\boxed{2.705278\ \ 18}$ which means 2.705278×10^{18}.

SCIENTIFIC NOTATION AND SMALL NUMBERS

We can also use scientific notation to express very small numbers.

Example 5

Evaluate $0.00025 \div 5,000,000$.

Solution

On your calculator, enter 0.00025 $\boxed{\div}$ 5,000,000 $\boxed{=}$. The calculator will display $\boxed{5.\ \ ^{-11}}$. This means 5×10^{-11}. The negative exponent (-11) indicates that we are dividing by a power of 10 instead of multiplying by it. So $5 \times 10^{-11} = 5 \times \frac{1}{10^{11}} = \frac{5}{10^{11}} = 0.00000000005$.

Sample Problems

Problem 1 A light-year is the distance that light travels in one year. About how many centimeters are in a light-year?

Solution The speed of light is about 3×10^{10} centimeters per second. To approximate the number of centimeters in a light-year, we multiply the number of seconds in a year by the speed of light.

Since there are 365 days in a year, 24 hours in a day, 60 minutes in an hour, and 60 seconds in a minute, there are (365)(24)(60)(60), or 31,536,000, seconds in one year.

$$(31{,}536{,}000)(3 \times 10^{10}) = 9.4608 \times 10^{17}$$
$$\approx 9.5 \times 10^{17}$$

Light travels about 9.5×10^{17} centimeters in one year.

Problem 2 Evaluate $987{,}234.4 \div 10^8$, and express the answer in scientific notation.

102

Think and Discuss

1 Why do we use scientific notation?

2 What is true about all the expressions in Example 1?

3 Which number is greater?
   a -2 or -3 **b** 10^{-2} or 10^{-3} **c** 9.87×10^5 or 1.2×10^6

In problems 4–6, is the statement *true* or *false?*

4 $3591 \times 10^2 = 359.1$ 5 $0.00123 = \dfrac{1.23}{1000}$ 6 $5 \times 10^2 = 50^2$

7 Express 43,000 in scientific notation.

8 Express 8.135×10^9 in standard form.

9 Evaluate each expression.
   a $10^5 + 10^7$ **b** $10^5 \cdot 10^7$ **c** $10^7 \div 10^5$
   d $10^5 \div 10^7$ **e** $10^5 - 10^7$ **f** $10^7 - 10^5$

Problems and Applications

In problems 10–13, express each number in scientific notation.

10 $93,4$ 11 $385,12$ 12 0.01234 13 5647

14 **Science** In chemistry, a mole is a unit of measure equal to 6.02×10^{23} molecules of a substance. Write this number in standard form.

15 Which side of the triangle is the longest?

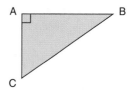

In problems 16 and 17, write each number in scientific notation.

16 52×10^6 17 0.52×10^6

In problems 18–21, write each expression in standard form.

18 3.05×10^4

19 23.4×10^{-2}

20 3.15648×10^3

21 8.7643×10^1

22 Arrange the numbers 130×10^7, 92.5×10^8, and 8.27×10^9 in order, from least to greatest.

23 In poker, there are 2,598,960 possible 5-card hands. Of these, 4 are royal flushes. What is the probability of getting a royal flush? Express your answer in scientific notation.

24 Science How long does it take sunlight to reach the Earth?

25 **a** What percent of 8×10^{30} is 2×10^{30}?
  b What percent of 8×10^{-2} is 8×10^{-3}?
  c What percent of 10^{23} is 10^{21}?

In problems 26–29, find the value of each expression. Express each answer in scientific notation.

26 $(3.5 \times 10^{14})(8.13 \times 10^{27})$

27 $\dfrac{9.52 \times 10^{44}}{4.12 \times 10^{12}}$

28 $5.1 \times 10^3 + 6.2 \times 10^4$

29 $95,476 \div (3 \times 10^8)$

30 Environmental Science In 1990, about 50 million tons of paper was used in the United States. The U.S. population in 1990 was about 250 million. What was the average number of pounds of paper used by each person?

31 **a** What is the length of $\overline{AB}$?
  b Find the area of $\triangle ABC$.
  c Find the perimeter of $\triangle ABC$.

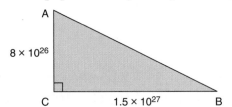

◀ LOOKING BACK **Spiral Learning** LOOKING AHEAD ▶

In problems 32 and 33, find a number that makes the equation true.

32 $\square^3 = 64$

33 $5 + 4 \cdot \triangle^2 = 41$

In problems 34–36, use a ruler to draw each polygon.

34 A rectangle measuring 4.5 centimeters by 5.6 centimeters

35 A rectangle with one 5-centimeter side and one 7-centimeter diagonal

36 A triangle with sides of 6 inches, 8 inches, and 10 inches

37 Write a square-root expression that has a value of 0.36.

38 A map legend indicates that 1 inch = 8.5 miles. What is the distance between two cities that are 6 inches apart on the map?

In problems 39–44, estimate the answer without using a calculator.

39 $\sqrt{85}$

40 $(9.9)^3$

41 $\sqrt{48}$

42 $4\sqrt{65}$

43 $\dfrac{18}{\sqrt{80}}$

44 $(9.1 - 4)^2$

45 **Health** In the state of Health, high school students are not allowed to wrestle unless 7% of their weight is body fat. Matt weighs 154 pounds, 10 pounds of which is body fat. Will Matt be allowed to wrestle, or will he need to increase his body fat?

46 Which of the expressions represent the area of rectangle ABCD? Why?
a $3 \cdot 4 + 3 \cdot 2 + 2 \cdot 4 + 2 \cdot 2$
b $3 + 2(4 + 2)$
c $(3 + 2)(4 + 2)$
d $4(3 + 2) + 2(3 + 2)$

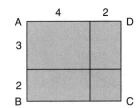

47 When this 10" × 10" × 10" cube is cut into 2" cubes as shown, exactly $5 \cdot 5 \cdot 5$, or 125, of the small cubes are produced. Copy the following table, indicating the greatest number of cubes of each size that can be cut from a 10" × 10" × 10" cube.

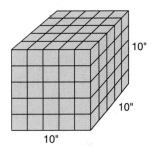

Size of cubes	1"	2"	3"	4"	5"	6"	7"	8"	9"
Number of cubes		125							

48 The pizza that Yogi, Ellie, and Mickey bought was cut into 12 slices. Yogi ate 6 slices, Ellie ate 3 slices, and Mickey ate 2 slices.
a What percent of the pizza did each person eat?
b What is the total percent of the pizza the three men ate?
c What percent of the pizza was not eaten?

49 What is the value of x if the perimeter of this polygon is 112 inches?

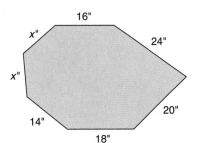

50 Use the digits 2, 3, 4, and 5 to make two 2-digit numbers whose product is as large as possible. Use each digit only once.

51 Evaluate each expression for $a = 4$, $b = 6$, and $c = 2$.
a b^2 **b** $4ac$ **c** $b^2 - 4ac$ **d** $\sqrt{b^2 - 4ac}$

52 **Communicating** What is the difference between a trapezoid and a parallelogram?

53 Margaret tosses a ring at random onto one of the numbered pegs on this pegboard.
a Find the probability that the number of the peg is a prime number.
b Find the probability that the number of the peg is a multiple of 2 or 3.

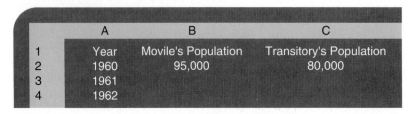

54 Arrange the numbers 4, 5, and 6 in the expression $\triangle \cdot \triangle^{\triangle}$ to make the greatest possible number.

55 Add parentheses and symbols ($+$, $-$, $\times$, $\div$) between the numbers 4 12 7 9 in the given order so that the value of the expression is
a 79   **b** 29   **c** 1   **d** 21

56 **Spreadsheets** Each year, 40% of the population of the town of Movile moves to Transitory, and the other 60% remains in Movile. Each year, 30% of the population of the town of Transitory moves to Movile, and the other 70% stays in Transitory. In 1960, the population of Movile was 95,000, and the population of Transitory was 80,000. Use a spreadsheet to make a table like the one shown.

	A	B	C
1	Year	Movile's Population	Transitory's Population
2	1960	95,000	80,000
3	1961		
4	1962		

Continue the spreadsheet through the present year. What happens to the populations over the years? (Hint: The formula for cell B3 is +0.6*B2+0.3*C2. Do you see why?)

Investigation

History Approximately how many minutes passed between the signing of the Declaration of Independence and the end of the American Civil War?

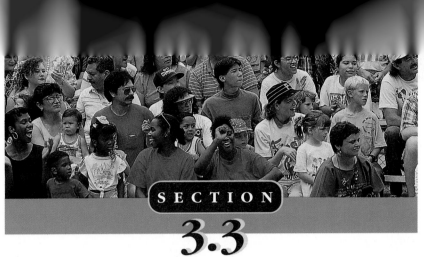

3.3
Estimation and Rounding

ACCURACY

The 1990 census gave the United States population as 248,709,873. Since the number is close to 249,000,000, we can say that in 1990, the population of the United States was 249 million, to the nearest million.

We often estimate a quantity to a reasonable accuracy. What is reasonable depends on the situation. For example, with a metric ruler, you can measure to within a millimeter, or one tenth of a centimeter. If a ruler has English units, you can round off to the nearest sixteenth of an inch. One general rule is that our result can be only as accurate as the least accurate measurement.

Example 1
What would be the most reasonable way to measure the height of a basketball player—to the nearest meter, to the nearest centimeter, or to the nearest millimeter?

Solution
Measuring to the nearest meter would not give a very accurate impression of the player's height, since all basketball players are about 2 meters tall. However, the height could not be measured accurately to the nearest millimeter. So in this case, the nearest centimeter is reasonable.

ROUNDING

We round a number to a specific place value. For example, rounding to the nearest ten-thousandth means leaving four numbers to the right of the decimal point.

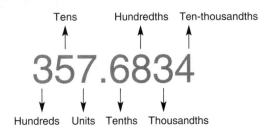

To help us decide whether to round a number up or down, we look at the value in the next lower decimal place and use the following rules.

1. If the value in the next decimal place is 5 or more, round up.
2. If the value in the next decimal place is less than 5, round down.

Example 2
Round 357.6834 to the nearest
a Ten   b Hundred   c Hundredth

Solution
a Since 7, the units digit, is greater than 5, we round up. Rounded to the nearest ten, 357.6834 is 360.
b Since the tens digit is 5, we round up. Rounded to the nearest hundred, 357.6834 is 400.
c Since 3, the thousandths digit, is less than 5, we round down. Rounded to the nearest hundredth, 357.6834 is 357.68.

However, there are some cases when it is necessary to revise the rules for rounding. Always make sure your answer is reasonable.

Example 3
There are 410 people going on a field trip. If the seating capacity of each bus is 44, how many buses are needed?

Solution
Since 410 ÷ 44 ≈ 9.32, we must round to 9 or 10. According to the rules for rounding, 9.32 should be rounded down to 9. However, if we do that, some people will not have a seat on the bus. In this case, it is necessary to revise the rules and round 9.32 up to 10. Therefore, 10 buses must be ordered.

Sample Problems

Problem 1 Barry has $10.00. How many burgers can he order?

BURGERS
$1.70 each

Solution   If we divide 10 by 1.7, we get about 5.88. In this case, we cannot round 5.88 up to 6 because Barry doesn't have enough money to buy the sixth burger. So Barry can buy only 5 burgers.

Problem 2 Maddy is painting the gutters that surround her house. How long is the ladder she is using?

11.25 ft

3.5 ft

Solution When rounding a number, always remember to round to a reasonable degree of accuracy. The top of the ladder is 11.25 feet above the ground, and the base of the ladder is 3.5 feet from the house. We can use the Pythagorean Theorem to solve this problem.

$$11.25^2 + 3.5^2 = (\text{hypotenuse})^2$$
$$126.5625 + 12.25 = (\text{hypotenuse})^2$$
$$138.8125 = (\text{hypotenuse})^2$$

So the ladder's length is $\sqrt{138.8125}$, or approximately 11.78187167, feet.
 This answer, however, suggests that we can determine the length of a ladder to the nearest hundred-millionth of a foot. Is this reasonable? Not even the most accurate ruler could be that precise. Furthermore, we cannot be sure that the original measurements were exact. It is more reasonable to round and say that the ladder is about 12 feet long.

Think and Discuss

1 Have someone record the time it takes you to perform a task. Then estimate how long it took. How accurate were you?

2 Have several people use rulers to measure the width of your teacher's desk. Then compare measurements. How accurate were you?

3 Estimate the height of the ceiling in your classroom. Then try to get an accurate measurement. How close was your estimate?

In problems 4–7, round each number to the nearest unit.

4 47.239   5 2.45   6 9.5   7 17.76

8 Jerome bought a pair of Atmosphere basketball shoes that cost $89.95. The sales tax was 7%. Estimate the cost of the shoes to the nearest dollar.

9 A survey in the 1800's determined the height of Mount Everest to be 29,000 feet (to the nearest foot). However, when the statistics were later published, the height was listed as 29,002 feet. Why do you think this was done?

Problems and Applications

In problems 10–12, round each number to the nearest ten-thousandth.

10 3.29681

11 4.2600

12 16.15936828

13 If you have $5.00, how many of each can you purchase?
  a Packages of gum at 65¢ each   **b** Boxes of candy at 50¢ each
  c Bags of chips at $1.29 each   **d** Newspapers at 45¢ each

14 A *right angle* is exactly 90°, an *acute angle* is less than 90°, and an *obtuse angle* is between 90° and 180°. Classify each angle as *right, acute,* or *obtuse.*

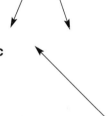

a   **b**

c   **d**

15 **Consumer Math**   The price of granola bars is 3 for $1. Gary bought one granola bar and was charged 34¢. How can you justify this method of rounding?

In problems 16–21, round each number to the nearest hundredth.

16 385.2865

17 475.391112

18 253.496

19 132.62

20 3.006

21 263.109

22 The shelves in Mr. Ditto's bookcase are 18 inches long. How many books can he put on each shelf if each book is
  a $\frac{3}{4}$ inch thick?   **b** $1\frac{1}{2}$ inches thick?
  c $1\frac{1}{3}$ inches thick?   **d** $\frac{3}{8}$ inch thick?

23 **Estimation**   Approximately how many seconds have you been alive?
  a 40,000   **b** 4,000,000
  c 400,000,000   **d** 400,000,000,000

24 **Communicating** Felix computed the length of the hypotenuse of the triangle to be 64.03124237 feet. Do you agree with his calculation?

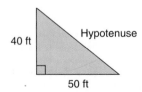

40 ft   Hypotenuse

50 ft

25 Discount Music Sales sells compact discs for $9.75 each. The sales tax is 6%. How many discs can Juanita buy for $50.00?

26 How many of the small cubes will fit inside the large cube?

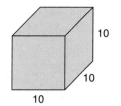

27 A newspaper reported that 53,000 people attended a ballgame. Assume that this number was rounded to the nearest thousand. What might have been the exact attendance? Give a range, from lowest to highest.

28 Kurt needs $2500.00 to buy a used car. He earns $9.75 per hour and works 40 hours per week. Assuming no pay deductions, how long would Kurt have to work in order to pay for the car?

29 **Consumer Math**   Victoria's Video has two plans for renting movies.

Plan 1   Rent one movie for one night for $3.
Plan 2   Pay an annual membership fee of $96; rent one movie for one night for $1.

How many movies would you need to rent annually to make the membership beneficial?

30 How many 16-ounce glasses of water will it take to fill a 10-gallon aquarium?

31 **Science**   A patient of Dr. J's has a heart rate of 36 beats every half minute.
a What is the average amount of time between two beats?
b How many beats occur per minute?

32 **Estimation**   The bases on a baseball diamond are 90 feet apart.
a Approximately how far did Babe Ruth run around the bases during his 714 home runs?
b Explain how you arrived at your estimated answer.

33 Using cruise control, Eddie can drive at a constant speed of 63 miles per hour. At that speed, his car gets 32.4 miles per gallon. If gasoline costs $1.32 per gallon and he travels 442 miles along an interstate highway,
a How long will the trip take?
b How much gasoline will he use?
c How much will the gasoline cost?

34 How many gallons of water are needed to fill a 24-inch-by-9-inch-by-18-inch aquarium if one cubic foot holds approximately 7.5 gallons of water?

35 **Spreadsheets**   Use a spreadsheet to create a table in which the numbers 1, 0.5, 0.25, 0.125, 0.0625, . . . are in the cells of column A. In column B, use formulas to list 30% of each value in column A.
a When does the spreadsheet begin to display the numbers in scientific notation?
b Set your spreadsheet to round to four decimal places. What happens to the entries in the table?

36 A rectangular container measuring 28 feet by 28 feet by 10 feet is filled with gasoline.

  a How much did it cost to fill the container if each cubic foot holds approximately 7.5 gallons of gasoline and each gallon costs $1.30?

  b How many miles could be driven using this gasoline if the drivers average 25 miles per gallon?

37 According to the U.S. Geological Survey, the Caspian Sea is 3363 feet deep. What does this mean?

◀ LOOKING BACK **Spiral Learning** LOOKING AHEAD ▶

---

38 Find the area of the trapezoid.

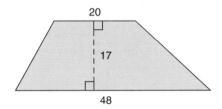

39 Stand and face north. Turn 90 degrees to the right. What direction are you facing?

40 Is each statement *true* or *false?*

  a $5 + 4^2 = 13$ **b** $5(4^2) = 400$

  c $5 \cdot 4^2 = 40$ **d** $5 \cdot 4^2 = 80$

41 The Furd Family owned two cars, five bicycles, two tricycles, and a motorcycle. What fraction of their tires belongs to vehicles with motors? (Don't forget that each car has a spare tire.)

42 Draw a triangle with sides of the following lengths.

  a 5 centimeters, 6 centimeters, 7 centimeters

  b 5 centimeters, 5 centimeters, 3 centimeters

  c 5 centimeters, 5 centimeters, 5 centimeters

43 Spreadsheets

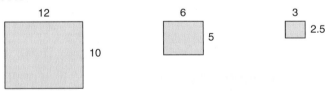

  a What is the perimeter of each figure?

  b Explain the pattern.

  c A spreadsheet was used to calculate the perimeters. What formula was probably entered in cell B4 to calculate the value in B4 in terms of the value in B3.

	A	B	C
1	Length	Width	Perimeter
2	12	10	44
3	6	5	22
4	3	2.5	11

44 Which angle is larger?

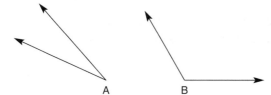

45 Find the value of each expression.

a $(3.7 \times 10^4) + (5.2 \times 10^3)$

b $\dfrac{3.7 \times 10^4}{5.2 \times 10^3}$

c $(3.7 \times 10^4) - (5.2 \times 10^3)$

d $(3.7 \times 10^4)(5.2 \times 10^3)$

46 Find the distance from A to B.

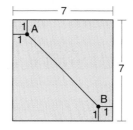

In problems 47–49, write each number in standard form.

47 5.23×10^1 **48** 5.23×10^{-4} **49** 5.23×10^6

In problems 50 and 51, is each statement *true* or *false?*

50 If $1 + a = 5$, then $a^2 + a = 30$.   **51** If $1 + x = 4$, then $x^x = 256$.

52 **Communicating**

a If $c = \sqrt{9^2 + 12^2}$, what's the value of c?
b Explain why this formula works.

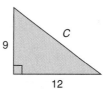

In problems 53–56, is each statement *true* or *false?*

53 If $x = 5$, then $x^x = 3125$.   **54** If $y = 2$, then $4 + 3y = 14$.

55 If $z = 9$, then $\sqrt{z} = 3$.   **56** $3.5^{3.5} \approx 80.21$

Investigation

In the News   Look through a newspaper and find several examples in which a rounded number is used to describe a situation. Then find several examples in which an exact number is used. Also find an example in which you cannot determine whether the number has been rounded or is exact.

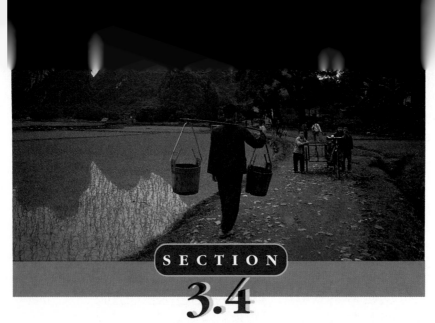

Understanding Equations

SOLVING AN EQUATION

We have solved many problems similar to ☐ + 7 = 15. In this equation, ☐ is a **variable.** A variable is a symbol that represents a number. If we replace the ☐ with 8, the equation will be true. By making this replacement, we have solved the equation. This type of equation is more commonly written as $x + 7 = 15$, with solution $x = 8$. In this case, x is the variable.

Example 1

Solve the equation $3x + 7 = 25$, choosing numbers from the set $\{4, 5, 6\}$.

Solution

We will substitute each number for the x to determine whether that number makes the equation true.

Try $x = 4$		**Try $x = 5$**		**Try $x = 6$**	
Left Side	**Right Side**	**Left Side**	**Right Side**	**Left Side**	**Right Side**
= 3(4) + 7	= 25	= 3(5) + 7	= 25	= 3(6) + 7	= 25
= 19		= 22		= 25	
False		False		True	

We say that 6 is a **solution** of the equation.

Example 2

Solve $c = 0.75 + 6(0.40)$ for c.

Solution

$c = 0.75 + 6(0.40)$
  $= 0.75 + 2.40$
  $= 3.15$

SINKIN DONUT SHOP

Doughnuts . . . . 40¢ each

Coffee . . . . 75¢

ESTIMATING SOLUTIONS

One good way to solve an equation is to guess and check—make a guess, check to see if the number is too large or too small, and revise the guess.

Example 3
Solve the equation $x^x = 8$.

Solution
Our goal is to find a number that when raised to itself equals 8. We know that $2^2 = 4$ and $3^3 = 27$, so the number we are looking for must be between 2 and 3.

Let's try $x = 2.4$. Enter 2.4 $\boxed{x^y}$ 2.4 $\boxed{=}$ on your calculator. Since $2.4^{2.4} \approx 8.175$, 2.4 is too large. Let's try 2.3. Since $2.3^{2.3} \approx 6.79$, 2.3 is too small. So the number we are looking for must be between 2.3 and 2.4, probably closer to 2.4. Let's try some more values.

$$2.38^{2.38} \approx 7.875$$
$$2.39^{2.39} \approx 8.0236$$

We now know that x is between 2.38 and 2.39. If we continue this process, we will get an even closer approximation.

INVERSE OPERATIONS

Inverse operations—operations that reverse the effect of each other—are commonly used to solve equations.

- Addition and subtraction are inverse operations.
- Multiplication and division are inverse operations.
- Taking the square root and squaring are inverse operations.

Example 4
Solve the equation $12x = 54$.

Solution
The first thing we may recognize is that the variable is being multiplied by 12. Therefore, to solve the equation, we will use the inverse operation of dividing by 12.

$$12 \cdot x = 54$$
$$x = 54 \div 12$$
$$= 4.5$$

It is always important to check the solution to see if it works. Since $12(4.5) = 54$, $x = 4.5$ is the answer.

Example 5

The area of the square is 72. Find the length, ℓ, of each side.

Solution

Recall that taking the square root of a number is the inverse operation of squaring the number. Therefore, if $\ell^2 = 72$, $\ell = \sqrt{72} \approx 8.5$.

Sample Problems

Problem 1

Solve the equation $x^2 + 15 = 8x$, choosing numbers from the set $\{1, 3, 5, 7\}$.

Solution

We will substitute each number for x to determine whether that number makes the equation a true statement.

Try $x = 1$		**Try $x = 3$**	
Left Side	**Right Side**	**Left Side**	**Right Side**
$1^2 + 15$	$= 8(1)$	$3^2 + 15$	$= 8(3)$
$= 1 + 15$	$= 8$	$= 9 + 15$	$= 24$
$= 16$		$= 24$	
	False		True

Try $x = 5$		**Try $x = 7$**	
Left Side	**Right Side**	**Left Side**	**Right Side**
$5^2 + 15$	$= 8(5)$	$7^2 + 15$	$= 8(7)$
$= 25 + 15$	$= 40$	$= 49 + 15$	$= 56$
$= 40$		$= 64$	
	True		False

We can say that both 3 and 5 are solutions of the equation.

Problem 2

Solve $y = 2 + 3x$ for y if $x = 7$.

Solution

If we substitute 7 for x in the equation, we get $y = 2 + 3(7) = 2 + 21 = 23$.

Problem 3

The base of a triangle with area 84 is 20. Find the height, h, of the triangle.

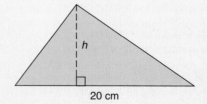

20 cm

Solution   Recall the formula for the area of a triangle.

$$\text{Area} = \tfrac{1}{2} \cdot \text{base} \cdot \text{height}$$
$$84 = \tfrac{1}{2} \cdot 20 \cdot h$$
$$84 = 10 \cdot h$$
$$8.4 = h$$

Since the variable is being multiplied by 10, we used the inverse operation of dividing by 10 to solve the equation. Since $84 = \tfrac{1}{2}(20)(8.4)$, the height of the triangle is 8.4.

Problem 4   Four blocks were put together to form a box. Find length ℓ.

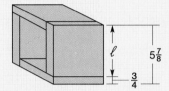

Solution   The length of the box can be represented by the equation

$$\ell + \tfrac{3}{4} = 5\tfrac{7}{8}$$

Since we are adding $\tfrac{3}{4}$ to the variable, we use the inverse operation, subtracting $\tfrac{3}{4}$, to solve for ℓ.

$$5\tfrac{7}{8} - \tfrac{3}{4} = 5\tfrac{7}{8} - \tfrac{6}{8} = 5\tfrac{1}{8}$$

Since $5\tfrac{1}{8} + \tfrac{3}{4} = 5\tfrac{7}{8}$, $\ell = 5\tfrac{1}{8}$ is the solution of the equation.

Think and Discuss

1 Solve the equation $4x + 10 = 38$, choosing numbers from the set $\{7, 9, 11\}$.

2 Solve for y if $y = 4 + 6x$ and $x = 3$.

3 List several pairs of values of x and y that make the equation $x + y = 10$ true.

In problems 4–7, solve each equation.

4 $x - 12 = 57$ **5** $x + 12 = 57$

6 $\dfrac{x}{12} = 57$ **7** $x(12) = 57$

8 Solve the equation $x^2 + 12 = 7x$, choosing numbers from the set $\{1, 2, 3, 4\}$.

9 Find the value of w that will make the perimeter of the rectangle 11.2.

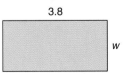

Problems and Applications

10 Solve for *a, b,* and *c.*

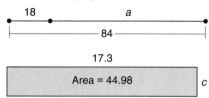

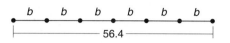

17.3

| Area = 44.98 | *c* |

In problems 11–16, solve each equation.

11 $x = 3 + 5(4)$

12 $x + 387 = 4129$

13 $\frac{x}{54} = 96$

14 $18.4x = 437.92$

15 $x - 23.5 = 90.1$

16 $12.3 = x - 11.2$

17 Find the value of *x* that will make the perimeter 53.4.

18 If $x = 3$ and $y = 3x + 4$, solve for *y*.

19 Find the length of each side of a square that has an area of 40.

20 If $x = 7$, $y = 5$, and $z = 16x - 8y$, solve for *z*.

21 Find as many values of *x* and *y* as you can for which $xy = 6$.

22 The height of a triangle with area 125 is 5. Find the length of the base of the triangle.

23 The area of a rectangle is 22,215.97 square inches. One side has length 684.20 inches. Find the length of the other side.

24 Solve the equations $19 + 8.4 = x$, $x + 13 = y$, and $\frac{y}{4} + \frac{x}{17} = z$ for *x, y,* and *z*.

25 **Spreadsheets** Examine the spreadsheet table. For what value(s) of *x* does $x^2 - 10 = 3x$?

	A	B	C
1	Value of X	X^2–10	3X
2	–5	15	–15
3	–4	6	–12
4	–3	–1	–9
5	–2	–6	–6
6	–1	–9	–3
7	0	–10	0
8	1	–9	3
9	2	–6	6
10	3	–1	9
11	4	6	12
12	5	15	15
13	6	26	18

26 The volume of a cube is 200. How long is each edge?

27 Solve $5w = w + 40$ for w.

28 **Communicating** The grape juice Jamie's little brother spilled on Jamie's homework covered part of this problem. Do you think $x = 1$ is a good estimate for the solution of this problem? Explain your answer.

$5x + 19.$ 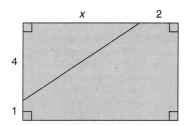 $= 24.$

29 The lengths of two sides of a triangle with a perimeter of 18 centimeters are 4.5 centimeters and 6 centimeters.
a Find the length of the third side.
b Draw the triangle accurately.
c If one angle of the triangle is selected at random, find the probability that it is acute.

30 Solve each equation for x.

a $\dfrac{1}{x} = \dfrac{3}{5}$ **b** $\dfrac{1}{x} = 6$ **c** $\dfrac{1}{x} = \dfrac{1}{3}$

In problems 31 and 32, approximate the solution of each equation to the nearest hundredth.

31 $x^x = 25$ **32** $8^x = 897$

33 Solve for N, M, and W.
a $78N + 4 = 160$ **b** $52M - 8 = 5$ **c** $512 - W = 437$

34 Solve the equations $a + b + c = 24$, $a + b = 11$, $a + c = 16$, and $b + c = 21$ for a, b, and c.

35 Find a value of x so that the area of the triangle is
a 20% of the area of the rectangle
b 30% of the area of the rectangle
c 40% of the area of the rectangle

◀ LOOKING BACK **Spiral Learning** LOOKING AHEAD ▶

---

36 Arrange angles A, B, and C in order, from smallest to largest.

37 Evaluate the expression $(v - x)(w - x)(x - x)(y - x)(z - x)$ for $v = 21$, $w = 19$, $x = 17$, $y = 15$, and $z = 13$.

$P \bullet \partial$ 1884

38 A right angle is exactly 90°, an acute angle is less than 90°, and an obtuse angle is between 90° and 180°. Classify each angle as *acute, right,* or *obtuse.*

39 The area of the rectangle is 25.6 square centimeters.
   a Find the lengths of the other three sides.
   b Draw the rectangle accurately.
   c Find the perimeter of the rectangle.

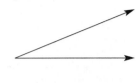

4.2 cm

40 Every day Jo Ger runs from his house to a circular track. The diameter of this track is 40 yards. He runs around the track 15 times, then back home. All together he runs about 3000 yards. How far is it from his home to the track?

$B \cdot 4$

In problems 41 and 42, solve each triangle for the length of the third side.

41
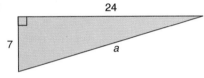

42
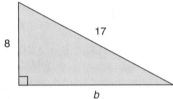

43 If the shaded area of the circle is greater than 100 cm², what is the length of the radius, to the nearest tenth of a centimeter?

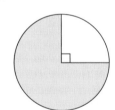

44 What percent of 8×10^7 is 3.2×10^6?
$0_{P0}0_{000}$ $\overline{60000}$

Investigation

Merchandising   Interview someone who works in a store. Find out what the average percent markup is on merchandise in that store. Give examples of two or three items, stating the cost to the store and the list price. Is the percent markup a percent of the cost or of the list price?

3.5

Angle Measurement

ROTATIONS

If you face any direction and turn all the way around in a complete circle so that you are facing the same direction as when you started, you have rotated 360°. If you turn halfway around (a half circle), you have rotated 180°. If you make a quarter turn, you have rotated 90°.

To represent a rotation, we begin with a **vertex,** the center of rotation. The **initial ray** shows the initial direction, and the rotation is represented by the curved arrow. The final position is shown by the **final ray.** Together, the two rays form an **angle.**

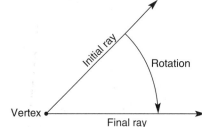

Example 1
What angle is formed by the hands of a clock at 5:00?

Solution
Recall that there are 360° in a circle. The numbers on the clock divide the 360° of the circular clock into twelve 30° intervals (360 ÷ 12 = 30). The rotation could be 150° (that is, 30° × 5) or 210° (that is, 30° × 7). We will agree to the following: When the problem does not say what the direction of the rotation is, we will give the smaller value. Therefore, we say that the hands of a clock form a 150° angle at 5:00.

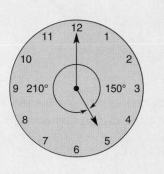

The symbol ∠ is used to represent the word *angle.* This angle can be named in three different ways. The vertex can be used to name the angle (∠A). Or one point from each ray, or **side,** of the angle can be used along with the vertex (∠BAC or ∠CAB). When three points are used, the vertex is always named in the middle.

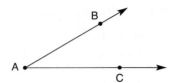

Example 2
Name three angles in the diagram.

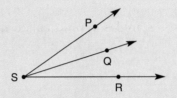

Solution
There are two smaller angles: ∠PSQ and ∠QSR. The largest angle is ∠PSR.

A **protractor** is an instrument used to measure angles. Here are some guidelines on how to use a protractor to measure an angle.

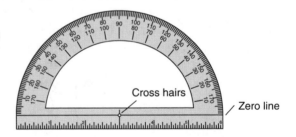

1. Estimate the measure of the angle.
   Is it acute, right, or obtuse?
   This is an acute angle.

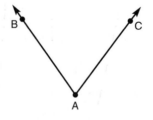

2. Locate the vertex and place the cross hairs on the vertex.

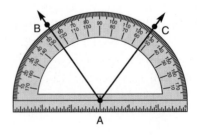

3. Rotate the protractor, keeping the cross hairs on the vertex, until one of the zero lines aligns with one side of the angle.

4. Read the angle measurement by determining the place where the other side of the angle crosses the row of numbers that corresponds to the zero line. We used the zero line on the right side of the protractor, so we will read the bottom row of numbers. (If we had used the zero

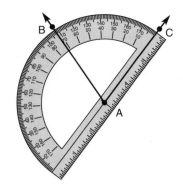

line on the left, we would have read the top row of numbers.) Since a protractor measures angles in units called *degrees*, we can say that ∠A is a 72° angle. We can also write m∠A = 72, which is read "the measure of ∠A is equal to 72."

Example 3
Find the measure of each angle.

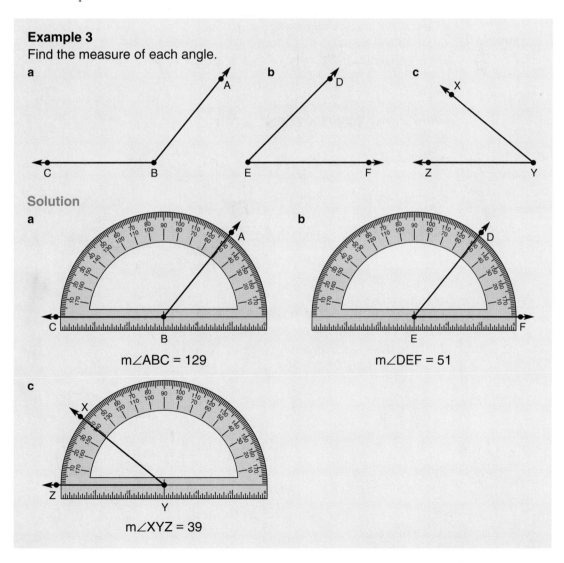

Solution

a   m∠ABC = 129

b   m∠DEF = 51

c   m∠XYZ = 39

Sample Problems

Problem 1

Two angles with measures that add up to 90 are **complementary angles.** Each of the two angles is called the **complement** of the other. Two angles with measures that add up to 180 are **supplementary angles.** Each of the two angles is called the **supplement** of the other.
a Of the angles in Example 3, which two are complementary?
b Of the angles in Example 3, which two are supplementary?

Solution

a ∠DEF and ∠XYZ are complementary because
m∠DEF + m∠XYZ = 51 + 39 = 90.
b ∠ABC and ∠DEF are supplementary because
m∠ABC + m∠DEF = 129 + 51 = 180.
Notice that a 180° angle is a straight line.

Problem 2

Draw an 80° angle and label it ∠ABC. Then draw ray BD inside the angle so that m∠DBC = 20. Find the ratio of the measure of ∠DBC to the measure of ∠ABD.

Solution

We begin drawing ∠ABC by marking its vertex B, then drawing one of its sides, ray BC.

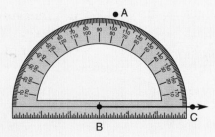

We align the protractor so that the cross hairs are at B and the zero line is on ray BC. We mark a point at 80° and label it A.

Then we draw ray BA so that m∠ABC = 80. Now we can repeat the process described above to draw ray BD on the inside of ∠ABC so that m∠DBC = 20.

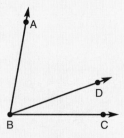

Since m∠ABC = 80 and m∠DBC = 20, m∠ABD = 80 − 20, or 60. The ratio of the measure of ∠DBC to the measure of ∠ABD is therefore $\frac{20}{60}$, or $\frac{1}{3}$.

Think and Discuss

1 If your initial direction is south and you rotate 90° to the right, what is your final direction?

2 Is the statement true *always, sometimes,* or *never?*
  a An acute angle has a supplement.
  b An acute angle has a complement.
  c An obtuse angle has a complement.
  d An obtuse angle has a supplement.

3 Why is it necessary to use three letters to name each angle in Example 2?

4 What is another name for each of the three angles in Example 2?

5 Identify the initial ray and the final ray of this angle.

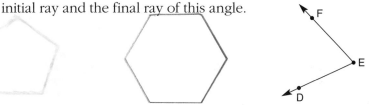

6 Name some situations in which it is important to know the measure of an angle.

7 If you rotated 120° to your left, then 70° to your right, at what angle, with respect to your original position, would you be facing?

In problems 8–11, find the measure of each angle. Then classify the angle as *acute, right,* or *obtuse*. (When you are asked to measure an angle, it is helpful to trace the angle onto another piece of paper and extend the angle's sides.)

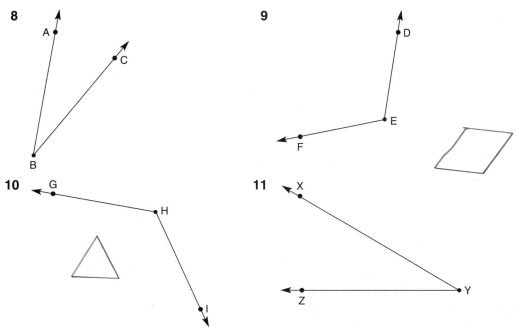

Problems and Applications

12 Find the angle formed by the hands of the clock at 4:00.

In problems 13–16, find the measure of each angle. Then classify the angle as *acute, right,* or *obtuse*.

13

14

15

16

In problems 17–20, draw an angle of the given number of degrees.

17 15°   **18** 105°   **19** 90°   **20** 180°

21 Name three angles in the diagram.

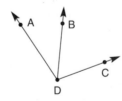

22 If you are facing west and rotate 90° to the left, then 180° to the right, in what direction are you facing?

23 If m∠A = 64,
   a What is the measure of the supplement of ∠A?
   b What is the measure of the complement of ∠A?

24 Find the value of n.

25 Draw an obtuse angle. Then draw a ray that divides it into two angles with equal measures.

26 a Find the measure of ∠ABC.
   b Draw an angle that is 80% of
      the measure of ∠ABC.

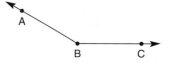

27 Draw a triangle with three 60° angles.

28 Communicating
   a If $a = 14°$, what is b?
   b If $a = 88°$, what is b?
   c Explain how to find b if you are given a.

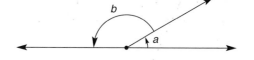

29 Draw a rectangle with dimensions 7 centimeters by 15 centimeters.

30 Find the value of $a + b + c$.

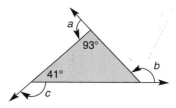

31 In triangle ABC, m∠A = 78 and the measure of ∠B is half the measure
of ∠A. What is the measure of ∠C?

32 If m∠ABC = 126, what is the
value of x?

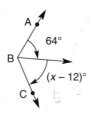

33 Estimating Costs   The blue segments
represent pipelines to the cities of Liberty
and Vernon. The cost of every two miles
of pipeline is $10,000,000.
   a Which pumping station, A, B, or C, will
      be the least expensive to pump from if
      costs for both cities are combined?
   b Estimate the cost of the pipelines from
      that station.

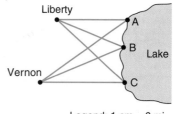

Legend: 1 cm = 2 mi

34 a Find the value of a.
   b Find the value of b.

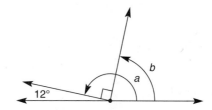

35 Draw a square with vertices A, B, C, and D, in that order. Put point E
midway between C and D. Connect A to E. Find the measure of ∠EAD.

36 Find the measure of each of
the supplementary angles.

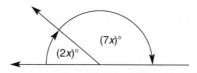

37 Solve each equation for x.

  a $x + 6 = 91.8$ **b** $6x = 91.8$

  c $x - 6 = 91.8$ **d** $\frac{x}{6} = 91.8$

38 Given that $\sqrt[3]{64} = 4$ and $\sqrt[3]{125} = 5$, estimate $\sqrt[3]{80}$ to the nearest thousandth.

39 What is the mean (average) measure of the angles of a triangle?

40 The Sunbirds have won 15 of their first 27 games. Find the least number of additional games they need to play and win so that they will have won 75% of their games.

In problems 41–44, write each number in scientific notation.

41 0.0392 **42** 41.2 **43** 3156 **44** 0.00002345

45 The perimeter of the pentagon is 71. Find the value of x.

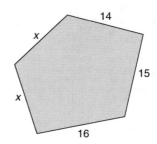

46 Evaluate each expression.

  a $\frac{1}{2} \cdot \frac{2}{3} \cdot \frac{3}{5} \cdot \frac{5}{7}$ **b** $\frac{3}{65} \cdot \frac{92}{7} \cdot \frac{65}{11} \cdot \frac{7}{31} \cdot \frac{31}{92}$

In problems 47–49, solve each equation for y.

47 $y - 312 = 587$ **48** $\frac{y}{2} = 36$ **49** $100y = 839.7$

50 Estimating The perimeter of the right triangle is 100 inches. Estimate, to the nearest tenth, the length of the shortest side of the triangle.

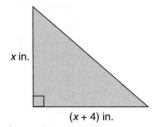

x in.

$(x + 4)$ in.

Investigation

Early Civilization Who decided that there were 360° in a circle? Why was that number chosen?

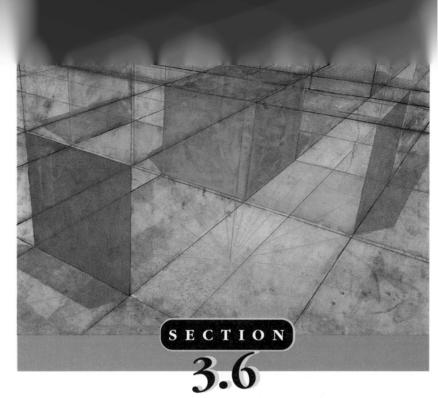

3.6

Constructions with Ruler and Protractor

In this section, you will learn how to draw figures accurately with a ruler and a protractor.

Example 1
Draw a triangle with a 65° angle between sides with lengths of 3.7 centimeters and 5.5 centimeters.

Solution
We can begin by drawing one of the sides of the triangle. In this case, we will draw a segment that is 3.7 centimeters long.

Then, using one endpoint of the segment as the vertex, we can use a protractor to construct a 65° angle.

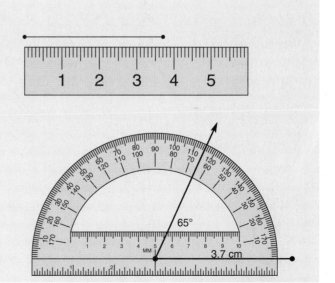

Now we can draw a segment 5.5 centimeters long for the other side of the angle. Then if we connect the ends of the segments, the triangle will be complete.

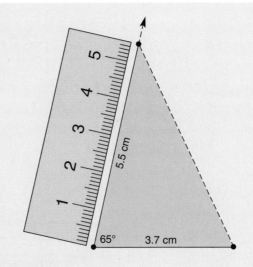

Example 2

Draw two parallel lines—one through point A and one through point B.

Solution

We begin by drawing any line through point A. Then we measure the angle.

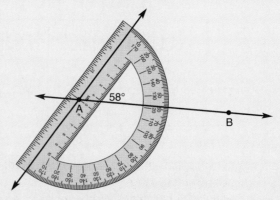

Now we construct the same size angle at the other point and draw the second line. The two lines are parallel. Can you figure out why?

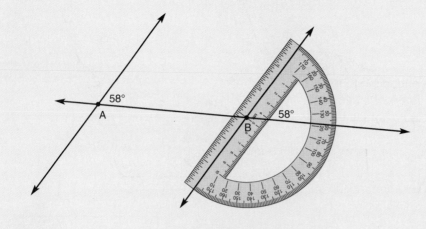

Sample Problem

Problem

Make an accurate drawing of this parallelogram.

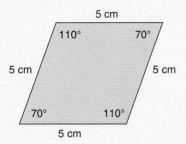

Solution

We will begin by drawing one of the sides. In this case, we will draw a horizontal segment 5 centimeters long. Then we will construct a 110° angle at an endpoint of this segment.

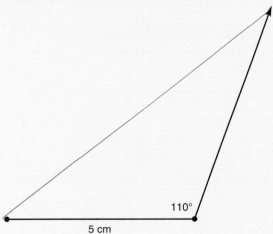

On the side of the angle, we can mark off a segment that is 5 centimeters long. Then we can construct a 70° angle at the other endpoint of the horizontal segment and mark off a 5-centimeter segment on the side of this angle.

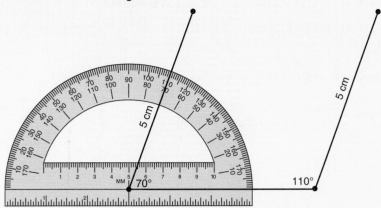

Finally, we connect the endpoints of the two segments to complete the parallelogram.

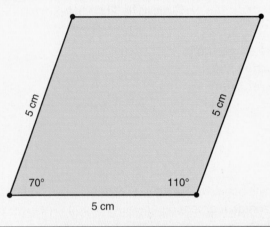

Think and Discuss

1 How is a trapezoid like a parallelogram? How is it different?

2 Draw a parallelogram with a 4-centimeter side, a 7-centimeter side, and a 60° angle between these sides. Draw a second parallelogram with the same dimensions. How do the two parallelograms compare?

3 Draw a trapezoid ABCD. Be sure $\overline{AB}$ and $\overline{CD}$ are parallel. Measure the four angles. What did you discover about
   a ∠A and ∠D?
   b ∠C and ∠B?

4 Explain how to draw a circle with a radius that is 6 centimeters long.

5 A method for drawing parallel lines is given in Example 2.
   a Explain why this method works.
   b Describe another method for drawing parallel lines.

6 Draw a triangle with angles of 50°, 50°, and 80°. Measure the lengths of the sides of the triangle. What did you discover?

In problems 7–9, accurately draw figures with the given dimensions.

7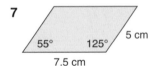

8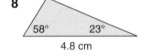

9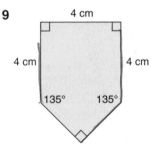

Problems and Applications

10 Draw an angle congruent to the one shown.
Use a protractor to construct
a Its complement
b Its supplement
c The supplement of its complement

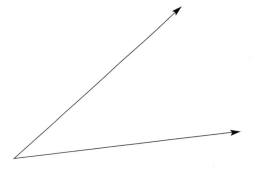

11 Construct a parallelogram with four congruent angles and with sides of 2.3 centimeters and 4.9 centimeters.

12 At least two sides of an isosceles triangle are equal in length. Draw an isosceles triangle and measure its three angles. What did you discover?

13 Accurately draw this figure using the given dimensions. Is each statement *true* or *false?*
(≅ means "is congruent to.")
a $\overline{AC} \cong \overline{BD}$
b $\angle A \cong \angle B$

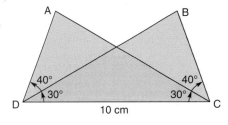

14 Make an accurate drawing of the figure, using the given dimensions. How many times longer is $\overline{AC}$ than $\overline{AB}$?

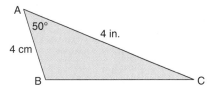

15 Draw a rectangle that has a length of 5 inches and a width of 12.7 centimeters.
a Find the ratio of the rectangle's length to its width.
b What is a special name for this kind of rectangle?

16 **Communicating** The area of the rectangle is 5050 square inches. The width is 68.3 inches. When the teacher asked for the length, Hal calculated that it is about 74 inches. Damon said it is 73.938506558 inches. With whom do you agree? Explain why.

17 Find the ratio of the complement of a 70° angle to the supplement of a 70° angle.

18 A stick 24 centimeters long is to be cut into four pieces to form a rectangle. The lengths of the sides are to be whole numbers. Draw and label the lengths of the sides of all such rectangles. Find the area of each rectangle.

19 Evaluate each expression.

    a $\sqrt{16 + 9}$ **b** $\sqrt{16} + \sqrt{9}$

20 **Estimating**   Sue buys four cans of soup at 89¢ per can, one loaf of bread at 97¢ per loaf, and three candy bars at 37¢ each.

    a Estimate whether $5 is enough to pay for her purchase.

    b If there is a 5% sales tax, will $6 be enough?

21 A circular region is divided into eight equal parts.

    a Find the ratio of the shaded area to the total area.

    b What percent of the circular region is shaded?

    c If a point is chosen at random inside the circle, what is the probability that it is in the shaded area?

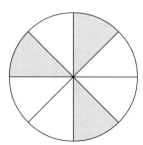

22 Solve each equation for n.

    a $\dfrac{2}{5} = \dfrac{n}{40}$ **b** $\dfrac{3}{11} = \dfrac{15}{n}$ **c** $\dfrac{n}{68} = \dfrac{8}{17}$ **d** $\dfrac{n}{17} = \dfrac{25}{85}$

23 **Spreadsheets**   A radiator contains four gallons of a mixture of water and antifreeze.

    a If the mixture is 50% antifreeze, how many gallons are water and how many are antifreeze?

    b If the mixture is 60% antifreeze, how many gallons are water and how many are antifreeze?

    c Use a spreadsheet to make a table showing how many gallons of antifreeze and water are in the radiator for mixtures containing from 40% to 100% antifreeze. Use intervals of 10% and a total amount of four gallons.

In problems 24–27, find the length of the third side of each triangle.

24
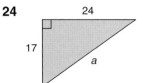

25
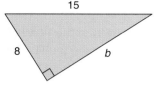

26
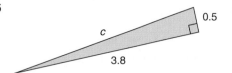

27

28 Tom set his cruise control at 57 miles per hour when he got on the interstate at 1:00 P.M. By 3:15 P.M. he had reached only the halfway point of his trip. How fast would he have to go to reach his destination by 5:00 P.M.?

29 Continue the pattern.

$$\left(\frac{1}{2}, \frac{1}{8}\right) \rightarrow \frac{3}{8}$$

$$\left(\frac{5}{12}, \frac{1}{4}\right) \rightarrow \frac{1}{6}$$

$$\left(\frac{2}{3}, \frac{1}{6}\right) \rightarrow \frac{1}{2}$$

$$\left(\frac{4}{5}, \frac{3}{10}\right) \rightarrow$$

30 **Spreadsheets** Using a spreadsheet, enter the formula @SQRT(A1^2+B1^2) in cell C1.
 a Try entering the values (3, 4), (5, 12), and (7, 24) in cells (A1, B1). What appears in cell C1 for each pair?
 b What does the formula do? What might A1, B1, and C1 represent?
 c What formula could you use to have the spreadsheet find A1 in terms of B1 and C1?

31 Is the statement true *always, sometimes,* or *never?*
 a The supplement of an obtuse angle is acute.
 b The complement of an obtuse angle is acute.
 c The supplement of an acute angle is acute.
 d The supplement of an acute angle is obtuse.
 e The complement of an acute angle is acute.

32 Is each statement *true* or *false?*
 a 4 inches = 4 feet
 b 3 feet + 1 foot = 4 feet

33 Write each number in lowest terms.
 a $\frac{15}{20}$
 b $\frac{25}{20}$
 c $\frac{9}{10}$

34 List several pairs of values of x and y for which the equation $3x + 4y = 48$ is true.

Investigation

Geometry In classical geometry constructions, what are the only two tools you are permitted to use? How is a straightedge different from a ruler? Learn how to bisect an angle by using a classical geometry construction. Demonstrate this construction to the class.

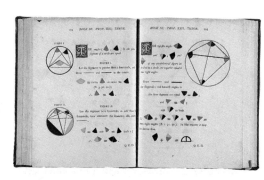

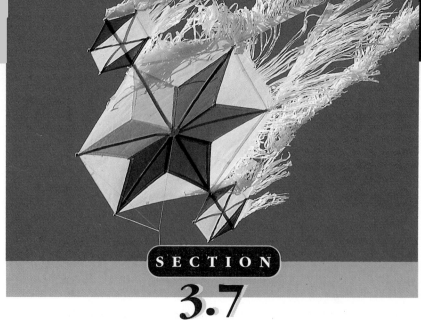

3.7
Geometric Properties

Draw a triangle, then tear off the corners of the triangle and rearrange them as shown below.

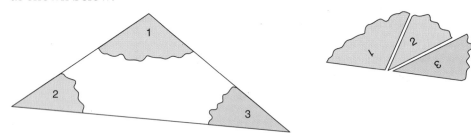

What did you discover?

Example 1

What is true about the sum of the measures of the angles of any triangle?

Solution

Let's draw some triangles and look for a pattern.

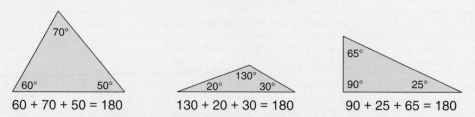

60 + 70 + 50 = 180   130 + 20 + 30 = 180   90 + 25 + 65 = 180

The sum of the measures of the angles in each triangle is 180. Do you think that this means that the sum of the measures of the angles of *any* triangle is 180°?

Example 2

What is the sum of the measures of the angles of a hexagon?

Solution

The diagonals drawn from one vertex of a hexagon divide the hexagon into four triangles. Therefore, the sum of the measures of the angles of the hexagon is 4 × 180, or 720.

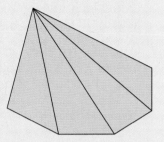

Example 3

An *equilateral* triangle has all sides congruent. What is true about the angles of an equilateral triangle?

Solution

If we measure the angles of several equilateral triangles, we find in each triangle that each angle has a measure of 60.

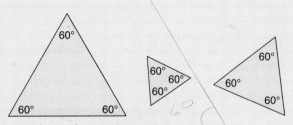

Figures like this, in which all angles are congruent, are called *equiangular.*

Sample Problem

Problem

Refer to the diagrams. What conclusions can you draw about parallelograms?

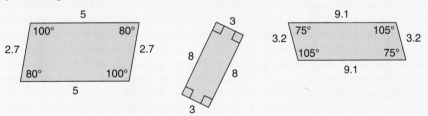

Solution

Here are some possible conclusions:
- Opposite sides of a parallelogram are congruent.
- Opposite angles of a parallelogram have equal measures.
- Consecutive angles of a parallelogram are supplementary.

Can you draw any more conclusions?

1 The measures of two angles of a triangle are given. What is the measure of the third angle?

a 90, 45   **b** 23, 72   **c** 106, 41   **d** 90, 53

2 Copy and complete the chart by filling in the sum of the measures of the interior angles of a polygon with the given number of sides.

Sides	3	4	5	6	7	8	9	10	11
Sum of angles									

In problems 3–5, find the sum of the measures of the angles of each polygon.

3 Quadrilateral   **4** Pentagon   **5** Octagon

In problems 6 and 7, is the statement true *always, sometimes,* or *never?*

6 An equilateral quadrilateral is equiangular.

7 An equilateral triangle is equiangular.

Problems and Applications

In problems 8–11, is the statement true *always, sometimes,* or *never?*

8 Two angles of a right triangle are acute.

9 If one angle of a triangle is obtuse, then the other two angles must be acute.

10 Two angles of a triangle are complementary.

11 Two angles of a triangle are supplementary.

12 The sides of the drawbridge rise to a 60° angle from horizontal. If these two sides are extended, what angle would be formed where they meet?

13 Draw $\triangle ABC$ so that $m\angle A = 55$, $m\angle B = 65$, and $m\angle C = 60$.
    a Which side is the longest?   **b** Which side is the shortest?

14 **Communicating** Draw several different isosceles triangles and measure their angles. What did you discover?

15 Is the statement *true* or *false?*
   a The diagonals of a rectangle are congruent.
   b The diagonals of any parallelogram are congruent.
   c A square is the only quadrilateral with four congruent sides.
   d Opposite angles of a parallelogram are congruent.
   e Each angle of a regular pentagon is 110°.

16 What is the mean (average) measure of the angles of a pentagon?

17 Find the number of degrees in ∠1, ∠2, and ∠3.

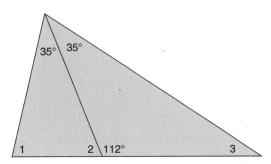

18 **Spreadsheets**
   a Use a spreadsheet to make a two-column table—one column with the numbers of sides of various polygons, the other column with the sum of the measures of the interior angles of each polygon.
   b What is the sum of the measures of the interior angles of a 15-sided polygon?

19 Lines *a* and *b* are parallel. What are the measures of the eight acute and obtuse angles in this figure?

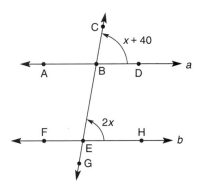

20 A polygon is ***convex*** if any two points in the interior of the polygon can be connected by a segment that lies entirely in the polygon's interior. Which of these polygons are convex?

   a   **b**   **c**   **d**

21 Draw two line segments that have different lengths and divide each other in half. Connect the endpoints of the segments to make a quadrilateral. What kind of quadrilateral is it?

22 Match each item in the first column with appropriate items in the other two columns.

A   2.54 centimeters   I   1 ton   1   Volume
B   144 square inches   II 1 cup   2   Length
C   2000 pounds   III 1 square foot   3   Weight
D   250 milliliters   IV 1 inch   4   Area

23 Evaluate each expression.

a $\frac{3}{5} \cdot \frac{5}{7} \cdot \frac{7}{11} \cdot \frac{11}{23} \cdot \frac{23}{41}$ **b** $4 \cdot \frac{3}{4} \cdot \frac{2}{3} \cdot \frac{7}{2}$

24 Jack loosely packed 8 ounces of feathers inside a box with a volume of 1 cubic foot (each edge was 1 foot long). Portia took the feathers and compressed them to fit into a cubical box with a volume of 27 cubic inches.
a How much do the feathers weigh in the smaller box?
b How many of the smaller boxes can fit into the larger box?

25 Draw each triangle and find its area. Which triangle has the greater area?

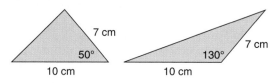

7 cm   50°   10 cm   7 cm   130°   10 cm

26 Solve each equation.

a $(0.78)x = 94$ **b** $\frac{2}{3} + x = \frac{8}{9}$
c $x^2 = 75$ **d** $x^x = 900$

27 Use the diagram to find each ratio.

a $\frac{BN}{NC}$ **b** $\frac{BT}{TM}$

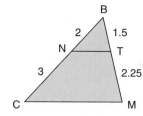

B   2   1.5   N   T   3   2.25   C   M

28 A large tree was struck by lightning and was broken as shown. About how tall was the tree before it was broken?

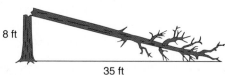

8 ft   35 ft

29 **a** Find the ratio of m∠ABD to m∠DBC.
b Find the ratio of m∠ABD to m∠ABC.
c What percent of m∠DBC is m∠ABD?
d What percent of m∠ABC is m∠ABD?

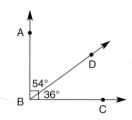

A   D   54°   36°   B   C

30 **Communicating** Explain how to find the center of a circle by using a ruler and protractor.

31 Determine the value of x.

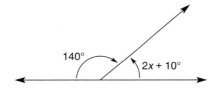

32 a Find some values of x and y for which $5x = 3y$.
  b For each pair of values, compute $\frac{x}{y}$.

33 If x is chosen from the set $\{0, 1, 2, 3, 4, 5\}$, what is the probability that x is a solution of $x^2 + 15 = 8x$?

34 Draw a triangle with sides 5 centimeters long, 7 centimeters long, and 8 centimeters long. Find the area of this triangle.

Investigation

Geometry Determine whether the three given lengths can be the lengths of the sides of a triangle. If they can, draw the triangle as accurately as possible. If they cannot, explain why not.

a 5 in., 8 in., 7 in.   **b** 10 cm, 20 cm, 8 cm
c 2 in., 5 in., 3 in.   **d** 220 mm, 70 mm, 190 mm

State a general rule for determining whether three lengths can be the lengths of the sides of a triangle.

Summary

CONCEPTS AND PROCEDURES

After studying this chapter, you should be able to

- Measure lengths, using both English and metric units (3.1)
- Recognize various polygons and investigate linear measurements associated with them (3.1)
- Use scientific notation to express large and small numbers (3.2)
- Recognize that different situations require different degrees of accuracy in measurement (3.3)
- Round a number to a specified number of decimal places (3.3)
- Express results to a reasonable degree of accuracy (3.3)
- Identify solutions of equations (3.4)
- Estimate the values of solutions of equations (3.4)
- Use inverse operations to solve equations (3.4)
- Interpret an angle as a rotation (3.5)
- Name angles (3.5)
- Use a protractor to measure angles (3.5)
- Use a ruler and a protractor to make accurate drawings of geometric figures (3.6)
- Discover some of the geometric properties of a figure (3.7)

VOCABULARY

acute angle (3.3)

angle (3.5)

complement (3.5)

complementary angles (3.5)

congruent (3.1)

convex (3.7)

degree (3.5)

diagonal (3.1)

equiangular (3.7)

equilateral (3.7)

final ray (3.5)

initial ray (3.5)

linear (3.1)

obtuse angle (3.3)

polygon (3.1)

protractor (3.5)

regular polygon (3.1)

right angle (3.3)

scientific notation (3.2)

side (3.1, 3.5)

solution (3.4)

supplement (3.5)

supplementary angles (3.5)

variable (3.4)

vertex (3.1, 3.5)

Review

1 Solve each equation for x.
  a $18 + x = 58.5$ **b** $18x = 58.5$
  c $x - 18 = 58.5$ **d** $\frac{x}{18} = 58.5$

In problems 2 and 3, express each number in scientific notation.

2 743,617   **3** 0.0041758

4 Construct a parallelogram with each side 4.7 centimeters long and with at least one 52° angle.

5 Find the length of $\overline{BC}$.

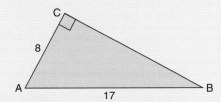

In problems 6 and 7, express each number in standard form.

6 3.86×10^{-2} **7** 6.44×10^5

8 Is $x = 4$ a solution of the equation?
  a $x^2 = 3x + 4$ **b** $2x + x^2 = 6x$
  c $x^x = 16x$ **d** $x^x = 256$

9 List some properties of a parallelogram.

10 What percent of the circular region is in the shaded sector?

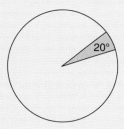

11 The measures of three angles of a pentagon are 60, 80, and 100. What is the sum of the measures of the other angles?

12 What percent of 6.5×10^7 is 3.25×10^6?

In problems 13–16, estimate the value of each expression.

13 $(4.1)(2.9)$ **14** $3.01^{1.99}$

15 $\frac{512}{10}$ **16** $788 \div 19$

17 Express the volume of the box in scientific notation.

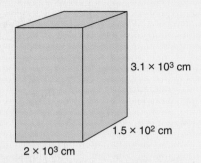

18 Draw three different triangles, each with a perimeter of 18 centimeters.

19 Solve for y if $x = 8$ and $y = 3x - 2$.

20 What are the measures of $\angle A$ and $\angle BCD$?

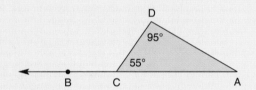

In problems 21–23, evaluate each expression.

21 $(10^6)(10^3)(10^{-4})$

22 $10^4 + 10^3 + 10^2 + 10^1$

23 $10^{-3} + 10^{-2} + 10^{-1}$

In problems 24 and 25, evaluate each expression.

24 60% of 50% of 40% of $250

25 12% of $250

26 Draw a line ℓ and locate a point P that is not on the line. Use a ruler and protractor to construct a line through point P parallel to line ℓ.

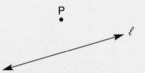

27 Give some examples of situations in which an approximation is preferable to an exact answer.

In problems 28 and 29, estimate the solution of each equation.

28 $x^2 = 18$

29 $x^x = 200$

30 Measure the top and the side of a piece of paper in centimeters. Find the ratio of the length of the top to the length of the side. Repeat the same procedure, using inches. What did you discover?

31 Find the value of x if $m\angle ABC = 60$.

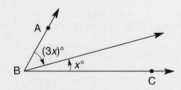

32 The length of one side of a triangle is 4.8 centimeters, the length of another side is 5.9 centimeters, and the perimeter of the triangle is 17 centimeters. Draw the triangle.

33 Draw a parallelogram in which the measures of one pair of opposite angles are 60. Measure the other angles. What did you discover?

34 Solve each equation for x.
  a $x + 7 = 10$ **b** $x + 10 = 7$

35 Use the figure to compute each ratio.

  a $\dfrac{a}{d}$ **b** $\dfrac{c}{f}$

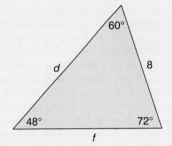

36 Draw a quadrilateral, other than a rectangle, with each side 2 inches long. Find the area of that quadrilateral.

37 Find the measure of each angle.
  a $\angle AOB$
  b $\angle COD$
  c $\angle DOB$

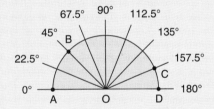

38 Which is greater, 0.036 or 3.6×10^{-3}?

39 Draw a line and pick a point on that line. Draw a 42° angle, using the point as its vertex. What is the measure of the obtuse angle in your diagram?

40 What is the ratio of the length of a shoelace that is 24 inches long to the length of a belt that is 3 feet long?

41 If r represents the radius of the circle and A represents its area, then $A = \pi r^2$, where $\pi \approx 3.1416$.
  a If $r = 7$, what is A?
  b If $r = 3.27$, what is A?
  c If $A = 153.86$, what is r?

42 Draw two line segments, each 4 inches long, that intersect at their midpoints. Connect the endpoints to form a quadrilateral.
  a Find the perimeter of the quadrilateral.
  b How can you do this problem so that the perimeter would be less or greater?

Test

1 Use a protractor to draw a triangle with angles of 27°, 68°, and 85°.

In problems 2–4, rewrite each number in scientific notation.

2 23,450

3 103.45

4 0.00791

5 Carefully trace a copy of the parallelogram shown. On the copy, label each angle with its measure and each side with its length. What do you notice about the angles and sides?

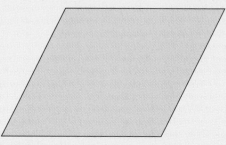

6 Solve the equation $\frac{4}{5} = \frac{x}{40}$ for x. Explain each step of your solution.

7 If you are facing east and you turn 90° to the left, 120° to the right, and 75° to the left, in what direction will you be facing?

8 If the perimeter of the triangle is $26\frac{1}{4}$ feet, what is the value of p?

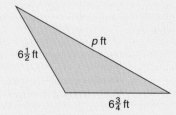

$6\frac{1}{2}$ ft

p ft

$6\frac{3}{4}$ ft

9 Which is shorter,
   a 30 yards or 100 feet?
   b $\frac{1}{2}$ mile or 100,000 inches?
   c 3.5×10^4 centimeters or 5.1×10^{-1} kilometer?

10 Find the measures of ∠BCA and ∠BCD.

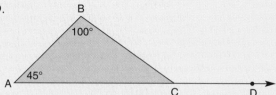

B

100°

45°

A   C   D

11 Estimate the solution of each equation.
   a $y^2 = 240$
   b $2^y = 240$

12 Rachel wants to draw a rectangle that has an area of 0.5 square meters. She starts by using a meterstick to draw a segment 80 centimeters long. How long should the other three sides of the rectangle be?

Draw each figure without lifting your pencil from the paper and without tracing any line twice.

1

2

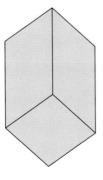

3

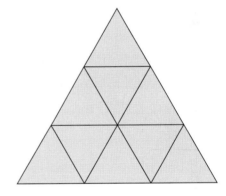

How many triangles are in each figure?

4

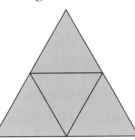

5

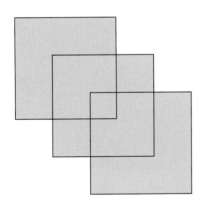

6 At the firm Dewey, Cheatem, and Howe, Inc., someone has been embezzling money. Each of the three executives made a statement to the police. Exactly one of them lied. Given the statements below, who was the guilty party?

Dewey: Cheatem did it.
Cheatem: Howe did it.
Howe: Cheatem lied when he said I did it.

Ratio
and
Proportion

AIRCRAFT DESIGNER Improvements are continually being made in the design of civilian and military aircraft. Aircraft are flying higher and faster and are becoming more automated. People who design these aircraft must be familiar with every aspect of aircraft construction and operation, including mechanics, guidance and control systems, propulsion systems, and communications. An aircraft designer must have a background in engineering, with studies in mathematics, physics, and materials science. Most aircraft designers are employed by private aerospace firms.

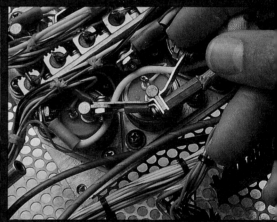

INVESTIGATION

Lift-to-Drag Ratios One important aspect of aircraft design is the creation of an efficient wing shape. The flow of air over an airplane's wing produces a force, called lift, that enables the plane to fly: the faster the flow, the greater the lift. On the other hand, any object that moves through the air is affected by a force known as drag, which slows down the object. Aircraft designers try to design wing shapes that will give planes a high *lift-to-drag ratio.* Do some research to find out about lift-to-drag ratios and how they are affected by the shapes of wings. What are the lift-to-drag ratios of various types of airplanes?

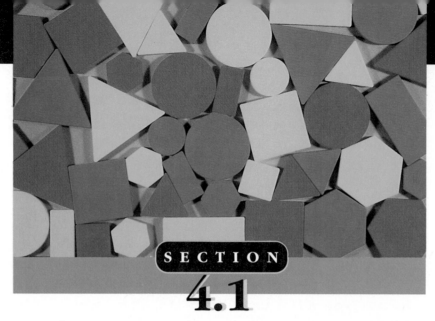

4.1

A Closer Look at Measurement

ATTRIBUTES AND UNITS

Young children are sometimes given blocks called attribute tiles to help them learn about shapes, colors, and sizes. An ***attribute*** is a characteristic, a quality that distinguishes an object from other objects. Some attributes, such as size, can be measured. In the preceding chapter, you learned about measuring one sort of size—length or distance. Size may also mean *area,* usually expressed in square units. Another sort of size is *volume,* the amount of space that an object takes up. It is usually expressed in cubic units.

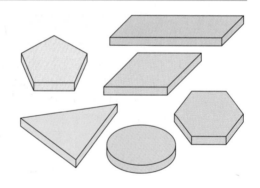

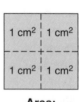

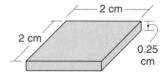

Linear Dimensions:
2 cm by 2 cm

Area:
4 cm²

Volume:
1 cm³

Notice how the exponents 2 and 3 are used to indicate square units and cubic units.

Units of capacity, such as quarts and liters, are used to measure the volume of liquids that a container can hold.

Many other attributes can be measured—mass, weight, time, temperature, speed, and cost are but a few—and a variety of units can be used to measure each. To avoid confusion, it is useful to ask yourself the following questions whenever you need to decide what unit you should use to express a measurement.

1. **Does the unit represent the attribute being measured?** It is impossible, for instance, to measure a distance in pints, since pints are units of capacity, not length. Similarly, we cannot measure temperatures in meters, lengths of time in ounces, or angles in square feet.

2. **Does the size of the unit fit the quantity being measured?** Although you could express your height in miles (it's about 0.001 mile), it is more reasonable to use a smaller unit, such as feet or centimeters. It would likewise be awkward (but not wrong) to express the weight of a dog in tons or the age of a friend in seconds.

Sometimes tradition makes a particular unit appropriate. For example, we measure speeds of ships in knots, lengths of horse races in furlongs, amounts of petroleum in barrels, and the area of land in acres.

METRIC UNITS

In Section 3.1, you learned about some metric units of length. The metric system is now the standard of measurement in most countries. It is also the basis for the units used in science. In the metric system, the basic unit of length is the meter, the basic unit of mass is the gram, and the basic unit of capacity is the liter. Larger and smaller units are obtained by multiplying and dividing these units by powers of 10. The following table shows how various prefixes—kilo-, centi-, etc. are used. You will use the units shown in bold face most frequently.

Attribute	Basic Unit	Other Units	Meaning
Length	*Meter*	*Kilometer*	1000 meters
		Hectometer	100 meters
		Dekameter	10 meters
		Decimeter	0.1 meter
		Centimeter	0.01 meter
		Millimeter	0.001 meter

The same prefixes are also used with grams and liters.

To see how metric units compare with English units, refer to the table of equivalent measurements in the back of this book.

When we want to compare or combine measurements of the same attribute, we usually need to express the measurements in the same units.

Example 1

On top of a 1-meter-high box is a box that is half a meter high. On top of that is a box that is 75 centimeters high. How high is the stack of boxes?

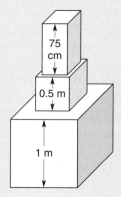

75 cm

0.5 m

1 m

Solution

In order to add the heights, we need to express them in the same units. The easiest way to do this is to rewrite centimeters as meters or rewrite meters as centimeters.

Method 1   1 m + 0.5 m + 75 cm
= 1 m + 0.5 m + 0.75 m
= 2.25 m

Method 2   1 m + 0.5 m + 75 cm
= 100 cm + 50 cm + 75 cm
= 225 cm

Since 2.25 m = 225 cm, the answers are the same.

Example 2

Evaluate each ratio of measurements.

a $\dfrac{9 \text{ feet}}{6 \text{ feet}}$

b $\dfrac{6 \text{ feet}}{2 \text{ yards}}$

Solution

Notice that in part **a** the units are the same, so they cancel. In part **b** we need to change the measurements to the same units.

a $\dfrac{9 \text{ feet}}{6 \text{ feet}} = \dfrac{3}{2}$

b $\dfrac{6 \text{ feet}}{2 \text{ yards}} = \dfrac{6 \text{ feet}}{6 \text{ feet}} = 1$

Sample Problems

Problem 1

Express 2 hours 12 minutes as a number of hours.

Solution

We need to change 12 minutes to hours. There are 60 minutes in an hour; so 1 minute is $\frac{1}{60}$ hour, and 12 minutes is $\frac{12}{60}$, or $\frac{1}{5}$, hour. Therefore, 2 hours 12 minutes is $2\frac{1}{5}$ hours.

Problem 2 If a speedboat travels at 65 kilometers per hour, how far can it travel in 2 hours 12 minutes?

Solution The boat travels 65 kilometers every hour. In the preceding problem, we found that 2 hours 12 minutes is equivalent to $2\frac{1}{5}$ hours.

$$1 \text{ hr } + 1 \text{ hr } + \frac{1}{5} \text{ hr } = 2\frac{1}{5} \text{ hr}$$

$$\downarrow \qquad \downarrow \qquad \downarrow$$

$$65 \text{ km} + 65 \text{ km} + \frac{1}{5}(65) \text{ km}$$

$$65 \text{ km} + 65 \text{ km} + 13 \text{ km} = 143 \text{ km}$$

Think and Discuss

In problems 1–8, choose from the box the units that would be most useful in measuring each attribute.

Quarts
Cents
Millimeters
Tons
Feet
Grams
Square centimeters
Fluidounces
Knots
Acres

1 The area of a postage stamp

2 The height of a building

3 The length of a housefly

4 The size of a lake

5 The amount of oil in a car's engine

6 The amount of scrap iron in a truck

7 The mass of a kernel of corn

8 The amount of root beer in a cup

9 Refer to the table of metric units in this section. What power of 10 seems to be indicated by each of these prefixes?
  a *Hecto-*   **b** *Deci-*   **c** *Milli-*
  d *Kilo-*   **e** *Centi-*   **f** *Deka-*

10 List as many attributes of this book as you can. Which of these attributes can be measured? What units might be used?

11 Would you use a 12-inch ruler, a meterstick, a 100-foot tape measure, or a car's odometer to measure
  a A vegetable garden?   **b** The length of a phone cord?
  c A baseball diamond?   **d** The distance between two cities?
  e A pencil?   **f** A poster hung on the wall?

12 Mr. Snackmeister can eat peanuts at a rate of 3 ounces per minute. If peanuts cost $2.88 per pound, how long would it take him to eat $4.50 worth of nuts?

13 A famous book by Jules Verne is titled *Twenty Thousand Leagues Under the Sea*. What do you think this title means?

Problems and Applications

14 Determine the value of n that makes the statement true.
 a n cm = 9 m **b** 5 yd = n in. **c** 5 yd = n ft

In problems 15–17, evaluate each ratio of measurements.

15 $\dfrac{2 \text{ feet}}{6 \text{ inches}}$ **16** $\dfrac{3 \text{ inches}}{1 \text{ foot}}$ **17** $\dfrac{4 \text{ feet}}{2 \text{ yards}}$

18 Find the area of a rectangle with the given dimensions. Be sure to include the proper units in your answer.
 a 3 cm by 5 cm **b** 4 in. by 6 in. **c** 5 m by 7 m

19 a What is the total length, in feet and inches, of segment AC?
 b Evaluate the sum $5\frac{8}{12} + 9\frac{7}{12}$.

A   B   C

5 ft 8 in.   9 ft 7 in.

20 **Consumer Math** If the cost of running an air conditioner is 10.4 cents per hour, how much does it cost to run the air conditioner for 250 hours?

21 Use the diagram to help you answer the following questions.
 a What fraction of a yard is a foot?
 b What fraction of a square yard is a square foot?
 c What fraction of a cubic yard is a cubic foot?

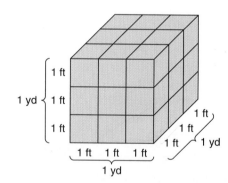

1 ft

1 yd 1 ft

1 ft

1 ft

1 ft

1 ft

1 yd

1 ft 1 ft 1 ft

1 yd

22 List two things you might measure with each unit.
 a Miles per hour **b** Meters per day **c** Inches per year

In problems 23–25, evaluate each ratio of amounts of money.

23 $\dfrac{3 \text{ quarters}}{5 \text{ dimes}}$ **24** $\dfrac{6 \text{ nickels}}{3 \text{ dimes}}$ **25** $\dfrac{4 \text{ quarters}}{15 \text{ dimes}}$

26 A gallon is equivalent to 4 quarts.
  a What percent of a gallon is a quart?
  b What percent of a quart is a gallon?

27 Find the difference between the heights of the buildings shown.

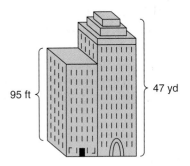

95 ft

47 yd

28 **Communicating**
  a Which is greater, 3 or 8?
  b Which is longer, 3 meters or 8 centimeters?
  c Explain why your answers to parts **a** and **b** were the same or were different.

29 Find the volume of a rectangular solid that measures 12 inches by 5 inches by 5 inches.

30 The criminal lawyer Dee Fender charges $125 per hour for her services. Use the picture of her billing notes to determine how much she earned on October 25.

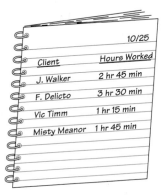

	10/25
Client	Hours Worked
J. Walker	2 hr 45 min
F. Delicto	3 hr 30 min
Vic Timm	1 hr 15 min
Misty Meanor	1 hr 45 min

31 Find the value of w for which the perimeter of the rectangle is 10 yards.

w

6 ft

32 **Consumer Math** A 12-ounce can of Meadowlark lemonade costs 60¢. How much does Meadowlark cost per ounce?

33 **Communicating**
  a Find the value of x.
  b Describe the situation that could be represented by the diagram.

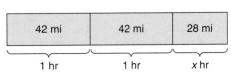

42 mi	42 mi	28 mi
1 hr	1 hr	x hr

34 Mickey is trying to estimate how much a trip to Florida will cost. One of the things he needs to calculate is the amount of gasoline he will need to buy. What kinds of measurements and units will he probably use in this calculation?

35 Di has 4 quarters, 3 dimes, and 2 nickels. Nick has 3 quarters, 5 dimes, and 2 nickels.
   a Determine the ratio of the number of coins that Di has to the number of coins that Nick has.
   b Determine the ratio of the value of Di's coins to the value of Nick's coins.

36 Six 1-by-1 squares can be joined edge to edge in various ways to form a figure with an area of 6. (Three possibilities are shown, but there are others.)
   a Find the perimeter of each figure shown.
   b What is the greatest possible perimeter of such a figure?
   c What is the least possible perimeter of such a figure?

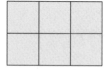 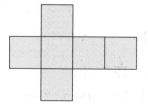 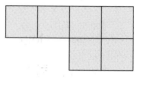

37 **Consumer Math**
   a A 19-inch television set is not 19 inches long or wide. To what might "19-inch" refer?
   b A spool of 6-pound-test fishing line does not weigh 6 pounds. To what might "6-pound" refer?

38 Rachel rode her bike for 2 hours at a speed of 12 mi/hr, then slowed down to 10 mi/hr for the next $1\frac{1}{2}$ hours. What was the total distance she traveled?

39 **Spreadsheets** The spreadsheet display shows that 1 mile per hour is equal to about 1.609 kilometers per hour. How could you use the copy feature of the spreadsheet to list speeds from 1 mi/hr to 100 mi/hr along with their equivalents in kilometers per hour?

B3: +A3*1.609		
	A	B
1	Mi/hr	Km/hr
2		
3	1	1.609
4		

40 Choose three of the units listed below, and write a description of each. Be sure to explain what the unit is used to measure, and give some examples of situations in which the unit might be used. (Look up the units in a dictionary or an encyclopedia if you need to.)
   a Angstrom   **b** Bushel   **c** Calorie   **d** Carat
   e Cord   **f** Decibel   **g** Fathom   **h** Furlong
   i Lumen   **j** Peck   **k** Roentgen   **l** Watt

41 Solve each equation for x.

a $x + 534 = 961.2$ **b** $x - 534 = 961.2$ **c** $534x = 961.2$

d $\frac{x}{534} = 961.2$ **e** $x + 961.2 = 534$ **f** $x + 534 = -961.2$

42 Which angle is greater, $\angle ACE$ or $\angle BCD$?

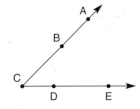

43 Evaluate each expression.

a $\frac{2}{3} \cdot \frac{3}{5} \cdot \frac{5}{7}$ **b** $\frac{a}{b} \cdot \frac{b}{c} \cdot \frac{c}{d}$

44 **Communicating** Greta added the fractions $\frac{1}{4}$ and $\frac{1}{6}$ in the following way.

$$\frac{1}{4} + \frac{1}{6} = \left(\frac{1}{4} \cdot \frac{3}{3}\right) + \left(\frac{1}{6} \cdot \frac{2}{2}\right) = \frac{3}{12} + \frac{2}{12} = \frac{5}{12}$$

Explain why she multiplied $\frac{1}{4}$ by $\frac{3}{3}$ and multiplied $\frac{1}{6}$ by $\frac{2}{2}$.

45 **Spreadsheets** Use a spreadsheet to make a table like the one shown. Continue the pattern to find the year when the ratio of Wally's age to Nancy's age was equal to 3.

Year	Wally's Age	Nancy's Age	Ratio
1991	48	24	2
1990	47	23	2.043
1989	46	22	2.09

46 Given that $\frac{3}{5} = \frac{6}{10}$, indicate whether each statement is *true* or *false*.

a $\frac{3}{10} = \frac{6}{5}$ **b** $3 \cdot 10 = 5 \cdot 6$ **c** $3 \cdot 6 = 5 \cdot 10$

47 Evaluate each expression.

a $\frac{3}{8} \cdot 8$ **b** $\frac{3 \cdot 8}{8}$ **c** $\frac{x}{y} \cdot y$ **d** $\frac{x \cdot y}{y}$

48 Arrange the four numbers 3.24×10^{-6}, 2×10^5, 2.13×10^{-7}, and 1.2×10^3 in order, from least to greatest.

Investigation

Mass and Weight Find out the scientific definitions of *mass* and *weight*. How do the attributes of mass and weight differ? In what kinds of situations would each be measured?

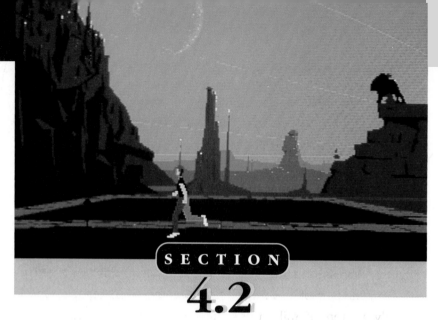

SECTION
4.2
Ratios of Measurements

RATIOS

A **ratio** is a way of comparing two values. The ratio of any value a to any value b can be written either in fraction form (that is, as $\frac{a}{b}$) or in the form $a{:}b$.

Example 1

While playing the video game Astroblaster, Luke fired 450 shots and destroyed 300 asteroids. What was the ratio of the number of destroyed asteroids to the number of shots fired?

Solution

We divide the number of destroyed asteroids by the number of shots. The ratio is $\frac{300}{450}$, or $\frac{2}{3}$, which can also be expressed in the form 2:3. This means that Luke destroyed, on the average, 2 asteroids with every 3 shots.

In Section 1.4 you saw that probabilities are ratios, but you may not realize that percents, speeds, averages, and many other quantities you encounter in your daily life are also based on ratios.

RATES

A ratio that compares measurements of two different attributes is called a **rate.** The word *per* is often a signal that a rate is being discussed.

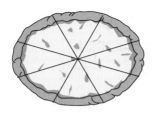

There are 4 pieces of pizza per person.

A bicycle wheel may make 100 revolutions per minute.

The gold sells for $396 per ounce.

A rate is usually expressed in terms of a **base unit** by rewriting the rate as a fraction with a denominator of 1. A rate of $\frac{135 \text{ miles}}{3 \text{ hours}}$, for example, can be reduced to $\frac{45 \text{ miles}}{1 \text{ hour}}$ (usually written "45 miles per hour," "45 mi/hr," or "45 mph").

Example 2
A boat traveled 126 kilometers in 4 hours. What was its average speed for the trip?

Solution
Speed is a kind of rate. It is calculated by evaluating the ratio $\frac{\text{distance}}{\text{time}}$.

$$\text{Speed} = \frac{\text{distance}}{\text{time}} = \frac{126 \text{ km}}{4 \text{ hr}} = \frac{31.5 \text{ km}}{1 \text{ hr}} = 31.5 \text{ km/hr}$$

The boat traveled at an average speed of 31.5 kilometers per hour. Notice that the units do not cancel when we evaluate a rate, since the measurements cannot be rewritten in terms of a common unit.

UNIT COSTS

People frequently want to compare similar products or services to determine which is cheapest. To do so, they may compare the items' **unit costs**—the costs of equal amounts of the items.

Example 3
If the box of Shreds costs $3.36 and the box of Flakes costs $2.64, which cereal is the better buy?

SHREDS
CEREAL

NET WEIGHT
16 OZ.

FLAKES
CEREAL

NET WEIGHT
12 OZ.

Since the boxes contain different amounts of cereal, it is difficult to make a direct comparison of the prices. We can, however, calculate the cost per ounce of each cereal.

Shreds: $\frac{\$3.36}{16 \text{ oz}} = \frac{\$0.21}{1 \text{ oz}}$, or $0.21 per ounce

Flakes: $\frac{\$2.64}{12 \text{ oz}} = \frac{\$0.22}{1 \text{ oz}}$, or $0.22 per ounce

An ounce of Shreds costs 1 cent less than an ounce of Flakes, so in terms of unit cost, Shreds is the better buy.

Sample Problems

Problem 1

Tito Tenspeed left home on his bicycle, traveling at a rate of 8 mi/hr. Half an hour later, his sister Tina rode off after him. If she averages 10 mi/hr, how long will it take her to catch Tito?

Solution

It is important to begin by thinking about the situation rather than just starting to do calculations. Since Tito travels 8 miles in one hour, he goes 4 miles in the half hour before Tina starts.

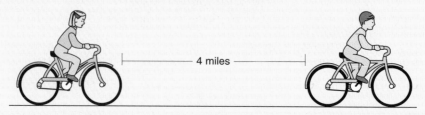
4 miles

Tina's speed of 10 mi/hr is 2 mi/hr faster than Tito's speed. She will therefore catch up to him by 2 miles every hour. Since Tito's head start is 4 miles, it will take Tina $\frac{4}{2}$, or 2, hours to overtake him.

Problem 2

The Dash Telephone Company's charge for a call between New York City and Chicago is $0.48 for the first minute and $0.19 for each additional minute. For the same call, the TT&T Company charges $0.75 for the first minute and $0.16 for each additional minute.
a Which company charges less for a 5-minute call between New York and Chicago?
b Which company charges less for a 20-minute call?

Solution　**a** A 5-minute call includes charges for the first minute and for 4 additional minutes.

Dash: $0.48 + 4($0.19) = $0.48 + $0.76 = $1.24
TT&T: $0.75 + 4($0.16) = $0.75 + $0.64 = $1.39

Dash charges $0.15 less for the call.

b A 20-minute call includes charges for the first minute and for 19 additional minutes.

Dash: $0.48 + 19($0.19) = $0.48 + $3.61 = $4.09
TT&T: $0.75 + 19($0.16) = $0.75 + $3.04 = $3.79

In this case, TT&T's charge is $0.30 less. So one company is less expensive for a 5-minute call, but the other company is less expensive for a 20-minute call.

Think and Discuss

1 Reduce each rate to a base unit.

a $\dfrac{200 \text{ miles}}{5 \text{ hours}}$　　　　**b** $\dfrac{75 \text{ dollars}}{5 \text{ books}}$　　　　**c** $\dfrac{720 \text{ miles}}{30 \text{ gallons}}$

2 The U.S. Postal Service handled 106,311,062,000 pieces of mail in 1980. There were about 227 million people in the United States at that time. Find the ratio of the number of pieces of mail to the number of people.

3 Is the statement *true* or *false?*

a Distance = speed + time　　　　　**b** Speed · distance = time

c $\dfrac{\text{Distance}}{\text{Speed}} = \text{time}$　　　　　　　**d** $\dfrac{\text{Distance}}{\text{Time}} = \text{speed}$

4 **Consumer Math**　　The makers of car B advertise that their car goes farther on a tank of gas than cars A, C, and D.

a Does the advertisement mean that car B is the most economical to drive? Why or why not?

b Which of the cars is the most economical to drive?

c Which is the least economical to drive?

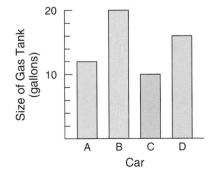

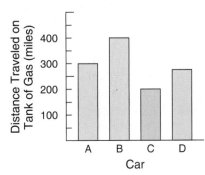

5 Consumer Math   In Example 3, on page 159, which cereal had the lower unit cost? What are some factors other than unit cost that help you determine the "better buy"?

6 Federico was bragging that he had received a raise of $80 a month. Katia said that she would not be impressed until she knew the ratio of his new salary to his old salary. Why?

Problems and Applications

7 Arrange the ratios $\frac{2}{3}, \frac{3}{5}, \frac{4}{7},$ and $\frac{5}{9}$ in order, from least to greatest.

.66   .6   .57   .55

8 Letitia can walk at a speed of 6.9 kilometers per hour. At that rate, how far could she walk in
   a 3 hours?   **b** 2 hours 20 minutes?

13.8

1.38

9 At Ed's Foods, the price of 10 pounds of potatoes is $4.50.
   a How much do the potatoes cost per pound?
   b How much do 25 pounds of potatoes cost?

10 a Determine the ratio $\frac{AC}{AB}$.

   b Determine the ratio $\frac{AC}{BC}$.

   c What is the perimeter of $\triangle ABC$?

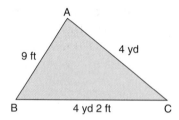

11 Bernice the bricklayer can set about 96 bricks per hour. If her workday is $7\frac{1}{2}$ hours long, about how many bricks can Bernice set in a day?

12 Consumer Math   If a 12-ounce bottle of shampoo costs $2.80 and an 18-ounce bottle of the same shampoo costs $4.00, which is the better buy?

13 A plane flew for 2 hours 45 minutes at a speed of 550 miles per hour. How far did the plane fly?

14 History   The first United States census was taken in 1790. According to this census, there were 3,172,006 white people and 757,208 black people. What was the ratio of black people to white people in the United States in 1790?

15 Farmer Fox raises corn on 120 acres of land. This year he expects a yield of about 185 bushels of corn per acre. About how many bushels of corn does he expect to harvest?

16 Consumer Math   In the Ticonderoga Boutique is a sign reading Erasers: 6 for a Dollar. How much would you expect to pay for one eraser?

17 Los Angeles and San Francisco are about 400 miles apart. If the speed limit on the highway connecting these cities is 65 miles per hour, what is the shortest time in which a person could drive from San Francisco to Los Angeles without breaking the law?

18 Billy Backstroke kept his head shaved while he was a member of his school's swimming team. After swimming season was over, he decided to let his hair grow out again. How long did it take his hair to reach a length of 4 inches? (Human hair grows about 0.01 inch per day.)

19 Find the ratio of m∠C to m∠B.

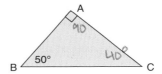

20 Annette drives 200 miles from her home to Bingo Beach in 4 hours. When she drove home, the trip took her 5 hours.
   a What was her average speed when she drove to the beach?
   b What was her average speed when she drove home?
   c What was her average speed for the round trip?

21 Two cars are directly opposite each other on a 1-mile oval track. One is traveling at 80 mph, the other at 95 mph. How long will it take the faster car to overtake the slower one?

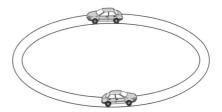

22 **Consumer Math** A 32-ounce bottle of Teucer cleaner costs $4.68. A 10-ounce bottle of Teucer concentrate costs $5.39. If it takes only a third as much concentrate as cleaner to do a cleaning job, which is the better buy?

23 When a person buys CD's from the Mayflower Compact Disc Club, the first disc costs $15.00, the second costs $7.50, and each additional disc costs $6.00. The Laser Trax store sells CD's for $9.75 each. If Aaron wants to buy three discs, where will he get the best price? Justify your answer.

24 **Spreadsheets** Use a spreadsheet to make a table showing the times needed to make a trip of 450 miles at speeds of 25, 30, 35, 40, 45, 50, 55, 60, and 65 miles per hour.

25 The graph shows numbers of magazine subscriptions sold during the annual fund-raising drive of the Yoknapatawpha School District. What is the ratio of the number sold by students in grades 9–12 to the number sold by students in grades 7–8?

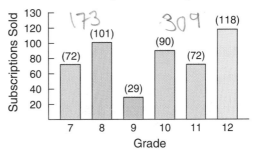

26 If $x = 3$ and $y = 3x + 4$, what is the value of y?

27 What percent of the tank is filled?

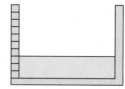

28 When Pinocchio was carved, his nose was 2 inches long. Each time he told a lie, his nose grew $\frac{1}{2}$ inch. How long was his nose after seven lies?

29 If $7 + (-4) = 3$ and $7 - (-4) = 11$, what is the value of each expression?

a $7 + (-6)$ **b** $7 - (-6)$ **c** $7 + (-7)$ **d** $3 - 7$

30 List six values of x and y for which $x \div y = 15$.

31 *Newspeak* magazine is offering a one-year subscription for $24.97. At a newsstand, each weekly issue of the magazine costs $1.50. What percent of the newsstand price is the subscription price?

32 Find the value of
  a $a + b$
  b $a + c$
  c $b + c$

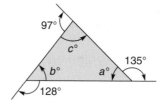

33 **Estimating** Julius, Leonard, Adolph, and Herbert went to a restaurant for dinner. The bill was $73.45, and they wanted to leave a 15% tip. Estimate the amount of the tip.

34 What is the ratio of the number of sides of a hexagon to the number of sides of a nonagon?

35 Suppose that the value of x is chosen at random from the set {2, 4, 6, 8, 10, 12}. What is the probability that the area of the small square will be more than 50% of the area of the large square?

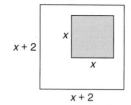

Investigation

Radar Guns Have you ever seen a "radar gun" being used to measure the speed of a car or the speed of a pitcher's fastball? Find out how this device works. How accurate are radar guns? If possible, interview a police officer to find out the margin for error in radar measurements of cars' speeds.

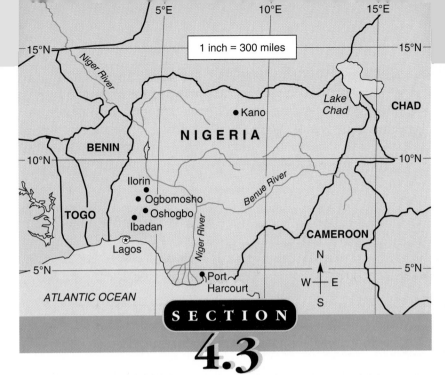

1 inch = 300 miles

SECTION 4.3

More Applications of Ratios

SCALE AND RATIOS

Most maps contain a legend telling how lengths on the map correspond to lengths in the real world. Each inch on the map above, for example, represents a length of 300 miles. The **scale** of a map is the ratio of distances on the map to real-world distances, so the scale of this map is 1 in. : 300 mi.

When units are the same, such as 1 ft:72 ft, you can give the scale without units, as in the following example.

Example 1

Orville built a 1:72 scale model of a jet plane. If the wingspan of the model is $9\frac{1}{2}$ inches, what is the wingspan of the real plane?

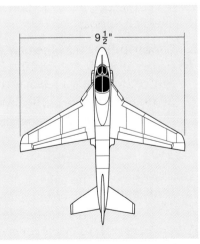

$9\frac{1}{2}$″

Solution

The scale of 1:72 means that each dimension of the real jet is 72 times the corresponding dimension of the model. Since the wingspan of the model is 9.5 inches, the wingspan of the jet is 9.5(72), or 684, inches. This is equivalent to 684 ÷ 12, or 57, feet.

DENSITY

Two objects can be exactly the same size but have different weights, or mass. That is because one is more *dense* than the other. A substance's **density** is the ratio of its mass to its volume.

$$\text{Density} = \frac{\text{mass}}{\text{volume}}$$

Example 2

If a 9-cubic-inch piece of granite has a mass of $14\frac{1}{2}$ ounces, what is the density of the granite?

Solution

We use the formula given above.

$$\text{Density} = \frac{\text{mass}}{\text{volume}} = \frac{14.5 \text{ oz}}{9 \text{ in.}^3} \approx \frac{1.61 \text{ oz}}{1 \text{ in.}^3}, \text{ or } 1.61 \text{ oz/in.}^3$$

The density of the granite is about 1.61 ounces per cubic inch.

This example shows that density is a kind of rate, expressed in units of mass per unit of volume. The table shows the densities of a few common substances in grams per cubic centimeter and in pounds per cubic foot. More densities are listed in the table of densities in the back of the book.

Substance	Density	
	g/cm³	lb/ft³
Liquid water	1.0	62.4
Ice	0.922	57.5
Steel	7.8	486.7
Aluminum	2.7	168.5
Wood (pine)	0.56	34.9

Sample Problems

Problem 1

Use the map of Nigeria on page 165 to find the distance, in miles, between Kano and Lagos.

Solution

If you use a ruler to measure the distance between Kano and Lagos on the map, you will find that they are about $1\frac{3}{4}$ inches apart. Since 1 inch on the map represents 300 miles, the cities are about $1\frac{3}{4} \cdot 300$, or 525, miles apart.

Problem 2

The cube on the left is made of ice.
The cube on the right is made of steel.
Which is heavier?

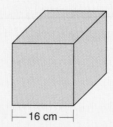

|— 16 cm —| |- 8 cm -|

Solution   The volume of the ice cube is 16^3, or 4096, cm^3. The volume of the steel cube is 8^3, or 512, cm^3. According to the table on page 166, the density of ice is 0.922 g/cm^3 and the density of steel is 7.8 g/cm^3.

Ice:

$$\text{Density} = \frac{\text{mass}}{\text{volume}}$$

$$0.922 \text{ g/cm}^3 = \frac{\text{mass}}{4096 \text{ cm}^3}$$

$$\frac{0.922 \text{ g}}{1 \text{ cm}^3}(4096 \text{ cm}^3) = \text{mass}$$

$$3777 \text{ g} \approx \text{mass}$$

Steel:

$$\text{Density} = \frac{\text{mass}}{\text{volume}}$$

$$7.8 \text{ g/cm}^3 = \frac{\text{mass}}{512 \text{ cm}^3}$$

$$\frac{7.8 \text{ g}}{1 \text{ cm}^3}(512 \text{ cm}^3) = \text{mass}$$

$$3994 \text{ g} \approx \text{mass}$$

The two cubes actually weigh about the same, with the steel cube being slightly heavier.

Think and Discuss

1 Estimating   Estimate the distance, by plane, between Thomasville and St. Henry.

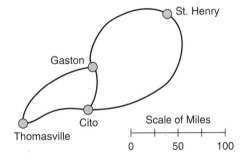

2   Why does ice float in water? (Hint: What are the densities of ice and water?)

3 a What is the scale of this house plan?
   b What are the dimensions of the kitchen? Of the master bedroom?

4 Balsa wood has a density of about 130 kg/m³.
  a How much does a 4-cubic-meter block of balsa wood weigh?
  b How many grams does a cubic centimeter of balsa wood weigh?

5 The land area of the state of Ohio is 41,004 square miles. In 1990, the population of Ohio was about 10,847,000. What was Ohio's population density (in people per square mile) in 1990?

Problems and Applications

In problems 6–8, find the density of a substance with the given mass and volume.

6 Mass: 150 g
Volume: 40 cm³

7 Mass: 4 lb
Volume: 29 in.³

8 Volume: 2.3 m³
Mass: 0.01 kg

9 The scale of a model airplane is 1:32. The tail fin of the model is 4 inches high. How high, in feet and inches, is the tail fin of the actual plane?

In problems 10–12, rewrite each map scale as a ratio of numbers.

10 1 in. : 50 mi

11 1 cm : 100 km

12 $1\frac{1}{2}$ in. : 100 ft

13 Science Gasoline has a density of 660 kilograms per cubic meter. A cubic meter of gasoline contains about 264 gallons. How much does a gallon of gasoline weigh?

14 The distance between two cities is 150 miles. On a map, the cities are represented by dots 3 inches apart. What is the scale of the map?

15 Estimating On the map shown, 1 inch represents 250 miles. Use the map to estimate the distance between
  a Milwaukee and Louisville
  b Indianapolis and Chicago

16 This 2-inch segment represents a distance of 5280 feet.

5280 ft

a Draw, to the same scale, a segment that represents 1760 yards.
b What is the ratio of the length of the segment shown to the length of the segment you drew in part **a**?

17 In Miss McPherson's classroom are two maps of the United States. The scale of one is 1:5,000,000, and the scale of the other is 1:3,500,000. Which map is larger?

18 The ratio between the height of the Empire State Building and its height in this picture is about 11,200:1. How tall is the Empire State Building?

19 **Science**   Water has a density of 1 g/cm³, and lubricating oil has a density of 0.9 g/cm³.
a Does oil float on water, or does water float on oil? Justify your answer.
b A container weighs 300 grams and has a capacity of 2.1×10^3 cm³. How much does the container weigh when filled with water? When filled with oil?

20 A map has a scale of 1 inch : 60 miles. What distance on the map represents 165 miles?

21 Phil wants to enlarge a photo that is 3 inches wide and 5 inches high to make a 24-inch-wide poster. How high will the poster be?

22 **Estimating**   Estimate the distance between Veronica Lodge and Pinepole Lodge.

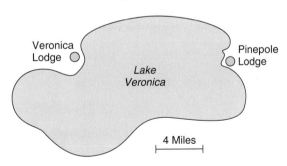

Veronica Lodge

Pinepole Lodge

Lake Veronica

4 Miles

23 The Abstract Concrete Company makes concrete blocks measuring 30 cm by 14 cm by 20 cm. If the concrete has a density of 2000 kg/m³, how much does a pallet of 128 blocks weigh?

24 **Architecture**   Lynn is making her niece Katy a dollhouse that is a scale model of Katy's real house. The living room of the dollhouse measures 18 inches by 12 inches. Katy's living room measures 24 feet by 16 feet. If the fireplace in Katy's living room is 8 feet wide and 5 feet high, what size should the fireplace in the dollhouse be?

25 Arnold is given a set of six balls, each having a radius of $\frac{1}{2}$ foot. The balls are made of different materials—steel, aluminum, copper, gold, oak, and glass. If the greatest weight Arnold can lift is 200 pounds, which of the balls could he lift? (Hint: Use the table of densities in the back of the book and the fact that the volume of a sphere with radius r is equal to $\frac{4}{3}\pi r^3$.)

26 Consumer Math Tony's car gets 24 miles to the gallon. If gas costs $1.20 per gallon, how much will Tony save by taking the direct route from Franklin to Accarda instead of going by way of Bolen?

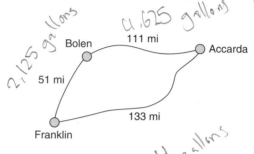

2.125 gallons

4.625 gallons

$8.40

51 mi

133 mi

5.54 gallons

$6.60

27

State	Population	Land Area (square miles)
Nevada	1,202,000	109,872
Connecticut	3,287,000	4,872

a Use the table to determine the population densities of Nevada and Connecticut.

b What would the population of Nevada have to be for its population density to be the same as Connecticut's?

c The Nevada cities of Las Vegas and Reno have populations of 258,000 and 134,000. If all the people in these two cities moved to Connecticut, what would the population densities of Nevada and Connecticut be?

◀ LOOKING BACK **Spiral Learning** LOOKING AHEAD ▶

---

28 Consumer Math A gallon of apple juice costs $4.25. A quart of apple juice costs $1.65. Which is a better buy?

29 On a 75-question test, Mandy answered 62 questions correctly. On a 70-question test, Sandy answered 59 questions correctly. Which student has the greater percent of correct answers?

30 Use a base and an exponent to write an expression for each measurement.
a The length of one side of the cube
b The area of one face of the cube
c The volume of the cube

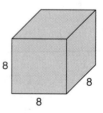

8

8

8

31 What is the ratio of the value of ten 29¢ stamps to the value of fifteen 25¢ stamps?

32 Which of the figures below represent figures the same shape as the 3-by-5 rectangle shown?

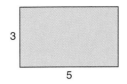

 a 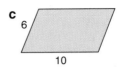 **b** **c** **d**

33 A freight train leaves New Orleans at noon, headed for Phoenix at 45 mph. At 2 P.M. an express train leaves New Orleans for Phoenix, traveling at 60 mph. At what time will the express train pass the freight train?

90 miles =

2 hours

34 Stopping distances of a car with good brakes on dry pavement are given in the graph. Estimate the stopping distance at a speed of
a 20 mph
b 40 mph
c 60 mph

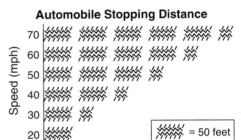

Automobile Stopping Distance

In problems 35–37, solve each equation for *x*.

35 $\dfrac{1}{x} = \dfrac{3}{5}$ **36** $\dfrac{1}{x} = 6$ **37** $\dfrac{1}{x} = \dfrac{1}{3}$

38 **Communicating**   Four students used four different methods to find the area of the unshaded part of this figure. Their calculations are shown below. Describe the method each student used, and explain why the method works.
Anna: $12(15) - 5(5) - 5(5) = 180 - 25 - 25 = 130$
Bert: $12(15) - 2(5)(5) = 180 - 50 = 130$
Carl: $10(5) + 2(5) + 10(7) = 50 + 10 + 70 = 130$
Dana: $12(5) + 10(7) = 60 + 70 = 130$

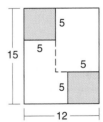

Investigation

Auto Trip   Holly Day is planning an automobile trip from Atlanta, Georgia, to Chicago, Illinois, to Minneapolis, Minnesota, to Portland, Oregon, to Los Angeles, California, to New Orleans, Louisiana, to Miami, Florida, then back to Atlanta. What information would you need in order to calculate her fuel expenses for the trip? Make some assumptions and estimate how much money she will spend on gasoline.

4.4
Working with Units

By now, you can probably figure out how many feet are in 5 yards or how many minutes are in 2 hours without too much trouble. But do you know how to convert from liters to gallons? Do you know the number of gallons in a cubic foot?

Example 1

The owner's manual for Mercedes's new sports car says that the car's gas tank holds 50 liters. The local gas station, however, sells gasoline by the gallon, not by the liter. How many gallons of gas does the tank hold?

Solution

We need to express 50 liters as a number of gallons. Looking at the table of equivalent measurements in the back of the book, we find that 1 gallon is about 3.785 liters, so $\frac{1 \text{ gallon}}{3.785 \text{ liters}} \approx 1$. We can therefore multiply 50 liters by this ratio to obtain an equivalent measurement.

$$50 \text{ liters} \approx 50 \text{ liters} \cdot \frac{1 \text{ gallon}}{3.785 \text{ liters}} \approx 13.2 \text{ gallons}$$

Notice that liters "canceled" and we were left with the desired units, gallons, after multiplying by a fraction equal to 1. This is an example of *dimensional analysis.*

Example 2

How many times does a person's heart beat in one day if it beats an average of 63 times per minute?

Solution

We are given that the person's heart beats 63 times per minute, and we know that there are 60 minutes in an hour and 24 hours in a day. Since we want our answer to be in beats per day, we can multiply by appropriate conversion factors so that all units will cancel except beats/day.

$$63 \text{ beats/minute} = \left(\frac{63 \text{ beats}}{1 \text{ minute}}\right)\left(\frac{60 \text{ minutes}}{1 \text{ hour}}\right)\left(\frac{24 \text{ hours}}{1 \text{ day}}\right)$$

$$= \frac{63 \cdot 60 \cdot 24 \text{ beats}}{1 \text{ day}}$$

$$= 90{,}720 \text{ beats/day}$$

Be sure to include units in all your calculations involving measurements. If the units don't come out right in the answer, go back and look for an error. A common error is for one of the fractions to be upside down. Since the numerator and the denominator of a conversion factor are equal, the fraction can be "flipped over" so that the correct units will be on the top.

Sample Problems

Problem 1   How many gallons of lime gelatin does it take to completely fill the wading pool shown?

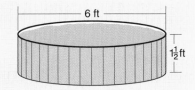

Solution   The pool is cylindrical, and we need to know the volume of space it encloses to determine the amount of liquid it will hold. According to the table of geometric formulas in the back of the book, the volume of a cylinder is equal to $\pi r^2 h$, where r represents the cylinder's radius and h represents its height. This pool has a radius of 3 feet and a height of 1.5 feet.

$$\text{Volume} = \pi \cdot r^2 \cdot h$$

$$= \pi \cdot 3^2 \cdot 1.5$$

Your calculator shows 42.41150082 , so the pool will hold about 42 cubic feet of lime gelatin. From the table of equivalent measurements in the back of the book, we find that 1 gallon is equal to 231 cubic inches. Furthermore, since there are 12 inches in a foot, there are 12^3, or 1728, cubic inches in a cubic foot. We can now convert the volume from cubic feet to cubic inches to gallons.

$$42 \text{ ft,}^3 = (42 \text{ ft}^3)\left(\frac{1728 \text{ in.}^3}{1 \text{ ft}^3}\right)\left(\frac{1 \text{ gal}}{231 \text{ in.}^3}\right)$$

$$= \frac{42 \cdot 1728}{231} \text{ gal}$$

$$\approx 314 \text{ gal}$$

It will take about 314 gallons of lime gelatin to fill the pool.

Problem 2 How many miles did a car travel in 3 hours if it was traveling at a speed of 50 km/hr?

Solution The speed of the car is given as 50 kilometers per hour. In 3 hours the car traveled $(3 \text{ hr}) \left(50 \frac{\text{km}}{\text{hr}}\right)$, or 150 km. But we need the answer in miles, so we multiply by 1 in the form $\frac{1 \text{ mi}}{1.61 \text{ km}}$, since 1 mi ≈ 1.61 km.

$$150 \text{ km} \approx 150 \text{ km} \cdot \frac{1 \text{ mi}}{1.61 \text{ km}}$$

$$\approx \frac{150}{1.61} \text{ mi}$$

$$\approx 93.2 \text{ mi}$$

The car traveled about 93.2 miles.

Think and Discuss

1 Which of the following ratios are equal to 1?

a $\frac{1 \text{ yd}}{3 \text{ ft}}$ **b** $\frac{5 \text{ gal}}{10 \text{ qt}}$ **c** $\frac{288 \text{ in.}^2}{2 \text{ ft}^2}$ **d** $\frac{100 \text{ cm}}{1 \text{ m}}$

2 **Estimating** The speed of sound is approximately 1100 feet per second.
  a About how many miles will the sound of thunder travel in 5 seconds?
  b Explain how to estimate how far away a storm is by counting the seconds between seeing the lightning and hearing the thunder.

3 **a** How many seconds are there in an hour?
  b If it takes a snail 10 seconds to travel an inch, how far could the snail travel in an hour?

4 Match each metric unit with the closest customary unit.
  a quart   I   meter
  b inch   II liter
  c mile   III centimeter
  d yard   IV kilometer

5 Copy each expression, filling in the missing number. Then simplify the expression, being sure to include the proper units, and describe a situation in which you might use the expression.

a $\frac{4 \text{ mi}}{1 \text{ min}} \cdot \frac{3 \text{ min}}{\_\_\_\_ \text{ sec}}$

b $\frac{34 \text{ mi}}{1 \text{ gal}} \cdot \frac{2 \text{ gal}}{1 \text{ hr}} \cdot \frac{\frac{1}{2} \text{ hr}}{\_\_\_\_ \text{ min}}$

6 In 1985, the A. C. Nielsen Company found that in the United States the average child spends 3 hours 54 minutes watching television each day. Estimate the number of hours of TV programs that the average child watches in a year.

Problems and Applications

7 Evaluate each product.

$\frac{4.2}{}$

a $\frac{7}{3} \cdot \frac{4}{4}$ $\frac{28}{12} \cdot \frac{7}{3}$ $1\frac{1}{3}$ **b** $\frac{7}{3} \cdot \frac{1.2}{1.2}$ $\frac{8.4}{36}$ $\overset{1.53}{=}$ **c** $\frac{7}{3} \cdot \frac{x}{x}$ **d** $\frac{7}{3} \cdot \frac{x^5}{x^5}$

8 Simplify each expression, being sure to include the correct units.

a $\frac{6 \text{ dollars}}{1 \text{ hour}} \cdot \frac{5 \text{ hours}}{1 \text{ workday}}$ $\frac{30 \text{ dollars}}{1 \text{ workday}}$ **b** $\frac{3 \text{ pounds}}{1 \text{ minute}} \cdot \frac{7 \text{ minutes}}{1 \text{ person}}$ $\frac{21 \text{ pound}}{1 \text{ person}}$

9 If a canoe is 17 feet long, how many canoe lengths are in a mile?

10 Lynda is 5 feet 3 inches tall, and Don is 6 feet 3 inches tall. What is the ratio of Lynda's height to Don's height?

11 Use dimensional analysis to express
   a 5 gallons as a number of quarts
   b 6 gallons as a number of pints
   c $2\frac{1}{2}$ pounds as a number of ounces

In problems 12 and 13, simplify each expression.

12 $\frac{4 \text{ ft}}{1 \text{ sec}} \cdot \frac{120 \text{ sec}}{2 \text{ min}}$

13 $\frac{5 \text{ yd}}{1 \text{ min}} \cdot \frac{1 \text{ min}}{60 \text{ sec}} \cdot \frac{36 \text{ in.}}{1 \text{ yd}}$

14 Express 32 pounds as a number of kilograms.

15 What is the volume of the cube in cubic feet?

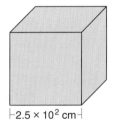

$\vdash 2.5 \times 10^2 \text{ cm} \dashv$

16 The printer that Carlo uses with his computer prints 160 characters per second. How many characters can the printer print in 10 minutes?

17 Maple syrup is delivered to Dr. Terror's House of Pancakes in 1-gallon cans. The syrup is served to customers in 8-ounce pitchers. How many pitchers can be filled from one can?

18 Danielle earns $5.50 per hour. She works $5\frac{1}{2}$ hours per day, 24 days per month.
   a How much does she earn per month?
   b How much does she earn for each 8 hours she works?

19 Olivia can maintain an average speed of 14 miles per hour when riding her bicycle.
   a How far can she cycle in 8 hours?
   b If she cycles 8 hours a day, how long will it take her to travel 2000 miles?

20 Mr. McCall knows that his truck, including its contents, weighs 6 tons. If he comes to a bridge in Canada that has a posted load limit of 5000 kilograms, should he drive across the bridge?

21 Pauline drove from Bodega Bay to Santa Mira by way of Hadleyville. She returned to Bodega Bay by way of Bedford Falls. How many kilometers long was the round trip?

498.79 km

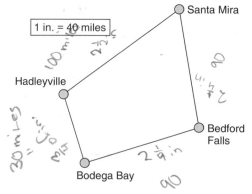

1 in. = 40 miles

Santa Mira
Hadleyville
Bedford Falls
Bodega Bay

22 The directions on a can of powdered lemonade mix say to use two scoops of mix to make an 8-ounce glass of lemonade. How many scoops of mix are needed to make

    a A quart?   **b** A 12-ounce glass?
    c A 10-ounce glass?   **d** A liter?

23 The scale of a map is 1 inch : 60 miles. Boris measured a journey on the map and found it to be $4\frac{1}{2}$ inches long. If Boris drives at an average speed of 50 miles per hour, how long will it take him to make the journey?

24 The rules of a 500-mile automobile race restrict each car's fuel supply to a maximum of 110 gallons.
    a How many miles per gallon must a car average for its driver to complete the race?
    b If a car averages 6 miles per gallon, how much of its fuel supply will be left at the end of the race?

25 Hilda planned to go hiking in a national forest. The government map of the region was too big to carry, however, so she decided to make her own map. On the government map, 6 inches represented 25 miles, and the distance from Jailhouse Rock to Blueberry Hill was 8 inches. If Hilda drew her map to a scale of 2 inches : 25 miles, how far apart were Jailhouse Rock and Blueberry Hill on her map?

26 **Communicating** A car going 60 miles per hour is traveling 88 feet per second. How can you use this information to compute the number of feet in a mile?

27 In the land of Decimalia, each day is divided into 10 gours, each gour into 10 linutes, and each linute into 10 reconds.
    a If a Decimalian tells you that it is 4 linutes past 6, what time is it according to our system?
    b How would a Decimalian express 10:15 A.M.?

In problems 28–30, find each ratio of lengths.

28 $\dfrac{8 \text{ feet}}{4 \text{ yards}}$

29 $\dfrac{9 \text{ feet}}{3 \text{ yards}}$

30 $\dfrac{36 \text{ inches}}{1 \text{ yard}}$

In problems 31 and 32, solve each equation for *x*.

31 $\dfrac{x}{4} = \dfrac{9}{12}$

32 $\dfrac{x}{18} = \dfrac{3}{2}$

33 Jasmine is 5'8" tall. Althea's shoulders are 4'9" off the ground. When Jasmine stands on Althea's shoulders, how far off the ground is the top of Jasmine's head?

34 Science Diamonds burn at temperatures between 1400°F and 1670°F. Express this range of temperature in degrees Celsius.

35 Use these three equations to find the values of *x, y,* and *z.*

$$19 + 8(4) = x \qquad x + 13 = y \qquad z = \dfrac{y}{4} + \dfrac{x}{17}$$

36 The Sears Tower in Chicago is 1454 feet high. What is the scale of this picture of the Sears Tower?

37 Technology Computer memory can be measured in kilobytes, but in this case *kilo-* does not mean exactly "one thousand." A kilobyte is actually 1024 bytes.
  a How many bytes are in 640 kilobytes?
  b Why might computer memory be measured in multiples of 1024 rather than multiples of 1000?

Investigation

Water Consumption How much water do you think you use in a day? Try to estimate the amount of water used by an average person on an average day. Then use your estimate to calculate, both in gallons and in cubic feet, the amount of water used in the United States during a year.

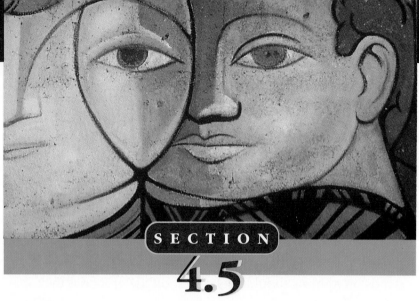

4.5
Proportions

WHAT IS A PROPORTION?

A *proportion* is an equation stating that two ratios are equal. The two forms of the proportion shown can both be read "*a* is to *b* as *c* is to *d*."

$$\frac{a}{b} = \frac{c}{d} \qquad a{:}b = c{:}d$$

If a line parallel to one side of a triangle intersects the other two sides of the triangle, it divides those two sides proportionally. For example, in triangle ABC the arrows indicate that $\overline{DE}$ is parallel to $\overline{AC}$. The ratios of the labeled parts of sides $\overline{BA}$ and $\overline{BC}$ are equal $\left(\frac{8}{6} = \frac{12}{9}\right)$, since each ratio is equal to $\frac{4}{3}$. Notice also that $8 \cdot 9 = 72$ and $6 \cdot 12 = 72$, so $8 \cdot 9 = 6 \cdot 12$.

SOLVING PROPORTIONS

Proportions are useful in solving many types of problems. When you want to solve a proportion, it is frequently useful to rewrite the equation by *cross multiplying*—that is, multiplying the numerator of each ratio by the denominator of the other.

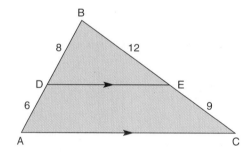

$$\frac{a}{b} = \frac{c}{d} \rightarrow a \cdot d = b \cdot c$$

Example 1

Find the value of n for which $\frac{n}{3} = \frac{5}{7}$.

Solution

We can use cross multiplication.

$$\frac{n}{3} = \frac{5}{7} \rightarrow 7n = 3(5) \rightarrow 7n = 15$$

Since n is multiplied by 7 in the rewritten equation, we can use the inverse operation, division, to solve the equation.

$$7n = 15$$
$$n = \frac{15}{7}, \text{ or about } 2.14$$

Example 2

The ratio of boys to girls at a party was 4:5. If there were 28 boys at the party, how many girls were at the party?

Solution

Let's use g to represent the number of girls. Since $\frac{\text{number of boys}}{\text{number of girls}} = \frac{4}{5}$ and there were 28 boys, we can write the proportion $\frac{28}{g} = \frac{4}{5}$. To solve it, you can cross multiply.

$$\frac{28}{g} = \frac{4}{5} \rightarrow 28(5) = 4g \rightarrow 140 = 4g$$
$$\frac{140}{4} = g$$
$$35 = g$$

There were 35 girls at the party. Notice that the proportion is written so that the numerators and denominators of the ratios correspond. If $\frac{\text{boys}}{\text{girls}}$ is on one side of the equation, the ratio on the other side must also be in the form $\frac{\text{boys}}{\text{girls}}$.

Sample Problems

Problem 1

The town council of Springfield decided to decorate a large wall in the center of town with a mural, so a contest was held to obtain a design for the artwork. Gloria won the contest with this 20-inch-by-28-inch drawing. The wall on which the mural is to be painted is 25 feet high and 42 feet wide. What is the largest mural that can be based on Gloria's drawing without changing its proportions?

20 in.

28 in.

We set up and solve a proportion.

$$\frac{\text{Height of drawing}}{\text{Width of drawing}} = \frac{\text{height of mural}}{\text{width of mural}}$$

$$\frac{20 \text{ in.}}{28 \text{ in.}} = \frac{25 \text{ ft}}{x \text{ ft}}$$

$$\frac{5}{7} = \frac{25}{x}$$

$$5x = 7(25)$$

$$5x = 175$$

$$x = \frac{175}{5} = 35$$

The largest possible mural is one 25 feet high by 35 feet wide. Since the wall is 42 feet wide, 7 feet of its width will remain unpainted. Can you figure out why we used 25 feet for the mural's height and x for its width instead of using x for its height and 42 feet for its width?

Problem 2 The recipe for a fruit punch says to mix 2 pints of fruit concentrate with enough water to make 3 gallons of the punch. How much concentrate is needed to make 10 gallons of punch?

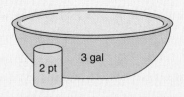

Solution Once again, we can solve this problem by using a proportion to compare like quantities. Notice that both ratios are in the form "concentrate:punch" and in the form "pints:gallons."

$$\frac{2 \text{ pints of concentrate}}{3 \text{ gallons of punch}} = \frac{x \text{ pints of concentrate}}{10 \text{ gallons of punch}}$$

$$\frac{2}{3} = \frac{x}{10}$$

$$20 = 3x$$

$$\frac{20}{3} = x$$

Since x represents the number of pints of concentrate that are needed, it would take $\frac{20}{3}$, or $6\frac{2}{3}$, pints of concentrate to make 10 gallons of punch. This result can also be obtained by solving the proportion $\frac{2 \text{ pints of concentrate}}{x \text{ pints of concentrate}} = \frac{3 \text{ gallons of punch}}{10 \text{ gallons of punch}}$. Do you see why?

Think and Discuss

1 Maude remembered that three of the four numbers in a proportion were 1, 3, and 4. She could not, however, remember the other number or the position of each number in the proportion. Help Maude to find all possible values of the missing number.

2 Solve each proportion for m. (Hint: Look for a pattern.)

a $\dfrac{8}{m} = \dfrac{2}{5}$ 　　　　**b** $\dfrac{8}{m} = \dfrac{4}{5}$ 　　　　**c** $\dfrac{8}{m} = \dfrac{8}{5}$

d $\dfrac{8}{m} = \dfrac{16}{5}$ 　　　**e** $\dfrac{8}{m} = \dfrac{32}{5}$ 　　　**f** $\dfrac{8}{m} = \dfrac{64}{5}$

3 $\overline{PQ}$ is parallel to $\overline{BC}$, AP = 4 in., PB = 8 in., and AQ = 5 in. Find length QC.

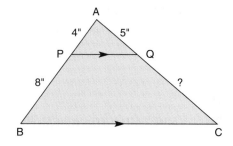

4 Explain why you cannot use the cross-multiplication technique to calculate $\dfrac{1}{5} + \dfrac{2}{3}$.

5 A photo measuring 6 inches by 8 inches is enlarged into a poster. The longer side of the poster is 3 feet long. How long is the shorter side?

6 On this bicycle, the pedal gear has 48 teeth, and the gear on the rear wheel has 18 teeth. Suppose we use P to stand for the number of times the pedals turn and R to stand for the number of times the rear wheel turns. Write a valid proportion involving 48, 18, P, and R. Explain why your proportion is valid.

Wheel gear　　Pedal gear

Problems and Applications

In problems 7–12, solve each proportion for x.

7 $\dfrac{12}{x} = \dfrac{3}{4}$ 　　　　**8** $\dfrac{12}{x} = \dfrac{4}{3}$ 　　　　**9** $\dfrac{12}{x} = \dfrac{6}{5}$

10 $\dfrac{12}{x} = \dfrac{2}{5}$ 　　　**11** $\dfrac{12}{x} = \dfrac{1}{5}$ 　　　**12** $\dfrac{12}{x} = \dfrac{12}{5}$

13 The ratio of the height of bar A to the height of bar B is 2:5.
  a What is the value of x?
  b What is the ratio of the height of bar C to the height of bar B?

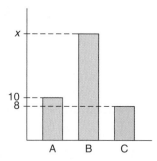

14 The directions on a can of lemonade mix say to use 8 tablespoons of mix to make 2 quarts of lemonade. Heathcliff wants to make 7 quarts of lemonade. How many tablespoons of mix should he use?

15 **Estimating** Use the gas gauge to estimate the number of gallons of gasoline left in the motorist's 20-gallon tank.

In problems 16–19, solve the proportions for w, x, y, and z.

16 $\dfrac{3.5}{8.4} = \dfrac{5.7}{w}$ **17** $\dfrac{2\frac{1}{2}}{3\frac{3}{4}} = \dfrac{4\frac{4}{5}}{x}$ **18** $\dfrac{2.75}{5.5} = \dfrac{y}{4.8}$ **19** $\dfrac{40\%}{60\%} = \dfrac{8}{z}$

20 For safety, a swimming pool should contain 2 parts of liquid chlorinator for each 1,000,000 parts of water. How much chlorinator should be added to a pool that contains 50,000 gallons of water?

21 In a recent year, the ratio of men to women in the United States armed forces was about 9 to 1.
  a If there were 90 men in a random group of military personnel, how many women would you expect to find in the group?
  b In a group of 90 military personnel, how many of them would you expect to be women?
  c What percent of armed-forces personnel were women in that year?

22 If the ratio of x to y in the diagram is 7:8, what are the values of x and y?

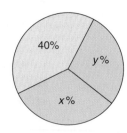

23 The ratio of the width to the length of a rectangle is 3:7. The shorter side is 9 inches long. What is the area of the rectangle?

24 Solve $\dfrac{x+4}{6} = \dfrac{9}{12}$ for x. $\left(\text{Hint: First solve } \dfrac{n}{6} = \dfrac{9}{12} \text{ for } n.\right)$

25 In the diagram, DI = 7, DA = 22, and NE = 8. Find AN.

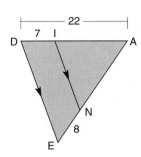

26 At Wassamatta U. the admissions office rejects nine applicants for every two that are accepted. If 1408 people applied for admission last year, how many were accepted?

27 The North Shore Blood Center has a goal of 3500 units of blood in its yearly blood drive. By September 1, the center has received 2000 units. If donations continue at the same rate, will the center reach its goal or fall short of it? By how much?

28 The ratio of officers to enlisted personnel in the United States Air Force is about 9:41. If there are about 606,000 people in the air force, how many of them are officers?

29 Solve each proportion for y.

a $\dfrac{y}{6} = \dfrac{6}{y}$ **b** $\dfrac{y}{2} = \dfrac{18}{y}$ **c** $\dfrac{y}{4} = \dfrac{16}{y}$ **d** $\dfrac{y}{3} = \dfrac{15}{y}$

30 At 3 P.M. on a sunny day, a 2-foot-high stick casts a shadow 3 feet long. At the same time, a telephone pole casts a shadow 50 feet long. How tall is the telephone pole? (Hint: Use a proportion to calculate the answer.)

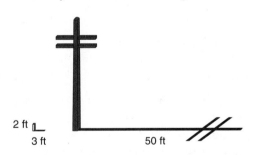

◀ LOOKING BACK **Spiral Learning** LOOKING AHEAD ▶

---

31 Find the ratio of 2 yards 2 feet 4 inches to 1 foot 8 inches.

32 In ⊙B, m∠ABC = 120. What percentage of the circular region is shaded?

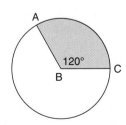

33 Jacob left his house, walking south at 4 miles per hour. Three hours later, his sister Danielle followed him on her bicycle at 12 miles per hour. How long did she ride before she caught up to him?

34 Architecture On this floor plan, 1 in. = 10 ft.

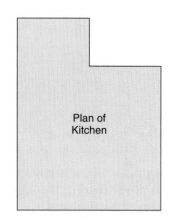

Plan of Kitchen

  a Make a sketch showing the lengths of all six sides of the actual room.
  b Find the area of the floor plan in square inches.
  c Find the area of the actual room in square feet.
  d Find the ratio of the area you found in part **b** to the area you found in part **c**.

35 Communicating Draw a circle and one of its diameters. Pick a point on the circle that is not an endpoint of the diameter. Draw segments connecting this point to each endpoint of the diameter. Then measure the angles formed. What do you notice?

36 The chances that a certain state lottery ticket costing $2 will be a winning ticket are 4 out of 11,543,672.
  a What is the probability that a ticket will be a winning one? (Express the probability in decimal form.)
  b If you spend $100 on these lottery tickets, what is the probability that you will win?

37 $\angle R$ is a right angle, and $\overline{QS} \parallel \overline{PT}$ (that is, $\overline{QS}$ is parallel to $\overline{PT}$).
  a Find PQ.
  b Find QS.
  c Find PT.

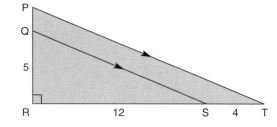

38 Estimate the distance from the tee to the flagstick on the golf hole shown.

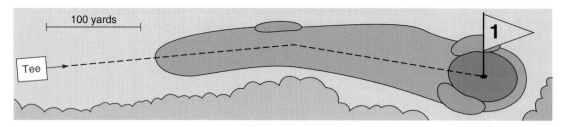

100 yards

Tee

1

Investigation

Floor Plans Draw, to scale, a floor plan of your home. Be sure that the plan includes a legend explaining the scale that you used. What is the total floor space, in square feet, represented by the plan?

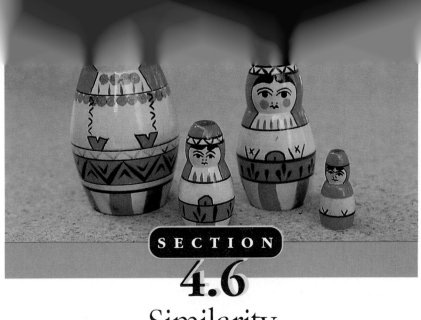

4.6
Similarity

ENLARGEMENTS AND REDUCTIONS

When a photographic slide is projected, the image on the screen is the same as the image on the slide, only larger. Maps, on the other hand, are smaller than what they represent.

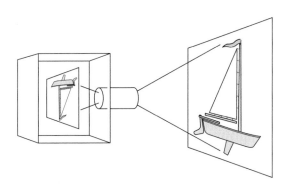

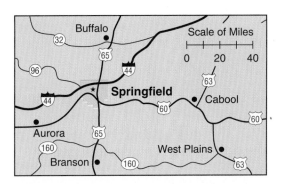

The slide and its image are *similar;* the map and the area it represents are also *similar.*

Let's reconsider the drawing and the mural discussed in Sample Problem 1 of the preceding section. These similar pictures show two characteristics that are shared by all pairs of similar objects.

1. The ratios of all dimensions of the drawing to the corresponding dimensions of the mural are the same.

$$\frac{\text{Width of drawing}}{\text{Width of mural}} = \frac{\text{height of drawing}}{\text{height of mural}}$$

$$\frac{20 \text{ in.}}{25 \text{ ft}} = \frac{28 \text{ in.}}{35 \text{ ft}}$$

$$\frac{4 \text{ in.}}{5 \text{ ft}} = \frac{4 \text{ in.}}{5 \text{ ft}}$$

In other words, any 4-inch length on the drawing will become a 5-foot length on the mural. If we express the ratio in terms of a common unit, we find that $\frac{4\text{ in.}}{5\text{ ft}} = \frac{4\text{ in.}}{60\text{ in.}} = \frac{1}{15}$. The drawing is therefore $\frac{1}{15}$ the size of the mural, and the mural is $\frac{15}{1}$, or 15, times the size of the drawing. The scale factor of the enlargement is 15:1.

2. The ratio of any two dimensions of the drawing is equal to the ratio of the corresponding dimensions of the mural.

$$\frac{\text{Height of drawing}}{\text{Width of drawing}} = \frac{\text{height of mural}}{\text{width of mural}}$$

$$\frac{20\text{ in.}}{28\text{ in.}} = \frac{25\text{ ft}}{35\text{ ft}}$$

$$\frac{5}{7} = \frac{5}{7}$$

Whenever a model or copy differs from its original in size but not in shape, the two objects are said to be **similar.** The ratio of linear measurements of the objects corresponds to the amount of enlargement or reduction and is sometimes called the **scale factor** of the change in size.

SIMILAR GEOMETRIC FIGURES

Similarity of polygons is like similarity of other objects. When polygons have exactly the same shape, they are similar even if their sizes are different.

In any pair of similar polygons, the ratios of the lengths of corresponding sides are equal, and the measures of corresponding angles are equal. The symbol ~ is used to indicate similarity.

Example

In the diagram, $\triangle ABC \sim \triangle PQR$.

a Find the ratios $\frac{AB}{PQ}$, $\frac{BC}{QR}$, and $\frac{AC}{PR}$.

b What can we conclude about the angle measures of the triangles?

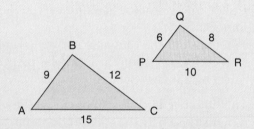

Solution

a $\frac{AB}{PQ} = \frac{9}{6} = \frac{3}{2}$ $\frac{BC}{QR} = \frac{12}{8} = \frac{3}{2}$ $\frac{AC}{PR} = \frac{15}{10} = \frac{3}{2}$

Notice that all three ratios are the same. In this pair of similar triangles, the ratio of corresponding lengths is 3:2.

b Since the triangles are similar, the measures of corresponding angles are equal: m∠A = m∠P, m∠B = m∠Q, and m∠C = m∠R.

Whenever each angle of one triangle is equal to the corresponding angle of another triangle, the two triangles are similar. (Although this is true of triangles, it usually is *not* true of other kinds of polygons.)

Sample Problem

Problem   Given that $\overline{AC} \perp \overline{BD}$ (segment AC is perpendicular to segment BD), m∠BAC = m∠DEC, and m∠B = m∠D, find length CD.

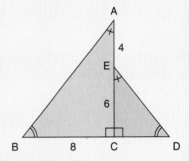

Solution $\overline{AC}$ is perpendicular to $\overline{BD}$, so ∠ACB and ∠ACD both have measures of 90. Since m∠BAC = m∠DEC and m∠B = m∠D, each angle of △ABC is equal to the corresponding angle of △EDC. Therefore, △ABC is similar to △EDC. Since $\overline{AC}$ corresponds to $\overline{EC}$ and $\overline{CB}$ corresponds to $\overline{CD}$,

$$\frac{AC}{EC} = \frac{CB}{CD}$$

$$\frac{10}{6} = \frac{8}{x}$$

$$10x = 48$$

$$x = \frac{48}{10} = 4.8$$

$\overline{CD}$ is 4.8 units long.

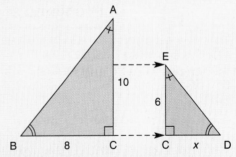

Think and Discuss

1 Felicia drew two triangles and said, "These two triangles are similar." Connie said that she didn't think they were similar. How could they decide?

2 Which of these rectangles are similar?

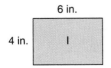

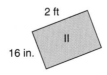

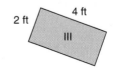

1 ft

6 in.   IV

3 If △ABC ~ △DEF, what are the values of *x* and *y*?

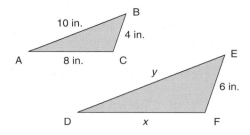

4 a Are the ratios of corresponding sides of these two figures equal?
b Are the two figures similar? Explain your answer.

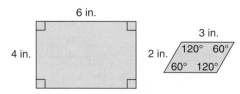

5 If the poster is an enlargement of the photo, what is the height of the poster?

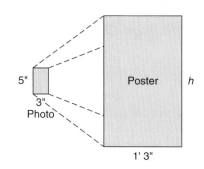

Problems and Applications

6 △ABC is similar to △PQR. Find lengths AC, QR, and PR.

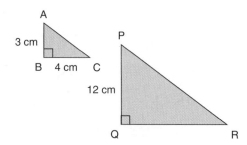

7 Draw a rectangle measuring 2 inches by 3 inches. Then draw another rectangle, measuring 2 inches by 6 inches.
a Do the two rectangles have equal angles?
b Do the two rectangles have the same shape? (That is, are they similar?)
c Are any two geometric figures with equal angles similar?

8 If $\overline{BC}$ is parallel to $\overline{DE}$, what is the ratio of AC to CE?

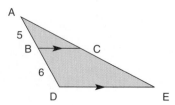

9 △ABC ~ △AFG, and AB = BD = DF.
   a Find the ratio AB:AF.
   b Find the ratio AC:AG.
   c Find the ratio BC:FG.
   d If the area of △ABC is 1, what is the area of △AFG?

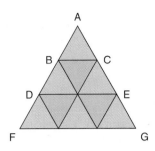

10 **Consumer Math**   A 4-acre parcel of property has an assessed value of $90,000. The taxes on the property are $3000 per year. A second parcel has an assessed value of $12,000. How much are the taxes on the second property if both are taxed at the same rate?

11 Compare the larger rectangle with the smaller rectangle. What is
   a The ratio of corresponding side lengths?
   b The ratio of the rectangles' areas?
   c The ratio of the rectangles' perimeters?

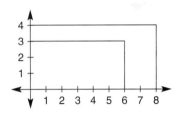

12 △RMW ~ △FAZ, RW = 18 ft, RM = 24 ft, MW = 12 ft, and FZ = 48 ft. Find FA and AZ.

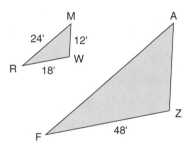

13 Rectangle SUZY is similar to rectangle KATE.
   a Find YZ.
   b Find TK to the nearest hundredth.

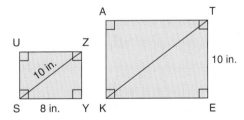

14 $\overline{DF}$ is an enlargement of $\overline{AC}$. If $\overline{AC}$ is 9 units long and $\overline{DF}$ is 30 units long, how long is $\overline{DE}$?

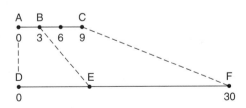

15 △BIG is similar to △TOP.
   a How long is $\overline{OP}$?
   b How long is $\overline{TP}$?
   c If $\overline{TO}$ were 10 feet long instead of 10 inches long, how long would $\overline{OP}$ and $\overline{TP}$ be?

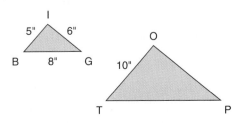

16 Spreadsheets A dollhouse is constructed so that each inch of the dollhouse corresponds to $2\frac{1}{2}$ feet of a real house.

a Use a spreadsheet to make a table listing "dollhouse lengths" of 1 in. to 20 in., in increments of $\frac{1}{4}$ in., along with the equivalent lengths in the real house.

b Now use the spreadsheet to make a table listing lengths of 1 ft to 20 ft, in increments of 1 ft, along with the equivalent dollhouse lengths.

c How might these conversion tables be useful?

17 △GOC ~ △ART, GO = 7, and AR = 3.

a If CO = 8, what is RT?

b If AT = 5, what is GC?

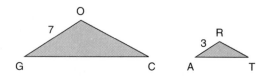

 18 Recall that the volume of a cylinder with radius r and height h is equal to $\pi r^2 h$.

a What is the volume of the cylindrical can?

b If a similar can has a diameter of 4 inches, what is its height? What is its volume?

c What is the ratio of the volumes of the cans in parts **a** and **b?**

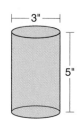

19 ABCD and EFGH are rectangles, AE = 3, AH = 1, and DG = 7. What is the area of rectangle EFGH?

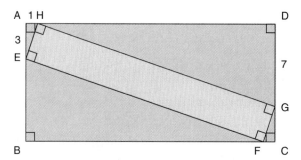

◀ LOOKING BACK **Spiral Learning** LOOKING AHEAD ▶

---

20 Solve each proportion for y.

a $\dfrac{y}{12} = \dfrac{3}{4}$ **b** $\dfrac{12}{y} = \dfrac{3}{4}$ **c** $\dfrac{12}{4} = \dfrac{3}{y}$ **d** $\dfrac{12}{3} = \dfrac{4}{y}$

21 In the circle graph shown, what is the value of x?

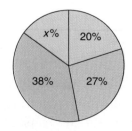

22 Aluminum has a density of 2700 kg/m³. If Billy cannot lift a weight greater than 23 kilograms, what is the size of the largest cube of aluminum that he can lift?

23 **Spreadsheets**   Consider the proportion $\frac{a}{b} = \frac{3}{7}$. Use a spreadsheet to make a table showing the values of b that correspond to whole-number values of a from 1 to 10.

24 In this diagram, 1 in. = 66 ft. How far apart are the house and the oak tree?

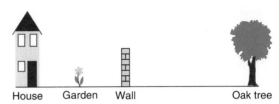

House   Garden   Wall   Oak tree

25 **Consumer Math**   A pack of ProStar baseball cards contains 16 cards and costs $0.59. A pack of Slugger cards contains 14 cards and costs $0.49. Which is the better buy? Why?

26 What is the value of y in the diagram?

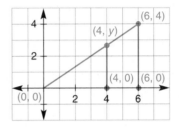

In problems 27–29, solve each proportion for w.

27 $\dfrac{w}{3.7} = \dfrac{8.9}{10.4}$ **28** $\dfrac{7.6}{w} = \dfrac{3.14}{180}$ **29** $\dfrac{11.7}{12.4} = \dfrac{w}{8.2}$

30 Suppose that $\frac{n^2}{9} = \frac{7}{3}$ and that $n > 0$. Find the value of n to the nearest hundredth.

31 **Environmental Science** If 6323.6 million barrels of petroleum were used in the United States in 1989, how much petroleum is represented by each part of the circle graph?

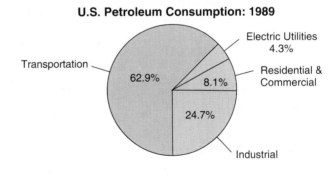

U.S. Petroleum Consumption: 1989

Transportation 62.9%
Electric Utilities 4.3%
Residential & Commercial 8.1%
Industrial 24.7%

Investigation

Similar Polygons   Draw two triangles that are similar, then draw two triangles that are not similar. Label the sides of each figure with their lengths, and label the angles of each figure with their measures. Repeat this process for quadrilaterals and for pentagons. What conclusions can you draw from your figures? Are all squares similar to one another? Why or why not?

Summary

CONCEPTS AND PROCEDURES

After studying this chapter, you should be able to

- Identify measurable attributes of objects and some of the units in which measurements of the attributes may be expressed (4.1)
- Recognize metric units of length, mass, and capacity (4.1)
- Add, subtract, multiply, and divide measurements of like attributes (4.1)
- Identify and evaluate ratios (4.2)
- Identify and evaluate rates (4.2)
- Calculate unit costs (4.2)
- Solve problems involving scale ratios (4.3)
- Solve problems involving densities (4.3)
- Use dimensional analysis to change the units in which measurements are expressed (4.4)
- Recognize proportions (4.5)
- Use proportions to solve problems (4.5)
- Understand the concept of similarity (4.6)
- Solve problems involving similar geometric figures (4.6)

VOCABULARY

attribute (4.1)

base unit (4.2)

centi– (4.1)

cross multiply (4.5)

density (4.3)

dimensional analysis (4.4)

gram (4.1)

kilo– (4.1)

meter (4.1)

milli– (4.1)

proportion (4.5)

rate (4.2)

ratio (4.2)

scale (4.3)

scale factor (4.6)

similar (4.6)

unit cost (4.2)

Review

1 What units might you use to express
 a The amount of cloth needed to make a dress?
 b The amount of baking soda needed to make a cake?
 c The amount of oil in an automobile's crankcase?
 d The amount of soda pop in a bottle?

2 Evaluate the ratio $\frac{84 \text{ in.}}{2\frac{1}{2} \text{ yd}}$.

3 Which is the better buy, a dozen daisies for $3 or 20 daisies for $5?

4 A storage tank holds 185 liters of liquid. How many gallons does it hold?

In problems 5–8, solve each proportion for x.

5 $\frac{x}{8} = \frac{6}{5}$ **6** $\frac{x}{8} = \frac{5}{6}$ **7** $\frac{x}{6} = \frac{8}{5}$ **8** $\frac{x}{6} = \frac{5}{8}$

9 A model limousine is 10 inches long and 3 inches wide. The scale of the model is 1:21. How long is the real car?

10 How many centimeters are in 5 kilometers?

11 Find the value of x.

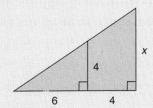

12 A photograph measuring 3 inches by 5 inches is to be enlarged so that the longer side of the enlargement will measure 11 inches. How long will the shorter side of the enlargement be?

13 Evaluate the ratio $\frac{1 \text{ hour}}{1 \text{ year}}$. Express your answer as a fraction, then rewrite the fraction in scientific notation.

14 A car traveled at a speed of 60 miles per hour for 100 miles, then at 40 miles per hour for 50 miles. How long did the trip take?

15 Express the area of the shaded region
 a In square meters
 b In square feet (Hint: 1 ft^2 ≈ 0.093 m^2.)

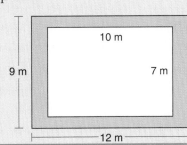

16 A pack of eight 16-ounce bottles of Coola Cola costs $5.60. A pack of six 12-ounce cans of Coola Cola costs $3.60. Which pack gives you more cola for your money?

17 List six attributes of a tree. Which of these attributes can be measured?

18 Given that $\overline{RA}$ is parallel to $\overline{DM}$, ER = 12, RD = 16, and EA = 15, find length EM.

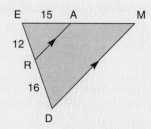

19 Bernie's car has a 12-gallon gas tank. He estimates that he can drive approximately 320 miles on a tank of gas. If his gas gauge indicates that his tank is about three-eighths full, about how far has he driven since he last filled his tank?

20 At a temperature of 25°C, a maximum of 36.2 grams of salt will dissolve in 100 milliliters of water. How much water is needed to dissolve 300 grams of salt at 25°C.

21 The Belmont Stakes is a $1\frac{1}{2}$-mile horse race. In 1941, Whirlaway won the race by running the course in 2 minutes 31 seconds. What was Whirlaway's average speed in miles per hour?

22 Rectangle BIRD is similar to rectangle BATH. If BI = 16, BD = 24, and BH = 18, what fraction of rectangle BIRD is shaded?

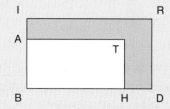

23 An ice sculptor is using a block of ice measuring 3 feet by 4 feet by 5 feet.
a What is the volume of the block?
b How many pounds does the block weigh?

24 Find the height of a building that casts a 75-foot shadow when a 4-foot fence post casts a 5-foot shadow.

25 The diagram represents the floor of a room. The scale of the diagram is 1:216. If carpeting sells for $15 per square yard, what is the price of the carpeting needed to cover the floor?

26 At Pies 'R' Round, a pizza 10 inches in diameter costs $6.50, and a pizza 14 inches in diameter costs $12.50. Which is the better buy?

27 △MTV ~ △VHI, TM = 5, MV = 8, and TV = 10. If HI = 15, what is the perimeter of △VHI?

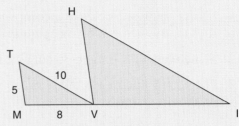

28 The maximum speed at which Tess Turtle can crawl is 20 feet per hour. Sidney Slug's top speed is 1 foot per hour. They decide to have a race, with Sidney getting a 100-foot head start because of his sluggishness. If both race at top speed, how long will it take Tess to catch Sidney?

29 Why is an 8-inch-by-10-inch "enlargement" of a $3\frac{1}{2}$-inch-by-5-inch photograph not a true enlargement?

30 Pam is planning to tile the floor of this L-shaped room. The tiles she wants to use measure 20 cm by 20 cm and are sold in boxes of 40 tiles. If each box costs $25, how much should Pam expect to spend on tiles?

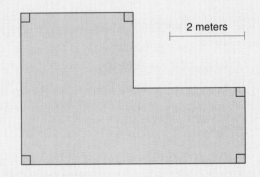

31 An acre is equal to 4840 square yards.
  a How many acres are in a rectangular lot that is 227 feet wide and 450 feet long?
  b The property tax on a 12.3-acre plot of land is $654. What is the tax rate per square yard?

32 Les Cargo the snail can travel at a speed of $\frac{1}{5}$ inch per minute. How long would it take Les to finish a 2500-mile cross-country snail race if he never stopped to rest?

33 The ratio of AB to BC is 4:9. The total length of $\overline{AC}$ is 195. Use a spreadsheet to make a table like the one shown, and extend the pattern to find the lengths of $\overline{AB}$ and $\overline{BC}$.

AB	BC	Total
4	9	13
8	18	26
12	27	39
.	.	.
.	.	.
.	.	.

Test

1 List as many attributes of a compact disc as you can think of. Which of these attributes can be measured?

2 Which length is longer, 30 cm or 2 m?

3 For what value of x is the perimeter of this rectangle 12 yards?

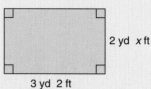

2 yd x ft

3 yd 2 ft

4 For the triangle shown, what is the ratio $\frac{AB}{BC}$?

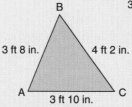

3 ft 8 in.   4 ft 2 in.

3 ft 10 in.

5 The driving distance between two towns is 250 miles. If the speed limit is 55 miles per hour, what is the least time in which a person could drive from one town to the other without breaking the law?

6 Which is the better buy, four 8-ounce cans of tomato paste for $4.12 or six 6-ounce cans of tomato paste for $4.50?

7 Rewrite the map scale 1 in. : 25 mi as a ratio of numbers.

8 If a 200-cubic-centimeter block of a substance has a mass of 450 grams, what is the density of the substance?

9 If a typist can type an average of 65 words per minute, how many words can he type in 8 hours?

10 Solve the proportion $\frac{4}{m} = \frac{20}{25}$ for m.

11 If $\triangle XYZ \sim \triangle MNO$, what are the values of p and q?

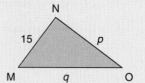

12   16

X   20   Z

15   p

M q O

12 $\triangle ABC \sim \triangle DEC$, $AB = 8$, $BC = 7$, $AC = 6$, and $DC = 4$. Find the ratio of the perimeter of $\triangle ABC$ to the perimeter of $\triangle DEC$.

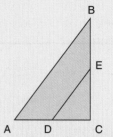

1 Using four straight lines, connect the nine dots without lifting your pencil from the paper.

```
•   •   •

•   •   •

•   •   •
```

2 Use exactly six toothpicks, each the same length, to create four equilateral triangles, each the same size.

3 Rearrange the letters in the word *elation* to spell a part of the body.

4 Figure out what rule was used to determine which letters in the diagram are above the line and which letters are below the line.

A E F H I K L M N T V W Y X Z
———————————————————
B C D G J O P Q R S U

5 Write a ten-digit number in which the first digit tells how many zeros are in the number, the next digit tells how many ones are in the number, the next digit tells how many twos, and so on.

Data
Analysis

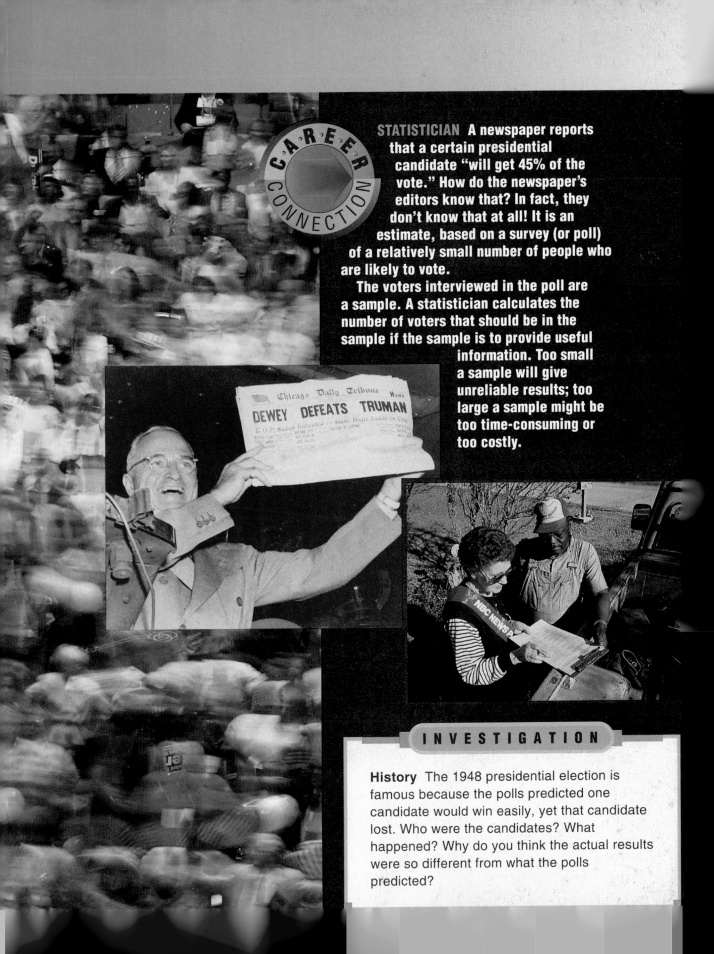

STATISTICIAN A newspaper reports that a certain presidential candidate "will get 45% of the vote." How do the newspaper's editors know that? In fact, they don't know that at all! It is an estimate, based on a survey (or poll) of a relatively small number of people who are likely to vote.

The voters interviewed in the poll are a sample. A statistician calculates the number of voters that should be in the sample if the sample is to provide useful information. Too small a sample will give unreliable results; too large a sample might be too time-consuming or too costly.

Chicago Daily Tribune
DEWEY DEFEATS TRUMAN

INVESTIGATION

History The 1948 presidential election is famous because the polls predicted one candidate would win easily, yet that candidate lost. Who were the candidates? What happened? Why do you think the actual results were so different from what the polls predicted?

SECTION

5.1

Circle Graphs

READING A CIRCLE GRAPH

Through a process called **data analysis,** we can collect, organize, display, and interpret data. To be meaningful, data must be collected in a fair and impartial manner, and the presentation of the data should be clear, accurate, and not misleading.

A **circle graph,** often referred to as a **pie chart,** relates portions of data to the total number of data. A circle represents the total number of data, and pie-shaped sectors represent portions of the data.

A circle graph is an appropriate graph to use when the data have the following attributes:

1. The sum of the data is known.
2. The groups of data are **disjoint**—that is, divisible into categories that do not overlap.

Example
The circle graph shows the results of a survey conducted at Hoday Junior High School. One of the survey questions asked students to list their favorite food. Of the total number of students surveyed, 154 students responded to the question and 23 did not. Determine the number of students in each category.

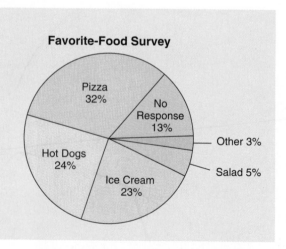

Favorite-Food Survey

Solution

Since 154 students responded to the favorite-food question and 23 did not, we know that a total of 177 students took the survey. We use this total and the percent from the graph to determine the number of students in each category.

Favorite Food	Percentage	Number of Students
Pizza	32% of 177 = 0.32 × 177 = 56.64	57
Hot dogs	24% of 177 = 0.24 × 177 = 42.48	42
Ice cream	23% of 177 = 0.23 × 177 = 40.71	41
Salad	5% of 177 = 0.05 × 177 = 8.85	9
Other	3% of 177 = 0.03 × 177 = 5.31	5
No response	13% of 177 = 0.13 × 177 = 23.01	23

DRAWING A CIRCLE GRAPH

To draw a circle graph, we need to

1. Identify the whole
2. Determine the number of parts
3. Calculate the percent of the circle represented by each part
4. Determine the measures of the angles that correspond to the percents
5. Draw and title the graph, labeling each pie-shaped sector with a category and a percent

Sample Problem

Problem Look at a map of the United States. Determine the number of states that border each state. (States that share only corners are not considered bordering states.) Make a circle graph, with each pie-shaped sector showing the percent of states with a given number of bordering states.

Solution
1. The entire set of data is the 50 states.
2. The number of states bordering each state is shown in the map at the top of the next page. We can see that some states are bordered by as many as eight states, and some states are not bordered by any other state. Therefore, the circle will be divided into nine parts.

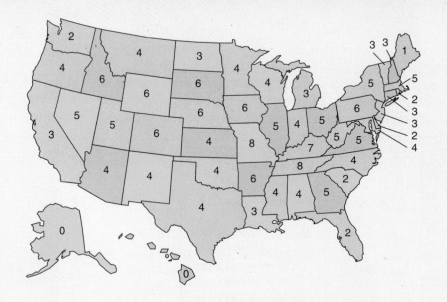

The table summarizes the data displayed on the map.

Number of bordering states	0	1	2	3	4	5	6	7	8
Number of states	2	1	5	8	13	9	9	1	2

3 and 4. We can now calculate the percent and angle measures.

Number of Bordering States	Percent of States with the Given Number(s) of Bordering States	Angle Measure
0 or 8	$\frac{2}{50}(100) = 4\%$	4% of 360° = 0.04 x 360 ≈ 14°
1 or 7	$\frac{1}{50}(100) = 2\%$	2% of 360° = 0.02 x 360 ≈ 7°
2	$\frac{5}{50}(100) = 10\%$	10% of 360° = 0.10 x 360 = 36°
3	$\frac{8}{50}(100) = 16\%$	16% of 360° = 0.16 x 360 ≈ 58°
4	$\frac{13}{50}(100) = 26\%$	26% of 360° = 0.26 x 360 ≈ 94°
5 or 6	$\frac{9}{50}(100) = 18\%$	18% of 360° = 0.18 x 360 ≈ 65°

5. Here is the completed circle graph with all labels.

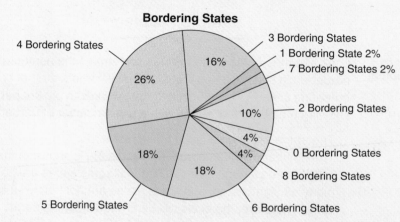

Think and Discuss

1 What does a circle graph represent?

2 Explain how to make a circle graph.

3 What is the sum of the measures of all the angles that make up the pie-shaped sectors of a circle graph?

4 What is the sum of the percent represented by the pie-shaped sectors into which a circle graph is divided?

In problems 5–7, refer to the example on pages 200–201.

5 Why is the number of "no responses" included on the graph?

6 List possible reasons that students did not respond to the question.

7 Can we conclude that less than one fourth of the students identified hot dogs as their favorite food?

8 Poll your class to determine students' favorite lunch foods. Make a pie chart representing the data.

Problems and Applications

9 In a given year, U.S. radio stations were polled to determine the most popular kinds of programming. The data are displayed on the graph. Can you conclude that country music and adult-contemporary music were the most popular kinds of programming that year?

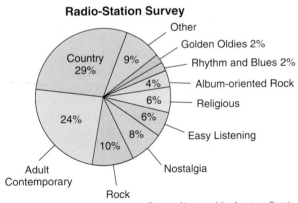

Radio-Station Survey

Other
Country 29%
9%
Golden Oldies 2%
Rhythm and Blues 2%
4%
Album-oriented Rock
6%
Religious
24%
6%
8%
Easy Listening
10%
Nostalgia
Adult Contemporary
Rock

Source: *Almanac of the American People*

In problems 10 and 11, refer to the survey that shows how U.S. consumers spent money to purchase albums, tapes, and compact discs.

10 Make a circle graph to display this information.

11 Compare the circle graph you drew for problem **10** to the one in problem **9**.

Type of Music	Percent of Money Spent
Rock	46.6%
Pop	14.2%
Disco	10.1%
Country	9.7%
Classical	5.9%
Jazz	3.9%
Gospel	3.0%
Other	6.6%

Source: *Almanac of the American People*

12 Communicating Problem **9** seems to imply that country music and adult-contemporary music are the most popular kinds of music in the United States. Problems **10** and **11** seem to imply that rock music is far more popular than any other kind of music. Discuss this apparent contradiction.

In problems 13 and 14, refer to the graph.

13 Find the angle measure of each of the four parts of the circle.

14 Determine the percent of the graph for each of the four parts.

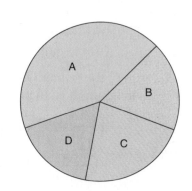

In problems 15–17, the graphs show U.S. petroleum use in 1970 and 1989.

15 In 1989, the United States used 6,323,600,000 barrels of petroleum. How many barrels of petroleum were used for transportation?

16 The United States had 25,900,000,000 barrels of petroleum in reserve on January 1, 1990. How long could that reserve last if petroleum was not used for transportation and the level of consumption remained the same?

17 Did the amount of petroleum used for industrial purposes go up or down from 1970 to 1989?

United States Petroleum Consumption

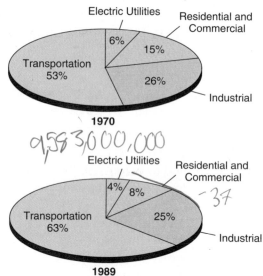

Source: *The World Almanac and Book of Facts*

18 A recent survey done at the House of Pizza revealed that the following numbers of pizzas were sold during the second week in February.

  a How many pizzas were sold during the second week of February?

  b What percent of the total is each type of pizza?

  c If a circle graph were constructed for the data, how many degrees would be in each pie-shaped sector?

  d Draw the circle graph.

Type of Pizza	Number Sold
Cheese only	96
Cheese and sausage	108
Cheese and mushroom	79
Cheese and pepperoni	125
Other combinations	143

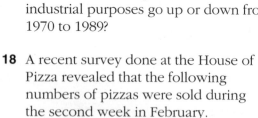

19 Spreadsheets The table displays the ages of cars being used in the United States.

a Enter the two columns of data on a spreadsheet.

b Find the total number of cars represented.

c Make a third column on the spreadsheet for the percent each entry represents. (Hint: Use a formula and the copy function.)

d Make a fourth column to show the angle measure of each portion of a pie chart. (Hint: Use a formula and the copy function.)

e Make a pie chart of the data by hand or with the spreadsheet.

Age of Car	Number of Cars on the Road
Less than 1 year	7,812,000
1–5 years	47,569,500
5–10 years	42,687,000
10–15 years	27,760,500
15 years or older	13,671,000

Source: *The Unofficial U.S. Census*

◀ LOOKING BACK **Spiral Learning** LOOKING AHEAD ▶

20 Continue the pattern.

$$5 + (3 \cdot 6) = 23$$
$$8 + (4 \cdot 6) = 32$$
$$11 + (5 \cdot 6) = 41$$
$$14 + (6 \cdot 6) = 50$$
$$17 + (7 \cdot 6) = 59$$

21 Explain the pattern in problem **20**. Why does it work?

22 $\triangle ACB \sim \triangle DEF$. Determine x and y.

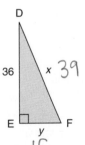

23 Sports The Mildcats' football team had the ball at their 28 yard line. On the first play, they gained 7 yards. On the next play, they gained 4 more yards. On the third play, they lost 8 yards. On the fourth play, they gained 2 yards. What was the team's net gain after the four plays?

24 Find lengths a, b, and c.

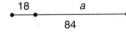

25 Jim Shu walked 8 miles in a direction 30° east of north and then walked 10 miles in a direction 70⁶ east of north. If Jim is facing in the direction he last walked, how many degrees should he rotate clockwise to face his starting point?

In problems 26 and 27, refer to the graph.

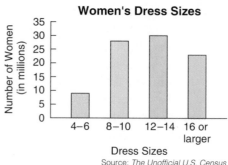

Women's Dress Sizes

Source: *The Unofficial U.S. Census*

26 If a woman is chosen at random from the total number of women selected to provide data for the graph, what is the probability that she wears a size 4–6 dress?

27 If a woman is chosen at random from the group in problem **26**, what is the probability that her dress size is 14 or smaller?

28 A board 6 feet 10 inches long is to be cut into 5 boards of equal length. Find the length of each board.

29 How many different routes run from A to B? (Notice the one-way arrows.)

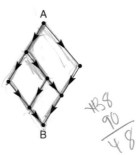

30 Mr. Matt Hematics's class took a test. The scores were

98, 96, 95, 94, 94, 90, 89, 88, 85, 79, 79, 79, 78, 76, 74, 73, 70, 69, 69, 65, 61, 60, 58, 51, 43

a Which score occurred most often?
b Millie Middle's score was exactly in the middle, with 12 students receiving higher scores and 12 students receiving lower scores. What was Millie's score?
c Find the mean (average) student score.
d Find the range of values.
e What is the difference between the highest score and the lowest score?

Investigation

Communications   Listen to one radio station continuously for at least an hour. Keep track of the different programming segments—commercials, music, talk, and news—and the amount of time spent on each. Make a circle graph to display your results. Be sure that the graph includes the name of the radio station and the length of time you listened to the radio. Will everyone in your class have similar graphs?

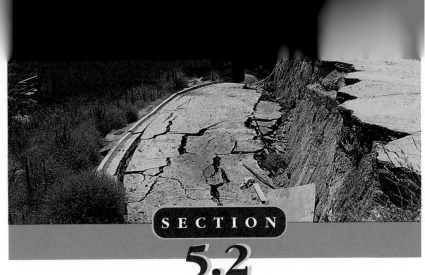

SECTION
5.2
Bar Graphs and Line Graphs

READING BAR GRAPHS AND LINE GRAPHS

A *bar graph* is a graph in which data can be displayed as vertical or horizontal parallel bars of appropriate length. Each of the axes of a bar graph is labeled with appropriate units. Bar graphs allow us to make quick comparisons.

Example 1

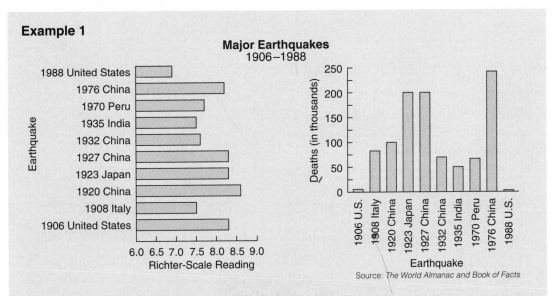

Major Earthquakes
1906–1988

Source: *The World Almanac and Book of Facts*

a Where and when did the quake that caused the fewest number of deaths occur? What was the Richter-scale reading for this quake?

b Where and when did the quake with the highest Richter-scale reading occur? How many deaths resulted from that quake?

c What country was hit by four major quakes? What is the difference between the largest and the smallest number of resulting deaths?

d Is there a relationship between the Richter-scale magnitude of an earthquake and the number of resulting deaths?

Solution

a The quake occurred in the United States in 1988. The Richter-scale reading was about 6.9.

b The quake occurred in China in 1920. There were about 100,000 deaths.

c China was hit by four major quakes. The difference between the largest and the smallest number of resulting deaths is about 170,000.

d There seems to be very little relationship between the Richter-scale magnitude of a quake and the number of resulting deaths. However, a smaller quake would probably cause fewer casualties. We need more data to draw a valid conclusion.

A **line graph** is a graph in which data are displayed as points that are connected by segments. Both axes on a line graph are also labeled. A line graph allows us to show trends.

Example 2

Do you think the women's Olympic high-jump record will reach 7 feet by the year 2000? Why?

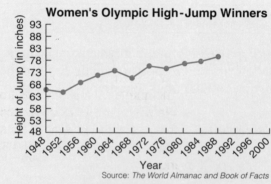

Women's Olympic High-Jump Winners

Source: *The World Almanac and Book of Facts*

Solution

If we lay a ruler along the graph and estimate an average rate of increase, it appears that the women's Olympic high-jump record will have reached 7 feet by the year 2000.

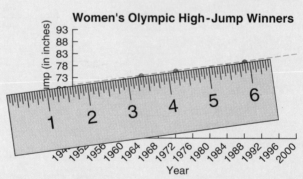

Women's Olympic High-Jump Winners

DRAWING BAR GRAPHS AND LINE GRAPHS

To make a bar graph or a line graph,

1. Decide what data to graph along each axis
2. Find the range of values
3. Label each axis with appropriate units
4. Draw the bars for a bar graph, or plot and connect the points for a line graph
5. Title the graph

Sample Problem

Problem

Mrs. Kur E. Uss surveyed her class to find out the types and numbers of pets her students owned. The table summarizes the results of the survey.

Pet	Number of Students Owning Pets	Total Number of Pets
Cat	8	13
Dog	10	12
Fish	6	68
Gerbil	5	8
Bird	3	4
Guinea pig	2	2
Other	2	4
No pet	3	0

Make a bar graph showing the total number of each type of pet owned by students.

Solution

1. We will label the horizontal axis with the number of pets and the vertical axis with the types of pets.
2. The number of pets ranges from 0 ("no pet") to 68 ("fish").
3. We will label the horizontal axis in increments of 10—each division of this axis will represent 10 pets. Since there are 8 types of pets, 1 type will be named in each of the 8 divisions of the vertical axis.
4 and 5.

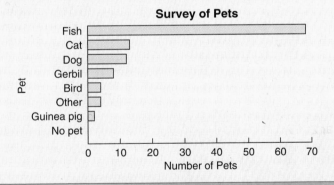

Think and Discuss

1 What would you need to do to change the horizontal bar graph in Example 1 into a vertical bar graph?

2 What would you need to do to change the vertical bar graph in Example 1 into a horizontal bar graph?

3 What conclusion was suggested by the data in Example 2? How certain are you about your conclusion?

4 Why is a circle graph not appropriate for the data in the sample problem on page 209?

5 **a** What kinds of data are best displayed in a circle graph?
b What kinds of data are best displayed in a bar graph?

Problems and Applications

6 **Science** Make a line graph using the following data.

Days after planting	0	10	20	30	40	50	60	70	80	90
Height of plant (in inches)	0	0	4	9	20	40	64	80	84	84

7 Refer to the sample problem on page 209.
a Make a bar graph that shows the number of students owning each type of pet.
b Is a fish or a cat the more popular pet among the students in Mrs. Kur E. Uss's class?

8 **Business** The value of Solar Plexus stock was $39.00 on Monday. The value of the stock rose by $1.50 on Tuesday, fell by $4.00 on Wednesday, rose by $1.75 on Thursday, and fell by $5.50 on Friday. Display this information in a line graph.

9 The chart displays weekly statistics for BCA stock.
a What do the numbers in the value column represent?
b What was the change in value of the stock from Monday to Friday?
c What was the range of values for the week?
d On which day was recorded the greatest change from the previous day?
e Make a line graph of this data.

Day	Value at Close
Monday	$35\frac{7}{8}$
Tuesday	$33\frac{1}{2}$
Wednesday	$35\frac{1}{4}$
Thursday	$37\frac{1}{8}$
Friday	$36\frac{3}{4}$

10 The following is a list of test scores for a geology test:

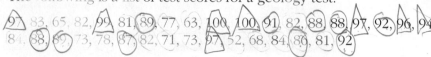

97, 83, 65, 82, 99, 81, 89, 77, 63, 100, 100, 91, 82, 88, 88, 97, 92, 96, 94,
84, 88, 89, 73, 78, 87, 82, 71, 73, 97, 52, 68, 84, 86, 81, 92

The given grading scale is used. Make a bar graph that shows the number of students that earned each grade.

Grade	Range
A	100 – 93
B	92 – 85
C	84 – 77
D	76 – 68
F	67 – 0

11 Social Science

a What percent of people got married in 1960?

b What percent of people got married in 1970?

c What percent of people got married in 1975?

d Did more people get married in 1970 or in 1975?

e What is the ratio of marriages to divorces, rounded to the nearest hundredth, in 1960? 1965? 1975? 1980? 1988?

Marriage Rates and Divorce Rates in the U.S.
1960–1988 (per 1,000 of population)

Source: *The Universal Almanac, 1991*

12 A study of deaths over a 25-year period revealed data on the average number of annual deaths from various weather-related conditions.

a Display the data in a bar graph.

b Explain why a circle graph is not an appropriate way to display the data.

Weather Condition	Average Annual Deaths
Heat	200
Floods	151
Lightning	94
Tornadoes	87
Hurricanes	31

13 Communicating Write a story about what the graph might represent.

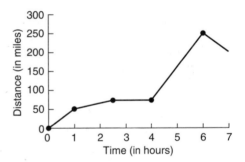

14 Communicating

a About how many times larger were farms in 1989 than in 1940?

b What may have happened to the number of farms from 1940 to 1989?

c Explain your response to part **b**.

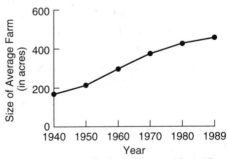

Source: *The World Almanac and Book of Facts*

15 For a basketball player to slam dunk, the sum of the vertical reach and the vertical jump of the player must be 10 feet 6 inches. Copy and complete the bar graph to show the vertical jump needed to slam dunk.

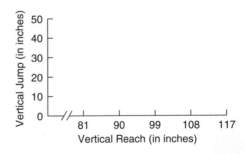

16 Classify each angle as *acute, right,* or *obtuse.*

a

b

c

17 In a surveyor's drawing, $\frac{1}{8}$ inch represents 12 feet. What is the actual perimeter of a rectangle if the dimensions in the drawing are 2 feet by $1\frac{1}{2}$ feet?

18 If $v = 21$, $w = 19$, $x = 17$, $y = 15$, and $z = 13$, what is the value of $(v - x)(w - x)(x - x)(y - x)(z - x)$?

19 The small rectangles are congruent. How many gallons does the red region represent?

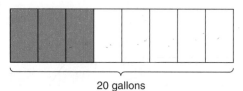

20 gallons

20 a Find the value of x.
b Why is the value of x close to the length of one of the legs of the triangle?

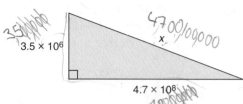

3.5×10^6

x

4.7×10^8

21 Science Ice (at 0°C) has a density of 922 kg/m³.
a If the edge of a cube of ice is 4 cm, what is the mass of the cube?
b Check your answer to part **a** by actually weighing such an ice cube.

22 a How many U.S. homes have four or fewer phones?
b Make a circle graph of the data.
c Based on the given data, what is the total number of phones in the U.S.?

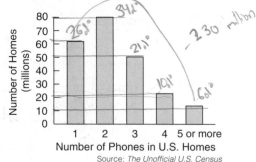

Number of Homes (millions)

Number of Phones in U.S. Homes

Source: *The Unofficial U.S. Census*

Investigation

Sports The winning women's high jump in the 1968 Olympics in Mexico City was surprisingly low. Research the history of the 1968 Olympic Games to find possible explanations.

SECTION

5.3
Other Data Displays

SCATTERGRAMS

In a **scattergram,** data are graphed along vertical and horizontal axes but cannot be connected by a line. The data in a scattergram often follow a pattern from which we can derive a trend or draw some conclusions.

Example 1

Ms. Anna Liss gathered data on the length of time that students studied for a science test and the resulting test scores. What trend do you see?

Study Time (minutes)	Scores
0 – 15	0, 20, 24, 30
16 – 30	20, 30, 40
31 – 45	36, 38, 40, 42, 46
46 – 60	34, 38, 40, 42, 44, 50
More than 60	38, 40, 44, 46, 48, 49, 50

Solution

We can draw a scattergram with the test scores graphed along the vertical axis and the lengths of study time graphed along the horizontal axis.

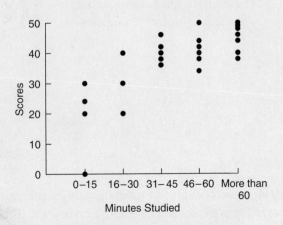

The scattergram shows a trend of better scores for students who studied longer.

HISTOGRAMS

A ***histogram*** (or ***line plot*** if data are graphed on a number line) indicates the number of times that a value or range of values occurs in a set of data. Histograms are similar to bar graphs with respect to the type of information they can display. A histogram can be drawn vertically or horizontally, but in line plots the number line is usually horizontal.

Example 2
Display the scores from Ms. Anna Liss's class in a line plot.

Solution

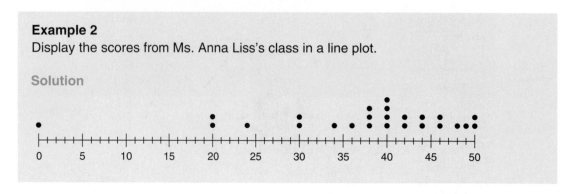

PICTOGRAPHS

A ***pictograph*** is used to represent data that would be difficult to display in a histogram. Pictographs use symbols related to the nature of the data.

Example 3
How much petroleum did the United States use in 1989?

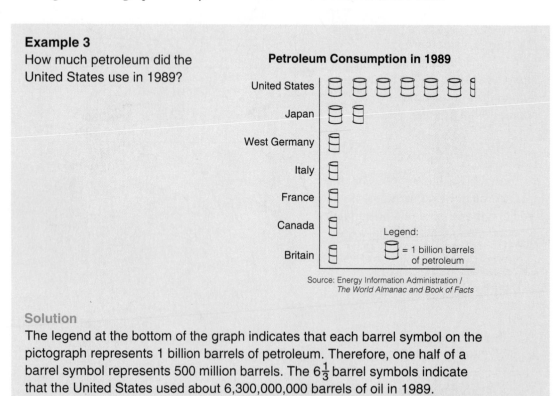

Solution
The legend at the bottom of the graph indicates that each barrel symbol on the pictograph represents 1 billion barrels of petroleum. Therefore, one half of a barrel symbol represents 500 million barrels. The $6\frac{1}{3}$ barrel symbols indicate that the United States used about 6,300,000,000 barrels of oil in 1989.

ARTISTIC GRAPHS

Sometimes information can be represented by an ***artistic graph.*** Artistic graphs vary greatly and usually manage to depict a great deal of information within a small space. Sometimes artistic graphs give impressions that are not exactly correct.

Example 4

Much information about the depletion of the world's rain forests is presented in this artistic graph. What might you conclude by looking at this graph?

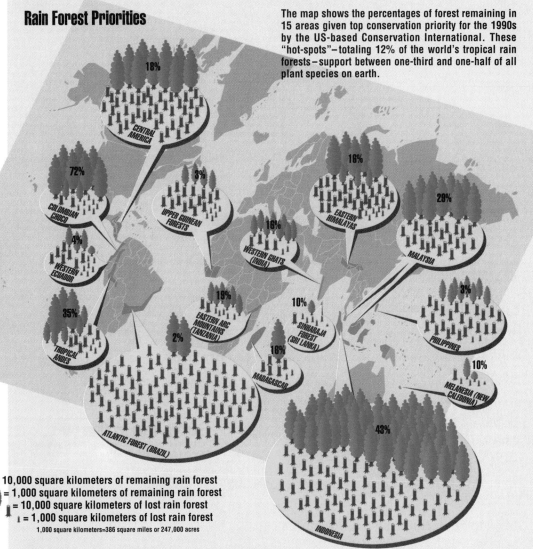

Rain Forest Priorities

The map shows the percentages of forest remaining in 15 areas given top conservation priority for the 1990s by the US-based Conservation International. These "hot-spots"—totaling 12% of the world's tropical rain forests—support between one-third and one-half of all plant species on earth.

= 10,000 square kilometers of remaining rain forest
= 1,000 square kilometers of remaining rain forest
= 10,000 square kilometers of lost rain forest
= 1,000 square kilometers of lost rain forest
1,000 square kilometers=386 square miles or 247,000 acres

Solution

We might conclude that most of the world's rain forests have been heavily depleted. However, if we read carefully, we learn that only 12% of the world's rain forests are depicted in this artistic graph and that these are the 15 rain forests that need the most help. If the artist had included all rain forests, our impressions might be different.

215

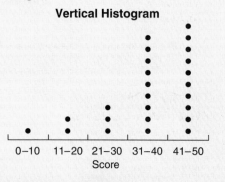
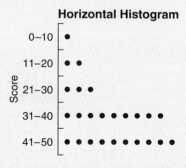
Think and Discuss

1 How does a histogram differ from a bar graph?

2 What is the difference between a histogram and a line plot?

3 How would you decide whether to use a scattergram or a bar graph?

4 What advantages does a pictograph have over a bar graph?

5 What advantage does a bar graph have over a pictograph?

In problems 6 and 7, refer to the graph.

6 What is the average number of years of experience for all 28 NFL coaches?

7 If we do not include the 6 head coaches listed, what is the average tenure of a head coach?

Source: NFL/Rod Little, USA TODAY

8 This is a histogram of the scoring of the Chicago Bulls in their first home game of the 1991 season against the Philadelphia 76ers.

a How many points did Scottie Pippen score?

b How many points did Michael Jordan score?

c What was the team score?

d The 76ers scored 90 points. Which team won?

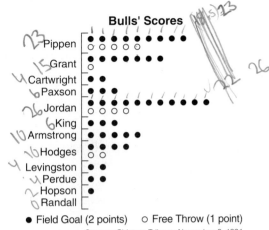

Bulls' Scores

Pippen
Grant
Cartwright
Paxson
Jordan
King
Armstrong
Hodges
Levingston
Perdue
Hopson
Randall

● Field Goal (2 points)   ○ Free Throw (1 point)

Source: *Chicago Tribune*, November 2, 1991

Problems and Applications

In problems 9–11, refer to the graph.

9 Find the ratio of noodles sold to long goods sold.

10 For every 5 ounces of noodles sold, what quantity of short goods is sold?

11 Why do you think long goods are the most popular type of pasta?

41%

31%

Picking pasta
Retail sales by shape of pasta:

15%

13%

| Long goods (spaghetti, linguini) | Short goods (elbows, twists, etc.) | Noodles (egg added) | Specialties (lasagne, jumbo shells, manicotti, flavored shapes) |

Source: National Pasta Association/Ron Coddington, USA TODAY

12 Adam rolled a pair of dice 116 times. Each time he rolled the dice, he wrote down the sum of the dots on the faces. The table summarizes the results. Represent the data in a histogram.

Sum of dots	2	3	4	5	6	7	8	9	10	11	12
Number of times	3	5	9	14	16	22	18	14	8	5	2

13 **Science** Draw a pictograph that displays the data in this table.

City	Snowfall (inches)
Juneau, Alaska	103
Buffalo, New York	92
Burlington, Vermont	78
Duluth, Minnesota	77
Portland, Maine	72
Denver, Colorado	60

14 **Science** Mr. Lewis had each student in his class run the 100-meter dash. The students' times were measured in seconds, and their hip heights were measured in inches. The data are displayed in a chart.

Hip height	30	31	28	34	26	29	32	22	26	33	32
Time	16.2	16.0	18.3	15.6	19.1	17.4	16.1	19.9	18.7	15.7	16.3

a Present the data in a scattergram.
b Find the average hip height of the students in Mr. Lewis's class.
c Find the average time it takes the students in Mr. Lewis's class to run the 100-meter dash.
d Describe a relationship between hip height and the time it takes to run the 100-meter dash.

Agriculture **In problems 15–18, refer to the graph, which shows the annual milk production of U.S. dairy cows.**

15 How many gallons of milk were produced in 1970? In 1990?

16 What is the percent of increase in annual milk production per cow between 1970 and 1990?

17 Which is greater, the percent of increase from 1970 to 1980 or the percent of increase from 1980 to 1990?

18 How much milk per day did cows give in 1970? In 1990?

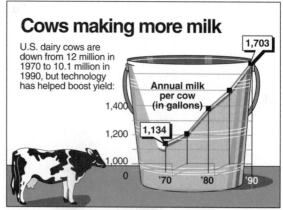

Source: United Dairy Industry Association, USDA./Suzy Parker, USA TODAY

19 Make a circle graph of the data showing the distribution of landfill garbage by volume.

Miscellaneous
20 percent by volume
Includes construction and demolition debris, tires, textiles, rubber, and disposable diapers.

Paper
50 percent
Includes packaging, newspapers, telephone books, glossy magazines, and mail-order catalogs.

Plastic
10 percent
Includes milk jugs, soda bottles, food packaging, garbage bags, and polystyrene foam.

Metal
6 percent
Includes iron as well as aluminium and steel cans for food and beverages.

Glass
1 percent
Includes beverage bottles, food containers, and cosmetics jars.

Organic
13 percent
Includes wood, yard waste, and food scraps.

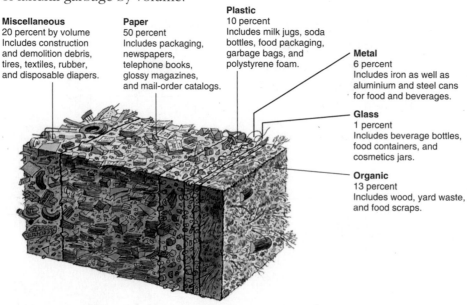

In problems 20 and 21, refer to the table, which displays the high temperatures in Frostbite Falls during the first week in January.

20 Display these data in a pictograph or an artistic graph.

21 **Communicating** Explain your choice of graph in problem **20**.

Day	Temperature
Monday	−27° F
Tuesday	−18°
Wednesday	−7°
Thursday	−12°
Friday	−19°
Saturday	−21°
Sunday	−25°

22 Solve each equation for x.
a $13x = 1352$ **b** $13 + x = 1352$

23 Halfback Crazy Legs carried the ball seven times in last week's game. The following changes in yardage took place: +4, −7, −3, +5, −2, 0, +3. What was his average gain?

24

A number line from −5 to 5 with points A at −3, B at −1, C at 1, and D at 4.

How many units apart are
a A and B? **b** B and C? **c** A and C? **d** A and D?

25 If you study the signs of the zodiac, you will see that $\frac{4}{12}$ of the signs represent people and $\frac{7}{12}$ of the signs represent animals. What fraction of the signs represent neither people nor animals?

26 Draw △ABC. Draw $\overline{PQ}$ parallel to $\overline{BC}$, where P is on $\overline{AB}$ and Q is on $\overline{AC}$. Measure $\overline{AP}$, $\overline{PB}$, $\overline{AQ}$, and $\overline{QC}$.
a Find the ratio of the length of $\overline{AP}$ to the length of $\overline{PB}$.
b Find the ratio of the length of $\overline{AQ}$ to the length of $\overline{QC}$.

27 **a** Calculate the area of each polygon to the left of the numbers 1 through 7.
b Make a bar graph of the data.

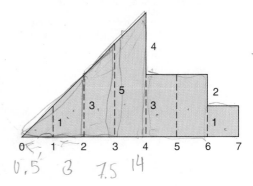

28 Evaluate each of the following.
a 42.63×10^3 **b** $523,609 \div 10^4$

29 a Compare the perimeters of the two rectangles.
b Compare the areas of the two rectangles.

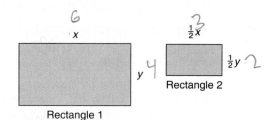

Rectangle 1

Rectangle 2

30 a List these seven people in order of height. Who is in the middle?
b Explain your answer to part **a**.

Alan — 5'4"
Cindy — 5'6"
Ellen — 5'3"
Greg — 5'7"
Bob — 5'8"
David — 5'2"
Fionnuala — 5'5"

31 a Measure each section of the pie chart with a protractor and use your results to calculate the approximate number of dogs in each category.
b Each year of a dog's life is equivalent to about seven years of a human's life. Calculate the equivalent human ages for each category.

Ages of 50.5 Million Dogs in the United States

Between 1 and 5 Years

Less Than 1 Year

More Than 15 Years

Between 5 and 10 Years

Between 10 and 15 Years

Source: *The Unofficial U.S. Census*

32 Solve for *n, m,* and *w*.
a $78n + 4 = 160$ **b** $52m - 8 = 5$ **c** $512 - w = 437$

33 The data for this problem were gathered from a 1991 survey.
a In 1991, if a science teacher were selected at random, what is the probability the teacher would have had a science degree?
b In 1991, if a mathematics teacher were selected at random, what is the probability the teacher would have had a mathematics degree?

Teachers Who Have a Degree in the Field in Which They Teach

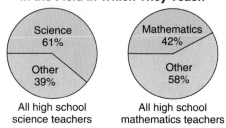

Science 61%

Other 39%

Mathematics 42%

Other 58%

All high school science teachers

All high school mathematics teachers

Source: *National Center for Education Statistics*

Investigation

Data Analysis   Find several examples of graphs from magazines or newspapers. Describe the main point(s) being made by each graph. Is some of this information misleading? Explain how graphs are sometimes used to mislead the reader. Produce examples if possible.

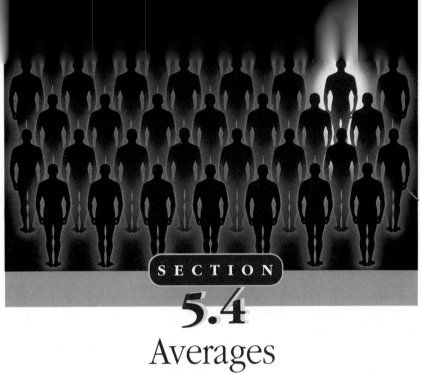

5.4
Averages

THE MEAN

An average tells us something about an entire set of data we are trying to analyze. As you will see, there are several kinds of averages. One kind, with which you are already familiar, is called the **mean.** In everyday life, when people talk about an average, they are usually referring to a mean. The mean is actually a ratio—the sum of the data values divided by the number of values.

Example 1

Here is a set of test scores from Miss Riley's third-period class. What is the mean test score?

65	76	84	93	69
87	95	92	79	72
82	86	88	94	66
82	77	74	82	95
97	82	91	89	73

Solution

$$\text{Mean} = \frac{\text{sum of test scores}}{\text{number of test scores}} = \frac{2070}{25} = 82.8$$

The mean test score is 82.8.

THE MEDIAN

The **median,** another kind of average, is the value in the middle of the data. To determine the median, you may put the data in order, either from least to greatest or from greatest to least. The value in the middle is the median. If the number of data items is even, the median is the mean of the two middle values.

Example 2

Find the median of the test scores in Example 1.

We will organize the data from least to greatest, then find the middle test score. Since there are 25 scores, the middle value of the data is the thirteenth score, 82. Therefore, the median is 82.

65	66	69	72	73
74	76	77	79	82
82	82	82	84	86
87	88	89	91	92
93	94	95	95	97

THE MODE

The **mode** is the data value that occurs most often.

Example 3

What is the mode of the data in Example 2?

In the set of scores, 82 occurs four times, more than any other score. The mode is 82.

The three averages—mean, median, and mode—are also called **measures of central tendency** because they are different ways of locating the center of a set of data.

Sample Problems

Problem 1

The Micro-Bitts Computer Company (MBCC) has 20 employees with the following annual salaries. Find the average salary at MBCC.

  1 President $100,000
  2 Vice-presidents..................$ 80,000 each
  1 Plant Manager ....$ 40,000
16 Assembly workers ....$ 15,000 each

Solution

To answer this question, we will find three kinds of averages—the mean, the median, and the mode.

$$\text{Mean} = \frac{\text{total of salaries}}{\text{number of employees}}$$

$$= \frac{\$100,000 + 2(\$80,000) + \$40,000 + 16(\$15,000)}{20}$$

$$= \frac{\$540,000}{20}$$

$$= \$27,000$$

There are 20 employees, so the median will be the mean of the tenth and eleventh salaries. The amounts of the tenth and eleventh salaries are each $15,000 because 16 of the 20 salaries are $15,000.

$$\text{Median} = \frac{\text{sum of the tenth and eleventh values}}{2}$$

$$= \frac{\$15,000 + \$15,000}{2}$$

$$= \$15,000$$

The mode is $15,000, the salary that occurs most often.

Problem 2

The list contains the sales volume for Top Ten compact discs sold at Seady's Record Store last week. Find the mode of the sales.

Pistols and Posies.....15   Snow Leopards 32
Twigs..........................19   Cellophane Rappers...45
Yukon II....................25   Madora 50
Nebraska...................25   Jack Michaelson.........52
Keen Teens..............28   A and J 52

Solution

There are two modes in this set of data, 25 and 52.

Problem 3

The mean of Jeremy's first three test scores is 88 points. How many points must he earn on the fourth test to have a mean score of 90?

Solutions

Method 1

Because the mean of the first three scores is 88, the total number of points Jeremy scored must be the same as if he had received an 88 on each test. Here is one way to determine the number of points he needs on the fourth test.

Calculate points earned: $88 \times 3 = 264$
Calculate necessary points: $90 \times 4 = 360$
Find the difference: $360 - 264 = 96$

Jeremy needs 96 points.

Method 2

We can also determine the number of points Jeremy needs on the fourth test by using a graph. On the first three tests, Jeremy's scores were a total of 6 points below a mean of 90. Therefore, he would need to score 90 + 6, or 96, on the last test to have a score of 90 on all four tests.

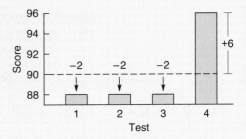

Think and Discuss

1 Find the mode, the median, and the mean of 13, 21, 35, 35, 48, 56, 65, 74, and 88.

2 **a** Find the mean of the data.
b Find the median of the data.
c Find the mode of the data.
d Explain the results of parts **a–c**.

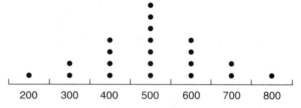

3 Sample Problem 1 on page 222 refers to an average. Why might it be important to specify which of the three averages is to be calculated?

4 The measures of the angles of a pentagon are 108, 108, 108, 78, and 138.
a Find the mean measure of the angles.
b What is the measure of any angle of a regular pentagon?

5 Tenna Pin bowled 120, 125, 130, 136, and 170 in the first five games of the Latin Club bowling tournament. She bowled 212 in the sixth game.
a Find the mean and the median of the first five games.
b Find the mean and the median of all six games.
c What is the change in the mean and the median between the first five games and all six games?

6 During the first nine weeks of the summer, Chip earned an average of $35 per week mowing lawns. How much would he need to earn during the tenth week to have a mean weekly income of $40?

7 **Spreadsheets** Here are some test scores from Mr. X's math class.

38, 43, 98, 96, 55, 95, 95, 56, 62, 63, 89, 87, 65

a Find the mean. (Use a spreadsheet if one is available.)
b Find the median. (If you use a spreadsheet, try the sorting function.)
c What is the mode of the data? Is the mode a good measure of central tendency for the data? Explain your response.
d Can we use the data to draw any meaningful conclusions?

Problems and Applications

8 Find the mean and the median for each set of data.
a 3, 8, 24, 35, 90
b 0, 20, 20, 40, 80
c 30, 30, 30, 30, 40
d 0, 0, 50, 50, 60

9 **a** Find the mean of 56, 94, 62, 75, and 83.
b Find the sum of all the differences of the data from the mean in part **a**.

10 The table shows the income of each member of the Mint family. Which of the following statements is correct?

Person	Income
S. Pierre Mint	$110,000
"Pepper" Mint	50,000
Merry Mint	35,000
Bela Mint	10,000
Horace Mint	10,000

   a The average income of the Mint family is $43,000.
   b The average income of the Mint family is $10,000.
   c The average income of the Mint family is $35,000.

11 Here are Pete's scores on video games.

21, 18, 19, 39, 26, 36, 28, 17, 19, 34, 36, 18, 21, 19, 29, 28, 24, 21, 13, 18, 29, 36, 29, 22, 29, 26, 27, 28, 21, 38, 23, 39, 32, 37, 39, 18, 12, 28, 31, 27, 32, 35, 37, 18

   a How many scores are between 10 and 19?
   b How many scores are between 20 and 29?
   c How many scores are between 30 and 39?

12 Spreadsheets Here are some test scores from Mr. X's math class.

85, 78, 87, 93, 67, 54, 67, 77, 88, 95, 93, 79, 56

   a Enter the data into cells A1–A13 of a spreadsheet.
   b Calculate the mean in cell A14 by using the function @Avg(A1..A13).
   c Was Mr. X's test a difficult one? Why or why not?
   d Use the spreadsheet to sort the data. What is the median?

13 The table displays the results of a survey taken to determine the average number of pieces of jewelry worn by women. What is the average?

Number of pieces	0	1	2	3	4	5 or more
Percent of women	30%	5%	14%	19%	14%	18%

14 Communicating Copy the "ruler" onto your paper. Mark 44 and 47. How did you determine where the two marks should go?

|———————————————————————————————|
40   50

15 In the Big Raffle, 125 people won nothing, 4 people won $50 each, and 1 person won $1000.
   a Find the mean of the people's winnings.
   b Find the median of the people's winnings.
   c Find the mode of the people's winnings.

16 The graph displays ten popular adult activities and the percent of adults that participate in them.
   a What is the sum of the percents?
   b Why can the sum of the percent exceed 100%?
   c Is it possible to determine the most popular activity for the average person in the United States?

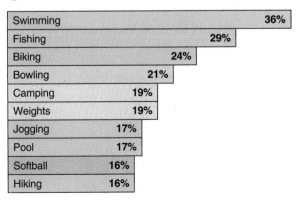

Swimming	36%
Fishing	29%
Biking	24%
Bowling	21%
Camping	19%
Weights	19%
Jogging	17%
Pool	17%
Softball	16%
Hiking	16%

17

10   22   35   53 57   72 78 85   95 102   113   130

a Find the mean of the numbers on the number line.
b Copy the number line onto your paper, marking only the extremes, 10 and 130.
c Mark the mean in the appropriate place.

18 During lunch hour at a compact-disc store, the employees kept track of the number of discs bought by each customer who entered the store. The results are listed in the table.

Number of customers	2	3	10	8	16	27
Number of discs purchased	5	4	3	2	1	0

a How many discs were sold?
b How many discs did the average person buy?
c If the average price of a disc is $14.00, how much money did the store make?
d How much did the average customer spend?

19

6 10 14 18 22 27   60   120

16 21 25 29

a Find the mean and the median of the numbers plotted.
b Copy the number line onto your paper. Plot 6, 120, the mean, and the median.

◀ LOOKING BACK **Spiral Learning** LOOKING AHEAD ▶

---

20 Find the measure of ∠D in pentagon ABCDE.

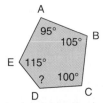

21 **a** How many personnel managers were surveyed?
b How many of them felt that health care will be a major concern in the year 2000?
c According to the managers surveyed, which issue was a major concern in 1990 but will not be in 2000? Which issues were not major concerns in 1990 but will be in 2000?

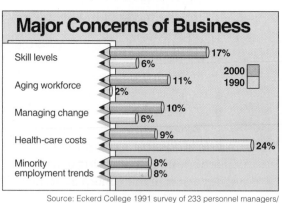

Source: Eckerd College 1991 survey of 233 personnel managers/ Elys A. McLean, USA TODAY

22 Mr. E. Ficcient organized his test scores into this table. Four of the scores, 92, 93, 97, and 99, are in the 90's.

Tens	Units
9	2 3 7 9
8	1 4 7 7 7
7	0 9
6	4 5 8

  a List all the scores.
  b Find the mean of the scores.
  c Find the median score.
  d Find the mode of the scores.

23 Enter 7 [+/−] [×] 8 [=] into your calculator. What did you get? Why?

24 Find the ratio of the values of six quarters to five dimes.

25 **Communicating**
  a What trend does the scattergram show?
  b If someone had a neck size of about 53 centimeters, what would you predict the person's wrist size to be?
  c Explain why the scales do not start with zero.

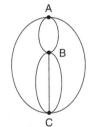

26 **a** How many paths run from A to C, traveling downward?
  b What percent of the paths go through B?

27 **a** Does the graph mean that Oakland has been the best team since 1969?
  b What does the fact that Oakland has won so many division titles suggest?
  c Cincinnati and Los Angeles have each been 5-2 in play-off series. Do some research and find out how they did in the World Series.

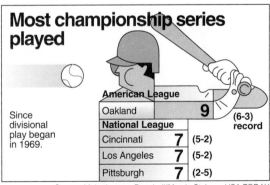

Most championship series played

Since divisional play began in 1969.

American League		
Oakland	9	(6-3) record

National League		
Cincinnati	7	(5-2)
Los Angeles	7	(5-2)
Pittsburgh	7	(2-5)

Source: Major League Baseball/Marcia Staimer, USA TODAY

Investigation

Baseball How is a batting average calculated in baseball? How is a pitcher's earned run average calculated? Are these averages examples of a mean, a median, or a mode? Explain your answer. Then write formulas that can be used to calculate a batting average and an earned run average.

5.5
Organizing Data

STEM–AND–LEAF PLOTS

When data are collected, they are often unsorted or are sorted in a way that does not meet our needs. In this section, we will use a **stem-and-leaf plot** to organize data.

Example 1

Below is a list of the score margins for the top 25 college football teams on October 18, 1991. Two teams did not play, so we ignore them. Four teams lost, so their margins are negative.

Florida State 32	Florida...............16	Alabama............46
Washington.......54	California............3	Illinois................21
Miami 37	Ohio State.........15	Texas A & M 23
Tennessee ....—	Pittsburgh............4	Georgia 15
Michigan 19	Syracuse.........–32	Mississippi 21
Oklahoma 21	N.C. State 7	Arizona State 6
Notre Dame 16	Iowa ....–19	Auburn ....–1
Baylor................17	Nebraska...........—	
Penn State........17	Clemson..........–15	

Organize these data in a stem-and-leaf plot.

Solution

The greatest and least values in a set of data are called the **extremes** of the data, and the difference between these values is the **range** of the data. The extremes of these data are 54 and –32, so the range of the data is 86. We will use the tens digits of the numbers –32 through 54 as the stems in our plot.

We add leaves to the stems by writing each unit's digit next to the corresponding stem. For example, Alabama had a score margin of 46, so we write a 6 to the right of 4. Similarly, we write a 1 next to −0 for Auburn's margin of −1.

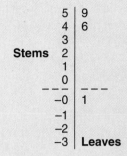

```
        5 │ 9
        4 │ 6
        3 │
Stems   2 │
        1 │
        0 │
       ─ ─ ┼ ─ ─ ─
       −0 │ 1
       −1 │
       −2 │
       −3 │ Leaves
```

Here is the completed stem-and-leaf plot. There are 23 data values, so the median is the twelfth value in the list (the value with 11 values greater and 11 values less). The median of these data is 16.

```
        5 │ 4
        4 │ 6
        3 │ 2 7
Stems   2 │ 1 1 1 3
        1 │ 5 5 6 6 7 7 9
        0 │ 3 4 6 7
       ─ ─ ┼ ─ ─ ─
       −0 │ 1
       −1 │ 5 9
       −2 │
       −3 │ 2    Leaves
```

BOX–AND–WHISKER PLOTS

A ***box-and-whisker plot*** is a visual representation of data that shows the middle 50% of the data relative to the extremes.

Example 2
Draw a box-and-whisker plot of the data in Example 1.

Solution
First we draw a segment whose length represents the range of the data. The range of the data in Example 1 is 86, so we can draw a segment 86 millimeters long. Each 1 millimeter of the segment will represent 1 point of a score margin. Next, we plot the median of the data. The median of these data is 16, and the difference between 54 and 16 is 38, so we plot the median 38 millimeters from the 54.

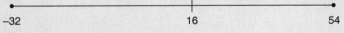

```
−32              16              54
```

The median divides the data into two equal parts. The median of the upper part is called the ***upper quartile*** of the data. In this case, the upper quartile is 21, the value from the top of the stem-and-leaf plot (or the sixth value above the median). It should be plotted 5 millimeters to the right of the median, since 21 − 16 = 5. Similarly, the ***lower quartile,*** 4, is the median of the lower part of the data. It should be plotted 12 millimeters to the left of the median.

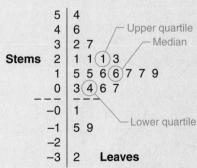

```
        5 │ 4
        4 │ 6                    ⌐ Upper quartile
        3 │ 2 7                  ⌐ Median
Stems   2 │ 1 1 ①3
        1 │ 5 5 6 ⑥ 7 7 9
        0 │ 3 ④ 6 7
       ─ ─ ┼ ─ ─ ─
       −0 │ 1
       −1 │ 5 9                  ⌐ Lower quartile
       −2 │
       −3 │ 2    Leaves
```

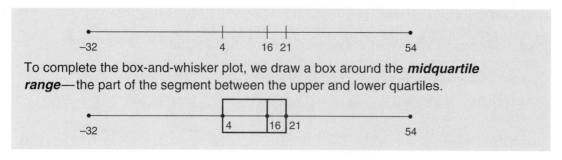

To complete the box-and-whisker plot, we draw a box around the **midquartile range**—the part of the segment between the upper and lower quartiles.

A box-and-whisker plot gives a pictorial view of a central tendency of a set of data. The midquartile range, corresponding to the middle 50% of the data, can be used to locate **outliers.** Outliers are data values that are more than 1.5 times the midquartile range above the upper quartile or below the lower quartile.

Sample Problem

Problem Use the box-and-whisker plot in Example 2 to determine whether the value 54 is an outlier of the data presented in the plot.

Solution The midquartile range of the data is the difference between the upper quartile and the lower quartile, so it is 21 – 4, or 17. If we multiply 17 by 1.5, we get a result of 25.5. Since 54 is more than 25.5 units above the upper quartile (it is 54 – 21, or 33, units above the quartile), it is an outlier of the set of data.

Think and Discuss

1 a Organize the data for average wind speeds into a stem-and-leaf plot.
b Which of the data values is an obvious outlier? Explain why this number is an outlier.

Location	Average Speed (mph)
Mt. Washington, N.H.	35.3
New Orleans, La.	8.2
New York, N.Y.	9.4
Omaha, Neb.	10.6
Philadelphia, Pa.	9.5
Phoenix, Ariz.	6.3
Pittsburgh, Pa.	9.1
Portland, Ore.	7.9
St. Louis, Mo.	9.7
Salt Lake City, Ut.	8.8
San Diego, Cal.	6.9
Seattle, Wash.	9.0
Washington, D.C.	9.3

Source: *World Almanac and Book of Facts, 1991*

2 Is the value −32 an outlier of the data in Example 1?

3 What percent of the data values are in each of the four sections of a box-and-whisker plot?

4 Coach Bradley recorded the number of seconds it took her students to do 50 sit-ups. Then she drew a box-and-whisker plot to represent the data she collected.

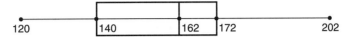

The next day she did the same thing and drew this box-and-whisker plot.

Explain how the students' performances changed.

5 In a box-and-whisker plot, data are divided into quarters, which are separated by quartiles. Standardized-test data are often divided into percentiles. Explain the difference between percentiles and quartiles.

6

Explain how the test data in the first box-and-whisker plot differ from the data in the second.

7 **a** Find the range of the data in the stem-and-leaf plot.
b Find the median of the data.
c Find the mode of the data.
d Find the lower quartile of the data.
e Find the upper quartile of the data.
f Make a box-and-whisker plot for the data.

Stems	Leaves
0	
1	5
2	
3	2
4	3 5
5	1 7 8
6	2 3 5 8 8 8 8 9
7	0 0 4 7 9
8	2 4 4 8
9	3 4 5 8 8

Problems and Applications

8 56, 68, 15, 98, 84, 38, 100, 95, 61, 46, 99, 81, 63, 49, 55, 100, 75, 91, 84, 56, 99, 71, 84, 64, 63, 84, 56

a Find the median, M, of the given test scores.
b Find the median of the data less than M. What is this number called?
c Find the median of the data greater than M. What is this number called?

9 a Make a stem-and-leaf plot for the data.
  b Find the median, the lower quartile, the upper quartile, the extremes, and the range for the data.
  c Make a box-and-whisker plot for the data.
  d Are there any outliers? Justify your answer.

Forest and Range Fires: Acres Burned, 1981–90 (in millions)			
Year	Acreage	Year	Acreage
1981	4.8	1986	3.3
1982	2.3	1987	4.2
1983	5.1	1988	7.4
1984	2.3	1989	3.3
1985	4.4	1990	5.5

Source: Boise Interagency Fire Center, 1992

10 Science

Major California Earthquakes, 1900–1989								
Year	Location	Richter-scale reading	Year	Location	Richter-scale reading	Year	Location	Richter-scale reading
1906	San Francisco	8.3	1980	Eureka	7.0	1971	San Francisco	6.4
1952	Tehachapi-Bakersfield	7.8	1940	Imperial Valley	6.7	1933	Long Beach	6.3
			1911	Coyote	6.6	1925	Santa Barbara	6.3
1927	Offshore San Luis Obispo	7.7	1980	Mammoth Lakes	6.6	1984	Morgan Hill	6.2
			1983	Coalinga	6.5	1987	Los Angeles	6.1
1923	North Coast	7.2	1979	Imperial Valley	6.4	1986	Palm Springs	6.0
1989	San Francisco	7.0	1968	Anza-Borrego Mountains	6.4			

a Make a stem-and-leaf plot for the data.
b Find the median of the data.
c Find the lower and upper quartiles.
d Make a box-and-whisker plot for the data.

11 Communicating
  a Arrange the data values from least to greatest.
  b Find the median, the lower quartile, the upper quartile, and the extremes of the data.
  c Compare the mean and the median of the data. Why is the median a better choice as an average of these data?
  d Draw a box-and-whisker plot for the data.
  e What are the outliers? Explain why these numbers are outliers.
  f Why, do you think, is much more fish caught in Alaska than in any other state?

Fisheries—Quantity of Catch, by State, (millions of pounds, live weight)	
State	1988
U.S. total	**7,155**
Alabama	24
Alaska	2,639
California	496
Connecticut	9
Delaware	6
Florida (east coast)	56
Florida (west coast)	126
Georgia	17
Hawaii	21
Louisiana	1,356
Maine	157
Maryland	80
Massachusetts	287
Mississippi	336
New Hampshire	11
New Jersey	113
New York	38
North Carolina	191
Oregon	149
Rhode Island	106
South Carolina	16
Texas	96
Virginia	651
Washington	174

Source: *Universal Almanac*

12 a Find the mean and the median of 3, 6, 8, 9, 10, 12, and 15.
   b What number would you add to the list of numbers in part **a** to make 30 the mean of the data?
   c Find the median of the new list of numbers.

13 The legs of a right triangle are 2.5 centimeters long and 4 centimeters long. How long is the hypotenuse?

14 Communicating   C.D. can press the < symbol on her tape player to rewind the tape and the > symbol to fast-forward the tape. C.D. was surprised when she saw the expressions 15 > 9 and 9 < 15 in her math book. What do the symbols > and < represent in her math book?

15 Determine whether each statement is *true* or *false*.
   a $8 + 5 > 9 + 4$ **b** $8 + 5 \leq 9 + 4$ **c** $8 + 5 < 9 + 4$
   d $8 + 5 \geq 9 + 4$ **e** $8 + 5 \neq 9 + 4$

16 Business   Here is an inventory sheet from Suzhanna's Dress Shop. A zero (0) entry means there are no dresses of the given size from that manufacturer in the store. A dash (–) entry means that dresses in the given size are not available.

Manufacturer Account Number

	#1023	**#1203**	**#1312**	**#1332**
Size 4	2	1	0	–
Size 6	2	2	1	1
Size 8	3	5	4	2
Size 10	3	4	6	5
Size 12	2	5	4	6
Size 14	1	3	6	5
Size 16	0	2	4	6
Size 18	–	0	2	3

   a How many dresses from #1312 are there in size 12?
   b What manufacturer does not produce size-4 dresses?
   c What two manufacturers produce all of the sizes?
   d How many size-8 dresses are in stock?
   e What sizes are most heavily stocked?

Investigation

Statistics   Gather data on how your favorite athlete performed during a three-year period. Organize the data, and present the data to the class. Decide whether or not the athlete's performance is improving, and explain your decision.

5.6
Matrices

ORGANIZING DATA IN A MATRIX

One of the most common ways of organizing data is in a ***matrix.*** This is a two-dimensional table in which the rows (the horizontal groups of entries) and the columns (the vertical groups of entries) are labeled to indicate the meaning of the data. The plural form of *matrix* is *matrices.*

The following matrix contains data about the U.S. recording industry in the years 1986–1989. The entries represent approximate numbers of records, CD's, and tape cassettes shipped to stores, in millions.

	Records	CD's	Cassettes
1986	125	53	345
1987	107	102	410
1988	72	150	450
1989	35	207	446

The entries in the first row, for example, indicate how many of each item were shipped in 1986. The entries in the first column represent the number of records shipped each year. What do you think the entry 150 (in the third row and the second column) represents?

DIMENSIONS OF A MATRIX

The size of a matrix is expressed by giving its ***dimensions***—the number of rows by the number of columns. The matrix above, for instance, is a 4-by-3, or 4×3, matrix. (The number of rows is always given first.) The individual entries can be referred to by their row and column numbers—in the matrix above, the entry in row 2, column 3, is 410. Sometimes subscripts are used to identify entries: The entry in row 2, column 3, can be called $e_{2,3}$, and we can write $e_{2,3} = 410$.

234   **Chapter 5**   Data Analysis

Example

This matrix gives information about some rectangles.

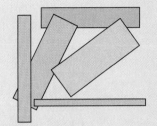

	Length	Width	Perimeter	Area
Rectangle 1	17	1	36	17
Rectangle 2	16	2	36	32
Rectangle 3	15	3	36	45
Rectangle 4	14	4	36	56
Rectangle 5	13	5	36	65

a What is the size of the matrix?

b What is entry $e_{2, 4}$?

c What is the location of the entry that represents an area of 45?

d What are the dimensions of the rectangle with the greatest area?

Solution

a 5 by 4, or 5 × 4

b 32

c $e_{3, 4}$

d 13 by 5, or 13 × 5

EQUAL MATRICES

A capital letter is often used to name a matrix. Let's take a look at two matrices—matrix A and matrix B. Do you notice anything special about the entries in these two matrices?

$$A = \begin{bmatrix} 1 & \frac{1}{2} & \frac{1}{3} & \frac{1}{4} & \frac{1}{5} \\ \frac{1}{6} & \frac{1}{8} & \frac{1}{9} & \frac{1}{10} & \frac{1}{20} \\ \frac{2}{3} & \frac{3}{4} & \frac{2}{5} & \frac{3}{5} & \frac{4}{5} \\ \frac{3}{8} & \frac{5}{8} & \frac{7}{8} & \frac{3}{10} & \frac{3}{20} \end{bmatrix}$$

$$B = \begin{bmatrix} 1 & 0.5 & 0.\overline{3} & 0.25 & 0.2 \\ 0.1\overline{6} & 0.125 & 0.\overline{1} & 0.1 & 0.05 \\ 0.\overline{6} & 0.75 & 0.4 & 0.6 & 0.8 \\ 0.375 & 0.625 & 0.875 & 0.3 & 0.15 \end{bmatrix}$$

We observe that corresponding entries in matrix A and matrix B have equal values. For example, $a_{1, 4}$ of matrix A and $b_{1, 4}$ of matrix B are equal— $\frac{1}{4} = 0.25$. Matrices whose corresponding entries are equal are called ***equal matrices.***

Sample Problems

Problem 1

In this matrix of tennis matches of players A, B, C, D, and E, each entry represents the number of games the player listed in the row won against the player listed in the column.

Player C won 6 matches against player B.

$$
\begin{array}{c c}
 & \begin{array}{c c c c c} \text{A} & \text{B} & \text{C} & \text{D} & \text{E} \end{array} \\
\begin{array}{c} \text{A} \\ \text{B} \\ \text{C} \\ \text{D} \\ \text{E} \end{array} &
\left[\begin{array}{c c c c c}
- & 4 & 6 & 7 & 3 \\
6 & - & 4 & 2 & 1 \\
4 & 6 & - & 5 & 9 \\
3 & 8 & 5 & - & 6 \\
7 & 9 & 1 & 4 & -
\end{array}\right]
\end{array}
$$

a Why are there five missing entries in the matrix?
b How many times did each pair of players meet?
c Who is the best player?

Solution

a A player cannot play against himself or herself.
b For any pair of players, the total number of wins is ten. Therefore, each pair of players met ten times.
c Who is best is a matter of interpretation. Player C won the most games—24. However, player A beat player C 6 out of 10 times, and player D won half of the matches with C.

Problem 2

In this diagram, called a *digraph*, a route is defined as a road that travels through a city at most one time. Construct a matrix that shows the number of routes from the city listed in the row to the city listed in the column.

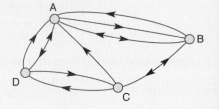

Solution

$$
\begin{array}{c c}
 & \begin{array}{c c c c} \text{A} & \text{B} & \text{C} & \text{D} \end{array} \\
\begin{array}{c} \text{A} \\ \text{B} \\ \text{C} \\ \text{D} \end{array} &
\left[\begin{array}{c c c c}
0 & 3 & 3 & 3 \\
5 & 0 & 3 & 4 \\
5 & 7 & 0 & 4 \\
5 & 7 & 5 & 0
\end{array}\right]
\end{array}
$$

Think and Discuss

1 What is a matrix?

2 Why is a matrix used?

3 What are the dimensions of the matrix $\begin{bmatrix} 3 & 6 & 8 \\ 4 & 5 & 1 \end{bmatrix}$?

4 Is matrix A equal to matrix B? Explain your answer.

$$A = \begin{bmatrix} 2 & 3 \\ 4 & 5 \end{bmatrix} \qquad B = \begin{bmatrix} 3 & 2 \\ 5 & 4 \end{bmatrix}$$

5 Construct a matrix with entries $e_{1,1} = 12$, $e_{2,1} = 15$, $e_{1,2} = 18$, and $e_{2,2} = 20$.

6 **Sports** Refer to the table showing 1990 National League records.
   a Which team had the best record?
   b What was the total number of games won by the teams in the Western Division?
   c Which team scored the least number of runs?
   d Which team scored the greatest number of runs?
   e How is the table similar to a matrix?

National League Records in 1990 Final Standings				
			Runs	
Eastern Division	W	L	Avg	vs.
Pittsburgh	95	67	4.5	3.8
New York	91	71	4.8	3.8
Montreal	85	77	4.1	3.7
Philadelphia	77	85	4.0	4.5
Chicago	77	85	4.3	4.8
St. Louis	70	92	3.7	4.3
			Runs	
Western Division	W	L	Avg	vs.
Cincinnati	91	71	4.3	3.7
Los Angeles	86	76	4.5	4.2
San Francisco	85	77	4.4	4.4
Houston	75	87	3.5	4.0
San Diego	75	87	4.2	4.2
Atlanta	65	97	4.2	5.1

Source: *World Almanac and Book of Facts*

7 Construct a 4-by-4 matrix in which $e_{a,b} = a + b$.

Problems and Applications

8 Consider the matrix $\begin{bmatrix} 5 & 2 & 1 \\ 2 & 15 & 10 \\ 4 & 21 & 22 \end{bmatrix}$.

   a What are the dimensions of the matrix?
   b What is entry $e_{3,2}$?
   c What is the sum of the elements in column 2?
   d What is the sum of the elements in row 3?

9 Consider the matrix $\begin{bmatrix} 3 & -4 & 8 \\ -9 & 5 & -4 \end{bmatrix}$.

   a In what locations are the entries negative?
   b In what locations are the entries even?

10 **Consumer Math** Create a matrix that displays your weekly expenses. Label the rows with the days of the week. For the columns, choose labels like *Food, Clothes, Entertainment,* and *Savings*.

11 Complete the matrix by finding the perimeter and the area of a rectangle with each given length and width.

Length	Width	Perimeter	Area
1	2		
2	4		
3	6		
4	8		
5	10		
6	12		

12 Create one 4-by-4 matrix in which
    1. The only entries are 1, 2, 3, and 4
    2. Every column contains 1, 2, 3, and 4
    3. Every row contains 1, 2, 3, and 4

13 What values of w, x, y, z, and t will make these matrices equal?

$$\begin{bmatrix} 2 & x-2 & w \\ 3y & z+5 & 4-t \end{bmatrix} = \begin{bmatrix} 2 & 7 & 6 \\ 18 & 4 & 2 \end{bmatrix}$$

14 The labels of the rows and columns of the matrix below correspond to the vertices of the digraph. The matrix has an entry of 1 if there is an arrow leaving the row vertex and going to the column vertex. A zero is placed in all other entry locations. Complete the matrix.

$$\begin{array}{c c} & \begin{array}{c c c c c} \mathbf{A} & \mathbf{B} & \mathbf{C} & \mathbf{D} & \mathbf{E} \end{array} \\ \begin{array}{c} \mathbf{A} \\ \mathbf{B} \\ \mathbf{C} \\ \mathbf{D} \\ \mathbf{E} \end{array} & \begin{bmatrix} 0 & 1 & 0 & 0 & 1 \\ & & & & \\ & & & & \\ & & & & \\ & & & & \end{bmatrix} \end{array}$$

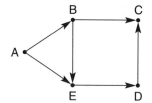

15 Create a matrix in which $e_{a,\,b} = a \cdot b$.

16 **Science** In the windchill table, the rows represent wind speed and the columns represent temperature.

	Determining the Windchill Factor																	
Wind speed	Actual temperature (°F)																	
	35°	30°	25°	20°	15°	10°	5°	0°	−5°	−10°	−15°	−20°	−25°	−30°	−35°	−40°	−45°
5 mph	33°	27°	21°	16°	12°	7°	0°	−5°	−10°	−15°	−21°	−26°	−31°	−36°	−42°	−47°	−52°
10 mph	22	16	10	3	−3	−9	−15	−22	−27	−34	−40	−46	−52	−58	−64	−71	−77
15 mph	16	9	2	−5	−11	−18	−25	−31	−38	−45	−51	−58	−65	−72	−78	−85	−92
20 mph	12	4	−3	−10	−17	−24	−31	−39	−46	−53	−60	−67	−74	−81	−88	−95	−102
25 mph	8	1	−7	−15	−22	−29	−36	−44	−51	−59	−66	−74	−81	−88	−96	−103	−110
30 mph	6	−2	−10	−18	−25	−33	−41	−49	−56	−64	−71	−79	−86	−93	−101	−109	−116
35 mph	4	−4	−12	−20	−27	−35	−43	−52	−58	−67	−74	−82	−89	−97	−105	−113	−120
40 mph	3	−5	−13	−21	−29	−37	−45	−53	−60	−69	−76	−84	−92	−100	−107	−115	−123
45 mph	2	−6	−14	−22	−30	−38	−46	−54	−62	−70	−78	−85	−93	−102	−109	−117	−125

    a If the temperature is 0°F and the wind is blowing 35 miles per hour, what is the windchill?

    b A windchill below −40°F is very dangerous. What combinations of wind speed and temperature are dangerous?

17 Use the following matrix to determine who should be assigned jobs A, B, and C so that the jobs will be done in the minimum time. (The people cannot share jobs, and each must do one of the jobs.)

	Job A	Job B	Job C
Arti	6 hr	5 hr	4 hr
Rita	5 hr	4 hr	2 hr
Tria	6 hr	3 hr	5 hr

18 The matrix represents a digraph. What is a possible graph for this matrix?

	A	B	C	D	E
A	0	1	1	1	1
B	0	0	1	0	0
C	0	0	0	0	0
D	0	0	0	0	1
E	0	0	1	1	0

19 Create a matrix showing the number of routes from point to point.

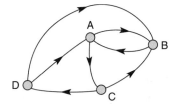

◄ LOOKING BACK **Spiral Learning** LOOKING AHEAD ►

20 If $x = 7$, $y = 5$, and $z = 16x - 8y$, what is the value of z?

21 The salary schedule for employees at Dominique's Food Store is summarized in the matrix. (The entries represent dollars per hour.)

Years Experience	Bagger	Stockboy	Cashier
1	4.50	4.75	7.35
2	4.90	5.25	8.00
3	5.35	5.85	8.70
4	5.70	6.15	9.50
5	6.25	6.75	10.45

In the new contract signed by the grocer's union, the salary in each category is increased by 6.7%. What is the new salary matrix?

22 Find the measures $\angle 1$, $\angle 2$, and $\angle 3$.

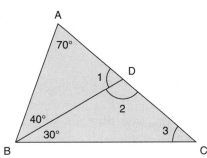

23 Ernest had an urn that contained some red marbles and some green marbles. He picked 20 marbles out of the urn, counted the number of red marbles, then returned all marbles to the urn. He did this ten times. Here are the numbers of red marbles he chose: 8, 4, 10, 9, 6, 7, 9, 6, 11, 8.
  a Make a box-and-whisker plot of these data.
  b Find the mean of the data, rounded to the nearest whole number.
  c What fraction of the marbles probably are red?
  d If Ernest's urn contains 300 marbles, about how many are red?

24 Business
  a The matrix represents data on the first week's sales of compact discs at Abby Rhodes's Music Store. Represent this data in a bar graph.

	Mon.	Tues.	Wed.	Thurs.	Fri.	Sat.	Sun.
Rock	18	11	13	19	16	38	8
Classical	6	5	8	11	9	22	3
Country	14	18	9	10	7	10	4
Jazz	4	2	0	3	4	6	1
Blues	9	1	3	0	2	7	4

  b This matrix represents data on the second week's sales of compact discs at Abby Rhodes's Music Store. Construct a matrix representing the total sales for both weeks.

	Mon.	Tues.	Wed.	Thurs.	Fri.	Sat.	Sun.
Rock	23	8	15	17	12	33	15
Classical	8	11	7	8	12	28	6
Country	12	15	12	8	6	15	7
Jazz	8	3	2	5	2	3	0
Blues	7	4	2	8	5	0	0

In problems 25–30, use the number line to find the distance between each pair of numbers.

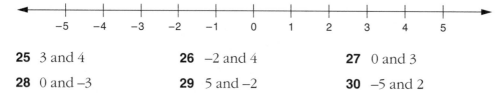

25 3 and 4   **26** −2 and 4   **27** 0 and 3

28 0 and −3   **29** 5 and −2   **30** −5 and 2

31

	Inventory Matrix				Price Matrix	
	Kix	**Trox**	**Soggies**			**Cost**
Store A	10	5	30		**Kix**	3.25
Store B	9	14	6		**Trox**	2.75
Store C	12	12	7		**Soggies**	4.25
Store D	25	3	18			

  a What is the total dollar amount of inventory at Stores A–D of Kix? Of Trox? Of Soggies?
  b What is the value of the cereal inventory at each store?
  c Which store has the greatest dollar amount of cereal inventory?

In problems 32–34, solve each equation. Round answers to the nearest hundredth.

32 $17x = -543$

33 $853y = 97$

34 $\dfrac{z}{-15.2} = 0.913$

35 Complete the matrix with the least common multiples (LCM) of the numbers in columns 1 and 2.

Value	Value	LCM
5	8	
6	10	
1	6	
14	21	
5	2	
6	8	

36 What percent of the area of the rectangle is the area of the triangle?

18

18

10

25

In problems 37–40, evaluate each expression.

37 $6 + 3 \div 9 \cdot 6$

38 $\dfrac{6+3}{9 \cdot 6}$

39 $6 + \dfrac{3}{9} \cdot 6$

40 $\dfrac{6+3}{9} \cdot 6$

Investigation

Language Arts The word *matrix* has different meanings in different fields. Find out what a matrix is in each of the following disciplines: model making, geology, printing, and anatomy. Do these uses of the word have anything in common? Do they relate to the mathematical meaning of matrix? Explain your answer.

CHAPTER 5

Summary

CONCEPTS AND PROCEDURES

After studying this chapter, you should be able to

- Read a circle graph (5.1)
- Draw a circle graph (5.1)
- Read a bar graph and a line graph (5.2)
- Draw a bar graph and a line graph (5.2)
- Interpret scattergrams, histograms, pictographs, and artistic graphs (5.3)
- Draw a scattergram, a histogram, a pictograph, and an artistic graph (5.3)
- Find the mean, the median, and the mode of a set of data (5.4)
- Interpret a stem-and-leaf plot and a box-and-whisker plot (5.5)
- Draw a stem-and-leaf plot and a box-and-whisker plot (5.5)
- Identify the entries in a matrix (5.6)
- Determine the dimensions of a matrix (5.6)
- Identify equal matrices (5.6)

VOCABULARY

artistic graph (5.3)
bar graph (5.2)
box-and-whisker plot (5.5)
circle graph (5.1)
data analysis (5.1)
digraph (5.6)
dimensions (5.6)
disjoint (5.1)
equal matrices (5.6)
extremes (5.5)
histogram (5.3)
line graph (5.2)
line plot (5.3)
lower quartile (5.5)
matrix (5.6)
mean (5.4)
measure of central tendency (5.4)
median (5.4)
midquartile range (5.5)
mode (5.4)
outlier (5.5)
pictograph (5.3)
pie chart (5.1)
range (5.5)
scattergram (5.3)
stem and leaf plot (5.5)
upper qaurtile (5.5)

Review

1 a How many days (on average) did each of the top 32 fifth-grade students miss?

b How many days (on average) did each of the bottom 32 fifth-grade students miss?

c Find the ratio of days missed by the bottom 32 seventh-grade students to days missed by the top 32 seventh-grade students.

d What conclusion would you draw from the data?

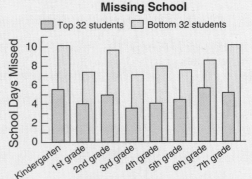

Missing School

☐ Top 32 students   ☐ Bottom 32 students

School Days Missed

Kindergarten · 1st grade · 2nd grade · 3rd grade · 4th grade · 5th grade · 6th grade · 7th grade

Average number of days missed over the last eight years by students who are now eighth graders

Source: *Chicago Sun-Times*

2 Mr. Ed's students scored 75, 80, 85, 74, 49, 63, 41, 91, 98, 71, 85, 81, 91, 66, 95, 91, 88, 91, and 83 on a test about horses.

a Make a stem-and-leaf plot for the data.

b Find the mean of the data.

c Find the median of the data.

d Find the mode of the data.

e Find the lower and upper quartiles of the data.

f Make a box-and-whisker plot for the data.

3 Construct a matrix with entries $e_{1,\,1} = 5$, $e_{1,\,2} = 7$, $e_{2,\,1} = 9$, and $e_{2,\,2} = 11$.

4 a What percent does each pie-shaped sector of the circle graph represent?

b Find the number of degrees for each pie-shaped sector of the circle graph.

c Use a protractor to measure each pie-shaped sector of the circle graph. Do the measurements agree with the calculations you made in part **b**?

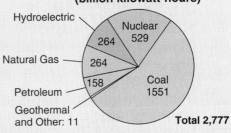

Sources of U.S. Electricity, 1989 (billion kilowatt-hours)

Hydroelectric — 264
Nuclear 529
Natural Gas — 264
Petroleum — 158
Geothermal and Other: 11
Coal 1551

Total 2,777

Source: Energy Information Administration

5 Watch a half-hour television news broadcast. Keep track of how much time is devoted to international news, national news, local news, sports, weather, special features, commercials, and other items (such as introduction, logo, and entertainment). Draw a circle graph to represent the data you have collected.

6 The table displays Super Bowl television ratings and the costs of advertising during the Super Bowl game. Use the data in the chart to draw a line graph in which

a The year is graphed against ad costs

b The year is graphed against ratings

c The ratings are graphed against ad costs

Year	Rating	Ad Cost (30 seconds)
1967	41.1	$40,000
1968	36.8	$54,500
1969	36.0	$55,000
1970	39.7	$78,200
1971	39.9	$72,500
1972	44.2	$86,700
1973	42.7	$88,100
1974	41.6	$103,500
1975	42.4	$107,000
1976	42.3	$110,000
1977	44.4	$125,000
1978	47.2	$162,300
1979	47.1	$185,000
1980	46.3	$222,000
1981	44.4	$275,000
1982	49.1	$324,300
1983	48.6	$400,000
1984	46.4	$368,200
1985	46.4	$525,000
1986	48.3	$550,000
1987	45.8	$600,000
1988	41.9	$645,000
1989	43.5	$675,000
1990	39.0	$700,000

Source: *Daily Herald*

7 Each week, Bill, Sue, and Harry work the given numbers of hours in each of three different jobs.

	Bagger	**Clerk**	**Cashier**
Hourly wage	5.25	4.75	8.25

	Bill	**Sue**	**Harry**
Bagger	10	5	4
Clerk	20	18	4
Cashier	5	13	25

a How much money does each person make per week?

b How many additional hours per week would Bill need to work in order to earn more than Sue?

8 a What percent of degrees earned in 1959–60 were bachelor's degrees? In 1969–70? In 1979–80? In 1984–85? In 1985–86?

b Why, do you think, does the number of advanced degrees seem to level off after 1979–80?

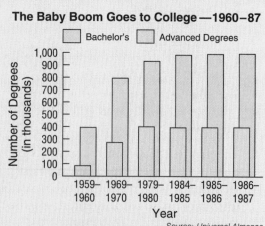

The Baby Boom Goes to College —1960–87

Source: *Universal Almanac*

9 Telly surveyed his classmates to find out how many hours of television they watched on a given day. Here are their responses. 3, 2.5, 4, 3, 2.5, 1.5, 0, 1, 0, 4, 2.5, 1, 2, 1, 0, 2.5, 3, 1, 0, 2.5, 3, 4, 2 Make a line plot of the data.

10

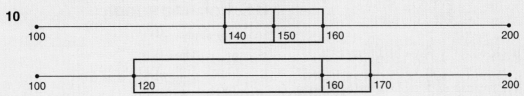

Explain the differences between the sets of data represented by the two box-and-whisker plots.

11 a Which team had the best home record in each division?
  b Which team had the best away record in each division?
  c Which team scored fewer runs than its opposition but still won more than half of its games?
  d Which team won the American League title?

American League Records in 1990 Final Standings						
Eastern Division	W	L	Home	Away	Runs Avg	Runs vs.
Boston	88	74	51-30	37-44	4.3	4.1
Toronto	86	76	44-37	42-39	4.7	4.1
Detroit	79	83	39-42	40-41	4.6	4.6
Cleveland	77	85	41-40	36-45	4.5	4.5
Baltimore	76	85	40-40	36-45	4.2	4.3
Milwaukee	74	88	39-42	35-46	4.5	4.7
New York	67	95	37-44	30-51	3.7	4.6
Western Division	W	L	Home	Away	Runs Avg	Runs vs.
Oakland	103	59	51-30	52-29	4.5	3.6
Chicago	94	68	49-31	45-37	4.2	3.9
Texas	83	79	47-35	36-44	4.2	4.3
California	80	82	42-39	38-43	4.3	4.4
Seattle	77	85	38-43	39-42	3.9	4.2
Kansas City	75	86	45-36	30-50	4.4	4.4
Minnesota	74	88	41-40	33-48	4.1	4.4
American League Championship Series						
Oakland 9, Boston 1 Oakland 4, Boston 1						
Oakland 4, Boston 1 Oakland 3, Boston 1						

Source: *The World Almanac and Book of Facts*

12 A town's population of 40,000 is decreasing by 8% each year. Of the total population, 1.5% is junior-high age, and 60% of these students attend Antelope Valley Junior High School.
  a Use a spreadsheet to copy and complete the table showing the change in the population over the next 15 years.
  b What will the population of Antelope Junior High School be in 2007?

Year	Town Population	Junior-High Age	Attend Antelope Valley
1992	40,000		
1993			
1994			
.			
.			
.			
2007			

13 Look at newspapers and magazines. What kinds of data displays are the most prevalent? Why do you suppose this is true?

14 a Which housing category increased the most from 1980 to 1990?

b How many detached houses were there in 1980?

c How many detached houses were there in 1990?

d Did the number of detached houses increase or decrease?

e Did the percent of detached houses increase or decrease?

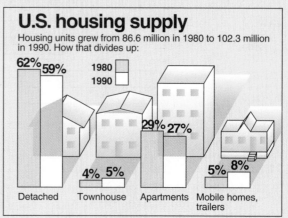

U.S. housing supply
Housing units grew from 86.6 million in 1980 to 102.3 million in 1990. How that divides up:

Source: Census Bureau/Elys A. McLean, USA TODAY

15 The map shows the 12 states with the greatest potential for wind-generated electricity. The numbers represent the percent of potential U.S. wind-generated electricity for each state.

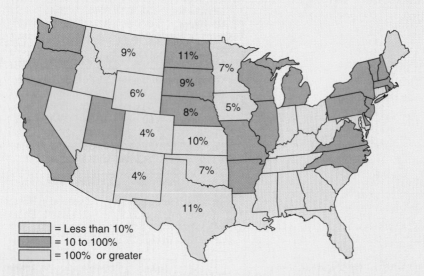

☐ = Less than 10%
▨ = 10 to 100%
▤ = 100% or greater

a Which states have the greatest potential for wind-generated electricity?

b What fraction of potential wind-generated electricity is in Iowa?

c Which states each have $\frac{1}{25}$ of the U.S. potential for wind-generated electricity?

Test

1. In a survey, 450 people identified their favorite color. Draw a circle graph to represent the data in the table.

Color	Number of People
Red	82
Blue	92
Yellow	66
Green	58
Purple	70
Pink	82

2. The stem-and-leaf plot shows the numbers of books read by the students in Mr. Reed's class during the first semester.
   a What are the extremes of the data?
   b Draw a box-and-whisker plot for the data.
   c Between what two numbers are 50% of the data values located?

```
1 | 5 5 6 8 9
2 | 0 0 3 4 4 5 7
3 | 0 2 5
```

3. a What is the mean number of hours worked by the students each week?
   b What is the median number of hours worked by the students each week?
   c What is the mode of the data?

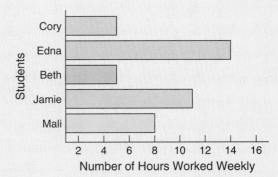

Number of Hours Worked Weekly

4. Consider the matrix A = $\begin{bmatrix} 2 & -1 & 3 \\ 4 & 2 & 6 \end{bmatrix}$

   a What are the dimensions of matrix A
   b What is $e_{1,3}$?

5. a What percent of the households surveyed have more than three telephones?
   b How many households were surveyed?

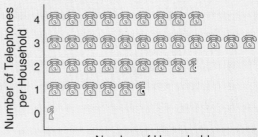

Number of Households

Legend: 📞 = 10 households

6 a Draw a vertical histogram using the data, which consist of the scores from Mr. Miske's history test.

Score	50	55	60	65	70	75	80	85	90	95	100
Number	2	1	3	2	5	6	8	4	3	1	2

b What percent of the students received a score of 90% or better?

7 Solve $\begin{bmatrix} 2 & 13-w \\ x+7 & 3y \end{bmatrix} = \begin{bmatrix} 2 & 5 \\ 14 & 9 \end{bmatrix}$ for w, x, and y.

8 Draw a pictograph to represent the number of strokes Debbie took per hole during a round of golf.

Hole	1	2	3	4	5	6	7	8	9
Strokes	2	4	4	6	4	8	2	6	4

9 a Draw a line graph for the data.
b What trend do you see in the graph?

Day	Number of Absences
Monday	56
Tuesday	28
Wednesday	18
Thursday	21
Friday	49

10 What conclusion can you draw from this scattergram?

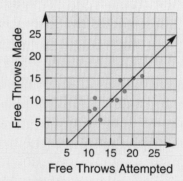

11 Mr. Litt E. Rature gave an English test. His students' test scores were 42, 87, 62, 94, 88, 82, 91, 85, 86, 92, 91, 95, 81, 79, 74, 65, 33, 98, 91
a Organize the data into a stem-and-leaf plot.
b Find the range of scores.
c Find the median.
d Find the lower quartile.
e Make a box-and-whisker plot.
f Which values are outliers?

1 Using operation signs, we can arrange four 4's to obtain various numbers. For example:

$$\frac{44}{44} = 1$$

$$\frac{4}{4} + \frac{4}{4} = 2$$

$$\frac{4 + 4 + 4}{4} = 3$$

$$\frac{4}{\sqrt{4}} + \frac{4}{\sqrt{4}} = 4$$

$$4 + \sqrt{4} - \frac{4}{4} = 5$$

Come up with ways to use four 4's to obtain 6, 7, 8, and 9.

2 Here is one way to use six 9's to obtain 100.

$$9 + 9 + 9 \times 9 + \frac{9}{9}$$

Find another way to use six 9's to obtain 100.

3 Arrange the numbers 1 through 9 in the squares so that the sums of the numbers in all the rows, columns, and diagonals are the same. This is called a *magic square*.

4 Find a two-digit number in which
  a. The number is twice the product of its digits
  b. The number is three times the sum of its digits
  c. The number is the square of its units digit
  d. The number exceeds its reversal by 20%
  e. The number and its reversal add to a perfect square

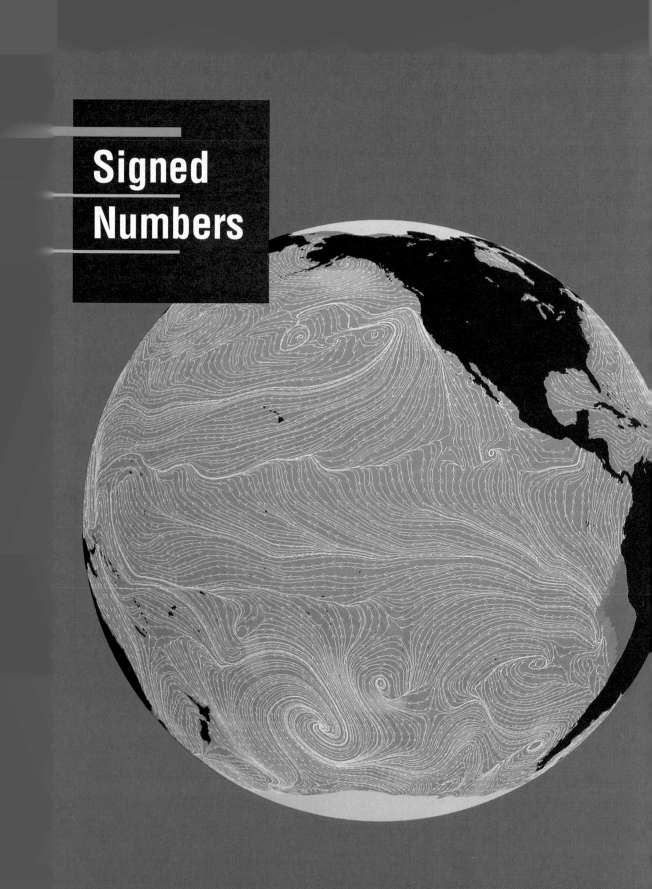

Signed
Numbers

INVESTIGATION

Map Coloring Four families own an island. They plan to divide the entire island into four separate lots by building fences at the boundaries. They have agreed to the following conditions:

- Each lot must share a boundary with each of the other three lots. ■ Each lot must have its own beach. ■ The lots can be irregular in shape and need not be equal in size.

The families need your help. Draw a map of an island, and construct boundaries according to the conditions stated above. Make each lot a different color. Explain your results to the class.

6.1
The Number Line

NUMBER LINES AND SIGNED NUMBERS

A new roller coaster has just opened at Great Flags Amusement Park. This ride runs partly above ground and partly below ground. The vertical number line shows the height and the depth the roller coaster reaches in feet.

Ground level is represented by zero on the number line. **Positive (+) signed numbers** represent distances above ground and **negative (–) signed numbers** represent distances below ground. Zero is neither positive nor negative. A nonzero number written without a sign is a positive number. Notice that the roller coaster rises 160 feet above ground (160) and descends 75 feet below ground (–75).

Example 1
If the roller coaster descends 45 feet below ground and then rises 30 feet, what is its location?

Solution

If we begin at −45 on the number line and move 30 units upward, we reach −15. The roller coaster is 15 feet below ground.

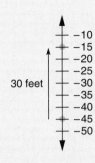

Example 2

What is the distance between the lowest point (75 feet below ground) and the highest point (160 feet above ground) on the roller coaster?

Solution

From 75 feet below ground to ground level is a distance of 75 feet. From ground level to 160 feet above ground is a distance of 160 feet. Therefore, the distance between the lowest and the highest point is 75 + 160, or 235, feet.

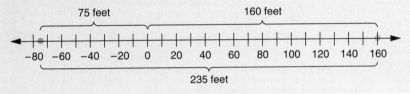

You may have noticed that on a horizontal number line the negative numbers are to the left of zero and the positive numbers are to the right of zero. To save space, we usually use a horizontal number line rather than a vertical one.

The circular number line used on some outdoor thermometers is another type of number line. Notice that the negative numbers are arranged in a counter-clockwise sequence and the positive numbers in a clockwise sequence.

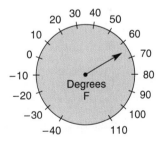

OPPOSITES

Two nonzero numbers are ***opposites*** if the numbers are the same distance from zero on the number line but one of the numbers is positive and the other is negative. For example, −30° and 30° are opposites on the thermometer scale, as are −20 and 20 on this horizontal number line.

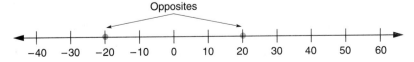

Example 3
Use a calculator to
a Add 33 and −33
b Subtract −33 from 33

Solution
Many calculators have a $\boxed{+/-}$ key for entering signed numbers.
a To add, enter 33 $\boxed{+}$ 33 $\boxed{+/-}$ $\boxed{=}$. The display shows ▮▮▮▮ 0.
b To subtract, enter 33 $\boxed{-}$ 33 $\boxed{+/-}$ $\boxed{=}$. The display shows ▮▮▮▮ 66.

ORIGIN AND COORDINATES

The number associated with a point on a number line is the **coordinate** of the point. The point on the number line assigned to 0 is called the **origin.** When we draw a number line, we usually label the divisions of the line with **integers**—... , −3, −2, −1, 0, 1, 2, 3, ...

Example 4
Draw a number line and locate the points with the coordinates −3.5, $-1\frac{7}{8}$, 2.6, and −π.

Solution
First we draw a number line and label the origin and several integer coordinates.

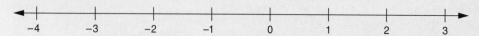

Then we label the four points.

1. The point with the coordinate −3.5 is located halfway between −3 and −4.
2. To locate the point with the coordinate $-1\frac{7}{8}$, we subdivide the interval between −1 and −2 into eight equal parts and locate $-1\frac{7}{8}$ at the mark nearest to −2.
3. To locate the point with the coordinate 2.6, we subdivide the interval between 2 and 3 into ten equal parts and locate 2.6 at the sixth mark to the right of 2.
4. Since −π ≈ −3.14, we can find an approximate location for it by subdividing the interval between −3 and −4 into ten equal parts and locating −π near the middle of the second subdivision to the left of −3.

Sample Problem

Tellie Fone calls friends in the other five time zones of the United States from her home in San Francisco. To reach her friends at the right times, she needs a fast way to calculate the time of day in each location.

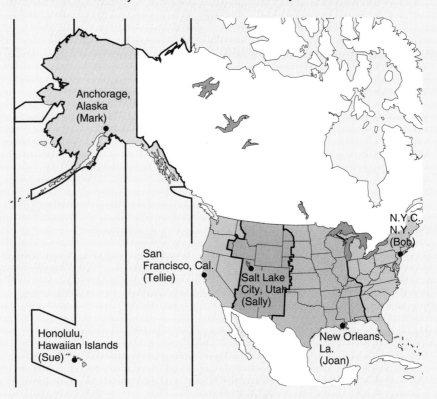

a Use a number line to show the time differences of the six zones.

b If Tellie's clock reads 7:00 P.M., how can she find the time in Bob's time zone? In Sue's time zone?

c Which of her friends are in time zones with opposite values?

d Mark needs to get up at 6:00 A.M. At what time must Bob set his own alarm if he has to give Mark a wake-up call?

Solution

a We will place Tellie at the origin. To the east of her, the time becomes one hour later in each successive zone. To the west, the time becomes one hour earlier in each successive zone. We therefore place zones to the east of Tellie at positive integer coordinates and zones to the west at negative integer coordinates. Each coordinate shows how much a friend's time differs from Tellie's.

	Sue: Honolulu	Mark: Anchorage	Tellie: San Francisco	Sally: Salt Lake City	Joan: New Orleans	Bob: New York City
	-2	-1	0	1	2	3

b Bob lives three time zones to the east, so Tellie must add three hours to her time to determine the time in Bob's time zone (10:00 P.M.). Sue lives two time zones to the west, so Tellie must subtract two hours to determine the time in Sue's time zone (5:00 P.M.).

c Mark (−1) and Sally (1) are in time zones with opposite values on the number line. So are Sue (−2) and Joan (2).

d Bob is four time zones to the east of, or four hours later than, Mark. So Bob must add four hours to Mark's wake-up time and set his own alarm for 10:00 A.M.

Think and Discuss

1 What is the sum of two opposite numbers?

2 Why do we need signed numbers?

3 What are some ways to define *integers?*

4 On a number line, what is the coordinate of the origin?

5 **Science** In a countdown for a space flight, the numbers before blast-off are negative and the numbers after blast-off are positive. If T stands for the time of blast-off, how many seconds pass from T − 15 seconds to T + 30 seconds?

6 Use a calculator to evaluate each sum.
  a −55 + 55   **b** −55 + 56   **c** −55 + 57

7 What is the opposite of each number?
  a −3.6   **b** 102   **c** 0

8 If −8°F is really cold, is 8°F really hot? Explain your response.

9 Suppose point A on the number line is moved five units and point B is moved four units.

a Find all possible locations for points A and B after they are moved.
b How far apart are the points in each possible pair of locations?

Problems and Applications

10 Draw a number line and locate each point at the given coordinate.
  a Point A: 3.5   **b** Point B: $-1\frac{2}{3}$
  c Point C: $-1\frac{1}{2}$ **d** Point D: −4

11 The temperature rose from −6°F to 10°F. What was the change in temperature?

12 Refer to the sample problem on page 255. Sue wants to call Bob to wish him a happy birthday. If she wants to reach him at 6:00 P.M., what time should she place her call?

13 There are 15 levels below ground in a mine shaft. The levels are numbered from top to bottom as follows: −1, −2, −3, . . ., −15.
a A miner is at level −3 and goes down 8 levels. On what level is she?
b If a mine inspector starts at level −13 and goes up 3 levels, then up 3 more levels, at what level is she?

14 Draw a number line and locate the points with the given coordinates.
a 2   **b** $\frac{2}{5}$ **c** 7.3   **d** −4.5   **e** $-3\frac{5}{6}$ **f** $-\sqrt{2}$

15 Write the opposite of each number.
a 14   **b** π **c** $-\sqrt{2}$ **d** 0   **e** −1   **f** $-\frac{3}{4}$

16 For each pair of numbers, determine which number is greater (further to the right on a number line).
a 8 or 0   **b** 3.6 or 3.7   **c** −3.6 or −3.7
d −7 or 0   **e** −1 or −3   **f** $-2\frac{1}{2}$ or $-2\frac{5}{8}$

17 For each pair of numbers, determine which number is less (further to the left on a number line).
a 4 or 2   **b** 0 or −9   **c** −8 or 1
d −4 or −2   **e** −3.4 or −3.5   **f** $-4\frac{5}{9}$ or $-4\frac{2}{3}$

18 Use a calculator to find each sum.
a 12 + (−8)   **b** 12 + (−9)   **c** 12 + (−10)   **d** 12 + (−11)
e 12 + (−12)   **f** 12 + (−13)   **g** 12 + (−14)   **h** 12 + (−15)

19 Find each difference.
a 5 − 3   **b** 5 − 4   **c** 5 − 5   **d** 5 − 6
e 5 − 7   **f** 5 − 8   **g** 5 − 9

20 **Sports** The data shown represent goals scored by our hockey team and the opposition during the time each of our players was on the ice.

Our Player	Our Goals	Opponents' Goals	Our Player Index
#1	35	41	−6
#2	16	8	+8
#3	19	17	2
#4	47	43	4
#5	40	52	−8
#6	29	31	−2
#7	38	32	6
#8	22	17	5

a Determine the player index for the remaining players.
b In a close game, which player(s) should be used?

21 Locate $\frac{-3}{4}$, –1, 6, –2.43, 2.3, –π, 4.7, $\frac{-\sqrt{2}}{2}$, 0, and –7 on a number line.

22 **a** Locate points 6, 8, 10, 17, 22, and 26 on a number line.
b Locate the mean and median of the numbers in part **a** on the same number line.

23 At 9:00 A.M. the temperature was 11°C. The table describes the temperature changes over the next 13 hours.

Time	Temperature Behavior
9:00 — 10:00 A.M.	Dropped 4°
10:00 — 2:00 P.M.	Remained steady
2:00 — 4:00 P.M.	Dropped 3°
4:00 — 6:00 P.M.	Dropped 5°
6:00 — 10:00 P.M.	Dropped 3°

a Graph the temperatures from 9:00 A.M. to 10:00 P.M.
b What was the temperature at 10:00 P.M.?

24 Perform the following operations on a calculator. Record your results.

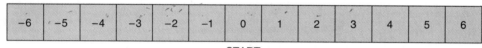

a 9 [+/–] [+] 15 [+/–] [=]   **b** 9 [+/–] [×] 15 [+/–] [=]
c 9 [+/–] [–] 15 [+/–] [=]   **d** 9 [+/–] [÷] 15 [+/–] [=]

25 Suppose that Bill stands on square 0 and tosses a die seven times. On the first, third, fifth, and seventh tosses, he moves to the right the number of squares indicated by the die. On the second, fourth, and sixth tosses, he moves to the left the number of squares indicated by the die.

| –6 | –5 | –4 | –3 | –2 | –1 | 0 | 1 | 2 | 3 | 4 | 5 | 6 |

START

a If Bill's first three tosses are 3, 6, and 1, on which square will he be standing?
b If Bill's next four tosses are 1, 2, 5, and 4, on which square will he be standing?

26

A number line showing points A at –4, B at –2, C at –1, D at 1, E at 3, F at 5, with labels from –5 to 5.

Find the length of the segment from
a D to F   **b** C to D   **c** A to B
d A to F   **e** B to E   **f** B to C

27 Point A is the midpoint of segment BC. What is the coordinate of A if the coordinates of B and C are
a 16 and 36?   **b** 0 and 20?
c –12 and 8?   **d** $-\frac{2}{3}$ and $4\frac{2}{3}$?

28 Every day, Roger tries to run a mile in 4 minutes 30 seconds. He records the difference between his target time and his actual time in seconds, using a + if it takes more time and a – if it takes less time. His goal is for the sum of the numbers for each week to be 0. One week his records showed –3, +5, +7, –2, –1, and 0 for the first six days. What must his running time be on the seventh day if he is to meet his goal?

29 Use your calculator to find each product.
a (−3) (−2)   **b** (−3) (−1)   **c** (−3) (0)
d (−3) (1)   **e** (−3) (2)   **f** (−3) (3)

30

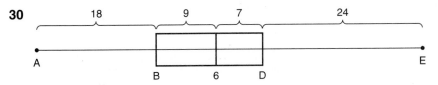

The coordinate of the median in the box-and-whisker plot is 6. Determine the coordinates of A, B, D, and E.

31 Find the mean of −8, −6, −3, 0, 3, 6, and 8.

32 Evaluate each expression for $x = 5$ and $y = 3$.
a $11x$ **b** $4x + 7x$ **c** $17y$
d $9y + 8y$ **e** $2x + 3y + 4x + 5y$ **f** $6x + 8y$

33 **Consumer Math** Stocky Dealer bought 40 shares of Widget stock at $57.50 a share. He later sold 25 of these shares at $49.25 a share. How much money did Stocky lose on these 25 shares of stock?

34 The perimeter of a triangle is 18 centimeters. The lengths of two sides of the triangle are 4.5 centimeters and 6 centimeters.
a Find the length of the third side of the triangle.
b Draw an accurate picture of this triangle.
c If one angle of the triangle is selected at random, what is the probability that the angle is acute?

35 **a** If $x = 8$ and $y = 24$, what is the value of $\frac{x + y}{2}$?

b If $x, y,$ and your answer to part **a** are placed on a number line, what conclusion can you draw about the answer to part **a**?

36 Point B is 20% of the way from A to C. Find the coordinate of B.

37 **Technology** When a spreadsheet is instructed to display numbers in dollars and cents, how does it show negative amounts of money?

Investigation

Temperature Scales Who were Fahrenheit and Celsius? Where and when did they live? Which of the two temperature scales do you find more convenient, and why? If you could invent your own temperature scale, how might it be different?

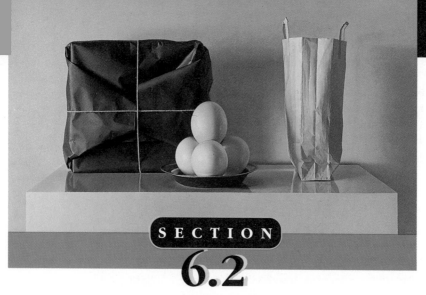

6.2
Inequalities

GRAPHING AND WRITING INEQUALITIES

United Shipping People (USP) will ship a package only if it meets the following three conditions:

Condition 1:   The package is no more than 70 pounds in weight.

Condition 2:   The package is no more than 130 inches in combined length and girth.

Condition 3:   The package is no more than 108 inches in length.

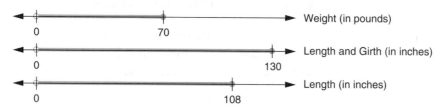

These three conditions can be described graphically.

A solid endpoint indicates that the coordinate of that point is included in the graph. An open endpoint indicates that the coordinate is not included in the graph. The shaded region indicates that all the numbers between the endpoints are included in the graph. The maximum values allowed by USP are represented by the solid endpoints at 70, 130, and 108. Why are all the endpoints at 0 open?

Example 1
A package has a length of 84 inches. Graph the possible values of the girth.

A package must have a girth greater than zero, but the sum of the girth and the length cannot exceed 130 inches. Since the length of the package is 84 inches, the girth can be at most 130 − 84, or 46 inches. The graph of the solution is

Girth (in inches)

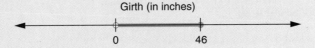

$$0 \qquad 46$$

For example, a 36-inch girth is acceptable, but a 60-inch girth is not.

We can also express the USP conditions in mathematical symbols, as an *inequality*—a statement containing one of the following symbols.

Symbol	Meaning
<	is less than
>	is greater than
≤	is less than or equal to
≥	is greater than or equal to
≠	is not equal to

Example 2
Express each USP condition as an inequality.

Condition 1:
$0 < \text{weight} \leq 70$

Condition 2:
$0 < \text{length} + \text{girth} \leq 130$

Condition 3:
$0 < \text{length} \leq 108$

AND INEQUALITIES AND OR INEQUALITIES

Graphs that are shaded between two numbers can be represented by two inequalities joined by the word *and*. For example, the inequality that describes condition 1 of the USP guidelines for mailing can be written as

$$0 < \text{weight and weight} \leq 70.$$

This statement is read "0 is less than the weight *and* the weight is less than or equal to 70."

Example 3
A computer needs at least 90 volts of electricity to work. It is damaged, however, if the voltage is 140 volts or more.
a Express the safe voltage range as an inequality.
b Graph the inequality in part **a**.

a Here are two ways to write the inequality:

1. Voltage ≥ 90 and voltage < 140
2. 90 ≤ voltage < 140

b This is the graph of the inequality.

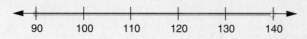

Some graphs have two or more separate sections. The inequalities that represent these graphs are joined by the word *or*.

Example 4

Refer to the set of "All numbers that are more than three units from zero on the number line."
a Draw a graph that represents this set.
b Describe the set using an inequality.

a

The numbers 3 and –3 are not included in the graph because they are not more than three units from zero on the number line—they are *exactly* three units from zero. We indicate this with the open endpoints. The arrowheads indicate that the numbers go on forever—all the numbers greater than 3 and all the numbers less than –3 are included in the graph.

b Number > 3 or number < –3

This inequality is read "The number is greater than 3 or the number is less than –3."

Example 5

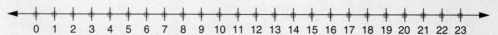

a Write an inequality that corresponds to this graph.
b What could this graph represent?

a 0 ≤ whole number ≤ 23
b This graph could represent the set of possible numbers in the hour portion of a 24-hour digital clock display.

Sample Problem

Problem For what values of N is it possible to compute the value of $\sqrt{N+7}$?

Solution Let's try some values for N. A spreadsheet is useful.

Although we are trying only a few numbers, we can see a pattern. It appears that no number less than –7 will work. A number less than –7 would result in the square root of a negative number, which we cannot compute. Therefore, N must be greater than or equal to –7.

	A	B
1	N	SQRT(N + 7)
2		
3	3	3.1622776602
4	2	3
5	1	2.8284271247
6	0	2.6457513111
7	–1	2.4494897428
8	–2	2.2360679775
9	–3	2
10	–4	1.7320508076
11	–5	1.4142135624
12	–6	1
13	–7	0
14	–8	ERR
15	–9	ERR

Using mathematical symbols, we can express all possible values of N as $N \geq -7$. We can also express the answers in a graph.

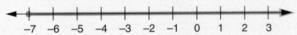

Think and Discuss

1 Match each set of numbers with the appropriate graph.
 a The nonnegative numbers
 b The negative integers
 c Integers between –4 and 4
 d The positive numbers
 e All numbers between –4 and 4

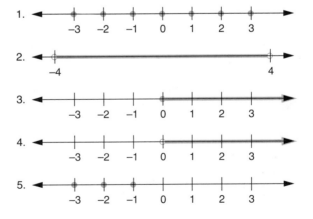

2 What is the difference between an equation and an inequality?

3 What does a shaded endpoint on the graph of an inequality represent?

4 What does an open endpoint on the graph of an inequality represent?

5 What does an arrowhead on the graph of an inequality represent?

6 What is the difference between the symbols < and ≤?

7 What is the difference between an *and* inequality and an *or* inequality?

Problems and Applications

8 Communicating
  a Why do you think USP uses girth and length instead of length, width, and height?
  b Why do you think USP sets a maximum weight?
  c Why do you think USP sets a maximum length?

9 a What is the first integer to the left of −3.8 on the number line?
  b Is your answer to part **a** less than or greater than −3.8?

10 Graph all integers between −3.4 and 3.9.

11 Communicating   Will USP deliver a pair of cross-country skis that are 215 centimeters long? Explain your answer.

12 Graph each inequality.
  a $x > -4$ **b** $x < 2$ **c** $x \geq -6$ **d** $x \leq 1$

13 a Between which two integers is $\sqrt{39}$ located on the number line?
  b Between which two integers is $-\sqrt{39}$ located on the number line?

14 Assuming each box weighs less than 70 pounds, which ones will USP deliver?

  a

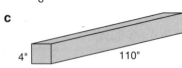

10"   75"
8"

  b

24"
18"   50"

  c

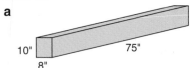

4"   110"
4"

  d

40"
20"   15"

15 Graph each inequality.
  a $x < -2$ or $x \geq 3$ **b** $x \geq -2$ and $x < 3$ **c** $-1 < x$ or $-4 > x$

16 Write an inequality for each graph.
  a

−4 −3 −2 −1 0 1 2 3 4

  b

−3 −2 −1 0 1 2 3 4 5

  c

−5 −4 −3 −2 −1 0 1 2 3

17 Communicating The inequality 3 < number < −3 represents this graph.

-3   3

   a Why is this the wrong inequality?   **b** What is the correct inequality?

18 If A < 7, 12 < B, and C > A, which inequalities must be true?

   a A < B   **b** C < 7   **c** C < B   **d** B > 7   **e** C > B

19 The perimeter of the rectangle is less than 50. Write an inequality for $L + W$.

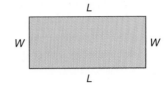

L

W   W

L

20 Communicating Will USP accept a package with a girth of 10 inches and a combined girth and length of 130 inches? Why or why not?

21 Write an inequality for each graph.

   a

   -4   -3   -2   -1   0   1   2   3   4

   b
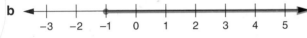

   -3   -2   -1   0   1   2   3   4   5

   c

   -4   -3   -2   -1   0   1   2   3   4

22 Graph each inequality on a number line.

   a −3 < x < 4   **b** −3 < x < 4, and x is an integer

   c −3 < x < 4, and x is a whole number

23 What is the difference between the graph of x < −2 or x > −1 and the graph of x < −2 and x > −1?

24 Spreadsheets

   a Use a spreadsheet to evaluate the expression $\sqrt{9 - x^2}$ for integer values of x ranging from −6 to 6.

   b What numbers seem to work?

   c Draw a number line that shows all the possible values of x.

◀ LOOKING BACK **Spiral Learning** LOOKING AHEAD ▶

25 Communicating Explain whether each number line is properly constructed.

   a
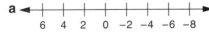

   6   4   2   0   -2   -4   -6   -8

   b
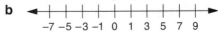

   -7 -5 -3 -1 0 1 3 5 7 9

26 For x = 7, determine whether each statement is *true* or *false*.

   a 3x + x = 4x   **b** 5x + 6x = 11x²   **c** 4x² + 8x² = 12x²

   d 5x · 3x = 15x   **e** 5x · 3x = 15x²

27 Draw a number line that shows all the possible measures of an obtuse angle.

28 How many paths are there from A to G? Follow the directions indicated by the arrows.

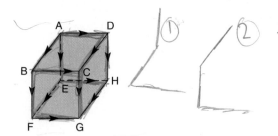

29 All 27 students in a class took a test, and no two students got the same score. The box-and-whisker plot represents the scores.

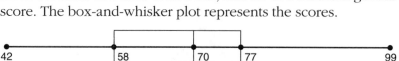

42   58   70   77   99

   a How many students scored over 70?
   b How many students scored at least 58 but less than 70?
   c How many students scored more than 77?

30 a Draw a parallelogram with one side 3 centimeters long, another side 5 centimeters long, and one 70° angle.
   b Measure the other three angles of the parallelogram and record your results.

31 Complete the following pattern, using a spreadsheet if possible.

$$6 \cdot 4 = 24 \qquad 6 \cdot 0 \ \ = \underline{\hphantom{000}}$$
$$6 \cdot 3 = 18 \qquad 6 \cdot (-1) = \underline{\hphantom{000}}$$
$$6 \cdot 2 = \underline{\hphantom{000}} \qquad 6 \cdot (-2) = \underline{\hphantom{000}}$$
$$6 \cdot 1 = \underline{\hphantom{000}} \qquad 6 \cdot (-3) = \underline{\hphantom{000}}$$

32 Find all whole numbers, N, for which $\frac{18}{N}$ is a whole number.

33 Ty Isle is making a rectangular kitchen counter using all 24 of his tiles. He wants a design where *no* tiles have to be cut.
   a Sketch the rectangular designs he could possibly use.
   b Graph all the possible lengths and widths.

34 Refer to a number line.
   a Start at 3 and move 7 units to the left. On which number do you land?
   b Start at −2 and move 5 units to the right. On which number do you land?
   c Start at −18 and move 39 units to the right. On which number do you land?

Investigation

Equilibrium   Investigate the operation of a refrigerator, furnace, air conditioner, or other appliance that is designed to maintain a particular temperature. How is the temperature equilibrium maintained? How many degrees above or below the preset temperature does the appliance tolerate before the unit kicks on or off? Report your findings.

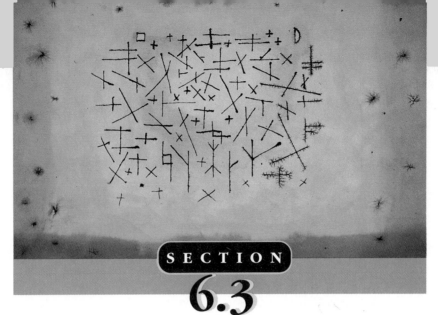

6.3
Adding Signed Numbers

ADDING SIGNED NUMBERS ON THE NUMBER LINE

We can use a number line to model the addition of signed numbers. When signed numbers are added, the signs indicate the directions to move on the number line. On horizontal number lines, a positive sign (+) indicates a move to the right and a negative sign (−) indicates a move to the left.

Example 1
Add two positive numbers, (+3) + (+6).

Solution
We start at zero and move three units to the right. Then we go six more units to the right. The sum is +9.

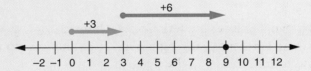

Example 2
Add a positive and a negative number, (+4) + (−6).

Solution

If we study the pattern shown, we see that as consecutively smaller integers are added to +4, the sums decrease by one. We can continue the pattern until we see that (+4) + (−6) = −2.

+4 + (+3) = +7	+4 + (−2) = +2
+4 + (+2) = +6	+4 + (−3) = +1
+4 + (+1) = +5	+4 + (−4) = 0
+4 + (0) = +4	+4 + (−5) = −1
+4 + (−1) = +3	+4 + (−6) = −2

To use a number line to show this addition, we begin at the point with coordinate 0 and move four units to the right to the point with coordinate +4. Then, from +4 we move six units to the left. The sum is −2.

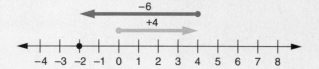

USING A CALCULATOR TO ADD SIGNED NUMBERS

A calculator can also be used to add signed numbers.

Example 3

At 8:00 P.M. the temperature was −2° Celsius. By 7:00 the next morning, the temperature had dropped 15 degrees. What was the temperature at 7 A.M.?

Solution

The expression (−2) + (−15) models the problem. We can use a number line to help us add.

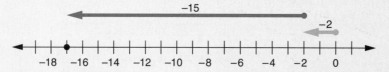

We can also use a calculator:

$$2 \;\boxed{+/-}\; \boxed{+}\; 15 \;\boxed{+/-}\; \boxed{=} \qquad -17$$

Using either method, we find that the temperature at 7 A.M. was −17°C.

Example 4

BCA computer stock sold for $18\frac{7}{8}$ dollars per share on Tuesday morning, but by noon its value had dropped $1\frac{1}{2}$ dollars per share. By closing time, its value had risen $\frac{5}{8}$ dollar per share. What was the closing value of the stock?

Solution

If you choose to use a calculator to solve this problem, it may be helpful to first write an expression that models the problem.

$$+18\tfrac{7}{8} + \left(-1\tfrac{1}{2}\right) + \left(+\tfrac{5}{8}\right)$$

If your calculator has a fraction key, you can enter the problem directly. If not, you could use the decimal equivalents for the fractions. If you enter 18.875 $\boxed{+}$ 1.5 $\boxed{+/-}$ $\boxed{+}$ 0.625 $\boxed{=}$, the display shows 18. Notice that the $\boxed{+/-}$ key is used to obtain the negative number.

Sample Problem

Tiana and Ping each had money in a piggy bank, in a checking account, and in a savings account. The money they had at the end of November is represented by this 2 × 3 matrix.

	Piggy Bank	Checking Account	Savings Account
Tiana	37.50	125.00	368.27
Ping	18.74	145.00	547.19

In December, Ping deposited money (+) in one account, and both Tiana and Ping withdrew money (–) from other accounts. Again, the data are represented in a 2 × 3 matrix.

	Piggy Bank	Checking Account	Savings Account
Tiana	–24.25	–76.87	0
Ping	–10.47	–165.43	+125

How much money did each person have in each of the three accounts at the end of December?

Solution
To answer this question, we need to add the two matrices. Two or more matrices can be added only if all the matrices have the same dimensions. To add matrices, we add corresponding entries.

$$\begin{bmatrix} 37.50 & 125.00 & 368.27 \\ 18.74 & 145.00 & 547.19 \end{bmatrix} + \begin{bmatrix} -24.25 & -76.87 & 0 \\ -10.47 & -165.43 & 125 \end{bmatrix}$$

$$= \begin{bmatrix} 13.25 & 48.13 & 368.27 \\ 8.27 & -20.43 & 672.19 \end{bmatrix}$$

The answer matrix gives the amounts of money in each person's accounts at the end of December. Why should Ping transfer some money from his savings account into his checking account?

Think and Discuss

1 In the sample problem above, two 2-by-3 matrices were added. Can you add a 4-by-3 matrix and a 3-by-4 matrix? Explain.

2 When a number line is used to add signed numbers, why is the endpoint of the first arrow at zero?

3 If your calculator has the fraction key $\boxed{a^b/c}$, use this key to help you find the sum $2\frac{2}{3} + \left(-3\frac{1}{2}\right) + 1\frac{5}{8}$.

4 In the expression (+2) + (−5) − (−7), how is the use of the plus and minus symbols outside the parentheses different from the use of the plus and minus symbols within the parentheses?

5 Add four pairs of positive signed numbers. Add four pairs of negative signed numbers. Can you draw any conclusions about the addition of numbers with the same sign?

6 What addition problem is suggested by each of the following diagrams?

a

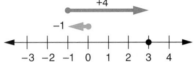

b

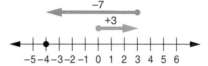

c

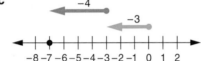

7 Use a number line to find each sum.
a 3 + 5   **b** −3 + 6   **c** −3 + (−4)   **d** 5 + (−7)

8 **Budgeting**   Sue and Juan's budgeted money (+) and actual expenses (−) for a month are arranged by categories in two matrices.

	Budget	**Expenses**
Food	250.00	−275.00
Housing	745.00	−745.00
Utilities	140.00	−130.00
Auto	210.00	−300.00
Entertainment	75.00	−10.00
Miscellaneous	100.00	−50.00

a Add the two matrices. Then explain the meaning of the answer matrix.
b Did Sue and Juan stay within their budget? Explain your answer.

Problems and Applications

9 What addition problem is represented by the diagram? Find the answer to the addition problem.

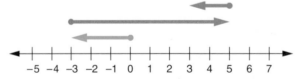

10 Find each sum.
a 7 + 91
b −4 + (−16)
c −86 + 35
d −42 + (−73) + 2
e 19 + (−30) + 79
f 19 + (−30) + (−19)
g 15 + (−5) + 12 + (−10) + (−12)

11 Is the sum of a nonzero number and itself farther from zero on the number line than the number itself?

12 Find each sum.
  a $(-8) + (-3)$
  b $-7 + 12 + 7 + (-12)$
  c $19 + (-5) + (-19)$
  d $38.6 + (-15.2) + (-29) + (-38.6) + 29$
  e $-93.92 + 15 + 38.6 + (-15) + (-93.92)$

13 Is the statement true *always, sometimes,* or *never?*
  a The sum of two negative numbers is greater than either number.
  b The sum of two positive numbers is greater than either number.
  c The sum of two numbers is equal to one of the numbers.

14 Find each sum.
  a $3\frac{1}{5} + \left(-4\frac{3}{5}\right)$ **b** $-6.8 + (-9.3)$ **c** $-4\frac{1}{2} + 6\frac{1}{4}$

15 Find the sum of the matrices.

$$\begin{bmatrix} -4 & -16 & 10 \\ -22 & 9 & 16 \end{bmatrix} + \begin{bmatrix} -7 & 6 & -5 \\ -17 & 12 & -3 \end{bmatrix}$$

16 Fill in the blank with a number that makes the equation true.
  a $19 + \underline{\hspace{1cm}} = -2$ **b** $-15 + \underline{\hspace{1cm}} = -13$ **c** $-11 + \underline{\hspace{1cm}} = -35$

17 Find the mean of $2\frac{2}{5}, -4\frac{5}{8}, 7\frac{1}{2}, 2.78, -3.69,$ and $4\frac{7}{8}$.

18 Evaluate the expression $3 + x$ for each number in the set $\{-1, -2, -3, -4, -5\}$.

19 If one of the expressions $3 + (-9), -10 + 2, -6 + 12, 15 + (-14.3),$ $19 + (-21), 75.5 + (-75.6), 18 + (-18),$ and $-4 + 4$ is chosen at random, what is the probability that the value of the expression is
  a Positive?   **b** Negative?   **c** Neither positive nor negative?

20 Find the sum of the matrices.

  a $\begin{bmatrix} 19 & 3.5 \\ -6 & -8 \end{bmatrix} + \begin{bmatrix} -7 & 4.3 \\ 6 & -12 \end{bmatrix}$ **b** $\begin{bmatrix} 11 & -4 \\ -8 & -3.1 \\ 6.3 & -10 \end{bmatrix} + \begin{bmatrix} -15 & 6 \\ -2.5 & 4.2 \\ -9 & 10 \end{bmatrix}$

21 **Communicating** Perform the indicated operations. What did you discover?
  a $18 + (-3)$ **b** $18 - 3$
  c $24.5 + (-18.2)$ **d** $24.5 - 18.2$

22 Find the sum of the matrices.

$$\begin{bmatrix} -2 & 3 \\ 5 & 0 \\ -9 & -1 \end{bmatrix} + \begin{bmatrix} -6 & -7 \\ -2 & -8 \\ 3 & 4 \end{bmatrix} + \begin{bmatrix} -2 & -1 \\ -7 & 3 \\ 2 & -1 \end{bmatrix}$$

23 If one of the expressions $12.47 + (-8.53), -\frac{2}{3} + \left(-\frac{5}{8}\right), -1\frac{2}{3} + 4\frac{5}{6},$ and $-2.5 + 3.95$ is chosen at random, what is the probability that the value of the expression is greater than 2?

24 Spreadsheets The spreadsheet display shows some of the formulas hidden in the cells. The pattern of these formulas is continued in the rows below.

	A	B	C
1	−4	18	−20
2	A1 + 1	B1 + (−5)	C1 + (−2.5)
3	A2 + 1	B2 + (−5)	C2 + (−2.5)

a What formula is in cell A5? In cell B5? In cell C5?
b What number will appear in cell A5? In cell B5? In cell C5?

25 Perform the indicated operation. Then graph each sum or difference on a number line.

a $\frac{7}{3} + \frac{8}{21}$ 　　　　　　**b** $2\frac{3}{4} - 1\frac{1}{3}$ 　　　　　　**c** $-7\frac{5}{8} + 2\frac{2}{3}$

26 Communicating
a Find the sum.

$$\begin{array}{r} -4215 \\ +\ \ \ 2363 \\ \hline \end{array}$$

b Explain why you actually *subtract* to find the sum of the numbers in part **a.**
c Find the sum.

$$\begin{array}{r} 2363 \\ +\ -4215 \\ \hline \end{array}$$

27 Communicating Joey owed Mandy 45 cents. He borrowed another quarter from her and later paid her back four dimes. The next day he forgot what he owed Mandy and gave her six nickels. How much change should Mandy give him back? Explain your answer.

28 Find the sum of the matrices.

$$\begin{bmatrix} \frac{-3}{8} & \frac{7}{3} \\ \frac{5}{12} & \frac{-14}{15} \end{bmatrix} + \begin{bmatrix} \frac{2}{5} & \frac{-4}{3} \\ \frac{2}{3} & \frac{-5}{21} \end{bmatrix}$$

29 Banking The balance of Tom's checking account was $140.00. Then he wrote some checks.
a Create a third column that shows the balance of the checking account after each check was written. You may want to use a spreadsheet.
b Make a bar graph to display the data.

Check	Amount
105	$74.47
106	32.53
107	24.18
108	16.42
109	5.49
110	19.25

◄ LOOKING BACK **Spiral Learning** LOOKING AHEAD ►

30 Solve each equation for x.
a $x + 98.3 = 0$ 　　　　　　**b** $-15.27 + x = 0$
c $93.16 + x = 0$ 　　　　　　**d** $x + (-113.96) = 0$

31 Find all numbers on the number line that are 8.4 units away from 3.1.

32 a Solve for h.
b Solve for h when the base of the ladder is 2 feet from the wall.

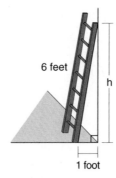

6 feet

h

1 foot

33 Matrix addition is needed to change the Start triangle into the Finish triangle. What matrix should be added to the ordered pairs (x, y) of the Start matrix to give the ordered pairs of the Finish matrix?

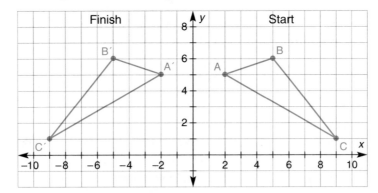

	Start	+	?	=	Finish	

$$\begin{array}{c} \\ \textbf{A} \\ \textbf{B} \\ \textbf{C} \end{array} \begin{array}{cc} x & y \end{array} \begin{bmatrix} 2 & 5 \\ 5 & 6 \\ 9 & 1 \end{bmatrix} + \begin{bmatrix} & \\ & \\ & \end{bmatrix} = \begin{array}{c} \\ \textbf{A}' \\ \textbf{B}' \\ \textbf{C}' \end{array} \begin{array}{cc} x & y \end{array} \begin{bmatrix} -2 & 5 \\ -5 & 6 \\ -9 & 1 \end{bmatrix}$$

34 The table contains time and temperature data for Denver, Colorado.
a Display the data in a bar graph.
b What was the greatest temperature change in a two-hour period?

Time	Temperature (°F)
6 A.M.	−12
8	−4
10	−2
12 P.M.	7
2	12
4	18
6	12
8	−4
10	−6
12 A.M.	−9

35 Communicating   Is the number line drawn correctly? Explain your answer.

−1 −2 −3 −4 −5 −6 0 1 2 3 4 5 6

36 Graph each inequality.
a $w \geq -2$ **b** $w < -2$ **c** $-2 < w$ **d** $-2 \geq w$

37 Use the Pythagorean Theorem to find the length of the third side of each triangle.

a
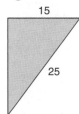
15
25

b
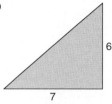
6
7

c
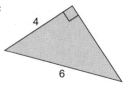
4
6

38 Use a calculator to find each quotient.

a $\dfrac{-42}{-7}$　　　　**b** $\dfrac{-42}{-21}$　　　　**c** $\dfrac{42}{-7}$　　　　**d** $\dfrac{42}{21}$

e What do you think is the rule for determining the sign of the quotient of signed numbers?

39 Use your calculator to perform the indicated operations in parts **a–f.**

a $-7 + (-7) + (-7) + (-7)$

b $(-4) + (-4) + (-4) + (-4) + (-4) + (-4)$

c $2 + 2 + 2 + 2 + 2 + 2 + 2 + 2 + 2 + 2$

d $(-7)(4)$

e $(-4)6$

f $(2)(10)$

40 If a number, x, is chosen at random so that $-5 \le x \le 6$, what is the probability that $-2 < x < 1$?

41 **Communicating**　The table indicates the sports in which Antelope High School students participate and the number of participants in each sport.

a Make a bar graph to display the data.

b Why is a circle graph not an appropriate way to display the data?

Sport	Number of Participants
Track	182
Soccer	156
Football	149
Swimming	123
Baseball	111
Basketball	106
Wrestling	70
Tennis	54
Cross country	52
Gymnastics	52
Volleyball	49
Golf	23

Investigation

Banking　How are signed numbers used in fields such as accounting, banking, and investing? Find out the meaning and use of the terms *credit, debit, payment, receipt, deposit, withdrawal, profit, loss, asset, liability, loan, interest,* and *overhead.* Which of these terms could be described as "positive," and which could be described as "negative"?

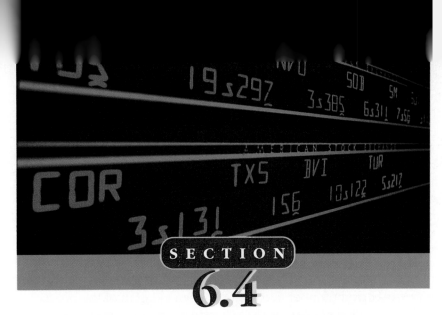

SECTION

6.4

Multiplying and Dividing Signed Numbers

MULTIPLICATION OF SIGNED NUMBERS

The patterns shown below will help us discover the rules for multiplying signed numbers.

$$3 \cdot \quad 4 = 12$$
$$3 \cdot \quad 3 = 9$$
$$3 \cdot \quad 2 = 6$$
$$3 \cdot \quad 1 = 3$$
$$3 \cdot \quad 0 = 0$$
$$3 \cdot (-1) = -3$$
$$3 \cdot (-2) = -6$$
$$3 \cdot (-3) = -9$$
$$3 \cdot (-4) = -12$$

$$3 \cdot (-4) = -12$$
$$2 \cdot (-4) = -8$$
$$1 \cdot (-4) = -4$$
$$0 \cdot (-4) = 0$$
$$-1 \cdot (-4) = 4$$
$$-2 \cdot (-4) = 8$$
$$-3 \cdot (-4) = 12$$
$$-4 \cdot (-4) = 16$$
$$-5 \cdot (-4) = 20$$

The patterns suggest three rules for multiplying signed numbers.

1. The product of two positive numbers is positive.
2. The product of a positive number and a negative number is negative.
3. The product of two negative numbers is positive.

Example 1

Find each product.

a $4 \cdot (-7)$ b $-5 \cdot 3$ c $-7 \cdot (-3)$

Solution

a $4 \cdot (-7) = -28$ b $-5 \cdot 3 = -15$ c $-7 \cdot (-3) = 21$

Example 2

Solve the equation $-8x = 40$ for x.

Solution

We can experiment with our calculator. First we try 5 and find that $-8(5) = -40$. It then seems logical to try –5. Since $-8(-5) = 40$, the solution of the equation is –5. On a calculator, 8 [+/−] [×] 5 [+/−] [=] results in a display of ▮▮▮▮ 40 . Therefore, $x = -5$.

SCALAR MULTIPLICATION

To multiply a matrix by a number, we multiply each element of the matrix by the number. This is called **scalar multiplication,** and the number we multiply by is called a **scalar.**

Example 3

Multiply $-3 \begin{bmatrix} 5 & -1 & 2 \\ -2 & 3 & 6 \end{bmatrix}$.

Solution

$$-3 \begin{bmatrix} 5 & -1 & 2 \\ -2 & 3 & 6 \end{bmatrix} = \begin{bmatrix} (-3)(5) & (-3)(-1) & (-3)(2) \\ (-3)(-2) & (-3)(3) & (-3)(6) \end{bmatrix} = \begin{bmatrix} -15 & 3 & -6 \\ 6 & -9 & -18 \end{bmatrix}$$

POWERS OF SIGNED NUMBERS

We apply the rules for multiplying signed numbers when we evaluate powers of signed numbers.

Example 4

Evaluate each expression.

a $(-3)^4$ **b** -3^4

Solution

a In the expression $(-3)^4$, the base is –3 and the exponent is 4. Therefore, –3 is used as a factor four times.

$$(-3)^4 = (-3)(-3)(-3)(-3) = 9 \cdot 9 = 81$$

b In the expression -3^4, the base is 3 and the exponent is 4. The value of this expression is the opposite of the number we get when we use 3 as a factor four times.

$$-3^4 = -(3)(3)(3)(3) = -81$$

DIVISION OF SIGNED NUMBERS

Dividing by a number gives the same result as multiplying by the reciprocal of the number. Keep this in mind as you study the next example.

Example 5

Find each quotient.

a $-4.5 \div 2$

b $\dfrac{-12}{-8}$

Solution

a $-4.5 \div 2 = -4.5 \cdot \dfrac{1}{2} = -4.5 \cdot 0.5 = -2.25$

b $\dfrac{-12}{-8} = -12 \cdot \left(\dfrac{1}{-8}\right) = -12 \cdot (-0.125) = 1.5$

The equation in Example 2 on the previous page, $-8x = 40$, can also be solved by using division, the inverse operation of multiplication. For example, if $-8x = 40$, then $x = 40 \div (-8)$.

Using a calculator, we get the same result.

$$40 \boxed{\div} \; 8 \boxed{+/-} \boxed{=} \qquad\qquad -5$$

Since dividing has the same result as multiplying by a reciprocal, the rules for dividing are the same as those for multiplying.

1. The quotient of two positive numbers is positive.
2. The quotient of a positive and a negative number is negative.
3. The quotient of two negative numbers is positive.

Sample Problems

Problem 1

Wally Street has 157 shares of Zenox stock. The stock's value was $32.75 per share on Tuesday morning. At the close of Tuesday's trading, the stock was down $1.50 per share.

a How much money did Wally lose on his Zenox stock on Tuesday?

b By what percent did the stock decrease in value?

Solution

a We indicate "down $1.50" by -1.5 and multiply to find Wally's total loss on the stock. Since $(-1.5) \cdot 157 = -235.50$, Wally's loss was $235.50.

b **Method 1**

From part **a** we know that the total loss was $235.50 out of a total value of 157($32.75), or $5141.75. Therefore, the percent of change was

$$\frac{-235.50}{5141.75} \approx -0.046, \text{ or } \approx -4.6\%$$

Therefore, the value of the stock decreased 4.6%.

Method 2

The percent of change for all 157 shares of stock is the same as the percent of change for a single share of the stock. Therefore, we can divide the loss per share by the value of one share of the stock.

$$\frac{-1.5}{32.75} \approx -0.046, \text{ or } \approx -4.6\%$$

Problem 2

The matrix shows the average number of miles per gallon of gasoline for three Major Motors cars. Included are figures for both city and highway driving.

Miles per Gallon

	City	Highway
Guzzle Mobile	14	17
Family Auto	24	30
Mini Mite	35	47

If an engineering breakthrough raises mileages on all three cars for both types of driving by 23%, what will each car's new mileage figures be?

Solution

To determine the result of the 23% increase, we first use scalar multiplication to find 23% of each number in the matrix, then add these results to the original numbers in the matrix.

$$0.23 \cdot \begin{bmatrix} 14 & 17 \\ 24 & 30 \\ 35 & 47 \end{bmatrix} + \begin{bmatrix} 14 & 17 \\ 24 & 30 \\ 35 & 47 \end{bmatrix} = \begin{bmatrix} 0.23(14) & 0.23(17) \\ 0.23(24) & 0.23(30) \\ 0.23(35) & 0.23(47) \end{bmatrix} + \begin{bmatrix} 14 & 17 \\ 24 & 30 \\ 35 & 47 \end{bmatrix}$$

$$\approx \begin{bmatrix} 3.22 & 3.91 \\ 5.52 & 6.90 \\ 8.05 & 10.8 \end{bmatrix} + \begin{bmatrix} 14 & 17 \\ 24 & 30 \\ 35 & 47 \end{bmatrix}$$

$$= \begin{bmatrix} 17.22 & 20.91 \\ 29.52 & 36.9 \\ 43.05 & 57.8 \end{bmatrix} \approx \begin{bmatrix} 17 & 21 \\ 30 & 37 \\ 43 & 58 \end{bmatrix}$$

Think and Discuss

1 Find each product.

   a $-3(6)$ **b** $3(-6)$ **c** $6(-3)$ **d** $-6(3)$

2 Condense the three rules for multiplying signed numbers into two rules—one for multiplying numbers with the same sign and one for multiplying numbers with different signs.

3 **a** Write a definition of the term *scalar*.
   b Why do you think the term *scalar* is used?

4 Find the products by using scalar multiplication.

a $-2 \cdot \begin{bmatrix} 2 & -4 \\ -6 & 8 \end{bmatrix}$

b $\frac{1}{2} \cdot \begin{bmatrix} -2 & -4 \\ 6 & 8 \end{bmatrix}$

5 **a** Evaluate $(-2)^2$.   **b** Evaluate -2^2.
  c Explain why the answers in parts **a** and **b** have different signs.
  d Evaluate $(-2)^3$.   **e** Evaluate -2^3.
  f Explain why the answers in parts **d** and **e** have the same sign.

6 What is a reciprocal? Find the reciprocals of these numbers.
  a 2   **b** $-\frac{1}{3}$ **c** $\frac{3}{4}$ **d** -2.5

7 What is the relationship between reciprocals and division?

8 Find each quotient, then explain why $-\frac{a}{b} = \frac{-a}{b} = \frac{a}{-b}$.
  a $-\frac{20}{5}$ **b** $\frac{-20}{5}$ **c** $\frac{20}{-5}$

Problems and Applications

9 **Communicating** Find each product. Then graph the products on a number line. What pattern do you see in the graph?
  a $(-5)4$ **b** $(-5)3$ **c** $(-5)2$ **d** $(-5)1$ **e** $(-5)0$
  f $(-5)(-1)$ **g** $(-5)(-2)$ **h** $(-5)(-3)$ **i** $(-5)(-4)$

10 Perform each operation. Arrange the answers in order, from least to greatest.
  a $(-5)(-7)$ **b** $\frac{-50}{-5}$ **c** $\frac{-50}{5}$ **d** $(-5)(7)$
  e $\frac{20}{-4}$ **f** $(9)(-5)$ **g** $3(4)$

11 Solve each equation for x.
  a $-4x = 32$ **b** $-4x = -32$ **c** $4x = 32$ **d** $4x = -32$

12 Is the statement true *always, sometimes,* or *never?*
  a A negative number added to a negative number is a positive number.
  b A negative number added to a positive number is a positive number.
  c A negative number multiplied by a negative number is a positive number.
  d A negative number divided by a negative number is a positive number.
  e A negative number added to a positive number is a negative number.

13 Evaluate each expression.   **a** $\dfrac{(-5)^2(-3) + 4(-3)}{(-1)(-3)}$ **b** $\dfrac{-12^2}{-24 + (-2)(-4)}$

14 **Communicating** Study the pattern in column A. Then determine which powers in column B will be negative. Explain your answer.

Column A	Column B
$(-2)^2 = \quad 4$	$(-2)^{77}$
$(-2)^3 = \quad -8$	$(-2)^{88}$
$(-2)^4 = \quad 16$	$(-2)^{36}$
$(-2)^5 = -32$	$(-2)^{100}$

15 Four employees at Joe's Burger Barn will receive a 7% raise. The matrix shows their current wages.

	Current Hourly Wage
Raul	4.95
Pablo	5.65
Sue	4.85
Melissa	5.75

  a Write a matrix problem that can be used to determine the new hourly wage for each employee.
  b Compute the new salary for each of the four employees.

16 Business Jan has 47 shares of Libom Oil stock. One share was worth $37.75 on Tuesday and $36.85 on Wednesday.
  a How much did she lose on a single share of the stock?
  b What was the percent of loss per share?
  c How much did she lose on all 47 shares?
  d What was the percent of loss on all 47 shares?

17 The area of the rectangle is 320. Solve for x.

20

$-4x$

18 Five wooden squares are numbered as indicated.

If two of the squares are chosen at random, what is the probability that
  a Their product is negative?   **b** Their product is positive?
  c Their sum is negative?

19 Perform each scalar multiplication.

  a $-2\begin{bmatrix} -3 & 4 \\ -9 & 18 \\ 6 & -2 \end{bmatrix}$
  b $-3.5\begin{bmatrix} -1.2 & -6 \\ 3.4 & -9 \\ 11.1 & 0 \end{bmatrix}$

20 Solve each equation.
  a $-6x = 30$ **b** $-7x = -49$ **c** $-4x + 3 = 31$ **d** $12 - 18 = -2x$

21 In 1990 the dollar values of five homes were $175,000, $98,000, $112,000, $145,000, and $205,000. In 1991 the value of each home decreased 14%.
  a Write a scalar matrix multiplication problem that represents the values of the homes at the end of 1991.
  b Solve the problem you wrote in part **a**.

22 Spreadsheets The students' scores in Mrs. Quadratic's algebra class are 97, 84, 69, 42, 79, 84, 86, 77, 62, 71, and 55. If possible, use a spreadsheet to answer these questions.
  a What are the new scores for all the students if Mrs. Quadratic increases each student's score by 5%? By 10%? By 12%? By 15%?
  b What percent of increase is necessary to have no scores below 60? What would be the highest score after that increase?

23 Graph each inequality.

a $n > 3$ **b** $n \geq 3$ **c** $n < 3$ **d** $n \leq 3$

e $3 > n$ **f** $3 \leq n$ **g** $3 \geq n$ **h** $3 < n$

24 The x-coordinates, and the y-coordinates, of vertices A, B, and C of the triangle are arranged in a matrix.

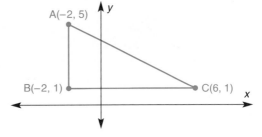

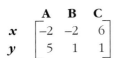

a If this matrix is multiplied by 2, what is the new matrix?

b Determine the vertices of the triangle represented by the matrix in part **a,** and draw the triangle.

c Compare the area of the original triangle with the area of the new triangle.

25 If one of the following expressions is selected at random, what is the probability that the expression has a negative answer?

a $-1732 + 1492$ **b** $(-81)(759)$ **c** $\frac{-1001}{-13}$

d $-8118 + 1881$ **e** $-4224 + (-8448)$ **f** $-37 \cdot [847 + (-847)]$

26 Find the sum of the matrices.

$$\begin{bmatrix} 7 & 12 & 15 \\ 8 & 10 & 19 \\ 6 & 14 & 8 \end{bmatrix} + \begin{bmatrix} -8 & -13 & -16 \\ -7 & -9 & -18 \\ -7 & -13 & -7 \end{bmatrix}$$

27 A rectangular field with dimensions of 30 meters by 50 meters is to be surrounded by a fence. Posts are placed every 2 meters.

a How many posts are needed?

b How many posts are needed if one 50-meter side is not fenced?

c How many posts are needed if one 30-meter side is not fenced?

28 **Consumer Math** If a hamburger costs $2.00, an order of fries costs $0.75, and a soft drink costs $0.60, how much is each person's bill?

	Hamburgers	Fries	Drinks
Alf	4	3	5
Betty	2	4	2
Grandma	1	3	5
Del	3	2	4

Investigation

Physics Find out the meaning of the term *half-life* as it applies to nuclear science. Draw a graph to help you explain the term to the class.

Matrix Multiplication

In the last section we looked at scalar multiplication—multiplying a matrix by a number. In this section you will learn how to multiply two matrices.

Example 1

Alpha, Beta, Gamma, and Delta want to buy burgers, soft drinks, and fries. The quantity matrix shows the number of items each person wants to buy.

Quantity Matrix

	Burgers	Soft Drinks	Fries
Alpha	4	4	4
Beta	6	1	1
Gamma	2	10	2
Delta	3	2	4

The price of each item at three fast-food restaurants— McDuck's, Burger Barn, and Wanda's—is shown in the price matrix.

Price Matrix

	McDuck's	Burger Barn	Wanda's
Burger	$1.69	$1.85	$1.75
Drink	0.79	0.59	0.65
Fries	0.69	0.75	0.59

a How much will each person pay at McDuck's? At Burger Barn? At Wanda's?
b Which fast-food restaurant has the best prices?

Solution

a There are 12 values to calculate because each of the 4 people could buy from any of the 3 restaurants. To calculate any of these values, we first choose a row from the quantity matrix and a column from the price matrix. Let's try the Alpha row and the Wanda's column to find out how much Alpha would pay at Wanda's.

4 burgers × $1.75 each + 4 drinks × $0.65 each + 4 fries × $0.59 each
= $7.00 + $2.60 + $2.36
= $11.96

The total cost for Alpha to purchase four burgers, four soft drinks, and four fries at Wanda's is $11.96.

The $11.96 it costs Alpha to buy at Wanda's is placed in the product matrix at the intersection of row 1 and column 3.

Product Matrix

	McDuck's	Burger Barn	Wanda's
Alpha			$11.96
Beta			
Gamma			
Delta			

Since each of the four people can make her purchase at any of the three fast-food restaurants, we will repeat this procedure 4 · 3, or 12, times.

Product Matrix

	McDuck's	Burger Barn	Wanda's
Alpha	$12.68	$12.76	$11.96
Beta	11.62	12.44	11.74
Gamma	12.66	11.10	11.18
Delta	9.41	9.73	8.91

b Determining the fast-food restaurant with the best prices depends on what items are ordered. Some people might say that Wanda's has the best price because it has the lowest-priced fries and the lowest combined price for the three menu items. The entries in the product matrix indicate that Alpha should go to Wanda's, Beta should go to McDuck's, Gamma should go to Burger Barn, and Delta should go to Wanda's.

Notice that in the preceding example it was important that the number of elements in a row of the first matrix matched the number of elements in a column of the second matrix. Also notice that the values in the product matrix were not found by simply multiplying corresponding elements of the two matrices.

Example 2

Multiply $\begin{bmatrix} -12 & 2.5 & -3 \\ 7 & -5 & 4.2 \end{bmatrix} \cdot \begin{bmatrix} 2 & -6 \\ 4 & 3 \\ -5 & -1 \end{bmatrix}$.

Solution

Column 1

Row 1 $\begin{bmatrix} -12 & 2.5 & -3 \end{bmatrix} \cdot \begin{bmatrix} 2 \\ 4 \\ -5 \end{bmatrix}$

$(-12)(2) + 2.5(4) + (-3)(-5) = \boxed{1}$

Column 2

Row 1 $\begin{bmatrix} -12 & 2.5 & -3 \end{bmatrix} \cdot \begin{bmatrix} -6 \\ 3 \\ -1 \end{bmatrix}$

$(-12)(-6) + 2.5(3) + (-3)(-1) = \boxed{82.5}$

Column 1

Row 2 $\begin{bmatrix} 7 & -5 & 4.2 \end{bmatrix} \cdot \begin{bmatrix} 2 \\ 4 \\ -5 \end{bmatrix}$

$7(2) + (-5)(4) + 4.2(-5) = \boxed{-27}$

Column 2

Row 2 $\begin{bmatrix} 7 & -5 & 4.2 \end{bmatrix} \cdot \begin{bmatrix} -6 \\ 3 \\ -1 \end{bmatrix}$

$7(-6) + (-5)(3) + 4.2(-1) = \boxed{-61.2}$

The product matrix is $\begin{bmatrix} 1 & 82.5 \\ -27 & -61.2 \end{bmatrix}$ Row 1 Row 2 (Column 1, Column 2)

Sample Problems

Problem 1 Suppose that $A = \begin{bmatrix} 2 & 4 \\ -5 & 3 \end{bmatrix}$ and $B = \begin{bmatrix} -6 & 12 \\ 3 & -7 \end{bmatrix}$. Find $A \cdot B$ and $B \cdot A$.

Solution

$$A \cdot B = \begin{bmatrix} 2 & 4 \\ -5 & 3 \end{bmatrix} \cdot \begin{bmatrix} -6 & 12 \\ 3 & -7 \end{bmatrix} = \begin{bmatrix} 0 & -4 \\ 39 & -81 \end{bmatrix}$$

$$B \cdot A = \begin{bmatrix} -6 & 12 \\ 3 & -7 \end{bmatrix} \cdot \begin{bmatrix} 2 & 4 \\ -5 & 3 \end{bmatrix} = \begin{bmatrix} -72 & 12 \\ 41 & -9 \end{bmatrix}$$

By looking at these results, we can see that the order in which the matrices are multiplied is important. Sometimes matrices that can be multiplied in one order cannot even be multiplied when their order is reversed. You will see an example of such matrices in the Think and Discuss problems of this section.

Problem 2 The shareholders' matrix gives the number of shares of three stocks owned by four stockholders.

Shareholders' Matrix

		Juan	Ali	Samir	Rachel
	ADE	15	5	9	7
Stock	**CAR**	12	13	4	34
	ING	9	24	7	5

On Tuesday, stock ADE lost $5.00 per share, stock CAR gained $2.00 per share, and stock ING lost $2.50 per share.

a Write a matrix multiplication problem to find the total losses or gains for each person's portfolio.

b Evaluate the matrix product you wrote in part **a**. How much did each person gain or lose on his or her stocks?

Solution

a The dollar gain or loss for each type of stock is displayed in the 1 × 3 gain/loss matrix. The product of the gain/loss matrix and the shareholders' matrix will be a matrix that displays the total gain or loss in each person's portfolio.

Gain/Loss Matrix

ADE	CAR	ING
-5	2	-2.5

Shareholders' Matrix

Juan	Ali	Samir	Rachel
15	5	9	7
12	13	4	34
9	24	7	5

b To evaluate the product matrix we wrote in part **a,** we multiply each column of the second matrix by the single row of the first matrix.

Juan: −5(15) + 2(12) + (−2.5)(9) = −73.5
Ali: −5(5) + 2(13) + (−2.5)(24) = −59
Samir: −5(9) + 2(4) + (−2.5)(7) = −54.5
Rachel: −5(7) + 2(34) + (−2.5)(5) = 20.5

Shareholders' Gain/Loss Matrix

Juan	Ali	Samir	Rachel
−73.5	−59	−54.5	20.5

Note that everyone but Rachel lost money on Tuesday.

Think and Discuss

1 Find the product in parts **a** and **b.**

a $\begin{bmatrix} 3 & -1 \\ 2 & -4 \end{bmatrix} \cdot \begin{bmatrix} -2 & 3 \\ 1 & -2 \end{bmatrix}$

b $\begin{bmatrix} -2 & 3 \\ 1 & -2 \end{bmatrix} \cdot \begin{bmatrix} 3 & -1 \\ 2 & -4 \end{bmatrix}$

c What conclusion can you draw about matrix multiplication from the results in parts **a** and **b?**

2 Find the product in parts **a** and **b.**

a $\begin{bmatrix} 2 & 1 \\ 1 & -1 \end{bmatrix} \cdot \begin{bmatrix} 4 & 3 & 2 \\ -2 & 4 & 5 \end{bmatrix}$

b $\begin{bmatrix} 4 & 3 & 2 \\ -2 & 4 & 5 \end{bmatrix} \cdot \begin{bmatrix} 2 & 1 \\ 1 & -1 \end{bmatrix}$

c What conclusion can you draw about matrix multiplication from the results in parts **a** and **b?**

3 Give an example of dimensions of two matrices that can be multiplied.

4 Give an example of dimensions of two matrices that cannot be multiplied.

5 If you multiply a 4 × 6 matrix by a 6 × 3 matrix, what will the dimensions of the product matrix be?

6 In matrix multiplication, if you multiply row 3 of the first matrix by column 5 of the second matrix, where is the result placed in the product matrix?

Problems and Applications

7 Find each product.

a $\begin{bmatrix} -3 & -4 \end{bmatrix} \cdot \begin{bmatrix} 2 \\ -7 \end{bmatrix}$

b $\begin{bmatrix} 2 \\ -7 \end{bmatrix} \cdot \begin{bmatrix} -3 & -4 \end{bmatrix}$

8 Possible dimensions of matrix A and matrix B are given. Copy and complete the table, determining the dimensions of each product matrix A · B.

Matrix B

Matrix A ×	2 × 4	2 × 2	2 × 5
3 × 2			
2 × 2			
5 × 2			

9 Find each product.

a $\begin{bmatrix} 3 & 1 & 5 \\ 2 & 0 & 6 \end{bmatrix} \cdot \begin{bmatrix} 4 \\ 8 \\ 9 \end{bmatrix}$

b $\begin{bmatrix} 3 & -1 & -5 \\ -2 & 0 & 6 \end{bmatrix} \cdot \begin{bmatrix} -4 \\ 8 \\ -9 \end{bmatrix}$

10 **Communicating** Write a procedure for multiplying two matrices. Read it to someone and have that person use your procedure to multiply two matrices.

11 The product of two matrices is given, but three of the elements are missing. Fill in the missing elements so that the product matrix will be correct.

$$\begin{bmatrix} 2 & \underline{} \\ \underline{} & 4 \end{bmatrix} \cdot \begin{bmatrix} 5 & -3 \\ -2 & \underline{} \end{bmatrix} = \begin{bmatrix} 6 & -12 \\ -3 & -15 \end{bmatrix}$$

12 Find each product.

a $\begin{bmatrix} 1 & 0 \\ 0 & 1 \end{bmatrix} \cdot \begin{bmatrix} 3 & 2 \\ 3 & 9 \end{bmatrix}$

b $\begin{bmatrix} 3 & 2 \\ 13 & 9 \end{bmatrix} \cdot \begin{bmatrix} 1 & 0 \\ 0 & 1 \end{bmatrix}$

c $\begin{bmatrix} 3 & 2 \\ 13 & 9 \end{bmatrix} \cdot \begin{bmatrix} 9 & -2 \\ -13 & 3 \end{bmatrix}$

13 Is the following statement true *always, sometimes,* or *never?*

For matrix C and matrix D, C · D = D · C.

14 Matrix A has 5 rows and 9 columns. Matrix B has 12 columns. We want to find the product A · B.

a How many rows must matrix B have? Explain your answer.

b If matrix B has the number of rows indicated in your answer to part **a,** how many rows does the product matrix have?

c How many columns does the product matrix have?

15 Find each product. What conclusion about matrix multiplication do your results suggest?

a $\begin{bmatrix} 3 & 1 \\ 4 & 2 \end{bmatrix} \cdot \begin{bmatrix} 5 & 6 \\ 9 & 8 \end{bmatrix}$

b $\begin{bmatrix} 3 & -1 \\ -4 & 2 \end{bmatrix} \cdot \begin{bmatrix} 5 & -6 \\ -9 & 8 \end{bmatrix}$

16 **Consumer Math** The shares matrix gives the number of shares of MBI stock and PI stock held by Peter, Kathy, and Bob. MBI stock lost $2.25 per share and PI gained $1.50 per share.

Shares Matrix

	Peter	Kathy	Bob
MBI	72	58	39
PI	14	47	81

    a Write a matrix multiplication problem that can be used to determine how much money each person's portfolio gained or lost.

    b Find the product of the matrices in part **a** to determine the actual gains and losses.

    c Who lost the most?

17 **Business** The wage matrix represents the hourly wage Clyde and Chloe earn working at Mickey Dees and Burger Barn. The time matrix shows that each person worked 10 hours at Mickey Dees and 8 hours at Burger Barn. Use matrix multiplication to find the total amount each person earned.

Wage Matrix

	Mickey Dees	Burger Barn
Clyde	$3.80	$4.10
Chloe	4.00	3.90

Time Matrix

	Hours
Mickey Dees	10
Burger Barn	8

18 **Environmental Science** Four conservationists want to purchase three types of evergreen trees. The trees are available at three nurseries.

Quantity Matrix

	Spruce	Red Pine	White Pine
George	25	35	14
Wally	45	50	32
Chuck	18	35	75
Bill	20	40	18

Price Matrix

Nursery	A	B	C
Spruce	1.45	1.53	1.62
Red pine	1.50	1.42	1.38
White pine	1.25	1.60	1.35

    a How much would it cost each person to purchase the given numbers of trees at each of the nurseries?

    b Which nursery offers the best overall deal for each person?

19 The number matrix for the Alsip Expressway's three toll booths gives the throughput numbers for three types of vehicles in one week. The toll matrix lists the toll fee per vehicle.

Number Matrix

	Cars	Trailers	Trucks
Booth 1	72,000	8,000	12,500
Booth 2	84,000	9,756	8,750
Booth 3	68,000	6,540	9,984

Toll Matrix

Fee per Vehicle	
Car	0.40
Trailer	0.60
Truck	0.95

    a Find the total amount collected at each toll booth for the week.

    b What was the total amount collected during the week at all the toll booths combined?

    c Why do you think tollways charge more for trucks and for trailers than for cars?

20 Find the missing numbers so that each side of the triangle will have the same sum.

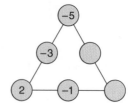

21 Evaluate each expression.

a $-16^2 + (-10)^2$ **b** $(-16)^2 - 10^2$

22 Solve each equation for x.

a $-8x = -120$ **b** $5x = -60$ **c** $-1.5x = 90$

23 Compute the product. Express your answer in scientific notation.

$$(-3.67 \times 10^{18})(4.00 \times 10^{10})$$

24 Which is greater, 20% of -6 or 40% of -8?

25 Find the area of the circle.

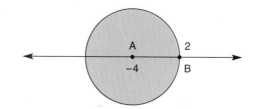

26 Write a mathematical expression that represents each phrase. Then evaluate the expression.

a The sum of -18, 7, and -4
b The product of -5, 3, and -2
c The sum of 3 times -4 and -2 times -5
d The product of the sum of 3 and -8 and the sum of -7 and -8
e The product of -8 and the sum of 3 and -7

27 Evaluate each expression for $x = -3$ and $y = -5$.

a $3x + 2y$ **b** $x \cdot y^2$ **c** $-5x + x \cdot y$

28 **Sports** The table shows the field-goal statistics in the Fumbler's Football League for last year. The data for attempted and completed field goals is broken down by the distance of the kicks.

Distance (yards)	Number Attempted	Number Made
Under 20	42	39
20–29	477	456
30–39	626	454
40–49	625	319
50–59	167	59
60 or more	5	0

a Make a circle graph using the distance and number attempted.
b Make a circle graph using the distance and the number made.

29 Solve for a.

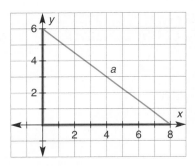

30 Solve each equation for n.

a $\dfrac{n}{-2} = \dfrac{12}{-3}$

b $\dfrac{7}{n} = \dfrac{14}{-6}$

31 Evaluate each expression.

a $\dfrac{(-48)(-3)}{-6}$

b $-9 + (-5) \cdot 3$

c $[-9 + (-5)] \cdot 3$

Investigation

Using a Matrix   Interview one or more of the following: a scientist, an engineer, a computer programmer, or a business owner. Discuss at least one example of how matrices are used in a job situation. Explain your findings.

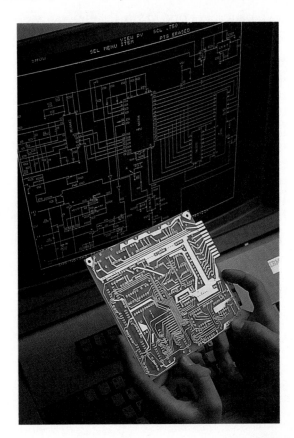

6.6

Subtracting Signed Numbers

DEFINITION OF SUBTRACTION

The number −4 can be read "the opposite of the number 4." Similarly, −(−4) can be interpreted as the opposite of −4.

Let's take a look at two patterns—one in which numbers are subtracted from 10 and one in which the opposites of these numbers are added to ten.

Subtraction		Addition	
$10 - 7$	$= 3$	$10 + (-7)$	$= 3$
$10 - 8$	$= 2$	$10 + (-8)$	$= 2$
$10 - 9$	$= 1$	$10 + (-9)$	$= 1$
$10 - 10$	$= 0$	$10 + (-10)$	$= 0$
$10 - 11$	$= -1$	$10 + (-11)$	$= -1$
$10 - 12$	$= -2$	$10 + (-12)$	$= -2$
$10 - 13$	$= -3$	$10 + (-13)$	$= -3$
$10 - 14$	$= -4$	$10 + (-14)$	$= -4$
$10 - 15$	$= -5$	$10 + (-15)$	$= -5$

The patterns help us understand why subtracting a signed number is the same as adding its opposite.

➤ **For any two numbers a and b, $a - b = a + (-b)$.**

Example 1
Find each difference.

a $5 - 9$ **b** $-5 - 9$ **c** $5 - (-9)$ **d** $-5 - (-9)$

Solution

a $5 - 9 = 5 + (-9) = -4$

b $-5 - 9 = -5 + (-9) = -14$

c $5 - (-9) = 5 + [-(-9)]$
$= 5 + 9$
$= 14$

d $-5 - (-9) = -5 + [-(-9)]$
$= -5 + 9$
$= 4$

Example 2

Friday at 5:00 P.M. the temperature was $-4°F$. At 5:00 A.M. Saturday the temperature was $-22°F$. What was the change in temperature?

Solution

To find the change in temperature, we subtract the 5:00 P.M. temperature from the 5:00 A.M. temperature.

$$-22 - (-4) = -22 + 4$$
$$= -18$$

The temperature decreased by 18 degrees Fahrenheit.

If we use a number line to represent the problem in Example 2, we see that the definition of subtraction makes sense.

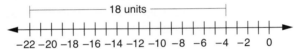

The number line shows that -22 is 18 units to the left of -4.

SUBTRACTING MATRICES

To subtract matrices, we subtract corresponding entries.

Example 3

Subtract $\begin{bmatrix} 2 & -4 \\ -5 & 9 \end{bmatrix} - \begin{bmatrix} -14 & 12 \\ -4 & -6 \end{bmatrix}$.

Solution

We will subtract each entry of the second matrix from the corresponding entry of the first matrix.

$$\begin{bmatrix} 2 & -4 \\ -5 & 9 \end{bmatrix} - \begin{bmatrix} -14 & 12 \\ -4 & -6 \end{bmatrix} = \begin{bmatrix} 2 - (-14) & -4 - 12 \\ -5 - (-4) & 9 - (-6) \end{bmatrix}$$

$$= \begin{bmatrix} 2 + 14 & -4 + (-12) \\ -5 + 4 & 9 + 6 \end{bmatrix}$$

$$= \begin{bmatrix} 16 & -16 \\ -1 & 15 \end{bmatrix}$$

Problem 1 How many integers are in the set {–15, –14, –13, . . . , 5, 6}?

Solution **Method 1**

From –15 to –1 there are 15 numbers.
Counting 0 adds 1 number.
From 1 to 6 there are 6 numbers.
Total: 22 numbers

Method 2
We can also subtract the number with the smallest value from the number with the largest value, then add 1.

$$6 - (-15) = 6 + [-(-15)] = 6 + 15 = 21$$

Adding 1, we have 21 + 1, or 22 numbers.

Problem 2 Sally and Tom were asked to solve the equation $x + 12 = 19$. Sally said she would subtract 12 from both sides of the equation to solve it. Tom said he would add –12 to both sides of the equation to solve it. Who was right? Explain your answer.

Solution Let's try Sally's approach:
If $x + 12 = 19$, then $x + 12 - 12 = 19 - 12$ and $x = 7$.
If we replace x with 7, we see that Sally is correct because $7 + 12 = 19$.

Now let's try Tom's approach:
If $x + 12 = 19$, then $x + 12 + (-12) = 19 + (-12)$ and $x = 7$.
Tom's answer is the same as Sally's.

Both Sally's approach and Tom's approach are correct. Subtracting 12 gives the same result as adding –12.

Think and Discuss

1 How do we find the opposite of a number?

2 What is the opposite of 5? Of 0? Of –7?

3 **a** How would you read the expression $-(-100)$?
b Evaluate the expression in part **a**.

4 Which difference has the smallest value? Which has the largest value? How could you arrange the differences from smallest to largest without doing any computation?
  a $-6 - 8$ **b** $6 - 8$ **c** $6 - (-8)$ **d** $-6 - (-8)$

5 Match each expression in the column on the left with an equivalent expression in the column on the right.

   a $4 - (-3)$ 1. $-4 + (-3)$

   b $-4 - 3$ 2. $-4 - (-3)$

   c $4 + (-3)$ 3. $4 + 3$

   d $-4 + 3$ 4. $4 - 3$

6 Refer to Sample Problem 1. Does method 2 work if the set has only positive numbers? Only negative numbers? Explain your answers.

7 Subtract $\begin{bmatrix} -4 & 6 & 0 \\ 3 & -2 & 5 \end{bmatrix} - \begin{bmatrix} 2 & 5 & -7 \\ -3 & 0 & 7 \end{bmatrix}$.

8 How many units apart on the number line are the numbers in each pair?

   a -12 and 7 **b** -18 and -11 **c** 8 and -17

Problems and Applications

9 Find each difference.

   a $5 - 8$ **b** $-5 - 8$ **c** $5 - (-8)$ **d** $-5 - (-8)$

10 Find the numbers that will complete the pattern.

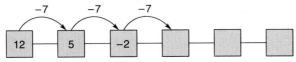

11 Copy and complete the table if $y = 4 - x$.

x	-8	-6	-4	-2	0	2	4	6	8
y									

12 For each diagram, write a subtraction expression that represents length of segment AB.

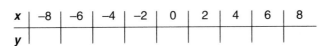

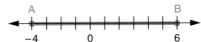

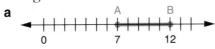

13 Evaluate the expression $x - y$ for the given values.

   a $x = 6, y = 2$ **b** $x = -2, y = 4$ **c** $x = 35, y = -2$

   d $x = -11, y = -6.5$ **e** $x = -8.36, y = 4.2$ **f** $x = 19.31, y = -4.58$

14 Subtract $\begin{bmatrix} -4 & 7 & -1 \\ 3 & -8 & 0 \end{bmatrix} - \begin{bmatrix} 8 & -2 & -5 \\ 9 & -3 & -11 \end{bmatrix}$.

15 Solve each equation for n.

   a $n - 23 = -12$ **b** $n - (-5) = 3$ **c** $n + 18 = 6$

16 Evaluate $\begin{bmatrix} -2 & 0 \\ -4 & 5 \\ 3 & -6 \end{bmatrix} - \begin{bmatrix} 10 & -8 \\ 7 & 5 \\ -2 & 3 \end{bmatrix}$.

17 How many numbers are in each set?
 a $\{-7, -6, -5, \ldots, 4\}$ **b** $\{-7, -6, -5, \ldots, 12\}$
 c $\{-100, -99, -98, \ldots, 100\}$ **d** $\{0, 1, 2, 3, \ldots, 100\}$

18 Arrange these differences in order from least value to greatest value.
 a $-8579 - 3654$ **b** $-8579 - (-3654)$
 c $8579 - 3654$ **d** $8579 - (-3654)$

19 Each number in the second row is obtained by subtracting the number to the
 right above it from the number to the left above it. Use this rule to form
 additional rows until there is a row at the bottom with only one number.

1		−7		21		−35		35		−21		7		−1
	8		−28		56		−70		56		−28		8	

20 Find each difference.
 a $3.7 - 4.8$ **b** $4.95 - (-15.28)$ **c** $3\frac{1}{2} - 4\frac{7}{8}$ **d** $-4\frac{3}{5} - \left(-2\frac{5}{8}\right)$

21 Evaluate each expression.
 a $-4 + (-3)(-2) - (-5)(-6)$ **b** $[-4 + (-3)](-2) - (-5)(-6)$
 c $-4 + (-3)[-2 - (-5)] - 6$ **d** $-4 + (-3)[-2 - (-5)] (-6)$

22 Subtract $\begin{bmatrix} 2.9 & -4.7 \\ -3.6 & 4.58 \end{bmatrix} - \begin{bmatrix} 6.9 & 2.4 \\ -4.6 & -2.76 \end{bmatrix}$.

23 Tommy Toad hopped
 from point A to point B.
 How far did he hop?

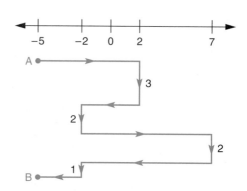

24 Refer to the set $\{10, 11, 12, \ldots, 20, 21, 22\}$.
 a How many numbers are in this set?
 b Subtract 14 from all numbers in the set, and list the resulting set.
 c Find the sum of the numbers in the original set.
 d Using your answers in parts **a** and **c,** find the sum of all the numbers in
  the set in part **b.**

25 Find the distance between these numbers on the number line.
 a 0 and 35   **b** 0 and −35   **c** 12 and 0   **d** −12 and 0

26 If the set $\{-11, -10, -9, -8, \ldots, x\}$ contains 34 integers, what is x?

27 The first matrix gives the number of grades earned last quarter by four students in five grade categories. The second matrix gives the points awarded for each grade.

<table>
<tr><td colspan="6" align="center">**Grades**</td></tr>
<tr><td></td><td>**A**</td><td>**B**</td><td>**C**</td><td>**D**</td><td>**F**</td></tr>
<tr><td>**Ted**</td><td>2</td><td>1</td><td>0</td><td>1</td><td>0</td></tr>
<tr><td>**Bill**</td><td>0</td><td>3</td><td>1</td><td>1</td><td>1</td></tr>
<tr><td>**Laura**</td><td>1</td><td>1</td><td>1</td><td>1</td><td>1</td></tr>
<tr><td>**Kim**</td><td>3</td><td>1</td><td>2</td><td>0</td><td>0</td></tr>
</table>

Points Earned for Each Grade

A	4.0
B	3.0
C	2.0
D	1.0
F	0.0

   a Use matrix multiplication to determine the number of points each person earned for the quarter.

   b Use your results from part **a** to determine each student's grade-point average.

28 a Subtract 5 from each x-coordinate and -3 from each y-coordinate of the triangle. Then graph and label the resulting triangle.

   b How has the position of the triangle shifted from its original placement?

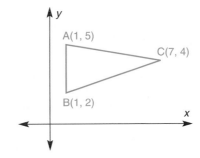

29 List all pairs of integers that have a product of -18.

30 The Game of -12 involves using one or more operation symbols $(+, -, \times, \div)$ along with three numbers to write an expression having a value of -12. For example, for the numbers 2, 42, and 3 the expression would be $2 - 42 \div 3 = -12$. Play this game with
   a 1, -3, 4   **b** 3, 8, -2 **c** 2, 1, 7   **d** -15, 2, 9

31 If $a = -5$ and $b = -3$, are the statements below *true* or *false*?
   a $2a + 7a = 9a$
   c $14a - 3a - 2a = 9a$
   b $9a + 6b + 4b + 3a = 12a + 10b$
   d $9a + 4b + 6a - b = 15a + 3b$

Investigation

Time Differences   List a dozen or so major cities from around the world. Assign to each city a positive or negative integer to indicate the time difference from your home.

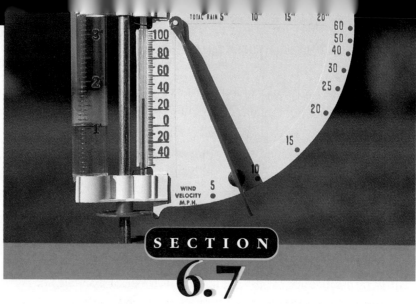

6.7

Absolute Value

DISTANCE FROM ZERO

Two temperatures, 6°C and −6°C, are both 6 degrees from 0° Celsius. If we use a number line to display this information, we see that −6 and 6 are each six units from 0 but located in opposite directions.

We call the distance of a number from zero, regardless of its direction from zero, the ***absolute value*** of the number. The mathematical symbol | | (vertical bars) represents the absolute value of a number. This symbol is read "the absolute value of."

Example 1
Evaluate each expression.

a $|6|$ **b** $|-6|$

Solution
a Since the number 6 is six units from 0 on the number line, $|6| = 6$.
b Since the number −6 is six units from 0 on the number line, $|-6| = 6$.

Example 2
Solve each absolute-value equation for all values of x.

a $|x| = 12$ **b** $|x| = -2$

a To solve the equation $|x| = 12$, we need to determine what values of x have an absolute value of 12—that is, what numbers are 12 units away from zero on the number line. The numbers -12 and 12 fit both descriptions. Notice that the solutions to the equation are opposites.

b The absolute value of a number is its distance from 0 on a number line. Since this distance is either a positive number or 0, the equation $|x| = -2$ has no solutions.

DISTANCE BETWEEN TWO NUMBERS

Now let's see what happens when we put the difference of two numbers within the absolute-value symbol. The absolute-value symbol is a grouping symbol.

$$|10 - 4| = |6| = 6$$
$$|4 - 10| = |-6| = 6$$

The result, 6, is the same in both cases. Notice that 6 is also the number of units between the numbers 10 and 4 on the number line.

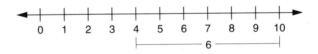

▶ **The distance between two numbers, a and b, on the number line is equal to $|a - b|$ or $|b - a|$.**

Example 3
Find the distance between -20 and 6 on the number line.

Solution
We can evaluate the expression $|-20 - 6|$.

$$|-20 - 6| = |-20 + (-6)| = |-26| = 26$$

Or we can evaluate the expression $|6 - (-20)|$.

$$|6 - (-20)| = |6 + 20| = |26| = 26$$

Both expressions result in the same answer. The numbers are 26 units apart on the number line.

Sample Problems

Solve the equation $|x - 6| = 7$ for all possible values of x.

Solution   The solutions of the equation are the numbers that are 7 units from 6 on the number line.

Check   If $x = 13$, $|x - 6| = |13 - 6| = |7| = 7$.

If $x = -1$, $|x - 6| = |-1 - 6| = |-1 + (-6)| = |-7| = 7$.

Therefore, the solutions to the equation are 13 and −1.

Problem 2   Write an inequality to represent the diagram.

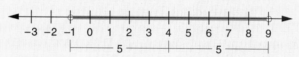

Solution   The midpoint of the shaded region is the point with a coordinate of 4. The shaded region represents all numbers that are less than five units away from 4. The distance from any number x to 4 can be written as $|x - 4|$. Since this distance must be less than 5 units, the inequality that describes the graph is $|x - 4| < 5$.

Think and Discuss

1 Evaluate each expression.
   a $|-5|$ **b** $|0|$ **c** $|6.23|$ **d** $\left|-3\frac{2}{3}\right|$

2 What points are 22 units from zero on the number line?

3 Solve each absolute-value equation.
   a $|x| = 10$ **b** $|x| = 1.3$ **c** $|x| = 0$

4 Is the statement true *always, sometimes,* or *never?*
   a The absolute value of a number is negative.
   b Opposite numbers have the same absolute value.

5 Evaluate each expression.   **a** $|-12 + 8|$ **b** $|-12| + |8|$

6 Use absolute-value symbols to express the distance between 3 and 6 in two ways.

7 Explain why $|x - y| = |y - x|$.

8 Point A is five units from zero on the number line and point B is three units from zero on the number line.
  a How far apart are point A and point B? Explain your answer.
  b What is the coordinate of the midpoint of segment AB?

9 Find a number for each box so that the inequality represents the graph. Explain how you solved each problem.

  a $|x - 7| \le \boxed{}$

  b $|x - \boxed{}| < 6$

10 Solve for x.   **a** $|x - 2| = 8$ **b** $|x + 6| = 3$

11 Graph $|x - 3| = 2$, $|x - 3| < 2$, and $|x - 3| > 2$. Discuss the differences among these three expressions.

Problems and Applications

12 Evaluate each expression.
  a $|-7|$ **b** $|24|$ **c** $\left|\frac{3}{4}\right|$ **d** $|8.3|$

13 Solve each equation.
  a $|x| = 8$ **b** $|x| = 0$ **c** $|x| = -9$

14 Evaluate each expression.
  a $|8 - 15|$ **b** $|8 + 15|$ **c** $|-8 - 15|$ **d** $|15 - 8|$

15 Arrange the expressions $|18 + (-7)|$, $|-18 + 7|$, $|7 - 18|$, $|-7 - 18|$, $|-7 - (-18)|$, and $|-7| - |18|$ in order from smallest value to largest value.

16 Find the value of each expression.
  a $|6| - |2|$ **b** $|-8| - |-10|$ **c** $|-8 - (-10)|$
  d $|-8| - (-|10|)$ **e** $-|8| - |-10|$ **f** $-|8 - (-10)|$

17 **a** If $|\text{number}| = 5$, what are the possible values of the number?
  b If $|x - 9| = 5$, what are the possible values of $x - 9$?
  c If $|x - 9| = 5$, what are the possible values of x?

18 Find all numbers that are $5\frac{1}{4}$ units away from $-7\frac{1}{2}$ on the number line.

19 Evaluate each expression for $a = -3$, $b = 4$, and $c = -6$.
  a $|ab|$ **b** $|a||b|$ **c** $|ac|$ **d** $|a||c|$

20 Write an absolute-value inequality to represent the graph.

  a
    -4 4

  b
    1 9

  c
    -6 2

21 Which of the numbers $-7, -4, -2, 0, 3,$ and 5 are solutions of $|x + 2| < 3$?

22 The midpoint of segment AB is point C. If you slide segment AB along the number line until the coordinate of C is 0, what will be the new coordinates of points A and B?

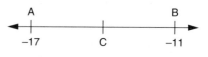

23 Substitute numbers for a and b so that the statement is true. Repeat this process three times for different values of a and b.

a $|a + b| = |a| + |b|$ **b** $|a + b| < |a| + |b|$ **c** $|a + b| > |a| + |b|$

24 Graph each solution on a number line.

a $|x| > 5$ **b** $|x - 3| > 5$

c $|x + 3| > 5$ [Hint: Remember that $x + 3 = x - (-3)$.]

25 If $|4 - y| = 11$, solve for all possible values of y.

26 If one of the numbers $|-15|, |5 - 8|, -|-21|, |0|,$ and $|0 - 1|$ is selected at random, what is the probability that the number is negative?

27 Find, to the nearest tenth, the distance between $\sqrt{31}$ and 5.5.

28 Consider the line segment on the number line.

a What percent of the segment contains solutions of the inequality $|x| \le 8$?

b What percent of the segment contains solutions of the inequality $|x - 5| \le 3$?

29 Point M is midway between -12 and 30.

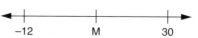

a What is the coordinate of M?

b What is the distance between M and -12? Between M and 30?

c Use the results of parts **a** and **b** to write an absolute-value equation that has the solutions -12 and 30.

30 If x is a number between 6 and -8 inclusive, what is the probability that $|x| < 3$?

31 Write an absolute-value equation to describe each statement.

a The distance between 3 and a number x is 12.

b The distance between -5 and a number x is 8.

───────────────────────────────

◀ LOOKING BACK   **Spiral Learning**   LOOKING AHEAD ▶

───────────────────────────────

32 Subtract $\begin{bmatrix} 3 & -6 \\ -2 & -4 \\ 10 & 0 \end{bmatrix} - \begin{bmatrix} 5 & -2 \\ 4 & 3 \\ 0 & -7 \end{bmatrix}$.

33 Find the mean, the median, and the mode of $-12, -34, -12, 6, -26, -1,$ $-10, 18, 2, 5, -3,$ and 0.

34 Evaluate the expression $(-3) \cdot \begin{bmatrix} -5 & 4 \\ -2 & -6 \end{bmatrix} + (-2) \cdot \begin{bmatrix} 6 & -8 \\ 7 & 3 \end{bmatrix}.$

35 In the following pattern, each number in the second row is found by subtracting the number to its right in the row above from the number to its left in the row above. Continue this pattern until there is a row at the bottom with only one number.

$$\begin{array}{ccccccccc} -25 & & 15 & & -10 & & 5 & & -20 \\ & -40 & & 25 & & -15 & & 25 & \end{array}$$

36 Write a mathematical expression that represents each phrase. Then evaluate each expression.
a The sum of -4 and -6 and 2
b The product of -4 and -3 and -2
c Subtract -7 from 8
d 3 times -5 is subtracted from -6
e Subtract the sum of -3 and -1 from -10

37 Multiply $\begin{bmatrix} 3 & -4 \\ -2 & 6 \end{bmatrix} \cdot \begin{bmatrix} -4 \\ 5 \end{bmatrix}.$

38 Using only movements to the right and down, how many routes are there from
a A to B?
b A to C?
c A to D?

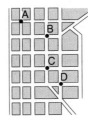

39 Solve for P.
a $-7 \cdot P = 28$ **b** $\dfrac{P}{-4} = \dfrac{5}{2}$ **c** $-7 - P = 5$

40 Solve $\dfrac{n}{-8} = \dfrac{21}{4}$ for n.

41 Copy and complete the multiplication table.

*	−3	−7	+4	−2
+2				
−5				
−6				

Investigation

Gasoline Mileage Choose a make and model car. Find out how many gallons of gas the tank holds and the average miles per gallon for this car. Obtain a map of your region and indicate the approximate location of your home. Now mark the areas you could reach on one tankful of gas or less. What shape is your travel region? What places in this region would you like to visit?

6.8

Two-Dimensional Graphs

THE RECTANGULAR COORDINATE SYSTEM

A **rectangular coordinate system** is formed by drawing two number lines that are perpendicular to each other and that intersect at their zero points. This point of intersection is the origin of the coordinate system.

The horizontal number line is the **x-axis,** with positive numbers to the right. The vertical number line is the **y-axis,** with positive numbers upward. The two number lines divide the coordinate system into four regions, called **quadrants,** numbered I, II, III, and IV as in the diagram.

Each point on the coordinate plane corrresponds to a unique **ordered pair** of numbers (x, y). For example, the point $(-4, 5)$ is located 4 units to the left of the y-axis and 5 units above the x-axis. The point $(5, -4)$, on the other hand, is located 5 units to the right of the y-axis and 4 units below the x-axis. The first number in the ordered pair (the **x-coordinate**) indicates how far to move to the left or right of the y-axis. The second number (the **y-coordinate**) indicates how far to move above or below the x-axis.

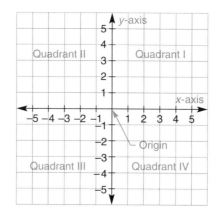

Example 1

What are the coordinates of points A and B in the coordinate system shown?

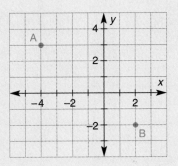

Solution

To reach point A from the origin, we can move 4 units to the left along the x-axis, then 3 units upward. The point's coordinates are therefore (−4, 3). (Notice that point A is directly above the −4 point of the x-axis and directly to the left of the 3 point of the y-axis.) Point B is 2 units to the right of the y-axis and 2 units below the x-axis, so its coordinates are (2, −2).

Example 2

a Plot points C(1, 3) and D(−4, −2) on a coordinate system.

b What are the coordinates of the point that is 3 units to the left of and 2 units below point C?

Solution

a To locate point C, we start at the origin and move 1 unit to the right, then 3 units up. We locate point D in a similar manner—starting at the origin and moving 4 units to the left, then 2 units down.

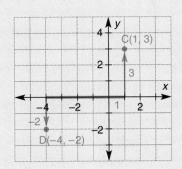

b Method 1: If we start at point C and move 3 units to the left, then 2 units down, we end up at the point with coordinates (−2, 1).

Method 2: We can add −3 (3 units in the negative direction) to the x-coordinate of point C and add −2 (2 units in the negative direction) to the y-coordinate of point C.

$$[1 + (−3), 3 + (−2)] = (−2, 1)$$

GRAPHING GEOMETRIC FIGURES

Drawing geometric figures on a coordinate system can often help us to identify some of the characteristics of the figures.

Example 3

a What are the coordinates of the vertices of rectangle RECT?

b Find the perimeter and the area of RECT.

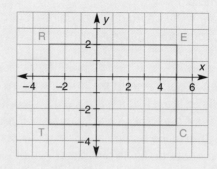

Solution

a The vertices are R(–3, 2), E(5, 2), C(5, –3) and T(–3, –3).

b Since $\overline{RE}$ is horizontal, its length is the difference between the x-coordinates of R and E. This length is $|-3 - 5|$, or 8, units. Since $\overline{RT}$ is vertical, its length is the difference between the y-coordinates of R and T. This is $|2 - (-3)|$, or 5, units. The perimeter is 2(RE) + 2(RT) = 2(8) + 2(5) = 26 units, and the area is (RE)(RT) = 8(5) = 40 square units. (Try counting the unit squares inside RECT. Are there 40 of them?)

Sample Problem

Problem

In the figure shown, point J is the **midpoint** of $\overline{GH}$—that is, it is halfway between points G and H.

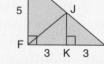

a Draw the figure on a coordinate system, labeling F, G, H, and K with their coordinates.

b What are the coordinates of point J?

c What is length FJ?

Solution

a There are many ways of placing the figure on a coordinate system. We will put F at the origin, so that $\overline{FG}$ lies on the y-axis and $\overline{FH}$ lies on the x-axis. From the given lengths, we can see that the coordinates of F, G, H, and K are (0, 0), (0, 5), (6, 0), and (3, 0).

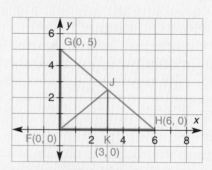

b When a point is the midpoint of a segment on the coordinate plane, the point's x-coordinate is the mean of the x-coordinates of the segment's endpoints, and the point's y-coordinate is the mean of the y-coordinates of the segment's endpoints.

Coordinates of J = $\left(\frac{0+6}{2}, \frac{5+0}{2}\right)$ = (3, 2.5)

c Since $\overline{JK}$ is vertical, its length is $|\,2.5 - 0\,|$, or 2.5, units. $\overline{FJ}$ is the hypotenuse of right triangle FJK, so we can use the Pythagorean Theorem to find the length of $\overline{FJ}$.

$$(FK)^2 + (JK)^2 = (FJ)^2$$
$$3^2 + 2.5^2 = (FJ)^2$$
$$9 + 6.25 = (FJ)^2$$
$$15.25 = (FJ)^2$$

Since $(FJ)^2 = 15.25$, length FJ must be $\sqrt{15.25}$, or ≈ 3.9, units.

Think and Discuss

1 What are the coordinates of points A, B, C, D, E, and F?

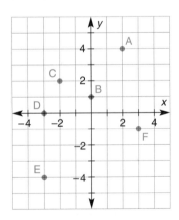

2 Why, do you think, are pairs of coordinates, such as (5, 3) and (3, 5), called *ordered* pairs?

3 How can you tell what quadrant a point is in just by looking at the signs of its coordinates? Write a rule that can be used to identify the quadrant of any given ordered pair.

4 Find the lengths labeled *a*, *b*, and *c* in the diagram.

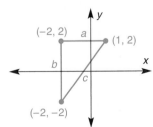

5 If point Y is the midpoint of $\overline{XZ}$, what are the coordinates of Y?

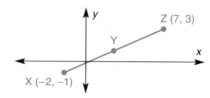

6 In this section's sample problem, a figure was placed on a coordinate system in a specific manner. Discuss some other ways of positioning the figure on a coordinate system. Which way is best? Why?

Problems and Applications

7 Create a rectangular coordinate system on graph paper. Then locate and label each of the following points and indicate which quadrant the point is in.
  a A(6, 2)   **b** B(8, 0)   **c** C(4, −6)
  d D(−1, 3)   **e** E(−3, −4)   **f** F(0, −2)

8 Is the following statement true *always, sometimes,* or *never?*
  A segment with one endpoint in Quadrant I and the other endpoint in Quadrant III passes through Quadrant II.

9 What are the coordinates of points G, H, J, K, and L?

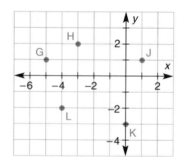

10 Point N is the midpoint of horizontal segment MP, and N is 15 units to the right of point M.
  a What are the coordinates of N and P?
  b What are lengths MN, NP, and MP?

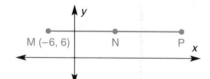

11 **Communicating** Create a coordinate system and locate the points with coordinates (3, 2), (3, −2), (−3, 2), and (−3, −2). Describe how the points are related to one another.

12 Each segment in the diagram is either vertical or horizontal. What are the coordinates of points T, U, F, E, and N?

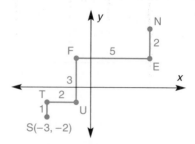

13 Locate points S(−4, 8), T(−4, −4), and U(1, −4) on a rectangular coordinate system. Connect the points to form △STU. What are the lengths of sides $\overline{ST}$, $\overline{TU}$, and $\overline{SU}$?

14 If $\overline{QR}$ is moved 3 units horizontally to the right, what will be the new coordinates of points Q and R?

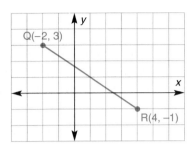

15 RECT is a rectangle.
  a What are the coordinates of the vertices of RECT?
  b What is the area of RECT?
  c What is the length of diagonal $\overline{ET}$?

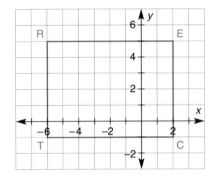

16 a What are lengths TR and RY?
  b What are the coordinates of the midpoints of $\overline{TR}$ and $\overline{TY}$?

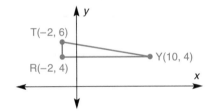

17 Communicating
  a Describe three ways in which this figure can be placed on a coordinate system.
  b Which of the three ways do you think is most convenient? Why?
  c Position the figure on a coordinate system in one of the ways you described, labeling each vertex with its coordinates.

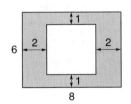

18 Each segment in the diagram is either horizontal or vertical. Find the coordinates of each lettered point.

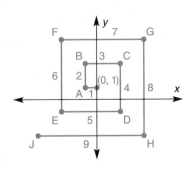

19 If this figure is placed on a coordinate system so that point P is at $(-29, -4)$ and point A is at $(-13, -4)$, what will be the coordinates of point R?

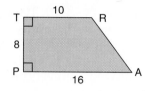

20 What are the areas of the circle and the triangle?

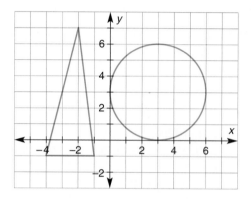

21 Find the coordinates of points A, B, and C.

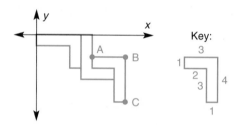

22 QUAD is a square. If point U is moved 3 units up and D is moved 3 units down,
   a What will be the new coordinates of U and D?
   b What will lengths QD, UA, QU, and DA become?

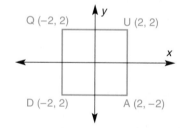

23 The shaded region in the diagram represents all ordered pairs (x, y) in which $-3 \le x \le 8$ and $-4 \le y \le 4$.
   a Find the area of rectangle RECT.
   b What percentage of the shaded region is in Quadrant II?

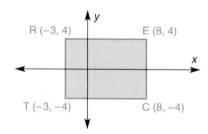

24 List five ordered pairs (x, y) in which $x - y = 2$. On a rectangular coordinate system, locate the points corresponding to these ordered pairs. What do you notice?

25 Express 60 mi/hr as a number of feet per second.

26 How many numbers are in each set?
   a {−4, −3, −2, . . . , 10}   **b** {0, 1, 2, 3, . . . , 14}   **c** {−8, −6, −4, . . . , 20}

In problems 27 and 28, graph each inequality.

27 $|x| < 8$

28 $|x − 3| < 8$

29 Each point of △A′B′C′ is the same distance from the y-axis as the corresponding point of △ABC. What are the coordinates of A′, B′, and C′?

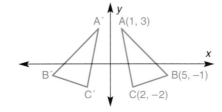

In problems 30–33, solve each equation for z.

30 $z + 1432 = 976$

31 $\dfrac{z}{−93} = 58$

32 $z − 349.7 = 41.26$

33 $25.1z = 921.17$

34 Copy and complete the diagram so that the sums of the numbers lying along the five segments are the same.

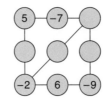

In problems 35–38, solve each equation for x.

35 $|x| = 2$ **36** $|x| = −2$ **37** $|x − 1| = 3$ **38** $|2x| = 3$

In problems 39 and 40, write an absolute-value inequality that is represented by the graph.

39

40

Investigation

Floor Plan   Using a coordinate system, draw to scale a floor plan of your classroom. Label several important positions in the floor plan (doors, windows, and so on) with their coordinates. Use the floor plan to determine some distances that you have not measured, then check your findings. What scale did you choose for your floor plan, and why?

Summary

After studying this chapter, you should be able to

■ Associate signed numbers with points on a number line (6.1)

■ Determine the opposite of a signed number (6.1)

■ Graph signed numbers on a number line (6.1)

■ Write inequalities and graph them on a number line (6.2)

■ Write and graph inequalities joined by *and* or *or* (6.2)

■ Use a number line to model the addition of signed numbers (6.3)

■ Use a calculator to add signed numbers (6.3)

■ Add matrices (6.3)

■ Multiply signed numbers (6.4)

■ Multiply matrices by scalars (6.4)

■ Calculate powers of signed numbers (6.4)

■ Divide signed numbers (6.4)

■ Multiply two matrices (6.5)

■ Subtract signed numbers (6.6)

■ Subtract matrices (6.6)

■ Determine the absolute values of numbers (6.7)

■ Recognize that the distance between two numbers on the number line is the absolute value of the difference of the numbers (6.7)

■ Create a rectangular coordinate system (6.8)

■ Graph geometric figures on a rectangular coordinate system (6.8)

VOCABULARY

absolute value (6.7)	positive signed number (6.1)
coordinate (6.1)	quadrant (6.8)
inequality (6.2)	rectangular coordinate system (6.8)
integer (6.1)	scalar (6.4)
midpoint (6.8)	scalar multiplication (6.4)
negative signed number (6.1)	x-axis (6.8)
opposite (6.1)	x-coordinate (6.8)
ordered pair (6.8)	y-axis (6.8)
origin (6.1)	y-coordinate (6.8)

CHAPTER 6

Review

1 Perform each operation.

a $-246 - (-93)$ **b** $\frac{9432}{-12}$ **c** $|-16| - (-42)$

d $|-3 - (-9)|$ **e** $(413)(-6)(-2)$ **f** $-15 - (-4 - 3)$

2 The area of square AUQS is 400.

a Find the coordinates of points S and Q.

b Move point Q along diagonal $\overline{AQ}$ to coordinates (12, 12). (Remember to move points S and U.) By what percent has the area of the square been reduced?

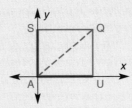

3 How far from zero on the number line is each number?

a -8 **b** $-3\frac{1}{2}$ **c** 7 **d** -5.34

4 List all pairs of integers that have a product of 24.

5 Write an inequality that represents the number line.

a  **b**

6 If -7 is subtracted from each of the numbers in the set $\{-10, -5, -1, 1, 5, 10\}$, what is the probability that a number selected at random from the new set will be greater than 0?

7 A scuba diver swims to a depth of -42 feet. How many feet must she rise to reach a depth of -24 feet?

8 Find the mean of each set of numbers.

a $2, 4, 6, 8$ **b** $-8, -6, -4, -2$ **c** $8, -6, -4, 2$

9 Evaluate each expression for $x = -8$, $y = -2$, and $z = 4$.

a $x + y$ **b** $x - y$ **c** xy **d** $\frac{x}{y}$

e $x + z$ **f** $x - z$ **g** x^z **h** $\frac{x}{z}$

10 Is the statement *true* or *false*? If it is false, give a counterexample.

a The sum of a negative number and a positive number is a negative number.

b The product of two integers is an integer.

11 Refer to rectangle ECTR. Solve for $w, x, y,$ and z.

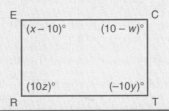

12 Companies that deliver heating oil calculate "degree days" to estimate when their customers will require an oil delivery. The degree-day number is calculated each day by subtracting the average temperature for the day from 68°. For example, if the average temperature on a given day was 35°, the calculation yields 68 − 35, or 33 degree days. The matrix gives the average temperatures over a one-week period in two towns.

a Use the average-temperature matrix to write a degree-day matrix.

b What do negative numbers represent in the degree-day matrix? What do positive numbers represent?

c How many degree days did each town have for the week?

d If the oil company fills the tanks of all customers after 1000 degree days have accumulated, estimate the length of time between fills for the customers in Cold Town. Assume all weekly data weeks are similar to the data that you have for one week.

Average-Temperature Matrix		
	Cold Town	Warm Ville
Monday	35	64
Tuesday	18	68
Wednesday	37	72
Thursday	42	54
Friday	33	76
Saturday	28	89
Sunday	10	62

13 If $(-2)^3 = -8$ and $(-2)^4 = 16$, evaluate each expression.
a $(-3)^3$ **b** $(-4)^3$ **c** $(-5)^3$ **d** $(-3)^4$ **e** $(-4)^4$ **f** $(-5)^4$

14 Evaluate each expression.
a $3 \cdot (-4) - 5 \cdot (-3)$ **b** $8 \cdot (-6) - 9 \cdot (-7)$ **c** $-4^2 - (-4)^2$

15 Find the values of u, v, x, y, and z.
$$\begin{bmatrix} 2 & -5 & -4 \\ 1 & -6 & z \end{bmatrix} + \begin{bmatrix} -5 & -8 & 12 \\ -2 & y & 10 \end{bmatrix} = \begin{bmatrix} x & u & v \\ -1 & 0 & -10 \end{bmatrix}$$

16 Find a pair of numbers for which each of the following statements is true and a pair of numbers for which each is false.
a The sum of the two numbers is a positive number.
b The sum of the two numbers is greater in value than either number.
c The difference of the two numbers is a positive number.
d The product of the two numbers is greater in value than either number.
e The quotient of the two numbers is smaller in value than either number.
f The product of the two numbers is equal to −1.

17 Write a mathematical expression that represents each phrase. Then evaluate the expression.
a Multiply the sum of 5 and 2 by (-6).
b Add the product of -9 and 5 to the product of -9 and 2.
c The product of -3 and the sum of 4 and -9.

18 a Plot points A(−2, 4) and B(3, −8)
b Find the coordinates of the midpoint of segment AB

19 **a** Determine the area of △ABC.
b If △A′B′C′ is the result of reflecting △ABC over the x-axis, what are the coordinates of A′, B′, and C′?

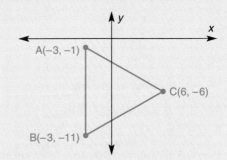

20 Multiply $\begin{bmatrix} -2 & 6 \\ 4 & 3 \end{bmatrix} \cdot \begin{bmatrix} 9 & -3 \\ -2 & -1 \end{bmatrix}$.

21 The sum of two numbers is −29, and one of the numbers is 13. What is the other number?

22 Find values for x and y that make each equation true. Then find values for x and y that make each equation false.
a $|x + y| = |x| + |y|$ **b** $|x| = -(x)$ **c** $|x - y| = |x + y|$

23 Is the statement *true* or *false?* If the statement is false, give a counterexample.
a The product of two negative numbers is a negative number.
b The sum of two negative numbers is a positive number.

24 **a** In rectangle ABCD each coordinate of each vertex is increased by 20%. Find the new coordinates of A, B, C, and D.
b If the new coordinates are called A′, B′, C′, and D′, respectively, compare the areas of rectangle ABCD and rectangle A′B′C′D′.

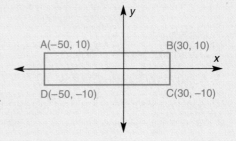

25 Evaluate each expression.
a $(-1)(2^6)$ **b** -2^6 **c** $(-2)^6$ **d** $(-1)^6(2)^6$

26 **a** Plot -6, π, -4.3, $\frac{22}{7}$, $\sqrt{11}$, $-\sqrt{35}$, and $-4\frac{1}{3}$ on a number line.
b Arrange the numbers in part **a** in order, from least to greatest in value.

27 If $y = -4$, solve for x.
a $-2x = 7y$ **b** $x - 3y = 4$ **c** $12 - x = y$

28 Find the next three terms in each pattern.
a $\frac{8}{9}$, $\frac{4}{3}$, 2, ___, ___, ___   **b** 81, 27, 9, ___, ___, ___

29 Solve for w.
a $|w - 5| = 8$ **b** $|w + 5| = 8$ **c** $|w - 5| \le 8$

30 Evaluate $b^2 - 4ac$, for $a = 2$, $b = -7$, and $c = -3$.

Test

1 Which number is greater in value, -8 or 6?

2 What is the opposite of the given number?
   a -5 **b** -7 **c** 0

3 Point A is the midpoint of $\overline{BC}$. What is the coordinate of point A on the number line if the coordinate of point B is -8 and the coordinate of point C is 16?

4 Graph each inequality.
   a $x \le -3$ or $x \ge 4$ **b** $x \ge -4$ and $x < 5$ **c** $-2 < x < 5$, x is an integer

5 Perform the indicated operation.
   a $28 + 56 + (-43)$ **b** $-18.7 + 9(-29.6)$
   c $3(-15)(2)$ **d** $18(-3)(0)$
   e $53 - 96$ **f** $-42 - (-18)$
   g $\dfrac{-56}{-8}$ **h** $\dfrac{-3(-4)^2}{2}$

6 Perform the indicated matrix operation.
   a $\begin{bmatrix} 2 & -3 & 0 \\ 4 & 5 & -9 \end{bmatrix} + \begin{bmatrix} -6 & 12 & 15 \\ 4 & 3 & -1 \end{bmatrix}$ **b** $\begin{bmatrix} 2 & 3 \\ -1 & 4 \end{bmatrix} \cdot \begin{bmatrix} 1 \\ 6 \end{bmatrix}$ **c** $-4 \begin{bmatrix} -3 & 2 & -6 \\ 0 & 4 & -7 \end{bmatrix}$

7 Solve $-9x = 180$ for x.

8 Evaluate $|-14 - (-9)|$.

9 Graph the solution of $|x - 2| > 3$ on a number line.

10 Draw a number line and label the points with the given coordinates.
    a -4 **b** 0 **c** 5 **d** $-1\frac{3}{4}$ **e** $2\frac{1}{3}$

11 Write the inequality that describes the graph.

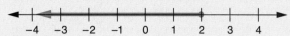

12 NCB stock sold for $19\frac{1}{2}$ dollars per share on Monday morning, but by noon its value had dropped $2\frac{1}{2}$ dollars per share. By closing time the same day, the stock has risen $\frac{3}{4}$ of a dollar per share. What was the closing value of the stock?

In problems 13–16, evaluate each expression.

13 -4^2 14 $(-4)^2$ 15 $|-19|$ 16 $|0|$

17 What is the distance between -214 and 16 on the number line?

18 Locate points A(-3, 2), B(-3, -5), and C(1, -5) on a coordinate plane. Connect the points to form a triangle. Find the length of $\overline{AB}$, $\overline{BC}$, and $\overline{AC}$.

1 If 78 players enter a singles tennis tournament, how many matches must be played for a winner to be determined?

2 A bear left its den and went due south for a mile. Then it turned 90° to the left and walked straight ahead for some distance. Then the bear turned 90° to the left and walked for one mile. It had arrived back at its den. What color is the bear?

3 In chess, a knight moves in an L-shaped manner, two spaces in one direction and one space in a direction perpendicular to the first direction.

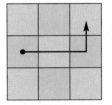

In the 3-by-3 square shown, we have numbered the squares to show the order in which the knight moved from square to square, ultimately landing in 8 of the 9 squares but never visiting the same square twice.

1	4	7
6		2
3	8	5

In the 4-by-4 square, the knight starts in the upper left-hand corner and visits 15 of the 16 squares, again never visiting the same square twice.

1	4	11	8
10	7	14	3
5	2	9	12
	13	6	15

In the 5-by-5 square, how can the knight start in the upper left-hand corner and visit at least 22 of the 25 squares, never visiting the same square twice?

7 Exploring Geometry

SPORTS PERFORMANCE A spherical basketball flies through the air in a symmetrical arc above a rectangular court and into a circular hoop with 1.6 seconds left in the game. Then, even as the 17,308 fans are still cheering, the players' statistics are updated. Mathematics pervades the world of sports! In recent years, mathematical studies of the geometry of motion and the performance of the human body have led to improved training techniques, helping athletes move faster, jump higher, and throw farther. A lot of mathematics also goes into the design of sports equipment. A racing bicycle, for example, must be sturdy but light. By analyzing the properties of various materials and making refinements in shape and construction, designers have been able to develop bicycles that go faster with less effort than ever before.

INVESTIGATION

Equipment Design Choose a sport and explain in detail how changes in the design of equipment have had an impact on that sport.

7.1
Line and Angle Relationships

Geometry is concerned with the size, shape, and location of objects. These attributes are often determined by the intended use of the object. Consider, for example, a loudspeaker. If the loudspeaker is intended for use at a rock concert, the speaker will have to be quite large. Small speakers cannot produce loud, distortion-free sound. If speakers are to be placed on a bookshelf, loudness is not critical, so the speakers can be smaller, but appearance and shape become important. Most people do not want unattractive objects on their bookshelves. If speakers are designed to fit in a person's ear, appearance becomes less important, but shape and size become critical.

PARALLEL AND PERPENDICULAR LINES

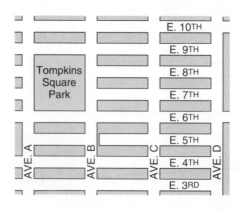

Picture a line and another line beside it. If the two lines are the same distance apart, so that they never meet, the lines are **parallel.** The symbol ∥ means "is parallel to." The rails of a straight railroad track are parallel.

If one of a pair of parallel lines is rotated 90°, the lines become **perpendicular.** The symbol ⊥ means "is perpendicular to." The top and side of a rectangular doorway are perpendicular.

In the portion of New York City shown, the numbered streets are parallel to one another, and the lettered avenues are parallel to one another. Each of the streets is perpendicular to each of the avenues.

Example 1

Refer to the map of a portion of New York City on the previous page.

a Suppose Juan is standing at the corner of B Avenue and 4th Street and René is standing at the corner of D Avenue and 10th Street. If they have agreed to meet at the corner of C Avenue and 7th Street, who will walk farther?

b From the corner of C Avenue and 7th Street, Juan will walk to the corner of A Avenue and 6th Street and René will walk to the corner of D Avenue and 10th Street. Who will walk farther?

Solution

a Both Juan and René will walk one long block and three short blocks. Since the streets are parallel and the avenues are parallel, all of the long blocks are the same distance and all of the short blocks are the same distance. Therefore, Juan and René will walk the same distance.

b Juan will walk two long blocks and one short block. René will walk one long block and four short blocks. Since we don't have a scale for the map, we are unable to answer the question. If we estimate that the length of three short blocks is equal to the length of one long block, Juan walks seven short blocks and René walks seven short blocks, so assume they will travel the same distance.

ADJACENT AND VERTICAL ANGLES

Consider three rays—$\overrightarrow{PA}$, $\overrightarrow{PB}$, and $\overrightarrow{PC}$—that have a common endpoint, P. Three angles are formed: ∠APB, ∠BPC, and ∠APC. ∠APB and ∠BPC are ***adjacent angles,*** since (1) they have the same vertex, (2) they have a side ($\overrightarrow{PB}$) in common, and (3) neither has a side that lies within the other.

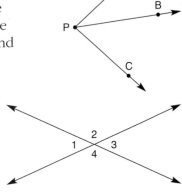

Now consider these two intersecting lines and the four numbered angles. Two pairs of these angles—angles 1 and 3 and angles 2 and 4—are not adjacent. These pairs of angles are called ***vertical angles.*** Vertical angles have the same vertex, and their sides form two straight lines.

Example 2

Are ∠AFT and ∠AFM adjacent angles?

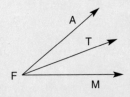

Solution

No, ∠AFT and ∠AFM are not adjacent angles because $\overrightarrow{FT}$ is inside ∠AFM. However, ∠AFT and ∠TFM are adjacent angles.

Problem In the diagram, m∠SOT = 57. What is the measure of
a ∠SOP? **b** ∠TOX? **c** ∠POX?

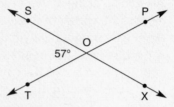

Solution **a** $\overleftrightarrow{TP}$ is a straight line, so ∠TOP is a 180° angle. Therefore, m∠SOP = 180 − 57 = 123.
b $\overleftrightarrow{SX}$ is another straight line, so m∠TOX = 180 − 57 = 123.
c Since adjacent angles SOP and POX form a 180° angle, m∠POX = 180 − 123 = 57.

Like two segments with the same length, two angles with the same measure are said to be congruent. The symbol ≅ means "is congruent to," so we can write ∠SOT ≅ ∠POX and ∠SOP ≅ ∠TOX. Draw a few other pairs of vertical angles and measure them. What can you conclude about vertical angles?

Think and Discuss

1 Find several examples of parallelism and perpendicularity in your classroom. Are there reasons why the objects involved are parallel or perpendicular?

2 $\overline{DE}$ is parallel to the y-axis, and $\overline{EF}$ is parallel to the x-axis.
a What are the coordinates of point E?
b How far is it from D to E?
c How far is it from E to F?
d How long is $\overline{DF}$?

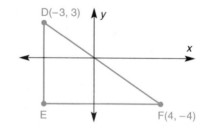

3 If m∠4 = 33, what is the measure of
a ∠2? **b** ∠1? **c** ∠3?

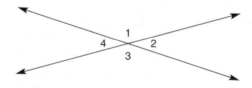

4 The shape and size of most objects is determined by their intended use. Think about the following questions and explain your answers.
   a Why are books rectangular?
   b Why are soft-drink cans round and cereal boxes rectangular?
   c Why are most houses and office buildings rectangular and most large stadiums round?
   d Why are computer disks, compact discs, and records round, yet stored in square cases?
   e Why do road signs have different shapes (circular, rectangular, triangular, and so on)?

Problems and Applications

Communicating   **In problems 5–7, identify the pair of angles indicated by blue arrows as *adjacent* or *not adjacent*. If the angles are not adjacent, explain why they are not.**

5 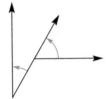   **6** 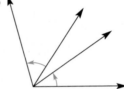   **7**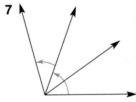

8 In the diagram, m∠VZW = 23, m∠WZX = 45, and m∠XZY = 31. What is
   a m∠VZX?
   b m∠WZY?
   c m∠VZY?

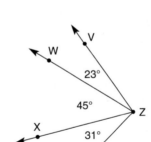

9 If m∠LJM = 129, what is
   a m∠KJL?
   b m∠KJN?
   c m∠NJM?

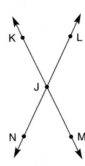

10 ABCD is a rectangle with its sides parallel to the axes. What are the coordinates of points A and C?

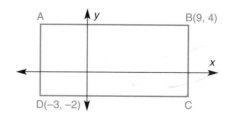

11 On a rectangular coordinate system, draw the line that passes through (−2, 5) and (6, 5). Label this line ℓ. Then draw a line that is parallel to line ℓ, a line that is perpendicular to line ℓ, and a line that is neither parallel nor perpendicular to line ℓ. Label each line by identifying the coordinates of two points on it.

12 a List all the pairs of adjacent angles in the figure.
  b List all the pairs of complementary angles in the figure.
  c List all the pairs of supplementary angles in the figure.

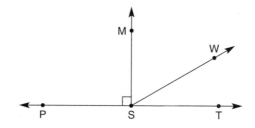

13 Carefully copy this graph of points A, B, C, and D. Draw $\overleftrightarrow{AB}$ and $\overleftrightarrow{CD}$. Are they parallel?

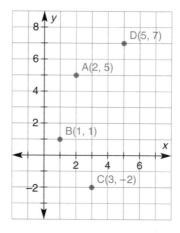

14 Can two supplementary angles have the same vertex without being adjacent? If so, draw an example of two such angles.

15 List all the pairs of parallel segments and all the pairs of perpendicular segments in polygon SQRE.

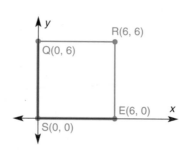

16 What is the length of $\overline{AB}$?

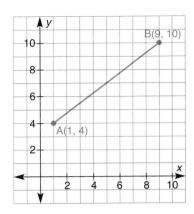

17 On a rectangular coordinate system, locate the points A(2, 5), B(–1, 3), C(6, 1), and D(6, –1). Then use a protractor to find
a m∠BAD **b** m∠BAC **c** m∠BDA **d** m∠ABD

18 What is the measure of the supplement of the complement of a 35° angle?

19 a Find the measures of the eight numbered angles.
b Which of the angles are congruent?
c Which of the angles are complementary?
d Which of the angles are supplementary?

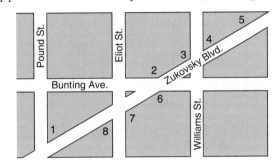

◄LOOKING BACK **Spiral Learning** LOOKING AHEAD ►

20 If one of the points in the diagram is picked at random, what is the probability that it is
a In Quadrant I?
b In Quadrant III?
c On the x-axis?

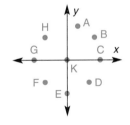

21

a How many units apart are the numbers –10 and –4?
b Evaluate –4 – (–10).
c How many units apart are the numbers –8 and 12?
d Evaluate 12 – (–8).

22 Evaluate $\begin{bmatrix} -7 & 2 & 4 \\ 15 & 9 & -31 \end{bmatrix} + \begin{bmatrix} -6 & -8 & -1 \\ -18 & -12 & 31 \end{bmatrix}$.

23 What are the lengths of $\overline{AB}$, $\overline{BC}$, $\overline{CD}$, and $\overline{DA}$?

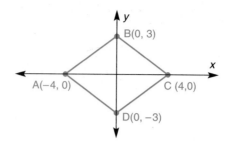

24 Evaluate $\begin{bmatrix} -6 & 4 \\ 3 & -6 \end{bmatrix} \cdot \begin{bmatrix} 12 & -3 \\ -5 & -2 \end{bmatrix}$.

25 Study the figures shown. Then copy and complete the table.

Figure	Number of Rays	Number of Angles
A		
B		
C		
D		
E		

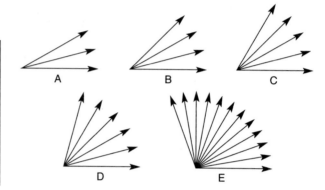

26 **Spreadsheets**   Use a spreadsheet to make a table listing (1) integer values of a from 1 to 20, (2) the lengths of $\overline{AC}$, $\overline{CB}$, and $\overline{AB}$ for each value of a, (3) the perimeter of $\triangle ABC$ for each value of a, and (4) the area of $\triangle ABC$ for each value of a.

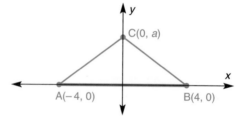

In problems 27–29, name the two consecutive integers that the given number is between.

27 $\dfrac{16}{3}$

28 -8.2

29 $-\dfrac{12}{5}$

Investigation

Architecture   When a skyscraper is built with vertical sides, the opposite sides are almost parallel, but not quite. Why is this? Draw a picture or build a model to show why the sides must be designed to be a little farther apart at the top than at the bottom.

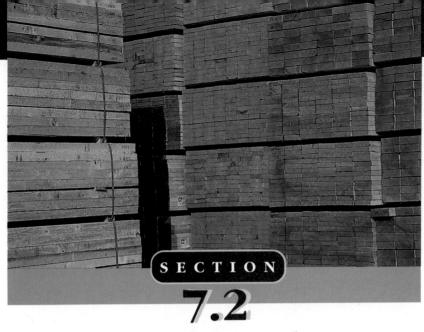

SECTION 7.2
Quadrilaterals

SQUARES, RECTANGLES, AND PARALLELOGRAMS

As you saw in Chapter 3, a **quadrilateral** is a polygon with four sides. By using the concepts of parallelism, perpendicularity, and congruence, we can identify some special kinds of quadrilaterals. You are already familiar with squares, like the one shown here. All four sides of a square are congruent. Adjacent sides are perpendicular and opposite sides are parallel.

Example 1

Suppose that side $\overline{UA}$ of square QUAD above is moved to the right in such a way that its length is not changed, it is kept parallel to side $\overline{QD}$, and sides $\overline{QU}$ and $\overline{DA}$ are allowed to stretch. What kind of figure will QUAD become?

Solution

Let's try moving $\overline{UA}$ three units to the right, so that vertex U moves from (4, 4) to (7, 4) and vertex A moves from (4, 0) to (7, 0). All four angles are still right angles, and the opposite sides are still congruent and parallel. The only change is that adjacent sides are no longer congruent. The result is a rectangle.

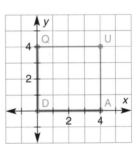

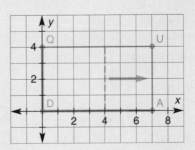

Example 2

Consider the rectangle produced in Example 1. Suppose that side $\overline{DA}$ is moved to the right along the x-axis. If its length is not changed and sides $\overline{QD}$ and $\overline{UA}$ are allowed to stretch, what kind of figure will QUAD become?

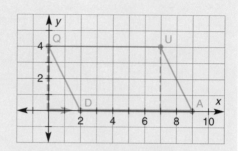

Solution

Let's try moving $\overline{DA}$ two units to the right, so that D moves from (0, 0) to (2, 0) and A moves from (7, 0) to (9, 0). The opposite sides remain parallel and congruent, but the figure's angles are no longer right angles. The quadrilateral has become a ***parallelogram***.

RHOMBUSES AND TRAPEZOIDS

There are two other kinds of special quadrilaterals you should know about.

Example 3

Figure RMBS is a square. Suppose that vertices R and B are moved the same distance in opposite directions along the x-axis, with all four sides being allowed to stretch. What kind of figure will RMBS become?

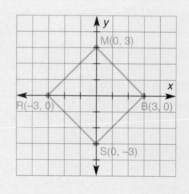

Solution

Let's move R two units to the left, from (–3, 0) to (–5, 0), and B two units to the right, from (3, 0) to (5, 0). The four sides are still congruent, and opposite sides are still parallel. This quadrilateral is a ***rhombus***.

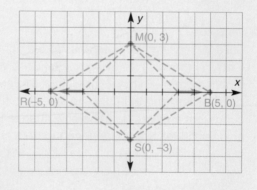

Example 4

Suppose that vertex A of parallelogram DRAG is moved to the right along the x-axis. If the other vertices remain fixed and sides $\overline{GA}$ and $\overline{RA}$ are allowed to stretch, what kind of figure will DRAG become?

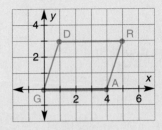

Solution

Let's move A three units to the right, to (7, 0). $\overline{DR}$ and $\overline{GA}$ are still parallel, but $\overline{DG}$ and $\overline{RA}$ are not. A quadrilateral such as this, with one pair of parallel sides, is called a *trapezoid*.

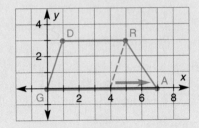

Quadrilaterals have four vertices. The quadrilateral on the right has vertices A, B, C, and D. If two vertices are the endpoints of an edge (A and B), they are said to be ***consecutive vertices.*** If they are not consecutive, like (A and C), they are ***opposite vertices.*** If two opposite vertices are connected, the segment formed is a ***diagonal.*** So far our discussion has focused on the sides and angles of quadrilaterals.

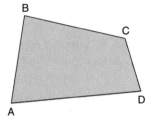

Sample Problem

Problem

a What kind of quadrilateral is figure AREH?
b What is the area of AREH?
c What is the length of $\overline{AR}$?
d What is the perimeter of AREH?

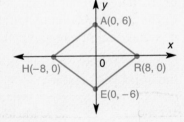

Solution

a AREH is a rhombus.
b Since OA = 6 and OR = 8, the area of $\triangle$ AOR is $\frac{1}{2} \cdot 6 \cdot 8$, or 24. Similarly, each of the triangles ROE, EOH, and HOA has an area of 24, so the area of AREH is 4(24), or 96.
c We use the Pythagorean Theorem.

$$(AR)^2 = 6^2 + 8^2 = 36 + 64 = 100$$

Since $(AR)^2 = 100$, AR must be $\sqrt{100}$, or 10.
d Since a rhombus has four congruent sides, the perimeter of AREH is 4(10), or 40.

Think and Discuss

In problems 1–6, is the statement true *always, sometimes*, or *never*?

1 A square is a rectangle.   **2** A rectangle is a square.

3 A rhombus is a trapezoid.   **4** A rhombus is a parallelogram.

5 A rhombus is a rectangle.   **6** A rhombus is a square.

7 Explain why a square is a rectangle, a rhombus, and a parallelogram, but not a trapezoid.

8 a Explain why quadrilateral DQUA is a rhombus.
   b Explain why quadrilateral DQUA is not a square.

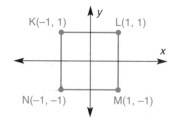

9 a What kind of quadrilateral is KLMN?
   b How could points K and N be moved so that KLMN would become a rectangle that is not a square?
   c How could points K and L be moved so that KLMN would become a rectangle that is not a square?

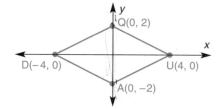

10 Is the statement true *always, sometimes,* or *never*?
   a The diagonals of a rectangle are perpendicular.
   b The diagonals of a rectangle are congruent.
   c The diagonals of a rectangle are parallel.
   d A diagonal of a rectangle is perpendicular to a side of the rectangle.

11 Copy the following table, then classify the polygons below by checking the appropriate boxes.

	Quadrilateral	Trapezoid	Parallelogram	Rhombus	Rectangle
a					
b					
c					
d					

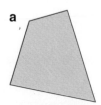   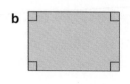      

Problems and Applications

In problems 12 and 13, refer to quadrilateral WHAT.

12 Classify each pair of vertices as *consecutive* or *opposite*.
a H and T
b A and T
c A and H
d A and W

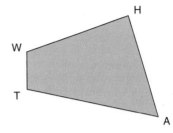

13 Classify each pair of sides as *adjacent* or *opposite*.
a $\overline{TW}$ and $\overline{AT}$
b $\overline{TW}$ and $\overline{HW}$
c $\overline{TA}$ and $\overline{HW}$
d $\overline{HA}$ and $\overline{HW}$

14 ABCD is a square. If you move $\overline{BC}$ to the right, keeping it parallel to $\overline{AD}$ and allowing $\overline{AB}$, $\overline{DB}$, and $\overline{DC}$ to stretch, what will happen to the value of
a w?
b z?
c w + z?

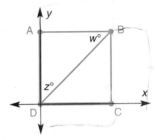

In problems 15–18, sketch an example of each figure described. If no such figure exists, write *impossible*.

15 A rectangle that is not a trapezoid

16 A rectangle that is not a parallelogram

17 A rectangle that is not a rhombus

18 A rectangle that is not a square

19 **Communicating**
a What kind of quadrilateral is QUAD?
b How could Q and U be moved to make QUAD a parallelogram that is not a rectangle?
c How could U and A be moved to make QUAD a parallelogram that is not a rectangle?
d How could D and U be moved to make QUAD a parallelogram that is not a rectangle?

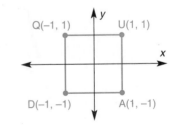

20 Determine the area of trapezoid TRAP.

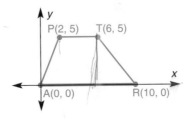

21 If BLUE is a parallelogram, what are the coordinates of point L?

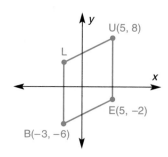

22 **Language Arts** Look up the words *quadrilateral, rectangle,* and *parallelogram* in a dictionary. What languages are the sources of these words? To what characteristics of the three polygons do the words refer?

23 Use a protractor to measure ∠F, ∠R, ∠E, and ∠D of this parallelogram. (You may need to trace the figure and extend its sides.) What do you notice?

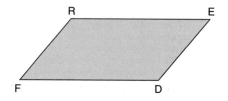

24 **a** What is the area of SPQR?
   b What is the perimeter of SPQR?
   c Draw a new quadrilateral by moving S to (10, 6) and R to (4, 6).
   d What is the area of the new quadrilateral?
   e What is the perimeter of the new quadrilateral?

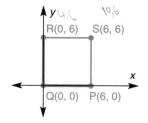

25 **Geography** Look at a map of the United States. Which states appear to be shaped like quadrilaterals? What kinds of quadrilaterals do they resemble?

26 **Spreadsheets** Use a spreadsheet to make a table listing (1) integer values of *a* from 1 to 20, (2) the lengths of $\overline{AB}, \overline{BC}, \overline{AD},$ and $\overline{DC}$ for each value of *a*, (3) the perimeter of quadrilateral ABCD for each value of *a*, and (4) the area of ABCD for each value of *a*. For what values of *a* is AB = DC?

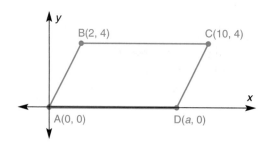

27 On a sheet of paper, draw a triangle with sides of different lengths. Then put another sheet of paper under your drawing and cut along the segments you drew so that you get two identical triangles. How many different parallelograms can you make by putting the two triangles together?

28 If you slide points Y and R so that quadrilateral GRAY becomes a square, what will the new coordinates of Y and R be?

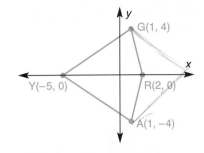

◀ LOOKING BACK **Spiral Learning** LOOKING AHEAD ▶

29 **a** What is 20% of −40?
   b What percent of −45 is −90?
   c If a value decreases from 40 to 30, by what percent has the value decreased?

In problems 30 and 31, write an absolute-value equation or inequality that is represented by the graph.

30

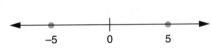

31

In problems 32–34, solve the proportions for *a*, *b*, and *c*.

32 $\dfrac{a}{-12} = \dfrac{-6}{-9}$ **33** $\dfrac{-14}{-3} = \dfrac{b}{-6}$ **34** $\dfrac{-2+5}{-6-1} = \dfrac{-15}{c}$

35 Suppose that ∠FOG and ∠GOH are complementary, and m∠GOH = 34. Find the measures of ∠FOH and ∠FOG.

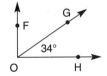

36 Imagine that the shaded rectangular region is balanced on the origin, so that it can be spun around like a phonograph record. If it is turned 90° clockwise, what will the coordinates of its vertices be?

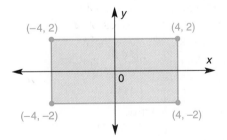

Investigation

Tessellations   From a sheet of paper, cut a square, a rectangle, a rhombus, a parallelogram, a trapezoid, and a quadrilateral having no parallel sides. If you had a large number of copies of each figure, which could you use to tile a floor, without leaving gaps or overlapping tiles? What other kinds of polygons could be used to tile floors?

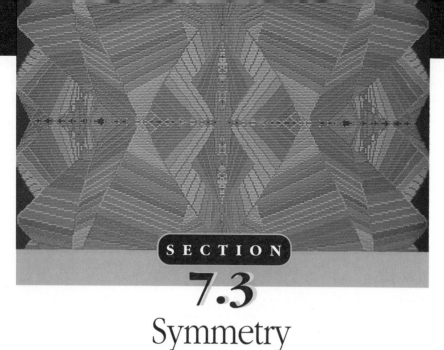

Symmetry

WHAT IS SYMMETRY?

In the pictures below, the objects on the left have an attribute that the objects on the right do not. That attribute is **symmetry.**

Symmetric	Not Symmetric

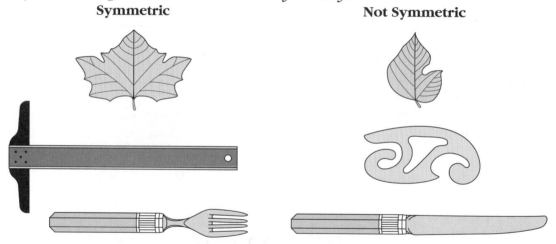

Basically, symmetry involves balance. The objects on the left appear balanced because parts of their shape correspond exactly to other parts. This is not true of the objects on the right.

Symmetry is widespread in nature, and it also plays an important role in manufacturing and design. Here are a few examples:

- Artists, architects, and photographers make use of symmetry (and of carefully planned departures from symmetry) to make visually pleasing designs and to draw attention to certain parts of their works.
- Containers are often made to be symmetric so that they are easier to handle and to stack.

- Symmetric tools can be used as easily by left-handed people as by right-handed people, but nonsymmetric tools (most kinds of scissors, for example) are usually designed for right-handed people and are difficult for lefties to use.
- Mathematicians find symmetry useful because it helps them understand properties of complex figures and it can reduce the effort required to solve difficult problems.

REFLECTION SYMMETRY

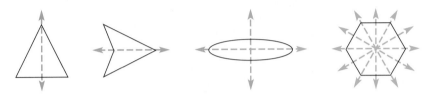

Each of these figures possesses *reflection symmetry.* A figure has this kind of symmetry if you can draw a line dividing the figure into two halves that are mirror images of each other. The figure is said to be symmetric about this *line of symmetry.* Figures may have only one line of symmetry, or they may have two, or they may have many.

A rectangle is drawn on a sheet of stiff paper, as shown on the right. If we fold the paper along one of the rectangle's lines of symmetry, the two halves of the rectangle will fit together perfectly. And if we cut the rectangle out, the line of symmetry will serve as a "balance line"— the rectangle will balance on a ruler placed along the line.

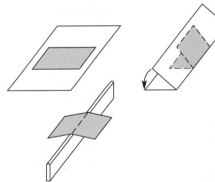

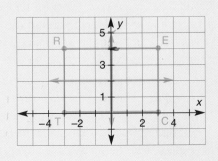

Example 1
A rectangle has vertices R(−3, 4), E(3, 4), C(3, 0), and T(−3, 0). Locate the lines of symmetry of the rectangle.

Solution
First, we draw the figure described. We notice that for each point of the rectangle on one side of the y-axis, there is a corresponding point the same distance on the other side of the y-axis. Therefore, the y-axis is a line of symmetry of the rectangle. For the same reason, a line parallel to the x-axis and two units above it is a line of symmetry of the rectangle.

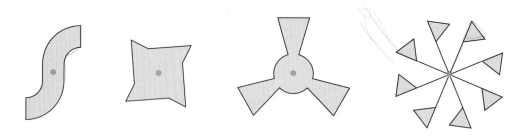

These figures all possess **rotation symmetry.** When each figure is rotated a certain number of degrees about a center point, the figure fits perfectly on top of its original position. (For each figure, try turning this book until the figure looks exactly as it does now. How much do you have to turn the book? Is it the same amount in each case?) If the amount of rotation is greater than zero and less than or equal to 180°, the figure has rotation symmetry.

Example 2

Identify the rotation symmetry of the figure shown.

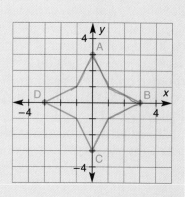

Solution

The figure's center of rotation is the origin. When the figure is rotated 90° about this point, it lies on its original position. The figure therefore has 90° rotation symmetry about the origin. Notice that the figure can also be rotated 180° and 270° to obtain the original figure.

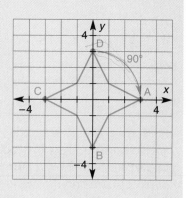

Sample Problem

Problem

What kinds of symmetry does each figure have?

a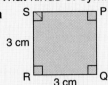

b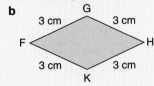

c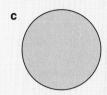

Solution

a The square has reflection symmetry about both diagonals and about lines through the midpoints of opposite sides. It also has rotation symmetry about the point where its diagonals intersect.

    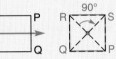

b The rhombus has reflection symmetry about both diagonals. It also has 180° rotation symmetry about the point where its diagonals intersect.

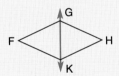 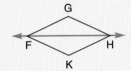 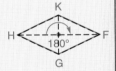

c Do you see that the circle has infinitely many line symmetries, since it is symmetrical about *any* diameter? It also has rotation symmetry, since no matter how much it is rotated about its center, it will always lie on its original position.

Think and Discuss

In problems 1–4, indicate whether the figure has reflection symmetry, rotation symmetry, both kinds of symmetry, or neither kind of symmetry.

1  **2** 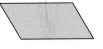 **3**   **4**

5 Is the statement true *always, sometimes,* or *never?*
  a A balance line is a line of symmetry.
  b A line of symmetry is a balance line.
  c A center of rotation symmetry is on a balance line.

6 Sports   Discuss the kinds of symmetry possessed by
  a A football field   **b** A baseball field
  c A tennis court   **d** A golf course

In problems 7–10, copy each figure. Then draw all the figure's lines of symmetry.

7   **8**   **9**   **10**

11 Is the statement *true* or *false?* Explain your answer.
  a A figure can have exactly three lines of symmetry.
  b A figure can have rotation symmetry about two different centers.

Problems and Applications

12 Of lines a, b, c, d, and e, which are lines of symmetry of the rectangle?

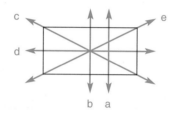

In problems 13 and 14, each diagram shows part of a figure that has reflection symmetry about the dashed line. Copy the diagram and complete the figure.

13    **14**

15 What kind of symmetry, if any, does figure JKLMNOPQ have?

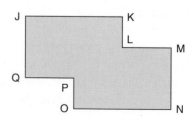

16 a How would you go about finding the center of symmetry of parallelogram PARL?
b How many degrees must PARL be rotated before it lies atop its original position?
c When PARL is rotated that number of degrees, which parts of the rotated figure will lie on the positions now occupied by $\overline{PL}$, $\overline{RL}$, and $\angle A$?

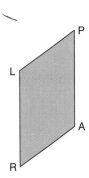

In problems 17–20, sketch each figure and draw all of the polygon's lines of symmetry.

17    **18**    **19**    **20**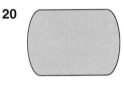

In problems 21–27, sketch an example of the figure described. If no such figure exists, write *impossible*.

21 A trapezoid without reflection symmetry

22 A rectangle without reflection symmetry

23 A rectangle without rotation symmetry

24 A parallelogram without reflection symmetry

25 A parallelogram without rotation symmetry

26 A rhombus without reflection symmetry

27 A rhombus without rotation symmetry

28 Quadrilateral ABCD has 180° rotation symmetry about point P. If m∠A = 58, AB = 8 cm, and AD = 6 cm, what is
a DC?   **b** BC?   **c** m∠C?

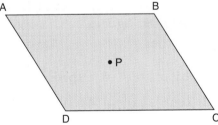

29 Industrial Arts Many bolt heads and nuts are hexagonal in shape.
a What advantage does a hexagonal nut have over a square nut?
b Why are octagonal nuts not used?
c Why are pentagonal nuts not used?
d See if you can find an example of a pentagonal bolt head.

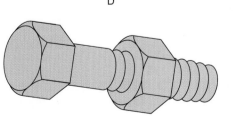

30 Classify the 26 capital letters of the alphabet according to the kinds of symmetry they have.

31 Both axes are lines of symmetry of the figure.
  a What are the coordinates of points A, B, C, D, and E?
  b Does the figure have rotation symmetry? If so, what point is the center of rotation, and what is the least rotation that will make the figure lie atop its original position?

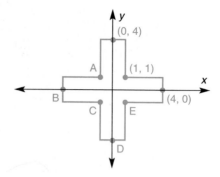

32 What kinds of quadrilateral always have reflection symmetry over each of their diagonals?

33 **Communicating**   Discuss some examples of symmetry that occur in nature.

◄ LOOKING BACK   **Spiral Learning**   LOOKING AHEAD ►

---

34 Of the three expressions $9 - 8(5 + 3)$, $9 - 8(5) + 8(3)$, and $9 - 8(5) - 8(3)$, which are equal?

In problems 35–38, evaluate each expression.

35 $-8(-7)$ **36** $-8 + (-7)$ **37** $\frac{-42}{7}$ **38** $3 - (-1)$

A diagonal of a quadrilateral divides the quadrilateral into two triangles. In problems 39–42, what can be concluded about the triangles formed by the diagonals of each quadrilateral?

39
Rectangle

40
Trapezoid

41
Rhombus

42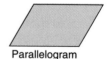
Parallelogram

In problems 43–46, express each length as a number of meters.

43 245 cm **44** 1.33 km **45** 10 ft **46** 2 mi

Investigation

Logos   Many corporate logos (the symbols the companies use on their products and in their advertising) are symmetric. One that you may be familiar with is the CBS "eye." Find some other examples of symmetric logos—both ones with reflection symmetry and ones with rotation symmetry. Then design a logo that you can use as your personal symbol.

SECTION
7.4

Rigid Transformations

Triangle ABC has been "flipped" over line ℓ to produce triangle A´B´C´. Each point of the original figure has a corresponding point in triangle A´B´C´.

This "flip" is an example of a **reflection.** The new figure has the same size and shape as the original figure, but the new figure has a different position.

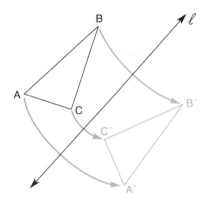

Example 1

Reflect figure TERASF over the x-axis.

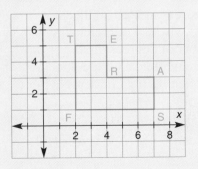

Solution

Notice that when TERASF is reflected over the x-axis, another figure, T′E′R′A′S′F′, is formed. Each point of the original figure is transformed into a point of the new figure. Each new point is called the **image** of an original point. Each original point is called the **preimage** of a new point. In order to distinguish between the image and the preimage, we will label an image point with the same letter as the preimage point and the additional symbol ′. In the example, the image of T is T′, read "T prime."

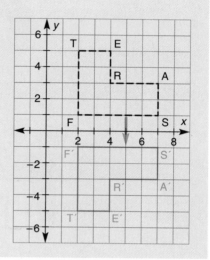

ROTATIONS

Let's revisit figure TERASF from Example 1.

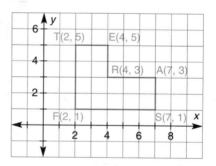

Select a point, in this case point S, and rotate the figure 90° in a clockwise direction about S. This movement transforms the figure into T′E′R′A′S′F′. The transformation is a **rotation** about S. To rotate a figure, we need a point about which the figure is rotated, a direction of rotation (clockwise or counterclockwise), and the number of degrees the figure is rotated. We then rotate all the points of the figure by that number of degrees around the point of rotation.

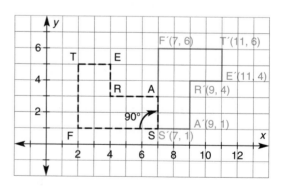

Example 2

Draw the image of the figure after a rotation of 90 degrees in a clockwise direction about the point (2, 3), and label its vertices using prime notation. Give the coordinates of the image's vertices.

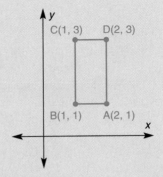

Solution

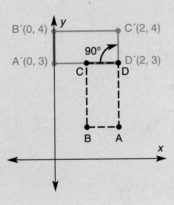

TRANSLATIONS

A third kind of transformation is a ***translation,*** or ***slide.***

Without turning or flipping, each point of the figure has been moved the same distance in the same direction, or translated. If we do the translation on a coordinate plane, we can find the image of a point by adding the ***translation numbers*** to the coordinates of the point being translated.

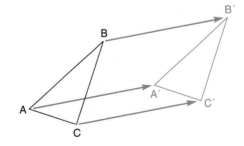

Translation Numbers

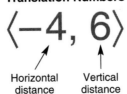

$$\langle -4, 6 \rangle$$

Horizontal distance   Vertical distance

Example 3
Translate △STU
a 3 units to the right
b 1 unit to the left and 4 units down

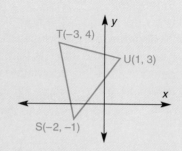

Solution
We write translation numbers and add them to the corresponding coordinates of the vertices.

Slide   **Translation Numbers**

a +3 units to the right   <3, 0>
   0 units up

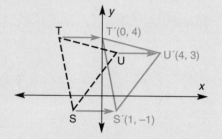

b 1 units to the left   <−1, −4>
   4 units down

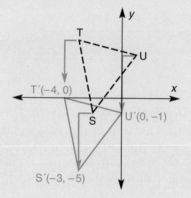

Sample Problem

Problem   The coordinates of the vertices of a triangle are A(2, 5), B(6, 1) and C(4, −3). Find the coordinates of the image after a translation of <−6, 4>.

Solution You can use a matrix to help you organize the information.

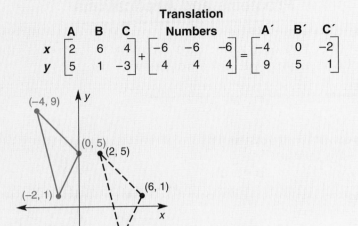

$$\begin{array}{c} x \\ y \end{array} \begin{array}{ccc} A & B & C \end{array} \\ \begin{bmatrix} 2 & 6 & 4 \\ 5 & 1 & -3 \end{bmatrix} + \begin{bmatrix} -6 & -6 & -6 \\ 4 & 4 & 4 \end{bmatrix} = \begin{bmatrix} -4 & 0 & -2 \\ 9 & 5 & 1 \end{bmatrix}$$

Think and Discuss

1 If points A, B, and C are rotated 120° clockwise about the center of the clock, where will their images be?

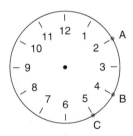

2 △ABC has vertices A(0, 5), B(4, 2), and C(0, 0). Reflect this triangle over the y-axis to produce △A′B′C′. Is there a translation that would slide △ABC onto △A′B′C′? Why or why not?

3 Copy figure TERASF in Example 1. Then draw its image after each of the following transformations. Label the vertices of each image with their coordinates.
   a A reflection over the y-axis
   b A 180° clockwise rotation about the origin
   c A 90° counterclockwise rotation about point T
   d A translation of <−4, −8>

4 Suppose that a triangle with vertices D(0, 8), R(6, 3), and Y(0, 0) is rotated 180° clockwise about the origin to produce the image △D′R′Y′.
   a If △DRY had been rotated 180° counterclockwise about the origin, would the image have been the same? Why or why not?
   b Is there a translation that will slide △DRY onto △D′R′Y′? Why or why not?

5 How is symmetry related to transformations?

Problems and Applications

6 Suppose that $\overline{AB}$ is translated along the number line to form $\overline{A'B'}$. If the coordinate of A' is 4, what will the coordinate of B' be?

7 Draw the image produced when the triangle shown is translated
  a <−3, 5>   **b** <2, 6>

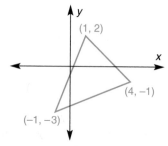

8 What are the coordinates of the image of P(−2, 7) after
  a A reflection over the x-axis?
  b A reflection over the y-axis?
  c A 90° clockwise rotation about the origin?

9 Sketch the image produced when this "propeller" is rotated 60° clockwise about the origin.

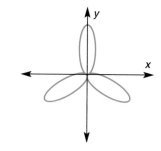

10 If △ARM is reflected over the x-axis to produce △A'R'M', what will lengths RR' and A'M' be?

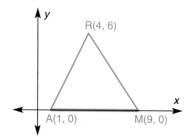

11 If rectangle RECT is rotated 90° clockwise about the origin, what will be the coordinates of the vertices of the image?

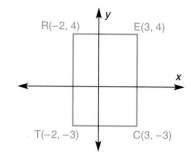

12 Draw the image produced when
quadrilateral BONE is reflected over
the y-axis. Label the vertices of the
image with their coordinates.

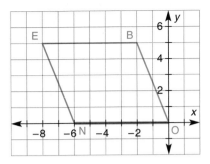

13 If $\overrightarrow{AB}$ is rotated 50° clockwise about
point A to form $\overrightarrow{A'B'}$, what will the measure
of $\angle DA'B'$ be?

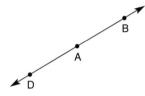

14 If figure MANDIBLE is translated
<−4, −6>, what will the coordinates
of the image's vertices be?

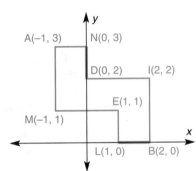

15 Rotate PMRV 180° clockwise
about the origin to produce
P′M′R′V′. What kind of quadrilateral
is PV′P′V?

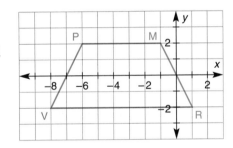

16 If line ℓ is a 180° rotation of
line m about point A, what are
m∠1, m∠2, m∠3, and m∠4?

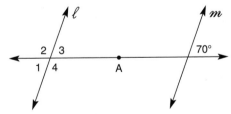

17 The matrix shows the coordinates
of the vertices of △LEG.

	L	**E**	**G**
x-coordinate	5	3	−1
y-coordinate	9	−2	7

   a Draw △LEG on a
coordinate system.

   b Translate △LEG <4, −7> and label the vertices of the image, △L′E′G′,
with their coordinates.

   c What matrix could you add to the given matrix to produce a matrix
containing the coordinates of L′, E′, and G′?

18 Design When drawing plans for a symmetrical object, a designer sometimes draws only part of the object, since reflections can be used to complete the plans accurately. This diagram shows one fourth of an electrical-outlet cover.

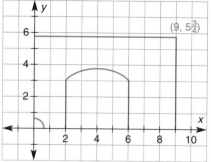

a Copy the diagram, reflect the figure over the x-axis, then reflect the figure and its image over the y-axis to complete the cover.

b If each unit of the coordinate system represents $\frac{1}{4}$ inch, what are the dimensions of the cover?

19 a If point B were moved 2 units to the right and point C were moved 2 units down, by what percent would length BC increase?

b If point B were moved 3 units to the right and point C were moved 3 units down, by what percent would length BC increase?

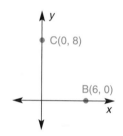

◀ LOOKING BACK **Spiral Learning** LOOKING AHEAD ▶

---

20 a What is the area of region A?

b What is the area of region B?

c What is the total area of the figure?

d How does the diagram show that $3(2 + 5) = 3(2) + 3(5)$?

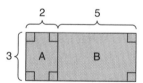

Communicating In problems 21 and 22, indicate whether the statement is *true* or *false*. Explain your answer.

21 10 is less than 5 less than 20.

22 5 less than 20 is greater than 15.

In problems 23–26, indicate whether the statement is *true* or *false*.

23 $7(3 - 5) = 7(3) - 7(5)$

24 $\sqrt{25 - 9} = \sqrt{25} - \sqrt{9}$

25 $-2(7 + 11) = -2(7) + (-2)(11)$

26 $(3 + 5)^2 = 3^2 + 5^2$

27 a Evaluate the ratio $\frac{2x}{5x}$ for $x = 4$.   **b** Evaluate the ratio $\frac{3k}{4k}$ for $k = -7$.

Investigation

M. C. Escher Find a book containing some examples of the works of the Dutch artist Maurits Cornelis Escher. Examine the pictures carefully. What are some of the ways in which Escher made use of transformations?

Discovering Properties

Recognizing symmetries and performing transformations can help you find useful properties of geometric figures. The three examples in this section show some ways in which properties can be discovered. In the problems that follow, you will have an opportunity to apply these properties and discover some other properties.

Example 1
A triangle with two congruent sides is called an *isosceles triangle*. △ABC is isosceles, with congruent legs $\overline{AB}$ and $\overline{BC}$ and base $\overline{AC}$. From the symmetry of this triangle, what can you conclude about base angles A and C?

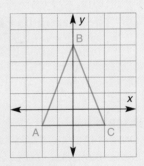

Solution
△ABC possesses reflection symmetry about the y-axis. When we reflect the triangle about its line of symmetry, the image (△A′B′C′) matches the preimage exactly. We observe that ∠C ≅ ∠A′ and that ∠A ≅ ∠C′. So, ∠A ≅ ∠C. Since every isosceles triangle has reflection symmetry, we can generalize this conclusion in the statement below.

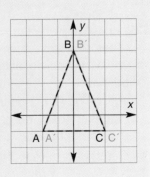

▶ **In an isosceles triangle, the base angles are congruent.**

Example 2

Think about the symmetry of a parallelogram. What parts of the parallelogram are congruent?

Solution

First, we draw a general parallelogram, GRAM. We know that the opposite sides of GRAM are congruent and that GRAM has a rotation symmetry of 180° about the intersection of its diagonals. When we rotate the parallelogram GRAM 180° about its center of symmetry, we see that each side matches its opposite side exactly. We also notice that ∠A′ matches ∠G, ∠M′ matches ∠R, ∠G′ matches ∠A, and ∠R′ matches ∠M. Since there is nothing special about this particular parallelogram, we generalize our observation in the statement below.

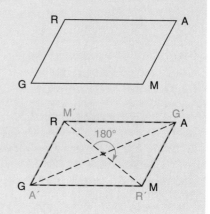

➤ **Opposite angles of a parallelogram are congruent.**

If we include the diagonals in the rotation, we see that $\overline{P'A'}$ matches $\overline{PG}$ and $\overline{P'M'}$ matches $\overline{PR}$. This means that $\overline{PA} \cong \overline{PG}$ and $\overline{PM} \cong \overline{PR}$. When a segment is divided into two congruent parts, it is said to be **bisected,** so we can draw the following general conclusion:

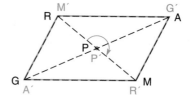

➤ **The diagonals of a parallelogram bisect each other.**

Since squares, rectangles, and rhombuses are kinds of parallelograms, these properties of parallelograms apply to them, too. Do the rotations we performed suggest any other congruences?

Example 3

Draw a rectangle and its diagonals. From the reflection symmetry of the rectangle, what can you conclude about its diagonals?

Solution

When we draw rectangle RECT and reflect it over one of its lines of symmetry, the image R′E′C′T′ matches the original rectangle exactly. Notice also that the image of diagonal $\overline{RC}$ ($\overline{R'C'}$) matches $\overline{ET}$ and that the image of diagonal $\overline{TE}$ ($\overline{T'E'}$) matches $\overline{CR}$. The diagonals are therefore congruent. Again, we generalize the conclusion in the statement below.

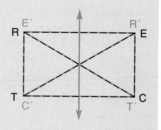

➤ **The diagonals of a rectangle are congruent.**

Think and Discuss

1 Suppose that the diagonals of a quadrilateral bisect each other and are perpendicular to each other, like $\overline{AC}$ and $\overline{BD}$ in the diagram. By using reflections, what can you conclude about quadrilateral ABCD?

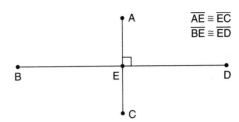

$\overline{AE} \cong \overline{EC}$
$\overline{BE} \cong \overline{ED}$

2 An *isosceles trapezoid* is a trapezoid in which the nonparallel sides are congruent. In isosceles trapezoid TRAP, $\overline{TR} \parallel \overline{PA}$ and $\overline{TP} \cong \overline{RA}$.

  a Reflect TRAP over line of symmetry $\overleftrightarrow{EZ}$. What properties do you notice?

  b If diagonals $\overline{PR}$ and $\overline{TA}$ are drawn, what additional properties do you notice from the reflection in part **a?**

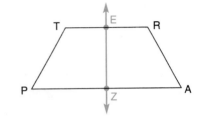

3 In your mathematics studies, you will frequently encounter triangles with angles of 30°, 60°, and 90°.

  a Describe how, with one reflection of $\triangle$TSN, you can create an equilateral triangle.

  b What can you conclude about the lengths of $\overline{TS}$ and $\overline{SN}$?

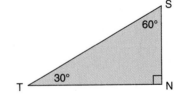

4 From the symmetries of a rhombus, what conclusions can you draw about

  a Its diagonals?

  b Its angles?

  c Its sides?

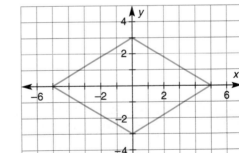

5 A quadrilateral that has two pairs of congruent adjacent sides is called a *kite*. In the kite shown, $\overline{EK} \cong \overline{KI}$ and $\overline{ET} \cong \overline{TI}$. Reflect kite KITE over its line of symmetry, $\overleftrightarrow{KT}$. What properties of the kite do you see?

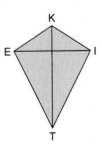

Problems and Applications

6 If AMRV is a rectangle and AR = 24, what is length VM?

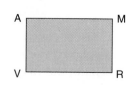

7 FAST is a parallelogram, and m∠A = 74. What is m∠T?

8 In this triangle, $\overline{AB} \cong \overline{AC}$ and m∠B = 52. What are m∠A and m∠C?

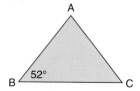

9 $\overline{AL}$ and $\overline{PF}$ are parallel to the x-axis, and $\overline{PA}$ and $\overline{FL}$ are parallel to the y-axis. What are the coordinates of points P and L?

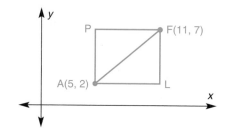

10 If this trapezoid is symmetric about the y-axis, what are the coordinates of points C and W?

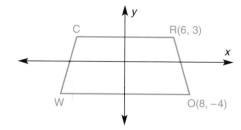

11 VOLE is a rectangle, and VL = 18. What is length PO?

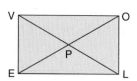

12 Parallelogram WREN can be translated as shown so that point W′ lies on N and point R′ lies on E. From this translation, what can be concluded about the consecutive angles of a parallelogram?

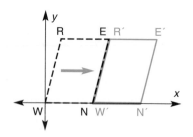

In problems 13–16, carefully draw each of the polygons described.

13 A quadrilateral that has angles of 35°, 35°, 145°, and 145° but is not a parallelogram

14 A parallelogram that has angles of 35°, 35°, 145°, and 145° but is not a rhombus

15 A quadrilateral that has angles of 35°, 35°, 145°, and 145° and is both a parallelogram and a rhombus

16 A rhombus that has angles of 35°, 35°, 145°, and 145° but is not a parallelogram

17 SMOU is a parallelogram. If MU = 31 and EO = 17, what are lengths EU and SE?

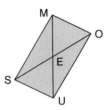

18 a If points C, O, N, and Y are connected by segments to form a quadrilateral, what kind of quadrilateral will CONY be?
b If the quadrilateral is translated <3, –2>, what will be the coordinates of the vertices of the image?
c What kind of quadrilateral will the image be?

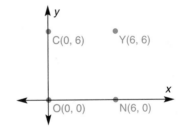

19 If $\overline{TC} \cong \overline{AC}$ and m∠C = 44, what are m∠A and m∠T?

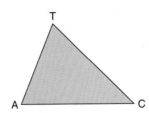

20 Find the area of △BUG for each of the values of *k*.
   a –6   **b** 0   **c** 4

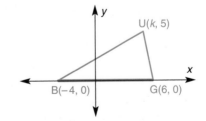

21 PICA is a parallelogram, with PA = 18 and CA = 7. What is the perimeter of PICA?

22 What kind of quadrilateral does square SQUA become if

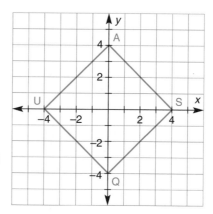

    a S is moved to (4, 4) and U is moved to (−4, −4)?

    b S is moved to (9, 0) and U is moved to (−9, 0)?

    c S is moved to (2, 0) and U is moved to (−2, 0)?

    d S is moved to (−2, −3) and Q is moved to (−2, 7)?

23 Parallelogram JETS has 180° rotation symmetry about point P. If JE = 20, JS = 21.2, JP = 17, and SP = 12, what are JT, SE, ET, and ST?

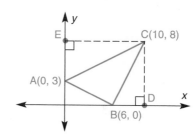

24 **a** Draw an equilateral triangle with side length 1 inch.

    b Keeping one vertex stationary, reflect the triangle over a side five times in a counterclockwise pattern. What kind of polygon is formed by the original triangle and the reflections?

    c What is the perimeter of the new figure?

    d List some properties of the new figure.

◀ LOOKING BACK **Spiral Learning** LOOKING AHEAD ▶

25 In this diagram, what are the coordinates of points D and E?

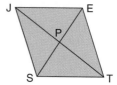

26 **a** Evaluate $\begin{bmatrix} 1 & 0 \\ 0 & -1 \end{bmatrix} \cdot \begin{bmatrix} 3 & 2 & 7 \\ 5 & 4 & 1 \end{bmatrix}$.

    b Evaluate $\begin{bmatrix} -1 & 0 \\ 0 & 1 \end{bmatrix} \cdot \begin{bmatrix} 3 & 2 & 7 \\ 5 & 4 & 1 \end{bmatrix}$.

    c Describe the effects of multiplication by $\begin{bmatrix} 1 & 0 \\ 0 & -1 \end{bmatrix}$ and of multiplication by $\begin{bmatrix} -1 & 0 \\ 0 & 1 \end{bmatrix}$ on a matrix having two rows.

27 Of a square, a rectangle, a rhombus, a parallelogram, and a trapezoid, which figures always are symmetric about a line through the midpoints of opposite sides?

28

Suppose that on the number line, points A and B are reflected over D to form A′ and B′, then points A′, B′, and D are reflected over C to form A″, B″, and D′. What will the coordinates of A″, B″, and D′ be?

29 Spreadsheets Use a spreadsheet to make a table showing the distances between A and B for k = 1, 2, 3, ... , 24.

1.8

Science The formula $F = \frac{9}{5}C + 32$ can be used to calculate the Fahrenheit equivalent of a temperature expressed in degrees Celsius. In problems 30–33, convert each temperature to degrees Fahrenheit.

30 20°C   **31** 0°C   **32** −8.4°C   **33** −32°C

34 Without using a calculator, evaluate the expressions on both sides of the equal sign. Which expression is easier to evaluate?

$$17(34) + 17(66) = 17(34 + 66)$$

35 Communicating
  a What is the length of $\overline{PQ}$?
  b What is the area of rectangle RSTU?
  c Would it make sense to calculate the sum of your answers to parts **a** and **b**? Why or why not?

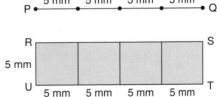

Investigation

Playing-Card Symmetries Look closely at the playing cards in a standard 52-card deck. What kind of symmetry do most of the cards have? Why are they designed to have this kind of symmetry? Which of the cards are not symmetric? Why aren't these cards symmetric?

7.6

Transformations and Matrices

THE VERTEX MATRIX

In this section, you will see how your knowledge of matrix addition and multiplication can help you transform geometric figures. As you study the examples and the sample problem, look for patterns and try to figure out why the methods presented here work.

Example 1

Create a matrix to represent this quadrilateral.

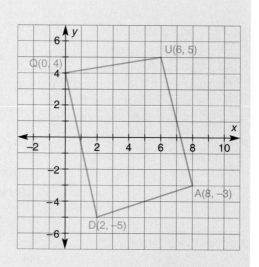

Solution

The vertices of the quadrilateral are Q(0, 4), U(6, 5), A(8, −3), and D(2, −5). Here are three possible ways of organizing the coordinates of the vertices in a matrix:

	Q	U	A	D
x	0	6	8	2
y	4	5	−3	−5

	A	D	Q	U
x	8	2	0	6
y	−3	−5	4	5

	A	U	Q	D
x	8	6	0	2
y	−3	5	4	−5

Each of these matrices is called a **vertex matrix** of the quadrilateral. Notice that the x-coordinates are always in the first row and the y-coordinates are always in the second row. The coordinates of the points are entered in order, going clockwise or counterclockwise around the figure from any of its vertices.

TRANSLATIONS

After writing a vertex matrix for a figure, you can use matrix addition to model a translation of the figure.

Example 2
The diagram shows a triangle being translated <3, −4>—that is, 3 units to the right and 4 units down. Use matrix addition to find the coordinates of A′, B′, and C′.

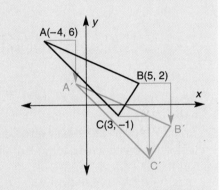

Solution
To translate the vertices, we need to add 3 to each x-coordinate and −4 to each y-coordinate.

Vertices of Preimage   Translation Matrix   Vertices of Image

$$\begin{array}{c}x\\y\end{array}\begin{array}{ccc}\mathbf{A}&\mathbf{B}&\mathbf{C}\\\begin{bmatrix}-4&5&3\\6&2&-1\end{bmatrix}\end{array} + \begin{bmatrix}3&3&3\\-4&-4&-4\end{bmatrix} = \begin{array}{ccc}\mathbf{A'}&\mathbf{B'}&\mathbf{C'}\\\begin{bmatrix}-1&8&6\\2&-2&-5\end{bmatrix}\end{array}$$

Notice that in the translation matrix we entered the translation numbers vertically so that we could add them to the corresponding x- and y-coordinates. The vertices of the image are A′ (−1, 2), B′ (8, −2), and C′ (6, −5).

REFLECTIONS AND ROTATIONS

To model reflections, we use matrix multiplication. Two key reflection matrices are

$$\begin{bmatrix}-1&0\\0&1\end{bmatrix} \qquad\qquad \begin{bmatrix}1&0\\0&-1\end{bmatrix}$$

For a reflection
over the y-axis

For a reflection
over the x-axis

Example 3

Use matrix multiplication to locate the vertices of the image produced by reflecting △DEF over the y-axis.

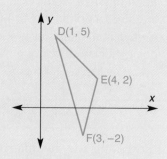

Solution

The reflection is over the y-axis, so we multiply the vertex matrix of △DEF by
$$\begin{bmatrix} -1 & 0 \\ 0 & 1 \end{bmatrix}$$

$$\begin{bmatrix} -1 & 0 \\ 0 & 1 \end{bmatrix} \cdot \begin{matrix} D & E & F \\ \begin{bmatrix} 1 & 4 & 3 \\ 5 & 2 & -2 \end{bmatrix} \end{matrix} = \begin{matrix} D' & E' & F' \\ \begin{bmatrix} -1 & -4 & -3 \\ 5 & 2 & -2 \end{bmatrix} \end{matrix}$$

The vertices of the image are D′ (−1, 5), E′ (−4, 2), and F′ (−3, −2). Draw the image to check this solution.

Matrix multiplication can also be used to rotate figures, but the mathematics involved is complicated for all but the simplest rotations.

Example 4

Locate the vertices of the image produced by rotating △GHK 90° counterclockwise about the origin.

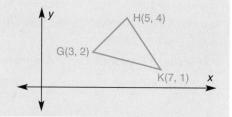

Solution

To rotate 90° counterclockwise, multiply the vertex matrix by $\begin{bmatrix} 0 & -1 \\ 1 & 0 \end{bmatrix}$.

$$\begin{bmatrix} 0 & -1 \\ 1 & 0 \end{bmatrix} \cdot \begin{matrix} G & H & K \\ \begin{bmatrix} 3 & 5 & 7 \\ 2 & 4 & 1 \end{bmatrix} \end{matrix} = \begin{matrix} G' & H' & K' \\ \begin{bmatrix} -2 & -4 & -1 \\ 3 & 5 & 7 \end{bmatrix} \end{matrix}$$

The vertices of the image are G′ (−2, 3), H′ (−4, 5), and K′ (−1, 7).

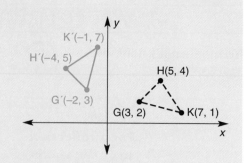

Sample Problem

Suppose △DIL has vertex matrix

$$\begin{array}{c} x \\ y \end{array} \begin{array}{ccc} \mathbf{D} & \mathbf{I} & \mathbf{L} \\ \begin{bmatrix} 0 & 5 & 7 \\ 3 & 8 & 2 \end{bmatrix} \end{array}.$$

Solution Find the area of △DIL.

We will begin by graphing △DIL. Then we will encase the triangle in a rectangle. The area of △DIL is the area of the rectangle minus the area of the three shaded triangles: △A_1, △A_2, and △A_3. This procedure is called **encasement.**

Area of rectangle: 7 · 6, or 42

Area of △A_1: $\frac{1}{2}$ · 5 · 5, or 12.5

Area of △A_2: $\frac{1}{2}$ · 2 · 6, or 6

Area of △A_3: $\frac{1}{2}$ · 7 · 1, or 3.5

Area of △DIL: 42 − (12.5 + 6 + 3.5), or 20

The area of △DIL is 20 square units.

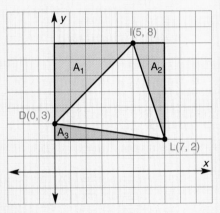

Think and Discuss

1 Which of these matrices is not a vertex matrix for quadrilateral MIRO?

a $\begin{bmatrix} -5 & -6 & 0 & 1 \\ 5 & -1 & 0 & 6 \end{bmatrix}$ **b** $\begin{bmatrix} -6 & -5 & 1 & 0 \\ -1 & 5 & 6 & 0 \end{bmatrix}$

c $\begin{bmatrix} 0 & -5 & 1 & -6 \\ 0 & 5 & 6 & -1 \end{bmatrix}$ **d** $\begin{bmatrix} 0 & 1 & -5 & -6 \\ 0 & 6 & 5 & -1 \end{bmatrix}$

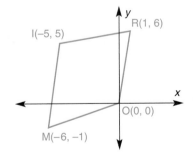

2 What is the area of △ABC?

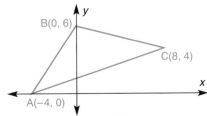

3 Refer to △DIL in the sample problem.

  a Multiply the vertex matrix of △DIL by $\begin{bmatrix} 2 & 0 \\ 0 & 2 \end{bmatrix}$ to find the vertex

  matrix of another triangle: △D′I′L′.

  b Find the area of △D′I′L′.

  c Find the ratio of the area of △DIL to the area of △D′I′L′.

4 Refer to the diagram of △STP.

  a Write a vertex matrix for the triangle.

  b Add $\begin{bmatrix} 5 & 5 & 5 \\ 6 & 6 & 6 \end{bmatrix}$ to the vertex matrix and draw the

  figure represented by the sum. What transformation
  did the addition produce?

  c Multiply the vertex matrix of △STP by

  $\begin{bmatrix} -1 & 0 \\ 0 & -1 \end{bmatrix}$ and draw the figure represented by the

  product. What transformation did the
  multiplication produce?

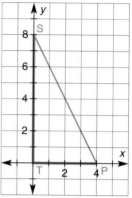

  d Multiply the vertex matrix of △STP by $\begin{bmatrix} -1 & 0 \\ 0 & 1 \end{bmatrix}$ and draw the figure

  represented by the product. What transformation did the
  multiplication produce?

  e Multiply the vertex matrix of △STP by $\begin{bmatrix} 1 & 0 \\ 0 & -1 \end{bmatrix}$ and draw the

  figure represented by the product. What transformation did the
  multiplication produce?

Problems and Applications

5 Write a vertex matrix for the triangle.

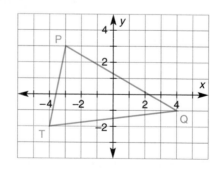

6 **a** Write a vertex matrix for △MUD.

  b Multiply the matrix by $\begin{bmatrix} 1 & 0 \\ 0 & -1 \end{bmatrix}$

  and draw the image represented
  by the product.

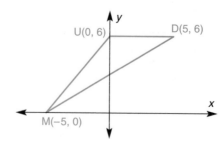

7 A triangle has vertices A(0, −6), B(4, −4), and C(6, 6). Use matrix addition to find the coordinates of the vertices of △A′B′C′, the image of △ABC after a translation of <0, −1>.

8 What is the area of quadrilateral SQUA?

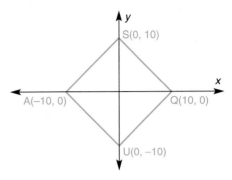

9 Communicating

   a Describe what happens to the x- and y-coordinates of F, U, and R when △FUR is reflected over the y-axis.

   b Evaluate $\begin{bmatrix} -1 & 0 \\ 0 & 1 \end{bmatrix} \cdot \begin{bmatrix} -6 & 5 & -8 \\ 4 & 3 & 2 \end{bmatrix}$.

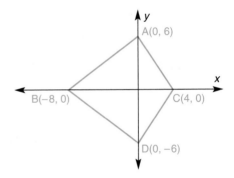

10 If points B and C are both moved 4 units to the right to form a new quadrilateral, by how much will the area of the new quadrilateral differ from the area of the one shown?

11 This vertex matrix represents △YES.

   a Multiply the matrix by $\begin{bmatrix} -1 & 0 \\ 0 & -1 \end{bmatrix}$ to produce the vertex matrix of △Y′E′S′.

$$\begin{array}{ccc} \mathbf{Y} & \mathbf{E} & \mathbf{S} \\ \begin{bmatrix} -6 & 4 & 10 \\ -10 & -8 & -10 \end{bmatrix} \end{array}$$

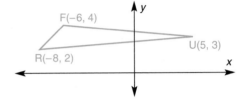

   b Draw △YES and △Y′E′S′. What transformation did the multiplication produce?

12 Suppose that points Y and X are moved to the right so that the lengths of $\overline{BY}$ and $\overline{OX}$ increase by 20%. By what percent will the lengths of the figure's diagonals change?

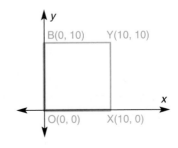

13 a Write a vertex matrix for △SAM.
  b If △S′A′M′ is the image of △SAM after a translation of <*p, q*>, what are the values of *p* and *q* and the coordinates of S′ and A′?

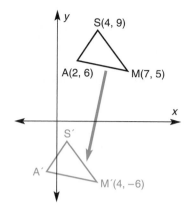

14 Using the vertex matrix shown, determine the area of △XYZ for
  a $k = 0$ **b** $k = 4$

$$\begin{array}{ccc} \mathbf{X} & \mathbf{Y} & \mathbf{Z} \end{array}$$
$$\begin{bmatrix} k + 2 & 0 & k + 10 \\ 0 & k + 8 & 0 \end{bmatrix}$$

In problems 15–17, refer to the diagram of △HAT.

15 Use matrix addition to locate the vertices of the image of △HAT after a translation of <−3, 5>.

16 Use matrix multiplication to locate the vertices of the image of △HAT after a reflection over the y-axis.

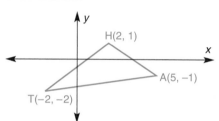

17 Use matrix multiplication to locate the vertices of the image of △HAT after a 90° counterclockwise rotation about the origin.

18 For what values of *w* and *z* will the quadrilateral represented by the following vertex matrix be a square?

$$\begin{bmatrix} -8 + w & 0 & 2 + z & 0 \\ 0 & -5 & 0 & 5 \end{bmatrix}$$

19 a Write a vertex matrix for △REV.

  b Multiply the vertex matrix by $\begin{bmatrix} -1 & 0 \\ 0 & 1 \end{bmatrix}$ and draw the image represented by the product.

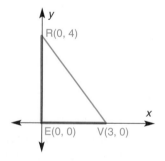

  c Multiply the product matrix from part **b** by $\begin{bmatrix} 1 & 0 \\ 0 & -1 \end{bmatrix}$ and draw the new image.

  d Evaluate $\begin{bmatrix} -1 & 0 \\ 0 & 1 \end{bmatrix} \cdot \begin{bmatrix} 1 & 0 \\ 0 & -1 \end{bmatrix}$.

  e Multiply the original vertex matrix of △REV by your answer to part **d**. What do you notice?

20 Indicate whether the statement is an *equation*, an *expression*, or an *inequality*.

a $9x - 3y + 7\sqrt{3}\,z^5$

b $9x = 3y + 7\sqrt{3}\,z^5$

c $9x - 3y + 7 = \sqrt{3}\,z^5$

d $9x - 3y < 7\sqrt{3}\,x^5$

e $9x - 3y = 7\sqrt{3}\,z^5$

21 Evaluate $\begin{bmatrix} 1 & 0 \\ 0 & 1 \end{bmatrix} \cdot \begin{bmatrix} 2 & -1 & 1 \\ 3 & -4 & 6 \end{bmatrix}$. What do you notice about the product?

22 Elsie, Lacie, and Tillie are sisters. Their mean age is 11, and their median age is 10. If Elsie is 15 years old, how old are the other two girls?

23

Suppose that $\overline{AB}$ is translated along the number line to form $\overline{A'B'}$. If the coordinate of A′ is 0,

a What will the coordinate of B′ be?

b What will the length of $\overline{A'B'}$ be?

In problems 24–27, solve each equation for x.

24 $x + 31.8 = 47.136$

25 $9.6x = -34.416$

26 $x - 39 = -42$

27 $\dfrac{x}{-4.36} = -91.3$

28 Communicating PENTA is a regular pentagon.

a Describe the reflection symmetries of the pentagon.

b Describe the rotation symmetries of the pentagon.

c List as many properties of the pentagon and its diagonals as you can, justifying each by a rotation or reflection.

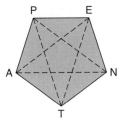

29 Suppose that point P(−6, −5) is translated <4, 2> to P′, then the translation is repeated four more times to produce P″, P‴, P⁗, and P‴‴. What are the coordinates of each of the images?

Investigation

Origami Do you know what origami is? Try to find a person (perhaps an art teacher) or a book that can teach you about origami, then construct an origami figure of your own. How are symmetries and transformations important in origami?

CHAPTER 7

Summary

CONCEPTS AND PROCEDURES

After studying this chapter, you should be able to

- Recognize parallel lines and perpendicular lines (7.1)
- Recognize adjacent angles and vertical angles (7.1)
- Identify squares, rectangles, parallelograms, rhombuses, and trapezoids (7.2)
- Identify figures that possess reflection symmetry (7.3)
- Identify figures that possess rotation symmetry (7.3)
- Transform a figure by means of reflection (7.4)
- Transform a figure by means of rotation (7.4)
- Transform a figure by means of translation (7.4)
- Discover and apply properties of polygons (7.5)
- Represent a figure by means of a vertex matrix (7.6)
- Use matrix addition to model translations (7.6)
- Use matrix multiplication to model reflections and rotations (7.6)

VOCABULARY

adjacent angles (7.1)
bisect (7.5)
consecutive vertices (7.2)
diagonal (7.2)
encasement (7.6)
image (7.4)
isosceles triangle (7.5)
line of symmetry (7.3)
opposite vertices (7.2)
parallel (7.1)
parallelogram (7.2)
perpendicular (7.1)
preimage (7.4)
quadrilateral (7.2)
reflection (7.4)
reflection symmetry (7.3)
rhombus (7.2)
rotation (7.4)
rotation symmetry (7.3)
slide (7.4)
symmetry (7.3)
translation (7.4)
translation numbers (7.4)
trapezoid (7.2)
vertex matrix (7.6)
vertical angles (7.1)

Review

1 One angle of a triangle is a 70° angle. The other two angles have equal measures. What are the measures of those two angles?

2 Which of the following pairs of angles are adjacent?
a ∠PBQ and ∠SBQ
b ∠RBS and ∠QBP
c ∠RBQ and ∠SBR
d ∠PBR and ∠QBR

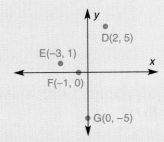

3 If points D, E, F, and G are reflected over the y-axis, what will the coordinates of their images be?

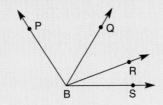

In problems 4–7, copy each polygon, indicating whether it has rotation symmetry, reflection symmetry, or both. If it has reflection symmetry, draw all of its lines of symmetry. If it has rotation symmetry, indicate the center of symmetry and the angle(s) of rotation for the symmetry.

4 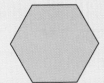 5 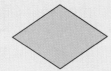 6 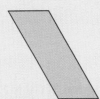 7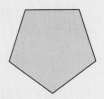

8 The coordinates of the vertices of a triangle are E(–6, –8), F(–2, 10), and G(4, 0). Suppose that △EFG is translated <–5, 3> to form △E´F´G´. Write a vertex matrix for △E´F´G´.

9 a What kind of quadrilateral is QUAD?
b How could $\overline{UA}$ be moved to make QUAD a square?
c How could $\overline{QU}$ be moved to make QUAD a square?
d How could $\overline{DA}$ be moved to make QUAD a square?

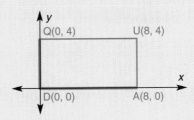

10 a Copy the diagram and reflect $\overline{RN}$ over the x-axis to form $\overline{R'N'}$. What are the coordinates of R′ and N′?
b What are the lengths of $\overline{RN}$ and $\overline{R'N'}$?

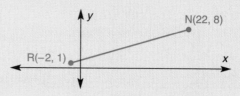

11 Draw the image of figure TRANSFIG after a 180° rotation about point F. Use prime notation to label the vertices of the image.

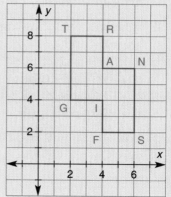

12 If $\overline{MT} \cong \overline{MV}$ and m∠T = 72, what are m∠M and m∠V?

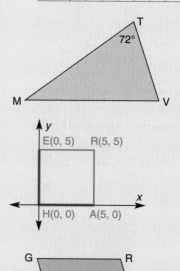

13 If vertex R were moved to (8, 5), how could you move another vertex to make quadrilateral ERAH
a A rectangle?
b A parallelogram?

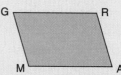

14 GRAM is a parallelogram. If $\overline{GR}$ is 12 cm long and $\overline{RA}$ is 8 cm long, how long are $\overline{GM}$ and $\overline{MA}$?

In problems 15–17, draw the image of this figure after the given transformation.

15 Reflection over the y-axis

16 Reflection over the x-axis

17 Rotation of 180° counterclockwise about the origin

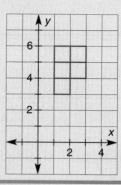

18 If △TRY is rotated 180° clockwise about the origin, what will be the coordinates of the vertices of the image?

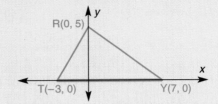

19 Describe the similarities and differences between
  a A square and a rhombus   **b** A rectangle and a parallelogram

20 If point F is translated 3 units to the right to form F´ and point L is translated 5 units to the left to form L´,
  a What will the coordinates of F´ and L´ be?
  b What will the area of trapezoid F´L´EX be?

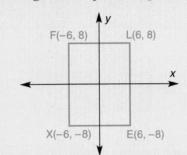

21 What is the area of △JST?

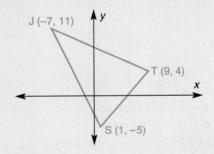

22 a Write a vertex matrix for rectangle RECT.
   b Multiply the vertex matrix by $\begin{bmatrix} -1 & 0 \\ 0 & -1 \end{bmatrix}$.
   c Draw the quadrilateral represented by your answer to part **b.** What transformation did the multiplication produce?

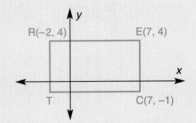

23 A quadrilateral has vertices K(–1, 5), I(1, 7), T(3, 5), and E(1, 0). Use matrix multiplication to locate the vertices of the image of KITE after a reflection over
  a The x-axis   **b** The y-axis

24 FIRM is a rectangle, $\overline{FI}$ is 6 inches long, and $\overline{FM}$ is 8 inches long. How long are $\overline{IR}$, $\overline{MR}$, $\overline{FR}$, and $\overline{IM}$?

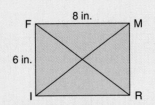

Test

In problems 1–3, refer to quadrilateral ABCD.

1 Identify all pairs of parallel segments and all pairs of perpendicular segments in the quadrilateral.

2 Describe all the symmetries of the quadrilateral.

3 What kind of quadrilateral is ABCD?

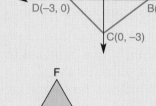

4 △EFG is equilateral. Copy the triangle and draw all its lines of symmetry.

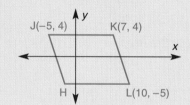

5 What are the coordinates of vertex H of parallelogram HJKL?

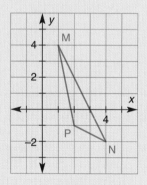

In problems 6–8, refer to △MNP. Find the coordinates of the vertices of the triangle's image after the given transformation.

6 A reflection over the y-axis

7 A translation of <–5, 2>

8 A 90° counterclockwise rotation about the origin

9 What is the area of △QRS?

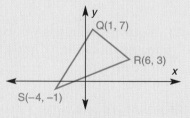

10 TUVW is a rhombus, with WV = 4.5 and m∠V = 72. What are UV, TW, m∠T, and m∠U?

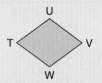

1 A **word chain** is a list of words, in order, where each word is made from the previous word by changing one letter. All words in a chain must be legitimate English words.

Example: A word chain can change JACK to KING with the following list: JACK, BACK, BANK, RANK, RINK, RING, KING

Find word chains for the following:

a Change MAST to SPAR.

b Change CENT to DIME.

c Change FAST to SLOW.

d Change WORK to PLAY.

e Change SHAVE to CLEAN.

f Change MEAT to FISH.

g Change WOK to FRY.

h Change WISH to HOPE.

2 Put 3 pennies, 3 dimes, 1 quarter, and 1 nickel into a 3-by-3 grid as shown. Slide the coins around, one at a time and one to a square. A coin can be moved only into an adjacent open space. Each move may be only left, right, up, or down. The idea is to end up with the same configuration, except that the nickel and quarter are switched. What is the fewest number of moves it takes for you to do this?

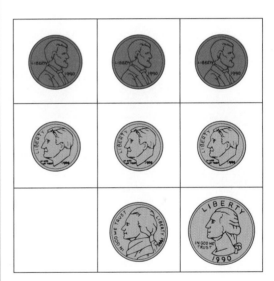

8

The Language of Algebra

AUTOMOTIVE DESIGN Why are today's cars so different from earlier models? Were changes made over the years just to make cars *look* different?

Some design changes are strictly for appearance, but others are for safety. At one time, for example, few cars had either seat belts or safety glass, and dashboards were made of steel. Air bags are a relatively recent safety feature.

Automotive designers use computers that can display three-dimensional designs. These designs can be altered by a few keystrokes. In addition to affecting safety and appearance, decisions about design can help to determine how long the car will last, how often it will need repairs, how much it will cost, and how much gas mileage it will get.

INVESTIGATION

Fuel Efficiency Ask a friend or relative how many miles per gallon his or her car gets. Does the type of driving affect the mileage? Explain the steps you would follow in order to determine a car's gas mileage. Will you get the same answer every time you follow these steps? Explain.

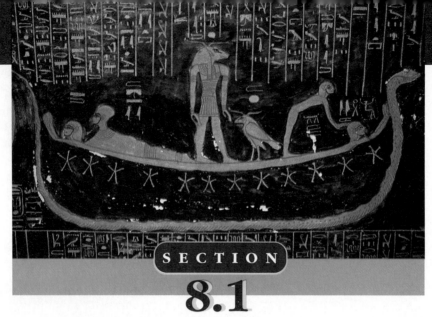

8.1
Simplifying Expressions

EQUIVALENT EXPRESSIONS

Ms. Perry asked her class to find the perimeter of triangle ABC for $x = 4$.

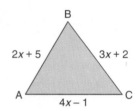

Subina wrote the expression for the length of each side and substituted 4 for x.

$$
\begin{array}{lll}
AB &= 2x + 5 & \\
&= 2(4) + 5 & \\
&= 13 &
\end{array}
\qquad
\begin{array}{l}
BC = 3x + 2 \\
= 3(4) + 2 \\
= 14
\end{array}
\qquad
\begin{array}{l}
AC = 4x - 1 \\
= 4(4) - 1 \\
= 15
\end{array}
$$

She added the lengths of the sides.

$$
\begin{aligned}
\text{Perimeter} &= 13 + 14 + 15 \\
&= 42
\end{aligned}
$$

Addem wrote an expression for the perimeter and substituted 4 for x.

$$
\begin{aligned}
\text{Perimeter} &= 9x + 6 \\
\text{Perimeter} &= 9(4) + 6 \\
&= 42
\end{aligned}
$$

Both students used different methods and found the same perimeter.

Example 1

Evaluate the two expressions $2x + 5 + 3x + 2 + 4x - 1$ and $9x + 6$ for five different values of x. What do you observe?

Solution
We can set up a table and choose five values.

Value of x	$2x + 5 + 3x + 2 + 4x - 1$	$9x + 6$
2.5	28.5	28.5
10	96	96
2	24	24
3.5	37.5	37.5
7	69	69

It isn't practical to substitute every possible value for x. The five values we used show that the two expressions $2x + 5 + 3x + 2 + 4x - 1$ and $9x + 6$ produce the same value for a replacement of x.

If two expressions produce the same value for all replacements of the variable(s), the two expressions are called **equivalent expressions.** We indicate this by connecting the two expressions with =, an equal sign.

The expression $9x + 6$ is shorter and simpler than $2x + 5 + 3x + 2 + 4x - 1$. When we work with an expression, we usually try to simplify the expression by finding its simplest equivalent form.

ADDING AND SUBTRACTING LIKE TERMS

How did Addem arrive at the simpler form $9x + 6$?

Rewrite the expression Subina used. $2x + 5 + 3x + 2 + 4x - 1$

Group the x-terms and the terms without x, the **numerical terms.** $2x + 3x + 4x + 5 + 2 - 1$

We call terms that have the same variable raised to the same power **like terms.** In this problem, $2x$, $3x$, and $4x$ are like terms. Like terms can be added or subtracted.

$$(2 + 3 + 4)x + (5 + 2 - 1)$$

Add the like terms. $$= 9x + 6$$

The result is the expression Addem used. Addem **simplified** the expression.

Example 2
Simplify the expression $3xy + 8xy - 5xy$.

Solution
Method 1 In this expression, all the terms are like terms. They have the same variable, xy.

Add and subtract the coefficients of xy
$$3xy + 8xy - 5xy$$
$$= (3 + 8 - 5)xy$$
$$= 6xy$$

Method 2 We can model the problem using rectangles with sides
 x and y and area xy.

Start with $3xy$.

Add $8xy$.

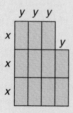

Subtract $5xy$.

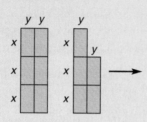

There are $6xy$ left.

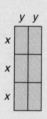

Example 3

Simplify the following expressions.

a $14x + 9x^2 - 3x^2 + 13y - 18x - 2x^2 + 8y$

b $3x + 8y + 5x^2$

Solution

a This expression contains x-terms, x^2-terms, and y-terms.

$$14x + 9x^2 - 3x^2 + 13y - 18x - 2x^2 + 8y$$

First, group like terms $= 14x - 18x + 9x^2 - 3x^2 - 2x^2 + 13y + 8y$

Combine like terms $= (14 - 18)x + (9 - 3 - 2)x^2 + (13 + 8)y$

$$= -4x + 4x^2 + 21y$$

b The expression $3x + 8y + 5x^2$ cannot be simplified because it has no like
terms. The simplest form is $3x + 8y + 5x^2$.

THE DISTRIBUTIVE PROPERTY

You have simplified expressions such as $-3x + 5x$ and $14y - 6y$.

$$-3x + 5x = (-3 + 5)x \text{ and } 14y - 6y = (14 - 6)y$$

The general form of these expressions is $ax + bx = (a + b)x$ or $ax - bx = (a - b)x$. These statements are true for any values of a, b, and x and are examples of one of the most important properties in algebra.

▶ **The Distributive Property of Multiplication over Addition or Subtraction:** For all numbers a, b, and c, $a(b + c) = ab + ac$ and $a(b - c) = ab - ac$.

Example 4
Multiply the quantity $34(2x + 6y)$.

Solution
We distribute the multiplication by 34.

Multiply $2x$ by 34 and $6y$ by 34

$$34(2x + 6y)$$
$$= 34(2x) + 34(6y)$$
$$= (34)(2)x + (34)(6)y$$
$$= 68x + 204y$$

Example 5
Multiply the quantity $-3(5x - 7y)$.

Solution
We distribute the multiplication by (-3). Be careful to keep track of the negative and subtraction signs.

$$-3(5x - 7y)$$
$$= (-3)(5x) - (-3)(7y)$$
$$= (-3)(5)x - (-3)(7)y$$
$$= -15x - (-21)y$$
$$= -15x + 21y$$

Sample Problems

Problem 1

Simplify the expression $6x + x$.

Solution Remember that $x = 1x$. Therefore, $6x + x = 7x$.

Problem 2 ____

Simplify the expression $12(3x - 5y) - 14(2 - 8y)$.

Solution

$$12(3x - 5y) - 14(2 - 8y)$$

Use the distributive property

Multiply

$$= 12(3x) - 12(5y) - 14(2) - 14(-8y)$$
$$= 36x - 60y - 28 + 112y$$
$$= 36x - 60y + 112y - 28$$

Combine like terms

$$= 36x + 52y - 28$$

Problem 3 ____

Find the area of the figure.

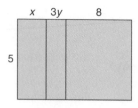

Solution   **Method 1**   The area of rectangle I is $8x$.
The area of rectangle II is $8y$.
The total area will be $8x + 8y$.

Method 2   The total length of the top is $x + y$.
The area is $8(x + y)$.

Because $8x + 8y$ and $8(x + y)$ are equivalent, both forms of the answer are equally valid.

Think and Discuss

1 Are $4x + 3 + 2x$ and $6x - 3$ equivalent expressions? Explain your answer.

2 Simplify $5x + 2 - x^2 + 3x^2 - 4x + 3$.

3 Explain why $8x + x = 9x$.

4 Explain why $7(5x) = 35x$.

5 Johnny said, "Terms with x and terms with x^2 should be like terms. They both include x's." Susie said, "They aren't like terms. If x represented length, x^2 would represent area." Who do you think was right and why?

6 a Express the total area of the figure in two different ways.
b Are the expressions equivalent?
c Defend your answer to the question in part **b**.

7 Use the equation $a(b + c) = ab + ac$.
  a Evaluate each side for $(a, b, c) = (5, 20, 7)$.
  b Which side was easier to evaluate?
  c Evaluate each side for $(a, b, c) = (27, 13, 7)$.
  d Which side was easier to evaluate?
  e When will the left side be easier to evaluate? When will the right side be easier to evaluate?

8 Is it always appropriate to change $\frac{9}{12}$ to $\frac{3}{4}$? Explain your answer.

9 The = sign in $3x + 4x = 7x$ means something different from the = sign in $x + 5 = 8$. Explain the difference between these two equations.

10 Nikita said, "Subtracting a positive number is just like adding a negative number." Explain why you think Nikita is or isn't correct.

Problems and Applications

11 Simplify each expression.
  a $8x + 5x + x$ **b** $5x + 3x - 8x$
  c $3x + 6y + 9x + y - x$ **d** $4x - 9 - 10x + 6$
  e $4x^2 + x - 8x^2 - 6x$ **f** $3(2x + 5y) - 8(3y - 5x)$

12 Write each expression in simplest form by combining like terms.
  a $x + x + x$ **b** $2xy + 9xy - xy$
  c $xy + x + y$ **d** $ab - ab$
  e $2xy + 5xy - x$

13 Write an algebraic statement to describe the drawings.

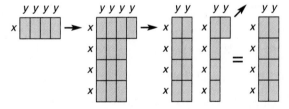

14 Match each item in the column on the left with an item in the column on the right.
  a x **i** $99x$
  b $2x + 3x$ **ii** $3(x + 2)$
  c $9x + 11x$ **iii** $5x$
  d $9(11x)$ **iv** $3x + 18$
  e $3(x + 6)$ **v** $9(x + 11)$
  f $3x + 6$ **vi** $1x$
  g $10(3x - x)$ **vii** $30x - 10x$

15 Is the statement *true* or *false* for $x = 4$ and $y = 9$?
  a $2x + 5x = 7x^2$ **b** $3y + 5y = 8y$
  c $36x + 14x = 50x$ **d** $2x + 7y + 9x + 11y = 29xy$

16 Write an expression in simplest form to represent

a The area of the rectangle

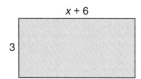

b The perimeter of the triangle

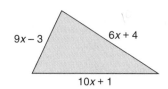

c The coordinates of points A, B, and C

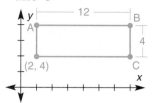

17 Simplify each expression.

a $\dfrac{-3}{4} + \dfrac{1}{2}$ 　　**b** $\dfrac{-3}{4}x + \dfrac{1}{2}x$ 　　**c** $\dfrac{-3}{4}xy + \dfrac{1}{2}x^2$

18 Simplify each expression.

a $3x + 6y$ 　　**b** $9x^2 - 6x$ 　　**c** $6x^2 + 3x - 4y + 2$

19 The lengths of line segments AB and CD are equal.

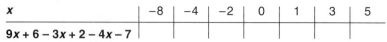

a Write an expression for the length of segment AB.

b Write an expression for the length of segment CD.

c If the lengths of segments AB and CD are each 16, what are the values of x and y?

d What would be the lengths of segments AB and CD if $(x, y) = (6, 9)$?

20 Complete the table.

x	−8	−4	−2	0	1	3	5
$9x + 6 - 3x + 2 - 4x - 7$							

21 **Communicating**　Explain why we write $3x - 3x = 0$, rather than $3x - 3x = 0x$.

22 Simplify each expression.

a $8(6.5) - 16\left(\dfrac{3}{4}\right) + 100(3.15)$ 　　**b** $14(2x - 6y) - 9(4 - 3x)$

c $19x + (-6x)$

23 **a** Write an expression for the length of the segment.

b Find the length of the segment for $x = 0.1$.

24 Simplify each expression.

a $-2(3x - 8y) - (4y + 2x)$ 　　**b** $5(2x - 6y^2) + 3(5x - 8x^2)$

$-6x + 16y - 4y - 2x$

25 **a** Write an expression to represent the perimeter of triangle TRI.

b Use the values $x \geq 1$. Create a spreadsheet to calculate the length of each side of the triangle, the sum of the sides, and the simplified form of the expression for the perimeter.

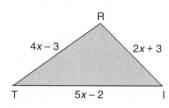

26 Mental Math Without using a calculator or a pencil and paper, evaluate each expression.

a $37 \cdot 2 + 37 \cdot 5 + 37 \cdot 3$ **b** $8 \cdot 23 + 23 \cdot 3 - 23 \cdot 11$

c $137 \cdot 93 - 37 \cdot 93$

27 Find the value of x and y if $5x + 5y = 30$ and $x + y = 6$.

28 Communicating The two expressions $18 + (-5)$ and $18 + -5$ mean the same thing. Why might someone want to use one form or the other?

◀ LOOKING BACK **Spiral Learning** LOOKING AHEAD ▶

---

29 Indicate whether each statement is *true* or *false*.

a If $x = 8$, then $x^2 - x = 56$. **b** If $x = 1$, then $x^0 + x^1 = 1$.

30 Write an expression to represent each phrase.

a 5 more than 27 **b** The product of 7 and 11 **c** 3 less than 56

31 Evaluate $2x - y$ for the following values.

a $(x, y) = (-5, 7)$ **b** $(x, y) = (-3, -8)$

32 Solve each equation for x.

a $x - 12 = 57$ **b** $\frac{x}{12} = 57$ **c** $12x = 57$

33 Evaluate each expression and divide the result by -9.

a $-859 + 958$ **b** $-813 + 318$ **c** $-512 + 215$

34 Find the next three terms in the pattern. $\frac{1}{3}, \frac{3}{5}, \frac{5}{7}, \frac{7}{9}$

35 Fill in each blank with one of the symbols $<$, $>$, or $=$.

a $3(5)$ _____ $3(4)$ **b** $0(5)$ _____ $0(4)$ **c** $-2(5)$ _____ $-2(4)$

Investigation

The Fibonacci Sequence The first two numbers in the following pattern are both 1. Each number after that is the sum of the two numbers that precede it. Continuing in this manner, you form the Fibonacci sequence.

$$1, 1, 2, 3, 5, 8, 13, 21, \ldots$$

You can generate some Fibonacci-like sequences by starting with two numbers that aren't both 1. For example, write several terms of the sequences whose first two terms are

1. 3, 3,… **2.** 2, 1,… **3.** x, x,…

Try some of your own. Then, for both the Fibonacci sequence and for your Fibonacci-like sequences, use your calculator to investigate the pattern of the ratios of one term to the next.

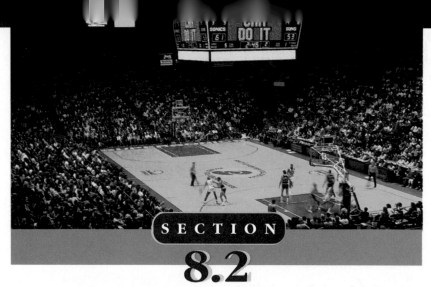

SECTION

8.2

Using Variables

EXPRESSIONS TO DESCRIBE PHRASES

Many math problems start as a situation described in words. The first step in solving these problems is to translate the words into symbols.

The phrase "2 more than 47" can be written as $47 + 2$.
The phrase "2 less than a number" can be written as $n - 2$.
The phrase "half of a number" can be written as $\frac{n}{2}$.

Example 1
Translate each phrase into an expression.
a The product of 4 and a number
b The quotient of 16 divided by a number

Solution
We can use any variable to represent the number.
a $4 \cdot x$ or $4x$
b $16 \div y$ or $\frac{16}{y}$

EXPRESSIONS TO DESCRIBE SITUATIONS

Many problems are based on physical situations, such as a drawing. In these problems, using symbols to represent the situation is the first step in solving the problem.

Example 2

a Write an expression for the area of each rectangle.

b Write an expression for the perimeter of each rectangle.

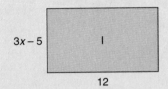

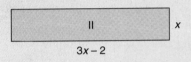

Solution

a The formula for the area of a rectangle is $A = \ell w$.

For rectangle I, $A = 12(3x - 5)$
For rectangle II, $A = x(3x - 2)$

b A formula for the perimeter is $P = 2\ell + 2w$.

For rectangle I, $P = 2(3x - 5) + 2(12) = 6x + 14$
For rectangle II, $P = 2(x) + 2(3x - 2) = 8x - 4$

EQUATIONS TO REPRESENT PROBLEMS

If we know that two or more expressions represent equal quantities, we use an equation to find out more about the problem.

Example 3

In the previous example, suppose the area of rectangle I is equal to the area of rectangle II. Write an equation to represent this equality.

Solution

From the previous example, we know the following:

$$\text{Area of rectangle I} = 12(3x - 5)$$
$$\text{Area of rectangle II} = x(3x - 2)$$

Since the areas are equal, $12(3x - 5) = x(3x - 2)$.

Example 4

Write an equation suggested by the figure.

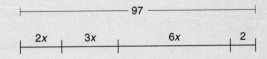

Solution

The total length is described in two ways.

$$\text{Total length} = 97$$
$$\text{Total length} = 2x + 3x + 6x + 2$$

An equation is $2x + 3x + 6x + 2 = 97$.

Problem 1   Lydia has drawn and labeled a line segment.

$$\vdash\!\!\overset{3x}{\rule{2.5cm}{0pt}}\!\!\!\vdash\!\!\overset{x-5}{\rule{2.5cm}{0pt}}\!\!\!\vdash\!\!\overset{6x-8}{\rule{2.5cm}{0pt}}\!\!\dashv$$

Write an expression to represent the segment.

Solution   The length of the segment is $3x + x - 5 + 6x - 8$. This expression can be simplified to $10x - 13$.

Problem 2   In Friday's basketball game, Al made six more baskets than Barry. Barry made twice as many baskets as Carl. Together, the three players made 56 baskets. Write an equation to represent this situation.

Solution   **Method 1**   Let A = the number of baskets Al made, B = the number of baskets Barry made, and C = the number of baskets Carl made. An equation is $A + B + C = 56$.

This equation has three variables. For this problem, it will be easier to use only one variable.

Method 2   Start with the equation $A + B + C = 56$. We know that Al made six more baskets than Barry ($A = B + 6$). Barry made twice as many baskets as Carl ($B = 2C$). Substitute equal quantities:

$$A + B + C = 56$$

$A = B + 6$ $B + 6 + B + C = 56$
$B = 2C$ $2C + 6 + 2C + C = 56$
Combine like terms $(2 + 2 + 1)C + 6 = 56$
                              $5C + 6 = 56$

Method 3   We know how many baskets Carl made, and we can work backward to find the number of baskets Bob and Al made.

Let x = the number of baskets Carl made.
Barry made twice as many baskets as Carl.
Let $2x$ = the number of baskets Barry made.
Al made six more baskets than Barry.
Let $2x + 6$ = the number of baskets Al made.
The three made a total of 56 baskets.

$$x + 2x + (2x + 6) = 56$$

Combine like terms $5x + 6 = 56$

Think and Discuss

1 Write an expression to represent each phrase. Simplify the expression.
  a The sum of 8 and its opposite
  b The product of $\frac{2}{3}$ and its reciprocal
  c The sum of x and its opposite
  d The product of y and its reciprocal (assume $y \neq 0$)

2 Write a phrase that represents each expression.
  a $x + 4$ **b** $9 - x$ **c** $x - 9$
  d $9 < x$ **e** $x < 9$ **f** $3x + 5$

3 Demonstrate that $5x - 12 = 5x - 12$ is true for all values of x.

4 The area of the rectangle is equal to the area of the triangle.

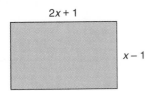
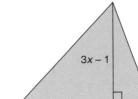

  a Write an expression to represent the area of the rectangle.
  b Write an expression to represent the area of the triangle.
  c Write an equation to express the equality.

5 **Business** Sally sells seashells at Seashore Susie's. Sally's salary is $3 per hour plus a 12% commission on her sales.
  a If Sally works 8 hours and sells shells worth $60, what is her pay?
  b If Sally works b hours and sells seashells worth d, what is her pay?

6 A box has length ℓ, width w, and height h.
  a Write an expression to represent the volume of the box.
  b Write an expression to represent the surface area of the box.

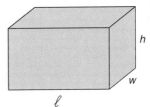

7 Write several expressions to represent the total length of the segment. Explain which form is simplest.

8 Match each phrase with its algebraic representation.
  a $2(N - 3)$ **i**   3 more than twice a number
  b $3 - N$ **ii**   3 is greater than twice a number
  c $3 > 2N$ **iii** Twice the difference of 3 and a number
  d $2N + 3$ **iv**   3 less than a number
  e $N - 3$ **v**   The product of 3 and a number
  f $3N$ **vi**   3 decreased by a number

Problems and Applications

9 Translate each phrase into an algebraic expression and each algebraic expression into a phrase.

a 6 less than a number

b $\frac{x}{2}$

c Twice the sum of a number and 3

d $5 - n$

10 Segment AB is equal in length to segment CD. Write an equation to represent this equality.

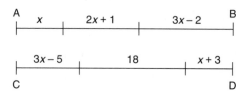

11 **Consumer Math** Rich bought an item that cost P and had a 6% sales tax added to the price. Write a formula for the total cost C of the item

12 In the figure, $\ell \| m$. Write an equation suggested by the figure.

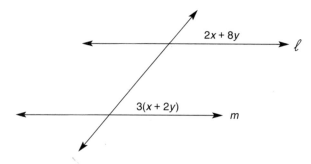

13 Andy is paid $4 per hour plus 9% commission on his sales.
a If he works 6 hours and sells $850 worth of goods, write an expression for his earnings.
b If he works H hours and sells D dollars of goods, write an expression for his income.

14 Write at least two equations that can represent the parallelogram.

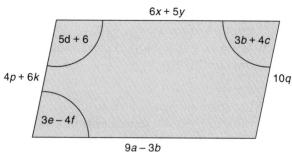

15 Yogi, Mickey, and Casey have a total of 63 hits. In the baseball season to date, Mickey has 14 more hits than Yogi. Yogi has 3 times as many hits as Casey. Use one or more variables and write one or more equations.

16 **Communicating** Explain the difference between the phrases "13 more than 10" and "13 is more than 10."

17 Write an equation for each right triangle.

a

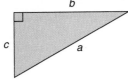

b

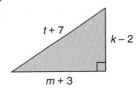

18 There are 2 inches of snow on the ground. Then its starts snowing at a rate of $\frac{1}{2}$ inch per hour. Write an expession for the depth of the snow after it has been snowing for

a 1 hour   **b** 2 hours   **c** 3 hours   **d** h hours

19 Write an equation to represent that AB = CD.

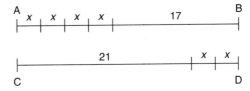

20 In $\triangle ABC$, the length of $\overline{AC}$ is twice the length of $\overline{AB}$ and the length of $\overline{BC}$ is 9 more than the length of $\overline{AB}$.

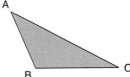

   a Write an expression for the perimeter of $\triangle ABC$ using only one variable.
   b If the perimeter of the triangle is 91, write an equation that represents the perimeter of the triangle in terms of the expression you wrote for part **a.**

21 A plane is at 33,000 feet. It descends 400 feet per minute. Find an expression for the plane's altitude after the plane has descended for

   a 1 minute   **b** 2 minutes
   c 3 minutes   **d** 4 minutes
   e m minutes

22 Write an expression for
   a The area of the base of the box
   b The volume of the box
   c The perimeter of the base of the box

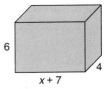

23 The length of one diagonal of a quadrilateral is $2x + 4y$ and the length of the other diagonal is $6x + 3$.
   a If the figure is a rectangle, can an equation describe the diagonals? If so, what is the equation?
   b If the figure is a trapezoid, can an equation describe the diagonals? If so, what is the equation?

24 If A = apples, B = basket and P = pear, the B had a total of $10A$ and at least one P. Carlos took $2A$ and $1P$. There are 12 pieces of fruit left. How many pears were in the basket originally?

25 Simplify each expression.

a $x - (3x + 5)$ **b** $3(x + y) + 12(x + y) - 4(x + y)$

26 a If $7(a + b) = 84$, what is $a + b$?   **b** If $p + q = 5$, what is $7(p + q) - 8$?

27 Find the perimeter of the quadrilateral if $(x, y) = (3, -2)$.

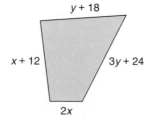

28 Evaluate each expression.

a $-3(5 - 12)$ **b** $-3(5) - 12$ **c** $-35 - 12$

29 Fill in each blank with one of the symbols <, >, or =.

a -3 _____ 15 **b** $-3 + 2$ _____ $15 + 2$

c $(-3)(2)$ _____ $(15)(2)$ **d** $-3 - 2$ _____ $15 - 2$

e $(-3)(-2)$ _____ $(15)(-2)$ **f** $\frac{-3}{-2}$ _____ $\frac{15}{-2}$

30 Draw a pentagon with the segments of the sides extended as shown. Measure the five marked angles. Find the sum of the measures of the five angles.

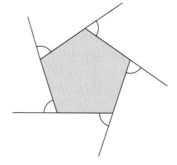

31 Communicating   Explain in detail the steps that must be taken to

a Evaluate $3x + 7$ for $x = 4$

b Solve the equation $2x + 5 = 35$ without using a calculator or pencil and paper

32 If $2x + 2y = 12$, what is the value of $6x + 6y$?

Investigation

Science   What shape is a single soap bubble as it floats in the air? What shape is a raindrop as its falls through the air? Find out why these shapes are formed naturally. Give some other examples.

SECTION 8.3

Solving Equations

In Section 3.4, we learned that we could use inverse operations to solve equations.

Example 1

Solve the equation $x + 57 = 126$ for x.

Solution

Since 57 added to x equals 126, we can find x by subtracting 57 from 126.

$$126 - 57 = 69$$

To see if 69 is the correct answer, check:

$$\text{Does } 69 + 57 = 126? \text{ Yes.}$$

So the answer is $x = 69$.

Example 2

Solve $y - 34.9 = 66.6$ for y.

Solution

Since 34.9 is subtracted from y, add 34.9 to each side of the equation. On the next page, you will see two different forms that can be used to solve the equation.

Horizontal Form	Vertical Form
$y - 34.9 = 66.6$	$y - 34.9 = 66.6$
$y - 34.9 + 34.9 = 66.6 + 34.9$	$+ 34.9 \quad +34.9$
$y = 101.5$	$y + 0 = 101.5$
	$y = 101.5$

Check the answer. $y - 34.9 = 101.5 - 34.9$
                              $= 66.6$

The correct answer is $y = 101.5$.

In general, using inverse operations can help you solve many equations. In Example 1, 57 is added to x, so you subtracted 57 from both sides of the equation. In Example 2, 34.9 is subtracted from y, so you added 34.9 to both sides of the equation.

EQUATIONS WITH SEVERAL OPERATIONS

In many equations, more than one operation is used with the variable. When this happens, we need to remember the order of operations we learned in Section 2.1.

Example 3
Write an equation to represent the diagram, and find the value of x.

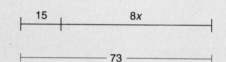

Solution
We can write the equation $15 + 8x = 73$ and solve for x.

Remember the order of operations. First, the variable x is multiplied by 8. Then, 15 is added to $8x$. To solve the equation, we will do the inverse operations in reverse order. First subtract 15 from each side of the equation, then divide each side of the equation by 8.

	$15 + 8x = 73$
First, subtract 15	$-15 \qquad -15$
	$8x = 58$
Then divide by 8	$\dfrac{8x}{8} = \dfrac{58}{8}$
	$x = 7.25$
Check the answer	$15 + 8x = 15 + 8(7.25)$
	$= 15 + 58$
	$= 73$

The answer is $x = 7.25$.

Example 4

Solve the equation $6y - 12 = 42$.

Solution

Method 1

Add 12 to each side

$$\begin{array}{rcl} 6y - 12 &=& 42 \\ +12 && +12 \\ \hline 6y &=& 54 \end{array}$$

Divide each side by 6

$$\frac{6y}{6} = \frac{54}{6}$$

$$y = 9$$

Check the answer

$$6 \cdot 9 - 12 = 54 - 12 = 42$$

Method 2

First let's divide each side by 6

$$6y - 12 = 42$$

$$\frac{6y - 12}{6} = \frac{42}{6}$$

$$\frac{6y}{6} - \frac{12}{6} = \frac{42}{6}$$

$$y - 2 = 7$$

Add 2 to each side

$$\begin{array}{rcl} y - 2 &=& 7 \\ +2 && +2 \\ \hline y &=& 9 \end{array}$$

We arrive at the same solution using either method.

Sample Problem

Problem Assume the measure of each of the 15 angles is k. Find k.

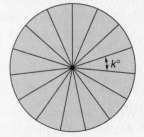

Solution There are 15 congruent angles, each $k°$, in the circle. The total number of degrees in all the angles in the center of the circle is $15k$. We also know that the sum of the measures of the fifteen angles will be 360. Therefore, we can use these two facts to write the equation $15k = 360$. Since k is multiplied by 15, we use the inverse operation, dividing by 15, to solve the equation.

Divide by 15

$$\frac{15k}{15} = \frac{360}{15}$$

$$\frac{15}{15} = 1$$

$$1k = k$$

$$1k = 24$$

$$k = 24$$

Check the answer

$$15k = 15(24)$$

$$= 360$$

The measure of each central angle k is 24.

Think and Discuss

1 To get dressed, we put on socks, then shoes. Later, we remove the shoes first, then the socks. This is an example of using inverse operations in reverse order. Give two more examples.

2 Identify each statement as an equation or an expression. If it is an equation, solve it. If it is an expression, simplify it.
 a $3x - 82 + 53$ **b** $3x - 82 = 53$
 c $12 - 5x = -18$ **d** $12 - 5x - 18$
 e $12 = 5x - 18$ **f** $6 - (x - 2)$

3 Each equation in the first column can be solved by using one of the steps in the second column. Match each equation with its step. Explain why you made each match and how you would apply the step.
 a $x + 17 = 34$ **i**   add 17
 b $x - 17 = 34$ **ii**   subtract 17
 c $17x = 34$ **iii**   multiply by 17
 d $\frac{x}{17} = 34$ **iv**   divide by 17

4 **a** Write an equation that represents that the length of $\overline{AB}$ is equal to the length of $\overline{CD}$.
 b Solve the equation in part **a**.
 c Does your answer make sense? Explain why.

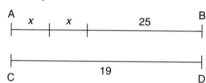

5 Write each statement as an equation or as an expression.
 a Seven is three more than a number
 b Seven more than a number
 c Seven more than three times a number
 d Seven more than three times a number is twelve
 e Seven more than three is a number

6 When Moe and Curly solved the equation $3x + 15 = 57$, they each found that $x = 14$. Explain the different forms they used.

Moe's Solution	**Curly's Solution**
$3x + 15 = 57$	$3x + 15 = 57$
$3x + 15 = 57$	$\dfrac{3x + 15}{3} = \dfrac{57}{3}$
$\dfrac{-15 \quad -15}{3x \qquad = 42}$	$x + 5 = 19$
	$\dfrac{-5 \quad -5}{x \qquad = 14}$
$\dfrac{3x}{3} = \dfrac{42}{3}$	
$x = 14$	

Problems and Applications

7 Solve each equation for x.
  a $12x = 66$
  b $3x + 5x = 7(6)$
  c $3x + 2y = -6$, if $y = 9$

8 Solve each equation for y.
  a $-19 - 6y = -43$
  b $7y - 3 = 53$
  c $19 + 8y = 47$
  d $3y + 42 = 21$

9 Solve each equation or simplify each expression.
  a $2 + 5x - 3 - 2x + 8$
  b $2 = 5x - 3 - 2x + 8$
  c $2 + 5x - 3 - 2x = 8$
  d $2 - 5x - 3 - 2(x + 8)$

10 **Communicating** Segment AB is equal in length to segment CD.
  a Write an equation that describes the equality.
  b Solve the equation for x.
  c Does the answer make sense? Explain why you think it does or does not.

A $x + 18$ $13 - x$ $7 - x$ B

C 42 D

11 Solve each equation or simplify each expression.
  a $19x = 85.5$
  b $x + 349 = 156$
  c $a + b + 3a - 4b$
  d $y - 43.25 = 103.26$
  e $92 = 4t - 16$
  f $24k = 463.2$
  g $45 = 19 - 2k$
  h $m - 392 + m$
  i $5x - 10x^2$
  j $d + d + d = 963$
  k $6 - 5t = -129$
  l $10 - (3x - 5)$

12 Karen taped a key to an index card and placed it in an envelope. Then she put the envelope in a box. Next she wrapped the box in paper and mailed it to Kitty. Describe the correct order of the process Kitty must use to get the key.

13 This figure is a regular octagon. All of its angles have the same measure. The sum of the measure of the angles is 1080. Find the measure of each angle.

14 **Aviation** An airplane is at 14,000 feet when the pilot is told by air traffic control to ascend to 24,000 feet. The pilot puts the plane into a climb rate of 425 feet/minute.
  a Write an expression for the height of the plane after it has ascended for t minutes.
  b Write an equation for the time it takes the plane to reach its assigned height.
  c Solve the equation in part **b**. What does your answer represent?

15 The area of the figure is 57 square units.
  a Write an equation that describes the area of the figure.
  b Solve the equation for x.

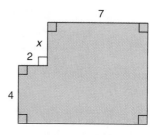

16 **Business**   Juan works at the Higgly-Piggly. He is paid $5.75 per hour Monday through Saturday. On Sunday he is paid time and a half (one and one half times his hourly pay). Let w = the number of Juan's Monday-through-Saturday hours and s = the number of Juan's Sunday hours.
  a Write an expression for his total pay for the week.
  b If Juan worked 35 hours Monday through Saturday and had a total weekly pay of $280, how many hours did he work on Sunday?

17 In $\triangle ABC$, $\angle A = (12x + 5)°$, $\angle B = (9x + 15)°$, and $\angle C = (2x - 1)°$.

  a Write an equation to describe the sum of the measures of the angles. (Hint: The sum of the angles in a triangle is 180°.)
  b Solve the equation for x.
  c Find the measures of angles A, B, and C.

18 **Communicating**   Bertha buys a box of beeswax and pays 6% sales tax. The total cost is $25.97.
  a Explain what each term of the equation $x + 0.06x = 25.97$ represents.
  b Solve the equation for x. What does x represent?

19 ABCD is a parallelogram.
  a Write an equation that can be used to determine a.
  b Solve the equation for a.
  c The perimeter of ABCD is 34. How long is $\overline{AD}$? How long is $\overline{BC}$?
  d What is the value of b?

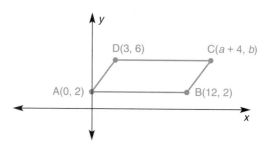

20 **Health**   To determine your target heart rate for one minute of aerobic exercise, subtract your age from 220 and multiply the result by 75%.
  a Compute your target heart rate.
  b If a represents age, write an expression for target heart rate.
  c Use a spreadsheet to calculate target heart rates for ages 10 through 60.

21 The probability a dart that lands on the figure will be in the shaded square is .4.
  a Write an equation, in terms of x, that describes this situation.
  b Find the value of x.

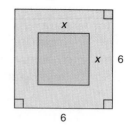

22 Evaluate each expression.
   a $\sqrt{36}$ **b** $\sqrt{25 + 144}$ **c** $\sqrt{5}$ **d** $\sqrt{25} + \sqrt{144}$

23 Evaluate each expression.
   a $|8| - |5|$ **b** $|5 - 8|$ **c** $|8 - 5|$ **d** $|5| - |8|$

24 **Communicating** Sticks can be used to make a "raft." Discuss the symmetries of the "raft" shown.

25 Evaluate each expression.
   a $-2(6 - 3 - 5)$ **b** $\frac{-3}{8}(-8 + 16 - 32 + 64 - 128)$

26 An angle has measure x. Write an expression for the measure of
   a The complement of the angle   **b** The supplement of the angle

27 Graph each inequality.
   a $-2 < x$ **b** $x \geq 7$ **c** $-5 < x \leq 2$

28 If $8x - 8y = 12$, find the value of $6x - 6y$.

29 Copy the diagram and shade each region described.
   a $4 \leq x \leq 7$ using ▨
   b $2 \leq y \leq 4$ using ▨
   c What is the area of the region that is shaded both ways ▨?

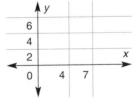

30 Perform the indicated operation.
   a $8.7 - 9.16$ **b** $\frac{3}{5} + \frac{1}{2}$ **c** $\frac{3}{5} - \frac{1}{2}$ **d** $\frac{1}{3} - \frac{1}{2}$

Investigation

Consumer Mathematics A store advertises a sale with a sign that reads, "20% off!" However, the store must add 5% tax to the price of your purchase. Will you pay more if the clerk calculates the tax first or the discount first? Use expressions from algebra to support your argument.

8.4
Some Special Equations

ABSOLUTE-VALUE EQUATIONS

To solve an equation that contains an absolute value, we apply the definition of absolute value.

Example 1
Solve the equation $|x| + 8 = 36$ for x.

Solution
Subtract 8 from each side or add −8 to each side.

$$\begin{array}{rcl} |x| + 8 & = & 36 \\ -8 & & -8 \\ \hline |x| & & = 28 \end{array}$$

In solving an equation, we try to find all values that work. There are two numbers, −28 and 28, that have an absolute value of 28. The equation has two solutions, $x = 28$ or $x = -28$.

Example 2
Solve the equation $|q| = -35$ for q.

Solution
Recall that the absolute value of a number cannot be negative. This equation has no solution.

EQUATIONS WITH SQUARE ROOTS

Squaring and finding the square root are inverse operations. You can use this idea in Examples 3 and 4.

Example 3

Solve the equation $\sqrt{r} = 4$ for r.

Solution

The inverse operation of taking the square root is squaring (raising to the second power).

Square both sides of the equation
$$\sqrt{r} = 4$$
$$\left(\sqrt{r}\right)^2 = (4)^2$$
$$r = 16$$

Check to see that the answer is correct.

Example 4

Solve the equation $y^2 = 25$ for y.

Solution

In the equation, y is squared, and the inverse of squaring is taking the square root. So you can find one answer by taking the square root of 25.

$$\text{If } y^2 = 25, \text{ then } y = 5.$$

But is 5 the only answer? What if y is negative? Since $(-5)^2$ also equals 25, the equation has two answers.

$$\text{If } y^2 = 25, \text{ then } y = 5 \text{ or } y = -5.$$

Always look for two answers in an equation with an x^2 term..

SIMPLIFYING TO SOLVE EQUATIONS

Sometimes one or both sides of an equation have expressions that must be simplified before we can solve the equation.

Example 5

Solve the equation $3(-5n + 8) = 237$ for n.

Solution

To solve the equation in Example 5, start by distributing multiplication over addition on the left side of the equation.

$$3(-5n + 8) = 237$$

Subtract 24 on each side $\qquad$ $-15n + 24 = 237$

$$\underline{-24 \quad -24}$$

Divide both sides by -15 $\qquad$ $-15n = 213$

$$\frac{-15n}{-15} = \frac{213}{-15}$$

$$n = -14.2$$

If we check the answer, we will see that $n = -14.2$ is the correct answer.

Sample Problems

Problem 1   Solve $|x - 3| = 5$ for x. Graph the solution on the number line. Explain where the points are in relation to the number 3.

Solution   We know that the absolute value of the number $x - 3$ is 5, so $x - 3$ can be either 5 or -5. Let's try both numbers.

$$x - 3 = 5 \qquad \text{or} \qquad x - 3 = -5$$
$$x = 8 \qquad\qquad\qquad x = -2$$

Check the answers $\qquad |8 - 3| = |5| = 5$

$$|-2 - 3| = |-5| = 5$$

The solutions of the equation are 8 and -2.

$$-3 \; -2 \; -1 \;\; 0 \;\; 1 \;\; 2 \;\; 3 \;\; 4 \;\; 5 \;\; 6 \;\; 7 \;\; 8$$

Both points are exactly five units from 3 on the number line.

Problem 2   Solve the equation $\sqrt{x} + 8 = 19$ for x.

Solution   Subtract 8 from both sides $\qquad \sqrt{x} + 8 = 19$

$$\underline{\phantom{\sqrt{x} +} -8 \quad -8}$$

Square both sides $\qquad\qquad\qquad \sqrt{x} = 11$

$$(\sqrt{x})^2 = 11^2$$

$$x = 121$$

Check the answer $\qquad\qquad\qquad \sqrt{x} + 8$
$$= \sqrt{121} + 8$$
$$= 11 + 8$$
$$= 19$$

The correct answer is $x = 121$.

1 Solve each equation for x.

a $|x| + 4 = 21$ **b** $|x + 4| = 21$

c $|x + 4| = 0$ **d** $|x| + 4 = 0$

e Explain the difference between parts **a** and **b**.

f Explain why there is only one answer to part **c**.

2 Is the equation $x(x + 3) = x^2 + 3x$ true for

a $x = 1$?   **b** $x = 4$?   **c** $x = -6$?

d $x = \frac{3}{5}$?   **e** $x = 0$?

f For how many values of x can the equation $x(x + 3) = x^2 + 3x$ be true?

3 Ms. E. Kwayshun gave her class the problem

$$3x + 5x + 9 - 2 = 5 + 8$$

Kwami said, "First, we combine the like terms on the left and get $8x + 7$. Then, we do the arithmetic on the right to get 13. Now it's $8x + 7 = 13$." Gyo argued, "That can't be right. We didn't do the same thing on each side." Who was right, Kwami or Gyo? Why?

4 Discuss what types of equations have more than one solution.

5 Is the statement true *always, sometimes,* or *never?*

a $|x| = x$ **b** $|x| = -x$

c $|x| \geq 0$ **d** $|x - 10| < 0$

6 Solve each equation for y.

a $-4(\sqrt{y} - 6) = 12$ **b** $y^2 = 49$

c $\sqrt{y} = -6$

Problems and Applications

7 For each equation, tell how many values of x are solutions. Find the solutions.

a $\sqrt{x} = 16$ **b** $x^2 = 16$

c $x^2 = x$ **d** $2(x + 4) = 2x + 8$

8 Solve each equation for k.

a $|k| = -3$ **b** $|k| - 9 = -2$

c $|k - 1| = 5$

9 Solve each equation for x.

a $\sqrt{x} = 9$ **b** $\sqrt{x} = -9$ **c** $x^2 = 9$

10 Solve each equation for n.

a $5(3n - 7) = 55$ **b** $5(3n - 7) = 4$

11 Jeff wants to enlarge a room so that it will have an area of 162 square feet, as in the diagram. He needs to find the value of x. He wrote the formula $A = 12(8 + x)$ for the area.

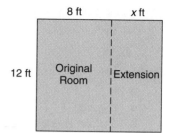

a Use Jeff's formula and solve for x.

b Find a way to find the size of the extension without using Jeff's area formula.

12 Solve each equation or simplify each expression.

a $3(7n - 38) = 138$

b $|a - 5| = 13$

c $\sqrt{x} + 3\sqrt{x} - 5$

d $\sqrt{x} - 3 = 5$

e $2\sqrt{y} - 9 = 13$

f $3x^2 - 6(4 - x^2)$

g $3x^2 + 6x^2 = 36$

h $4x - (3 - x)$

13 Find the value of x that makes 50 the perimeter of the triangle.

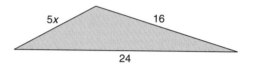

14 Find the value of w, x, y, and z in the equation $\begin{bmatrix} 2x - 10 & 3y \\ \frac{1}{2}w & 4 - z \end{bmatrix} = \begin{bmatrix} 22 & -24 \\ 40 & 30 \end{bmatrix}$

15 **Business** The cost of producing an open-top cubical container is \$5 per square foot of base and \$8 per square foot of the sides.

a Write a formula for the cost C of the entire container.

b Find the difference in the cost of a container with edges that are 3 feet long and the cost of a container with edges that are 4 feet long.

16 Solve each equation or simplify each expression.

a $3[4 + (3)(-2)] = 3x - (x - 10)$

b $3[4 + 5(-6)] + 3x - (x - 10)$

c $15 - (9 - p) = 14\left(\frac{1}{2}\right) - 3\left(\frac{2}{3}\right)$

d $\frac{1}{4}(8x) - 2(15 - \frac{1}{2}x)$

e $\frac{2}{3}(6 - 12y) + 5\left(\frac{1}{5} + 2y\right)$

f $5(-3m + 6) = 660$

g $3a + 6 = 90$

17 The area of rectangle ABCD is 42. Find the value of a.

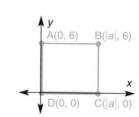

18 Find the value of x so that the perimeter of the square is equal to the perimeter of the triangle.

19 Refer to the expressions $x + 75$, $x + 5$, $x - 10$, x, and $x + 100$.
a Arrange the data from smallest to largest.
b What is x if the median is 200?

20 Use a number line to graph the values of x for which $|x| = x$.

21 The diagonals of a rhombus are 12 and 16. Determine the value of x if the length of each side is $4x - 2$.

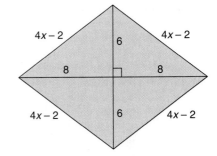

22 Solve the equation $(0.2)(0.3)(0.4)x = (0.5)(0.6)$.

23 Write an inequality to represent each graph.

a

b

24 a List the operations, in order, that should be used to evaluate the expression $\sqrt{x^2 - 25}$ for $x = 13$.

b List the operations, in order, that should be used to solve the equation $\sqrt{x^2 - 9} = 5$.

25 **Spreadsheets** Set up a spreadsheet like the one shown, using values for x from -10 to 10. (Note: Different spreadsheets use different notations for square root and absolute value.) What do you notice about columns $|x|$ and $\sqrt{x^2}$?

	A	B	C	D
1	x	x^2	$|x|$	$\sqrt{x^2}$
2				
3	-10			
4	-9			
	.			
	.			
	.			
	.			
	.			
23	10			

26 Find the value(s) of t that describe the indicated length of the number line.

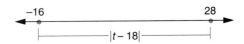

27 Indicate whether the statement is *true* or *false*.

a $15 > 10$ **b** $15 + 7 > 10 + 7$ **c** $15 - 7 > 10 - 7$

d $15(7) > 10(7)$ **e** $15(-7) > 10(-7)$ **f** $\frac{15}{-5} > \frac{10}{-5}$

28 Communicating   Explain why $5 > 2$, but $-5 < -2$.

29 a Find the area of rectangle ABCD.

b Move C and D three units to the right and three units down. What are the coordinates of the new points?

c Find the area of the new quadrilateral.

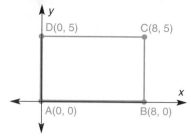

30 Find the value of x, y, and z if $2x = 12$, $y = x + 8$, and $3z - 1 = y$.

31 Solve each equation for x.

a $x(b + c) = 2(b + c)$ **b** $3x + ax = 5(a + 3)$

32 Simplify each expression.

a $-42 + 16$ **b** $-11 - 16$ **c** $(-11)(-16)$

d $(-11) - (-16)$ **e** $\frac{-11}{16} + \frac{1}{2}$ **f** $\frac{-8}{-4} - \frac{-4}{-2}$

33 Find the coordinates of the images of points A, B, and C when $\triangle$ABC is reflected over line ℓ.

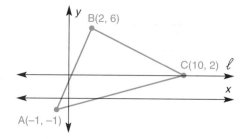

34 Find the number that will make the equation true if the number replaces the box.

a $\frac{1}{8} + \boxed{} = \frac{3}{4}$ **b** $\frac{3}{4} - \frac{\boxed{}}{3} = \frac{1}{12}$ **c** $\frac{5}{6} + \boxed{} = \frac{5}{4}$

Investigation

Science   What is the absolute, or Kelvin, temperature scale? What is absolute zero? Explain any connection between this use of the word *absolute* and the concept of absolute value. Write a formula showing how to convert a temperature from Celsius (C) to Kelvin (K).

SECTION

8.5

Solving Inequalities

ADDING AND SUBTRACTING

What happens when we add the same value to each side of the inequality $12 > -9$? What happens when we subtract the same value from each side?

Add 3 to each side.
$$12 + 3 > -9 + 3$$

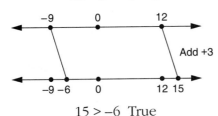

$15 > -6$ True

Add –3 to each side.
$$12 + (-3) > -9 + (-3)$$

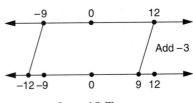

$9 > -12$ True

Subtract 3 from each side.
$$12 - 3 > -9 - 3$$

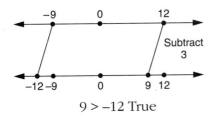

$9 > -12$ True

Subtract –3 from each side.
$$12 - (-3) > -9 - (-3)$$

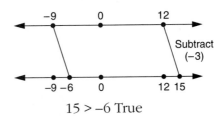

$15 > -6$ True

When the same value was added to or subtracted from both sides of the inequality, the order of the numbers stayed the same. This result leads to a rule for inequalities.

▶ **Addition and Subtraction Rule for Solving Inequalities**
If the same number is added to or subtracted from both sides of an inequality, an equivalent inequality results.

Inequalities involving addition and subtraction are solved in a way similar to the way we solve equations. We use the inverse operation.

Example 1

Solve the inequality $x + 315 > 296$ for x.

Solution

Subtract 315 from each side

$$\begin{array}{rcr} x + 315 & > & 296 \\ -315 & & -315 \\ \hline x & > & -19 \end{array}$$

Any number greater than -19 (-18.4, 234, 0, -15, or many others) makes the original inequality true. You may want to check some values.

MULTIPLYING AND DIVIDING

What happens to the inequality $12 > -9$ when we multiply or divide each side of the inequality by the same value?

Multiply each side by 3.
$$3(12) > 3(-9)$$

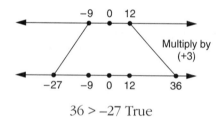

$36 > -27$ True

Multiply each side by -3.
$$-3(12) > -3(-9)$$

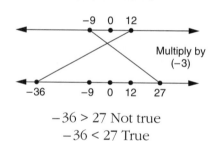

$-36 > 27$ Not true
$-36 < 27$ True

Divide each side by 3.
$$\frac{12}{3} > \frac{-9}{3}$$

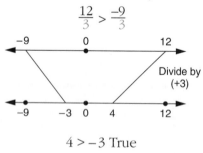

$4 > -3$ True

Divide each side by -3.
$$\frac{12}{-3} > \frac{-9}{-3}$$

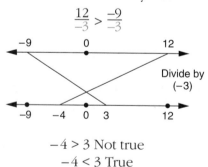

$-4 > 3$ Not true
$-4 < 3$ True

When we multiply or divide by a negative number, both numbers are reflected over the origin on the number line, and the order (direction of inequality) is reversed. This illustrates an important rule for solving inequalities.

▶ Multiplication and Division Rules for Solving Inequalities

If both sides of an inequality are multiplied or divided by a positive number, the result is an equivalent inequality with the same order.

If both sides of an inequality are multiplied or divided by a negative number, the result is an inequality with the order reversed.

Example 2

Solve the inequality $-4x > 34$ for x.

Solution

When we divide by -4, we reverse the order of the inequality.

$$-4x > 34$$

$$\frac{-4x}{-4} < \frac{34}{-4}$$

$$x < -8.5$$

Sample Problems

Problem 1

Solve the inequality $-19 + 8p \geq 37$ for p.

Solution   The symbol $\geq$ means "is greater than or equal to." It is a way to combine two separate statements: the equation $-19 + 8p = 37$ and the inequality $-19 + 8p > 37$.

Add 19 to each side

$$\begin{array}{r} -19 + 8p \geq 37 \\ +19 \qquad +19 \\ \hline 8p \geq 56 \end{array}$$

Divide each side by 8

$$\frac{8p}{8} \geq \frac{56}{8}$$

$$p \geq 7$$

Problem 2

Solve the inequality $5 - 8y \leq -35$ for y and graph the solution.

Solution   First, subtract 5 from each side of the inequality. This has the same effect as adding -5 to each side.

$$\begin{array}{r} 5 - 8y \leq -35 \\ -5 \qquad -5 \\ \hline -8y \leq -40 \end{array}$$

Divide by -8

$$\frac{-8y}{-8} \geq \frac{-40}{-8}$$

Change $\leq$ to $\geq$

$$y \geq 5$$

Graph this solution on a number line.

5

Problem 3 Write an inequality to represent the diagram.

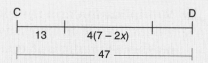

Solution   The length of $\overline{CD}$ is $13 + 4(7 - 2x)$ plus an unknown amount. The length is also 47. An inequality that represents this is $13 + 4(7 - 2x) < 47$.

Think and Discuss

1 Which of the following operations require reversing the order of an inequality? Explain your answer.
   a Add a positive number to each side
   b Add a negative number to each side
   c Multiply by a positive number on each side
   d Multiply by a negative number on each side
   e Subtract a positive number from each side
   f Subtract a negative number from each side
   g Divide by a positive number on each side
   h Divide by a negative number on each side

2 Explain the difference between $x > 7$ and $x \geq 7$.

3 Why does subtracting 5 have the same effect as adding -5?

4 If $y \not< 8$ (y is not less than 8) and $y \neq 8$, what do we know about y?

5 Use the inequality $13 + 4(7 - 2x) < 47$ from Sample Problem 3.
   a What are the possible values for x?
   b Explain why $13 + 4(7 - 2x) < 47$ represents the diagram in Sample Problem 3.

6 Is the statement true *always, sometimes,* or *never?*
   a If $x < 0$, then $x < -2$ **b** If $x > 3$, then $x > 0$ **c** $|x| < 0$

7 Is the inequality $x > -34.8$ *true* or *false* for the following values of x?
   a -40 **b** -34.08 **c** -34.80 **d** -34

Problems and Applications

8 Is the inequality $x \geq 31.7$ *true* or *false* for the following values of x?
   a -1 **b** 31.70 **c** 31.71 **d** 3.17
   e 31 **f** 31.07 **g** 37.1 **h** -30.7

9 If $z \not< 5$, what do we know about z?

10 Solve each inequality. Graph the solution on a number line.
   a $2x - 15 < 37$ **b** $-12 - 3x \geq -48$
   c $x + 43.6 > -91.7$ **d** $14 \geq 9x - 13$

11 Find the smallest integer that solves each inequality.
   a $3x - 6 > 23$ **b** $2x + 5 \geq -22$ **c** $10 - 3x \leq 56$

12 The mean of $3x$, $2x + 5$, $4x - 11$, and $18 - x$ is less than 21.
   a Write an inequality to represent this.
   b Solve the inequality for x.

13 Solve each inequality.
   a $3x + 52 > 13$ **b** $-14 - 6x \leq -98$
   c $-2x - 53 > 47$ **d** $9 > 3 + 2x$

14 Solve each equation or inequality. Simplify each expression.
   a $3 - 8x > 27$ **b** $3 - 8x + 27$
   c $-5(x + 3) > -10$ **d** $-5(x + 3) - 10$
   e $-4(3 - 2x) - (6 - 8x)$ **f** $-3(6 - 2x) \leq 15$
   g $4(3 - 2x) = 62$ **h** $\frac{-2}{3}x < \frac{-4}{5}$

15 Refer to the drawing.
   a Write an inequality to describe the figure.
   b Solve for x.
   c Graph the solutions for x on a number line.

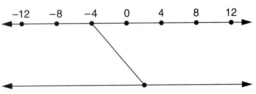

16 Copy the figure. Multiply $-\frac{1}{2}$ by the coordinate of each point shown on the top number line. Plot the results on the bottom number line, and draw segments connecting each point on the bottom number line with its corresponding point on the top number line. An example is shown.

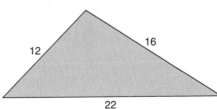

17 The perimeter of the square is at least 70% of the perimeter of the triangle. Find the value of x.

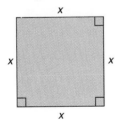

18 If $10° \leq y \leq 40°$, what is the range of x?

19 Solve each inequality for k.
 a $2(4k + 3k) > 56$ **b** $-2(4k + 3k) > 84$
 c $2k - 5k < -24$

20 For each statement, decide which symbol, <, >, or =, should replace the box.

 a $-6 \boxed{} 4$ **b** $\dfrac{-5}{8} \boxed{} \dfrac{(-5)(1)}{(8)(-1)}$

 c $(-3)(-6) \boxed{} (-3)(4)$ **d** $-\dfrac{-3}{-7} \boxed{} \dfrac{-3}{7}$

21 Find the value(s) of x.

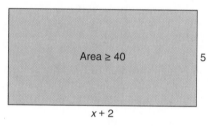

Area ≥ 40   5

$x + 2$

22 **Business** Jon's sales commission ranges from 2% to 7% depending on the items he sells. What is the range of possible commissions on the sale of a $650 item?

23 The coordinates of the set of points shown are each divided by -4. Show the new graph on a number line.

-8 -4

24 **Science** The high temperatures on the first six days of January were $-4°$, $6°$, $1°$, $11°$, $7°$, and $-2°$. What must be the high temperature on January 7 in order for the first week of January to have an average high temperature greater than 5°?

25 **Business** Yang receives an $8 bonus for every CD player she sells. Her CD sales bonus for December exceeded $150. What can we conclude about the number of CD players she sold in December?

26 Write an inequality having the form $nx \geq 20$ and having a solution given by the graph.

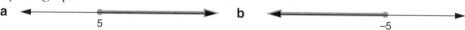

 a   5   **b** -5

27 Is the inequality $|x| > 5$ *true* or *false* for the following values of x?
 a 5.1 **b** -5.1
 c 5 **d** -5
 e 4.8 **f** -4.8
 g 7 **h** -7

28 The mean of -10, 6, x, 15, and 31 is greater than 5. Find the value of x.

29 **Communicating** Penny had a balance scale, but the left side was heavier than the right. She put the same type of coin on each side, and the left side remained heavier than the right side. She put more coins, the same number and the same type on each side. The left side was still heavier than the right side. Explain why Penny didn't get the scale to change position.

30 Solve each equation for x.
  a $|x| - 3 = 15$ **b** $|x - 3| = 15$
  c $\sqrt{x} = 36$ **d** $x^2 = 36$

31 Multiply $\begin{bmatrix} -4 & 13 \\ 16 & -2 \end{bmatrix} \cdot \begin{bmatrix} -2 & 3 \\ -1 & 1 \end{bmatrix}$.

32 a Solve $3y + 18 = 12$ for y.
  b Solve $3(a + b) + 18 = 12$ for $a + b$.
  c Solve $3(2x + 8) + 18 = 12$ for $2x + 8$.
  d Solve $3(2x + 8) + 18 = 12$ for x.

33 Segment AB is 8 units long. It is to be placed on a number line. Either A or B could be on the left.
  a If A is placed at -2, where is B?
  b If $\overline{AB}$ is centered at the origin, what are the coordinates of A and B?

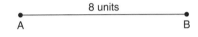

34 Which of the following are possible?
  a A trapezoid with rotation symmetry
  b A parallelogram with reflection symmetry
  c A rectangle with rotation symmetry
  d A rhombus with rotation symmetry
  e A trapezoid with reflection symmetry

35 ABCD is a square with its diagonals drawn as shown.
  a Name all pairs of segments that are parallel.
  b Name all pairs of segments that are perpendicular.

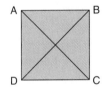

Investigation

The Triangle Inequality

1 Can you draw a triangle that has sides with the following dimensions? Explain your answer.
  a 4 in., 2 in., 7 in.   **b** 8 cm, 5 cm, 15 cm
  c 9 in., 1 in., 9 in.

2 The sides of one triangle are 3, 5, and x. Write an inequality that describes the possible values of x.

3 Find out what is meant by the triangle inequality in geometry.

8.6
Substitution

SPECIAL SUBSTITUTIONS

We have substituted values for variables in earlier sections. Now let's look at some special kinds of substitution.

Example 1

If $(x, y) = (12, -7)$, find the area of the parallelogram.

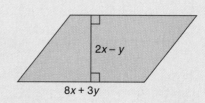

Solution

The base of the parallelogram is

$$8x + 3y$$
$$= 8(12) + 3(-7)$$
$$= 75$$

The height is

$$2x - y$$
$$= 2(12) - (-7)$$
$$= 31$$

The area is (base) × (height)

$$= (75)(31)$$
$$= 2325$$

Notice that when we substituted values for variables in Example 1, we used parentheses ( ). You will find parentheses to be a valuable tool when doing substitutions. Sometimes we substitute expressions for variables in order to solve equations.

Example 2

If $3x + 5y = 47$ and $x = 2y + 1$, find x and y.

Solution

$$3x + 5y = 47$$

Substitute $(2y + 1)$ for x $3(2y + 1) + 5y = 47$
Use the distributive property $6y + 3 + 5y = 47$
Combine like terms $11y + 3 = 47$
Subtract 3 $11y = 44$
Divide by 11 $y = 4$

Now that we know $y = 4$, we can find x.
$$x = 2y + 1$$
$$= 2(4) + 1$$
$$= 9$$

The answers are $x = 9$ and $y = 4$.

In Example 2, we again used parentheses around $2y + 1$ when we substituted for x. If we had not used parentheses, we could have distributed the multiplication incorrectly.

VARIABLES FOR EXPRESSIONS

You have simplified expressions like $3x + 5x = 8x$. The variable, x, can be any value.

Example 3

Simplify the expression $4(3x - 2) - 7(3x - 2) + 6(3x - 2)$.

Solution
Method 1
Using familiar techniques,

$$4(3x - 2) - 7(3x - 2) + 6(3x - 2)$$
$$= 12x - 8 - 21x + 14 + 18x - 12$$
$$= 12x - 21x + 18x - 8 + 14 - 12$$
$$= 9x - 6$$

Method 2
Think of $3x - 2$ as a single value.

$$4(3x - 2) - 7(3x - 2) + 6(3x - 2)$$
$$= (4 - 7 + 6)(3x - 2)$$
$$= 3(3x - 2)$$
$$= 9x - 6$$

Treating an expression as a single value can make some problems easier to solve.

Example 4

Simplify the expression $4(NUM) - 7(NUM) + 6(NUM)$.

Solution

$$4(NUM) - 7(NUM) + 6(NUM)$$
$$= (4 - 7 + 6)NUM$$
$$= 3(NUM)$$

Sample Problems

Problem 1

Find two numbers that have a ratio of 1:3 and a sum of 92.

Solution

Method 1 Call the numbers a and b. We know two facts: $\frac{a}{b} = \frac{1}{3}$ and $a + b = 92$. Using cross multiplication, $b = 3a$.

In the equation $a + b = 92$, we substitute $3a$ for b.

$$a + b = 92$$

Substitute $\qquad a + 3a = 92$

$$4a = 92$$
$$a = 23$$

If $a = 23$ and $b = 3a$, $b = 3(23)$, or 69.
The numbers are 23 and 69.

Method 2 Since the numbers are in the ratio 1:3, we can call the numbers $1x$ and $3x$. The sum of the numbers is 92, so

$$1x + 3x = 92$$
$$4x = 92$$
$$x = 23$$
$$3x = 69$$

Using either method, the numbers are 23 and 69.

Problem 2

The angles of a triangle are in the ratio 2:3:4. Find their measures.

Solution

If the numbers are in the ratio 2:3:4, we can call the angle measures $2x$, $3x$, and $4x$. We also know that the sum of the measures of the angles of a triangle are 180. We can write an equation.

$$2x + 3x + 4x = 180$$
$$9x = 180$$
$$x = 20$$

The measures of the angles are 2(20), or 40; 3(20), or 60; and 4(20), or 80.

Think and Discuss

1 Solve each equation.
   a Solve $3x + 8 = 26$ for x.
   b Solve $3 \cdot NUM + 8 = 26$ for NUM.
   c Solve $3(a + b) + 8 = 26$ for $a + b$.
   d Solve $3(5x - 9) + 8 = 26$ for $5x - 9$.
   e Solve $3(5x - 9) + 8 = 26$ for x. Use at least two methods.

2 a Describe how to solve for x and y if $2x - 6y = -8$ and $x = 9y - 6$.
   b Find x and y.

3 The word *substitute* is commonly used in conversation, as in a substitute teacher, a substitute player in sports, a substitute ingredient in a recipe, or a substitute part in a machine.
   a Give several other examples of substitutes.
   b Discuss similarities and differences between these uses of the word *substitute* and the mathematical use of the word.

4 The following procedure converts 8 feet to inches.

$$8 \text{ ft} = 8 \text{ ft } (1)$$
$$= 8 \text{ ft} \left(\frac{12 \text{ in.}}{1 \text{ ft}} \right)$$
$$= 96 \text{ inches}$$

Explain the substitution that took place.

5 Ben and Frank were evaluating the expression $\frac{1}{3} \cdot 10$. They both reached for their calculators, entered 1 ÷ 3 =, and got the result 0.3333333. Ben left the number on his screen, then entered × 10 = and got 3.3333333. Frank cleared his calculator, entered 0.3333333 × 10 = and got 3.333333. Explain why they got different results.

6 Triangle EQU is equilateral. Find the length of a side and find the perimeter.

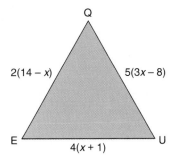

7 If $-2x + 3y = 12$ and $y = 6$, find the value of x.

8 If $5(x + 2y) + 3(x + 2y) - 2(x + 2y) = 36$, find the value of $x + 2y$.

9 Two numbers, a and b, have a ratio $a{:}b = 5{:}2$. Find a if $6a + 10b = 200$.

10 If $(b_1, b_2, h) = (10, 24, 6)$, find the area of the trapezoid.

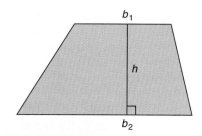

Problems and Applications

11 Find the value of x if $4x + y = 8$ and $y = 10$.

12 Find the value of x and y if $2x + 3y = 8$ and $y = x - 9$.

13 Simplify the expression $9(2x - 7) - 15(2x - 7) + 11(2x - 7)$ in two different ways.

14 Find two numbers that have a ratio of 3:5 and a sum of 52.

15 Which of the following values can be substituted for 25%?

    a 0.025   **b** $\frac{5}{20}$ **c** 0.25%   **d** $\frac{1}{4}$

    e $\frac{2}{5}$ **f** $\frac{75}{300}$ **g** 0.25   **h** $\frac{25}{100}$

16 Communicating Explain why $5 \cdot \left(\frac{3}{8}\right) = 5 \cdot (0.375)$.

17 The angles of a quadrilateral are in the ratio 2:3:3:4. Find their measures.

18 Two complementary angles have a ratio 2:3. Find the measure of the larger angle.

19 Communicating Explain how Edna used substitution to simplify the fraction $\frac{18}{24}$.

$$\frac{18}{24} = \frac{6 \cdot 3}{6 \cdot 4} = \frac{6}{6} \cdot \frac{3}{4} = 1 \cdot \frac{3}{4} = \frac{3}{4}$$

20 The lengths of the sides of the triangle are in the ratio $a:b:c = 5:6:7$. The perimeter is less than 135. What are the possible lengths of sides a, b, and c?

21 Solve each equation or inequality and simplify each expression.

    a $3(x + 5) + 8(x + 5) = 11$ **b** $3(x + 5) + 8(x + 5) + 11$

    c $3(x + 5) + 8(x + 5) \geq 11$ **d** $3(x + 5) + 8(x + 5) - 11(x + 5)$

    e $3(x + 5) + 8(x + 5) = 11(x + 5)$

22 On the planet Sram, a dyme is worth 12 centts and a nickall is worth 6 centts. On Sram, how many packages of guum, which cost 28 centts each, can be purchased with a total of 11 dymes and 9 nickalls?

23 The lengths of segments AB and BC have the ratio AB:BC = 3:2, and AC = 60. Find the length of segment AB.

24 Franklin remembered that a rod is a unit of measurement equal to about $16\frac{1}{2}$ feet. On a canoe trip, the map showed a portage that was 13 rods long. How many feet long was the portage?

25 Find the coordinate of point P on the number line if $a{:}b = 1{:}4$.

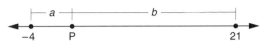

26 If $(x_1, y_1) = (3, -9)$ and $(x_2, y_2) = (1, 7)$, evaluate the expression $\frac{y_2 - y_1}{x_2 - x_1}$.

27 Business A company had a profit of $78,000 in a given year. The three owners of the business divided the profits in a ratio of 4:4:5. How much did each owner receive?

28 In triangle ABC, AB = AC. The ratio of $\angle B$ to $\angle A$ is 2:1. Find the measure of $\angle C$.

29 Solve each inequality.
  a $30 - 8x \le 126$
  b $15 + 2x > 9$
  c $x + 382.16 \le -15.05$
  d $15 - 6x \ge -18$

30 Spreadsheets Make a spreadsheet to complete the table.

x	y	2x + 3y
4	2	
3	1	
2	0	
.	.	.
.	.	.
.	.	.
−8	−10	
−9	−11	

31 Simplify each expression and solve each equation or inequality.
  a $2(x + 1) + 5$
  b $2(y + 1) = 5$
  c $2(z - 2) - (3 - z)$
  d $2 < 8 - 4a$
  e $10(q + 10q)$
  f $10 = q + 10q$

32 In the figure, $\angle ABC \cong \angle DEF$. Find the measure of $\angle DEG$.

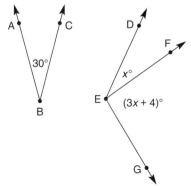

33 Ace earned the same score on every one of his five tests. Bee scored 81, 68, 96, 91, and 89 on her five tests. Bee and Ace had the same mean score. What did Ace score on each of his tests?

34 Use a ruler to find the area of the parallelogram. What dimensions do you need to measure?

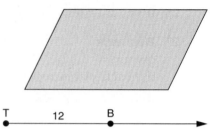

35 Tom starts riding his bicycle at point T. Bill, who is 12 miles east of Tom, starts at point B. Tom rides 18 miles per hour and Bill rides 13 miles per hour. They both start riding east at the same time. Let x = the number of hours they have been riding.

T   12   B

a Write an expression for Tom's distance from point T.
b Write an expression for Bill's distance from point T.
c Write an equation for when the distances in parts **a** and **b** are equal. What does this mean?
d Solve for x. What does this solution mean?

36 The length of the sides of a square is x. The perimeter of the square is between 12 and 28. What are the possible values of x?

37 a How many angles are in each figure?
   b If a similar figure has five rays, how many angles would there be?

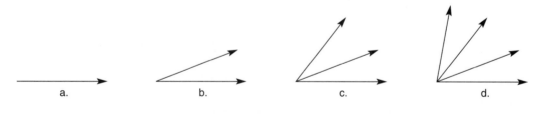

a.   b.   c.   d.

Investigation

Decimals vs. Fractions   Why doesn't $\frac{1}{3} + \frac{2}{3}$ equal the same quantity as $0.333\ldots + 0.666\ldots$, or does it? Explain.

$$\begin{array}{ccc} \frac{1}{3} & = & 0.333\ldots \\ +\frac{2}{3} & = & +\,0.666\ldots \\ \hline 1 & = & 0.999\ldots \end{array}$$

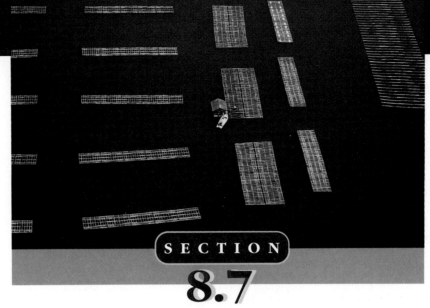

WHAT IS A FUNCTION?

In order to find the area of a rectangle, we need to know the rectangle's length and width. To find out how long a trip will take, we need to know the distance (how far we will travel), and the speed (how fast we will travel).

A ***function*** describes a relationship in which one value depends on the other values. In a rectangle, the area depends on the length and the width. The area is a function of the length and the width. For a trip, the time depends on the distance and the speed. The time is a function of the distance and the speed.

We write a function by naming the function, placing parentheses around what we need to know, and giving a formula, equation, or a set of instructions that shows how to find what we need to know. We call the information in parentheses the ***input,*** and the result of the formula or equation the ***output.***

Example 1

Express the perimeter of the rectangle as a function.

Solution

The perimeter of the rectangle depends on the length and the width. We can write a function for the perimeter.

$$\text{Perimeter (Length, Width)} = 2 \cdot \text{Length} + 2 \cdot \text{Width}$$

The function would be much shorter if we used single variables like P for perimeter, ℓ for length, and w for width.

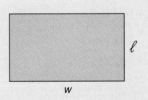

$$P(\ell, w) = 2\ell + 2w$$

Name of function   Inputs   Formula to compute outputs

Example 2
Write a function for the surface area of a cube.

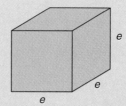

Solution
Let S represent the surface area of a cube and e represent the length of each edge of a cube. The length of an edge is the only input we need. Each face of the cube has area e^2, and there are six faces, so the formula will be $6e^2$.

The function for the surface area of a cube is $S(e) = 6e^2$.

Example 3
Using the function from Example 2, evaluate $S(5)$. What does $S(5)$ mean?

Solution
$S(5)$ means that $e = 5$ in the formula $6e^2$. We use the function and the input 5 to find the output.

Use 5 as an input for e

$$S(e) = 6e^2$$
$$S(5) = 6 \cdot 5^2$$
$$= 6 \cdot 25$$
$$= 150$$

For the input 5, the output is 150. This means that 150 is the surface area of a cube with an edge length of 5.

EVALUATING FUNCTIONS

Letters like f and g are often used to name functions. In the case of perimeter or area, we will use P or A to name a function. Usually, x or y is used for inputs. It makes sense to use ℓ for length, w for width, or e for edge.

Example 4
If $f(x) = 4x^2 + 7x$, evaluate $f(5)$.

Solution
For the function $f(x) = 4x^2 + 7x$, $f(5)$ means that the value of x is 5. To evaluate the function at 5, we substitute 5 in place of x in the formula or equation.

$$f(5) = 4(5)^2 + 7(5)$$
$$= 4(25) + 7(5)$$
$$= 100 + 35$$
$$= 135$$
$$f(5) = 135$$

We read the result as "f of 5 equals 135."

Sample Problems

Problem 1   Evaluate $g(x, y) = -3x - 7y$ for $g(-4, 11)$.

Solution   Substitute -4 for x and 11 for y in the formula.

$$g(x, y) = -3x - 7y$$
$$g(-4, 11) = -3(-4) - 7(11)$$
$$= 12 - 77$$
$$= -65$$

Problem 2   If $f(x) = 8x - 43$, find x so that $f(x) = 97$.

Solution

	$f(x) = 8x - 43$
Find x so that	$f(x) = 97$
Substitute $8x - 43$ for $f(x)$	$8x - 43 = 97$
and solve	$\underline{+43 \quad +43}$
	$8x = 140$
	$\dfrac{8x}{8} = \dfrac{140}{8}$
When $x = 17.5$, $f(x) = 97$.	$x = 17.5$

Problem 3   How much is the total simple interest received if \$5000 is invested for 3 years at an annual interest rate of 8%?

Solution   The total interest, I, depends on the amount of principal invested, P; the interest rate, r; and the number of years, t. The formula is $I = Prt$. As a function we write $I(P, r, t) = Prt$.

In this problem, $I(5000, 0.08, 3) = (5000)(0.08)(3)$
$$= 1200$$

The total interest is \$1200.

Problem 4   Tandy is a salesperson at TV Shack. She is paid \$4 per hour and an 8% commission on whatever she sells. Write a function to express Tandy's earnings.

Solution   Since we are computing earnings, let's call this function E. We need two inputs to compute the salary.

Let h = the number of hours Tandy works and
let d = the total dollar amount of Tandy's sales.

To compute Tandy's earnings, we use the formula $4h + 0.08d$.
Now we can write the function $E(h, d) = 4h + 0.08d$.

1 What is the difference between a formula and a function?

2 Given the function $f(x) = 2x + 7$, evaluate
   a $f(3)$ **b** $f(6)$ **c** $f(9)$ **d** $f(3 + 6)$

3 Explain the different meanings of parentheses in each of the following.
   a $3(5)$ **b** $f(5)$ **c** $4(5 + 2)$

4 For the figure shown, $V(r, h) = \pi r^2 h$.
   a What do V, r, and h represent?
   b Compute $V(3, 4)$.
   c Compute $V(4, 3)$.
   d Explain the meaning of the result in parts **b** and **c**.

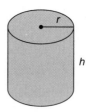

5 Define the operation $\otimes$ as $a \otimes b = a + 2b - 3$. Evaluate $5 \otimes 7$.

6 Use the function $f(x) = x + 2x + 3x + 4x + 5x + 6$ and find
   a $f(0)$ **b** $f(1)$ **c** $f(2)$ **d** $f(7.36)$

7 Use the function $f(x, y) = x^2 + y$ and find
   a $f(1, 0)$ **b** $f(0, 1)$ **c** $f(2, 3)$ **d** $f(3, 2)$

8 **Sports**   Play Skicker is a field-goal and extra-point kicker for his football team. He tries F field goals and E extra points during the season. He is 65% successful on field goals and 98% successful on extra points. Write a function P for his point total during the season. [Note: A field goal is worth three points and an extra point is worth one point.]

9 Evaluate the functions $f(x) = 3x + 4$ and $g(x) = x^2 + x$ for each of the following values.
   a $f(5)$ **b** $g(5)$ **c** $f(1) + g(3)$ **d** $g(1) + f(3)$
   e $g(1.5)$ **f** $f\left(\frac{1}{3}\right)$ **g** $g(0)$ **h** $f(0)$

10 If $Batting\ Average\ (At\ Bats,\ Hits) = \dfrac{Hits}{At\ Bats}$, find the value of $Batting\ Average\ (20, 7)$. Explain what your answer means.

11 Find the interest received if $6000 is invested for one year at 6% simple interest.

12 **Finance**   How much simple interest is received from an investment of $8000 for 4 years at an annual interest rate of 8%?

13 Write a function for the perimeter of each figure.

a Square

b Rectangle

c Parallelogram

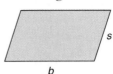

d Kite

e Isosceles trapezoid

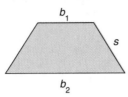

14 Complete the following table for $f(x) = 3x + 5$.

x	−5	−4	−3	−2	−1	0	1	2	3	4	5	6
f(x)			−4				8					

Explain the pattern in the results.

15 Write a function for the volume of a box. Be sure to explain what is represented by any letters you use.

16 **Business** How much is the commission on $1700 of sales if the commission rate is 4%?

17 Write a function for the area of each figure.

a Square

b Triangle

c Parallelogram

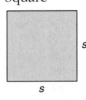
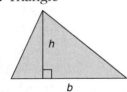
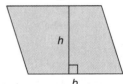

d Kite

e Trapezoid

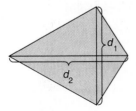
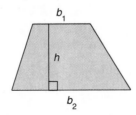

18 Biff is a waiter at the Let Us Eat Lettuce restaurant. He is paid $5.50 per hour and receives tips that average 18% of each bill. If he works b hours and earns t dollars in tips, write a function for how much he earns.

19 For the functions $f(x) = 3x^2$ and $g(x) = (3x)^2$,
   a Evaluate $f(4)$ and $g(4)$
   b Evaluate $f\left(\frac{1}{3}\right)$ and $g\left(\frac{1}{3}\right)$
   c Evaluate $f(-2)$ and $g(-2)$
   d Find the value(s) of x so that $f(x) = g(x)$

20 Write a formula to represent the function
Value(nickels, dimes, quarters).

21 For each of the following inputs, the function f gives the following outputs. Write function f for input x and output y.

Inputs	Output	Inputs	Output
(3, 4)	10	(1, 5)	7
(0, 4)	4	(0, 11)	11
(6, 1)	13	(5, 0)	10

22 Evaluate $f(2)$ if $f(x) = \begin{bmatrix} 2x & 3x-6 \\ x^2 & 5-x \end{bmatrix}$

23 Solve each of the following for y if $g(y) = 3y - 11$.
a $g(y) = 49$ **b** $g(y) > 4$

24 If $f(x) = 3x - 2$ and $g(x) = 4^x$, find
a $f(5)$ **b** $g(3)$ **c** $f(5) + g(3)$

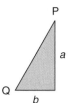

25 Evaluate the function $f(x) = 8(3^x)$ for each input.
a $f(2)$ **b** $f(0)$
c $f(1.7)$ **d** $f(2.6)$

26 Write a function $L(a,\ b)$ for the length of segment PQ.

27 If $A(b,\ h) = \frac{1}{2}\,bh$, and $A(b,\ 6) = 84$, find b.

28 The function $M(x + 2) = 3x$. Evaluate $M(5)$.

◄ LOOKING BACK **Spiral Learning** LOOKING AHEAD ►

29 **Spreadsheets** Make a spreadsheet that resembles the diagram.

Use the spreadsheet to solve $x^2 + 88 = 21x - 20$ by copying down until the values in columns B and C are equal.
(Hint: There are two answers.)

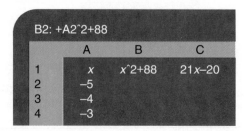

30 List the set of all even integers between -7 and 3.

31 What set of points lies in both triangle ABE and quadrilateral DEBC?

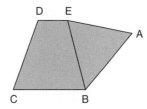

32 Write an expression for
  a The sum of p and q
  b The product of p and q
  c The quotient of p and q
  d The difference of p and q

33 The sides of a quadrilateral have a ratio of 3:6:8:9. The quadrilateral's perimeter is 91. Find the lengths of the sides.

34 If $8x - 3y = 1$ and $y = 3x - 2$, find x and y.

35 Evaluate each expression.
  a $\frac{-3}{8} \cdot \frac{5}{7} \cdot \frac{-7}{11}$
  b $\frac{-3}{5} + \frac{1}{2}$
  c $-8 \cdot \frac{-4}{5} \cdot \frac{-1}{16}$
  d $\frac{-2}{3} - \frac{3}{4}$

36 The perimeter of the figure is less than 25. Write an inequality for x and solve the inequality.

37 How many integers are between $-\sqrt{51}$ and $\sqrt{55}$ on the number line?

38 △ABC is reflected across the y-axis. What are the coordinates of the new vertices?

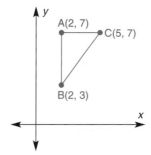

Investigation

Rent Costs   What is the monthly rent for an apartment in your area? The answer certainly depends on the size of the apartment. (We can say that the monthly rent is a function of its size.) But the cost also depends on many other factors.

   Report on the range in rents for typical apartments or houses in your area. Include evidence such as newspaper ads. List all the factors you can think of that influence rent prices.

Summary

After studying this chapter, you should be able to

- Recognize equivalent expressions (8.1)
- Add and subtract like terms (8.1)
- Use the Distributive Property of Multiplication over Addition and Subtraction (8.1)
- Use expressions to describe phrases and situations (8.2)
- Use equations to represent problems (8.2)
- Use inverse operations to solve equations (8.3)
- Solve equations with several operations (8.3)
- Solve absolute-value equations (8.4)
- Solve equations with square roots (8.4)
- Simplify expressions to solve equations (8.4)
- Use addition and subtraction to solve an inequality (8.5)
- Use multiplication and division to solve an inequality (8.5)
- Use substitution to solve equations (8.6)
- Use a quantity as a single term (8.6)
- Recognize a function (8.7)
- Calculate the value of a function (8.7)

equivalent expressions (8.1)

function (8.7)

input (8.7)

like terms (8.1)

numerical term (8.1)

output (8.7)

simplify (8.1)

Review

1 Evaluate each expression for $x = -7$ and $y = 12$.

   a $3(x + 2y) - 2(x - 3y)$ **b** $x + 12y$

   c $2x^2 + y$ **d** $\dfrac{(2x)^2}{y}$

2 Solve each equation and simplify each expression.

   a $3y - (2 + 3y) = 40$ **b** $3y - (2 + 3y) - 40$

   c $\frac{1}{3}(6a - 5) + \frac{2}{3}$ **d** $\frac{1}{3}(6a - 5) = 7$

3 Add $\begin{bmatrix} 4x & 2y & 3z \\ 5x & y & -z \\ 7x & 3y & 2z \end{bmatrix} + \begin{bmatrix} x & 3y & 2z \\ 0 & 4y & 6z \\ -2x & 2y & 2z \end{bmatrix}$

4 Complete the table.

x		−18	−15	−13	−5	0	3	8
8x − 4x + 2x − 6x								

5 If $x = -3$ and $y = \frac{2}{3}$, which of the following are true?

   a $3x + 4y = 12xy$ **b** $x + 2x + 3x + 4x = 10x$

   c $2x + 2y = 2(x + y)$ **d** $xy = 1 + x$

6 Find x.

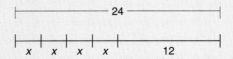

7 Simplify each expression.

   a $3 + x + 4x + 5$ **b** $2x^2 + x + x^2 + 3$

8 Write an expression, an equation, or an inequality for each of the following.

   a 17 less than four times a number

   b The square of a number is less than 25

   c The average of x and 12

   d The area of a given rectangle is numerically the same as its perimeter.

9 Write a sentence or phrase to represent each of the following.

   a $3x + 9$

   b $3(x + 9)$

   c $\frac{2}{3} = \frac{5}{x}$

10 Carlo sells cameras at Photo World. He earns \$15 per hour plus a 10% commission on camera purchases. Find his earnings if he

   a Works 8 hours and sells \$350 worth of cameras

   b Works h hours and sells \$$d$ worth of cameras

11 Find the perimeter of the triangle in terms of x and y.

12 Write a function $Ave(a, b, c)$ to find the average of the numbers a, b, and c.

13 The appliance repairer in Pleasantville charges $30 for a service call plus $20 per hour. Find the total cost for a service call if the repairer works

    a $2\frac{1}{2}$ hours   **b** b hours

14 A train travels 45 miles per hour for t hours and 50 miles per hour for 4 hours. Find the value of t if the entire trip covered 520 miles.

15 The mean of 80, 64, 94, 96, and x is 84. Find the value of x.

16 **a** Write an equation to represent the measures of angles ABD and DBC.
    b Solve for x.
    c Determine the measure of $\angle$ABD.

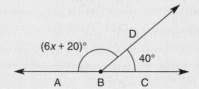

17 The measures of the four angles of a quadrilateral have a ratio of 3:4:5:6. Find the measures of the angles.

18 Solve each equation.
    a $40 - 4x = -32$ **b** $\frac{8}{5}x + \frac{4}{5} = \frac{2}{5}$
    c $-6(y + 4) = 39$

19 In the triangle, AB = BC. Write a function, in simplest form, for the perimeter of the triangle.

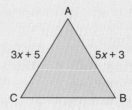

20 Solve $9(3y - 2) + 4(3 - 6y) = \frac{14 + 22}{4}$ for y.

21 Solve each equation for x.
    a $|x| + 3 = 8$ **b** $|x + 3| = 8$
    c $|x| + 8 = 3$ **d** $|x + 8| = 3$

22 Write a function V for the volume of a cone with base radius r and height b.

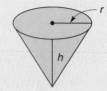

23 The perimeter of the triangle is 40. Find the value of x.

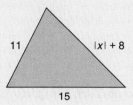

24 Solve each equation for x.

a $\sqrt{x} = 81$ **b** $x^2 = 81$

c $\sqrt{x} = -81$ **d** $x^2 = -81$

25 Write the symbol, >, <, or =, that should be in each ☐.

a $\frac{7}{8}$ ☐ $\frac{8}{7}$ **b** $\frac{-3}{5}$ ☐ $\frac{-5}{3}$

c 0.125 ☐ $\frac{1}{8}$ **d** 40% ☐ $\frac{3}{5}$

26 Solve $3x + y > -10$ for x if $y = 5$.

27 Refer to the diagram.
 a Write an inequality to represent the diagram.
 b Solve the inequality.

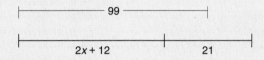

28 Solve $3x + 8y = 39$ for y if $x = 5$.

29 What two different methods can be used to simplify the expression $5(2x + 4) - 18(2x + 4) + 7(2x + 4) + 9(2x + 4)$?

30 Two numbers have a ratio of 4:3. The sum of the two numbers is greater than 21. What must be true about the smaller of the two numbers?

31 Evaluate the functions $f(x, y) = 4x - 7y$, $g(x) = x^2$, and $h(x) = 3^x$ for each of the following inputs.

a $f(3, 1)$ **b** $f(1, 3)$ **c** $g(4)$ **d** $g(-4)$

e $h(2)$ **f** $h(-2)$ **g** $f(7, 4)$ **h** $f(4, 7)$

32 The function $f(x, y) = \begin{bmatrix} 6 \\ 2 \end{bmatrix} + \begin{bmatrix} x \\ y \end{bmatrix}$. Evaluate $f(3, -4)$.

33 Describe what happens to the value of a if b is increased by 3 and the perimeter stays the same.

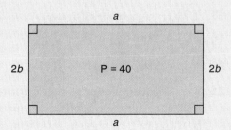

34 a If $x < \frac{2}{3}$, is it always true that $\frac{1}{x} > \frac{2}{3}$?

b If $x > \frac{2}{3}$, is it always true that $\frac{1}{x} < \frac{2}{3}$?

Test

In problems 1–3, simplify each expression.

1 $4x + 6 - 3x - 9$ **2** $3(2x + 5) + 4(7x - 1)$ **3** $-4(3x - 2y)$

4 Add $\begin{bmatrix} 3xy & -2x & -4y \\ -5x & 5xy & -6y \end{bmatrix} + \begin{bmatrix} -4xy & -6x & 3y \\ 7y & -3xy & 6x \end{bmatrix}$.

5 Write an algebraic expression that represents the phrase "three less than a number."

6 Write an equation that shows that the area of the rectangle is equal to the area of the triangle.

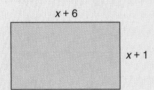

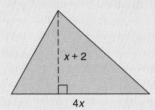

In problems 7–12, solve each equation.

7 $17x = 20.4$ **8** $2b + 1 = 5b - 9$ **9** $2x + x = 15$

10 $5(3x + 4) = 125$ **11** $|a - 2| = 8$ **12** $\sqrt{m} + 2 = 9$

In problems 13–15, solve each inequality.

13 $3x + 1 < 10$ **14** $8 - 3x \geq 17$ **15** $5(2x - 7) > 120$

16 If Megan sells from 10 to 20 items at $50 each, she earns a 6% commission. What is the possible range of Megan's commission in this situation?

17 If $3x - 4y = 18$ and $y = -3$, solve for x.

18 If $m:n = 5:3$, solve the equation $2m + 3n = 76$ for m.

19 If $3x + 4y = 17$ and $y = x - 1$, solve for x and y.

20 If $f(x, y) = x^2 - 2xy + y^2$, evaluate $f(2, -1)$.

21 A $4000 investment is made for two years at a 6% annual interest rate.
   a Write a function using one variable for this situation.
   b What will be the actual dollar amount of interest earned?

22 Find the value of x that makes the perimeter of the rectangle 40.

$3x - 2$ | $4x + 1$

1 Find an English word in which all five vowels (a, e, i, o, u) appear in alphabetical order, and each vowel appears only once.

2 Find a common English word in which three pairs of double letters appear one after another.

3 Continue this pattern for two more rows.

```
              1
            1   1
          1   2   1
        1   3   3   1
      1   4   6   4   1
    1   5   10   10   5   1
```

4 Carl is standing by a river with a 7-quart bottle and a 4-quart bottle. Explain how he can bring home exactly 5 quarts of water.

5 Interpret the phrase each puzzle suggests.

a

b

W A G O N
N O
O N
G W
O A
G G
A O
W N

c S r P a A i l n N

d S A F E

FIRST

9 Real Numbers

CAREER CONNECTION

OPTICS Optics is the study of light and vision. Careers in optics may fall into either of two categories: physical optics or geometrical optics.

Physical optics deals with the physics of light waves, and may involve the design and the energy-efficiency of different types of lights such as neon or fluorescent, for example.

Geometrical optics, on the other hand, deals with the reflection and refraction (bending) of light rays, and may be applied to the development and improvement of equipment such as eyeglasses.

INVESTIGATION

Optical Illusion When you put an oar in the water, the part that is under water appears to bend. Explain why this happens. If the water were some other clear liquid, would the amount of "bending" be affected? Why?

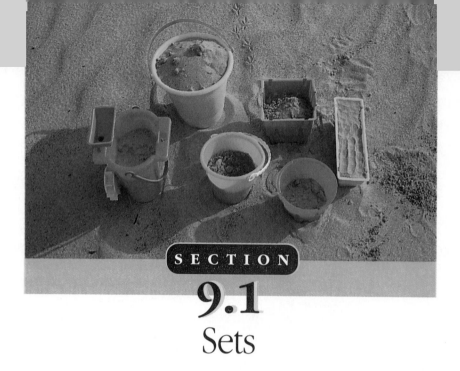

9.1
Sets

DESCRIBING SETS

A *set* is any collection of objects. Usually we will be considering sets of numbers or sets of geometric figures. Capital letters are often used to name sets. A single member of a set is called an *element* of the set. The set, I, of integers can be written as follows:

$$I = \{\ldots, -3, -2, -1, 0, 1, 2, 3, \ldots\}$$

Example 1

A cassette tape deck has a three-digit tape counter. The tape counter was set at 200 at the start of a tape, and it reads 486 at the end of the tape. In four different ways, describe the set of numbers that appeared on the tape counter during the playing of the tape.

Solution

1. In words: The counter showed every integer from 200 to 486 inclusive.
2. By listing the elements: {200, 201, 202, ... , 486}
3. By using **set-builder notation:** $\{x : 200 \leq x \leq 486 \text{ and } x \text{ is an integer}\}$. This notation is read "the set of all values of x such that x is greater than or equal to 200 and less than or equal to 486 and is an integer."
4. By graphing:

198 199 200 201 202 203 484 485 486 487 488 489

Example 1 shows several different ways of representing a set. We can describe a set in words. We can make a list or a partial list that shows how the set continues. We can make a rule. We can draw a graph.

Example 2

A circle has its center at the origin of the coordinate system, and the circle has a radius of 2 units. In three different ways, describe the set of points where the circle intersects the axes of the coordinate system.

Solution

Here are three possible ways:

1. By graphing: The points are shown on the coordinate system.
2. By listing: {(2, 0), (0, 2), (–2, 0), (0, –2)}
3. In words: The set of points on the coordinate axes are 2 units from the origin.

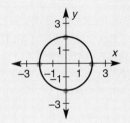

SUBSETS

Set B is a **subset** of a set A if every element in set B is also an element of set A. We write this as B⊂A, which is read, "B is a subset of A." Or we can write {1, 2}⊂{1, 2, 3}, which is read, "The set containing the elements 1 and 2 is a subset of the set containing the elements 1, 2, and 3." Every set is a subset of itself.

Example 3

Amy Planter purchases 20 feet of fence to border a rectangular garden. She wants the length of each side of the garden to be a whole number of feet.
a Find the set of possible areas of the garden.
b Find the set of possible areas for which the garden will be at least 3 feet wide.
c Find the set of possible areas greater than 30 square feet.

Solution

a The figure shows the rectangles that have dimensions that are whole numbers of feet and perimeters of 20 feet. The set of areas is {9, 16, 21, 24, 25}.

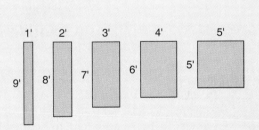

b The set of areas for which the garden is at least 3 feet wide is {21, 24, 25}.

c There are no dimensions for which the area is greater than 30 square feet. The set with no elements in it is called the **empty set.** The empty set can be written { }. The empty set is a subset of every set.

Example 4

a By listing coordinates, identify the set of vertices of this figure.

b Reflect the figure over the x-axis. Which vertices of the image form a subset of the vertices of the preimage?

c Reflect the figure over the y-axis. Which vertices of the image form a subset of the vertices of the preimage?

d Translate the figure 1 unit to the left and 2 units up. Which vertices of the image form a subset of the vertices of the preimage?

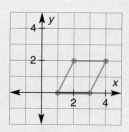

Solution

a {(1, 0), (3, 0), (4, 2), (2, 2)}   **b** {(1, 0), (3, 0)}

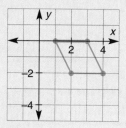

c { }   **d** {(2, 2)}

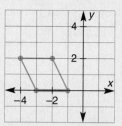 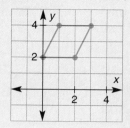

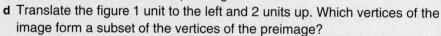

Sample Problems

Problem 1   List all the subsets of the set {1, 2, 3}. How many are there?

Solution   { }, {1}, {2}, {3}, {1, 2}, {1, 3}, {2, 3}, {1, 2, 3}
There are a total of eight subsets.

Problem 2   The perimeter of the figure is less than 20 units. Describe all possible values of *x* as a set. (This is known as a **solution set.**)

Solution
$$2(x + 2) + 2x < 20$$
$$2x + 4 + 2x < 20$$
$$4x + 4 < 20$$
$$4x < 16$$
$$x < 4$$

We know that the lengths of the rectangle's sides must be positive. This means that $x > 0$. Here are two ways to show the set:

1. Graph:

0   4

2. Set-builder notation: $\{x : 0 < x < 4\}$

Think and Discuss

1 A set of numbers is represented on the number line. Describe the set of numbers in words and in set-builder notation. Why can't you list the elements in the set?

−8   2

2 Suppose that $P = \left\{-2, 17, \frac{3}{5}, -\frac{4}{9}, \pi, \sqrt{5}, 0\right\}$. Explain why listing is the only method that can be used to describe set P.

3 If $R = \{x : 200 \le x \le 486\}$, is the statement *true* or *false?* Explain your answer.
   a 300 is an element of R.   b −300 is an element of R.
   c 203.5 is an element of R.   d 486 is an element of R.

4 Describe the shaded set in several ways. Which method seems easiest? Why?

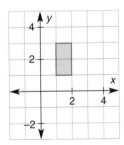

5 If $A = \{x : x > 4\}$, is 5 the smallest element of A? Why or why not?

6 a List all subsets of each of the sets {a}, {a, b}, and {a, b, c}.
   b Do you see a pattern that can be used to determine the number of subsets a set has if you know the number of elements in the set? What is the pattern?
   c How many subsets do you think {a, b, c, d} has?

Problems and Applications

7 Communicating Suppose that A = {−4, −2, 0, 2, 4, 6, 8, 10, 12, 14, 16}.
a Describe A in words.
b Represent A by graphing.
c Describe A in set-builder notation.
d Which is the best method?

8 If B = {b:−5 < b < 5 and b is an integer}, which of the following values of b are in B?
a $b = \frac{1}{2}$
b $b = -5$
c $b = 0$

9 A circle with center at (2, 0) has a radius of 2 units. Describe in two ways the set of points where the circle intersects the coordinate axes.

10 Undistributed Middle School is expecting between 80 and 100 students for a ski trip. Students will be transported by minivans that hold 7 students each. Use set-builder notation to show the set of possible numbers of minivans that will be needed for the trip.

11 If all of the subsets of set X are { }, {5}, {10}, {a}, {5, 10}, {5, a}, {10, a}, and {5, 10, a}, what are the elements of X?

12 a By listing coordinates, identify the set of vertices of the figure shown.
b Reflect the figure over the y-axis. Which vertices of the image form a subset of the vertices of the preimage?
c Reflect the figure over the x-axis. Which vertices of the image form a subset of the vertices of the preimage?

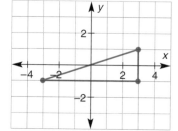

d Translate the figure ⟨6,2⟩. Which vertices of the image form a subset of the vertices of the preimage?

In problems 13–16, indicate whether the statement is *true* or *false*.

13 {1, 2, 3}⊂{1, 3, 5, 7, 9, 11}

14 {4, 7}⊂{4, 7}

15 {1, 3}⊂{0, 1, 3, 5, 7}

16 {1, 3, 5, 7, 9}⊂{2, 4, 6, 8, 10}

17 List the set of all angles in the figure.

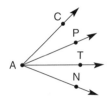

In problems 18–23, determine the number of elements in each set.

18 {1, 2, 3, 4, ... , 41}

19 {United States senators}

20 {Phases of matter}

21 {Even prime numbers}

22 {0}

23 { }

24 For what values of x chosen from $\{-4, -3, \ldots, 4, 5, 6\}$ is $2x - 1 < 3$?

25 If the perimeter of the parallelogram is less than 43 units, what is the set of all possible integer values of x?

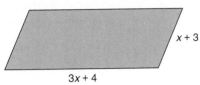

26 **a** List the set of perfect squares less than or equal to 100.
b List the subset of the set in part **a** that consists of even numbers.
c What else do you notice about all the numbers in part **b**?

In problems 27–29, determine the number of elements in each set.

27 $\{y : y^2 = 9\}$ **28** $\{y : y = 1, 2, 3, 4, 5\}$

29 $\{(x, y) : x = 1, 2, \text{ or } 3; y = 1, 2, \text{ or } 3\}$

30 Suppose that A = {squares}, B = {rectangles}, C = {rhombuses}, and D = {parallelograms}. Indicate whether each statement is *true* or *false*.
  a $A \subset B$ **b** $A \subset C$ **c** $A \subset D$ **d** $B \subset C$
  e $B \subset D$ **f** $C \subset D$ **g** $B \subset A$ **h** $C \subset A$
  i $D \subset A$ **j** $C \subset B$ **k** $D \subset B$ **l** $D \subset C$

31 **Communicating** If $A \subset B$ and $B \subset D$, is it true that $A \subset D$? Explain your answer.

32 Write an equation for which the solution set is $\{-5, 5\}$.

33 In the figure, $AB = x + 5$. Find the set of integers that are possible values of x.

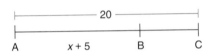

34 Suppose that A = $\{x : -8 < x \leq 6\}$, B = $\{x : -6 \leq x \leq 3\}$, and C = $\{x : -7 < x < 11\}$. Indicate which of the sets, if any, contains the given number.
  a -10 **b** -7 **c** -6 **d** 10
  e 7 **f** 2 **g** -6.5 **h** 5.4
  i 8.2 **j** 0 **k** -7.6 **l** -8

35 **Architecture** An office building is to be built with a height between 100 and 120 feet. Depending on the type of construction and the heights of the ceilings, each story will be between $9\frac{1}{2}$ and 12 feet high. List the possible numbers of stories that the building can have.

36 **Communicating** Describe and draw on a coordinate system the set of points that are
  a 4 units from the point $(1, 2)$ **b** Less than 4 units from $(1, 2)$
  c More than 4 units from $(1, 2)$

37 List the elements of each set.
  a {Numbers that are factors of 64}   **b** $\{x : x = 2^n, \text{ where } n = 1, 2, 3, 4, 5, 6\}$

38 **Communicating** Describe in words $\{x : -4 < x < 4\}$.

39 Some of the subsets of S are {15}, {3, 6, 9}, {9, 12}, {6, 9, 12}, and {9, 18}.
  a What is the smallest possible number of elements of S?
  b List as many subsets of S as you can for which {3, 6, 9, 12} is a subset.

40 Evaluate $\begin{bmatrix} 4 & -1 & 6 \\ -6 & 19 & -7 \end{bmatrix} - \begin{bmatrix} 5 & -7 & -3 \\ -3 & -14 & -7 \end{bmatrix}$.

41 There are 40 people at a costume party. Twenty-eight are wearing masks, 31 are wearing belts, and 23 are wearing both masks and belts. How many are wearing neither masks nor belts?

42 If $f(t) = 3t + 8$ and $g(t) = 4t^2 - t$, what is
  a $f(4)$? **b** $g(4)$? **c** $f(0)$?
  d $g(0)$? **e** $f(-3)$? **f** $g(-3)$?

43 At Elisha Cook Junior High School, the math club had 30 members and the science club had 21 members. (No one was a member of both clubs.) Some members left each of these clubs and formed a computer club. All three clubs now have the same number of members. How many members from the math club and how many from the science club transferred to the computer club?

44 If A = {1, 2, 3, 4} and B = {3, 5, 7, 9}, is the statement *true* or *false?*
  a 2 is an element of A. **b** 2 is an element of B.
  c 3 is an element of A. **d** 3 is an element of B.
  e 2 is an element of A or 2 is an element of B.
  f 3 is an element of A or 3 is an element of B.
  g 2 is an element of A and 2 is an element of B.
  h 3 is an element of A and 3 is an element of B.

45 Students at Rocky Mountain High School can win tickets to a ball game by having both an A average and perfect attendance. There are 366 students in the school. One hundred students have perfect attendance, 120 have an A average, and 186 have neither. How many students earned tickets to a ball game?

46 If $3t - 6y = 18$ and $t = -5$, what is the value of $y?$

47 **Communicating** Suppose that X = {multiples of 4}, Y = {multiples of 6}, and Z = {multiples of 8}.
  a Which set is a subset of another set?
  b Describe the set containing all the numbers that are in both X and Y.

Investigation

Infinite Sets Write down some examples of sets that have a finite number of elements. Then give some examples of sets that have an infinite number of elements. Write a convincing argument to show that there is an infinite set of points on any line segment.

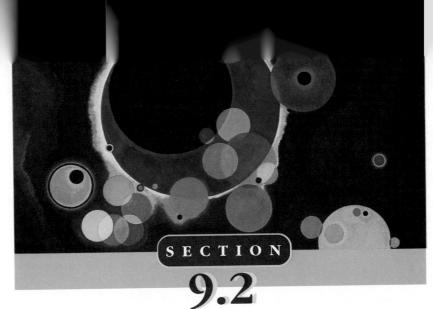

Intersection and Union

INTERSECTIONS AND UNIONS OF SETS

Sometimes the solution of a problem requires numbers that are in one set and also in another set. For instance, to be hired by the police department in Center City, a male candidate must be at least 66 inches tall but not more than 79 inches tall. His height must fall into both sets $A = \{x : x \geq 66\}$ and $B = \{x : x \leq 79\}$. The set $A \cap B$ is called the **intersection** of sets A and B. $A \cap B$ consists of all the numbers or objects the two sets have in common.

At other times a solution calls for things that are either in one set or in another set. For example, at the time of a flu epidemic, the local health department recommends flu shots for people over the age of 60 or people who have traveled outside the country in the past six months.

If we let $C = \{$those older than 60$\}$ and $D = \{$those who have traveled outside the country in the past six months$\}$, then any person who is in set C or in set D or in both sets should have the flu shot. The set $C \cup D$ is called the **union** of sets C and D. $C \cup D$ consists of all elements that are in set C or in set D. (An element that is in both of two sets is an element of both the union and the intersection of the sets.)

Example 1
Let A be the set of points on the circle and B be the set of points on the square. What are the elements of
a $A \cap B$? **b** $A \cup B$?

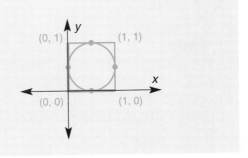

Solution

a The intersection consists of the points belonging to both figures. According to the graph, $A \cap B = \{(0.5, 0), (1, 0.5), (0.5, 1), (0, 0.5)\}$.

b $A \cup B$ consists of an infinite number of points. We can describe $A \cup B$ in words with the phrase "all the points on the square or on the circle." We can also describe the set by referring to the graph. The whole of the figure shown in blue represents the union of sets A and B.

Example 2

Suppose we define set A as $\{x : x = 3n + 1,$ where n is a natural number less than 7$\}$ and we define set B as {prime numbers less than 20}.
a List the elements in each set.
b Find $A \cap B$.
c Find $A \cup B$.

Solution

a $A = \{4, 7, 10, 13, 16, 19\}$, $B = \{2, 3, 7, 11, 13, 17, 19\}$
b $A \cap B = \{7, 13, 19\}$
c $A \cup B = \{2, 3, 4, 7, 10, 11, 13, 16, 17, 19\}$

VENN DIAGRAMS

A **Venn diagram** is a way to show the intersection or union of two or more sets.

The Venn diagram at the right shows the intersection of sets A and B from Example 2.

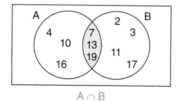

$A \cap B$

The Venn diagram at the right shows the union of sets A and B from Example 2.

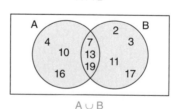

$A \cup B$

Example 3

Gerry Booker will work in the library every fourth day, starting on Monday, April 2. Draw a calendar for the month of April and circle the days he works. Underline the weekend days. If S is the set of days he will work and T is the set of weekend days, list the elements of S, T, and $S \cap T$.

In the calendar, the circled dates represent the elements of set S. The underlined dates represent the elements of set T.

S = {2, 6, 10, 14, 18, 22, 26, 30}

T = {1, 7, 8, 14, 15, 21, 22, 28, 29}

S∩T = {14, 22}

S	M	T	W	T	F	S
1	2	3	4	5	6	7
8	9	10	11	12	13	14
15	16	17	18	19	20	21
22	23	24	25	26	27	28
29	30					

In Example 3, we talked about the set T of weekend days. We might also refer to the set of weekdays. This is the set of all days that are not weekend days. It is designated by $\overline{\text{T}}$ and is called the complement of T.

▶ The **complement** of a set A is the set of all numbers or elements under discussion that are not in A. The complement of A is written $\overline{\text{A}}$.

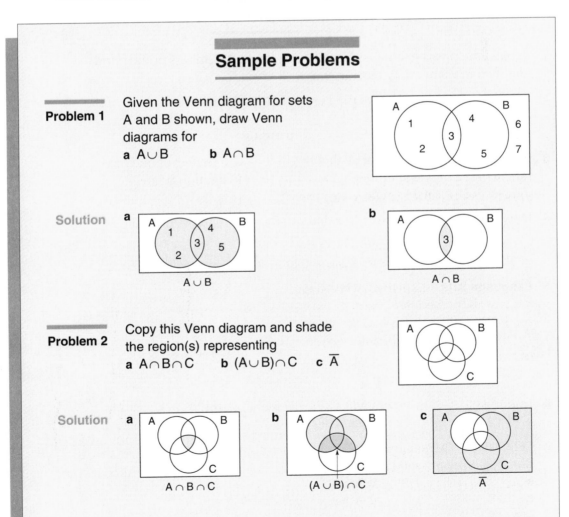

Sample Problems

Problem 1 Given the Venn diagram for sets A and B shown, draw Venn diagrams for
 a A∪B   **b** A∩B

Solution **a** A∪B   **b** A∩B

Problem 2 Copy this Venn diagram and shade the region(s) representing
 a A∩B∩C   **b** (A∪B)∩C   **c** $\overline{\text{A}}$

Solution **a** A∩B∩C   **b** (A∪B)∩C   **c** $\overline{\text{A}}$

437

Problem 3 If set A is the set of points on or below line ℓ_1 and set B is the set of points on or above line ℓ_2, what is
  a A∩B? **b** A∪B? **c** $\overline{A∪B}$?

Solution We can describe these sets by shading the diagram in three ways.

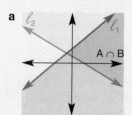 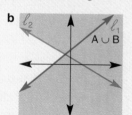 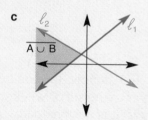

Think and Discuss

1 Explain the possible confusion in the statement, "Members of the band and the orchestra are to meet in the auditorium."

2 If B is the set of members of the band and O is the set of members of the orchestra, what is
  a B∪O? **b** B∩O?

3 An announcement says that all eighth graders with perfect attendance may watch a movie after lunch. Does this refer to a union or an intersection of sets? Explain your answer.

4 How do the uses of the word *or* differ in the following statements:

  I left my book in my locker or in the cafeteria.
  The number 8 belongs to A∪B—that is, it is in set A or in set B.

5 **Language Arts** In everyday language, we talk about the intersection of two roads. How does this use of the word *intersection* relate to the intersection of two sets?

6 Under what circumstances will each statement be true?
  a A∩B = A **b** A∪B = A **c** A∩B = B∩A

7 Refer to the diagram and list the numbers in each set.
  a A **b** $\overline{A}$
  c A∪B **d** A∩B
  e $\overline{A∪B}$

Problems and Applications

8 Given that A = {1, 3, 5, 7, 9}, B = {2, 3, 5, 7, 11, 13}, C = {5, 7, 9}, and
D = {6, 8, 10}, list the elements of each intersection or union.
  a A∩B   **b** A∩C   **c** B∩C   **d** A∪B
  e A∪C   **f** B∪C   **g** C∩D   **h** C∪D

9 Use symbols to describe
the shaded set.

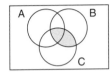

10 Draw four Venn diagrams
like the one shown. Shade
regions for
  a A∩B   **b** A∪B
  c $\overline{A∩B}$ **d** $\overline{A∪B}$

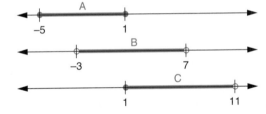

11 **a** List the elements of {x:x is a multiple of 3 and 1 < x < 41}.
  b List the elements of {x:x is a multiple of 4 and 1 < x < 41}.
  c List the elements of the intersection of the sets in parts **a** and **b**.
  d Use set-builder notation to represent your answer to part **c**.

12 Sets A, B, and C are graphed
on the number lines shown.
Draw a graph of
  a A∩B   **b** A∩C
  c B∩C   **d** A∪B
  e A∪C   **f** B∪C

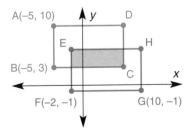

13 If A = {..., −4, −3, −2, −1, 0, 1, 2, 3,...} and B = {0, 1, 2, 3, 4, ...}, what is
  a A∩B?   **b** A∪B?

14 There are 71 students on the track team and 53 students on the
swimming team. Sixteen of the students are on both teams. Find the total
number of students on the two teams.

15 The two rectangular
regions are congruent.
  a Find the area of their
    intersection.
  b Find the area of the
    complement of their
    intersection.

16 Use a spreadsheet or a calculator to find the set of squares of the integers
from 1 to 50. Then find the subset of the squares that have
  a A units digit of 1   **b** A units digit of 5   **c** A units digit of 3

17 a Find the intersection of the interiors of rectangle ACFH and rectangle BDEG.
b Find the union of the interiors of rectangle ACFH and rectangle BGED.

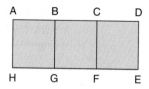

18 Give an example of two sets, A and B, such that A⊂B and B⊂A.

19 Reflect $\overline{AB}$ over the y-axis to form $\overline{A'B'}$. Use set-builder notation to represent
a $\overline{A'B'} \cap \overline{AB}$
b $\overline{A'B'} \cup \overline{AB}$

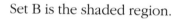

20 Q is the set of all quadrilaterals. Name at least four subsets of this set.

21 Set A is the shaded region.

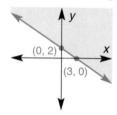

Set B is the shaded region.

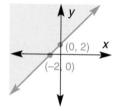

On a coordinate system, draw
a A∩B   **b** A∪B   **c** $\overline{A \cup B}$

22 ℓ is the line through (−3, 2) and (3, 2).
m is the line through (−4, −4) and (4, 4).
A is the region above ℓ. B is the region below m.
Of (8, 5), (0, 5), (−5, 0), and (5, 0), which are in
a A∩B?   **b** A∪B?

23 Suppose that A = {rectangles whose side lengths are a whole number of centimeters and whose perimeter is 10 centimeters} and D = {rectangles whose side lengths are a whole number of centimeters and whose area is 6 square centimeters}. What is
a A∩D?   **b** A∪D?

24 Draw Venn diagrams like the one shown and shade regions to show
a A∩B   **b** A∪B
c B∩C   **d** A∩B∩C
e (A∩B)∩$\overline{C}$ **f** (A∪B)∩$\overline{C}$

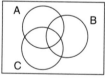

25 Suppose that A = {1, 4, 7, 10}, B = {2, 4, 6}, and C = {1, 3, 5}. List the elements of each of the following sets.
a A∩B   **b** (A∩B)∪C   **c** A∪C   **d** (A∪C)∩B
e A∩B∩C   **f** A∪B∪C   **g** (A∪C)∩(B∪C)   **h** (A∩B)∪(C∩B)

26 List all the subsets of the set of prime numbers less than 10.

27 Rewrite each number as a fraction:
    a 0.3   **b** 0.3333...   **c** 15%   **d** 9.2

28 **a** Find the length of $\overline{AB}$.
    b Find the length of $\overline{AC}$.
    c Find the length of $\overline{BC}$.
    d Find the area of $\triangle ABC$.
    e Find the perimeter of $\triangle ABC$.

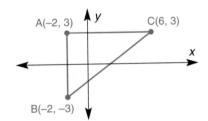

29 Find the solution set of each inequality.
    a $3x - 8 < 13$ **b** $10 - 4x \leq 14$

30 **a** Find the area and the circumference of
       the circle inscribed in the square.
    b Find the area of the region that is outside
       the circle but inside the square.

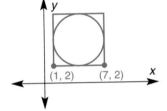

31 Find the solution set of each equation.
    a $x^2 = 36$ **b** $\sqrt{x} = 36$ **c** $x^2 = -36$ **d** $\sqrt{x^2} = x$

32 **Communicating** Describe the relationship between
sets A and B.

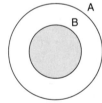

33 **a** Find several possible values
      of x, not necessarily integers.
    b Using set-builder notation,
      represent all values of x such
      that AB < BC.

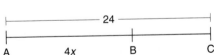

Investigation

Limits Using a calculator, enter any positive number greater than 1, then press the $\boxed{\sqrt{}}$ key repeatedly. Describe what happens. Now enter any positive number less than 1 and press the $\boxed{\sqrt{}}$ key repeatedly. Describe what happens. Try the procedure with some other numbers. Can you explain your results?

9.3

Important Sets of Numbers

THE RATIONAL NUMBERS

In mathematics we try to be as clear and precise as possible with vocabulary and notation. When you refer to a triangle, a circle, or a square, other people know just what you mean. In a similar way, we define important sets of numbers. We build these sets by starting with the **natural numbers,** which are also called the counting numbers.

Name	Set	Graph
Natural numbers	$\{1, 2, 3, \ldots\}$	
Whole numbers	$\{0, 1, 2, 3, \ldots\}$	
Integers	$\{\ldots, -3, -2, -1, 0, 1, 2, 3, \ldots\}$	

On the graph of the integers, there are many points that can be paired with numbers that are not integers. Points for numbers like $\frac{1}{2}$, -3.25, and 8.1 lie between the points representing the integers. These numbers, along with the integers, make up a fourth set of numbers.

▶ A **rational number** is any number that can be written in the form $\frac{a}{b}$, where a and b are integers and $b \neq 0$. In set-builder notation, $R = \left\{ \frac{a}{b} : a \text{ and } b \text{ are integers}, b \neq 0 \right\}$.

Example 1

Which of the following are rational numbers?

$2, \frac{3}{4}, -\frac{5}{8}, 3\frac{6}{7}, 2.54, 0, \sqrt{49}, 0.\overline{3}$

Solution

All of the numbers are rational numbers. We can show that each number can be written as a ratio of two integers. The numbers $\frac{3}{4}$ and $-\frac{5}{8}$ are already in fraction form. The other fraction forms are

$$2 = \frac{2}{1} \qquad 3\frac{6}{7} = \frac{27}{7} \qquad 2.54 = \frac{254}{100} \qquad 0 = \frac{0}{1} \qquad \sqrt{49} = \frac{7}{1} \qquad 0.\overline{3} = \frac{1}{3}$$

Any fraction can be converted to a decimal. Thus, any rational number can be written as a decimal. The decimal form of a rational number either terminates or repeats. In numbers such as 0.4545… and $3.2\overline{716}$, the ellipsis dots and the bar mean that the groups of digits repeat, in the same pattern, without end.

THE REAL NUMBERS

Not all of the points on the number line represent rational numbers. There is another set of numbers on the number line in addition to the rationals. This set contains numbers that cannot be written as a ratio of two integers and so cannot be written as terminating or repeating decimals.

▶ An **irrational number** is a number that is the coordinate of a point on the number line but is not a rational number. Some irrational numbers are $\sqrt{2}$, $\sqrt[3]{6}$, $-\sqrt{24}$, $2\sqrt{3}$, π, and 0.010010001…

Since no irrational number can be written as a ratio of two integers, the set of rational numbers and the set of irrational numbers have no numbers in common. In other words, {rational numbers} ∩ {irrational numbers} = { }. When two sets have an intersection that is empty, the two sets are called **disjoint sets.**

Rational	Irrational
2 $\quad \frac{13}{4}$	
-5	$\sqrt{2}$ $\quad \sqrt[3]{6}$
$\quad 2.54$	
$\frac{-5}{8}$	$-\sqrt{24}$
$\quad \sqrt{16}$	π
$3.\overline{6}$	$0.01001…$

▶ The union of the set of rational numbers and the set of irrational numbers is the set of **real numbers.**

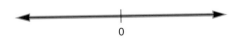

Every point on the number line has a coordinate that is a real number.

Example 2

On a number line, locate $\sqrt{5}$, π, and $-2\sqrt{3}$.

Solution

Using a calculator, we find that $\sqrt{5} \approx 2.2$, $\pi \approx 3.1$, and $-2\sqrt{3} \approx -3.5$.

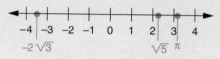

Sample Problems

Problem 1

Write $-2.\overline{57}$ as a ratio of two integers.

Solution Let $n = -2.5757\ldots$

Multiplying by 100 provides a way to eliminate the repeating decimal

$$100n = -257.5757\ldots$$
$$n = -2.5757\ldots$$

Subtract

Divide and simplify

$$99n = -255$$

$$n = \frac{-255}{99} = \frac{-85}{33}$$

Therefore, $-2.\overline{57} = \frac{-85}{33}$.

Problem 2

Indicate the sets of numbers containing each of the following:

$$8, -2, 0, \sqrt{25}, \tfrac{3}{4}, 2\pi, -5.2, 3.1\overline{7}, -\sqrt{5}$$

Solution

Natural numbers: $8, \sqrt{25}$
Whole numbers: $8, \sqrt{25}, 0$
Integers: $8, \sqrt{25}, 0, -2$
Rational numbers: $8, \sqrt{25}, 0, -2, \tfrac{3}{4}, -5.2, 3.1\overline{7}$
Irrational numbers: $2\pi, -\sqrt{5}$
Real numbers: $8, \sqrt{25}, 0, -2, \tfrac{3}{4}, -5.2, 3.1\overline{7}, 2\pi, -\sqrt{5}$

Think and Discuss

1 Indicate whether the statement is *true* or *false*.
  a The sum of two natural numbers is always a natural number.
  b The difference of two natural numbers is always a natural number.
  c The difference of two integers is always an integer.
  d The quotient of two integers is always an integer.

2 What is the intersection of the set of natural numbers and the set of whole numbers?

3 Which of the following numbers are integers?

  a $-764{,}002$ **b** $\frac{48}{6}$ **c** 4.2 **d** $\frac{1.2}{0.4}$ **e** $\sqrt{64}$

4 For which of the following will a calculator provide the exact value?

  a $2 \div 5$ **b** $\sqrt{3}$ **c** $\frac{4}{7}$ **d** $\frac{353}{120}$ **e** $\frac{17}{32}$

5 Which of the following are rational numbers?

  a 2.54789 **b** $-2.1717\ldots$ **c** $0.\overline{6}$ **d** 0.66 **e** $0.20020002\ldots$

6 Does a calculator display the exact values of all rational numbers?

7 Does a calculator display the exact values of all irrational numbers?

8 Explain the difference between $\{x: 0 < x < 10\}$ and $\{x: 0 < x < 10 \text{ and } x \text{ is an integer}\}$.

9 You know that $\frac{1}{3} = 0.\overline{3}$ and $\frac{2}{3} = 0.\overline{6}$. Explain why $1 = 0.\overline{9}$.

Problems and Applications

10 Write each number as a decimal.

  a $\frac{7}{8}$ **b** $1\frac{4}{11}$ **c** $-\frac{5}{6}$ **d** $\frac{3}{64}$

11 Write each number in fraction form.

  a 0.35 **b** $0.\overline{3}$ **c** $0.5555\ldots$ **d.** $0.\overline{6}$

12 Write each number as a ratio of two integers.

  a $0.\overline{15}$ **b** -2.456 **c** $4.111\ldots$ **d** 6

13 Which of the following are rational numbers?

  a $\sqrt{3} \cdot \sqrt{3}$ **b** $\sqrt{7} - \sqrt{7}$ **c** $\sqrt{14} \div 2\sqrt{14}$ **d** $2\sqrt{14}$

14 Locate the following values on a number line.

  a $2\sqrt{7}$ **b** $\sqrt{11} - 1$ **c** -1.2 **d** $-0.55\ldots$

15 Arrange the following numbers in order, from smallest to largest.

$$\frac{11}{10}, \frac{100}{99}, \sqrt{5} \div 2, 1.111\ldots$$

16 Find the values of *a, b,* and *c.* Indicate whether each is *rational* or *irrational.*

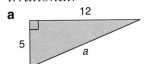
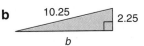
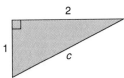

17 What points (x, y) satisfy the equation $x + y = 10$ if x and y must be natural numbers?

18 Is the statement true *always, sometimes,* or *never?*
  a An integer is a rational number.
  b A whole number is a natural number.
  c A rational number is an irrational number.
  d An irrational number is a real number.
  e A rational number is an integer.

19 Suppose that N = {natural numbers}, I = {integers}, Q = {rational numbers}, and R = {real numbers}. Is the statement *true* or *false?*
  a $N \subset I$ **b** $I \cap Q = Q$ **c** $I \cup Q = R$ **d** $I \cap R = I$

20 Copy the table, writing *yes* or *no* in each space to indicate the sets to which the numbers belong.

	Natural	Whole	Integer	Rational	Irrational	Real
13						
$\sqrt{5}$						
−7						
$-\frac{7}{2}$						
0						
$\sqrt{-4}$						
$-\frac{6}{2}$						

21 Draw a Venn diagram showing the relationship between the six sets of numbers discussed in this section.

22 a Use set-builder notation to describe the set of points shown.
  b If a point on this graph is selected at random, what is the probability that it will be in the third quadrant?

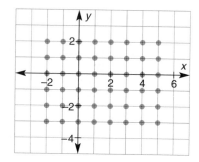

23 Which of the following pairs of sets are disjoint?
  a {Even integers} and {odd integers}
  b {Positive integers} and {negative integers}
  c {Prime numbers} and {even integers}
  d {Positive multiples of 5 less than 5} and {triangles with 5 sides}

24 **Spreadsheets** Suppose that *x* and *y* are both integers less than or equal to 12. Use a spreadsheet to find the set of all pairs (*x, y*) for which the hypotenuse of the triangle is an integer.

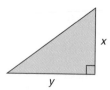

25 a Find the radius of the smallest circle that has its center at the origin and contains all of the points shown, either in its interior or on its circumference.
b What is the smallest radius that is an integer?

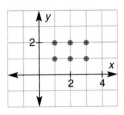

26 Evaluate each expression.
 a $(-3)(5 \times 7)$ **b** $(-3)(5)(7)$ **c** $19 - 4$ **d** $4 - 19$

27 Evaluate $\begin{bmatrix} 3 & -4 \\ -1 & 6 \\ 9 & -5 \end{bmatrix} \cdot \begin{bmatrix} -2 & 4 \\ 3 & -5 \end{bmatrix}$.

28 Technology Many calculators use arrays like the one shown to display numbers. By lighting up different parts of the array (lettered A–G in the diagram), a calculator can display any of the ten digits. For example, the set of lit parts for a 3 is {A, B, D, E, F}. What set of parts corresponds to each of the following?

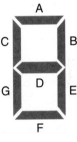

 a 2 **b** $3 \cap 2$
 c 4 **d** $1 \cap 5$

29 Communicating Suppose that A = {positive multiples of 4} and B = {positive multiples of 6}.
 a Describe in words $A \cap B$.
 b Find the least element in $A \cap B$.

30 Is the statement true *always, sometimes,* or *never?*
 a If $A \subset B$, then $B \subset A$.
 b If $A \cap B = \{\ \}$, then A and B are disjoint.

31 If $W = \{w : w$ is a multiple of 3$\}$ and $Z = \{z : z$ is a factor of 60$\}$, what is $W \cap Z$?

32 Given the irrational number $0.010010001\ldots$, find another irrational number that you can add to this number so that the sum will be a rational number.

Investigation

Fractions Use a calculator to investigate the decimal forms of fractions that have a denominator of 9. Then extend your investigation to fractions with denominators of 99, of 999, of 9999, and so forth. Write a description of the patterns you notice.

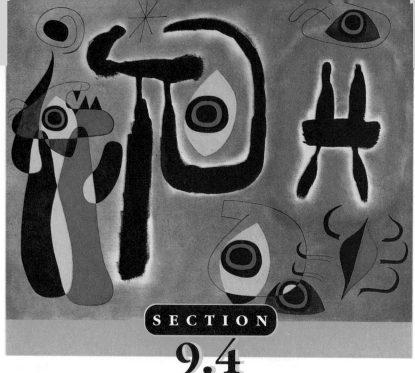

9.4
Pi and the Circle

THE MEANING OF π

A well known irrational number is π (pi). You have used this number to find circumferences and areas of circles. The symbol ⊙O (read "circle O") identifies a circle with center at point O.

$\overline{OA}$ is a radius of the circle. $\overline{CD}$ is a *chord.* The longest chord passes through the center and is a diameter of the circle. A diameter of a circle is twice as long as a radius of the circle. $\overline{RS}$ is a diameter.

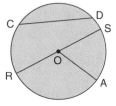

The people of many ancient civilizations discovered that dividing the circumference of a circle by the circle's diameter always results in the same number, regardless of the size of the circle. This ratio of the circumference to the diameter of a circle is the number π.

You can estimate the value of π by collecting several cans of different sizes. Use a string to measure their circumferences and diameters as accurately as possible. Divide each circumference by the corresponding diameter. Take the average of the ratios that you calculate. It should be close to 3.14.

The number π cannot be written as a ratio of two integers or as a terminating or repeating decimal. A close approximation of π can be found by pressing the π key on the calculator.

Example 1
If the distance around a circle is 34.7 centimeters, what is the circle's radius?

Solution
Based on the definition of π, $\frac{34.7}{\text{diameter}} = \pi$. Therefore,

$$\pi \times \text{diameter} = 34.7$$
$$\text{diameter} = \frac{34.7}{\pi} \approx 11.0 \text{ cm}$$

The radius is half the diameter, so the radius is ≈5.5 centimeters

Example 2
a Find the circumference of ⊙P.
b Find the area of ⊙P.

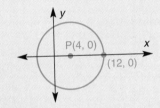

Solution
Since (4, 0) and (12, 0) are 8 units apart, the radius of the circle is 8.
a Circumference $= 2\pi r = 2 \cdot \pi \cdot 8 = 16\pi \approx 50.27$
b $A = \pi r^2 = \pi \cdot 8^2 = 64\pi \approx 201.06$
Sometimes an exact answer, such as 16π, is more useful than an approximation, such as 50.27, and sometimes not.

A PROPERTY OF CIRCLES

Circles have a number of interesting and useful properties. Draw several circles of different sizes, along with their diameters. Then draw a triangle in each circle such that the diameter is one side and the vertex opposite the diameter is on the circumference of the circle. In each figure, measure the angle opposite the diameter. You will find that the angle is a right angle. In the figure, $\overline{AC}$ is a diameter and ∠B is a right angle.

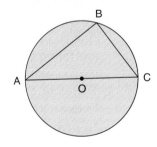

▶ **Right Angle Property:** If $\overline{AC}$ is a diameter of a circle and B is any point of the circle other than A or C, then ∠ABC is a right angle.

Sample Problems

Problem 1 Circle O has diameter $\overline{AC}$, AC = 10, and AB = 8. If a dart has an equal chance of landing on any point within the circle, what is the probability that the dart will land inside the triangle?

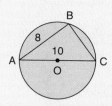

Solution By the Right Angle Property, $\angle ABC$ is a right angle. Using the Pythagorean Theorem, we find that $(BC)^2 + 64 = 100$, so BC = 6.

Area of $\triangle ABC = \frac{1}{2}bh = \frac{1}{2}(8)(6) = 24$
Area of $\odot O = \pi \cdot 5^2 = 25\pi$
Probability $= \frac{24}{25\pi} \approx .31$

The dart will land in the triangle about 31% of the time.

Problem 2 A circle with radius 2 rolls along the outside of the square without slipping. How far does the center of the circle travel when the circle makes one complete trip around the square?

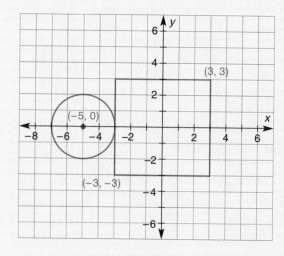

Solution The path of the center of the circle consists of four straight segments and four quarters of a circle with radius 2. Therefore, the distance traveled is $4(6) + 2 \cdot \pi \cdot 2$, or ≈ 36.57 units.

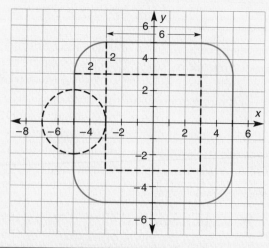

Think and Discuss

1 Can the ratio of two irrational numbers be a rational number? Explain your answer.

2 Can the ratio of two rational numbers be an irrational number? Explain your answer.

3 Press the π key on a scientific calculator. Does the display show a rational number or an irrational number?

4 Three values sometimes used for π are $\frac{22}{7}$, 3.14, and $\frac{355}{113}$.
  a Are any of these the exact value of π? Why or why not?
  b Which of the three is the closest to π?

5 In the diagram shown, AB = CD, BC = AD, and $\overline{AC}$ is a diameter.
  a What type of figure is ABCD? Why?
  b What is a way to find the center of a circle?

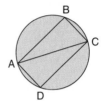

6 Explain what the letter π stands for.

7 Is the statement *true* or *false*?
  a 7π = 22   **b** 100π = 314   **c** π > 3.14

8 Let *r* = radius of a circle, *d* = diameter of the circle, *A* = area of the circle, and *C* = circumference of the circle. Write a function for
  a *d* in terms of *r*   **b** *r* in terms of *d*   **c** *A* in terms of *r*
  d *A* in terms of *d*   **e** *C* in terms of *r*   **f** *C* in terms of *d*
  g *d* in terms of *C*   **h** *r* in terms of *C*   **i** *r* in terms of *A*

9 These two circles are *concentric*—that is, they have the same center. If a dart has an equal chance of landing on any point within the outer circle, what is the probability that the dart will land within the inner circle?

10 In solving problem 9, Laura could not remember the value of π, so she used 5. Why did she still get the correct answer?

Problems and Applications

11 Determine the
  a Area of a circle with radius 7
  b Circumference of a circle with radius 8
  c Circumference of a circle with diameter 9
  d Area of a circle with diameter 10

12 What is this circle's
  a Diameter?
  b Radius?
  c Area?
  d Circumference?

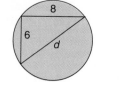

13 Circle O rolls along the line from A to B. How far does point O travel?

14 **Communicating** If $C(r) = 2\pi r$ and $A(r) = \pi r^2$, what are $C(5)$ and $A(4)$? Why does $C(-2)$ not make sense?

15 The circle rolls along the outside of the rectangle without slipping. How far has the center of the circle traveled after the circle has made one complete trip around the rectangle?

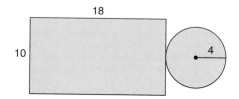

16 The circumference of a juice can is about 8.5 inches. Find the diameter of the can.

17 $\overline{AB}$ is a diameter of the circle. Find the coordinates of the endpoints of the diameter that is perpendicular to $\overline{AB}$.

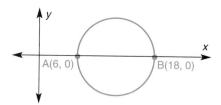

18 $\overline{AC}$ is a diameter of ⊙O. AC = 26 and AB = BC.
  a Find the area of △ABC.
  b Find AB.

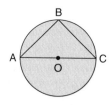

19 The circle is inscribed in the triangle.

  a Find the radius of the circle.
  b Which is greater, AB or the circumference of the circle?

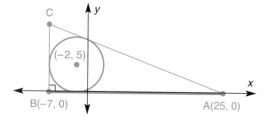

20 Circle O has diameter $\overline{BD}$. AB = 15, AD = 20, and DC = 7. Find BD and BC.

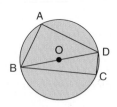

21 A wheel with a diameter of 3 feet rolls along a surface, making one complete revolution. How far does the center of the wheel travel?

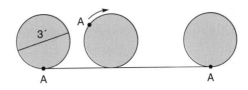

22 For the circle shown,
  a Find the length of the diameter
  b Find the area of the circle
  c If a dart has an equal chance of landing on any point within the circle, what is the probability that the dart will land in the square?

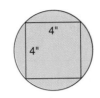

23 The circle rolls along the outside of the triangle without slipping. Find the distance that the center of the circle has traveled after one complete trip around the triangle.

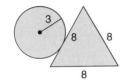

24 A bicycle wheel has a diameter of 27 inches.
  a When the wheel makes one revolution, how far does the bike travel?
  b How far is this in feet?
  c How many revolutions of the wheel are needed for the bike to travel one mile? (Hint: There are 5280 feet in a mile.)

25 **Science** The pedal gear of a bike has 48 teeth. The gear on the rear wheel has 14 teeth.
  a Which completes a revolution faster, the pedal gear or the gear on the rear wheel?
  b How many revolutions does the rear wheel make for each revolution of the pedals?

26 In problem 25, if the diameter of the rear wheel is 27 inches, how many revolutions of the pedals are needed to travel one mile?

◀ LOOKING BACK **Spiral Learning** LOOKING AHEAD ▶

---

27 Find the largest integer value of x for which the figure will have a perimeter of less than 27 inches.

x

$2x + 1$

28 In how many ways can eight students be arranged in a row of eight seats?

29 The following favorite fitness activities were reported in a survey of 397 people: running, 150; biking, 92; aerobics, 73; and walking, 82. Draw a circle graph to represent this information. Include an appropriate percent in each section.

30 Copy the table and complete it by writing *yes* or *no* in each space to indicate the sets to which each number belongs.

	Natural	Whole	Integer	Rational	Irrational	Real
-2.3						
π						
$-\frac{6}{2}$						
3						
$2.\overline{3}$						
0						
$\sqrt{2}$						

31 Draw three Venn diagrams like the one shown. Shade the regions that represent
a $A \cup B$ **b** $A \cap B$ **c** $(A \cap B) \cup C$

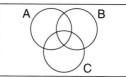

32 Solve each equation and simplify each expression.

a $3(x-2) - 4(2-x)$
c $9 - 3(4-x) = 18$
e $9 - 4(1 + 3x) - 76$

b $3(x+4) - 2x = 12$
d $-10 - 3x = -76$
f $4x - 2(x-3) - 6$

33 Write $12.\overline{39}$ as a fraction.

34 Write $4\frac{7}{11}$ as a decimal.

Investigation

Approximating π Mathematicians have discovered a number of expressions that can be used to approximate the value of π. One of them is

$$\sqrt{6\left(\frac{1}{1^2} + \frac{1}{2^2} + \frac{1}{3^2} + \frac{1}{4^2} + \ldots\right)}$$

The farther the pattern inside the parentheses is extended, the closer the value of the expression is to π. Use a calculator to evaluate the expression for the first three fractions in the pattern. How close is the resulting value to π? Then see if you can figure out a way to use a spreadsheet to continue the pattern. How many fractions do you have to use to approximate π to the nearest hundredth?

Properties of Real Numbers

ASSOCIATIVE PROPERTIES

Example 1
Find the area of the triangle.

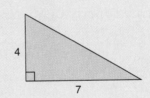

Solution
The formula for the area is $A = \frac{1}{2}bh$.

Method 1 $\frac{1}{2}(4 \cdot 7) = \frac{1}{2} \cdot 28 = 14$

Method 2 $\left(\frac{1}{2} \cdot 4\right)7 = 2 \cdot 7 = 14$

The answer is the same for both methods. It doesn't matter which two numbers you multiply first. We say that multiplication is ***associative.***

▶ **Associative Property of Multiplication:** $a(bc) = (ab)c$

Addition has a similar property: $4 + (5 + 7) = (4 + 5) + 7 = 16$. It doesn't matter which two numbers you add first.

▶ **Associative Property of Addition:** $a + (b + c) = (a + b) + c$

Example 2
Evaluate each pair of expressions.
a $36 \div (6 \div 2)$ and $(36 \div 6) \div 2$ **b** $12 - (7 - 2)$ and $(12 - 7) - 2$

Solution
a $36 \div (6 \div 2) = 36 \div 3 = 12$
$(36 \div 6) \div 2 = 6 \div 2 = 3$

b $12 - (7 - 2) = 12 - 5 = 7$
$(12 - 7) - 2 = 5 - 2 = 3$

Example 2 shows that division and subtraction are not associative.

COMMUTATIVE PROPERTIES

Example 3
Find the length of the hypotenuse in the figure shown.

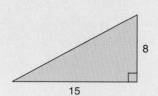

Solution
Method 1 $8^2 + 15^2 = 64 + 225 = 289; \sqrt{289} = 17$
Method 2 $15^2 + 8^2 = 225 + 64 = 289; \sqrt{289} = 17$

The order in which the numbers are added does not matter. We say that addition is **commutative.**

▶ **Commutative Property of Addition:** $a + b = b + a$

The order of multiplication also does not affect a result. The area of an 8-by-3 rectangle can be found by evaluating either $8 \cdot 3$ or $3 \cdot 8$.

▶ **Commutative Property of Multiplication:** $ab = ba$

Example 4
Evaluate each pair of expressions.
a $42.3 \div 6.2$ and $6.2 \div 42.3$ b $31.7 - 58.5$ and $58.5 - 31.7$

Solution
a $42.3 \div 6.2 = 6.8$ b $31.7 - 58.5 = -26.8$
   $6.2 \div 42.3 = 0.15$ $58.5 - 31.7 = 26.8$

Example 4 shows that division and subtraction are not commutative.

THE ZERO PRODUCT PROPERTY

Example 5
Find all values of x that solve each equation.
a $6x = 0$ b $x(5 - 9) = 0$ c $x(x - 2) = 0$ d $(x - 3)(x + 4) = 0$

Solution
The only number that can make a product equal to 0 is 0.
a $6x = 0$ will be true only if $x = 0$.

b $x(5 - 9) = x(-4) = 0$ will be true only if $x = 0$.

c $x(x - 2) = 0$ will be true if $x = 0$ or if $x - 2 = 0$.
Therefore, there are two solutions: $x = 0$ and $x = 2$.

Check: $0(0 - 2) = 0$; $2(2 - 2) = 2(0) = 0$

d $(x - 3)(x + 4) = 0$ will be true if $x - 3 = 0$ or if $x + 4 = 0$.
Therefore, $x = 3$ and $x = -4$ are solutions.

Check: $(3 - 3)(3 + 4) = 0(7) = 0$
$\quad\quad\quad (-4 - 3)(-4 + 4) = (-7)0 = 0$

▶ **Zero Product Property:** If $ab = 0$, then either $a = 0$ or $b = 0$.

Sample Problems

Problem 1 In finding the circumference of the circle, Walker and Maria used different formulas but got the same answer.

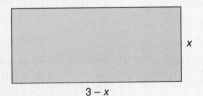

Walker: $C = 2\pi r = 2\pi(8) \approx 50.27$
Maria: $C = \pi d = \pi(16) \approx 50.27$

Use number properties to show that the formulas are equivalent.

Solution Commutative Property of Multiplication $2\pi r = \pi(2)(r)$
Associative Property of Multiplication $= \pi(2r)$
$\quad\quad\quad\quad\quad\quad\quad\quad\quad\quad\quad\quad\quad\quad\quad\quad\quad = \pi d$

Problem 2
a For what values of x will the area of the rectangle equal 0?
b On a number line, graph the possible values of x in this figure.

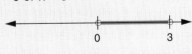

Solution **a** Area of a rectangle = bh $x(3 - x) = 0$
Zero Product Property $x = 0$ or $3 - x = 0$
$\quad\quad\quad\quad\quad\quad\quad\quad\quad\quad\quad\quad\quad\quad x = 0$ or $x = 3$

b The area of a rectangle must be positive. Testing values less than 0, between 0 and 3, and greater than 3 shows that a positive product is found only when x is between 0 and 3.

Think and Discuss

1 Rachel wants to know how many small cubes are in the large rectangular solid. Should she evaluate $(5 \times 4)3$ or $5(4 \times 3)$?

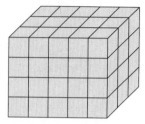

2 Match each equation with the property it illustrates.
  a $4(3 \cdot 5) = (4 \cdot 3) \cdot 5$ 1. Associative Property of Multiplication
  b $3 + 5 = 5 + 3$ 2. Associative Property of Addition
  c $(9 + 4) + 2 = (4 + 9) + 2$ 3. Commutative Property of Multiplication
  d $(4 + 7) \cdot 3 = 4 \cdot 3 + 7 \cdot 3$ 4. Commutative Property of Addition
  e $(4 + 7) \cdot 3 = 3 \cdot (4 + 7)$ 5. Distributive Property of Multiplication
  f $5 + (2 + 6) = (5 + 2) + 6$ over Addition

3 Without using a calculator, indicate whether $<$, $>$, or $=$ goes in the blank.
  a $(-81)(-59)$ _____ $(-59)(-81)$ **b** $-81 \div 3$ _____ $3 \div -81$
  c $-18 - 57$ _____ $-57 - (-18)$ **d** $(-49) + 87$ _____ $87 + (-49)$

4 For what set of values of x is $(x - 100)(x - 99)(x - 98)(x - 97) = 0$ a true equation?

5 Use several sets to determine if, for the intersection and union of sets,
  a $\cap$ is commutative   **b** $\cup$ is commutative
  c $\cap$ is associative   **d** $\cup$ is associative

6 If the empty set, { }, is like 0 and intersection is an operation, is there a zero intersection property—if $A \cap B = \{ \}$, then is $A = \{ \}$ or $B = \{ \}$? If not, give a counterexample.

7 Is the converse of the zero intersection property discussed in problem 6 true? (If $A = \{ \}$ or $B = \{ \}$, is $A \cap B = \{ \}$?) Explain your answer.

8 If $a \wedge b$ is defined to mean a^b, is the operation symbolized by $\wedge$ commutative? Why or why not?

Problems and Applications

9 Identify the property illustrated.
  a $(3 \cdot 4) \cdot 7 = (4 \cdot 3) \cdot 7$ **b** $(3 + 4) + 10 = 3 + (4 + 10)$
  c $7x = 0$, so $x = 0$ **d** $4(x + 2) = 4x + 8$
  e $4(x + 3) = 4(3 + x)$

10 Solve each equation for x.
  a $(x)6 = 0$ **b** $(x - 4)6 = 0$
  c $(x - 4)(6x) = 0$ **d** $(x - 2)(x + 9) = 0$

11 Without using a calculator, indicate whether <, >, or = goes in the blank.

    a $91 + (73 + 87)$ _____ $(91 + 73) + 87$

    b $77 + (41 - 82)$ _____ $(77 + 41) - 82$

    c $59 - (72 - 77)$ _____ $(59 - 72) - 77$

    d $37 - (18 + 15)$ _____ $(37 - 18) + 15$

12 State a property or operation for each step.

$$\frac{1}{2} \cdot 4(7 + 6) = \left(\frac{1}{2} \cdot 4\right)(7 + 6)$$
$$= 2(7 + 6)$$
$$= 14 + 12$$
$$= 26$$

13 The product of three consecutive integers is 0. What are the possible values of these three integers?

14 **Consumer Math**   For a $340 television set, Goodbuy offers a 10% clearance discount followed by a 15% holiday discount. On the same item, Cheapo offers a 15% seasonal discount followed by a 10% overstocked discount. How do the TV prices of the two stores compare?

15 Suppose that $A = \begin{bmatrix} 2 & 3 \\ 4 & 5 \end{bmatrix}$ and $B = \begin{bmatrix} -1 & 5 \\ 3 & 7 \end{bmatrix}$.

    a Is $A + B = B + A$?

    b Is $AB = BA$?

    c Do you think matrix addition is commutative?

    d Do you think matrix multiplication is commutative?

16 Use the number properties to evaluate each expression. Do not use a calculator.

    a $(0.06 \cdot 8)100$ **b** $(15 \cdot 7) \cdot \frac{2}{5}$

    c $(432 + 450) + 18$ **d** $98 + (576 + 2)$

17 **Communicating**   Two students computed the area of the trapezoid in different ways. Explain why each method works.

    Mandy: $A = \frac{1}{2} \cdot 6(4 + 7) = 3(4 + 7) = 3 \cdot 11 = 33$

    Carlos: $A = \frac{1}{2} \cdot 6(4 + 7) = \frac{1}{2} \cdot 6 \cdot 11 = \frac{1}{2}(66) = 33$

18 A "combination" is determined by multiplying all of the numbers in a row or column. Without multiplying, determine which row or column will have the greatest combination.

	1	2	3	4	5
A	0	9	17	4	3
B	6	21	0	2	19
C	18	0	5	3	6
D	4	11	12	8	2
E	1	18	6	4	0

19 If $r \# s = r\sqrt{s}$.

    a Is the operation symbolized by # commutative?

    b Is there a "zero property" for the operation?

20 If $a @ b = a + b - 2$, is the operation symbolized by @ commutative?

21 For 2 × 2 matrices, the zero matrix is $\begin{bmatrix} 0 & 0 \\ 0 & 0 \end{bmatrix}$.

  a Evaluate $\begin{bmatrix} 2 & 2 \\ 0 & 0 \end{bmatrix} \cdot \begin{bmatrix} 0 & -2 \\ 0 & 2 \end{bmatrix}$.

  b Is there a zero product property for matrices?

22 Solve each equation for x.
  a $2x(3x - 1) = 0$ **b** $(3x - 4)(2x + 7) = 0$
  c $5x(x - 7)(x + 11) = 0$ **d** $3(x + 2) + 0 = 15$

23 **a** Write a function $A(x)$ for the area of the figure.
  b What values of x give an area of zero?
  c What is the set of possible values of x?

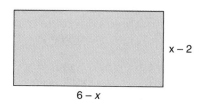

$x - 2$

$6 - x$

24 The digits of a three-digit number are all different. The product of the digits is 0 and the sum is 7. If the number is divided by 10, the result is a prime number. What might the three-digit number be?

25 Use the number properties to simplify each expression.
  a $\frac{2}{3}\left(5 \cdot \frac{3}{2}\right)$ **b** $\left(\frac{1}{7} \cdot 14\right)35$
  c $\frac{7}{5}\left(\frac{5}{7} \cdot 9\right)$ **d** $0.85 - \left(\frac{1}{2} + \frac{17}{20}\right)$

26 In the squares shown, lengths x and y are related by the equations $(6y - 3x) \cdot 10 = 0$ and $y = x - 2$. Find the perimeter of the smaller square.

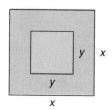

y x

y

x

◀ LOOKING BACK **Spiral Learning** LOOKING AHEAD ▶

27 For the points $(4, 9)$ and $(-2, 7)$,
  a Find the mean of the x-coordinates and the mean of the y-coordinates.
  b Graph the two given points and the point found in part **a.**
  c Discuss the relationships among the three points.

28 Find lengths a, b, and c.

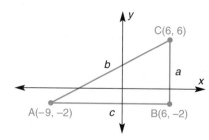

29 The measures of the angles of a triangle are in the ratio 2:5:8. Find the measures of the angles.

30 Copy and complete the table for the formula $A = \pi r^2$. Round to the nearest tenth.

r	2	4	6	8	10
A					

31 $\overline{AC}$ is a diameter and AB = 7 inches. The area of the triangle is 14 square inches. Find
   a BC
   b AC
   c The circumference of the circle

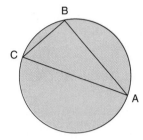

32 The Acme computer can be purchased with any one of 6 different disk drives, 9 different memory sizes, and 5 different monitors. How many different types of computer configurations are possible?

33 Technology   Most scientific calculators have a ⌊x!⌋ key, called a *factorial* key. What are the results of the following calculator operations?
   a 2 ⌊x!⌋
   c 3 ⌊x!⌋
   e 4 ⌊x!⌋
   g 5 ⌊x!⌋
   b 1 ⌊×⌋ 2 ⌊=⌋
   d 1 ⌊×⌋ 2 ⌊×⌋ 3 ⌊=⌋
   f 1 ⌊×⌋ 2 ⌊×⌋ 3 ⌊×⌋ 4 ⌊=⌋
   h 1 ⌊×⌋ 2 ⌊×⌋ 3 ⌊×⌋ 4 ⌊×⌋ 5 ⌊=⌋

34 a The square has side 4. A dart lands somewhere inside the square. What is the probability the dart has landed inside the circle?
   b Repeat part **a** for a square of side 8 and a circle that is proportionately larger than the circle in part **a**.

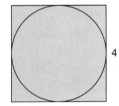

35 Find the values of *x* and *y* that solve the equations $x = 19 + 4y$ and $2x + 5y = 12$.

Investigation

Language   What meanings of the words *commute* and *associate* are most familiar to you? How are the everyday meanings of these words related to the mathematical meanings of *commutative* and *associative?* Consult a dictionary to find out the meanings of the Latin words that are the ancestors of these terms. Does knowing the meanings of the Latin words help you see how the English meanings are related?

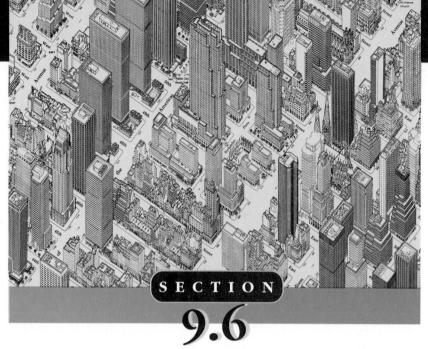

9.6
Two Coordinate Formulas

THE DISTANCE FORMULA

In the city of Fairview, the avenues run east-west and the streets run north-south—except for Main Street, which cuts diagonally across many streets and avenues. Fairview Middle School is located at the intersection of Second Avenue, Fifth Street, and Main Street. Fairview High School is located at the intersection of Eighth Avenue, Ninth Street, and Main Street. The distance between two consecutive streets or avenues is 0.1 mile.

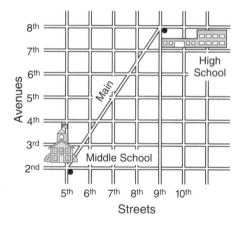

You can find the distance from the middle school to the high school by drawing a right triangle. The distance is 0.4 mile east-west and 0.6 mile north-south.

$$d = \sqrt{0.6^2 + 0.4^2} \approx 0.7 \text{ mi}$$

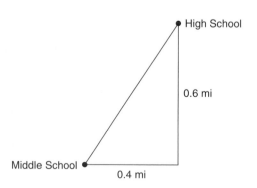

Example 1
Find the distance between points A and B.

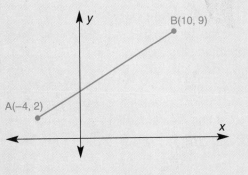

Solution
Form a right triangle. Find the lengths of the legs.

Horizontal leg: $|10 - (-4)| = 14$
Vertical leg: $|9 - 2| = 7$

By the Pythagorean Theorem,

$$AB = \sqrt{14^2 + 7^2} \approx 15.7$$

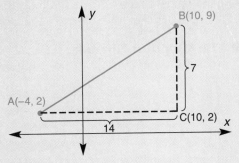

It is possible to find the distance by working directly with the coordinates. In Example 1, $AB = \sqrt{[10 - (-4)]^2 + (9 - 2)^2}$

> **The Distance Formula:** If (x_1, y_1) and (x_2, y_2) are the coordinates of any two points, then the distance between these two points is equal to

$$\sqrt{(x_2 - x_1)^2 + (y_2 - y_1)^2}$$

THE MIDPOINT FORMULA

Look again at the map of Fairview. Can you determine what intersection is midway between the middle school and the high school?

Example 2
Find the coordinates of the point midway between A(-3, 8) and B(15, 2).

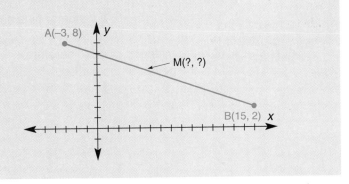

Solution

First, draw a right triangle. Find the coordinates of P by averaging the y-coordinates.

$$\left(-3, \frac{8 + 2}{2}\right) = (-3, 5)$$

Find the coordinates of Q by averaging the x-coordinates.

$$\left(\frac{-3 + 15}{2}, 2\right) = (6, 2)$$

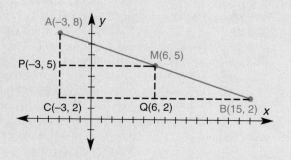

Using the x-coordinate from Q and the y-coordinate from P gives the midpoint M(6, 5).

▶ **The Midpoint Formula:** If (x_1, y_1) and (x_2, y_2) are the coordinates of two points, the point midway between the two points has the coordinates

$$\left(\frac{x_1 + x_2}{2}, \frac{y_1 + y_2}{2}\right)$$

Sample Problems

Problem 1

a Find the circumference of Circle O.
b Find the area of Circle O.

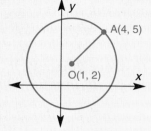

Solution　Find the radius of the circle by using the distance formula.

$$r = \sqrt{(4 - 1)^2 + (5 - 2)^2} = \sqrt{9 + 9} \approx 4.24$$

a $C = 2\pi r = 2\pi(4.24) \approx 26.6$　　　**b** $A = \pi r^2 = \pi(4.24)^2 \approx 56.5$

Problem 2

The endpoints of a diameter of a circle are A(−4, −3) and B(6, 15).
a Find the coordinates of the center of the circle.
b Is the point P(5, −3.4) inside or outside the circle?

Solution　**a** M is the midpoint of $\overline{AB}$. Therefore, M is the center of the circle.

$$M\left(\frac{-4 + 6}{2}, \frac{-3 + 15}{2}\right) = M(1, 6)$$

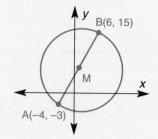

b The radius of the circle can be found by using the distance formula with B(6, 15) and M(1, 6).

$$r = \sqrt{(6-1)^2 + (15-6)^2} = \sqrt{5^2 + 9^2} \approx 10.296$$

We next want to find the distance from M(1, 6) to P(5, –3.4).

$$MP = \sqrt{(1-5)^2 + [6-(-3.4)]^2} = \sqrt{(-4)^2 + 9.4^2} \approx 10.216$$

Since the distance from M to P is less than the radius of the circle, point P lies inside the circle.

Think and Discuss

1 When you use the distance formula, does it matter which point you use as (x_1, y_1) and which you use as (x_2, y_2)? Why or why not?

2 Does the order of points matter in the midpoint formula?

3 Explain the connection between averages and the midpoint formula.

4 Find the coordinates of some points that are 5 units from the origin.

5 Knowing an endpoint, A, and the midpoint, M, of a segment, Jason used the figure shown to find the other endpoint.
a What are the coordinates of the other endpoint, B?
b Why does the figure work?

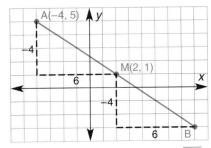

6 Given points A(–10, 2) and B(6, –10), find points that divide segment $\overline{AB}$ into four congruent segments.

7 a Find the distance AB for $a = 2$ and $b = 3$.
b Find AB for $a = 7$ and $b = 1$.
c Find AB for $a = -1$ and $b = 6$.
d Explain the results of parts **a**, **b**, and **c**.

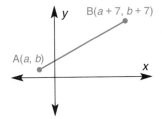

Problems and Applications

8 Find the distance between each pair of points.
a (–5, 6) and (8, 6)
b (4, –1) and (4, 12)
c (5, 0) and (0, –12)
d (6, –3) and (3, 1)

9 Find the midpoint of the segment joining each pair of points.
   a $(9, -4)$ and $(15, -10)$ **b** $(-8, 10)$ and $(16, 5)$
   c $(1.3, 5.8)$ and $(2.5, -6)$ **d** $(3.9, 2)$ and $(-4.7, 2)$

10 M is the midpoint of $\overline{AB}$. Find the coordinates of B.

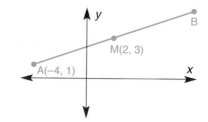

11 For the given circle, find
   a AO   **b** BO
   c CO   **d** FO

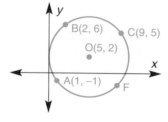

12 Given points $A(-8, -3)$ and $B(4, 13)$, find
   a The length of $\overline{AB}$
   b The midpoint of $\overline{AB}$
   c The distance from A to the midpoint

13 **Surveying**   A land surveyor for a housing development drew the grid shown. The side length of each small square represents 1000 feet. Find, to the nearest foot, the distance between points
   a B2 and B5   **b** C3 and F6
   c G1 and F5   **d** A2 and D6

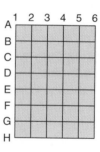

14 Find the distance from C to the midpoint of $\overline{AB}$.

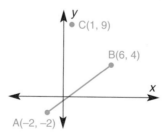

15 Find AB, BC, and AC. What kind of triangle is $\triangle ABC$?

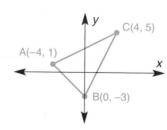

16 Pick three points on the coordinate plane that do not all lie on a straight line, and connect them to form a triangle. Locate the midpoints of two sides of the triangle.
  a Find the length of the segment joining the two midpoints.
  b Find the length of the side opposite the segment used in part **a**.
  c What is the ratio of the lengths found in parts **a** and **b**?

17 Find the midpoint of the segment joining each pair of points.
  a A($\sqrt{2}$, 3) and B($-\sqrt{2}$, 5)　　　　　　**b** C(0.5, -0.5) and D(-0.5, 1.5)

18 For circle O, find
  a The radius
  b The diameter
  c The area
  d The circumference

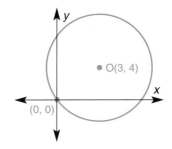

19 Draw a triangle with the given vertex matrix. Connect the midpoints of the sides of the triangle and find the vertex matrix for the smaller triangle. Could you have found the matrix without drawing the smaller triangle?

$$\mathbf{x} \begin{bmatrix} 3 & -4 & 8 \\ -9 & 5 & -4 \end{bmatrix}$$
$$\mathbf{y}$$

20 If A\$B means finding the midpoint of $\overline{AB}$, is A\$B = B\$A?

21 Locate the points A(3, 9), B(-5, 6), C(-3, -5), and D(5, -2) on a coordinate system.
  a Draw and name the quadrilateral having these four points as vertices.
  b Find the midpoint of $\overline{AC}$.
  c Find the midpoint of $\overline{BD}$.
  d Find the lengths of $\overline{AB}$ and $\overline{CD}$.
  e Find the lengths of $\overline{BC}$ and $\overline{AD}$.

22 Find the area of the shaded region, given that ABCD is a square.

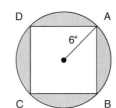

23 **a** Find the coordinates of the midpoint of $\overline{AC}$.
  b Find the coordinates of the midpoint of $\overline{BD}$.
  c What do you notice?

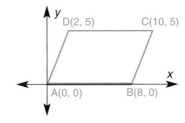

24 a Plot the points represented in the table below and connect them.

b What function F could have produced the values in the table—that is, if $y = F(x)$, what is $F(x)$?

x	−5	−4	−3	−2	−1	0	1	2	3	4	5
y	5	4	3	2	1	0	1	2	3	4	5

25 Consumer Math Mark bought six sandwiches at $1.64 each, four pieces of pie at $1.05 each, and four juices at $0.98 each. There is a 7% sales tax. Find the total bill.

26 Solve each equation, and simplify each expression.

a $9x(2x - 3) = 0$

b $9x + 6x - 3 = 2$

c $5x + 8 - 3(9 - 2x)$

d $-3x - 2(4 - x)$

27 Evaluate each expression.

a $9 - (3 - 7)$

b $2 - 3^2$

c $\dfrac{18 - 6}{-3} - (5)(-2)$

d $\sqrt{3^2} + \sqrt{4^2} - \sqrt{3^2 + 4^2}$

28 Express each number as a product of prime numbers.

a 46   **b** 180   **c** 363   **d** 462

29 If $(x, y) = (3, 8)$, $a = \frac{4}{3}$, and $y = ax + b$, what is the value of b?

30 If A = {9, 12, 15} and B = {−6, 0, 6, 12, 18}, what is

a A ∪ B?   **b** A ∩ B?

31 Name the property illustrated by each equation.

a $a + 7 = 7 + a$

b $(ab)c = a(bc)$

c $(a + b) + c = (b + a) + c$

d $p(q + r) = pq + pr$

e $3ab = 3ba$

f $a + (2 \cdot 3 + x) = (a + 3 \cdot 2) + x$

32 Suppose that 4 segments make 1 square, 7 segments make 2 squares, 10 segments make 3 squares, and 13 segments make 4 squares. Write a function for the number of segments needed to make n squares.

Investigation

Geography   On a flat surface, like the coordinate plane, distances are measured along straight line segments. How are distances measured on curved surfaces, like the surface of the earth? Select two cities that are at roughly the same latitude and are on different continents. Use a globe and a piece of string to find the length of the shortest route between the cities.

9.7
Graphs of Equations

There are a number of ways to show mathematical relationships. Pairs of values can be listed in a table. A graph can be used to provide a visual presentation of a direction or trend. An equation can be used to show the relationship between the values of two or more variables.

Li and Josh went for a 5-hour hike. They walked at a rate of 3 miles an hour. If we let h stand for hours and m for miles, then we can make a table showing the relationship between time and distance.

h	1	2	3	4	5
m	3	6	9	12	15

We can use the pairs of numbers as coordinates, and we can use the coordinates to plot points. Connecting the points will give the graph shown.

To find the number of miles traveled, you multiply the number of hours by 3. This can be shown by the equation $m = 3h$.

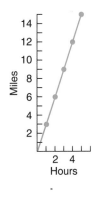

Example 1

Make a table and a graph for the equation $y = 2x - 5$.

Solution

We can select any values to substitute for x to find y values. We will substitute $\{-1, 0, 1, 2, 3, 4\}$.

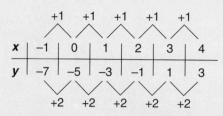

x	−1	0	1	2	3	4
y	−7	−5	−3	−1	1	3

Note that as the x values increase by 1, the y values increase by 2. The coefficient of x in the equation is 2 and causes this increase in y.

Also note that when $x = 0$, $y = -5$. The constant term in the equation is also −5.

We can use the pattern of x and y values to help us draw the graph. We start at any point in the table, say (0, −5), and move to the right 1 unit (thus increasing x by 1). Then we move upward 2 units (thus increasing y by 2) to arrive at another point on the graph, (1, −3). We repeat this process several times to locate several points on the graph, then draw a straight line through the points.

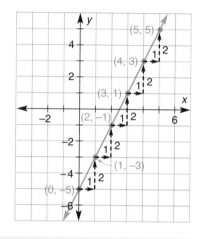

Example 2

Use the table to draw a graph. Then write an equation for the relationship.

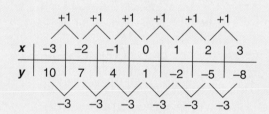

x	−3	−2	−1	0	1	2	3
y	10	7	4	1	−2	−5	−8

Solution

To draw the graph, we use the pattern from the table.

In determining the equation, we notice that each change of +1 in x corresponds to a change of −3 in y. So x must be multiplied by −3 in the equation. When $x = 0$, $y = 1$, so the constant term is 1. The equation is $y = -3x + 1$.

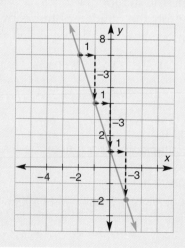

Example 3

Use the graph to create a table. Then write an equation for the relationship.

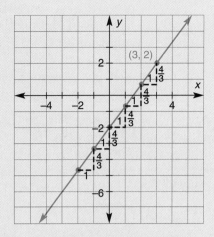

Solution

We notice that the point (3, 2) is on the graph. Also, for every increase of 1 in the value of *x*, there is an increase of $\frac{4}{3}$ in the value of *y*. With this information we can create the table shown.

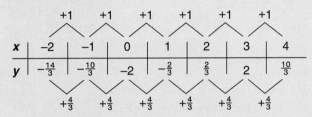

Using the pattern for the change in *y* values and the value of *y* when *x* = 0, we have the equation $y = \frac{4}{3}x + (-2)$.

Sample Problems

Problem 1

Write an equation that represents the graph.

(The solution to this problem appears on the next page.)

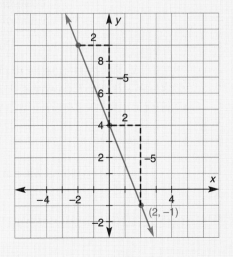

Solution   For each change of 2 in *x*, there is a change of –5 in *y*. So for a change of 1 in *x*, there is a change of –2.5 in *y*. The equation must have the form $y = -2.5x +$ constant. To find the constant, we substitute the coordinates, (2, –1).

$$-1 = -2.5(2) + \text{constant}$$
$$-1 = -5 + \text{constant}$$
$$4 = \text{constant}$$

The equation is $y = -2.5x + 4$.

Problem 2   The math class at Algebra High is planning a car wash to raise money for a $450 computer. The students' plans are based partly on the following:

Expenses (polish, cloths, sponges): $100
Income: washes, $3 each; polishes, $4 each

The students estimate that half of the customers will want a polish.
a What is the average income expected per customer?
b Complete the table.

Number of customers	0	10	20	30	40
Profit					

c Write an equation relating number of customers to profit.
d How many customers are needed for the math class to earn enough money to purchase the computer?

Solution   **a** Income for every two customers:

2 washes + 1 polish = $3 + $3 + $4 = $10

Therefore, the average income per customer is $5.

b

Number of customers	0	10	20	30	40
Profit	–100	–50	0	50	100

c For each increase of 10 customers, there is a $50 increase in profit. For each increase of 1 customer, there is a $5 increase in profit.

$$\text{Profit} = 5(\text{customers}) + (-100)$$

d For the students to purchase the computer, the ordered pair (*c*, 450) is needed, where *c* is the number of customers.

$$450 = 5c - 100$$
$$550 = 5c$$
$$110 = c$$

The students will earn enough money to purchase the computer if they have 110 or more customers.

Think and Discuss

1 Indicate which of the three groups of points lie on a line.
   a (1, 4), (2, 5), (3, 6), (4, 7)   **b** (−1, 1), (0, 0), (1, 1), (2, 4)
   c (0.5, 3.5), (4, 21), (7.5, 38.5)

2 In the equation $y = 2x + 3$,
   a Which number shows how much y changes for each increase of 1 in x?
   b Which number is called the constant?

3 If you know that the graph of an equation is a straight line, how many points should you plot before you draw the line?

4 Copy the table twice and fill in values for y such that
   a The points lie on a line
   b The points do not lie on a line

x	−4	−3	−2	−1	0	1	2	3
y								

5 For the equation $y = 5x + 1$, explain why when x increases by 1, y increases by 5.

6 The points represented by the values in the table all lie on the same line except one. Which coordinates represent a point not on the line? How can you change the coordinates so that the point is on the line?

x	−3	−2	−1	0	1	2	3	4	5
y	−8	−5	−2	1	4	8	10	13	16

7 **Business**   The students of the Math Club are selling mugs to raise money. They buy 500 mugs at $1.25 each. They are selling the mugs for $4.00 each.
   a What is the total expense?
   b What is the income per sale of each mug?
   c Copy and complete the table.

Mugs sold	0	1	2	3	4	5	6
Profit (dollars)	−625						

   d Write a profit equation.
   e How many mugs must be sold to make a profit of $400?

Problems and Applications

8 **Business**   Suppose that potatoes cost $0.59 a pound.
   a Copy and complete the table.

Pounds	0	1	2	3	4	5
Cost	0	0.59				

   b Write an equation for the cost, c, of p pounds of potatoes.

9 Copy and complete the table for the equation $y = 4x + 7$.

x	−5	−4	−3	−2	−1	0	1	2	3	4
y	−13	−9								

10 Make a table for each equation.

   a $y = 2x - 3$ **b** $y = 3x + 1$ **c** $y = \frac{1}{2}x + 1$

11 Draw a graph for each table.

  a

x	−3	−2	−1	0	1	2
y	10	7	4	1	−2	−5

  b

x	−3	−2	−1	0	1	2
y	18	16	14	12	10	8

12 Make a table and draw a graph for each equation.

   a $y = x - 2$ **b** $y = -\frac{2}{3}x + 1$

13 For the graph shown,
  a Find the increase in the value
     of y for each increase of 1 in x.
  b Find the value of y when $x = 0$.
  c Write an equation for the graph.

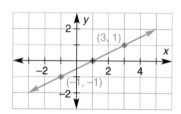

14 a Continue the pattern in the table and then graph the data.

x	−9	−7	−5	−3	−1	1	3	5
y	−5	−1	3					

  b How much does y change for each increase of 1 in x?

15 For each table, write an equation of the form $y = ax + b$.

  a

x	−3	−2	−1	0	1	2
y	−3	0	3	6	9	12

  b

x	−3	−2	−1	0	1	2
y	7	4	1	−2	−5	−8

16 Which of the following tables have graphs that are straight lines?

  a

x	−3	−2	−1	0	1	2
y	9	5	1	−3	−7	−11

  b

x	−3	−2	−1	0	1	2
y	9	4	1	0	1	4

  c

x	−3	−2	−1	0	1	2
y	$-\frac{1}{3}$	$-\frac{1}{2}$	−1	—	1	$\frac{1}{2}$

17 Sports The winning heights in the men's Olympic high jump from 1948 through 1988 were as follows. Heights are in inches.

Year	'48	'52	'56	'60	'64	'68	'72	'76	'80	'84	'88
Height	78	80.3	83.25	85	85.75	88.24	87.75	88.5	92.75	92.5	93.5

  a Plot the points, using the x-axis for years and the y-axis for inches.
  b Draw a line to approximate the data.
  c Predict the winning height in 2000.

18 Given the equation and point, determine the value of the constant. Then graph each equation.

   a $y = \frac{2}{3}x + $ constant; $(6, -2)$ **b** $y = -\frac{1}{4}x + $ constant; $(8, 5)$

19 Using x values from -3 to 3, make tables for
  a $y = 5x$ **b** $y = 9$

20 **Science** A plane is descending at a rate of 640 feet per minute. Right now (at time zero) its altitude is 30,000 feet. Negative time means minutes just past. Positive time means minutes to come.
  a Copy and complete the table.

Time	−3	−2	−1	0	1	2	3
Altitude				30,000			

  b Write an equation for this table.
  c When will the plane be at 5,000 feet?

21 Write an equation for each graph.

a

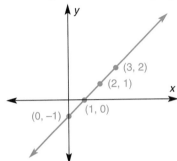

b

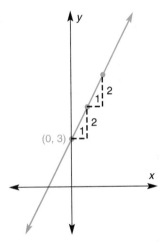

22 a Suppose that y is the area of the shaded portion of the rectangle. Use the given values of x to complete the table.

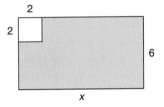

x	4	5	6	7	8	9	10
y							

  b Using the pattern from the table, complete the function

  Shaded area(x) = _____

  c Draw a graph of the data.
  d What is the set of possible values of x?

23 Copy and complete the table, and draw a graph, for the equation $y = 1 + \frac{3}{4}x$.

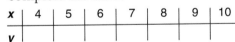

	A		B				C				
x	−4	−3	−2	−1	0	1	2	3	4	5	6
y											

Compute the distance between points A and B and between C and B.

24 If PQ = 18, find the area of the two semicircles with centers at P and Q.

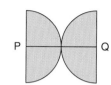

25 a Find the distance between the midpoints of $\overline{AB}$ and $\overline{BC}$.
   b Compare your answer in part **a** with the length of $\overline{AC}$.

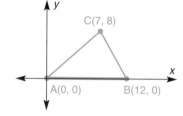

26 Given A $(-4, -2)$ and B $(10, -6)$, find the coordinates of
   a The point one fourth of the way from A to B
   b The point three fourths of the way from A to B

27 Find the area of the triangle that has the vertex matrix shown.

$$\begin{matrix} x \\ y \end{matrix} \begin{bmatrix} 3 & -1 & 5 \\ 7 & 1 & -6 \end{bmatrix}$$

28 Find the values of $(x-4)(x-3)(x-2)(x-1)(x)(x+1)(x+2)$ when x is taken from the set $\{-2, -1, 0, 1, 2, 3, 4\}$.

29 Evaluate $f(x) = 7 - 2(-4 + 3x)$ for $x = 5$.

30 Write $3.\overline{571428}$ as a ratio of integers. Reduce your answer to lowest terms.

31 Suppose that A = {whole-number divisors of 20}, B = {whole-number divisors of 36}, and C = {whole-number divisors of 30}. Make a Venn diagram of sets A, B, and C.

32 Find the next three numbers in the pattern $\sqrt{5}, \sqrt{20}, \sqrt{45}, \sqrt{80}, \ldots$

33 Point A has coordinates $(-3, 4)$. It is translated $<5, -8>$ to produce A′, then A′ is translated $<5, -8>$ to produce A″.
   a What are the coordinates of A′ and A″?
   b What are the coordinates of the midpoint of $\overline{AA''}$?

Investigation

Data Analysis   Find out the heights and the shoe sizes of at least eight people, all girls or all boys. Then draw a graph in which one axis represents height and the other represents shoe size. Plot the data you gathered. Does the graph suggest a linear relationship between height and shoe size? Try combining your data with your classmates' data in a class graph. Does the relationship (or lack of relationship) become clearer?

Summary

After studying this chapter, you should be able to

- Represent a set of numbers by listing, by using set-builder notation, and by graphing (9.1)
- Identify sets as subsets of other sets (9.1)
- Determine the intersection and the union of two sets (9.2)
- Use Venn diagrams to represent intersections and unions (9.2)
- Categorize numbers according to the number sets to which they belong (9.3)
- Recognize that π is the ratio of a circle's circumference to its diameter (9.4)
- Recognize that if the vertex of an angle is on a circle and the angle's rays pass through the endpoints of a diameter of the circle, the angle is a right angle (9.4)
- Apply the associative properties of real numbers (9.5)
- Apply the commutative properties of real numbers (9.5)
- Apply the Zero Product Property (9.5)
- Apply the distance and midpoint formulas (9.6)
- Recognize that the solution sets of many equations can be represented by straight lines on a coordinate system (9.7)

VOCABULARY

associative (9.5)

commutative (9.5)

chord (9.4)

complement (9.2)

disjoint sets (9.3)

element (9.1)

empty set (9.1)

intersection (9.2)

irrational number (9.3)

natural number (9.3)

rational number (9.3)

real number (9.3)

set (9.1)

set-builder notation (9.1)

solution set (9.1)

subset (9.1)

union (9.2)

Venn diagram (9.2)

Review

1 Using set-builder notation, express the solution set of each inequality.

    a $3x - 4 < 11$ **b** $-5x + 8 > 7$ **c** $12x + 4 \geq 16x$

2 Consider the points shown on the graph.
If A = {points such that $x \geq 2$ and $y \leq 5$} and
B = {points on the axes}, what points are in
the following sets?

    a $\overline{A}$ **b** $\overline{B}$ **c** $\overline{A \cup B}$

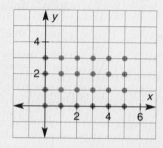

3 Suppose that M = {distances from O to each of the
other points}.

    a List all of the rational numbers in M.

    b If you were to continue the pattern by adding
point F, what would be its distance from O?

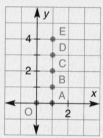

4 Indicate whether the statement is *true* or *false*.

    a $\pi = 3.14$ **b** $\pi = \frac{22}{7}$ **c** $\pi > 3.14$

    d $\pi < 3.15$ **e** $\pi > \frac{22}{7}$ **f** π is an irrational number.

5 Give examples to show that

    a There is no associative property of subtraction

    b There is no associative property of division

    c There is no commutative property of subtraction

    d There is no commutative property of division

6 For points A $(4, -3)$ and B (x, y), the midpoint of $\overline{AB}$ is $(6, 4)$.
Find (x, y).

7 Each table gives coordinates of points on a straight line. Copy and
complete the tables.

a

x	−3	−2	−1	0	1	2
y	4	6				

b

x	−3	−2	−1	0	1	2
y	5	2				

8 There are 270 students at Algebra High. On Friday, 194 students went to
the basketball game, 125 went to the dance held after the game, and 80
went to both the game and the dance. Use a Venn diagram to determine
how many students did not go to either the game or the dance.

9 Find the set of all values of *x* such that AB is a positive even integer.

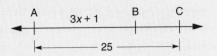

10 Is each statement *true* or *false?*
  a 0 is a rational number.
  b $-\sqrt{16}$ is a natural number.
  c The intersection of the rational and the irrational numbers is {0}.
  d The intersection of the integers and the whole numbers is the natural numbers.

11 Figure ABCD is a rectangle. AD = 6 and DC = 8. If ABCD is rotated 90° clockwise about the center of the circle, what is the probability that a randomly selected point inside the circle will be inside both the preimage and the image?

12 For real numbers *a*, *b*, and *c,* is each statement true *always, sometimes,* or *never?*
  a If $abc = 0$, then $a = 0$.
  b $a(b + c) = ab + ac$
  c $a(b + c) = ab + bc$
  d $(a + a)^b = a^b + a^b$
  e If $ab = 0$, then $a = 0$ or $b = 0$.
  f $|ab| = |a| \cdot |b|$

13 For circle A, find
  a The length of the diameter
  b The length of the radius
  c The area of the circle
  d The circumference of the circle

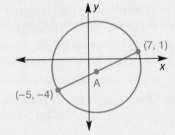

14 A boat can be rented for a fee of $23 plus $17 an hour.
  a Copy and complete the table.

Hours	0	1	2	3	4	5	6
Cost (dollars)							

  b Write an equation for the cost in terms of hours.

15 a List all subsets of {□, @}
  b List all subsets of {B, E, A, R}

16 A = {x:$2x < 21$ and x is a natural number}
  B = {x:$x^2 < 25$ and x is an integer}
  C = {x:$4x = 16$}
  a List the numbers in each of the sets.
  b Is $C \subset (A \cap B)$?
  c Is $C \cup B = B$?
  d Is $(C \cap B) \subset A$?

17 Copy the Venn diagram and place each
of following numbers in the proper section.

$-2, 0, \frac{3}{2}, \sqrt{49}, \sqrt{61}, \frac{-15}{6},$

$\frac{1}{\sqrt{2}}, 5\pi, 2.76, 0.010010001\ldots,$

$3.14, -15, -2\sqrt{3}$

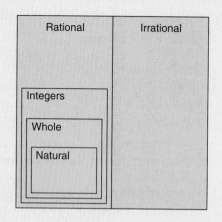

18 $\overline{AC}$ is a diameter of the circle shown.
AB = 6, BC = 8, and AD = 9.
Find CD.

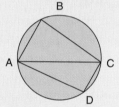

19 Find the set of all values of x for which $5x(x-4)(2x-3)(3x+7) = 0$.

20 P is a point on circle O.
  a Find the radius of the circle.
  b Find the area of the circle.

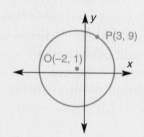

21 Use the relationship shown in the table to create another table in which
the x values increase by 1.

x	-4	-1	0	2	5
y	$\frac{8}{3}$	$\frac{11}{3}$	4	$\frac{14}{3}$	$\frac{17}{3}$

22 List the set of all times for which the digits are
consecutive integers. (Hint: The order of the
integers can be either smallest to largest or
largest to smallest.)

23 Suppose that A = {positive-integer divisors of 36} and
B = {positive-integer divisors of 30}.
  a Describe in words $A \cap B$.
  b Find the greatest number in $A \cap B$.

24 Convert each decimal to a fraction.
  a 2.76   **b** 3.94   **c** $5.8\overline{712}$

25 In rectangle PMTK, PK = 12, and the area of rectangle PMTK is 192 square units. If a point inside the circle is selected at random, what is the probability that it will be inside the rectangle?

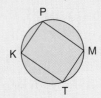

26 Match each property with the appropriate equation.
    a Commutative Property of Addition
    b Commutative Property of Multiplication
    c Associative Property of Addition
    d Distributive Property
    e Associative Property of Multiplication

    1. $9 + (7 + 4) = (9 + 7) + 4$
    2. $9(7 + 4) = 9 \cdot 7 + 9 \cdot 4$
    3. $9(7 \cdot 4) = (9 \cdot 7)4$
    4. $9 + (7 + 4) = 9 + (4 + 7)$
    5. $9(7 \cdot 4) = 9(4 \cdot 7)$

27 The midpoint of $\overline{AB}$ is on circle B. Find the area of the circle.

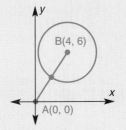

28 If $(-8, 11)$ and $(-2, -3)$ are the endpoints of a diameter of a circle, is $(1, 1)$ inside, on, or outside the circle?

29 How many elements are in each set?
    a $\{(x, y): x + y = 10$ and x and y are whole numbers$\}$
    b $\{(x, y): x + y = 10$ and x and y are integers$\}$

30 Copy the Venn diagram and shade the area representing
    a $A \cup (B \cap C)$ **b** $\overline{A} \cap \overline{B}$

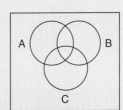

31 The circumference of circle A is 50 cm. The area of circle B is 50 cm². Find the ratio of the radius of circle A to the radius of circle B.

32 Point P is translated to P′ using the translation numbers <8, 15>. Find the distance from P to P′ if P has the coordinates
    a $(0, 0)$ **b** $(5, 8)$ **c** $(-11, 1)$

33 Copy and complete each table, assuming that the entries represent points on a line. Then write an equation for the table.

a

x	−3	−2	−1	0	1	2	3
y	4						16

b

x	−3	−2	−1	0	1	2	3
y	5						−4

Test

1 If $V = \{x : -4 < x \le 20\}$, is -5 an element of set V?

2 List all the subsets of $\{2, 4, 6\}$.

3 If values of x are chosen from $\{-3, -2, -1, \ldots, 6, 7\}$, for what subset of the values is $3x + 5 < 24$?

4 Suppose that $A = \{1, 3, 5, 7, 9\}$, $B = \{1, 4, 9, 16\}$, and $C = \{2, 3, 5, 7\}$. List the elements of each of the following sets.
  a $A \cap B$ 　　　　　　　　　　**b** $B \cup C$

5 Out of 90 freshman students, 47 are involved in sports and 53 are involved in clubs. How many students are involved in both sports and clubs?

6 If $N = \{\text{natural numbers}\}$, $I = \{\text{integers}\}$, $Q = \{\text{rational numbers}\}$, and $R = \{\text{real numbers}\}$, is the statement *true* or *false?*
  a $N \subset Q$ 　　　　　　　　　　**b** $I \cap R = R$

7 Write $1.\overline{23}$ as a ratio of two integers.

8 What is the area of a circle with a diameter of 8 meters?

9 What is the circumference of a circle with a radius of 10 inches?

10 If the circle rolls once around the rectangle without slipping, how far will the center of the circle travel?

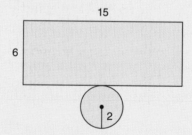

11 Solve $(x + 4)(x - 2) = 0$ for x.

12 Use number properties to evaluate $0.75 - (8.15 + 0.75)$ mentally.

13 What is the distance between the points $A(7, 5)$ and $B(-1, 12)$?

14 Given $C(-8, 12)$ and $D(2, -8)$, find the coordinates of the midpoint of $\overline{CD}$.

15 a In the following table, each pair (x, y) represents a point on a line. Copy and complete the table.

x	-3	-2	-1	0	1	2	3
y	-9	-7					

  b Draw a graph showing the relationship between x and y.
  c Write an equation that represents the graph you drew.

1 Divide this shape into four parts, each exactly congruent to the other three.

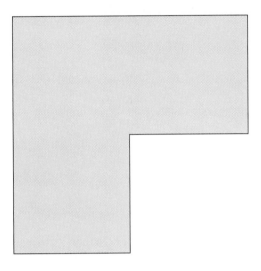

2 Point O is the center of this circle. OA = 3 and OB = 4. Find the radius of the circle.

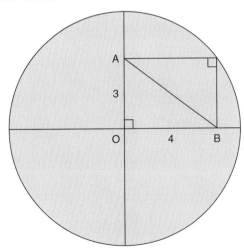

3 Who says that two WRONG's can't make a RIGHT? Solve the alphametic, where the letter O stands for the digit 0 and H stands for 8.

$$
\begin{array}{r}
\text{WRONG} \\
+ \text{WRONG} \\
\hline
\text{RIGHT}
\end{array}
$$

4 Mr. and Mrs. Smith went to a party with three other married couples. Several people shook hands with some other people. No one shook hands with himself or herself and no one shook hands with his or her spouse. No one shook hands with the same person twice. After all this handshaking took place, Mr. Smith asked each person, "How many handshakes did you make?" Each person gave him a different answer. How many handshakes did Mrs. Smith make?

Topics of
Number
Theory

AGRICULTURE If you pursue a career in agriculture, you may be growing crops for food or other uses, or you may be raising livestock. Either way, there will be plenty of mathematics involved. For crops, you will need to calculate yield per acre or the profit per bushel. You may want to weigh the costs and benefits of using fertilizers or weed killers.

A person raising livestock will need to be able to estimate the amount of feed to keep on hand, the costs of shipping animals to market, the number of animals that can be supported per acre, and the best time to sell.

CAREER CONNECTION

INVESTIGATION

Farming Choose a crop that is grown in your area. Find out the approximate yield per acre for that crop and the current or projected selling price for that crop. Also list some of the major costs involved in producing it.

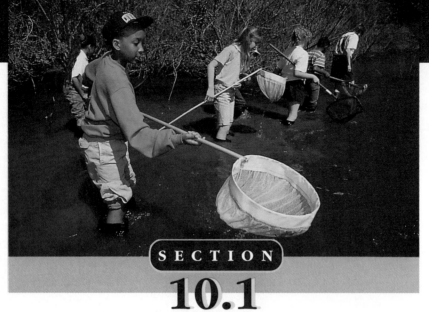

SECTION
10.1
Techniques of Counting

THE FUNDAMENTAL COUNTING PRINCIPLE

We have worked with different sets of numbers. In the study of number theory we will deal primarily with the set of natural or counting numbers—$\{1, 2, 3, 4, 5, \ldots\}$—and related subsets.

Example 1

Every camper attending Timber Lake Summer Camp is required to select two activities each day, one activity from Group I and one activity from Group II.

Group I	Group II
Scuba Diving (S)	Archery (A)
Horseback Riding (H)	Tennis (T)
Fishing (F)	Dance (D)
	Photography (P)

How many combinations of activities are possible?

Solution

There are three ways of selecting an activity from Group I and four ways of selecting an activity from Group II. Each activity in Group I can be paired with each activity in Group II. Thus, there are (3)(4), or 12, possible combinations for each camper.

Example 1 is a direct application of the ***Fundamental Counting Principle*** stated below:

> ▶ If Event I can happen in *m* ways and Event II can happen in *n* ways, then the number of ways that both Event I and Event II can happen is $m \cdot n$.

There are other ways we can view the solution to Example 1. Using letter abbreviations, we can list the possible arrangements in a display. For example, SA will represent the scuba diving and archery combination.

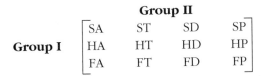

$$\text{Group I} \begin{bmatrix} SA & ST & SD & SP \\ HA & HT & HD & HP \\ FA & FT & FD & FP \end{bmatrix}$$

Notice that the list of all possibilities forms a 3 by 4 matrix. We see that there are (3)(4), or 12, entries in the display.

We can also use a horizontal or a vertical **tree diagram.**

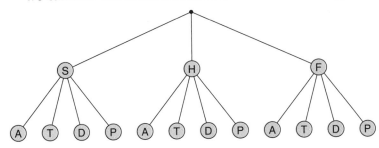

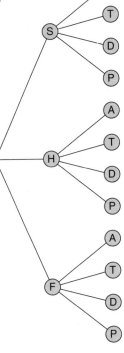

We can count 12 paths along the branches of the trees in each tree diagram. Again we see that a camper can choose from 12 different schedules.

COUNTING APPLICATIONS

Counting techniques can be used to solve a number of problems.

Example 2
How many three-digit even numbers can be formed using the digits 1, 2, 3, 4, and 5?

Solution
There are three blanks to be filled in a three-digit number:

$$\underset{\text{(hundreds)}}{\underline{\quad ? \quad}} \qquad \underset{\text{(tens)}}{\underline{\quad ? \quad}} \qquad \underset{\text{(units)}}{\underline{\quad ? \quad}}$$

Since there are two even digits, 2 and 4, we have two choices for filling in the units blank. There are five different numbers that we can select for both the tens and the hundreds blanks. Thus, we have 5 · 5 · 2, or 50, possible three-digit even numbers.

Example 3

Donisha has 12 songs on his compact disc. How many different ways can he program his compact disc player to play 3 of the 12 songs?

Solution

There are 12 choices for the first song, 11 choices for the second song, and 10 choices for the third song. By the Fundamental Counting Principle there are 12 · 11 · 10, or 1320, different ways 3 out of 12 songs can be programmed on the compact disc player.

Sample Problem

Problem

When Jordanne Michaels shoots two free throws, she makes 70% of her first free-throw attempts and 80% of her second free-throw attempts.

a What percent of the time does she make both of the free-throw attempts?

b What percent of the time does she make exactly one free-throw attempt?

Solution

We can draw a tree diagram to model Jordanne's shooting of two free throws.

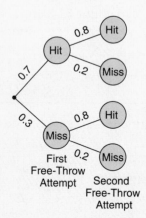

a To determine the percent of times Jordanne makes both free throws, we follow the path where both shots are made and multiply

(0.7)(0.8) = 0.56

She makes both shots 56% of the time.

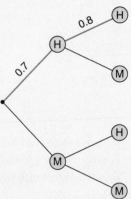

b To determine the percent of times Jordanne makes exactly one free throw, we follow both paths where one shot is made and one shot is missed. We multiply (0.7)(0.2) and (0.3)(0.8) and add the results for the two parts.

$$(0.7)(0.2) + (0.3)(0.8) = 0.14 + 0.24$$
$$= 0.38$$

Jordanne makes one shot 38% of the time.

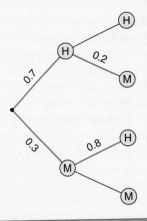

Think and Discuss

1 Suppose a camper in Example 1 was not allowed to choose horseback riding. How many choices would he or she have?

2 Pat can go either to the movies or to a concert on Friday night and can babysit or mow the lawn on Saturday. How many combinations of activities are possible?

3 State in your own words the Fundamental Counting Principle.

4 The weather forecast for the weekend is for a 60% chance of rain on Saturday and a 60% chance of rain on Sunday. Find the probability of
a Rain on both Saturday and Sunday
b No rain all weekend
c Rain on Saturday but no rain on Sunday
d No rain on Saturday but rain on Sunday
e Some rain all weekend

5 On each of three days, the probability of rain is listed as 50%.
a Find the probability that on two days it rains and on one day it does not rain.
b Find the probability that on two days it does not rain and on one day it does rain.

6 In the sample problem, what is the probability that Jordanne will make the first shot? The second shot? Both shots? Neither shot?

7 a Multiply each number in column A by each number in column B. How many different products are possible?
b Do the same problem for columns C and D.
c Explain why your answers are different.

A	B		C	D
2	11		1	3
3	13		2	5
5	17		4	6
7			8	

8 a What is the probability of getting a head on one toss of a coin?

   b Tokahama tossed a coin four times in a row and it came up heads each time. What is the probability the coin will come up heads on the next toss?

9 Use a tree diagram to find the probability of getting heads exactly three times when a coin is tossed four times.

10 Refer to the sample problem on pages 488–489.

   a What percent of the time does Jordanne miss both free throw attempts?

   b Jordanne makes both shots 56% of the time, makes exactly one out of two 38% of the time, and misses both shots 6% of the time. What is the sum of these three percents? Explain your answer.

Problems and Applications

11 Copy the tree diagram onto your paper. Then, complete the diagram.

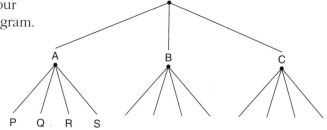

12 Set A_1 = {a, b, c, ... , w, x, y, z} and set A_2 = {A, B, C, ... , X, Y, Z}. How many ways can we pair one element from set A_1 with one element from set A_2?

13 How many line segments can be drawn between the points on the left and the points on the right?

A •
            • P
B •
            • Q
C •
            • R
D •

14 Suzanne has five blouses and three skirts that can be mixed and matched. How many different outfits can she make?

15 At a family restaurant, diners are given their choice of soup or salad; asparagus, carrots, or beets; and pasta, chicken, beef, or pork. How many different meals are possible if we assume one choice is made from each of the three categories?

16 The Savory Sandwich Shop allows customers to select one of five kinds of meat and one of three kinds of cheeses. How many different sandwiches can a person have if he or she orders a meat-and-cheese sandwich?

17 How many three-digit numbers can be formed using the digits 0, 1, 2, 3, 4, 5, 6, 7, 8, and 9?

18 Sports The tree diagram models Tom's shooting of two free throws. Find the probability that he will make exactly one free throw.

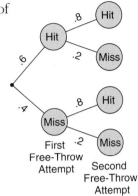

19 The coach of the girls' softball team is selecting a catcher and a pitcher for the starting lineup. How many combinations of catcher and pitcher can the coach select if there are three catchers and five pitchers on the team?

20 How many two-by-two matrices can be written if each entry is a single-digit prime number?

21 Sports Scottie Pitten has a 64% free throw average. What is the probability that he will make four free throws in a row?

22 A coin is tossed three times. What is the probability that it lands heads twice and tails once?

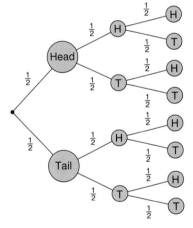

23 Business A clothing store is selling sweatshirts at 50% off. The store guarantees it will have a wide selection of sizes and colors. The colors are black, white, blue, red, green, brown, yellow, and purple. The sizes are small, medium, large, and extra-large. How many choices are available?

24 The notation 7!, read "7 factorial," means $7 \cdot 6 \cdot 5 \cdot 4 \cdot 3 \cdot 2 \cdot 1$. Evaluate the expression $4! + 3!$.

25 Communicating Write a problem that can be represented by the tree diagram.

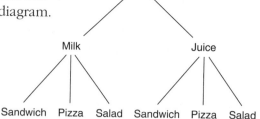

26 Science The weatherman says that the probability for rain today is 70% and for tomorrow is 40%.
a What is the probability that it rains both days?
b What is the probability that it rains only one of the days?
c What is the probability that it does not rain either day?

27 Suppose a line segment joins A to one of the other points on the circle. Then a third point is selected to be joined to the first two points. How many triangles are possible?

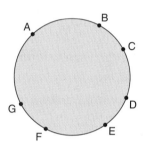

28 In a video game, a Victory missile has an 80% chance of hitting a Scum missile. Three Scum missiles are observed to be honing in on a target. A Victory missile is fired at each of the Scum missiles. Find the probability that the Victory missiles hit
a Exactly one Scum missile   **b** At least one Scum missile
c At least two Scum missiles   **d** No Scum missiles

29 a What is the probability of rolling a 5 on one toss of one fair die?
b What is the probability of rolling an even number on one toss of one fair die?
c What is the probability of rolling a 5 and then an even number if a fair die is tossed twice?
d What is the probability of rolling an even number and then a 5 if a fair die is tossed twice?
e What is the probability of rolling a 5 and an even number if a fair die is tossed twice?
f What is the probability of rolling an even number or a 5 if a fair die is tossed twice?

30 Technology A binary digit is either a zero or one. A binary number used by computers consists of a string of binary digits. For example, 100,110 is a six-digit binary number. One K is defined as "the number of different ten-digit binary numbers."
a How large is 1 K?
b How large is 640 K?
c One meg is 1000 K. How large is 1 meg?
d A computer has a 40-meg hard drive. How large is 40 meg?

◄ LOOKING BACK **Spiral Learning** LOOKING AHEAD ►

31 Each ticket for the school play costs $6.00. George totaled the sales for one night and wrote the number on a slip of paper. When he looked for this slip of paper, he found five slips of paper, with the numbers $576.00, $584.00, $596.00, $564.50, and $591.00. Which number represents the ticket sales for the school play?

32 Perform the indicated operation.
a $\frac{1}{4} - \frac{1}{6}$
b $\frac{1}{2} - \frac{1}{3} - \frac{1}{4}$

33 Spreadsheets Copy machine A makes 8 copies per minute, and copy machine B makes 12 copies per minute.
a Suppose each machine runs for an hour. Use a spreadsheet to list, minute by minute, the total number of copies made by each machine.
b List the numbers that appear in both columns.
c Why do these numbers appear in both columns?

34 How many different fractions can be made if the numerator of the fraction is selected from {1, 3, 5, 7} and the denominator of the fraction is selected from {1, 4, 7, 10}?

35 A solid rectangle is formed by using 20 tiles. Find all possible perimeters of the rectangles.

36 Find the smallest natural number that is divisible by
a 16 and 24
b 7 and 11

Investigation

Lotteries Does your state have a state lottery? If so, find out how it is played. If not, check out a lottery in some other state. What is the probability of winning? What percent of the money spent on tickets is actually paid out to the winners? On average, is playing the lottery profitable? Explain.

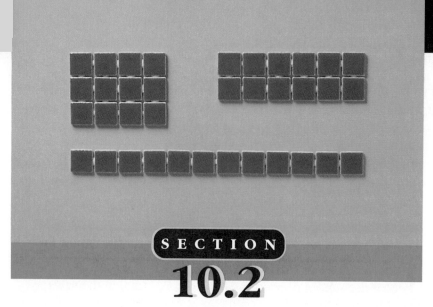

SECTION
10.2
Primes, Composites, and Multiples

PRIME NUMBERS AND COMPOSITE NUMBERS

We can use tiles to learn about prime numbers and composite numbers.

Example 1
a How many different rectangles can be formed using 12 tiles?
b How many different rectangles can be formed using 7 tiles?

Solution
a We can arrange the 12 tiles into three different rectangles.

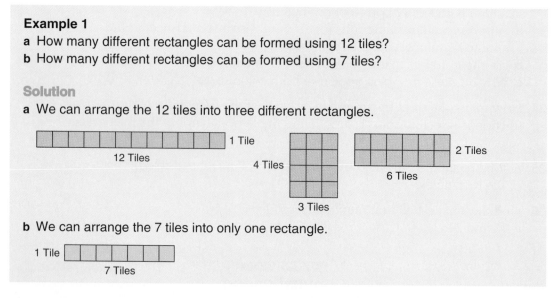

b We can arrange the 7 tiles into only one rectangle.

The example shows that the numbers 1, 12, 2, 6, 3, and 4 are *factors* of 12. Each number divides into 12 leaving a remainder of zero. The only factors of 7 are 1 and 7. A number greater than one is a *prime number* if it has exactly two factors, 1 and itself. Seven is a prime number. A natural number greater than one is a *composite number* if it has more than two factors. The number 12 is a composite number, since it has factors other than 1 and 12. Every prime number and every composite number have at least two different factors. The number 1 has only one factor; therefore, it is neither a prime number nor a composite number.

We can represent the natural numbers using a Venn diagram.

Natural Numbers

Prime Numbers 2, 3, 5, 7, 11, …	1 (Neither prime nor composite)	Composite Numbers 4, 6, 8, 9, 10, 12, …

Example 2

List the factors of each number and classify each number as *prime* or *composite*.

a 28   **b** 31   **c** 64

Solution

a The factors of 28 are 1, 2, 4, 7, 14, and 28. The number 28 is composite.

b The factors of 31 are 1 and 31. The number 31 is prime.

c The factors of 64 are 1, 2, 4, 8, 16, 32, and 64. The number 64 is composite.

MULTIPLES

Let's take a look at these two patterns.

$1 \cdot 4 = 4$	$1 \cdot 6 = 6$
$2 \cdot 4 = 8$	$2 \cdot 6 = 12$
$3 \cdot 4 = 12$	$3 \cdot 6 = 18$
$4 \cdot 4 = 16$	$4 \cdot 6 = 24$
$5 \cdot 4 = 20$	$5 \cdot 6 = 30$
$6 \cdot 4 = 24$	
$7 \cdot 4 = 28$	
$8 \cdot 4 = 32$	

The set A = {4, 8, 12, 16, 20, 24, 28, 32} contains the first eight natural-number multiples of 4. The set B = {6, 12, 18, 24, 30} contains the first five natural-number multiples of 6. The numbers 12 and 24 are common multiples of 4 and 6. The number 12 is the ***least common multiple (LCM)***—the common multiple with the smallest value—of 4 and 6.

We can represent set A and set B using a Venn diagram.

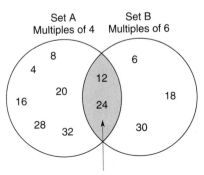

Multiples of Both 4 and 6
(multiples of 12)

Example 3

Draw a number line and graph all the natural numbers less than 100 that are

a Multiples of 9   **b** Multiples of 12   **c** Common multiples of 9 and 12

Solution

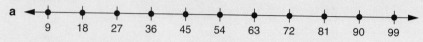

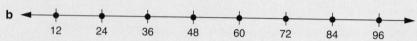

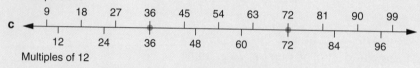

Notice that the least common multiple (LCM) of 9 and 12 is 36.

Sample Problems

Problem 1

We will define LCM(m, n) to be the least common multiple of m and n. Find LCM(4, 6) + LCM(6, 9).

Solution

We first evaluate LCM(4, 6) and then evaluate LCM(6, 9). The least common multiple of 4 and 6 is 12 and the least common multiple of 6 and 9 is 18. Thus, LCM(4, 6) + LCM(6, 9) = 12 + 18 = 30.

Problem 2

Find the value of n if $n = \frac{7}{8} - \left(\frac{1}{2} - \frac{1}{3}\right)$.

Solution

We will use the LCM of the denominators of the fractions as the common denominator of the fractions.

$$n = \frac{7}{8} - \left(\frac{1}{2} - \frac{1}{3}\right)$$

Rewrite $\frac{1}{2}$ as $\frac{3}{6}$ and $\frac{1}{3}$ as $\frac{2}{6}$

$$n = \frac{7}{8} - \left(\frac{3}{6} - \frac{2}{6}\right)$$

$$n = \frac{7}{8} - \frac{1}{6}$$

Rewrite $\frac{7}{8}$ as $\frac{21}{24}$ and $\frac{1}{6}$ as $\frac{4}{24}$

$$n = \frac{21}{24} - \frac{4}{24}$$

$$n = \frac{17}{24}$$

Note that the LCM of 2 and 3 is 6 and the least common denominator of $\frac{1}{2}$ and $\frac{1}{3}$ is 6. Also, the LCM of 6 and 8 is 24, and the least common denominator of $\frac{1}{6}$ and $\frac{7}{8}$ is 24.

Think and Discuss

1 What are the first five prime numbers?

2 What are the first five natural-number multiples of 3?

3 What is the least common multiple of 2 and 5?

4 Complete the table for the dimensions of all the rectangles that can be formed with each given number of tiles.

Number of Tiles	Dimensions of Rectangles
1	1 × 1
2	
3	
4	
5	
6	
7	
8	
9	
10	
11	
12	

5 For what natural numbers of tiles can exactly one rectangle be formed?

6 Ms. Monroe's class of ten students was using tiles to build a rectangle. Each of the students had a different number of tiles and each was able to build only one rectangle. Ms. Monroe's class did this with the least number of tiles. How many tiles did the students have?

7 Mr. Quincy's class was using tiles to build rectangles. He had six different groups, and each group had a different number of tiles. Each group was able to build exactly two rectangles. Mr. Quincy's class did this using the least number of tiles. How many tiles did each group use?

8 A given number of tiles can be arranged to form a 3-by-6 rectangle. What are the dimensions of the other rectangles that can be formed using the same tiles?

9 List the dimensions of the rectangles that can be formed using
  a 10 tiles   **b** 11 tiles   **c** 9 tiles

10 Find four numbers of tiles that will produce exactly
  a One rectangle   **b** Two rectangles   **c** Three rectangles

11 **a** List the first three multiples of 16.
   b List the first three multiples of 24.
   c What is the LCM of 16 and 24?

12 Which of the numbers 1, 2, 5, 9, and 12 is different from the others? Explain your answer.

13 Find the five numbers with the smallest values that are divisible by 10 and 15.

14 Is the statement true *always, sometimes,* or *never?*
    a The sum of two prime numbers is a prime number.
    b The sum of two composite numbers is a composite number.
    c The product of two prime numbers is a composite number.
    d The product of two composite numbers is a composite number.

Problems and Applications

15 Classify each number as *prime* or *composite.*
    a 31   **b** 51   **c** 72   **d** 43

16 List the first six natural-number multiples of
    a 4   **b** 7

17 Find the least common multiple of each pair of prime numbers.
    a 5 and 7   **b** 2 and 3   **c** 11 and 13

18 What three numbers with the smallest values belong in II?

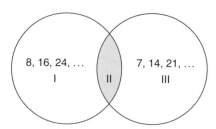

19 Find the least common multiple of
    a 5 and 7   **b** 12 and 3   **c** 8 and 6

20 List the first five common multiples of 6 and 8.

21 **a** Find the least common multiple of 12 and 8.
    b Find the least common multiple of 10 and 12.

22 How many solid rectangles can be formed using 40 tiles?

23 Find all natural numbers n so that $\frac{12}{n}$ is a natural number.

24 Draw a number line and graph all positive multiples of
    a 4 that are less than 50   **b** 3 that are less than 50
    c 3 and 4 that are less than 50

25 Draw the other rectangles that can be made with these tiles.

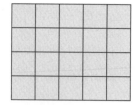

26 Toby arranged a set of tiles in a single row. The perimeter of the rectangle formed was 100. What is the perimeter of the square that can be constructed with these tiles?

27 a List the positive multiples of 7.
  b List the whole-number multiples of 7.
  c List the integer multiples of 7.

28 Two dice are tossed. The table is filled in by determining the LCM of the numbers on the faces of the two dice.
  a Copy and complete the table.
  b Find the probability that the LCM of the numbers on the faces of the two dice is a multiple of 6.
  c Find the probability that the LCM of the numbers on the faces of the two dice is a multiple of 5.

LCM	1	2	3	4	5	6
1	1					
2		2				
3				12		
4						
5						
6						

29 Let $a \# b = $ LCM $\{a, b\}$. Find the values of
  a $(4 \# 6) \# 8$
  b $4 \# (6 \# 8)$

30 Science Gear A rotates in a clockwise direction while Gear B rotates in a counter-clockwise direction. How many complete revolutions of Gear A and Gear B are necessary in order for the gears to align themselves at 0?

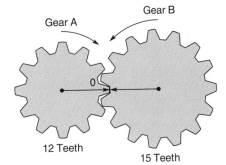

Gear A
Gear B
12 Teeth
15 Teeth

31 a Find LCM $(9, 12)$.
  b Use your answer in part **a** to write equivalent fractions for $\frac{1}{9}$ and $\frac{1}{12}$ that have a common denominator.
  c Use your answer to part **b** to find $\frac{1}{9} - \frac{1}{12}$.

32 Phyllis can run once around a certain field in 8 minutes. Tyred can run once around the same field in 12 minutes. If they begin at the same time and run in the same direction for an hour, when will Phyllis pass Tyred?

33 a Find the LCM $(18, 48)$.
  b Use your answer in part **a** to rewrite $\frac{17}{18} - \left(\frac{5}{18} + \frac{11}{48}\right)$ as an expression with a common denominator.
  c Evaluate the new expression you wrote in part **b**.

34 Spreadsheets
  a Write a spreadsheet to generate the first 100 multiples of 3 and the first 100 multiples of 5. How would you describe the common multiples in these two lists?
  b Repeat part **a** for 6 and 8.

35 Doralee rides 14 miles per hour on her bike. Annabelle rides 19 miles per hour. At noon, they begin to ride toward each other. If they start 80 miles apart, at what time will they meet?

36 The least common multiple of two different numbers *a* and *b* is *a*. What is true about *b*?

◀ LOOKING BACK **Spiral Learning** LOOKING AHEAD ▶

37 a How many three-digit multiples of 5 can be created using each of the digits 1, 2, 3, 4, 5, and 6 no more than once?
  b How many three-digit multiples of 5 can be created using each of the digits 0, 2, 3, 4, 5, and 6 no more than once?

38 Gil can mow $\frac{2}{15}$ of a large lawn in one hour. Juan can mow $\frac{1}{12}$ of the same lawn in an hour.
  a What fraction of the lawn can be mowed in an hour if Gil and Juan work together?
  b What fraction of the lawn can Gil mow in three hours?
  c What fraction of the lawn can Juan mow in three hours?
  d After Gil and Juan have worked together for three hours, what fraction of the lawn is mowed?
  e What percent of the lawn still needs to he mowed after Gil and Juan have worked together for three hours?

39 If Bill is able to paint a fence in six hours, how long must he work to complete 40% of the job?

40 Let # (*x*) be equal to the sum of all the factors of *x*. Find
  a # (28)   **b** # (17)

41 How many 2-by-2 matrices can be formed where the elements are different prime numbers less than 20?

42 How many four-digit numbers can be formed using the digits 0, 1, 2, 3, 4, 5, 6, 7, 8, and 9 once?

43 Chuck can shuck about 80 ears of corn in a half hour. How long would it take Chuck to shuck 1000 ears of corn?

Investigation

Tile Arrangements   Raúl took his tiles and made a picture frame as shown. How many different picture frames can he make with his tiles?

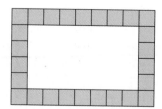

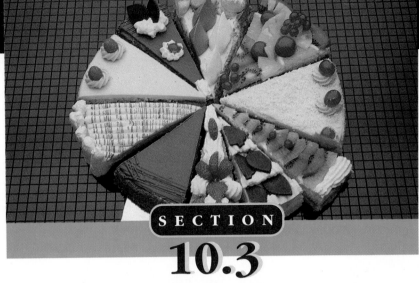

SECTION 10.3
Divisibility Tests

TESTS FOR 2, 3, 4, 5, 6, 8, 9, 10, AND 12

We can use a calculator to test whether a number is divisible by another number. Sometimes, however, it is preferable to use a divisibility test.

A natural number n is divisible by
- 2 if the last digit of the number is even
- 3 if the sum of the digits of the number is divisible by 3
- 4 if the number formed by the last two digits of the number is divisible by 4
- 5 if the last digit of the number is either 0 or 5
- 6 if the number is divisible by both 2 and 3
- 8 if the number formed by the last three digits of the number is divisible by 8
- 9 if the sum of the digits of the number is divisible by 9
- 10 if the last digit of the number is 0
- 12 if the number is divisible by both 3 and 4

Example 1
Test the number 6,392,124 for divisibility by
a 2   b 3   c 4   d 5   e 6   f 8   g 9   h 10   i 12

Solution
a The number is divisible by 2 because the last digit, 4, is even.
b The number is divisible by 3 because the sum of the digits, 27, is divisible by 3.
c The number is divisible by 4 because the number formed by the last two digits, 24, is divisible by 4.
d The number is not divisible by 5 because the last digit is not 0 or 5.
e The number is divisible by 6 because the number is divisible by both 2 and 3.
f The number is not divisible by 8 because the number formed by the last three digits, 124, is not divisible by 8.
g The number is divisible by 9 because the sum of the digits, 27, is divisible by 9.
h The number is not divisible by 10 because the last digit is not 0.
i The number is divisible by 12 because the number is divisible by both 3 and 4.

You may have noticed that divisibility tests for 7 and 11 have not been included. A divisibility test for 11 follows.

DIVISIBILITY TEST FOR 11

Example 2
Is 31,829,172,691,807 divisible by 11?

Solution
The number is too large to be displayed on most calculators, so use of the calculator is limited. Here is a test for the divisibility of the number 31,829,172,691,807 by 11.

List the digits of the number in order.	3 1 8 2 9 1 7 2 6 9 1 8 0 7
Add every other digit, beginning with the first digit on the left (the odd-positioned digits).	$3 + 8 + 9 + 7 + 6 + 1 + 0 = 34$
Add the remaining digits.	$1 + 2 + 1 + 2 + 9 + 8 + 7 = 30$
Find the absolute value of the difference of the two sums.	$|34 - 30| = 4$
Check whether the absolute value of the difference is divisible by 11.	Since 4 is not divisible by 11 31,829,172,691,807 is not divisible by 11.

What if the final absolute value for some number n was 0? Would the number n be divisible by 11? Since 0 is divisible by 11, the number n would be divisible by 11.

> A natural number is divisible by 11 if the absolute value of the sum of the odd-positioned digits minus the sum of the remaining digits is divisible by 11.

Sample Problem

Problem Find a value for n so that the number 619,4n2 will be divisible by

a 2   b 3   c 4   d 5   e 6

Solution   **a** 619,4*n*2 will be divisible by 2 if *n* = 0, 1, 2, 3, 4, 5, 6, 7, 8, or 9. Since the last digit of the number is 2, the number will always be an even number.

b 619,4*n*2 will be divisible by 3 if 6 + 1 + 9 + 4 + *n* + 2 = 22 + *n* is divisible by 3. This happens if *n* = 2, 5, or 8, because 24, 27, and 30 are divisible by 3.

c 619,4*n*2 will be divisible by 4 if the two-digit number *n*2 is divisible by 4. This will happen if *n* = 1, 3, 5, 7, or 9, because 12, 32, 52, 72, and 92 are divisible by 4.

d 619,4*n*2 will be divisible by 5 if the number ends in 0 or 5. This will never happen, so there is no value of *n* that will be a solution.

e 619,4*n*2 will be divisible by 6 if the number is a multiple of both 2 and 3. The only replacements of *n* that work for both 2 and 3 are 2, 5, and 8.

Think and Discuss

1 Is 2992 divisible by 2? Explain your answer.

2 Is 3516 divisible by 6? Explain your answer.

3 Explain how to test for divisibility on a calculator.

4 Why is it not always possible to use a calculator to test for divisibility?

5 The divisibility test for 3 says "add the digits and see whether the sum is divisible by 3." The divisibility test for 9 says "add the digits and see whether the sum is divisible by 9." Guess a divisibility test for 27 (which is 3^3). Does it work?

6 Which of the divisibility tests are easiest to use?

7 Is the statement *true* or *false?*
   a If a number is divisible by 4, then it is divisible by 8.
   b If a number is divisible by both 2 and 6, then it is divisible by 12.
   c If a number is divisible by 3 and 5, then it is divisible by 15.
   d If a number is divisible by 2, 3, and 5, then it is divisible by 5.

8 In part **a** of the sample problem on the previous page, why do all values of *n* work?

Problems and Applications

9 Is the number 7890 divisible by
  a 2?   **b** 3?   **c** 4?   **d** 5?

10 Which numbers are divisible by 3? By 9?
  a 108   **b** 355   **c** 828   **d** 633   **e** 552   **f** 981   **g** 3744

11 Is the number 4,316,280,948 divisible by
  a 2?   **b** 3?   **c** 4?   **d** 5?   **e** 6?
  f 8?   **g** 9?   **h** 10?   **i** 11?   **j** 12?

12 Which numbers are divisible by 2?
  a 8924   **b** 1735   **c** 2190   **d** 4000   **e** 2481
  f 5225   **g** 2222   **h** 7×10^3 **i** $\sqrt{144}$

13 Which numbers are divisible by 3?
  a 779,623,556,395   **b** 779,623,556,396   **c** 779,623,556,397
  d 779,623,556,398   **e** 779,623,556,399

14 Which numbers are divisible by 11?
  a 891   **b** 121   **c** 585   **d** 743
  e 9284   **f** 8778   **g** 5353   **h** 573,375

15 Which of the numbers are prime numbers?
  a 7713   **b** 4705   **c** 6318   **d** 9427   **e** 1871

16 If a number *n* is divisible by 36, by what other number is *n* divisible?

17 Is each of the three numbers 1257, 345, and 234 divisible by
  a 2?   **b** 3?   **c** 5?   **d** 9?   **e** 11?

18 Communicating   Is the area of the rectangle divisible by 12? Explain your answer.

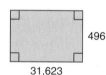

496

31,623

19 Communicating   Explain why the sum of two multiples of a number must be a multiple of the number.

20 Communicating   The numbers *a* and *b* are divisible by 2.
  a Is the sum of *a* and *b* divisible by 2? Explain your answer.
  b Is the difference of *a* and *b* divisible by 2? Explain your answer.
  c Is the product of *a* and *b* divisible by 2? Explain your answer.
  d Is the quotient of *a* and *b* divisible by 2? Explain your answer.

21 Which numbers are divisible by 9?
  a 25,727,577,360,705   **b** 25,727,577,360,706
  c 25,727,577,360,707   **d** 25,727,577,360,717
  e 25,727,577,361,717

22 **Communicating**   Explain why 32,768,325 is divisible by 15.

23 Find the values of *n* so that the number 32*n*5 is divisible by 15.

24 The number 823*n*45 is divisible by 11.
   a What is *n?*
   b Is the number divisible by 3?

25 Write a six-digit number in which all the digits are not the same. Then rearrange the digits of the number you wrote to form another six-digit number. Subtract one of the numbers from the other. Is your answer divisible by 9?

26 Of the three-digit numbers having three different digits from the set {1, 2, 3, 4}, which are divisible by 3?

27 The number 413*n* is divisible by 3 and it is an even number. What is the value of *n?*

28 On a coordinate system, graph the lattice points (*x, y*) that make the number *x*3*y*527 divisible by 11. (The point (*x, y*) is a lattice point if both *x* and *y* are integers.)

29 **Communicating**   Explain why 5! is divisible by 30.

30 Of the four-digit numbers having four different digits from the set {1, 2, 3, 4}, which numbers are divisible by 4?

31 Suppose that a number divided by 4 has a remainder of 2.
   a List five such numbers.
   b Show that when these numbers are divided by 2, the quotient is odd.

32 Find all values of *n* that make the number 1*nnnnnnnn*1 divisible by 11.

33 **Communicating**   The numbers 3625 and 5263 are a palindromic pair of numbers, since reversing the order of the digits of one number gives the other number. Explain why in a palindromic pair, if one number is divisible by 9, then so is the other number.

34 **a** A number is divisible by 11. The sum of all the odd-positioned digits of the number is 22. The sum of all but one of the even-positioned digits is 18. What is the missing digit?
   b A number is divisible by 11. The sum of all the even-positioned digits is 22. The sum of all but one of the odd-positioned digits is 12. What is the missing digit?
   c A number is divisible by 11. The sum of the odd-positioned digits is 22. One of the even-positioned digits is missing. Can you find two possible values for the missing digit?

35 Describe the graph, using set-builder notation.

36 An ordinary die is tossed three times. Find the probability that the number on the first toss is prime, the number on the second toss is a multiple of 2, and the number on the third toss is a multiple of 3.

37 Write an equation that generates the table.

x	−4	−3	−2	−1	0	1	2	3	4
y	−9	−7	−5	−3	−1	1	3	5	7

38 Beumont skis cross-country a distance of 1 kilometer in 180 strides. He takes 12 strides in 20 seconds. How long will it take Beumont to ski 12 kilometers?

39 a What is the least number of tiles needed to produce exactly one rectangle that is not a square?
b What is the least number of tiles needed to produce exactly one rectangle whose area is greater than 20?

40 Write each number in decimal form.
a $\frac{1}{6}$ **b** 315%   **c** $9\frac{1}{4}$ **d** $\sqrt{(0.05)^2 + (0.12)^2}$

41 Evaluate each expression.
a $\frac{5}{12} - \frac{2}{3}$ **b** $\frac{3}{5} + \frac{7}{4}$ **c** $\frac{5}{6} - \frac{3}{8}$

42 When running a race, Teng takes a swallow of water every 8 minutes and changes her stride every 10 minutes. How many minutes after she begins will she have to do both at the same time?

43 Breathing normally, Nathan takes 5 breaths every 28 seconds. Find his breathing rate in breaths/hour. How many breaths will he take in a day?

44 **Spreadsheets**   Make a spreadsheet consisting of 3 columns: column A—multiples of 3; column B—multiples of 15; column C—the quotient of the number in column A divided by the number in column B. Explain your results.

Investigation

Numeric Palindrome   A numeric palindrome is a natural number whose digits read the same forward or backward. For example, 375,573 is a numeric palindrome, as is 8228. The number 121 is a three-digit palindrome that is divisible by 11. Find other three-digit palindromes that are divisible by 11. List the numbers from least to greatest value. Can you find all the four-digit palindromes that are multiples of 11?

"DISCOVER ANY NEW PRIME NUMBERS LATELY?"

SECTION

10.4

Prime Factorization

PRIME-FACTORIZATION FORM

It's easy to find the prime factors of a number like 12.

$$12 = 2 \cdot 2 \cdot 3$$

But how do you factor a number like 4693? Or is 4693 prime? In this section we will introduce methods for determining the prime factorization of a natural number.

The **prime-factorization form** of a natural number shows the prime factors being multiplied. The prime-factorization form of 12 is shown above. We usually list prime factors in order from least to greatest.

Example 1
Write the prime-factorization form for the natural numbers 26, 27, 28, 29, 30, 31, and 32.

Solution

Natural Number	Prime-Factorization Form
26	$2 \cdot 13$
27	$3 \cdot 3 \cdot 3$ or 3^3
28	$2 \cdot 2 \cdot 7$ or $2^2 \cdot 7$
29	29 is prime.
30	$2 \cdot 3 \cdot 5$
31	31 is prime.
32	$2 \cdot 2 \cdot 2 \cdot 2 \cdot 2$ or 2^5

PRIME-FACTORIZATION TECHNIQUES

In earlier mathematics classes, you may have used factor trees to find the prime-factorization form of a natural number.

Example 2
Use a factor tree to find the prime-factorization form of 120.

Solution
We can begin with any two factors of 120.
Let's use 10 and 12.

We now factor 10 and 12 into two factors each.

Now we factor 6.

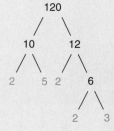

We observe that all the numbers at the ends of the factor-tree branches are prime numbers. The prime-factorization form of 120 is $2^3 \cdot 3 \cdot 5$.

Example 3
Factor 924 into its prime-factorization form without using a factor tree.

Solution
We use the divisibility rules for 3 and 4 to determine that 12 is a factor of 924.

$$924 = 12 \cdot 77$$
$$= (2 \cdot 6) \cdot (7 \cdot 11)$$
$$= 2 \cdot (2 \cdot 3) \cdot 7 \cdot 11$$
$$= 2^2 \cdot 3 \cdot 7 \cdot 11$$

GENERAL PRIME-FACTORIZATION PROCEDURE

Let's look at a process for determining the prime-factorization form of any natural number. We begin by listing the pairs of factors of 36 and 120.

The factors of 36 are

1 and 36
2 and 18
3 and 12
4 and 9
6 and 6

The factors of 120 are

1 and 120   5 and 24
2 and 60   6 and 20
3 and 40   8 and 15
4 and 30   10 and 12

We observe that each number in the last pair of factors of 36 and 120 is equal to or close in value to the square roots of 36 and 120. The numbers in the first columns of the pairs of factors are less than or equal to the square roots of the numbers 36 and 120. We will use these observations in the next example and the sample problem.

Example 4
Determine the prime-factorization form of 4693.

Solution
We will systematically check the primes, that is, 2, 3, 5, 7, 11, 13, ... , to determine whether any are factors of 4693.

We test 2, 3, 5, 7, and 11 and find that none of these prime numbers are factors of 4693.

If we check the next prime, 13, we find that it is a factor of 4693 because

$$4693 = 13 \cdot 361$$

We then check to see if 13 is a factor a second time. However, we find that 13 is not a factor of 361.

If we check the next prime, 17, we find that 17 is not a factor of 361.

However, the next prime, 19, is a factor of 361.

$$361 = 19 \cdot 19$$

Therefore, $4693 = 13 \cdot 19 \cdot 19 = 13 \cdot 19^2$.

You may be wondering how many consecutive primes we need to test. Since $\sqrt{4693} < 68.52$, we have to check whether the primes less than 68.52 are factors of 4693.

Sample Problem

Problem
Show that 317 is prime.

Solution
Since $\sqrt{317}$ is approximately 17.80, we need only to check whether the prime numbers less than 17.80 are factors of 317. The only such primes are 2, 3, 5, 7, 11, 13, and 17. None of these are factors of 317. Thus, 317 is a prime number.

Think and Discuss

1 Find the prime-factorization form of
 a 10   **b** 16   **c** 23   **d** 27

2 **a** Write the prime-factorization form of 2520.
 b Without actually doing the division, determine which of the following numbers divide evenly into 2520. Explain your answers.
 i 72   **ii** 45   **iii** 63

3 Faron was checking to see which numbers were factors of a given number. He used the divisibility test for 3 and found it did not work. He then announced that 3, 6, 9, 12, 15, 18, 21, 24, 27, and 30 did not divide the number. Was he correct? Explain your answer.

4 Is the statement *true* or *false?*
 a If a prime number divides evenly into the square of a number, then it divides evenly into the number.
 b Explain your reasoning for part **a.**

5 **a** What is the greatest possible prime factor of a number n?
 b In the sample problem, why was it necessary to check only numbers less than $\sqrt{317}$ when looking for prime factors of 317?

6 **a** Find two positive integers that cannot be written as the sum of two primes.
 b Find two positive integers that can be written as the sum of two primes.
 c Find two positive integers that can be written as the sum of two primes in two different ways.

Problems and Applications

7 Find the prime-factorization form of $9 \cdot 6 \cdot 4$.

8 Use the tree diagrams to factor 84 into its prime-factorization form.

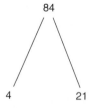
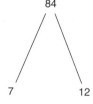
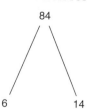

9 **Communicating** Explain why $2^3 \cdot 3^2 \cdot 25^3$ is not a prime-factorization form.

10 Completely factor each number into prime factors.
 a 4   **b** 36   **c** 121   **d** 25   **e** 64   **f** 100

11 List all the factors of 30.

12 Find the prime-factorization form of

    a 286   **b** 301   **c** 601

13 Which number has a prime-factorization form of $3^2 \cdot 2^3 \cdot 5$?

14 Use two tree diagrams to find the prime-factorization form of 380.

15 Find the prime-factorization form of 8463.

16 The prime-factorization form of 315 is $3^2 \cdot 5 \cdot 7$, and the prime-factorization form of 825 is $3 \cdot 5^2 \cdot 11$.

    a What is the greatest number that is a factor of both 315 and 825?

    b Write the answer to part **a** in prime-factorization form.

    c What is the smallest number that is a multiple of both 315 and 825?

    d Write the answer to part **c** in prime-factorization form.

17 a Copy the factor trees and fill in the missing numbers.

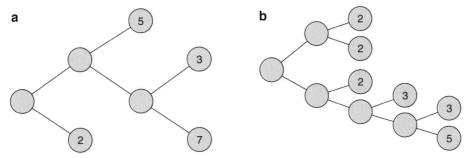

    c How could you have found the number at the beginning of the tree without filling in the entire tree?

18 a Simplify the expression $\frac{3 \cdot 5 \cdot 7 \cdot 11}{5 \cdot 7 \cdot 11 \cdot 13}$.

    b Express the numerator and the denominator of $\frac{2940}{945}$ in prime-factorization form.

19 a Find the prime-factorization forms of 225 and 150.

    b Find the product of the common prime factors of 225 and 150.

    c Find the greatest number that divides evenly into 225 and 150.

20 Solve $2^3 \cdot 3^4 \cdot 5^2 \cdot x = 2^5 \cdot 3^4 \cdot 5^3$ for x.

21 What is the probability that a number selected from the set $\{1, 2, 3, \ldots, 19, 20\}$ is prime?

22 **Communicating** If $2N = 2^6 \cdot 3^5 \cdot 5^4 \cdot 7^3 \cdot 11^7$, explain why $2 \cdot 3 \cdot 5 \cdot 7 \cdot 11$ is a factor of N.

23 If $2^a \cdot 3^b = 864$, find the values of a and b.

24 Which prime numbers need to be tested as possible factors in order to determine if 937 is prime?

25 Evaluate each expression.

    a $\sqrt{3^2}$ **b** $\sqrt{3^2 \cdot 2^2}$ **c** $\sqrt{5^2 \cdot 7^2}$ **d** $\sqrt{9 \cdot 36}$

26 Find the smallest number that can be divided by three different prime numbers.

27 Write the prime-factorization form of 7!.

28 **Communicating** Explain why 10,101 is not prime.

29 Take any six-digit number in which the first three digits are identical and in the same order as the last three digits—for example, 243,243. What prime numbers divide each of these numbers?

30 **Communicating** Explain why the product of two consecutive natural numbers is divisibleby 2.

◀ LOOKING BACK **Spiral Learning** LOOKING AHEAD ▶

31 A store sells eight different model airplanes and five choices of colored paints. How may different model planes can you make?

32 **a** Find the set of all factors of 24.
 b Find the set of all factors of 18.
 c Find the intersection of the two sets in parts **a** and **b.**
 d Find the greatest number in the intersection of the sets. What is this number called?

33 Find the distance between
 a A(−4, 5) and B(−2, 12) **b** A(5, 11) and B(−4, −8)

34 **a** Plot (10, 0), (0, 8), and (0,0).
 b Connect the points in part **a** and find the area of the triangle.
 c Find the midpoints of the sides of the triangle.
 d Connect the midpoints to form four triangles.
 e Find the area of the four triangles in part **d.**

35 A license plate from Bronkovia consists of two letters followed by four numbers. How many different license plates can Bronkovia have?

36 **Business** Hal O'Famer charges $5000 to appear at a sports show. He also receives $6 per autograph.
 a Write an expression to represent the amount of money Hal gets if he signs x autographs.
 b If Hal made $9740 at one show, write an equation that represents the number of autographs he signed.
 c Solve the equation in part **b** to find the number of autographs he signed.

Investigation

Number Game Find any three consecutive three-digit numbers, none of which is divisible by 3. Explain your results.

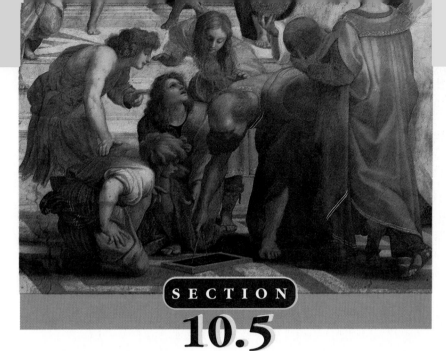

10.5
Factors and Common Factors

FACTORS OF A NATURAL NUMBER

We used tiles earlier to introduce prime numbers and composite numbers. We found the factors of a natural number n by listing the dimensions of the rectangles formed by n tiles. However, using rectangular tiles is not practical for large numbers. We need other methods of determining the factors of a number.

Example 1
Determine all the factors of 120.

Solution
Method 1
We list the factors in pairs—1 and 120, 2 and 60, 3 and 40, 4 and 30, 5 and 24, 6 and 20, 8 and 15, and 10 and 12.

Arranging the factors from least to greatest gives us

$$1, 2, 3, 4, 5, 6, 8, 10, 12, 15, 20, 24, 30, 40, 60, 120$$

Method 2
A second method involves a tree diagram.

Show the prime-factorization form of 120 $2^3 \cdot 3 \cdot 5$

List the factors of each term 2^3 (or 8): 1, 2, 4, 8
of the prime factorization   3: 1, 3
          5: 1, 5

The tree diagram is shown on the next page.

513

Now label the branches of a tree diagram. The first row of branches shows the factors of 8. The second row of branches shows the factors of 3; and the third row, the factors of 5. We multiply the numbers downward along the branches and write the products in the circles. The numbers in the circles at the end of the branches are the 16 factors of 120.

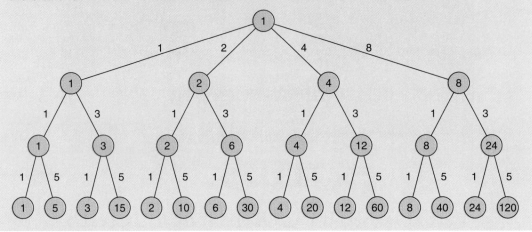

ABUNDANT, DEFICIENT, AND PERFECT NUMBERS

The early Greeks were interested in natural numbers and their related properties. The Greeks classified the natural numbers according to the sum of their factors. We will build from the Greeks' ideas.

Example 2
Find all the factors of each number. Then find the sum of the factors.
a 1   b 4   c 6   d 24   e 120

Solution

	Number	Factors	Sum of Factors
a	1	1	1
b	4	1, 2, 4	7
c	6	1, 2, 3, 6	12
d	24	1, 2, 3, 4, 6, 8, 12, 24	60
e	120	1, 2, 3, 4, 5, 6, 8, 10, 12, 15, 20, 24, 30, 40, 60, 120	360

To see whether a number n is a **perfect number**, we look at the ratio r, where

$$r = \frac{\text{Sum of the factors}}{\text{Number}}$$

If $r = 2$, the number n is a perfect number. There is only one perfect number in Example 2—the number 6 in part **c**

$$\frac{1 + 2 + 3 + 6}{6} = 2.$$

If $r < 2$, the number n is **deficient.** Thus, 4 is deficient because $\frac{1 + 2 + 4}{4} = 1.75$ and $1.75 < 2$. Is 1 deficient?

If $r > 2$, the number n is called **abundant.** Thus, 24 and 120 are abundant since their values of r exceed 2. A perfect number, such as 6, is neither abundant nor deficient.

We can use a Venn diagram to show the relationship among abundant, deficient, and perfect numbers.

Natural Numbers

Deficient Numbers	Perfect Numbers	Abundant Numbers

GREATEST COMMON FACTORS

Look at the factors of 6 (1, 2, 3, and 6) and the factors of 9 (1, 3, and 9). Do 6 and 9 have any factors in common? Yes—both 1 and 3 are common factors of 6 and 9.

Now we will find the common factors of 45 and 60.

Example 3
a List the factors of 45.
b List the factors of 60.
c List the common factors of 45 and 60.

Solution
a The factors of 45 are 1, 3, 5, 9, 15, and 45.
b The factors of 60 are 1, 2, 3, 4, 5, 6, 10, 12, 15, 20, 30, and 60.
c The common factors of 45 and 60 are 1, 3, 5, and 15.

The **greatest common factor (GCF)** of 45 and 60 is 15.

Sample Problem

Problem

Simplify the fraction $\frac{45}{60}$.

Solution

Method 1
We will use 15, the greatest common factor of 45 and 60, to simplify the fraction.

$$\frac{45}{60} = \frac{15 \cdot 3}{15 \cdot 4} = \frac{3}{4}$$

515

Method 2

We will use the prime-factorization forms of 45 and 60 to simplify the fractions.

$$\frac{45}{60} = \frac{3^2 \cdot 5}{2^2 \cdot 3 \cdot 5} = \frac{3 \cdot 3 \cdot 5}{2 \cdot 2 \cdot 3 \cdot 5} = \frac{15 \cdot 3}{15 \cdot 4} = \frac{3}{4}$$

Think and Discuss

1 a Name the one-digit natural numbers that have exactly two factors.
b What are these numbers called?

2 Name the one-digit natural numbers that have
a Exactly three factors
b Exactly four factors
c Exactly one factor

3 a Are all numbers less than 6 deficient?
b Are all numbers greater than 6 abundant?

4 Explain how to find the common factors of two natural numbers.

5 How do you find the greatest common factor of two numbers?

6 Explain why some numbers have an even number of distinct factors and why some numbers have an odd number of distinct factors.

7 Some textbooks define *perfect number* as follows:

A natural number is perfect if the sum of all its factors, except itself, adds up to the number.

Is this definition equivalent to the definition in this section? Explain your answer.

Problems and Applications

8 List all the factors of each number.
a 75 **b** 130 **c** 80

9 Make a tree diagram of all the factors of 18.

10 Copy and complete the table.

GCF	12	15	24
16			
31			
42	6		

11 Find the GCF and LCM of each pair of numbers.
   a 20 and 32   **b** $2^2 \cdot 3^3 \cdot 5$ and $2^4 \cdot 3^2 \cdot 5^3$

12 List all the factors of each number.
   a 48   **b** 84   **c** 484   **d** 848

13 Find the LCM and GCF of the prime numbers 71 and 73.

14 Classify each number as *abundant, deficient,* or *neither.*
   a 16   **b** 24   **c** 80

15 Copy and complete the table.

LCM	12	15	24
6		30	
8			
10			

16 Simplify each fraction.
   a $\dfrac{15}{21}$ **b** $\dfrac{156}{168}$ **c** $\dfrac{28}{40}$

17 The prime-factorization form of 36 is
   $2 \cdot 2 \cdot 3 \cdot 3$. The prime-factorization form
   of 40 is $2 \cdot 2 \cdot 2 \cdot 5$. You may find the
   diagram helpful.
   a Find the GCF of 36 and 40.
   b Find the LCM of 36 and 40.

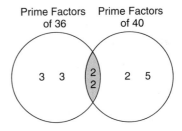

18 List all the factors of 320 that are multiples of 5.

19 Find the factors of 56 by using
   the factor tree. What percent
   of the factors are prime?

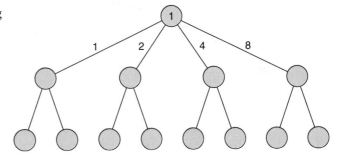

20 Let $r = \dfrac{\text{Sum of the factors of } n}{n}$ be the "r-value" of n. Find the "r-value" of n
   if n is
   a 6   **b** 9   **c** 28   **d** 120

21 The prime-factorization form of 32 is
   $2 \cdot 2 \cdot 2 \cdot 2 \cdot 2$. The prime-factorization form
   of 40 is $2 \cdot 2 \cdot 2 \cdot 5$. You may find the
   diagram helpful.
   a Find the LCM of 32 and 40.
   b Find the GCF of 32 and 40.

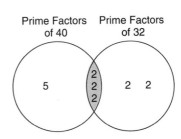

22 Find the smallest natural number that has a remainder of 2 when divided by 3, 5, or 7.

23 Use the diagram to help you list the factors of 54.

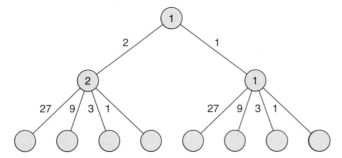

24 If a is a multiple of 7, then what are the next four multiples of 7 greater than a?

25 Is the greatest common factor of two numbers always a factor of their
   a Sum?   **b** Difference?   **c** Product?   **d** Quotient?

26 **Communicating**   How can you use these rectangles to draw a picture that will convince someone that 4 is a factor of 24 + 40 = 64?

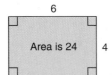

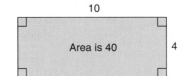

27 **Spreadsheets**   Using a spreadsheet, enter +B1 in cell A2 and +A1−B1*@INT(A1/B1) in cell B2. Then copy row 2 to rows 3–17.
   a Enter 75 in cell A1 and 27 in cell B1. As you look down column A, what is the last nonzero number you see?
   b Find the GCF of 75 and 27.
   c Try entering the other pairs of numbers in A1 and B1. What do you notice?

28 Make a table of positive integer x-values and y-values that solve the equation $xy = 30$.

29 If $600 = 2^3 \cdot 3 \cdot 5^2$, any factor of 600 must be a factor of $2^3 \cdot 3 \cdot 5^2$. How many factors does 600 have? A factor of the number 600 can have zero, one, two, or three 2's (four choices), zero or one 3's (two choices), and zero, one or two 5's (three choices). Therefore, the possible number of factors of 600 is $4 \cdot 2 \cdot 3$, or 24. Use this example to find the number of factors of each of the following numbers.
   a 70   **b** $2^4 \cdot 3^2 \cdot 5^7$ **c** $5^4 \cdot 11^3 \cdot 13$ **d** 36

30 Communicating Copy and fill in the multiplication matrix. Explain why the entries determine all possible factors of 144.

$$
\begin{array}{c}
 & \begin{array}{ccc} \mathbf{1} & \mathbf{3} & \mathbf{3^2} \end{array} \\
\begin{array}{c} \mathbf{1} \\ \mathbf{2} \\ \mathbf{2^2} \\ \mathbf{2^3} \\ \mathbf{2^4} \end{array}
\begin{bmatrix}
1 & & \\
 & 6 & \\
 & & 36 \\
 & 24 & \\
 & &
\end{bmatrix}
\end{array}
$$

31 Spreadsheets Create a spreadsheet in which column A contains the numbers from 1 to 100, cell C2 contains factors you want to identify, and cell B2 contains the formula $C$2/A2. Copy this formula down column B for 100 cells.
  a Describe how this spreadsheet can help you find factors.
  b Find the factors of
    i 140   **ii** 725   **iii** $2^3 \cdot 5^3 \cdot 7^3$

32 Simplify each expression.
  a $\dfrac{5}{12}$ **b** $-\dfrac{5}{6} - \dfrac{3}{4} - \dfrac{2}{3}$

33 There are a certain number of candies in a pile.
  a Tom eats one, divides the pile into thirds, takes one third for himself, and leaves the rest.
  b Bill takes the remaining pile, eats one candy, divides the pile into thirds, and takes one third for himself.
  c Sue follows the same procedure as Tom and Bill.
  d Juanita follows the same procedure as Sue and the others.
  e Ralph takes the remaining candies.
Write expressions that represent the number of candies in the original pile and the number of candies each person has.

34 The length of segment AB is 126. Find the lengths of segments AC, CD, and DB if their measures are three consecutive multiples of 14.

A   C   D   B

◄ LOOKING BACK **Spiral Learning** LOOKING AHEAD ▶

---

35 Let g(n) represent the greatest prime factor of n. Find
  a g(44)   **b** g(68)   **c** g(49)

36 Find all values of x so that
  a LCM(x, 14) = 42   **b** LCM(x, 7) = 35

37 The red car traveled 6 hours at 60 miles per hour from point A to point C. The blue car traveled 3 hours at 50 miles per hour from point A to point B. Find BC.

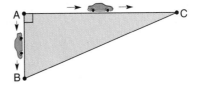

38 Barry's box contains 84 small marbles, of which 25% are blue. Bradley's box contains 240 large marbles, of which 40% are blue. Barry and Brad dump their boxes of marbles in a bucket. What percent of the marbles in the bucket will be blue?

39 In set A are the factors of a number. In set B are the factors of another number.

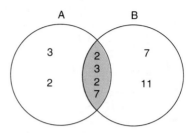

    a Find A ∩ B.
    b Find A ∪ B.
    c What are the two numbers?
    d What is the GCF of the numbers?
    e What is the LCM of the numbers?

40 Solve each inequality. Write your solution by using set-builder notation.
    a $3x - 8 < 10$ **b** $8 - 3x < 10$ **c** $|x - 8| < 10$

41 Silky ran the first $1\frac{1}{4}$ miles of a race at a speed of 30 miles per hour. How long did it take Silky to run this distance?

42 Lashaun observed that a group of bricklayers could lay 8 rows of bricks all the way around a building in one day. The walls were already 48 rows high, and she estimated that the building would require 710 rows. How many working days will be needed to finish the job?

43 Solve for all possible values of x.
    a $(x - 6)(x + 7)(x + 3)(2x) = 0$
    b $4x - 9 < 18$, x is an integer
    c $\frac{3}{4}x = \frac{7}{8}$

44 Bill leaves point A at 9 A.M., driving 45 miles per hour. Tom leaves point A at 10 A.M. traveling in the same direction as Bill at 55 miles per hour. At what time will Bill catch up to Tom?

Investigation

Relatively Prime Numbers   For two numbers to be "relatively prime," they don't have to be prime numbers at all. For example, the following pairs of numbers are relatively prime:

    a 4, 9   **b** 5, 6   **c** 8, 5   **d** 12, 7   **e** 10, 13

But the following pairs of numbers are *not* relatively prime.

    a 4, 6   **b** 9, 3   **c** 8, 12   **d** 15, 10   **e** 21, 28

What do you think relatively prime means? Where could you apply this concept?

SECTION 10.6
LCM and GCF Revisited

In this section we will further our understanding of the least common multiple (LCM) and the greatest common factor (GCF), and we will apply both to our work with fractions. We will look at several methods for determining the LCM or the GCF of two numbers.

Example 1
Find both the LCM and the GCF of 48 and 72.

Solution
We will investigate two methods of finding the LCM and the GCF of 48 and 72.

Method 1
Write the prime-factorization form of each number.

$$48 = 2 \cdot 2 \cdot 2 \cdot 2 \cdot 3$$

$$72 = 2 \cdot 2 \cdot 2 \cdot 3 \cdot 3$$

The GCF of 48 and 72 is the product of the prime factors common to both numbers: $2 \cdot 2 \cdot 2 \cdot 3$, or 24.

The LCM of 48 and 72 is the product of the GCF and the remaining prime factors of the two numbers: $2 \cdot 3 \cdot \text{GCF} = 2 \cdot 3 \cdot 24$, or 144.

The second method is on the next page.

GCF = $2 \cdot 2 \cdot 2 \cdot 3$ = 24

48 = 2 · ②·②·②·③
72 = ②·②·②·③ · 3

LCM = $2 \cdot 2 \cdot 2 \cdot 2 \cdot 3 \cdot 3 = 144$

Method 2

We can draw a Venn diagram. Fill in region II with the prime factors common to 48 and 72: 2, 2, 2, and 3. Fill in region I with the remaining factor of 48—2. Fill in region III with the remaining factor of 72—3.

The GCF is the product of the primes in region II, the intersection of the two circles. Thus, the GCF is 24.

The LCM is the product of the primes in regions I, II, and III—the union of the two circles. Thus, the LCM is 144.

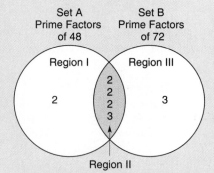

Product of factors in A $\cap$ B = $2^3 \cdot 3^1$, the GCF
Product of factors in A $\cup$ B = $2^4 \cdot 3^2$, the LCM

Example 2

Find the GCF and the LCM of 25 and 56.

Solution

The prime-factorization form of 25 is 5^2, and the prime-factorization form of 56 is $2^3 \cdot 7$. The Venn diagram shows that there are no common prime factors in region II. Since 25 and 56 have no prime factors in common, the GCF is 1. The LCM of 25 and 56 is 25 · 56, or 1400.

If the GCF of two numbers is 1, the two numbers are **_relatively prime._** Thus, 25 and 56 are relatively prime. When the GCF of two numbers is 1, the LCM is the product of the two numbers.

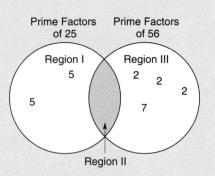

SIMPLIFYING FRACTIONS

The concepts of LCM and GCF are helpful when working with fractions.

Example 3

Simplify the expression $\frac{1}{2} \cdot \frac{7}{20} - \frac{3}{5} \cdot \frac{7}{10}$.

Solution

$$\frac{1}{2} \cdot \frac{7}{20} - \frac{3}{5} \cdot \frac{7}{10}$$

Multiply first

$$= \frac{7}{40} - \frac{21}{50}$$

LCM of 40 and 50 is 200

$$= \frac{5}{5} \cdot \frac{7}{40} - \frac{4}{4} \cdot \frac{21}{50}$$

$$= \frac{35}{200} - \frac{84}{200}$$

GCF of 49 and 200 is 1

$$= -\frac{49}{200}$$

Since the GCF of 49 and 200 is 1, the fraction cannot be further simplified.

If an equation contains a fraction, it may be helpful to multiply both sides of the equation by the LCM of the denominators of the fractions.

Example 4

Solve $\frac{1}{2} + \frac{2}{3}x = \frac{3}{4}$ for x.

Solution

The denominators of the fractions are 2, 3, and 4. The LCM of 2, 3, and 4 is 12. We multiply both sides of the equation by 12.

$$12\left(\frac{1}{2} + \frac{2}{3}x\right) = 12\left(\frac{3}{4}\right)$$

$$(12)\left(\frac{1}{2}\right) + (12)\left(\frac{2}{3}x\right) = 12\left(\frac{3}{4}\right)$$

$$6 + 8x = 9$$

$$\underline{-6 \qquad\quad -6}$$

$$8x = 3$$

$$x = \frac{3}{8}$$

Sample Problem

Problem

Painter Phil estimates that he can paint a certain fence by himself in 6 hours. He estimates that his son Scott can paint the fence by himself in 10 hours. Can they finish the job if they work together for $3\frac{1}{2}$ hours?

Solution

Phil can do $\frac{1}{6}$ of the job in one hour. Scott can do $\frac{1}{10}$ of the job in one hour. Each person is scheduled to work $3\frac{1}{2}$ hours.

Phil completes $\left(3\frac{1}{2}\right)\left(\frac{1}{6}\right) = \frac{7}{2} \cdot \frac{1}{6} = \frac{7}{12}$ of the job.

Scott completes $\left(3\frac{1}{2}\right)\left(\frac{1}{10}\right) = \frac{7}{2} \cdot \frac{1}{10} = \frac{7}{20}$ of the job.

Together they paint $\frac{7}{12} + \frac{7}{20} = \frac{35}{60} + \frac{21}{60} = \frac{56}{60}$ of the fence, which is a little short of completing the job.

Think and Discuss

1 **a** Find the greatest common factor of 12 and 8.

 b Find the least common multiple of 12 and 8.

2 a Explain why two consecutive integers greater than 1 will always be relatively prime.
  b Explain why three consecutive integers greater than 1 will always contain a multiple of 3.

3 Is it possible for the sum of the GCF and the LCM of two numbers to be odd?

4 Is the statement true *always, sometimes,* or *never?* If two numbers are relatively prime, then any factor of the first number and any factor of the second number will also be relatively prime. Explain your answer.

5 If you multiply two numbers, is the result always a common multiple of the two numbers? Is it always the LCM of the two numbers?

6 Explain why the product of three consecutive natural numbers is divisible by 6.

7 Is the statement true *always, sometimes,* or *never?*
  a The number 2 is relatively prime to an odd number.
  b The number 2 is relatively prime to an even number.
  c Two even numbers are relatively prime.
  d An odd number and an even number are relatively prime.
  e Two odd numbers are relatively prime.
  f Two integers with a last digit of 5 are relatively prime.
  g Two integers with a last digit of 7 are relatively prime.

8 Martin was asked to find the LCM of 12 and 9. He started by listing the multiples of 12 (12, 24, 36, …) until he found one, 36, that was divisible by 9. Is 36 the LCM of 12 and 9? Will this method always work?

Problems and Applications

9 The prime-factorization form of 120 is $2 \cdot 2 \cdot 2 \cdot 3 \cdot 5$. The prime-factorization form of 75 is $3 \cdot 5 \cdot 5$. You may find the diagram helpful. Find the LCM and the GCF of 120 and 75.

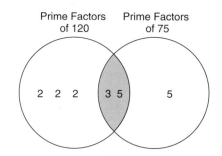

10 a Find the LCM of 3, 6, and 15.
   b Use the answer to part **a** to help you solve the equation $\frac{4}{5} + \frac{1}{6}x = \frac{7}{15}$.

11 Business Machine A can make 500 CD's per hour. Machine B can make 760 CD's per hour. The company has an order for 900,000 CD's. At 8 hours per day, how many days will it take to complete the order?

12 Suppose that there are ten hot dogs to a package and eight hot dog buns to a package. What is the fewest number of packages of hot dogs you can purchase so that you can purchase a whole number of packages of buns and have exactly the same number of hot dogs and buns?

13 The prime-factorization form of 45 is $3 \cdot 3 \cdot 5$. The prime-factorization form of 68 is $2 \cdot 2 \cdot 17$. You may find the diagram helpful. Find the LCM and the GCF of 45 and 68.

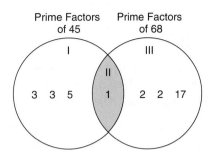

Prime Factors of 45   Prime Factors of 68

I   III

II

3 3 5   1   2 2 17

14 Solve each equation for x.

  a $\frac{1}{6}x + \frac{1}{4} = 1$ **b** $\frac{1}{6}x + \frac{1}{4}x - \frac{1}{3}x = 1$

15 a Copy and fill in the factor trees to find all the factors of 75 and 60 if $75 = 3 \cdot 5^2$ and $60 = 2^2 \cdot 3 \cdot 5$.

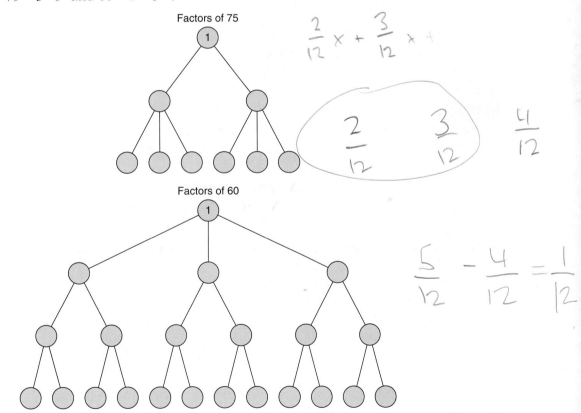

Factors of 75

Factors of 60

  b Find the GCF and the LCM of 75 and 60.

16 Solve each equation for x.

  a $\frac{2}{3} + \frac{3}{5}x = \frac{5}{7}$ **b** $1\frac{2}{3} + \frac{5}{9}x = 8$

17 Find the LCM and the GCF of 7! and 8!.

18 Pump 1 can pump 80 gallons of water per minute, pump 2 can pump 60 gallons of water per minute, and pump 3 can pump 45 gallons of water per minute. A flooded basement has approximately 2000 gallons of water that needs to be pumped out. What percent of the water will be pumped out per minute if the three pumps are used together?

19 Suppose that you are going to add $\frac{7}{36}$ and $\frac{19}{45}$.
 a Why do you need to know the LCM of 36 and 45?
 b Use the LCM to add the fractions.
 c What is the GCF of the numerator and the denominator before you simplify the sum? After you simplify the sum?

20 Kim can clean a fish in 2 minutes, while Ping Yo can clean 25 fish in an hour. If they have 180 fish to clean, how long will it take?

21 In 1992, February 29 was on a Saturday. What is the next year that February 29 will be on a Saturday? What does this have to do with LCM and GCF?

◄ LOOKING BACK **Spiral Learning** LOOKING AHEAD ►

22 If 80 is 40% of the quantity $x + 12$, what is x?

23 **Spreadsheets** Make a spreadsheet with three columns. Column A should show years, column B should show Tony's age if he was born in 1972, and column C should show the age of Tony's sister if she was born in 1982. In what year is Tony three times as old as his sister?

24 Solve each equation for x.
 a $0.5x + 0.7x = 1.68$ **b** $-0.8x + 0.2x = 2.46$

25 a Convert $186{,}000 \frac{\text{miles}}{\text{second}}$ to $\frac{\text{feet}}{\text{hour}}$. **b** Simplify $\frac{25 \text{ miles}}{10 \frac{\text{miles}}{\text{hr}}}$

26 **Science** Gear 1 has 40 teeth, gear 2 has 24 teeth, and gear 3 has 60 teeth. All of the teeth are the same size. How many revolutions must each gear make before the arrows are again lined up?

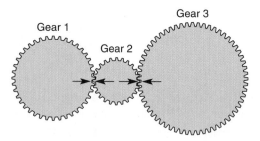

Gear 1 Gear 2 Gear 3

27 If 40 textbooks $2\frac{1}{2}$ inches thick can be stored on a shelf, then how many textbooks $1\frac{1}{4}$ inches thick can be stored on the same shelf?

28 Solve $\frac{2}{3} + \frac{3}{2}x = \frac{5}{6}$ for x.

29 The LCM of p and g is 48. The GCF of p and g is 4. Find all possible values of p and g.

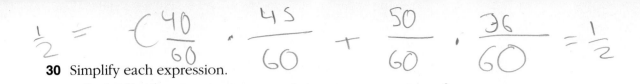

$$\frac{1}{2} = \left(\frac{40}{60} \cdot \frac{45}{60}\right) + \frac{50}{60} \cdot \frac{36}{60} = \frac{1}{2}$$

30 Simplify each expression.

a $\frac{2}{3} \cdot \frac{3}{4} + \frac{5}{6} \cdot \frac{6}{10}$ **b** $3.75 + 2\frac{1}{4}$ **c** $15\% + \frac{2}{5}$

31 You are playing a game with a pair of dice. You win if the numbers on the two dice are relatively prime; otherwise, you lose. What percent of the dice throws should be winning ones?

32 Fran drives her delivery truck at an average speed of 50 miles per hour and Fred drives his delivery truck at an average speed of 45 miles per hour.

  a At noon, the two trucks leave company headquarters and head in opposite directions. How far apart will the trucks be after $2\frac{1}{2}$ hours?

  b If the trucks head back to headquarters at 2:30 P.M., at what time will each truck arrive?

  c How many miles will each truck have traveled?

33 What are the first five perfect-square multiples of 5?

34 **Finance**   A car depreciates at a rate of 17% per year for the first four years after it is purchased. If the car originally cost $17,549, what is its value after four years?

35 Ten gallons of punch that is 60% ginger ale is mixed with 15 gallons of punch that is 70% ginger ale. What percent of the mixture is ginger ale?

36 How many different three-digit numbers can be formed using three different digits?

37 Find the GCF and the LCM of each pair of numbers.
  a 6 and 8   **b** 12 and 16   **c** 18 and 24

38 Let p be a prime number. List the factors of p^2.

39 What is the smallest square that can be made using rectangular 3-inch-by-4-inch tiles?

Investigation

Lattice Points   Lattice points are points with coordinates that are both integers. Plot the lattice points that have coordinates that are relatively prime. Describe some patterns that you observe.

10.7

Number-Theory Explorations

SYMMETRIC PRIMES

The number 25 is midway between the prime numbers 19 and 31. The numbers 19 and 31 are **symmetric primes** (also called Euler Primes) of 25 because both numbers are six units from 25 on the number line.

Example 1
Find all other pairs of symmetric primes of 25.

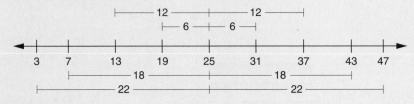

Solution
Other pairs of symmetric primes of 25 are 13 and 37, 7 and 43, and 3 and 47.

GOLDBACH'S CONJECTURES

Does every natural number have a pair of symmetric primes? The answer is no. The numbers 1, 2, and 3 do not have a pair of symmetric primes. Do all natural numbers greater than 3 have a pair of symmetric primes? The answer to this question is unknown at this time. If you could solve this problem, you would be able to prove the following conjectures by the Prussian mathematician Christian Goldbach.

▶ **Goldbach's First Conjecture**   Every even number greater than or equal to four can be represented as the sum of two primes.

▶ **Goldbach's Second Conjecture**   Every odd number greater than or equal to seven can be expressed as the sum of three primes.

Example 2
Test Goldbach's conjectures by expressing each number as the sum of primes.
a 42   **b** 23

Solution
a Since 42 is an even number greater than 4, we can express it as the sum of two primes, 5 + 37.
b Since 23 is an odd number greater than 7, we can express it as the sum of three primes, 3 + 7 + 13.

FIGURATE NUMBERS

The ancient Greeks were interested in *figurate numbers*—special numbers associated with geometric figures. The answers to many problems that require counting are figurate numbers. Triangular numbers, square numbers, pentagonal numbers, and hexagonal numbers are examples of figurate numbers.

Example 3
a The first four triangular numbers are 1, 3, 6, and 10.

  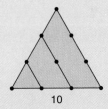

1   3   6   10

What is the next triangular number?

b The first four square numbers are 1, 4, 9, and 16.

  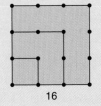

1   4   9   16

What is the next square number?

c The first four pentagonal numbers are 1, 5, 12, and 22.

What is the next pentagonal number?

d The first four hexagonal numbers are 1, 6, 15, and 28.

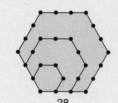

What is the next hexagonal number?

Solution

a The fifth triangular number is 10 + 5, or 15.
b The fifth square number is 16 + 9, or 25.
c The fifth pentagonal number is 22 + 13, or 35.
d The fifth hexagonal number is 28 + 17, or 45.

PYTHAGOREAN TRIPLES

Study the data displayed in the table.

a	b	c
1	0	1
3	4	5
5	12	13
7	24	25
9	40	41
11	60	61

The numbers in the chart satisfy the well-known equation $a^2 + b^2 = c^2$, which is associated with the Pythagorean Theorem. Except for the first line of data, (1, 0, 1), each line is a trio of natural numbers called ***Pythagorean Triples.***

Example 4

What pattern can be used to describe the numbers in columns **a, b**, and **c** in the preceding table?

Solution

Here is one description of the pattern:

In column **a,** the consecutive numbers differ by two. In column **b,** the numbers are multiples of 4 and the consecutive numbers differ by 4, 8, 12, 16, and 20. Each number in column **c** is one more than the corresponding value in column **b.**

Can you find other ways to describe the number relationships in columns **a, b,** and **c?**

Sample Problem

Problem Count the number of diagonals in each drawing. How do the number of diagonals in each geometric figure relate to the triangular numbers?

Triangle   Quadrilateral   Pentagon   Hexagon

Solution We can organize the answer in a table.

Figure	Number of Diagonals
Triangle	0
Quadrilateral	2
Pentagon	5
Hexagon	9

The number of diagonals in each figure is one less than a triangular number.

$$0 = 1 - 1$$
$$2 = 3 - 1$$
$$5 = 6 - 1$$
$$9 = 10 - 1$$

1 The prime numbers 5 and 23 are symmetric to what number?

2 What two pairs of primes are symmetric primes of 9?

3 Express 6 as the sum of two primes.

4 Refer to Example 2 on page 529.
  a Find other ways to express 42 as the sum of primes.
  b Find other ways to express 23 as the sum of primes.

5 Express 14 as the sum of two primes in two different ways.

6 Express 11 as the sum of three primes.

7 What is a triangular number?

8 What are figurate numbers?

9 Which of the following are Pythagorean triples?
  a 6, 8, 10   **b** 5, 11, 12   **c** 8, 15, 17

Problems and Applications

10 Write 86 as the sum of two prime numbers in three different ways.

11 Write 137 as the sum of three prime numbers in three different ways.

12 The LCM of a and b is 12. The GCF of a and b is 4.
  a Find ab.
  b Find the LCM of $2a$ and $2b$.
  c Find the GCF of $2a$ and $2b$.
  d Find the LCM of $3a$ and $3b$.
  e Find the GCF of $3a$ and $3b$.

13 Find all pairs of symmetric primes of 30.

14 In parts **a** and **b,** determine whether the statement is true *always, sometimes,* or *never.*
  a The product of two numbers divided by their LCM is their GCF.
  b The product of two numbers divided by their GCF is their LCM.
  c Find the LCM of 24, 36, and 45.

15 The figurate numbers 1, 5, 12, 22, and 35 are called pentagonal numbers. Represent each pentagonal number greater than 1 as the sum of a square number and a triangular number.

16 Communicating How might the rules for baseball change if the baseball field had five bases instead of four bases?

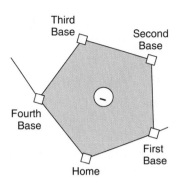

17 The numbers 20, 21, and 29 represent a Pythagorean Triple. Can you find other Pythagorean Triples in which the two smaller numbers differ by one? By two?

18 Copy the diagram and circle the primes. If the pattern were continued forever, would there be a prime in every row after the first row?

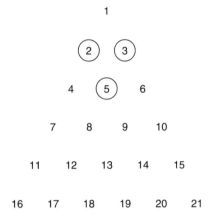

19 Sports How would bowling change if there were 15 pins instead of 10?

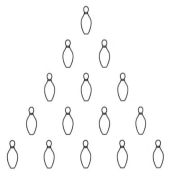

20 Observe that 41 and 61 are symmetric primes of 51. Also, $51 = \frac{41 + 61}{2}$ and $102 = 41 + 61$. How does this relate to Goldbach's First Conjecture?

21 Find the sum of the numbers in the fifteenth row of the triangle.

$$
\begin{array}{ccccccc}
 & & & 1 & & & \\
 & & 3 & & 5 & & \\
 & 7 & & 9 & & 11 & \\
13 & & 15 & & 17 & & 19
\end{array}
$$

22 Two primes of the form n and $2n$-1 are "almost-double primes" (ADP). Find the first five pairs of almost-double primes.

23 Pick a natural number.
Step 1: Divide the number by 2 if the number you chose is even. Repeat this procedure as long as the resulting number is even.
Step 2: Multiply the number by 3, add 1, and divide by 2 if the number you chose is odd.
Continue to repeat Step 1 or Step 2 on the resulting number. What happens?

24 Pick a prime number greater than 3, and double it. Now, look at the two integers that are one greater than and one less than your product. Can both numbers be prime? Explain.

25 Let $f(n)$ = the sum of the natural-number factors of n. Find $f(n)$ for each of the following.
a $f(24)$ **b** $f(31)$

◀ LOOKING BACK **Spiral Learning** LOOKING AHEAD ▶

---

26 Evaluate each expression.
a $(-4)^2$ **b** -4^2
c $-(-4)^2$ **d** $-(4^2)$

27 a Write an expression for the perimeter of the triangle.
b Find the perimeter if $x = 2.4$.

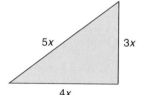

28 Multiply $\begin{bmatrix} -2 & 6 \\ -1 & 0 \end{bmatrix} \cdot \begin{bmatrix} 5 & -4 \\ 2 & -3 \end{bmatrix}$.

29 Solve $\frac{x-6}{4} = \frac{1}{2}$.

30 a How many points did Rick score?
b What is the mean number of points scored by the six players?

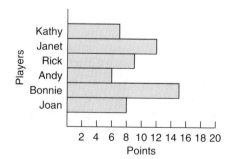

31 A.J. can mow the lawn in 30 minutes and J.R. can mow the lawn in 45 minutes. How long will it take if they work together?

32 Solve $|x - 4| = 9$ for x.

33 **a** Find the length of $\overline{AB}$.
   b Find the length of $\overline{BC}$.
   c Find the area of the rectangle.

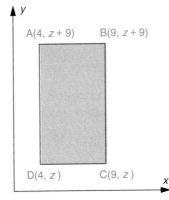

34 Two years ago, Mary was half her sister's age. If Mary's sister is 12 years old, how old is Mary?

35 Solve $x + 4 = 3x + 6$ for x.

36 What is the probability of randomly selecting a natural number from $(-4, -3, -2, -1, 0, 1, 2, 3, 4)$ that is 3 units or less from -2?

37 Find the area of square C.

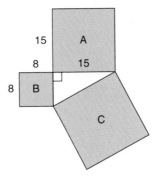

38 Solve each equation for x.
   a $3x = 0$ **b** $3(x - 4) = 0$ **c** $(x - 3)(x - 4) = 0$

39 Graph the equation $2x - 4 = 1$.

Investigation

Prime Numbers   Find all two-digit prime numbers that remain prime when the digits are reversed. Find a three-digit prime number that remains prime no matter how you rearrange the digits.

Summary

CONCEPTS AND PROCEDURES

After studying this chapter, you should be able to

■ Apply the Fundamental Counting Principle to solve problems (10.1)

■ Identify prime numbers and composite numbers (10.2)

■ Identify natural-number multiples of a number (10.2)

■ Identify the least common multiple of natural numbers (10.2)

■ Apply divisibility tests for 2, 3, 4, 5, 6, 8, 9, 11, and 12 (10.3)

■ Express a number in prime-factorization form (10.4)

■ Determine whether a number is prime (10.4)

■ Determine all factors of a natural number (10.5)

■ Determine whether a number is an abundant number, a deficient number, or a perfect number (10.5)

■ Determine the greatest common factor of a set of numbers (10.5)

■ Use Venn diagrams to determine the least common multiple and the greatest common factor of a set of numbers (10.6)

■ Determine whether numbers are relatively prime (10.6)

■ Use LCM and GCF to simplify fractions and solve equations (10.6)

■ Identify symmetric prime numbers (10.7)

■ Apply Goldbach's first and second conjectures (10.7)

■ Identify figurate numbers (10.7)

■ Identify Pythagorean triples (10.7)

VOCABULARY

abundant number (10.5)

composite number (10.2)

deficient number (10.5)

factor (10.2)

figurate numbers (10.7)

Fundamental Counting Principle (10.1)

greatest common factor (10.5)

least common multiple (10.2)

perfect number (10.5)

prime-factorization form (10.4)

prime number (10.2)

Pythagorean triple (10.7)

relatively prime numbers (10.6)

symmetric prime numbers (10.7)

tree diagram (10.1)

Review

1 Write the prime-factorization form of each number.
  a 27   **b** 16   **c** $16 \cdot 27$ **d** $8 \cdot 9 \cdot 5$ **e** 720

2 Coach Simon has eight pitchers and three catchers. How many combinations of one pitcher and one catcher can he select?

3 Camille has four blouses, five skirts, and six sweaters that can be mixed and matched. How many different outfits can Camille assemble?

4 Determine the perimeters of all rectangles with area 80 if the lengths of the sides of the rectangles are natural numbers.

5 When a ball comes down from the top of a pinball machine, it goes left 80% of the time and right 20% of the time. It then hits a bumper. The bumper on the left sends it to the left 30% of the time and to the middle 70% of the time. The bumper on the right sends it to the right 90% of the time and to the middle 10% of the time. Find the probability that, after the ball first hits a bumper, it goes to the
  a Left   **b** Middle   **c** Right

6 The diagram represents the probabilities connected with Bart shooting two free throws.
  a Find the probability that Bart will make at least one free throw.
  b Find the probability that Bart will make exactly one free throw.

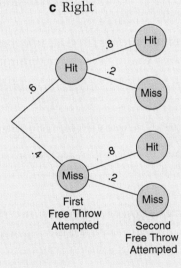

7 Boards come in 8-foot, 10-foot, and 12-foot lengths. You need seven 6-foot boards and eight 5-foot boards. What size boards should you buy to minimize waste?

8 Suppose x is a prime factor of 30 and y is a composite factor of 56.
  a What is the number of possible values for the volume of the box?
  b What is the greatest possible volume of the box?
  c What is the least possible volume of the box?

9 Use a spreadsheet to find the factors of 2477. How far down column B do you need to copy the formula to be sure that you have found all the factors?

	A	B
1	1	2477/A1
2	2	
3	3	

10 The five-digit number $n5n5n$ is divisible by 11. Determine the values of n.

11 Find all single-digit values of n so that $|n^2 - 3|$ is a multiple of 11.

12 The area of a rectangle is 140 and the base and height are both natural numbers. Find all possible values of the height if the height is greater than the base.

13 The PTO has $1000 for scholarships. Each of the people receiving a scholarship must receive the same amount of money. What scholarship amounts can be given to each person if the amount of the scholarship must be at least $50?

14 a List the natural-number factors of 18.
   b Find the sum of the reciprocals of the factors in part **a**.

15 a Find the least common denominator of $\frac{1}{4}$, $\frac{1}{8}$, and $\frac{5}{6}$.
   b Subtract the sum of the last two fractions in part **a** from the first fraction.

16 If a pair of numbers is randomly selected from 5, 18, 20, 27, and 36, what is the probability that the two numbers are relatively prime?

17 Classify each number as *abundant, deficient,* or *perfect.*
   a 28   **b** 58   **c** 36

18 Find the LCM and the GCF of 120 and 135.

19 Printing Press 1 is able to print 6000 magazines per hour. What percent of a printing job of 75,000 magazines has been completed after $3\frac{1}{2}$ hours of running time?

20 How many complete revolutions of Gear 2 are necessary for the arrows of the two gears to line up again?

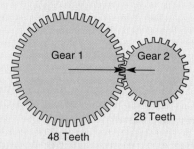

Gear 1   Gear 2

28 Teeth

48 Teeth

21 Evaluate each expression.
   a $\dfrac{12}{20} - \dfrac{9}{15}$ **b** $\dfrac{8}{12} + \dfrac{6}{9}$ **c** $\dfrac{5}{20} + \dfrac{6}{12}$

22 Locate the symmetric primes of 20 on a number line.

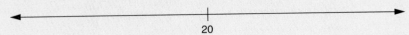

23 Bill comes to work at 6 A.M. and works for eight hours. He takes a five-minute break every three hours. Sue comes to work at 10 A.M. and works eight hours. Sue takes a break every two hours for five minutes. When will Bill and Sue have a break?

24 How many different combinations of three segments can be selected from the group shown?

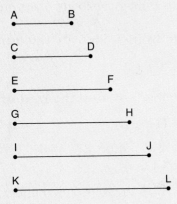

25 List all the factors of each number.
   a 1492   **b** 1776   **c** 1941

26 Make a spreadsheet consisting of these four columns:
A (multiples of 6)
B (multiples of 15)
C (multiples of 9)
D (multiples of 12)

   a What is the smallest number that appears in all four columns?
   b Explain why it is the first number that appears in all four columns.

27 **a** How many factors does 3^4 have?
   b How many factors does 2^3 have?
   c How many factors does $2^3 \cdot 3^4$ have?

28 **a** Factor 1001 into primes.
   b Factor 1,002,001 into primes.

29 List the perfect-square factors of 1800 if the prime-factorization form of 1800 is $2^3 \cdot 3^2 \cdot 5^2$.

30 List the set of all three-digit lock combinations that use only the digits 1, 2, and 3 without using any of these digits more than once.

31 Evaluate each expression.
   a $\frac{1}{4} + \frac{1}{2.5}$ **b** $\frac{2}{1.5} + \frac{1.5}{2.5}$ **c** $\frac{2}{3} + \frac{3}{2}$

Test

1 A restaurant offers four types of sandwiches, three types of salads, and four types of soup. How many different meals could Judy order if she wants a sandwich, a salad, and a bowl of soup?

2 On each of the next three days, the probability of snow is listed as 20%. Calculate the probability that it snows exactly two out of three days.

In problems 3–5, identify the number as *prime* or *composite*.

3 34   **4** 71   **5** 292

In problems 6–8, find the LCM of each pair of numbers.

6 3 and 13   **7** 4 and 18   **8** 42 and 36

9 Check the number 27,165,879,348 for divisibility by 2, 3, 4, 5, 6, 8, 9, 10, 11, and 12.

10 What is n if the four-digit number $513n$ is divisible by 4?

In problems 11 and 12, determine the prime-factorization form of each number.

11 18,000   **12** 560

In problems 13–15, determine whether each number is *abundant*, *deficient*, or *perfect*.

13 28   **14** 42   **15** 84

In problems 16 and 17, simplify each fraction.

16 $\dfrac{112}{196}$ **17** $\dfrac{1}{2} \cdot \dfrac{2}{5} + \dfrac{3}{4} \cdot \dfrac{1}{5}$

18 One hose can add 40 gallons of water per hour to an empty pool. Another hose can add 30 gallons of water per hour. If the pool can hold 12,000 gallons of water, what percent of the pool will be filled per hour if both hoses are used together?

19 Solve $\dfrac{5}{6}x + \dfrac{1}{4}x - \dfrac{2}{3}x = 3$ for x …

20 Is 391 a prime number?

21 Use one of Goldbach's conjectures to express 110 as the sum of primes.

22 What is the seventh triangular number?

23 What is a pair of symmetric primes of 36?

24 What number completes the Pythagorean triple (7, ___, 25)?

1 Create a 4-by-4 Magic Square. That is, put the integers 1 to 16 in the squares so that the sums of the four numbers in each row, each column, and each four-square diagonal are the same.

2 A palindrome is a word that reads the same forwards as backwards. Examples are tot, noon, radar, and hannah. See how many four-, five-, and six-letter palindromes you can find which are legitimate English words.

3 Palindromes can also be numbers (for example, 343 or 6776). In the multiplication problem (11)(181) = 1991, the product of a two-digit palindrome and a three-digit palindrome is a four-digit palindrome. Try to find other multiplication problems in which the product of a two-digit palindrome and a three-digit palindrome is a four-digit palindrome.

4 Some letters are missing from the word list below. Form a complete word by replacing each set of asterisks with a man's first name. For example, ad***tage plus *van* gives the complete word *advantage*.

a r****serie

b k****knack

c b****yard

d ***ichoke

e ****etplace

f aspara***

g flot***

h f*****

i ***ural

j ***esman

k *****le

l m***ge

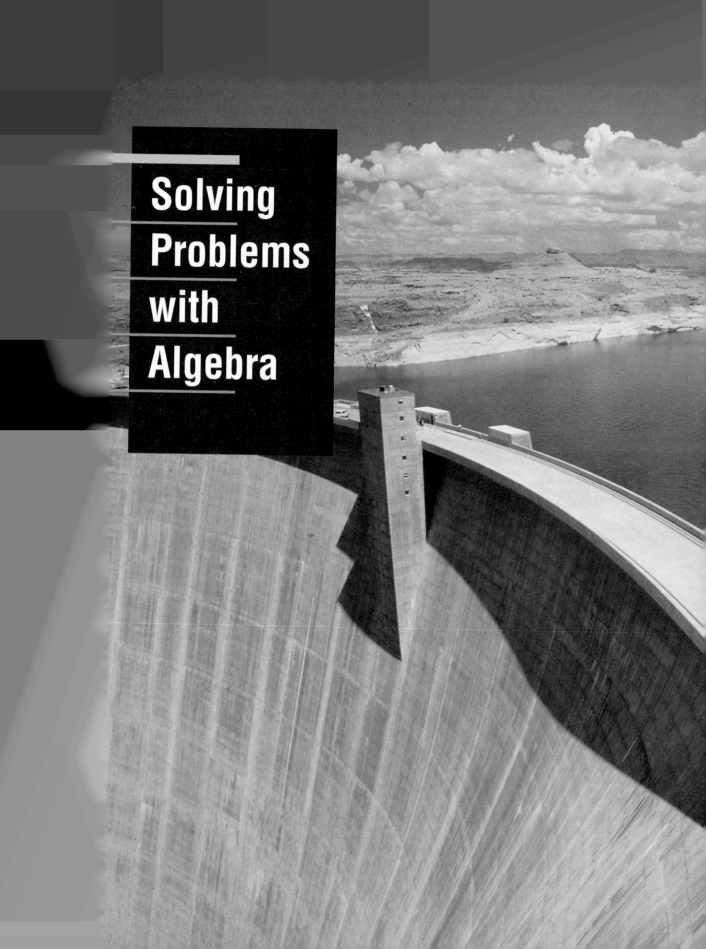

Solving Problems with Algebra

WATER ENGINEERING A water engineer gets involved in the management and distribution of supplies of fresh water from sources such as wells, rivers, and lakes. Needs for fresh water vary depending on whether the use is for home, industry, or agriculture.

Some water engineers devote their efforts to the problem of converting sea water to fresh water. This is called desalination.

Water engineers also deal with the purity of fresh water, by learning how to test for, and how to remove pollutants.

INVESTIGATION

Water Conservation Obtain a copy of a water bill. Use it to estimate the quantity of water used by a family in a year. What is the cost for a year's supply of water? List some ideas for conserving water, and estimate how much water each of your ideas would conserve if implemented.

Mathematics in Words

One reason mathematics is interesting and exciting is that there are many ways to solve most math problems. Solve each of the following problems, using logic, a drawing, or any other method that makes sense to you. See if you can find more than one way to solve each problem. Be prepared to discuss with the class how you reached your solutions.

PROBLEM 1: A Distance Problem

Cliff left his house at 8 A.M., walking at an average rate of 3 miles per hour. Two hours later, his sister, Heath, left home to catch her brother, bicycling at 12 miles per hour. How long did it take Heath to catch Cliff?

PROBLEM 2: Overlapping Data

At the annual watermelon convention, three farmers, Smith, Jones, and Squash, had the three largest melons. When the melons were weighed in pairs, each pair weighed more than 100 pounds.

- Smith's and Jones's melons together weighed 110 pounds.
- Jones's and Squash's melons together weighed 104 pounds.
- Smith's and Squash's melons together weighed 122 pounds.

Whose melon was the heaviest and how much did it weigh?

PROBLEM 3: Percent of Concentration

Mikey looked at the bottle of pancake syrup that his mother put on the table. The list of ingredients showed that the pancake syrup was 3% pure maple syrup and 1% butter. Sugar syrup was the only other ingredient. If the full bottle contained 24 ounces, how much of the full bottle was sugar syrup?

PROBLEM 4: An Age Puzzle

Five years ago, Jason was three times as old as Freddy. When Freddy was four years old, Jason was four times Freddy's age. How old are Jason and Freddy now?

PROBLEM 5: Counting Coins in a Fountain

There is a fountain in the center of a city. People like to toss coins in the fountain for luck. At the end of each day, the city cleans the fountain and donates the money to charity. On a given day, one fourth of the people tossed in a quarter, 40 people tossed in a dime, and the rest tossed in a penny. If there was a total of 200 coins tossed in the fountain that day, how much money did the city donate to charity?

PROBLEM 6: Work Rates

a A cold-water faucet fills two thirds of a water tank in one hour. How long must the faucet run in order to fill the whole tank?

b A hot-water faucet takes two hours to fill the same tank. What portion of the tank does it fill in one hour?

c If both faucets are used together, how long will it take them to fill the tank?

PROBLEM 7: A Combination Problem

Phylo won a $100 gift certificate that can be used to purchase tapes and CDs. He goes to a store where each tape costs $9 and each CD costs $12. He wants to use as much of the gift certificate as possible. How many tapes and CDs should he buy?

PROBLEM 8: A Range Problem

A small radio station is three miles from a straight highway. The station has a broadcasting range of five miles. If a car is driving down the highway, how long is the section of highway on which the car can receive the radio signal?

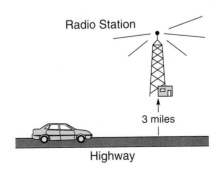

Radio Station

3 miles

Highway

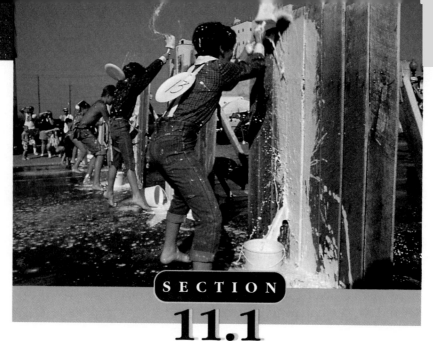

11.1

Presenting Solutions to Problems

Each time you come across a problem, you need to decide on a strategy to solve the problem. Remember,

> ➤ No one strategy works for all problems.
>   Most problems can be solved in many ways.

As you solve problems, you will develop your own strategies. We will show you some techniques that you may not have thought of trying. Try to solve each problem before you read the method we use. Then read our solution and see how it differs from yours.

Sample Problems

Problem 1
A Distance Problem

Carlos left home at 10 A.M. on a daylong bike trip, traveling at an average speed of 9 miles per hour. One hour later, his mother realized that Carlos had forgotten his lunch. She hopped on her moped and followed him, traveling 15 miles per hour. Did she catch up with him in time for lunch?

Solution

Carlos travels 9 miles per hour. Traveling at 15 miles per hour, his mother closes the gap by 6 miles each hour. Since she left at 11 A.M., by noon she has gained 6 miles. Carlos is still 3 miles ahead.

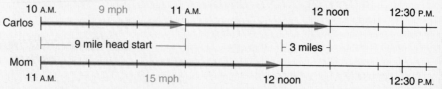

It will take another half hour for his mother to catch him at 12:30. You can decide if this was in time for lunch, since we don't know what time he usually eats lunch.

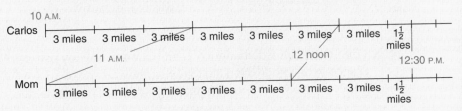

Problem 2
An Age Problem

When I was born, my father was eleven times as old as my sister, who had just turned three. How old was I when my father was

a Six times as old as my sister?

b Four times as old as my sister?

c Twice as old as my sister?

Solution

A spreadsheet provides a useful way of solving this problem. After the starting ages of 0, 3, and 33 are entered, each number in columns A, B, and C is one more than the preceding number. Each ratio in column D is found by dividing the number in column C by the number in column B.

a When my dad's age was six times my sister's, I was 3 years old.

b When my dad's age was four times my sister's, I was 7 years old.

c When my dad's age was twice my sister's, I was 27 years old.

	A	B	C	D
	Me	Sister	Dad	Dad/Sister
1				
2	0	3	33	11
3	1	4	34	8.5
4	2	5	35	7
5	3	6	36	6
6	4	7	37	5.28571429
7	5	8	38	4.75
8	6	9	39	4.33333333
9	7	10	40	4
10	8	11	41	3.72727273
11	9	12	42	3.5
12	10	13	43	3.30769231
13	11	14	44	3.14285714
14	12	15	45	3
15	13	16	46	2.875
16	14	17	47	2.76470588
17	15	18	48	2.66666667
18	16	19	49	2.57894737
19	17	20	50	2.5
20	18	21	51	2.42857143
21	19	22	52	2.36363636
22	20	23	53	2.30434783
23	21	24	54	2.25
24	22	25	55	2.2
25	23	26	56	2.15384615
26	24	27	57	2.11111111
27	25	28	58	2.07142857
28	26	29	59	2.03448276
29	27	30	60	2
30	28	31	61	1.96774194

Tom knows that Ben can whitewash a fence in six hours. Johney can do the job in eight hours. Tom talked them both into working together to whitewash the fence. How long will it take them?

Solution Ben can paint $\frac{1}{6}$ of the fence in an hour and Johney can paint $\frac{1}{8}$ of the fence in one hour. Working together, they can paint $\frac{1}{6} + \frac{1}{8} = \frac{4+3}{24} = \frac{7}{24}$ of the fence in an hour. Think of $\frac{7}{24}$ fence per hour as a rate.

$$(\text{Rate})(\text{time}) = \text{amount of work done}$$

$$\text{Time} = \frac{\text{amount of work done}}{\text{rate}}$$

$$= \frac{1 \text{ fence}}{\frac{7}{24} \frac{\text{fence}}{\text{hour}}}$$

$$= 1 \text{ fence} \cdot \frac{24}{7} \frac{\text{hour}}{\text{fence}}$$

$$= \frac{24}{7} \text{ hours}$$

Together they can paint the fence in a little less than $3\frac{1}{2}$ hours.

Problem 4
Probability

A 50-foot wire is strung between the tops of two 35-foot telephone poles. If the wire breaks at a random point between the poles, what is the probability that one end of the wire will hit the ground?

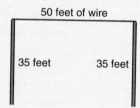

50 feet of wire

35 feet   35 feet

Solution Diagrams and number lines help model this problem.

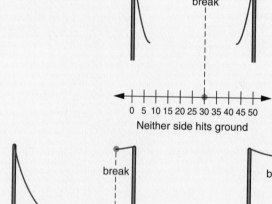

break

0 5 10 15 20 25 30 35 40 45 50

Neither side hits ground

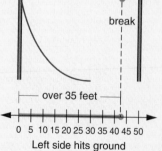

break

over 35 feet

0 5 10 15 20 25 30 35 40 45 50

Left side hits ground

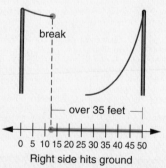

break

over 35 feet

0 5 10 15 20 25 30 35 40 45 50

Right side hits ground

If the wire breaks within 15 feet of either pole, then one end of the wire will hit the ground. The "winning" length is 15 + 15 = 30, out of the total of 50 feet.

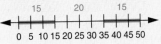

The probability that the wire will hit the ground is $\frac{30}{50}$, or $\frac{3}{5}$.

As you can see, there are different types of word problems and different ways to solve them. Were the methods you used different from the methods we showed? Try each of the sample problems again, using a method different from the one we used or the one you used before.

Think and Discuss

1 Ms. Word gave her class the following problem:

Moe can mow the lawn in 3 hours. Len can mow the lawn in 2 hours. How long will it take if they work together?

Adam said, "*Together* means add. So I added 2 and 3 and got 5 hours." Was Adam correct? Explain your answer.

2 The next day, Ms. Word gave her class another problem.

Mark walks five blocks north, turns left, and goes three blocks. How far has he walked?

Sal said, "Two blocks." Darren said, "That doesn't make any sense." Sal answered, "The problem uses the word *left*, so I subtracted." What is wrong with Sal's thinking?

3 A freight train, traveling 50 miles per hour, left Chicago at 9 A.M. and headed south. An express train, traveling 65 miles per hour, left Chicago at noon and headed south on the same track. At what time will the express train catch up to the freight train? Explain how to solve this problem in at least two different ways.

4 Jack went uphill at 6 miles per hour to meet Jill. After he reached the top of the hill, he fell downhill at 12 miles per hour. What was his average speed for the entire trip up and down?

5 Jack jogged up a hill at 10 miles per hour to meet Jill. How fast must Jack go downhill so that his average speed for the trip will be 20 miles per hour?

6 In the last part of 1992, Nancy is one-half of Sally's age. Copy and complete the chart to determine when this will happen again.

		1992	1993	1994	1995	1996
Jan. 1 – May 3	Sally	47				
	Nancy	23				
May 4 – June 29	Sally	48				
	Nancy	23				
June 30 – Dec. 31	Sally	48				
	Nancy	24				

Make a similiar chart and decide when you will be half of your mother's age. Will this occur more than once?

7 Athos said, "I have five racks of three-piece suits. How many suits do I have?" Porthos said, "Fifteen." Aramis said, "How did you get that?" Porthos replied, "*Of* means times, and five times three equals fifteen." Aramis objected, "That is nonsense." Why was Porthos wrong?

Problems and Applications

8 a What is the probability that a point chosen on the segment shown is within five units of 8?

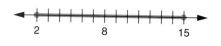

b What is the probability that the chosen point is within five units of one of the endpoints of the segment?

9 When I was two years old, my brother was double my age and my father was seven times my brother's age. How old was I when my father was three times my brother's age?

10 The area of the triangle is 45. Solve for x.

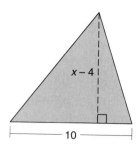

11 A quart of 4% butterfat milk is mixed with 3 quarts of 1% butterfat milk.
   a What fraction of a quart of the 4% milk is butterfat?
   b What fraction of a quart of the 1% milk is butterfat?
   c What fraction of the three quarts of 1% milk is butterfat?
   d What percent of the mixture is butterfat?

12 A point is chosen at random on the segment shown.

a What is the probability that the point chosen is more than four units from −3?

b What is the probability that the coordinate of the chosen point makes the inequality $2x - 5 \leq 1$ true?

13 Charlie's Chihuahua barks 42 times per minute. Lucia's Lhasa apso barks 28 times per minute. Silvie's springer spaniel barks 10 times per minute, and Lunyee's Labrador retriever barks 4 times per minute. If all the dogs start barking at the same time

a When will they all bark simultaneously?

b When will Lucia's and Lunyee's dogs bark at the same time?

14 Two numbers, x and y, are chosen at random. If $0 \leq x \leq 10$ and $0 \leq y \leq 7$, what is the probability that both numbers are at most 5?

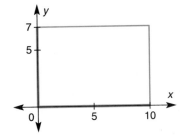

15 Michael can paint a wall in three hours. Angelo can paint the same wall in two hours. How long will it take if they work together?

16 The planets Tragedy, Comedy, and Variety orbit the star Serious. Every so often the planets line up on one side of Serious in a formation called a syzygy. Tragedy revolves around Serious once every 12 days, Comedy once every 18 days, and Variety once every 30 days. How many days is it from one Serious syzygy to the next?

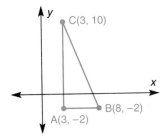

17 What is the probability that a number selected from the set {2, 3, 5, 7, 11, 13, 17, 19} is a prime number?

18 Find the area of the triangle.

19 How many integers are there between points A and B?

20 Evaluate each expression.

    a $\frac{-3}{5} + \frac{1}{2}$ **b** $3.6 - 9.4$ **c** $-0.25 + \frac{1}{3}$ **d** $\frac{-3}{2} + \frac{1}{4}$

21 Given the equation $3x + y = 10$,

    a Find all the pairs of whole numbers (x, y) that solve the equation.

    b Find all the pairs of natural numbers (x, y) that solve the equation.

22 **Spreadsheets**   Use a spreadsheet to find the value of x for which $5x - 40 = 3x - 15$.

23 Solve each equation for x.

    a $-6x = 30$ **b** $-30 = 6x$

24 **a** For what values of x and y is $xy = 0$?

    b Solve the equation $(2x + 18)(x - 12) = 0$ for x.

25 Suppose that $9x + 6 = 5x - 30$. Find the equation that results from performing each of the following operations.

    a Adding 30 to each side of the equation

    b Subtracting 6 from each side

    c Subtracting $5x$ from each side

    d Subtracting $9x$ from each side

26 Find all integer values of n for which $\frac{11}{2n + 3}$ is an integer.

27 Find the LCM of 6, 8, and 15.

28 Solve each equation for x.

    a $2(x + 17) = 24$ **b** $1571(x - 9.3) = 1571$

    c $2x + 4\frac{1}{2} = 1\frac{1}{4}$

29 Find the value(s) of n for which the five-digit number $52n36$ is divisible by 24.

30 Philip José, a farmer, has 430 feet of fencing. He wants to use it to fence in three sides of a rectangular field that borders a straight stretch of river.

    a What are the dimensions of the largest field that can be fenced?

    b What is its area?

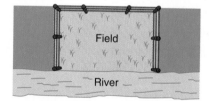

Investigation

Language   Look up the word *syzygy* and explain why it makes sense to use the word in problem 16. When would you be likely to read or hear about syzygy in the news?

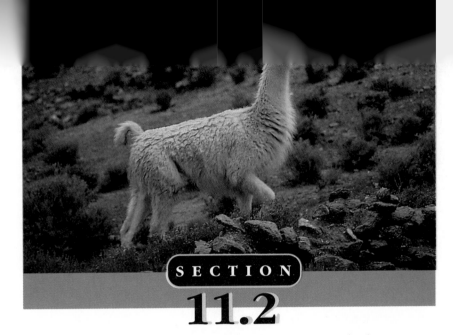

11.2

Equations with Variables on Both Sides

Example 1

Aacme Rent-an-Aardvark charges $30 plus $5 per hour to rent an aardvark. Lletme Rent-a-Llama charges $44 plus $3 per hour to rent a llama. Zzezze was planning a birthday party and found that it would cost the same amount to rent either animal for the time he needed them. For how long did Zzezze need an animal?

Solution

Let h represent the number of hours that Zzezze rents an animal. The rental charge from Aacme will be $30 + $5 \cdot h$. The rental charge from Lletme will be $44 + $3 \cdot h$. Since the total cost is the same, we set the two expressions equal to each other and solve the resulting equation, $30 + 5h = 44 + 3h$.

As we have done before when solving equations, we add the same quantity to both sides of the equation. In this case, we add $-3h$ to both sides.

Horizontal Method	Vertical Method
$30 + 5h = 44 + 3h$	$30 + 5h = 44 + 3h$
$30 + 5h - 3h = 44 + 3h - 3h$	$\underline{-3h \qquad -3h}$
$30 + 2h = 44 + 0$	$30 + 2h = 44 + 0$
$2h + 30 - 30 = 44 - 30$	$\underline{-30 \qquad -30}$
$2h = 14$	$2h = 14$
$h = 7$ hours	$h = 7$ hours

If Zzezze rented an aardvark or a llama for 7 hours, the rental would cost

$$30 + 5(7) = \$65 \qquad \text{or} \qquad 44 + 3(7) = \$65$$

The strategy we use for solving equations with variable terms on both sides of the equal sign is similar to strategies we have used earlier—add or subtract as necessary in order to have all variable terms on one side of the equation and all numerical terms on the other side of the equation.

Example 2

Solve the equation $2(19 - x) = 3 + 5x$.

Solution

$$2(19 - x) = 3 + 5x$$

Apply the distributive property $\quad 38 - 2x = 3 + 5x$

Now there are two methods we can use to solve the equation.

Method 1

$$38 - 2x = 3 + 5x$$

Add $2x$ to each side $\quad 38 - 2x + 2x = 3 + 5x + 2x$

$$38 = 3 + 7x$$

Subtract 3 from both sides $\quad 38 - 3 = 3 + 7x - 3$

$$35 = 7x$$

Divide both sides by 7 $\quad \dfrac{35}{7} = \dfrac{7x}{7}$

$$5 = x$$

Method 2

$$38 - 2x = 3 + 5x$$

Subtract $5x$ from both sides $\quad 38 - 2x - 5x = 3 + 5x - 5x$

$$38 - 7x = 3$$

Subtract 38 from both sides $\quad 38 - 7x - 38 = 3 - 38$

$$-7x = -35$$

Divide both sides by -7 $\quad \dfrac{-7x}{-7} = \dfrac{-35}{-7}$

$$x = 5$$

Either way, the solution is the same: $x = 5$. The variable can be eliminated from either side of the equation. Some students prefer to eliminate x terms from the right side so that the solution turns out in the form "$x =$." Others prefer to eliminate the negative terms. The choice is yours.

Sample Problems

Problem 1

Find the value of x if $\dfrac{x-6}{x} = \dfrac{2}{3}$.

Solution

The equation says that the ratio $\dfrac{x-6}{x}$ is equal to the ratio $\dfrac{2}{3}$. Thus, the equation is a proportion, and we can cross multiply.

$$\frac{x-6}{x} = \frac{2}{3}$$

$$3(x-6) = 2x$$

$$3x - 18 = 2x$$

$$\underline{+18 \qquad\qquad +18}$$

$$3x = 2x + 18$$

$$\underline{-2x \quad -2x}$$

$$x = 18$$

Check the solution: $\dfrac{18-6}{18} = \dfrac{12}{18} = \dfrac{2}{3}$.

Problem 2   The square and the rectangle shown have equal perimeters. Find the dimensions of both figures.

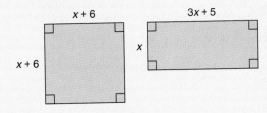

Solution   The perimeter of the square is

$$4(x+6)$$
$$= 4x + 24$$

The perimeter of the rectangle is

$$2x + 2(3x+5)$$
$$= 2x + 6x + 10$$
$$= 8x + 10$$

The two perimeters are equal, so we can write the equation $4x + 24 = 8x + 10$.

$$4x + 24 = 8x + 10$$

$$\underline{-4x \qquad\quad -4x}$$

$$24 = 4x + 10$$

$$\underline{-10 \qquad\quad -10}$$

$$14 = 4x$$

$$\frac{14}{4} = x$$

$$3\tfrac{1}{2} = x$$

The side of the square is

$$x + 6 = 3\tfrac{1}{2} + 6$$
$$= 9\tfrac{1}{2}$$

The length of the rectangle is

$$3x + 5 = 3\left(3\tfrac{1}{2}\right) + 5$$
$$= 10\tfrac{1}{2} + 5$$
$$= 15\tfrac{1}{2}$$

The rectangle is $3\tfrac{1}{2}$ by $15\tfrac{1}{2}$. Check to be sure that the perimeters are equal.

Think and Discuss

1 Solve $3(x + 2) = 12(x - 3)$ in two different ways.

2 Copy the following steps, filling in the missing coefficients and constants, to solve $28 + 4k = 7k - 14$ for k.

Step 1 $28 + 4k + \underline{\hphantom{xx}}k = 7k - 14 + \underline{\hphantom{xx}}k$
Step 2 $28 + \underline{\hphantom{xx}}k = -14$
Step 3 $28 + \underline{\hphantom{xx}}k - \underline{\hphantom{xx}} = -14 - \underline{\hphantom{xx}}$
Step 4 $\underline{\hphantom{xx}}k = \underline{\hphantom{xx}}$
Step 5 $k = \underline{\hphantom{xx}}$

3 Solve the equation $9x + 11 = 6x - 4$ in several ways.

4 Indicate whether the statement is *true* or *false*.
  a If $\frac{a}{b} = \frac{2}{3}$, then $a = 2$ and $b = 3$.   **b** If $\frac{a}{b} = \frac{2}{3}$, then $a = \frac{2}{3}b$.

Problems and Applications

5 Solve each equation for x.
  a $\dfrac{2x - 4}{4} = \dfrac{x - 2}{2}$ **b** $\dfrac{3}{x + 4} = \dfrac{2}{2x + 8}$

6 Solve each equation for x.
  a $\dfrac{x - 6}{2} = \dfrac{x}{3}$ **b** $\dfrac{2}{x - 6} = \dfrac{3}{x}$ **c** $\dfrac{x}{x - 6} = \dfrac{3}{2}$

7 If $2x + y = 8(x + y) + 13$ and $y = 5$, what is the value of x?

8 Copy the following steps, filling in the missing coefficients and constants, to solve $28 + 4k = 7k - 14$ for k.

Step 1 $28 + 4k + \underline{\hphantom{xx}}k = 7k - 14 + \underline{\hphantom{xx}}k$
Step 2 $\underline{\hphantom{xx}} = 3k - 14$
Step 3 $\underline{\hphantom{xx}} + \underline{\hphantom{xx}} = 3k - 14 + \underline{\hphantom{xx}}$
Step 4 $\underline{\hphantom{xx}} = 3k$
Step 5 $\underline{\hphantom{xx}} = k$

9 Solve the proportion $\frac{2x - 3}{x + 5} = \frac{3}{4}$ for x.

10 The perimeter of a square with a side $2x$ is equal to the perimeter of an equilateral triangle with a side length of $x + 10$. Solve for x.

11 The perimeter of the square equals the circumference of the circle. Find the diameter of the circle.

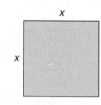
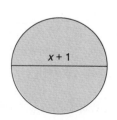

12 The circumference of circle A is three times the circumference of circle B. Find the radii of the circles.

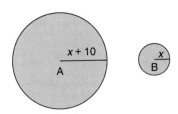

13 **Business** For routing roots from a sewer pipeline, Bob the plumber charges a $50 service fee per visit plus $75 per hour. Rob the router charges a $75 service fee plus $50 per hour for the same job. Is it cheaper to hire Rob? How long must a job take in order for it to be cheaper to hire Rob?

14 A stream is flowing at 4 miles per hour. A small motorboat can go $5y$ miles downstream in 3 hours. It takes 5.9 hours for the boat to return upstream to its starting place. How fast does the boat travel in still water?

15 $\triangle ABC$ is similar to $\triangle DEF$. Find the length of $\overline{AB}$.

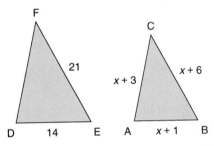

16 **Consumer Math** At Scratch and Dents Rent-a-Car, it costs $34.95 a day plus $0.23 per mile to rent a car. At Rent-a-Lemon, the charge is $25.00 a day plus $0.31 per mile. If you need to rent a car for three days, how many miles must you drive for a car from both agencies to cost the same amount?

17 The area of the triangle shown is $8x - 20$. Find the value of x.

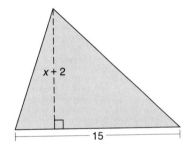

18 Candy Barr wanted to buy some big chocolate kisses that cost $0.50 each. She took them to the checkout counter and had just enough money for the kisses but forgot about the 8% tax. She put two kisses back and had just enough money. How many kisses did she buy?

19 **Business** Lo was hired as a salesperson. She was given her choice of two salary plans. She could earn either $300 per week plus 10% commission or $200 per week plus 20% commission. How much merchandise does Lo have to sell in order for the $200 plan to be in her best interest?

20 Solve each equation.
a $3x - 9 = 5x + 11$
b $-3x - 9 = 5x + 11$
c $-3x - 9 = 5x - 11$
d $-3x - 9 = -5x - 11$

21 Find the value of n if the three-digit number $nn2$ is 197 more than the three-digit number $2n5$.

22 **Business**   Willie was hired as a door-to-door salesperson. He had a choice of two salary plans. He could take a straight salary of \$375 per week or he could take a salary of \$200 per week plus 10% commission on his sales. How much merchandise would he have to sell in a week in order for the commission plan to be in his best interest?

23 Simplify each fraction. Then explain your results.

a $\dfrac{2+7}{3\cdot 3}$ **b** $\dfrac{8+5}{15-2}$ **c** $\dfrac{48}{50-2}$

◄ LOOKING BACK   **Spiral Learning**   LOOKING AHEAD ▶

24 Solve each equation and simplify each expression.
  a $3x-5=9x+4$ **b** $(3x-5)+(9x+4)$
  c $(3x-5)-(9x+4)$ **d** $3(x-5)=9(x+4)$
  e $3(x-5)=9x+4$ **f** $3(x-5)-9(x+4)$

25 Solve each equation.
  a $3(x-4)+2x=5x-12$ **b** $2(3x+1)=6x-4$

26 List the following values in order, from smallest to largest.

$$3.5\times 10^{-4},\ 3.5\times 10^{-3},\ -3.5\times 10^{-3},\ -3.5\times 10^{-4}$$

27 The area of the trapezoid is 80. Find the value of h.

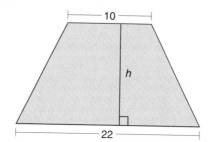

28 Solve each equation for x.
  a $x+\dfrac{2}{3}=\dfrac{4}{5}$ **b** $x+\dfrac{4}{5}=\dfrac{2}{3}$
  c $\dfrac{4}{5}x=\dfrac{2}{3}$ **d** $\dfrac{2}{3}x=\dfrac{4}{5}$

29 The smallest angle of a triangle measures 36 degrees. Find the average of the other two angles.

Investigation

Balance   Look up the meaning of *balance beam*, *balance scale*, and *fulcrum balance*. Explain the similarities and the differences. Also, explain how each device is used.

11.3
More Word Problems

Earlier in this chapter, we worked with several types of word problems. Now we will look at some additional types of word problems.

Example 1

Ye Olde Chocolate Shoppe makes chocolate bars that measure 5 centimeters by 12 centimeters by 0.5 centimeter. Wilbur Wanna, a chocolate maker, pours melted chocolate into molds at a rate of 10 milliliters per second. How long does it take Wilbur to fill 100 chocolate-bar molds?

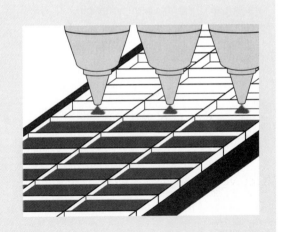

Solution

A milliliter is approximately equal to one cubic centimeter. The volume of each mold is 5(12)(0.5), or about 30 cubic centimeters, or 30 ml. Since Wilbur pours chocolate at a rate of 10 ml per second, it takes him 3 seconds to fill each mold. Wilbur fills 100 molds in 300 seconds, or 5 minutes.

Example 2

Minny Olta bought a camera. Mr. Cannon, the salesperson, agreed to sell her the camera for $50, including the 6% sales tax. He had trouble figuring out what amount to enter into the computerized cash register so that it would add the tax to the price of the camera and produce a total of exactly $50. What should the price of the camera have been before tax?

Solution

The total cost, C, of the camera should equal the selling price, P, plus 6% of P in sales tax.

$$C = P + (0.06)P$$
$$50 = P(1 + 0.06)$$
$$50 = 1.06P$$
$$\frac{50}{1.06} = \frac{1.06P}{1.06}$$

Priced to the nearest cent

$$47.17 \approx P$$

Check the solution

$$\text{Tax} = 0.06(47.17)$$
$$\approx 2.83$$

Total cost

$$\$47.17 + \$2.83 = \$50.00$$

Example 3

The areas of the two rectangles are equal. Find the perimeter of each rectangle.

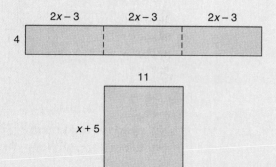

Solution

The area of the top rectangle is $3[4(2x - 3)]$.
The area of the bottom rectangle is $11(x + 5)$.

The areas are equal

$$3[4(2x - 3)] = 11(x + 5)$$
$$12(2x - 3) = 11(x + 5)$$
$$24x - 36 = 11x + 55$$
$$\underline{-11x \qquad -11x}$$
$$13x - 36 = 55$$
$$\underline{+ 36 \quad + 36}$$
$$13x = 91$$
$$\frac{13x}{13} = \frac{91}{13}$$
$$x = 7$$

The perimeters of the rectangles are

$$P_{top} = 2[4 + 3(2x - 3)]$$
$$= 2[4 + 3(2 \cdot 7 - 3)]$$
$$= 2[4 + 3(11)]$$
$$= 2(37)$$
$$= 74$$

$$P_{bottom} = 2[11 + (x + 5)]$$
$$= 2[11 + 7 + 5]$$
$$= 2(23)$$
$$= 46$$

Sample Problem

Problem   Scrooge wants to use $2500 for two investments. One of the investments earns 4% interest per year. The other investment earns 9% interest per year. Scrooge decides to put half his money in each account. How much interest does he earn after one year? How much money does he have after 3 years, with interest compounded annually?

Solution   A spreadsheet is helpful. If we don't have a spreadsheet, we can use a calculator and organize the results in a table similar to a spreadsheet's.

	A	B	C	D	E	F
		Investment at 4%		Investment at 9%		TOTAL
1	Time	Interest	Total $	Interest	Total $	ACCUMULATED
2	0 yr	0.00	1250.00	0.00	1250.00	2500.00
3	1 yr	50.00	1300.00	112.50	1362.50	2662.50
4	2 yr	52.00	1352.00	122.63	1485.13	2837.13
5	3 yr	54.08	1406.08	133.66	1618.79	3024.87

After one year, Scrooge has earned interest of $162.50. After 3 years, he has $3024.87.

Think and Discuss

1 Is it possible for 15% of a number to be greater than the number itself?

2 When a store discounts an item, does it matter whether the discount is computed before the tax is added or after the tax is added? Explain your answer.

3 What restrictions must be placed on x so that the dimensions of the rectangle will make sense?

$2x - 30$

$x + 5$

Problems and Applications

4 A one-cubic-foot container will hold approximately 7.5 gallons of water. How much water will a 16-inch-by-12-inch-by-8-inch aquarium hold?

5 **Business** At Buster Block's Video, Le, the owner, wants to charge $3.25 for video rental. If the price must include an 8% tax, what is the pre-tax price for each rental? (Round your answer to the nearest cent.)

6 The edge of a cube is 4 inches. Kuba contracts to make 1000 such cubes out of plastic. If each cube weighs 0.5 ounce per cubic inch, how many pounds of plastic must Kuba buy to fill the order?

7 If the sides of a square are doubled in length, the perimeter increases by 40 centimeters.
a How long are the sides of the original square?
b What is the perimeter of the original square?

8 The shaded area is what percent of the total area of the rectangle?

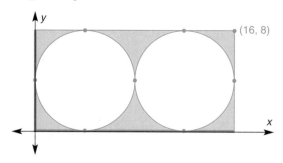

9 A machine produces 400 CD's per hour. A second machine produces 520 CD's per hour. On a given day, the first machine was started at 8 A.M. and the second machine was started at 11 A.M. Both machines were shut down at the same time, and they produced the same number of CD's.
a How long did each machine run?
b What was the total number of CD's produced?

10 A circular disc with a diameter of 6 is tossed onto a flat surface so that at least part of the disc is inside the circle. What is the probability that the disc lies entirely inside the circle?

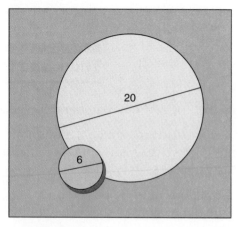

11 A pile contains 900 coins. Each day Penny Nichols takes 25% of the coins from the pile. Approximately how many coins remain in the pile after 10 days?

12 Business The manufacturer of Kukka Koola, a soft drink, decides to change from 12-ounce cans to $11\frac{1}{2}$-ounce cans. By what percent will the manufacturer's income increase for every 120 ounces of beverage sold?

13 Harold walked around a circle. Then he walked 5 feet farther from the center of the circle and walked around another circle. All together, he walked 2000 feet. What is the radius of the inner circle?

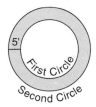

14 Finance Ole and Lars, twins from Minnesota, each inherited $10,000 from their great-uncle Calvin. Lars invested part of his money at 3% interest and part at 8%. Ole divided his money the same way Lars did, but invested one part at 4% and the other part at 6%. They ended the year with the same amount of interest. How did they divide their money?

15 Ace Plumbing charges $50 for a house call and $15 per hour for repairs. Deuce Plumbing charges $30 per visit and $17.50 per hour. Trey needed a plumber. Amazingly, both Ace and Deuce would have charged the same amount for the number of hours required to fix the problem. How many hours did it take to fix Trey's plumbing?

16 The perimeter of the triangle is twice the perimeter of the square. Find the value of x.

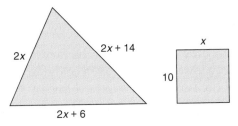

17 Business Mavis sells real estate. She recently sold a house for $225,000. That is 15% more than the house was worth last year. How much was the house worth last year?

18 At the Tex-Mex horseshoe-throwing contest, the winner is determined by the sum of the lengths of three tosses. A bonus of 10 feet is given for each ounce over 16 ounces that a horseshoe weighs. Red throws a $2\frac{1}{2}$-pound horseshoe and Slats throws a 20-ounce horseshoe. Both tied for first place. What is the difference, in feet, in the sum of their tosses?

19 Triangle ABC is similar to triangle DEF. Find the length of segment EF.

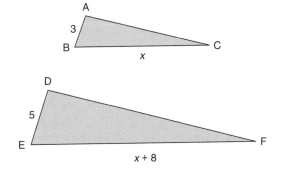

20 Find the value of W for which $5W = W + 40$.

21 The area of the triangle is $28x$. What is the height of the triangle?

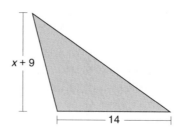

22 Solve each equation.
   a $3x - 15 = 23 + 7x$ **b** $16 - 4y = 4y - 8$
   c $\frac{3}{4}a + 6 = \frac{1}{4}a - 2$ **d** $6k + 8 = 8(k + 10)$

23 Write a function for the area A of a trapezoid with bases b_1 and b_2 and height h.

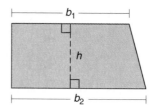

24 **Consumer Math** A dress originally priced at \$67.95 is marked down three successive times. The first markdown is 15%, the second is 8%, and the third is 15%. What is the final cost of the dress?

25 The area of the front of the box in the drawing is twice the area of the bottom of the box. What is the volume of the box?

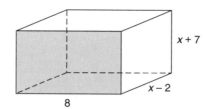

26 Sue gets paid \$7.50 an hour. One week she notices that she worked the same number of hours as her age. If this had happened four years ago, in order to make the same amount of money, she would have had to earn \$8.25 per hour. How old is Sue?

─────────────────────────────

◄ LOOKING BACK **Spiral Learning** LOOKING AHEAD ►

─────────────────────────────

27 **Science** A ball is dropped from 6 feet above the ground. It is allowed to bounce continuously. On each bounce, the ball rebounds to a height 85% as high as the previous bounce.
   a What is the maximum height of the ball after the fifth bounce?
   b What is the maximum height of the ball after the ninth bounce?
   c What is the total distance that the ball has traveled by the end of the ninth bounce? (Hint: Use a spreadsheet.)

28 Consumer Math Billi paid $15 down on a CD player and then paid $12 a month until she had paid a total of $231 for the player. How many monthly payments did she make?

29 Business Kirk started a business with a total investment of $6000. Then, friend Spock bought a 25% share in Kirk's business enterprise. How much did Spock invest?

30 The ratio of AB to AC is 3:5. What is the length of the diameter of the circle?

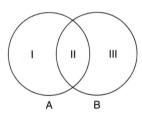

31 Find x so that the area of triangle ABC is 72.

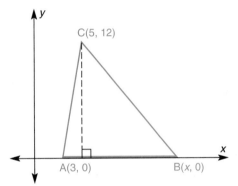

32 Region I contains 20 elements.
Region II contains x elements.
Region III contains $2x$ elements.
How many elements are in Region III if $A \cup B$ contains 74 elements?

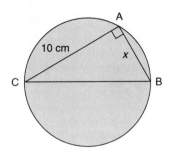

33 If $f(x) = 3x + 8$ and $g(x) = x^2 - 4$, what is
  a $f(2)$?   **b** $g(-2)$?
  c $f(3)$?   **d** $g(3)$?

Investigation

The Teeter-totter Principle Weights A and B are put on the ends of the scale to make it balance. What can you determine about the relationship between A and B?

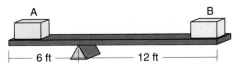

11.4

Equations with Several Variables

We have worked with formulas and functions that involve several inputs. For example, the area, A, of a triangle with base b and height h is found with the function

$$A(b, h) = \frac{1}{2}bh$$

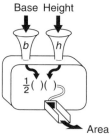

Base Height

Area

The perimeter of a rectangle is determined by its length, ℓ, and its width, w. The function that gives the perimeter of a rectangle is

$$P(\ell, w) = 2\ell + 2w$$

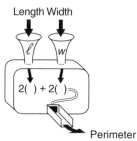

Length Width

Perimeter

Example 1

The perimeter of a rectangle is 58 centimeters. The length of the rectangle is twice its width. Find the dimensions of the rectangle.

Solution

Formula for perimeter	$P = 2\ell + 2w$
Substitute 58 for P	$58 = 2\ell + 2w$
Since $\ell = 2w$, we can substitute $2w$ for ℓ	$58 = 2(2w) + 2w$
	$58 = 4w + 2w$
	$58 = 6w$
	$\dfrac{58}{6} = \dfrac{6w}{6}$
	$\dfrac{29}{3} = w$

Since $w = 9\frac{2}{3}$ and $\ell = 2w$, $\ell = 2\left(\frac{29}{3}\right) = \frac{58}{3}$, or $19\frac{1}{3}$. The length of the rectangle is $19\frac{1}{3}$ centimeters, and the width is $9\frac{2}{3}$ centimeters.

Example 2

A stamp collector collects $2 stamps and $3 stamps. He has 12 more $2 stamps than $3 stamps. The total value of the stamps is $944. How many $3 stamps does the collector have?

Solution

Let a represent the number of $2 stamps and b represent the number of $3 stamps. The value of a $2 stamps is $2a$. The value of b $3 stamps is $3b$.
The total value of the stamps is $2a + 3b = 944$.
Since he has 12 more $2 stamps than $3 stamps, $a = b + 12$.

We can substitute $(b + 12)$ for a

$$2(b + 12) + 3b = 944$$
$$2b + 24 + 3b = 944$$
$$5b + 24 = 944$$
$$\underline{-24 \qquad -24}$$
$$5b \qquad = 920$$
$$b = 184$$

The collector has 184 three-dollar stamps (and 196 two-dollar stamps). Can you think of a way to do this problem without using algebraic equations?

Example 3

In a balance problem, the product of the mass on one end of the beam and its distance from the balance point (fulcrum) must equal the product of the mass at the other end of the beam and its distance from the fulcrum.

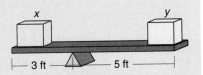

Mass x is 10 kilograms heavier than mass y. Mass x is 3 feet from the fulcrum, and mass y is 5 feet from the fulcrum. Find the mass of the heavier object.

Solution

The balance equation is $3x = 5y$.
Since mass x is 10 more than y, $x = y + 10$.

We can substitute $(y + 10)$ for x

$$3(y + 10) = 5y$$
$$3y + 30 = 5y$$
$$\underline{-3y \qquad \quad -3y}$$
$$30 = 2y$$
$$15 = y$$

The other object, x, has mass

$$y + 10 = (15) + 10$$
$$= 25$$

The heavier object has a mass of 25 kilograms.

Sample Problems

Problem 1 The area of the rectangle is numerically equal to its perimeter.

a Write an equation to describe this situation.

b Find the length of the rectangle if the width is 12 inches.

c Solve the equation you wrote in part **a** for ℓ in terms of w.

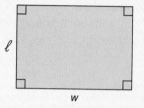

Solution The formula for the area of a rectangle is $A = \ell w$.
The formula for the perimeter of a rectangle is $P = 2\ell + 2w$.

a Since it is given that the area is numerically equal to the perimeter,
$2\ell + 2w = \ell w$.

b If the width is 12 inches,

$$2\ell + 2(12) = \ell(12)$$
$$2\ell + 24 = 12\ell$$
$$\underline{-2\ell \qquad\qquad -2\ell}$$
$$24 = 10\ell$$
$$2.4 = \ell$$

c To solve for ℓ in terms of w, we must have all of the ℓ terms on the same side of the equation.

$$2\ell + 2w = \ell w$$
$$2\ell - 2\ell + 2w = \ell w - 2\ell$$

Distributive property $\qquad\qquad\qquad\qquad 2w = \ell(w - 2)$

Divide both sides by
$(w - 2)$ to isolate the ℓ $\qquad\qquad\qquad\qquad \dfrac{2w}{w - 2} = \ell$

The variable ℓ is now expressed in terms of w.

Problem 2 Find all pairs of natural numbers (x, y) for which $\dfrac{14}{x + 2y}$ is a natural number.

Solution In order for the fraction to be a natural number, $x + 2y$ must be a factor of 14. It must be either 1, 2, 7, or 14. We organize our trials:

$x + 2y = 1$ No pairs of natural numbers work.

$x + 2y = 2$ If $y = 1$, then $x = 0$. No pairs of natural numbers work.

$x + 2y = 7$ (1, 3), (3, 2), and (5, 1) each work.

$x + 2y = 14$ (2, 6), (4, 5), (6, 4), (8, 3), (10, 2), (12, 1)

There are nine different pairs of natural numbers that satisfy the condition.

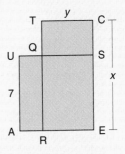

Problem 3 Each side of square SUAE is 7. Find the restrictions on the values of *x* and *y* for which rectangle RECT exists and for which Q is on $\overline{US}$ and T is outside of the square.

Solution In order for the rectangle to exist as shown, both *x* and *y* must be positive and *y* must be smaller than 7 and *x* must be larger than 7. In summary, *x* > 7 and 0 < *y* < 7.

Think and Discuss

1 A rectangle has length 12 and width 8. Which of the following is a correct method of computing the perimeter of the rectangle? Explain your choice(s).
a 12 + 8 + 12 + 8 = 40
b 24 + 16 = 40
c 2(20) = 40
d (12 − 8) · 10 = 40

2 The perimeter of a rectangle is 20 millimeters. If the length of the rectangle is increased by 2 millimeters and the width is decreased by 2 millimeters, the perimeter of the rectangle is still 20 millimeters. Find the length and width of the rectangle.

3 **a** If $Q(x, y) = 3x + 5y$, what is $Q(4, 3)$?
b If $Q(x, y) = 3x + 5y$, what is $Q(3, 4)$?
c Could $Q(a, b)$ ever be equal to $Q(b, a)$?

4 For what values of *x* will $\frac{43}{x + 9}$ be an integer?

5 If $G(x, y) = 3x + 4y$ and $x = y + 5$, find $G(x, y)$ for
a $y = 3$ **b** $y = 0$ **c** $x = 2$ **d** $y = 2x$

6 For what pairs of natural numbers is $\frac{24}{3x + 3y}$ a natural number? What do you notice about your answer?

Problems and Applications

7 For what natural-number values of *n* is $\frac{n + 7}{n}$ a natural number?

8 If $f(x, y) = x + 2y$, what is
a $f(3, 5)$?   **b** $f(5, 3)$?
c $f(a, b)$?   **d** $f(b, a)$?

9 The perimeter of the rectangle is 80 centimeters.
  a Find $x + y$.
  b Graph the lattice points (x, y) in Quadrant I. (A *lattice point* is a point whose coordinates are both integers.)

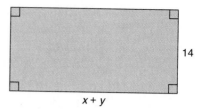

14

$x + y$

10 Find all ordered pairs of natural numbers (x, y) for which $\frac{21}{x + 2y}$ is a natural number.

11 **Science** One of the boxes weighs 15 kilograms more than the other.
  a Which box is heavier, A or B?
  b What must be the weight of each box so that the scale balances?

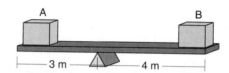

A   B

3 m   4 m

12 Mr. Coyne has some dimes and quarters. He has twice as many dimes as quarters. The total value of his coins is $8.10. How many dimes does he have?

13 The length of a rectangle is three times its width. The perimeter of the rectangle is 348. Find its length.

14 Sarah Alice has 14 identical diamond rings to display in the window of Diamonds Are Us. The window display has 12 sections. Sarah wants to place at least one ring in each section. In how many different ways can Sarah display the 14 rings?

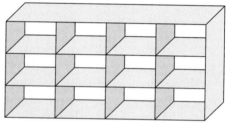

15 If $\frac{18}{x + 2y}$ is a natural number, and x and y are natural numbers, explain why $x + 2y$ must be equal to either 3, 6, 9, or 18.

16 At the Children's Little Theatre, admission is $8 for adults and $5 for children. Adrian spent $47 on tickets. How many tickets of each type did she buy?

17 The perimeter of an isosceles triangle is 48 inches. The length of the base of the triangle is 4 inches greater than the length of either leg. What is the length of the base of the triangle?

18 Pip buys 24 cans of soda at 25¢ each and 5 liters of soda at 75¢ each. How much did Pip pay for the soda?

19 Suppose the perimeter of the rectangle and the perimeter of the triangle are equal.
  a Write an equation in terms of x to represent this situation.
  b Solve the equation for x.
  c Find the length of the rectangle.
  d Find the length of each side of the triangle.

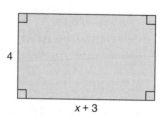

4

$x + 3$

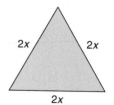

$2x$ $2x$

$2x$

20 **Sports** A National Football League kicker scores three points for each field goal made and one point for each extra point made.
  a Write a function for the number of points, P, a kicker gets for f field goals and e extra points.
  b During the 1990 season, Nick Lowery made 34 field goals and 37 extra points. How many points did he score?
  c During the 1990 season, Pete Stoyanovich scored 100 points, of which 37 were extra points. How many field goals did he kick?

21 **Sports** Jump Shot, a basketball player, can make either two-point baskets or three-point baskets. In his last game, he scored 20 points with no free throws. How many two- and three-point baskets could Jump Shot have made?

22 A six-pack of cans of Sparkly soda costs $3.75. An eight-bottle carton of Sparkly soda costs $4.25. Juanita bought some six-packs and some cartons of the soda. All together, she had a combination of 48 cans and bottles at a cost of $27.75. How many six-packs of cans and how many eight-bottle cartons did she buy?

23 The length of segment RE is 2 and the length of segment TR is 3. Find the restrictions on the radius r of circle C so that the area of the shaded region is at least one third the area of rectangle RECT.

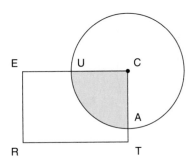

◀ LOOKING BACK **Spiral Learning** LOOKING AHEAD ▶

24 Find the least common multiple and the greatest common factor of 18 and 24.

25 Suppose that $f(x) = 3x + 2$. Peter let $x = 2$ and determined $f(2)$. He took his answer and put it back into the function. He repeated the process several times, using each output as the next input.
  a Find the first ten outputs of the function if $x = 2$ is the initial input.
  b Find the first ten outputs of the function if $x = 1$ is the initial input.

26 **Consumer Math** Connie bought identical ice-cream cones for herself, Van, and Illa. The total bill came to $4.41, including 5% sales tax. How much was each ice-cream cone?

27 Mike can mow the lawn in two hours and Sherry can mow the lawn in three hours. How long will it take to mow the lawn if they work together?

28 Draw the image resulting from
  a A 90° clockwise rotation about (0, 0)
  b A 90° clockwise rotation about (1, 2)

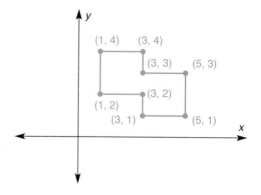

29 Solve each equation and simplify each expression.
  a $-\frac{2}{3}x + 4x^2 - 6x^2 + \frac{1}{4}x$ 　　　　**b** $\frac{3}{5}x + \frac{4}{9} = -\frac{1}{3}$
  c $9\left(\frac{1}{3}x - \frac{1}{6}\right) = 4\left(\frac{1}{2}x + \frac{1}{4}\right)$ 　　**d** $-9\left(\frac{1}{3}x - \frac{1}{6}\right) - 4\left(\frac{1}{2}x - \frac{1}{4}\right)$

30 **a** Write a function for the volume, V, of the box in terms of ℓ, w, and h.
  b Write a function for the surface area of the box.

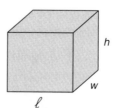

31 Suppose the figure is cut out and folded to make a box.
  a Find the area of the box.
  b Find the volume of the box.

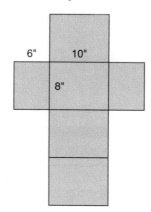

32 Multiply $-5\begin{bmatrix} -4 & 9 & -8 \\ 0 & 7 & -3 \end{bmatrix}$.

33 At Parker High School, the students raise money for the production of the school play by selling cookies. If the students receive 15% of total sales, how much money will they raise by selling $34,500 worth of cookies?

Investigation

Chemistry A very well known equation in chemistry is $PV = nRT$. Find out what the variables P, V, n, R, and T represent.

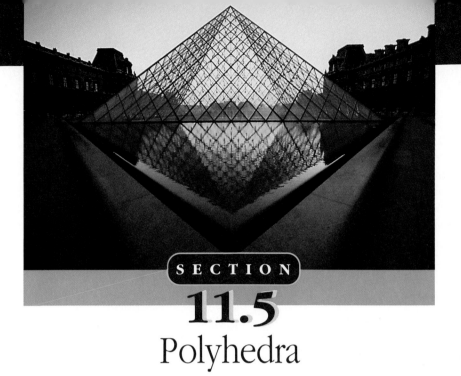

SECTION
11.5
Polyhedra

PRISMS

In this section we will study **polyhedra**—solids with flat faces. The word *polyhedra* means "many faces." The singular form of the word is *polyhedron*.

A rectangular box is a polyhedron. It has 6 **faces**, 12 **edges**, and 8 **vertices**. Each face is a polygon. Each edge is formed by the intersection of two faces. Each vertex is the point of intersection of several edges. We can compute the volume of a rectangular box by using the formula

Volume = (length)(width)(height)

Edges

Faces

Vertices

The rectangular box is an example of a type of polyhedron called a **prism**—a figure with two congruent parallel polygonal bases. Any cross section of a prism cut parallel to the bases is also congruent to the bases. Bases do not need to be on the "bottom" and "top" of a prism.

Bases are shaded green.

The formula for the volume of any prism is

$$\text{Volume}_{\text{prism}} = (\text{area of base})(\text{height})$$

The total surface area of a prism can be found by adding together the areas of the faces.

The faces of the prism that are not bases are called **lateral faces.** Often we need to know the surface area of the "sides" of a prism. The **lateral area** of a prism is the sum of the areas of the lateral faces—the surface area minus the area of the bases.

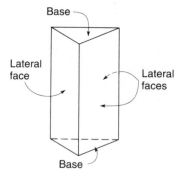

Base

Lateral face

Lateral faces

Base

Example 1
a Find the volume of the triangular prism.
b Find the total surface area of the triangular prism.

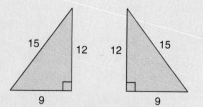

12 in.

9 in.

20 in.

Solution
a The base of this triangular prism is a right triangle that has an area of $\frac{1}{2}(9)(12) = 54$ square inches. Since we know the area of the base, we can find the volume by using the formula

$$\begin{aligned}
\text{Volume} &= (\text{area of base})(\text{height}) \\
&= (54)(20) \\
&= 1080
\end{aligned}$$

The volume of the triangular prism is 1080 cubic inches.

b The total surface area is equal to the sum of the areas of the two bases and the lateral area.

$$\begin{aligned}
\text{Area of bases} &= \tfrac{1}{2}(12)(9) + \tfrac{1}{2}(12)(9) \\
&= 54 + 54 \\
&= 108
\end{aligned}$$

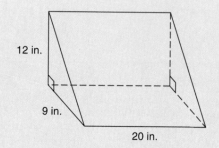

15   12   12   15

9   9

The area of the two bases of the triangular prism is 108 square inches.

The lateral area is equal to the sum of the areas of the three rectangular faces of the prism.

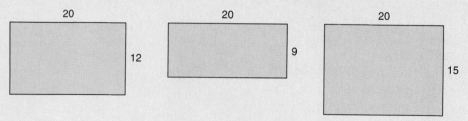

20

12

20

9

20

15

$$\text{Lateral area} = (9)(20) + (12)(20) + (15)(20)$$
$$= 180 + 240 + 300$$
$$= 720$$

The lateral area of the triangular prism is 720 square inches.

The total surface area of the triangular prism is the sum of the areas of the two bases and the lateral area.

$$\text{Total surface area} = 720 + 108$$
$$= 828$$

The total surface area of the triangular prism is 828 square inches.

PYRAMIDS

A **pyramid** is a polyhedron with several lateral faces, but only one base. The square-based pyramid shown has 4 lateral faces, 8 edges, and 5 vertices. The height of the pyramid is measured perpendicular to the base. A **slant height** is the height of one of the lateral faces.

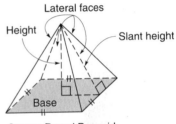

Square-Based Pyramid

The surface area of a pyramid is the sum of the areas of the lateral faces and the area of the base.

Clearly, the volume of a pyramid is less than the volume of a prism with the same base and height. In fact, the volume of a pyramid is one third the volume of a prism with the same base and height.

$$\text{Volume}_{\text{pyramid}} = \tfrac{1}{3}(\text{area of base})(\text{height})$$

Example 2

A solid stone pyramid is 4 feet tall and has a square base with a 6-foot side. What is the weight of the pyramid if the stone weighs 300 pounds per cubic foot?

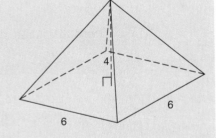

Solution

We will use the formula for the volume of a pyramid.

$$V = \tfrac{1}{3}(\text{area of base})(\text{height})$$
$$= \tfrac{1}{3}(6^2)(4)$$
$$= 48$$

The volume of the pyramid is 48 cubic feet. Since the weight of the material is 300 lb/ft^3 the weight of the solid pyramid is 48 ft$^3 \cdot \left(\dfrac{300 \text{ lb}}{1 \text{ ft}^3}\right)$, or 14,400 pounds.

Problem 1 The pentagonal base of the pyramid has an area of 12 square millimeters, and the pyramid has a height of 8 millimeters. Find its volume.

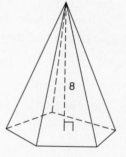

Solution The formula for the volume of a pyramid is

$$\text{Volume} = \frac{1}{3}(\text{area of base})(\text{height})$$

$$= \frac{1}{3}(12)(8)$$

$$= 32$$

The volume of the prism is 32 cubic millimeters.

Problem 2 A tower is built with a rectangular base. Find the volume of the tower.

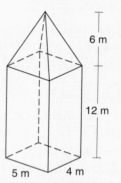

The easiest way to solve this problem is to "divide and conquer." First find the volume of the rectangular prism. Then find the volume of the pyramid. Finally, add the two volumes.

$$\text{Volume}_{\text{prism}} = (4)(5)(12)$$

$$= 240$$

The volume of the prism is 240 cubic meters.

$$\text{Volume}_{\text{pyramid}} = \frac{1}{3}(20)(6)$$

$$= 40$$

The volume of the pyramid is 40 cubic meters.

$$\text{Total volume} = 240 + 40$$

$$= 280$$

The total volume of the tower is 280 cubic meters.

Think and Discuss

1 Is a rectangular box a prism?

2 In part **b** of Example 1 on page 574, what does the number 15 represent in the calculation of the lateral area of the triangular prism?

3 What do the dashed lines in the figure represent?

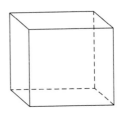

4 Explain why the figures in column I are prisms and why the figures in column II are not prisms.

Column I   Column II

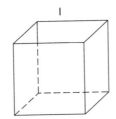
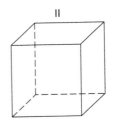

5 Explain the difference between the height of a pyramid and the slant height of a pyramid.

6 How would you calculate the surface area of a pyramid?

7 Explain the difference between figure I and figure II.

Problems and Applications

8 Find the volume of each figure.

a

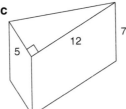

b

c

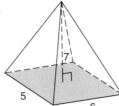

d

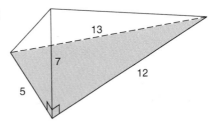

9 For the triangular prism, find the
  a Area of one base
  b Area of each lateral face
  c Lateral area
  d Total surface area
  e Volume

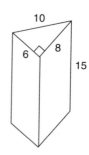

10 Find the lengths of edges $\overline{BC}$ and $\overline{DF}$.

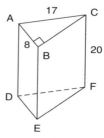

11 **Communicating** What does the diagram appear to represent?

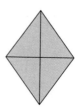

12 A rectangular prism has edges $(x - 8)$, x, and $(x + 2)$.
  a Write a formula for the volume of the prism in terms of x.
  b What is the volume of the prism for $x = 10$? $x = 8$? $x = 5$?

13 In the square-based pyramid, each edge of the base is 16, the height is 15, and the slant height is 17.
  a Find the area of the base.
  b Find the lateral area.
  c Find the total surface area.
  d Find the volume.

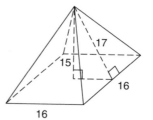

14 Bill knows the maximum number of marbles that can fit inside a pint jar. How would he determine the maximum number of marbles that can fit inside a gallon jar?

15 Which of the square-based pyramids shown has the greatest volume? The least volume?

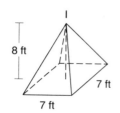
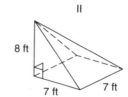
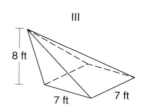

16 The Great Pyramid of Cheops measured 775.75 feet on each side of its square base, and it had a height of 481.4 feet.
   a Find the volume of the pyramid.
   b Tutt wants to build a model of the pyramid. He wants the model to have a height of 4 feet. How long should he make each edge of the base?

17 Find the volume of each triangular prism.

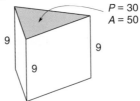

a 6
   12
   10

b 9   9   9 $P = 30$ $A = 50$

18 Science Which weighs more, a cubic foot of ice or a cubic foot of water? Explain your answer.

19 Find the volume and the surface area of the box. Explain why the volume and the surface area are not really equal.

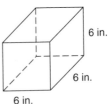

6 in.
6 in.
6 in.

20 Find the volume of the solid.

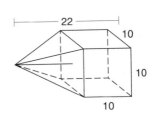

22
10
10
10

21 Science A hexagonal fish tank is filled with water. How much does the water weigh?

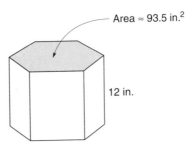

Area ≈ 93.5 in.²

12 in.

22 How many paths are there from A to B? The arrows indicate one-way paths.

a A

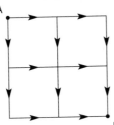

B

b

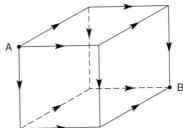

A   B

23 Two polyhedral dice are shaped like an octahedron and a dodecahedron. The faces of each die are numbered with consecutive natural numbers, starting with 1. If the two dice are tossed, what is the probability that the sum of the two top faces is

a 2?   b 7?   c 18?

Octahedron

Faces numbered
1–8

Dodecahedron

Faces numbered
1–12

◄ LOOKING BACK **Spiral Learning** LOOKING AHEAD ▶

---

24 In parts **a–d**, evaluate $f(x) = 3x - 1$ for each input.

a $f(4)$ b $f(-2)$ c $f\left(\frac{1}{3}\right)$ d $f\left(\frac{1}{2}\right)$

e Explain why $\frac{1}{2}$ could be called a "fixed point" of function f.

25 At Abie's CD's, you can choose 5 songs from a list of 20 songs, and the store will make you a custom-made CD. How many different custom-made CD's can be made?

26 Solve each equation for x.

a $\frac{x-4}{7} = \frac{x}{5}$ b $\frac{4}{x} = \frac{x}{9}$

27 Find all ordered pairs of natural numbers (x, y) for which the expression $\frac{18}{x + 5y}$ is a natural number.

28 Science   Find the value of y so that the scale balances.

40 kg   30 kg

9 ft   y ft

Investigation

Polyhedra   Make a table like the one shown, listing the number of faces (F), edges (E), and vertices (V) for a number of polyhedra, including the three pictured.

	F	E	V
Cube	6	12	8
Octahedron			
"House"			
.			
.			
.			

Examine your results and find a relationship between F, E, and V.

Solids with Circular Cross Sections

CYLINDERS

A **cylinder** is a geometric figure with two parallel congruent circular bases. You can think of a cylinder as being a prism with circular bases.

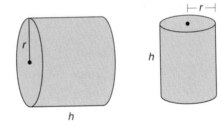

The formula for the volume of a cylinder is the same as the formula for the volume of a prism.

Volume = (area of base)(height)

Since the base of a cylinder is a circle, we can use the formula for the area of a circle to find the area of the base of a cylinder. Therefore, we can rewrite the formula for the volume of a cylinder as

$$\text{Volume}_{\text{cylinder}} = \pi r^2 h$$

The total surface area of a cylinder is found by adding the areas of the circular bases of the cylinder and the lateral area of the cylinder. If we think of a cylinder as a can, the lateral area is the area of the label.

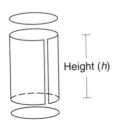

Height (*h*)

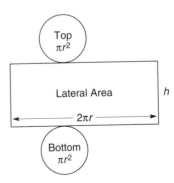

Top
πr^2

Lateral Area   *h*

2*πr*

Bottom
πr^2

When we lay the label flat, we see that it is a rectangle with a length equal to the circumference of the can and a width equal to the height of the can.

$$\text{Lateral area}_{\text{cylinder}} = (\text{circumference})(\text{height})$$
$$= 2\pi rh$$

$$\text{Total surface area}_{\text{cylinder}} = \text{lateral area} + \text{area}_{\text{base 1}} + \text{area}_{\text{base 2}}$$
$$= 2\pi rh + 2(\pi r^2)$$

Example 1

The height of a can is 6.4 inches, and the length of a diameter is 4.8 inches.

a How much liquid will this can hold?

b Find the area of the label of the can.

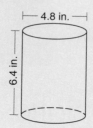

Solution

a First we will find the volume of the can. Since the radius of a circle is half the diameter, the radius of the base is 2.4 inches.

$$\text{Volume}_{\text{cylinder}} = \pi r^2 h$$
$$= \pi(2.4^2)(6.4)$$
$$\approx 116$$

The volume of the can is about 116 in.^{3}. Since a gallon is about 231 in.^{3}, this can holds about half a gallon.

b The label covers the lateral area of the can.

$$\text{Lateral area}_{\text{cylinder}} = 2\pi rh$$
$$= 2\pi(2.4)(6.4)$$
$$\approx 96.5$$

The lateral area of the can is about 96.5 in.^{2}.

CONES

Just as a cylinder is like a prism with circular bases, a **cone** is a pyramid with a circular base. The formula for the volume of a cone is like the formula for the volume of a pyramid. However, the area of the base of a cone is the area of a circle.

$$\text{Volume}_{\text{cone}} = \tfrac{1}{3}(\text{area of base})(\text{height})$$
$$= \tfrac{1}{3}\pi r^2 h$$

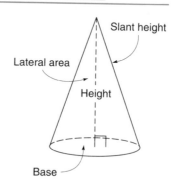

To find the surface area of a cone, we first need to determine the lateral area of the cone.

$$\text{Lateral area}_{\text{cone}} = \pi r L, \text{ where } L \text{ is the slant height}$$

The total surface area of the cone is the sum of the area of the circular base and the lateral area.

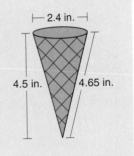

Example 2

An ice-cream cone has a diameter of 2.4 inches and a height of 4.5 inches. The slant height is about 4.65 inches.

a Find the volume of the cone.

b Find the lateral area of the cone.

Solution

a The radius of the cone's base is $\frac{2.4}{2}$, or 1.2, inches.

$$\begin{aligned}
\text{Volume}_{\text{cone}} &= \tfrac{1}{3}\pi r^2 h \\
&= \tfrac{1}{3}\pi(1.2^2)(4.5) \\
&= 2.16\pi \\
&\approx 6.8
\end{aligned}$$

The volume of the cone is about 6.79 in.^{3}.

b

$$\begin{aligned}
\text{Lateral area}_{\text{cone}} &= \pi r L \\
&= \pi(1.2)(4.65) \\
&\approx 17.5
\end{aligned}$$

The lateral area of the cone is about 17.5 in.^{2}.

SPHERES

A common geometric shape is a **sphere.** Baseballs, soap bubbles, and planets are all approximately spherical in shape. A sphere has a radius and a diameter, but it does not have any edges. The formula for the volume of a sphere is

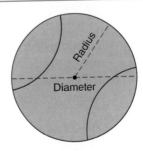

$$\text{Volume}_{\text{sphere}} = \tfrac{4}{3}\pi r^3$$

The formula for the total surface area of a sphere is

$$\text{Total surface area}_{\text{sphere}} = 4\pi r^2$$

Example 3

A spherical scoop of ice cream has a diameter of 2.4 in. If it is placed in the cone described in Example 2 and melts into the cone, will the melted ice cream overflow the cone?

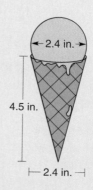

2.4 in.

4.5 in.

2.4 in.

Solution

In Example 2, we found that the volume of the cone is 6.79 in.^{3}. The radius of the scoop of ice cream is the same as the radius of the cone—1.2 in.

$$
\begin{aligned}
\text{Volume}_{\text{sphere}} &= \tfrac{4}{3}\pi r^3 \\
&= \tfrac{4}{3}\pi(1.2^3) \\
&= \tfrac{4}{3}\pi(1.728) \\
&= 7.24
\end{aligned}
$$

The volume of the scoop of ice cream is about 7.24 in.^{3}. Since the volume of the ice cream is greater than the volume of the cone, the ice cream will overflow the cone when it melts.

Sample Problem

Problem

A cone-shaped paper cup has a height of 8 cm and a radius of 4 cm. If you fill the cup with water to half of its depth, what portion of the volume of the cup is filled with water?

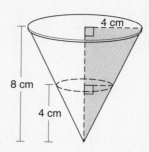

4 cm

8 cm

4 cm

Solution

In the drawing, the smaller triangle is similar to the larger triangle. The ratio of the corresponding sides is 1:2. Therefore, the cone of water has half the height and half the radius of the cup. We will find the ratio of the volume occupied by the water to the volume of the whole cone.

$$
\frac{\text{Volume of water}}{\text{Volume of cone}} = \frac{\tfrac{1}{3}\cdot\pi\cdot 2^2\cdot 4}{\tfrac{1}{3}\cdot\pi\cdot 4^2\cdot 8} = 0.125
$$

Think and Discuss

1 A tube is just large enough to contain three tennis balls. Which is greater, the height of the tube or the circumference of the tube? Explain your answer.

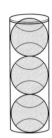

2 If the full glass of water is poured into the rectangular container shown, will the water overflow the container?

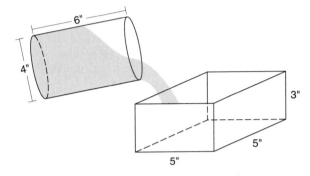

3 An egg is not a sphere. What are some possible ways to find the volume of an egg?

4 A sphere has a radius of 6 feet.
   a Find the volume and the total surface area of the sphere.
   b If the volume and the surface area of a sphere are numerically equal, what is the sphere's radius?

5 A cone is 10 cm in diameter and 12 cm in height.
   a Find the lateral area.
   b Find the area of the base.
   c Find the total surface area.
   d Find the volume.

Problems and Applications

6 A farmer carries liquid fertilizer in a cylindrical tank that is 12 feet long and 6 feet in diameter.
   a Find the volume of the tank in cubic feet.
   b Find the number of gallons that the tank will hold. (There are about 7.48 gal per ft^3.)

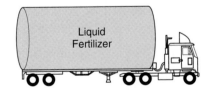

7 A cone is partially filled with water. The radius of the cone is 12". The height of the cone is 18". The radius of the surface of the water is 4".

   a How deep is the water in the cone?
   b What fraction of the cone is filled with water?

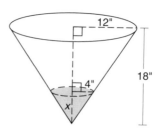

8 A 4" by 8" sheet of paper can be rolled into a cylinder in two ways. Circular caps can close off the ends.

   a Which cylinder has the greater lateral area?
   b Which cylinder has the greater total surface area?
   c Which cylinder has the greater volume?

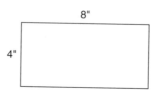

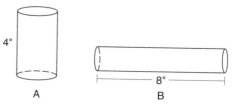

A   B

9 A scoop of ice cream has a diameter of 4.2 cm. It is placed in a cone with a diameter of 4 cm and a height of 6 cm. If the ice cream melts into the cone, will it overflow the cone?

10 One thousand gallons of water is pumped into a holding tank that is 20 ft in diameter and 30 ft tall. What is the approximate depth of the water in the tank?

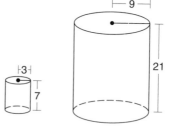

11 Consider the two cylinders shown.

   a Find the ratio of the radii of the two cylinders.
   b Find the ratio of the heights of the two cylinders.
   c Find the ratio of the volume of the smaller cylinder to the volume of the larger cylinder.

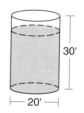

12 Science The earth is almost a sphere, with a diameter of 7920 miles. About 29% of the surface of the earth is land.

   a Find the volume of the earth.
   b Find the total surface area of the earth.
   c Find the approximate land area on the surface of the earth.

13 In Wet City each person uses approximately 100 gallons of water per day. The city reservoir is a cylinder 100 ft across and 30 ft deep. For how many people will the reservoir provide water in a day?

14 Which has the larger volume, a cube with sides of 3 units or a sphere with a radius of 2 units?

15 Science A cubical piece of ice and a spherical piece of ice have the same volume. The pieces are submerged in two identical glasses of Cool-Aid. The cooling rate of a piece of ice depends on the surface area of ice exposed to the liquid. Which piece do you think will cool the drink faster? Explain your response.

16 An ice machine makes 20-mm cubes that have a hole through the center. Each hole has a 6 mm diameter.
  a Find the total surface area of the ice cube shown, including the inside walls of the hole.
  b Find the volume of the ice in the cube shown.

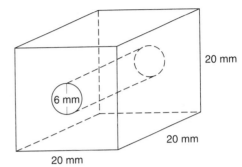

17 Can 50 marbles, each with a radius of 1 cm, be melted down to form a sphere with a radius of less than 4 cm?

18 The cylinder, the hemisphere, and the cone have the same radius r and height h. Find the ratio

$$\text{Volume}_{\text{cylinder}} : \text{Volume}_{\text{hemisphere}} : \text{Volume}_{\text{cone}}$$

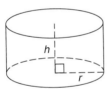

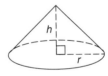

19 Science The fuel for this rocket takes up 40% of the volume of the rocket. The diameter of the rocket is 12 ft. (Hint: In this problem, divide and conquer.)
  a Find the volume of the rocket that can be used for the payload.
  b Find the lateral area of the nose cone.

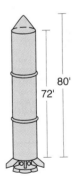

20 A piston cylinder has a diameter of 6 cm. If 60 cm³ of oil is pumped into the cylinder, how far does the oil push the piston rod?

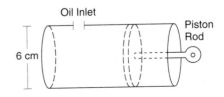

21 Find all whole number values of x for which $\frac{33}{2x-1}$ is a whole number.

22 A pyramid with a square base has a height of 6 and a volume of 32. What is the length of the sides of the square?

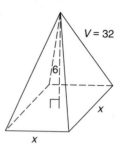

$V = 32$

23 Deb U. Tant wanted to rent a room for a dance. Holly's Day Inn charges $200 plus $80 per hour. Sherry's Tonn charges $300 plus $60 per hour. Amazingly, at either place the total cost would have been the same. For how many hours did Deb plan to rent the room?

24 Solve $x = 3y + 5$ for (x, y) if $6x - 2 = 4y$.

25 Solve each equation for x.
 a $2(x + 3) = 13 - 5x$
 b $x - 2x + 3x - 4x + 5x - 6x + 7x = 8x + 20$

26 **a** Evaluate $\sqrt{.04}$
 b Evaluate $\sqrt{\sqrt{.04}}$
 c Evaluate $\sqrt{\sqrt{\sqrt{.04}}}$
 d Continue the same process, taking the square root of the answer to each previous problem. What value do your answers seem to approach?

27 If $f(1) = 7$ and $f(n + 1) = f(n) + 4$, what is the value of each of the following?
 a $f(1)$　　　　　　　　　**b** $f(2)$
 c $f(3)$　　　　　　　　　**d** $f(4)$
 e $f(5)$

28 Arrange the following from least to greatest by weight.
 a A two-liter bottle of cola
 b A two-liter bottle of diet cola
 c A two-liter bottle of water

Investigation

Ratio　Find the ratio of the diameter of a 12-ounce soft drink can to the height of the can. Do the same for other cans. Are the ratios the same? What is the range of ratios that you find?

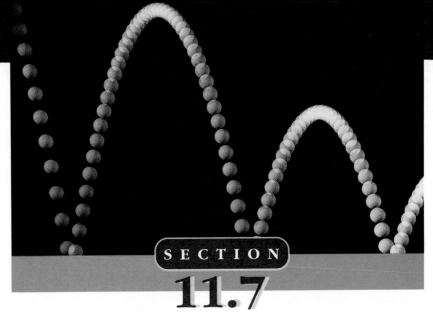

Reading Information from Graphs

As you have seen in earlier chapters, graphs can help us see information quickly. Let's look at some more examples.

Example 1

Solve the equation $2x - 8 = -4x + 7$ in the following two ways.

a By graphing the two equations $y = 2x - 8$ and $y = -4x + 7$

b Algebraically

Solution

a We can sketch the graphs of the two equations $y = 2x - 8$ and $y = -4x + 7$. Where do the two lines seem to intersect? They seem to intersect at $(2.5, -3)$. Thus, $x = 2.5$. We must test the value in the equation in order to verify that it is correct.

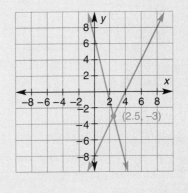

Left Side	**Right Side**
$2x - 8$	$-4x + 7$
$= 2(2.5) - 8$	$= -4(2.5) + 7$
$= 5 - 8$	$= -10 + 7$
$= -3$	$= -3$

Since the left side is equal to the right side, $x = 2.5$. Can you describe what the -3 represents in the ordered pair $(2.5, -3)$?

b

$$2x - 8 = -4x + 7$$
$$\underline{+4x \qquad\quad +4x}$$
$$6x - 8 = \qquad 7$$
$$\underline{+8 \qquad\quad +8}$$
$$6x \quad = \qquad 15$$

$$x = \frac{15}{6} = 2.5$$

Example 2
Cashe Box has a group of nickels and dimes with a total value of 55 cents. Cashe has 8 coins. How many nickels and dimes does Cashe have?

Solution
Although we could use trial and error to get an answer, let's look at another way to model this problem:

> Let D = the number of dimes.
> Let N = the number of nickels.
> We can now write the equation $D + N = 8$.

One way to solve this is with 8 dimes and no nickels. We graph this as (8, 0). He could also have 8 nickels and no dimes. We graph this as (0, 8). We then connect the two points. This is the graph of $D + N = 8$.

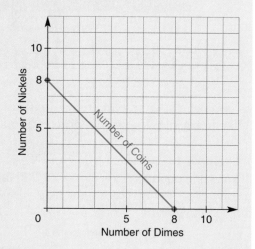

Now let's represent the value of the coins. Each dime is worth 10 cents and each nickel is worth 5 cents. The total value of the dimes is $10D$ and the total value of the nickels is $5N$. The total value of the coins is $10D + 5N = 55$.

If $D = 0$, there must be 11 nickels ($5N = 55$). We can graph this as (0, 11). If $N = 0$, there must be 5.5 dimes ($10D = 55$). Even though Cashe can't have half a dime, we can still use the point (5.5, 0) as a point on the graph.

The intersection of the two lines is (3, 5). This means that 3 dimes and 5 nickels are the 8 coins with a total value of 55 cents.

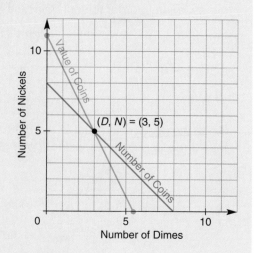

What if there were 9 coins? We can adjust the graph. Just slide the graph of the number of coins to the points (0, 9) and (9, 0) and look for the solution.

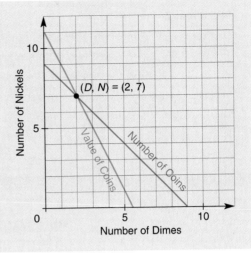

Calculators with graphing capabilities and computers with a graphing program enable us to examine graphs that are too complicated to draw.

Sample Problems

Problem 1

Graph the equation $h = 6 + 64t - 16t^2$. This equation gives the height in feet, h, of a rock that is tossed in the air at a time in seconds, t, after the rock is tossed.

a What is the maximum height that the rock will reach?

b The rock will reach a height of 54 feet twice, once going up and once coming down. Identify those two times (in seconds).

c After how many seconds will the rock hit the ground?

d From what height was the rock tossed?

Solution

With the aid of a graphing calculator or a computer graphing program, we can find the information.

a The maximum height is 70 feet.

b The rock reaches 54 feet at 1 second and at 3 seconds.

c The rock will hit the ground in approximately 4.1 seconds.

d The rock was tossed from a height of 6 feet.

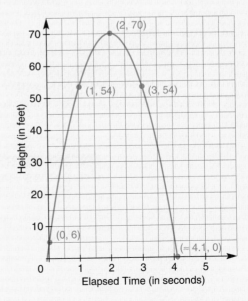

591

Problem 2

Solve the equation $2^x = 2x$.

Solution

Graph the two equations $y_1 = 2^x$ and $y_2 = 2x$. There are two points of intersection of the graphs. We are looking for the x-coordinates. They are at $x = 1$ and at $x = 2$.

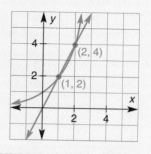

Think and Discuss

1 Use a graphing calculator or a computer to create the graphs of the equations $y = x^2$ and $y = 2^x$. Then use the trace or zoom feature to find the three points of intersection.

2 On graph paper, draw the graph of the equation $y = \frac{1+x}{4+x}$ for the whole-number values $x = 0, 1, 2, \ldots, 10$. For what values of x is $y \geq 0.6$?

3 Box-seat tickets cost $7 each, and grandstand seats cost $4 each.
   a Write a formula that represents the cost of B box seats and G grandstand seats.
   b Find all combinations (B, G) that could be bought with exactly $100.

4 Two angles are complementary. The measure of one angle is 4 times the measure of the other.
   a Write two equations to describe the two facts.
   b Graph the two equations on the same coordinate system and find the measures of the two angles.

5 Compute the area, A, of the rectangle for values of x greater than 0. Then sketch a graph of the area of the rectangle by plotting the ordered pairs (x, A). Check your result by writing a function for the area, $A(x)$, and graphing the function with a graphing calculator or computer.

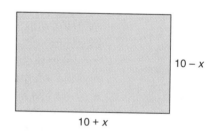

Problems and Applications

6 Graph the two equations $y = 6x$ and $y = -2x + 16$. Use the graphs to solve the equation $6x = -2x + 16$.

7 Draw the graph of the equation $A = \pi r^2$. (Hint: You may need to find values of A to the nearest tenth.)

8 For the equation $y = 16 - 4t - t^2$,

    a Find the values of y when $t = 0, 1, 2, 3, 4, 5,$ and 6. Graph the seven points (t, y).

    b What value of t gives the greatest value of y?

9 **Communicating** Explain how a graph can be used to determine the value in cents, y, of a number of dimes, x.

10 **Science** I shot an arrow into the air, with an initial vertical velocity of 48 feet per second. It left my hand at a height of about 5 feet. Its height-versus-time equation is $b = -16t^2 + 48t + 5$.

    a What is the maximum height the arrow will reach?

    b After how many seconds will it hit the ground?

11 Graph the two equations $y = 2^x - 3$ and $y = 3x + 1$.

    a Use the graph to solve the equation $2^x - 3 = 3x + 1$ for x.

    b Verify the result by substituting the value of x into the equation.

12 **Business** A company's profits for the years 1975 through 1990 are shown on the graph.

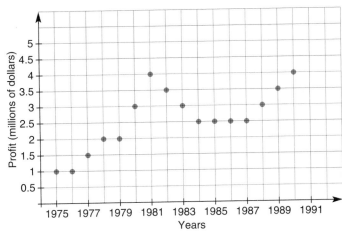

    a Between what years were the profits declining?

    b In what years were the profits at an all-time high?

    c Use the graph to project what the profits will be in the next two years. Explain your answer.

13 In the game of LegBall, it is possible to score 8 points with a touch-up and 5 points with a parkgoal.

    a Write a function for the value, V, of t touch-ups and p parkgoals.

    b In the Colossal Bowl, a team scored 34 points. Write an equation to represent this, and graph the result.

    c What point on the graph represents the kinds of scores made?

14 Let x be the number of gallons in a batch of punch. Ginger ale makes up 60% of the punch.

    a Write a formula to describe the number of gallons of ginger ale in x gallons of punch.

    b Draw the graph of the equation.

15 The length of the rectangle shown is 20 more than the width. The perimeter of the rectangle is 80.
  a Write two equations to describe the given conditions.
  b Graph the equations you wrote in part **a** and find ℓ and w.

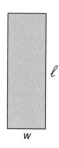

16 The Very Little Theater sold 17 tickets for a performance and took in $3.00. Adult tickets cost $0.30 and children's tickets cost $0.15. The manager, Joey, wrote the equations $A + C = 17$ and $30A + 15C = 300$, where A represents the number of adults and C represents the number of children. Joey used a graph to answer the following questions.
  a How many of each kind of tickets were sold to produce total sales of $3.00?
  b The next day Joey also made $3.00 but sold only 12 tickets. How many of each kind of ticket were sold?

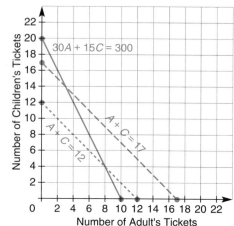

17 **Science** Use the values $F = 32, 41, 50, 59, 68, 77, 86, 95$, and 104 to draw the graph of the equation $C = \frac{5}{9}(F - 32)$. What does this equation represent?

18 **Communicating** Write a story that describes the graph shown.

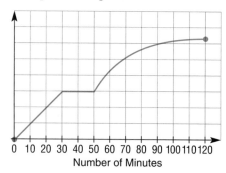

◄ LOOKING BACK **Spiral Learning** LOOKING AHEAD ►

---

19 A cone has a radius of 5 and a slant height of 13.
  a Find the height of the cone.
  b Find the lateral area of the cone.
  c Find the volume of the cone.

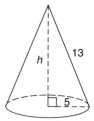

20 There are approximately 7.48 gallons in a cubic foot. How many gallons can a cylindrical barrel hold if it is 4 feet tall and 3 feet in diameter?

21 Which has the greatest volume, cylinder A, cylinder B, or cone C?

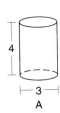
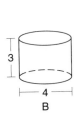
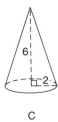

22 A cylindrical drainpipe is 60 feet long and has a diameter of 4 inches.
  a Find the lateral area of the drainpipe.
  b What volume of water can the pipe hold at one time?

23 Solve each equation for x.
  a $-2x - 7 = -4x + 13$ **b** $-\frac{2}{3}x + 5 = -\frac{1}{3}x + 10$

24 Find the value of  $\sqrt{3}$ to the nearest thousandth.

25 Find the surface area of a hemisphere that has a radius of 12 cm. (Hint: Be sure to include the flat face.)

26 Coina Clecter has 50 dimes for every 7 nickels she has. What is the value of her coins if she has 228 coins?

27 Find all pairs of whole numbers (x, y) for which the value of $\frac{17}{3x + 4y}$ is a whole number.

28 Solve each equation for x.
  a 20% of x = 12% of $(x + 20)$
  b $12 - 3x = 15\left(1 + \frac{1}{3}x\right)$

29 The total number of squares in an n-by-n checkerboard is given by the formula $f(n) = \frac{n(n + 1)(2n + 1)}{6}$. How many squares are in
  a A 4-by-4 checkerboard?
  b An 8-by-8 checkerboard?
  c A 12-by-12 checkerboard?

30 Evaluate each expression.
  a $(-3)(-4) + 5(-6)$ **b** $\left(-\frac{1}{2}\right)\left(-\frac{2}{3}\right)\left(-\frac{3}{4}\right)\left(-\frac{4}{5}\right)\left(-\frac{5}{6}\right)$
  c $\frac{-3}{5} + \frac{4}{7}$ **d** $\frac{1}{2} + \frac{1}{3} + \frac{1}{4}$

Investigation

Graphs   Interview people in various lines of work to find out how they use graphing calculators or computer graphics in their jobs.

Summary

CONCEPTS AND PROCEDURES

After studying this chapter, you should be able to

- Develop strategies for solving problems (11.1, 11.3)
- Solve equations with variables on both sides (11.2)
- Solve equations with several variables (11.4)
- Find the volume and the total surface area of a prism (11.5)
- Find the volume and the total surface area of a pyramid (11.5)
- Find the volume and the total surface area of a cylinder (11.6)
- Find the volume and the total surface area of a cone (11.6)
- Find the volume and the total surface area of a sphere (11.6)
- Read information from graphs (11.7)

VOCABULARY

cone (11.6)

cylinder (11.6)

edge (11.5)

face (11.5)

lateral area (11.5)

lateral face (11.5)

polyhedra (11.5)

prism (11.5)

pyramid (11.5)

slant height (11.5)

sphere (11.6)

vertex (11.5)

Review

1 If one of your friends didn't believe that the formula for the volume of a cone should include the factor $\frac{1}{3}$, how could you convince your friend that $V = \frac{1}{3}\pi r^2 h$ is correct?

2 The price of garbanzo beans increased 20%, to a cost of $45 per ton. What was the cost before the price increase?

3 A rectangle has a length of x meters and a width of 12 meters. A square with the same perimeter has a side of 17 meters. Find the length of the rectangle.

4 Mark Kett invests $1000 in each of two stocks. The value of the first stock increases 3% per month, and the value of the second increases 2% per month. What is the total value of the stocks for each month up to one year? (Hint: Use a spreadsheet.)

5 Find the value of x if the perimeters of the rectangle and the triangle are equal.

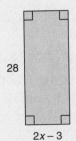

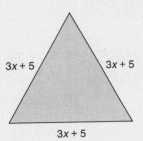

28

$3x + 5$ $3x + 5$

$2x - 3$ $3x + 5$

6 Freddy leaves his home on the corner of Maple Street and heads east on Forest Street. Jason leaves camp and heads west on Forest Street at exactly the same time, traveling 6 mph. They meet at Oak Street. How fast was Freddy traveling?

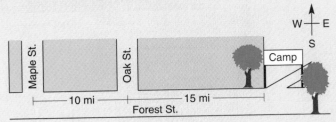

7 Simplify each expression and solve each equation.
   a $50 - 3x = 5(x + 18)$ b $50 - 3x - 5(x + 18)$
   c $\frac{1}{2}(2x + 8) + \frac{1}{4}(8x - 20)$ d $\frac{1}{2}(2x + 8) = \frac{1}{4}(8x - 20)$

8 Video Heaven rents movies for $3 per night. Video Heaven also offers a video club plan. The plan costs $100 per year and allows movie rentals at $1 per night plus two free rentals per month. How many movies must you rent per year to make the video club worthwhile?

9 Katrina earns $12.68 per hour for up to 8 hours a day. She earns time and a half for additional hours.
   a How much does she earn per hour of overtime?
   b If she works for 8 hours at regular pay and then works 3 hours overtime, what is her total earning for that day?
   c If she works the 11-hour day in part **b**, what is her average hourly wage for that day?

10 When I was a lad (9 years old), I worked for my dad (he was 5 times as old as I). My sister was born that year. Use a spreadsheet to determine
   a How old I was when my dad was 10 times as old as my sister
   b How old I was when my dad was twice as old as I

11 Triangle ABC is similar to triangle DEF. Use a proportion to find the value of x.

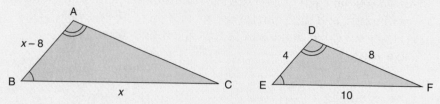

12 Find all pairs of natural numbers (x, y) for which $2x + 3y = 30$.

13 Cardy collects sets of baseball cards. He has 12 sets of 1992 Bottoms and 5 sets of 1992 Flairs. Their combined worth is $400. He buys 6 more sets of Flairs and sells 2 sets of Bottoms. The value of the cards he owns now is $470. Find the value of a set of Flairs cards.

14 The perimeter of a rectangle is 80 cm. Find the rectangle's length if its width is 300% of the length.

15 Find the value of x so that the lever will balance.

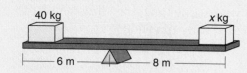

16 A house has the shape of a rectangular prism with a triangular prism on the top. Find the interior volume of the house.

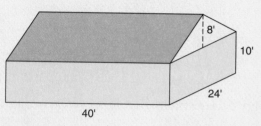

17 A pyramid has a square base with a side of 6 and a slant height of 5.
   a Find the lateral area of the pyramid.
   b Find the total surface area.
   c Find the volume.

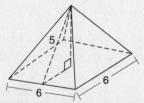

18 Use the trapezoidal pyramid shown.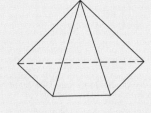
  a How many vertices, V, does the pyramid have?
  b How many edges, E, does the pyramid have?
  c How many faces, F, does the pyramid have?
  d Is the equation $F - E + V = 2$ *true* or *false?*

19 Find the volume and the total surface area of each of the following solids. If necessary, round your answer to the nearest tenth.
  a Sphere   **b** Cylinder   **c** Cone

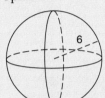
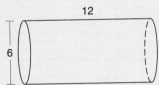
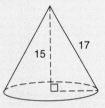

20 Find the ratio of the volume of the cone to the volume of the cylinder.

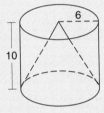

21 Graph the equations $y = 2x + 7$ and $y = -3x - 3$ and find the point where the graphs intersect.

22 An open-top box has a square base.
  a Find the lateral area of the box.
  b Find the total surface area.
  c Find the volume.
  d Convert the volume from cubic inches to cubic feet.

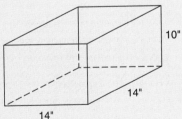

23 Mr. Mint has one more dime than he has quarters. The total value of his dimes and quarters is $4.30.
  a How many methods can you think of to find the number of dimes and quarters Mr. Mint has?
  b How many dimes and quarters does he have?

24 Use a graphing calculator or a computer to graph the equations $y = 3^x$ and $y = x^3$. Find the points of intersection of the graphs in order to solve $3^x = x^3$. If necessary, find your answer to the nearest tenth.

Test

In problems 1–3, solve each equation.

1 $3x - 8 = 7x - 20$

2 $\dfrac{x-4}{3x} = \dfrac{4}{9}$

3 $2(3x - 1) = 2x$

4 Today, Rita's father is three times her age. Six years ago, he was four times her age. How old are Rita and her father today?

In problems 5–7, find the volume of each figure.

5

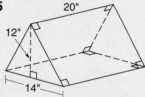

6

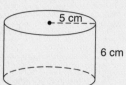

7

8 Ginny bought two tires for $120, including sales tax. If sales tax is 5%, what was the price of the tires before tax? Round your answer to the nearest cent.

9 The areas of the two rectangles are equal. Find the perimeter of each rectangle.

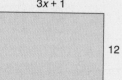

10 David decided to invest his $10,000 inheritance. He put half of the money in a savings account that pays 5% interest and the other half in a CD that pays 8% interest. How much interest will David earn in one year?

11 Graph the equations $y = 4x + 3$ and $y = 3x + 1$. Use the graphs to solve the equation $4x + 3 = 3x + 1$.

In problems 12–14, find the total surface area of each figure.

12

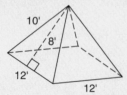

13

14

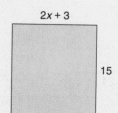

15 Juanita's piggy bank contains only quarters and dimes. The value of the coins is $5.75. If she has 32 coins, how many are quarters and how many are dimes?

1 Eric, Dave, and Carl are triplets. Each participates in two of the following six sports: baseball, football, soccer, basketball, hockey, and swimming. No two are in the same sport. From the facts below, deduce which two sports each participates in.

a Eric and the football player went to watch the basketball game.

b Dave doesn't wear any special kind of protective equipment in either of his sports, just special attire.

c The football player and the hockey player watched their brother set a swimming record.

d Soccer and football are played at the same time.

2 Can you read the two familiar proverbs printed at the right?

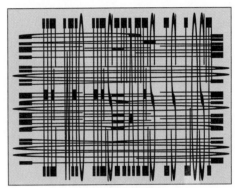

3 Match each item on the left with the one on the right that has a similar or related meaning. The relationships are disguised by the use of double meanings or altered spacing between words. For example, the word *avenue* (a venue) goes with "one location" since *venue* means "location." The word *holster* goes with "arm rest" since it is a place that an arm (gun) gets placed (rested). These puzzles, called "Mind Flexers" by their inventor, psychology professor Morgan Worthy, are meant to improve mental ingenuity. He says, "Do not take them too seriously, and you will quickly improve at seeing the relationships."

1	Avenue	**A**	Laugh at pigs' home
2	Pantry	**B**	Large flower
3	Mango	**C**	Bad ratio
4	Hasty	**D**	Promote music
5	Bumper	**E**	Attempt to cook
6	Meant	**F**	Adequate golfer
7	Fortune	**G**	I'm an insect
8	Parking	**H**	One location
9	Maximum	**I**	Do more work
10	Restless	**J**	He left
11	Holster	**K**	Arm rest

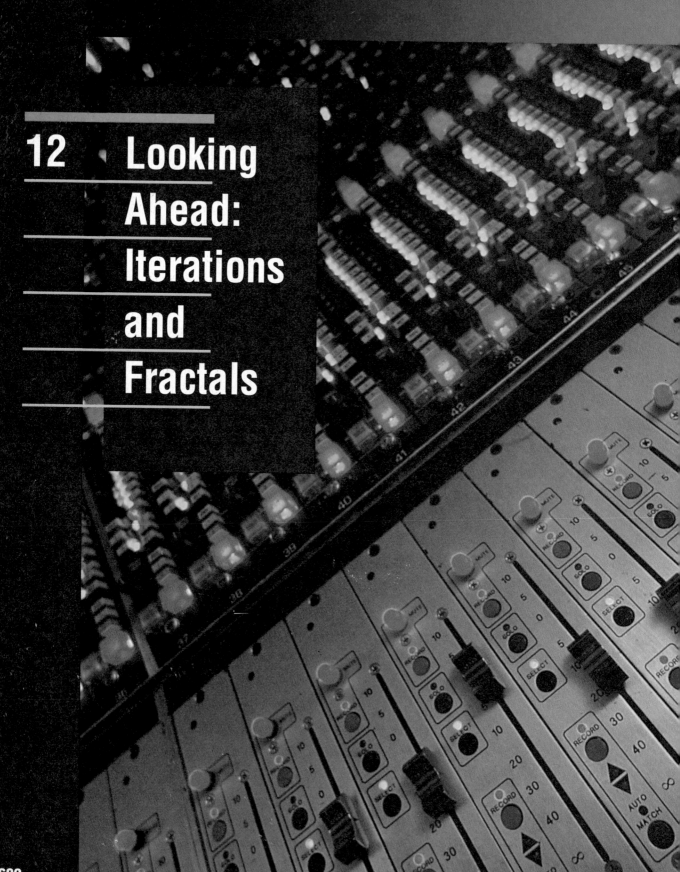

12

Looking Ahead: Iterations and Fractals

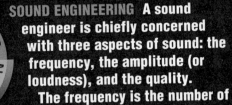

SOUND ENGINEERING A sound engineer is chiefly concerned with three aspects of sound: the frequency, the amplitude (or loudness), and the quality.

The frequency is the number of vibrations per second. Electronic equipment can produce sounds with a given frequency, and can vary the intensity. Sound engineers are continually working on ways to improve the quality of music, whether it be a live orchestra, a rock concert greatly amplified, or music recorded on a tape or a CD.

If you like both music and electronics, you could be headed for a career related to sound engineering.

PITAGORAS

INVESTIGATION

Music What is harmony? Explain in mathematical terms why some musical notes sound good when played together, and some combinations sound less pleasant.

REPEATED CALCULATIONS

The following example will help you to understand the meaning of *iteration.*

Example 1

If Mary puts $500 in a bank account that gives 6.5% interest per year figured once a year, how much will she have in the bank at the end of ten years?

Solution

Let's first just figure out how much she has after one year. This will be the original $500 plus the interest earned on the $500 calculated by multiplying the rate as a decimal 0.065 times $500.

Times	Amount in Bank at That Time
Start of Year 1	$500
End of Year 1	$500 + 0.065 ($500) = $532.50

Now we can figure the amount at the end of the second year by repeating the same calculations as used for the first year, only starting with $532.50 in the bank. That is, our result from the previous year is used as the starting value for the next year. We now use this idea to complete our table for ten years.

Year	Amount	End of Year	Amount in Bank at End of Year
1	$500	1	500.00 + 0.065 (500.00) = $532.50
2	532.50	2	532.50 + 0.065 (532.50) = 567.11
3	567.11	3	567.11 + 0.065 (567.11) = 603.97
4	603.97	4	603.97 + 0.065 (603.97) = 643.23
5	643.23	5	643.23 + 0.065 (643.23) = 685.04
6	685.04	6	685.04 + 0.065 (685.04) = 729.57
7	729.57	7	729.57 + 0.065 (729.57) = 776.99
8	776.99	8	776.99 + 0.065 (776.99) = 827.50
9	827.50	9	827.50 + 0.065 (827.50) = 881.29
10	881.29	10	881.29 + 0.065 (881.29) = 938.57

We see that Mary will have $938.57 in the bank at the end of ten years. **Note:** If you try these calculations, you might get slightly different answers because of rounding differences.

The repetitive process in Example 1 is called iteration. It is used when the next calculation to be done is exactly the same as the previous calculation, except that the next calculation uses the results of the previous calculation as its starting value.

ITERATION DIAGRAMS

One good way to model iterations is by means of an *iteration diagram* like the following.

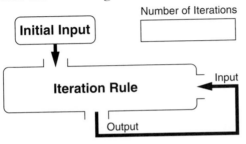
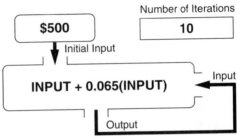

Notice the characteristics of an iteration diagram.

- There is always an initial input value. In Example 1, it was the $500 initially placed in the bank.
- There is an iteration rule to enable us to take any input and compute the output. In Example 1, it was INPUT + 0.065(INPUT).
- There is an arrow indicating that the previous output should be used as the next input. In Example 1, the money in the account at the end of each year is used as the input for the next year.
- There is a number of iterations, indicating the number of times to repeat the process. In Example 1, there were ten iterations, corresponding to the ten years.

Example 2
Consider the iteration diagram shown.
a Calculate the outputs for the indicated number of iterations.
b How is this problem different from the problem in Example 1?

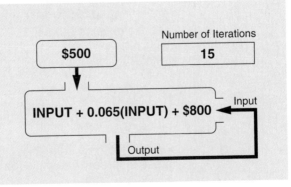

a Initial input value: $500
Iteration rule: INPUT + 0.065 (INPUT) + $800
Continue iterations 15 times.

Iteration	Amount ($)
0	500
1	1332.5
2	2219.113
3	3163.355
4	4168.973
5	5239.956
6	6380.553
7	7595.289
8	8888.983
9	10266.77
10	11734.11
11	13296.82
12	14961.12
13	16733.59
14	18621.27
15	20631.66

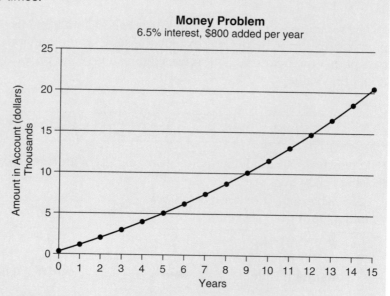

Money Problem
6.5% interest, $800 added per year

b This is the same problem as Example 1, only Mary adds an additional $800 to her account at the end of each year, and the iterations are done for 15 years instead of 10 years.

Sample Problems

Problem 1

A ball is dropped from a height of 12 feet, and each time it rebounds to a height that is 85% of the previous height. On which rebound will the ball first fail to reach a height of 1 foot?

Solution

Initial input value: 12 feet
Iteration rule: 0.85(INPUT)
Continue until the output is less than 1 foot.

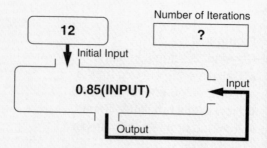

Spreadsheets are especially useful in solving problems using iteration. Here is a spreadsheet solution to the problem.

Bounce	Height (ft)
0	12
1	10.2
2	8.67
3	7.3695
4	6.264075
5	5.324464
6	4.525794
7	3.846925
8	3.269886
9	2.779403
10	2.362493
11	2.008119
12	1.706901
13	1.450866
14	1.233236
15	1.048251
16	0.891013

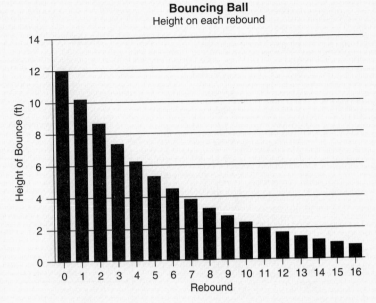

Bouncing Ball
Height on each rebound

On the sixteenth rebound the ball first bounces less than 1 foot high.

Note: Many graphing calculators have an [ANS] key, and this can be used to do iteration. For this problem, you would do the following:

Enter	Display
12 [EXE]	12
0.85 [×] [ANS] [EXE]	10.2
[EXE]	8.67
[EXE]	7.3695
⋮	⋮

On some calculators, the enter key or the [=] works like the [EXE] key.

Problem 2

Jake Whitehorse has just won a radio music quiz. The station gives Jake two possible options for his prize.

Option 1: A flat sum of $10,000
Option 2: $0.01 today, $0.02 tomorrow, $0.04 the third day, and so on for 24 days

Solution

Which option should Jake take?

Initial value: $0.01
Iteration rule: 2(INPUT)
Continue iterations 23 times.

We use a spreadsheet to help us quickly and painlessly get our answer. We make a third column to show the total of the money received by each day.

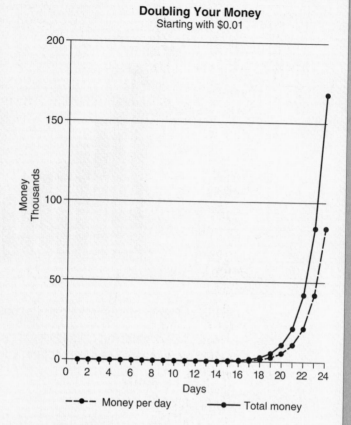

Day	Money/day	Total
1	$0.01	$0.01
2	$0.02	$0.03
3	$0.04	$0.07
4	$0.08	$0.15
5	$0.16	$0.31
6	$0.32	$0.63
7	$0.64	$1.27
8	$1.28	$2.55
9	$2.56	$5.11
10	$5.12	$10.23
11	$10.24	$20.47
12	$20.48	$40.95
13	$40.96	$81.91
14	$81.92	$163.83
15	$163.84	$327.67
16	$327.68	$655.35
17	$655.36	$1,310.71
18	$1,310.72	$2,621.43
19	$2,621.44	$5,242.87
20	$5,242.88	$10,485.75
21	$10,485.76	$20,971.51
22	$20,971.52	$41,943.03
23	$41,943.04	$83,886.07
24	$83,886.08	$167,772.15

Doubling Your Money
Starting with $0.01

Jake should definitely take option 2. (There is an interesting pattern involving the numbers in the second column and those in the third column. Describe this pattern.)

Think and Discuss

1

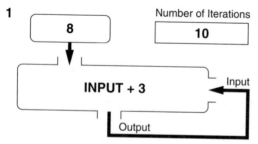

Number of Iterations
10

INPUT + 3

a Copy and complete the following table for the iteration diagram above.

Term	0	1	2	3	4	5	6	7	8	9	10
Output											

b Make a graph on a coordinate system for the table in part **a**.

c Write an equation that goes with the table and graph.

2 A lily pad on a pond doubles its area every day. If it will completely cover the pond at the end of 100 days, after how many days will it cover 50% of the pond?

3 There is a legend about a king who agreed to grant any wish to the subject who slew a giant. The subject who did this asked for a grain of wheat for the first square of a checkerboard, two for the second square, four for the third square, and so on, with the number of grains of wheat being doubled each time until all 64 squares of the checkerboard had been accounted for.

   a Draw an iteration diagram for this situation.

   b How many grains would go on the last square?

   c Explain why the king could not fulfill his promise.

Problems and Applications

4

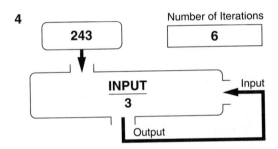

Number of Iterations

| 243 | | 6 |

   a Copy and complete the following table for the iteration diagram above.

Term	0	1	2	3	4	5	6
Output							

   b At what term will the output be less than 1?

5 **Business**   In 1960, the cost of a certain computer was $750,000. Every five years since then, the cost of an equivalent computer has been cut in half.

   a Draw an iteration diagram for this situation.

   b Make a table showing the cost of this computer every five years from 1960 to 2000.

   c When would the cost of this computer be less than $50?

6 **Spreadsheets**   In Example 1, Mary put $500 in a bank account that gives 6.5% interest per year for ten years.

   a How much money would she have if her original deposit had been $800 instead of $500?

   b How much would she have if the bank had paid 7.5% interest on her $500 for ten years?

7 A theater has 20 rows of seats and has 23 seats in the first row. In each successive row there are 4 more seats than in the row in front of it.
a Draw an iteration diagram to describe this situation.
b How many seats are in the twentieth row?

8 **Banking**   Ann puts $1000 into a bank account. She gets 5.1% interest per year. Each year, she adds another $600 to the account. How much will she have after ten years?

9

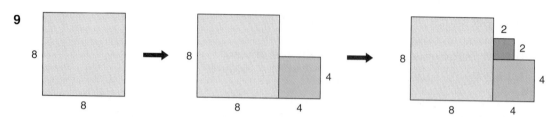

a What is the area of the smallest square when there are 12 squares in the figure?
b Continuing the pattern, what would be the total area of the entire figure after 12 iterations?

10 **Science**   S. Cargo started out with 32 snails in his aquarium. He discovered that every month the number of snails increased by one fourth of the number he had the previous month. For example, at the end of the first month he had $32 + \frac{1}{4}(32)$, or 40, snails. Assume that no snails die.
a Draw an iteration diagram for the number of snails S. Cargo has in any given month.
b When would S. Cargo have 1,000,000 snails in his aquarium?

11 A toy car is 12 feet from a wall. At each successive second it travels one half of the way to the wall.
a Copy the table, extending and completing it for the first 10 seconds.

Seconds	0	1	2	3
Distance from wall					...

b When is the car less than 3 inches from the wall?
c Does the car ever reach the wall? Explain.
d Describe the speed of the car as time increases.

12

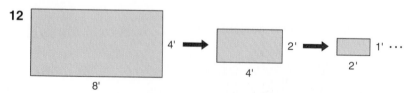

a Make an iteration diagram to figure the area of each successive rectangle in the pattern shown.
b What is the area of the tenth rectangle?

13 Consumer Math Larry takes out an auto loan for $9000 at 9.5% interest per year. He makes payments of $350 per month.

a What is the monthly interest rate?

b The following expression represents the amount Larry still owes after making his first $350 payment.

$$9000 + \frac{0.095}{12}(9000) - 350$$

Explain why this is the correct formula.

c Make an iteration diagram for the amount owed at the end of any month.

d How many months must Larry make payments?

14 Science A swimming pool has had chlorine added to it to raise the level of chlorine in the water to 3 parts per million. Each day 15% of the chlorine that was present the previous day is lost. A swimming pool must have at least 1 part per million of chlorine for safety. How many days will go by before more chlorine must be added?

15

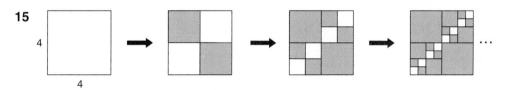

Find the shaded area of the sixth figure in the pattern shown above.

16 Consumer Math Tom takes out a $9000 loan for 48 months at 9.5% yearly interest. He makes monthly payments of $200. The iteration diagram can be used to find the amount of the loan remaining each month.

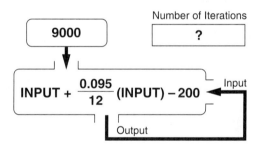

a Why is the 0.095 divided by 12?

b How much is owed at the end of one year? Two years? Three years? Four years?

c Experiment with changing the monthly payment until you find the correct monthly payment to pay off the loan in exactly four years.

Investigation

The Calendar Suppose that your birthday falls on a Saturday this year. On what day will your birthday fall next year? Explain why.

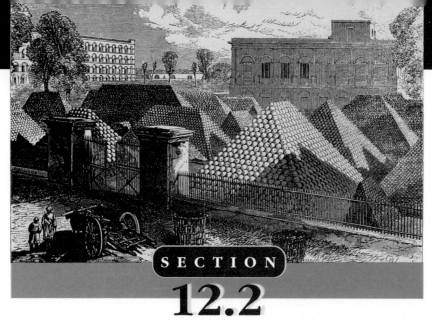

12.2
More About Iterations

RULES INVOLVING THE ITERATION COUNTER

In many iteration problems the iteration rule depends on both the input value and the number of iterations that have been performed. The following diagrams show such a situation.

Figure	Number of Dots in Bottom Row	Total Number of Dots
•	1	1
	2	1 + 2 = 3
	3	3 + 3 = 6
	4	6 + 4 = 10
	5	10 + 5 = 15
	6	15 + 6 = 21

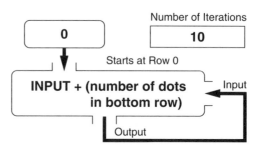

Notice that the total number of dots in each triangle depends on two things:

1. The number of dots in the previous triangle.
2. The number of dots in the new row.

Many iteration rules depend on two conditions such as those above.

FUNCTION NOTATION FOR ITERATION

It is convenient to use function notation to describe iteration problems. Consider the following example.

Example 1

If $f(0) = 10$ and $f(n) = f(n-1) + n$, what is $f(5)$?

Solution

We proceed one step at a time. We make a table of values for n, enter 10 as the first function entry, and then use the iteration formula $f(n) = f(n-1) + n$ to calculate each successive function entry.

n	$f(n)$
0	$f(0) = 10$
1	$f(1) = f(1-1) + 1 = f(0) + 1 = 10 + 1 = 11$
2	$f(2) = f(2-1) + 2 = f(1) + 2 = 11 + 2 = 13$
3	$f(3) = f(3-1) + 3 = f(2) + 3 = 13 + 3 = 16$
4	$f(4) = f(4-1) + 4 = f(3) + 4 = 16 + 4 = 20$

Notice that the function operates just like the iteration diagram: $f(0) = 10$ is the initial input, and the counter, n, starts at 0. The iteration rule, $f(n) = f(n-1) + n$, indicates that the next output is the sum of the previous output, $f(n-1)$, and the current value of the counter, n.

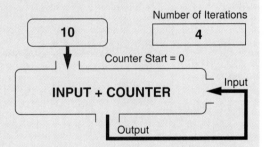

Example 2

Write an iterative function to describe the following situation:

Mary deposits $500 in a bank account that gives 6.5% interest per year. At the start of each year thereafter, she deposits an additional $300 in the account.

Solution

$M(0) = \$500$ — Money at start of first year.

$M(n) = M(n-1) + M(n-1)(0.065) + \$300$ — Money at end of each year equals money at start of that year, plus interest earned on that money for the year, plus $300 deposit.

Example 3

Convert the iteration diagram into function notation.

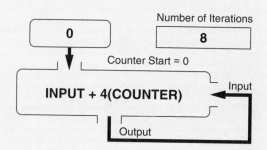

Solution

The initial input is 0, so we write $f(0) = 0$. Each time through the iteration diagram, the counter, which counts the number of iterations done so far, increases by 1. The iteration rule states that we find each output by adding 4 times the current value of the iteration counter to the preceding output. In function notation we write $f(n) = f(n-1) + 4n$. The complete function is $f(0) = 0$ and $f(n) = f(n-1) + 4n$.

Sample Problems

Problem 1

Consider the following pattern of angles. The next picture is formed from the previous picture by adding one more ray having the same endpoint as the previous rays. Count the number of different angles formed in each picture. How many angles would be formed with 11 rays?

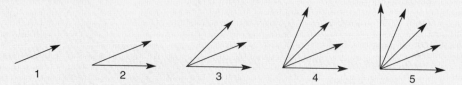

Solution
A good way to solve many of these problems is to jump right into the middle and think about how many new angles are formed when we add an additional ray.

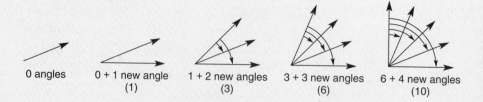

The additional ray makes a new angle with each of the rays that were in the preceding diagram. Therefore,

$A(1) = 0$ With one ray there are no angles.

$A(n) = A(n - 1) + (n - 1)$ With n rays there are all the angles previously there, plus the $(n - 1)$ new angles formed by adding the nth ray.

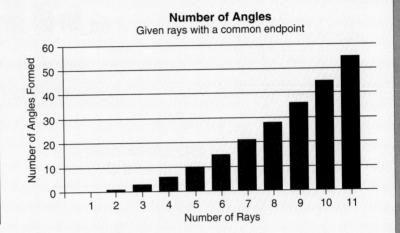

Number of Rays	Number of Angles
1	0
2	1
3	3
4	6
5	10
6	15
7	21
8	28
9	36
10	45
11	55

Number of Angles
Given rays with a common endpoint

Problem 2

It takes 4 toothpicks to make the 1 × 1 square shown. It takes 12 toothpicks for the 2 × 2 figure and 24 toothpicks for the 3 × 3 figure. How many toothpicks will it take for an 8 × 8 figure?

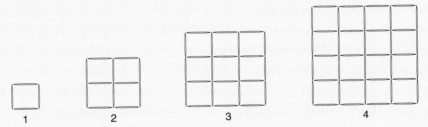

1   2   3   4

Solution

Again we jump in the middle and try to see how many toothpicks must be added to a given figure to produce the next figure.

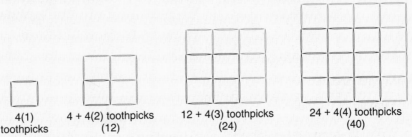

4(1) toothpicks   4 + 4(2) toothpicks   12 + 4(3) toothpicks   24 + 4(4) toothpicks
              (12)   (24)   (40)

We need to add $4n$ toothpicks, where $n \times n$ is the size of the figure. Therefore, for the next figure we need all the toothpicks for the previous figure plus $4n$ more. In function notation we write $S(1) = 4$ and $S(n) = S(n - 1) + 4n$. For an 8 × 8 figure, 144 toothpicks are needed.

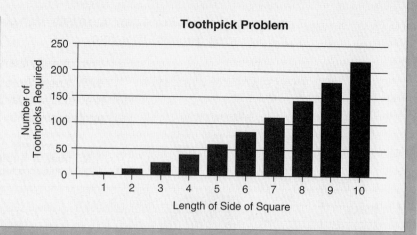

Side Length	Toothpicks
1	4
2	12
3	24
4	40
5	60
6	84
7	112
8	144
9	180
10	220

Toothpick Problem

Think and Discuss

1 Consider the following two functions.

$f(1) = 100$
$f(n + 1) = 2 \cdot f(n)$

$g(1) = 100$
$g(n + 1) = g(n) - 100$

Notice that as the value of n increases, the value of $f(n)$ increases rapidly and the value of $g(n)$ decreases rapidly. If $h(1) = 100$ and $h(n + 1) = 2 \cdot h(n) - 100$, does the value of $h(n)$ increase or decrease as the value of n increases?

2 Suppose that $f(n) = \sqrt{f(n - 1)}$.
  a Find $f(n)$ for $n = 1, 2, 3, \ldots, 12$ if $f(1) = 16$.
  b Find $f(n)$ for $n = 1, 2, 3, \ldots, 12$ if $f(1) = 0.16$.

3 Suppose we connect triangular numbers with toothpicks.

0

3

9

18

  a Copy and complete the following table.

Length of side	0	1	2	3	4	5	6
Number of toothpicks							

  b Write an iterative function to describe the number of toothpicks needed.
  c How many toothpicks would be needed for a triangle with 15 toothpicks on each side?

4 **a** Write an iterative function for this diagram.
b Make a table of outputs for the indicated number of iterations.

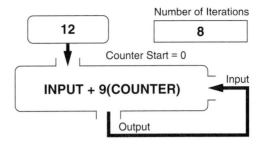

Problems and Applications

5 If $f(0) = 8$ and $f(n) = 2 \cdot f(n - 1) - 5$, what are $f(1), f(2), f(3)$, and $f(4)$?

6 If $f(1) = 5$ and $f(n + 1) = \frac{1}{2}\left(f(n) + \frac{1}{f(n)}\right)$, what are $f(2), f(3)$, and $f(4)$?

7 **Consumer Math** The iteration diagram is for a loan repayment where payments are made monthly.
a What is the original amount of the loan?
b What is the yearly interest rate?
c What is the monthly payment?
d Write the iteration in function notation.
e How many months will it take to repay the loan?

8 How many diagonals does an 18-sided polygon have? (Hint: Look at the pattern for several polygons. Write an iteration diagram for this pattern.)

9

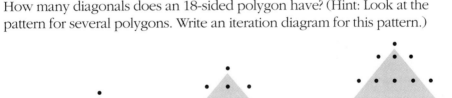

Write an iterative function to represent the total number of dots in the *n*th triangle.

10

If $f(1) = 1$, which of the following functions describes the iteration pictured in the figures above?
a $f(n + 1) = n^2$ **b** $f(n + 1) = 2n + f(n)$ **c** $f(n + 1) = 2n + 1 + f(n)$
d $f(n + 1) = 2n - 1 + f(n)$ **e** $f(n + 1) = n + 1 + f(n)$

11 It takes 12 toothpicks glued together to make a $1 \times 1 \times 1$ box.

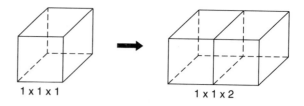

$1 \times 1 \times 1$ $1 \times 1 \times 2$

   a How many toothpicks are needed to make a $1 \times 1 \times 2$ box? A $1 \times 1 \times 3$ box? A $1 \times 1 \times 4$ box?

   b Write an iterative function for a $1 \times 1 \times n$ box.

   c Use your answer to part **b** to find the number of toothpicks needed for a $1 \times 1 \times 12$ box.

12 Suppose that $f(1) = 1$, $f(2) = 4$, $f(3) = 9$, $f(4) = 16$, $f(5) = 25$, and $f(6) = 36$.

   a Write a normal function for the pattern.

   b Write an iterative function for the pattern.

13

Chords = 0   Chords = 1 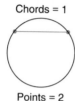 Chords = 3 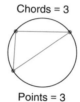 Chords = 6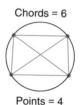

Points = 1   Points = 2   Points = 3   Points = 4

Write an iterative function for the total number of chords connecting n points on a circle. (Hint: When you add one more point, how many additional chords are added?)

14 Try using the numbers 4, 16, 11, 18 and 49 as initial inputs for the iteration diagram shown. What results do you get? It has been conjectured that for any input, this diagram will eventually produce an output of 1. Do you agree?

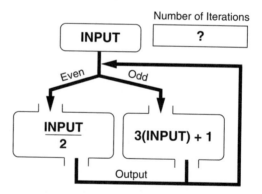

15 Copy the following table and use the iteration diagram to fill in the missing entries. What do you notice about the outputs?

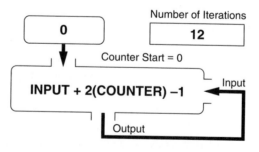

Counter	1	2	3	4	5	6	7	8	9	10	11	12
Output	1											

16 **Communicating**

a Make a table for this
iteration diagram.

b Evaluate $1 \cdot 2 \cdot 3 \cdot 4 \cdot \ldots \cdot 10$.

c Compare the result of the
tenth iteration in part **a**
with your answer in part **b**.
Why does this occur?

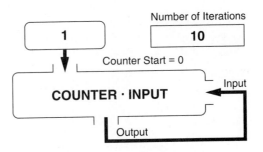

17 If $f(1) = 100$ and $f(n + 1) = 2 \cdot f(n)$, the value of $f(n)$ increases each time
the value of n increases. If $g(1) = 100$ and $g(n + 1) = g(n) - 150$, the
value of $g(n)$ decreases each time the value of n increases. If $h(1) = 100$
and $h(n + 1) = 2 \cdot h(n) - 150$, what happens to the value of $h(n)$ as the
value of n increases?

18

 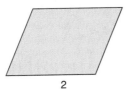

1   2   3

a What is the sum of the measures of the angles in figure 1?

b What is the sum of the measures of the angles in figure 2?

c What is the sum of the measures of the angles in figure 3?

d When a new side is added to the previous figure, by how much does
the sum of the angle measures increase?

e Write an iterative function to describe the sum of all the angles of an
n-sided figure.

f Copy and complete the table.

Number of sides	1	2	3	4	5	6	7	8	9	10
Sum of angles										

19 **Consumer Math**   At age 16, Bill deposits $10,000 in a bank account that
earns 6.5% interest per year, and he adds another $5000 each year thereafter.
At what age will Bill have a quarter of a million dollars in the bank?

20 Each day a writer writes 5% more than she did on the preceding day. If
she writes 2 pages the first day, when will she be writing more than 35
pages per day?

Investigation

Mental Math   Approximately how many years will it take to double the
money you invest if interest is compounded annually at a rate of

a 4%?   b 6%?   c 8%?   d 12%?

Find out what the "rule of 72" is and how it will allow you to solve the above
problems mentally.

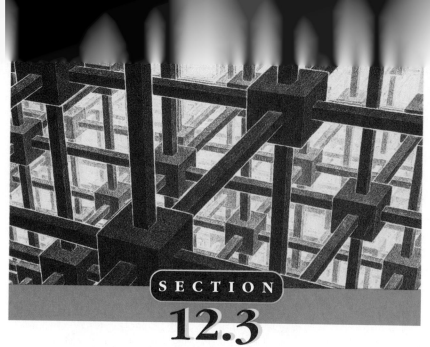

Geometric Iterations

In addition to iterating with numbers, it is possible to iterate with shapes. Consider the equilateral triangle shown, with points marked at the midpoint of each side.

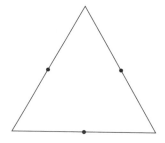

For our first iteration, we will connect the midpoints and mark the midpoints of the segments we drew. Notice that the triangle we just drew is similar to the original triangle.

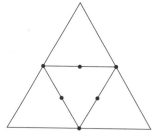

Theoretically, you can repeat this process forever, but in actual practice, after a few times the triangles become too small to draw.

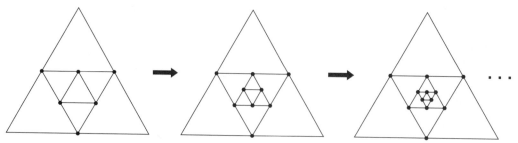

Example 1

Start with a square, ABCD. Locate a point one third of the way from A to B. Locate points in the same way on $\overline{BC}$, $\overline{CD}$, and $\overline{DA}$. Connect the points to form another square, and keep iterating in the same manner (clockwise).

Solution

We follow the instructions to form square ABCD and the square inside it.

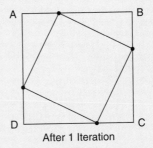

After 1 Iteration

Then we repeat the procedure with the inner square, selecting and connecting points one third of the way between consecutive vertices, in a clockwise pattern. We could repeat the process for as long as space allows.

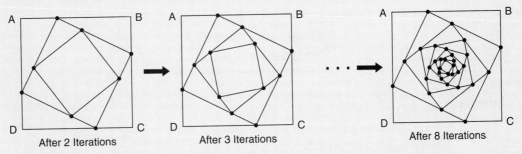

After 2 Iterations   After 3 Iterations   After 8 Iterations

What would happen if this iteration were tried on a triangle or a pentagon? What if the distance were something other than one third of the way to the next point?

In Example 1, we started with a polygon. We can also iterate with segments.

Example 2

Begin with a horizontal segment, $\overline{AB}$, as shown. At the right-hand endpoint (B), draw two segments that are the same length as $\overline{AB}$ and that form congruent (120°) angles all the way around, then draw segments parallel and congruent to $\overline{AB}$ at the right-hand endpoints of these two new segments. Repeat the process for a few iterations.

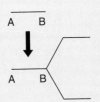

Solution

This time, the figure eventually gets too big to fit on the paper, not too small to draw.

Second Iteration   Third Iteration

How many new segments will there be in the twelfth iteration? How many segments will there be all together after 12 iterations?

Sample Problem

Problem

On a coordinate system, start at the origin, and draw a segment 1 unit long on the x-axis. Then turn left 90° and draw a segment 2 units long. For each subsequent iteration, turn left and draw a segment 1 unit longer than the one you drew last time. Continue for a while.

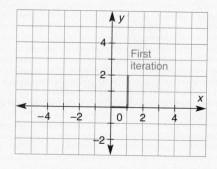

First iteration

Solution

The diagram shows the result of the first 5 iterations. Can you predict how long the segment will be that is added on at the eleventh iteration? Can you predict in which quadrant(s) it will lie? Can you predict the total length of the figure after 11 iterations? Will the fifteenth segment be horizontal? Will it be drawn from left to right?

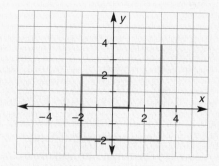

Think and Discuss

1 We are going to alter Example 2 by modifying the iteration rule. We will begin with a horizontal segment as before, and draw new segments as before, only this time their length will be half the length of the original segment. Do you think the segments will ever come together, as they did before? Will there be the same number of them as before? Will it stretch off the page if we do it enough times?

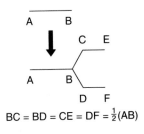

$BC = BD = CE = DF = \frac{1}{2}(AB)$

2 Suppose that the perimeter of the triangle shown at the beginning of this section is 3 units.
  a What is the perimeter of the triangle made on the first iteration? The second iteration? The third iteration?
  b Write an iterative function to describe the perimeter on the nth iteration.

3 Draw a circle. Draw a diameter. Draw two circles, each having a diameter half that of the original circle, so that the new circles are tangent to each other and to the original circle. Iterate this process several times.

4 Try the iteration procedure in Example 1 on an equilateral triangle. Start with an equilateral triangle ABC, select a point one third of the way from A to B, and repeat on $\overline{BC}$ and $\overline{CA}$. Connect these three points. Iterate several times.

Problems and Applications

5 Draw a rectangle. Locate the midpoints of all four sides. Connect them in order.
  a What shape do you get?
  b Now iterate several more times. What shapes do you get?

6 **Communicating** Consider this iteration performed on a coordinate system.
  a List the next six vertices of the right angles in the iteration.
  b What is the length of the first line segment? The second line segment? The third line segment? The fifty-fourth line segment?

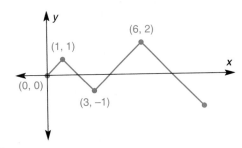

  c Does the ninety-seventh line segment slant / or \ ?
  d Is the ending vertex of the ninety-seventh line segment in the first quadrant? Explain.

7 Try the iteration scheme that generated the triangles at the beginning of this section, only this time begin with an isosceles right triangle instead of an equilateral triangle.

8 On graph paper make a large square 24 units on a side. Locate eight points on the sides that are one third of the distance from one vertex to the next vertex. Connect every other one of these to form another square. Connect the remaining four to form still another square. These two new squares intersect at eight new points. Connect every other one to form another new square and the remaining four to form yet another square. Continue this iteration process. Color the picture to form an interesting mosaic.

9 Starting at the origin of a coordinate system, draw a segment 1 unit long on the x-axis to (1, 0). Turn left 90° and draw a segment 2 units long. Turn left 90° and draw another segment 2 units long. Each iteration consists of 2 segments and 2 turns. The subsequent iterations increase the length of the segments by 1 unit. Draw ten iterations (20 segments). Which lattice points will be missed?

10 On a coordinate system, start at (0, 0) and iterate as shown. All the angles are right angles.
  a Find the coordinates of the next six points that are the vertices of the right angles.
  b What is the length of the first segment? The second segment? The third segment? The tenth segment?
  c In which direction does the seventeenth segment slant?
  d What is the total length of the first ten segments? Write an iteration diagram for this part of the problem.
  e What is the average length of the first ten segments?

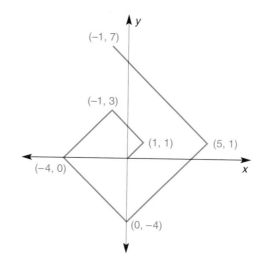

11 In this section's sample problem, which lattice points in the first quadrant does the figure pass through? Which lattice points in the first quadrant are missed? Can you think of a way to iterate that would pass through all of the first-quadrant lattice points? All of the lattice points?

Investigation

Snowflake Curve   Find out about the Koch snowflake curve. Show how it is iterated from an equilateral triangle.

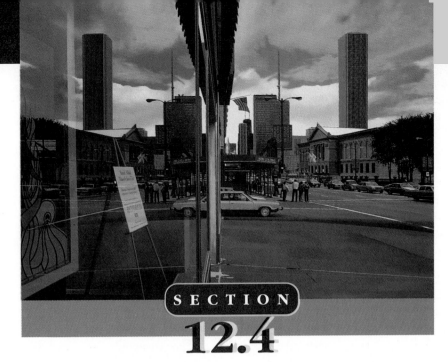

SECTION
12.4
Convergent Iterations

CONVERGENCE

Iterations that we have done thus far have been of two distinct types—those that approached closer and closer to a particular value and those that didn't. In this section, we will look more closely at those that approach a particular value. These are called **convergent** iterations.

Example 1

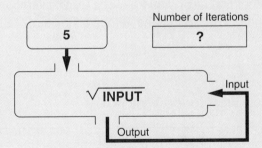

Consider the iteration diagram above. Each successive output is calculated by taking the square root of the previous output. In function notation, we can write

$$f(1) = 5$$
$$f(n) = \sqrt{f(n-1)}$$

What are the values of $f(1)$ through $f(21)$?

This could be done with a calculator, a graphing calculator, or a spreadsheet. Below are results from a spreadsheet.

Term	Value
1	5.00000
2	2.23607
3	1.49535
4	1.22284
5	1.10582
6	1.05158
7	1.02547
8	1.01265
9	1.00631
10	1.00315
11	1.00157
12	1.00079
13	1.00039
14	1.00020
15	1.00010
16	1.00005
17	1.00002
18	1.00001
19	1.00001
20	1.00000
21	1.00000

Iteration Using Square Root

Notice that as we continue iterating, the values get closer and closer to the number 1. In fact, the number we use for our initial input does not matter as long as we choose a number that has a square root. (Try this iteration with several other starting values.) We say that the iteration converges to the number 1.

We now give two intuitive ideas for convergence.

Convergence of Iterations

1. An iteration converges if after a while each output looks almost identical to the preceding output.
2. We also say an iteration converges if the input and the output become almost identical—in other words, if INPUT ≈ f(INPUT).

In some cases the convergence may happen very quickly, and in others it takes many iterations for this to occur. In some cases the iteration does not converge at all.

When an iteration converges, the number that the iteration converges to is called the **limiting value** of the iteration. The limiting value of the iteration in Example 1 was 1.

Example 2

A ball is dropped from a height of 6 feet, and each time it bounces, it rebounds to a height 75% of its preceding height.

a If we iterate the height of the bounce, does this height converge? If so, what is its limiting value?

b If we iterate the total (vertical) distance the ball travels, does this distance converge? If so, what is the limiting value?

Solution

a If we draw an iteration diagram for this problem, we see that each output is produced by multiplying the input by 0.75. We can use a spreadsheet to make a table for the first 25 bounces.

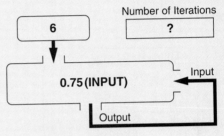

Bounce	Height (ft)
0	6.00
1	4.50
2	3.38
3	2.53
4	1.90
5	1.42
6	1.07
7	0.80
8	0.60
9	0.45
10	0.34
11	0.25
12	0.19
13	0.14
14	0.11
15	0.08
16	0.06
17	0.05
18	0.03
19	0.03
20	0.02
21	0.01
22	0.01
23	0.01
24	0.01
25	0.00

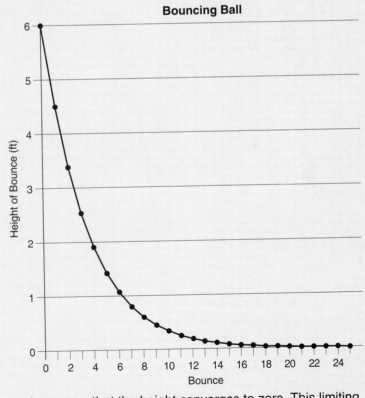

Bouncing Ball

It appears that the height converges to zero. This limiting value of zero makes sense, since the ball will eventually stop bouncing.

b The ball travels 6 feet when it is dropped. On any given bounce, it has traveled all the distance so far plus twice the height of that particular bounce.

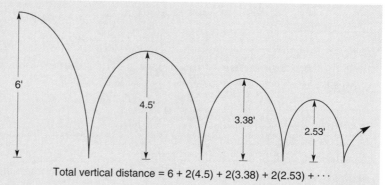

Total vertical distance = 6 + 2(4.5) + 2(3.38) + 2(2.53) + · · ·

We can add a third column to our table in part **a** to describe the results. The formula +C2+2*B3 was used to obtain the value 15.00 in cell C3.

Bounce	Height (ft)	Distance (ft)
0	6.00	6.00
1	4.50	15.00
2	3.38	21.75
3	2.53	26.81
4	1.90	30.61
5	1.42	33.46
6	1.07	35.59
7	0.80	37.19
8	0.60	38.40
9	0.45	39.30
10	0.34	39.97
11	0.25	40.48
12	0.19	40.86
13	0.14	41.14
14	0.11	41.36
15	0.08	41.52
16	0.06	41.64
17	0.05	41.73
18	0.03	41.80
19	0.03	41.85
20	0.02	41.89
21	0.01	41.91
22	0.01	41.94
23	0.01	41.95
24	0.01	41.96
25	0.00	41.97
26	0.00	41.98
27	0.00	41.98
28	0.00	41.99
29	0.00	41.99
30	0.00	41.99
31	0.00	42.00
32	0.00	42.00

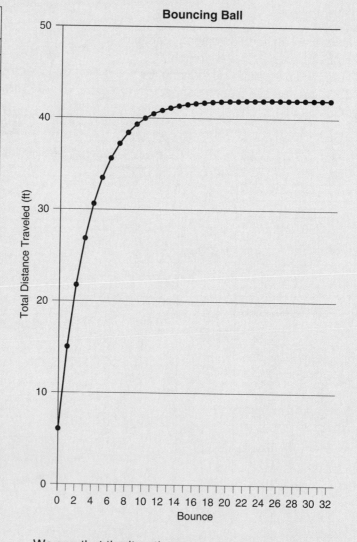

We see that the iterations seem to converge to 42 feet. The ball has a limiting distance of travel of 42 feet.

Sample Problem

Problem

Suppose you start with a ball of string at point A and unroll it along the segments. If the pattern continues in the same manner, how many meters of string must be in the ball for you to unroll it over the entire figure?

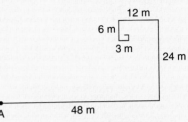

Solution

At any step, we need the amount of string we used before plus one half of the amount of string we used on the last straight piece we traced. Let's start by making a table.

Iteration	String for That Section	Total String Used
1	48 meters	48 meters
2	24 meters	72 meters = 48 + 24
3	12 meters	84 meters = 72 + 12
4	6 meters	90 meters = 84 + 6
.	.	.
.	.	.
.	.	.

We now employ a spreadsheet to simplify the work.

Segment	Length (m)	Total Length (m)
1	48.000	48.000
2	24.000	72.000
3	12.000	84.000
4	6.000	90.000
5	3.000	93.000
6	1.500	94.500
7	0.750	95.250
8	0.375	95.625
9	0.188	95.813
10	0.094	95.906
11	0.047	95.953
12	0.023	95.977
13	0.012	95.988
14	0.006	95.994
15	0.003	95.997
16	0.001	95.999
17	0.001	95.999
18	0.000	96.000
19	0.000	96.000

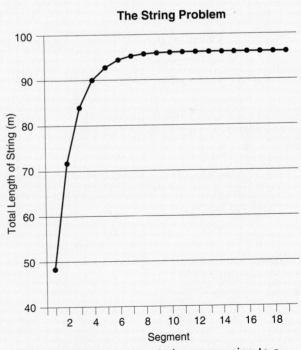

The total length seems to be converging to a limiting value of 96 meters. We need a ball that contains 96 meters of string.

Think and Discuss

1 a Use the iteration diagram to determine the outputs for ten iterations.

   b Repeat part **a** for a different positive initial input.

   c Change the 8 in the iteration rule to 64 and repeat parts **a** and **b.**

   d Try using various other positive numerators in place of the 8.

   e What does this iteration compute?

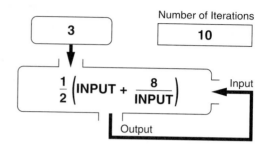

2 Repeat problem 1, but this time use negative numbers as the initial inputs. What do you notice about the convergence now?

3 a Perform iterations as shown in the diagram until you see what the limiting value is. To what value do the iterations converge?

   b Repeat part **a** with other initial inputs. Do the iterations converge to the same value as in part **a?**

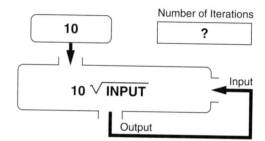

4 To what number does the following iteration function converge?

$$f(1) = 4$$
$$f(n) = f(n-1) + 3$$

5 a Duplicate this diagram on a sheet of graph paper. Then follow these steps:

   1. Put your pencil at (8, 0).
   2. Move vertically (drawing a segment) to the graph of $y = \frac{1}{2}x + 3$.
   3. Move horizontally (drawing a segment) to the graph of $y = x$.
   4. Repeat steps 2 and 3 for four iterations.
   Note: The figure of segments that you have just drawn is called a *web diagram.*

   b Make a table of the x and y values of the ordered pairs on the two lines that you "visited" in part **a.**

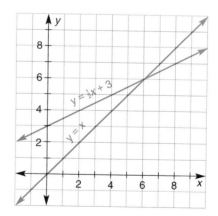

Problems and Applications

6 Repeat parts **a** and **b** of problem 5, using this diagram.

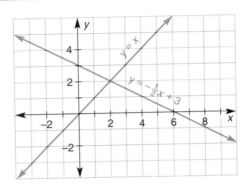

7 **Science** A swimming pool has had chlorine added to bring the chlorine concentration to 3 parts per million (3 ppm). Fifteen percent of the chlorine present on any day is lost by the next day.
a Iterate to see how much chlorine is left each day.
b The ideal concentration of chlorine in a pool is 2 ppm. If there are 3 ppm now, how much chlorine should be added each day to have the amount of chlorine converge to 2 ppm?

8 **Communicating** These are the directions on a bottle of shampoo:
   1. Put a small dab of shampoo in your hand.
   2. Work the shampoo into your hair.
   3. Rinse.
   4. Repeat.
Explain what these directions mean iteratively and what would happen if they were taken literally.

9 **Consumer Math** Bill borrows $7000 to be paid back monthly over 24 months. The yearly interest rate is 9.5%.
a What is the monthly interest rate?
b We do not know what his monthly payment is, so we do the following. We make a table of monthly payments and how much of the loan is left at the end of 24 months. Copy and complete the table.

Monthly payment	$100	$150	$200	$250	$300
Amount left at end of 24 months					

c Make a graph, using the data from part **b.** Use this graph to estimate the value of the monthly payment needed to repay the loan in 24 months.
d Use iteration to check your result in part **c.**

10 A man spent the first third of his life unmarried. After he had been married for 50 years, his wife died. Six years later, he died. How old was the man when he died? (Hint: Guess any age for an initial input and then iterate $\frac{1}{3}$(INPUT) + 50 + 6.)

11 Does this iteration converge? If so, what is the limiting value?

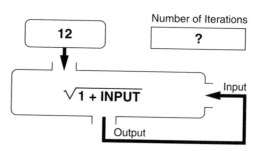

12 The imaginary substance antgrav rebounds to a height that is 115% of its height on the previous bounce. A ball of antgrav is dropped from a height of 5 feet.

   a When will it touch a ceiling that is 9 feet above the floor on which it bounces?

   b Does this iteration problem converge? Why or why not?

13 **Science** A certain prescription says to take two 500-milligram pills every 4 hours. If every 4 hours 80% of the medicine that is in the body is used up, what is the amount of medicine that remains in the body over a period of several days? (That is, what does the medicine level converge to?)

14 In each diagram, a ball begins at point A and is shot diagonally. At which point will it exit—A, B, C, or D?

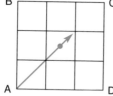

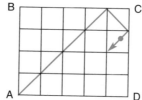

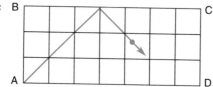

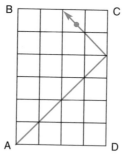

15 Draw some other diagrams like those in problem 14 and look for patterns. Try to predict conditions that will lead the ball to exit at point A, point B, point C, or point D.

16 **Science** A doctor prescribes an initial dosage of 2000 milligrams of a certain medicine. If 75% of the medicine is gone from the body one day later, what daily dosage should be given after the initial dosage in order to maintain an effective level of 1260 milligrams of medicine in the patient?

17 Sally wants to borrow $6000 and pay it back in payments of $275 per month. What is the greatest possible interest rate she could have and be able to repay the loan in 24 months?

18 Each side of the triangle is divided into equal thirds (trisected). A ball at point K is shot toward B and bounces toward F and so on. Trace the entire path of the ball. What happens?

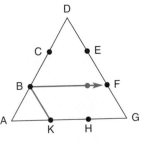

19 In the iteration diagram shown, to what value do the iterations converge?

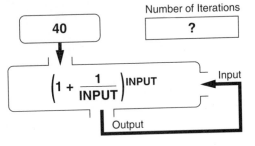

20 If the pattern of segments continues, how much string is needed to trace the entire diagram?

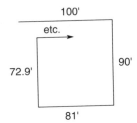

21 Consider the following two functions.

$f(1) = 47,000$
$f(n) = 0.8 \cdot f(n-1) + 0.15 \cdot g(n-1)$

$g(1) = 64,000$
$g(n) = 0.85 \cdot g(n-1) + 0.2 \cdot f(n-1)$

a Copy and complete the following table for values of n from 1 to 15.

n	1	2	3	4	5	6
f(n)						
g(n)						

b After many iterations, what do $f(n)$ and $g(n)$ converge to?

Investigation

Consumer Math   What is a mortgage? If a bank loans you money to buy a house, who is the mortgagor and who is the mortgagee? Obtain a copy of a mortgage payment schedule that shows principal and interest payments, and explain it to the class.

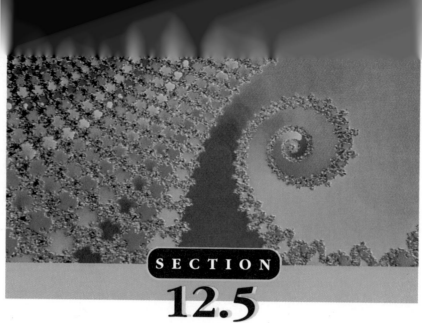

12.5
Introduction to Fractals

We now return to geometry for a look at a new and fascinating branch of mathematics. For our first example, we begin with an equilateral triangle and connect the three midpoints of its sides. This time, we also shade the center triangle.

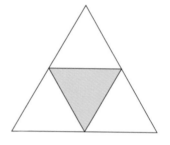

After the first iteration, there are three unshaded triangles. We now repeat the process, locating the midpoints of the sides of each unshaded triangle, connecting them, and shading each center triangle.

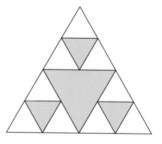

After the second iteration, there are nine unshaded triangles, so our third iteration will be done on each of these nine triangles.

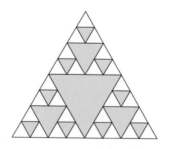

There are a few things to notice about the process.

- It is an iterative process.
- We could continue until the next set of triangles would be too small to draw. In our minds, it could continue forever. Theoretically, we could iterate infinitely many times.
- Part of the figure that is added each time an iteration is completed is similar to the previous picture. This property is called **self-similarity.** (Notice that the red portion of the third iteration is similar to the entire figure of the second iteration.)

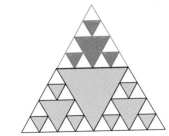

In general, if we continue this process on a figure that has the three properties listed above, the figure converges to a figure that is called a **fractal.** If we continue iterating, eventually the figure shown here appears. This figure is called the Sierpinski triangle, after the Polish mathematician, Waclaw Sierpinski, who first introduced it.

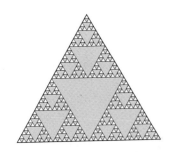

It is also possible to generate fractal curves by iterating line segments. For our example, we begin with a segment that has been divided into three congruent parts.

For our initial step, we remove the center segment and replace it with two segments that are equal in length to the segment removed. We place them as shown in the figure, to form two sides of an equilateral triangle. The segment we removed would have been the third side.

Now we iterate by repeating the same procedure on each of the four segments in the new diagram.

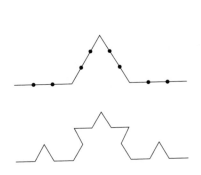

As before, we continue to iterate. Notice that the three properties of a fractal are present.

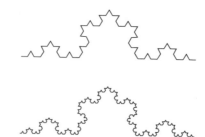

If we had started with an equilateral triangle and had iterated each side of the triangle in the same manner as the single segment, the curve generated would be the Koch snowflake, named after the Swedish mathematician, Helge von Koch.

The study of fractals began in about 1900 but did not become a major topic until the early 1970's, when computers made it possible to draw the complicated pictures in a reasonable period of time. Fractal geometry is closely connected with chaos theory, a rapidly developing branch of science.

The best way to learn about fractal geometry is to create your own fractal curve. Try this one. Draw a long line segment down the center of a sheet of paper. Find its midpoint and draw two segments from the midpoint, each half as long as the segment and making 120° angles with the bottom half of the segment. You should now have four congruent segments. Repeat the iterative process on each of these four, and then again on the new segments produced. Continue for as long as you can.

Sample Problem

Problem   What is the pattern for the number of shaded triangles in the Sierpinski triangle?

Solution   Going back and looking at successive pictures, we notice that the first few numbers are 1, 4, and 13. We could just play with the patterns as we did in Chapter 1. Perhaps a more effective approach is to think about what is happening each time we iterate.

We start with 1 triangle shaded and 3 unshaded. Each of the 3 unshaded triangles yields 1 shaded and 3 unshaded triangles. The shaded total is 1 + 3, or 4. The unshaded total is 3 · 3, or 9. At the next iteration, each of the 9 unshaded triangles again yields 1 shaded and 3 unshaded triangles. The shaded total is 4 + 9, or 13. The unshaded total is 3 · 9, or 27.

	Shaded	Total Shaded	Total Unshaded
Begin	1	1	3
Iterate	+3	4	9
Iterate	+9	13	27
Iterate	+27	40	81
Iterate	+81	121	243

It looks difficult to generate a single formula, but we can generate an iterative function for the number of shaded triangles after n iterations.

$$f(1) = 1$$
$$f(n) = f(n-1) + 3^n$$

Let's put it on a spreadsheet and see what happens. Notice that after only a few iterations, there is quite a large number of triangles. Perhaps you guessed a formula for the number of triangles after n iterations.

	A Step	B Shaded	C Unshaded
1	Step	Shaded	Unshaded
2	1	1	3
3	2	4	9
4	3	13	27
5	4	40	81
6	5	121	243
7	6	364	729
8	7	1093	2187
9	8	3280	6561
10	9	9841	19683
11	10	29524	59049
12	11	88573	177147
13	12	265720	531441
14	13	797161	1594323
15	14	2391484	4782969
16	15	7174453	14348907
17	16	21523360	43046721
18	17	64570081	129140163
19	18	193710244	387420489

Think and Discuss

1   Begin with the legs of an isosceles right triangle, $\overline{AB}$ and $\overline{BC}$. Locate the midpoints, M and N. Replace $\angle MBN$ with $\angle MDN$ as shown. Iterate on all the remaining right angles in the same manner. Repeat for at least two more iterations. Draw the resulting diagrams. If AB = 4, find the total length of the segments in each iteration.

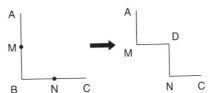

2   Draw a square. Divide it into nine congruent squares and color four of them as shown in the diagram. Iterate on the remaining noncolored squares. Do two more iterations.

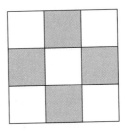

3 a Draw a regular pentagon. (Hint: Start with a circle and divide it into five equal parts.)

b Draw all five diagonals. Notice that you get another pentagon formed in the center of the original pentagon.

c Iterate by drawing the diagonals of this inner pentagon. Repeat one more time. Is this self-similar?

Problems and Applications

4 An L-shaped figure can be divided into four congruent L shapes as shown. Shade one of the four pieces as shown and iterate the unshaded L-shaped figures. Repeat several times. Is the figure self-similar?

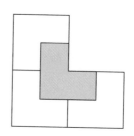

5 Do the Sierpinski triangle iteration scheme on an isosceles right triangle. Do three iterations.

6 Begin with a semicircle. Replace it with two semicircles as shown. If the length of the first semicircle is 16π, find the length of the curve formed on each iteration for the first five iterations.

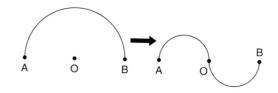

7 Do the Koch snowflake iteration using squares instead of triangles. The first iteration is shown.

8 a Find the missing sums.

b How are the numbers to the left of the equal signs related to the Sierpinski triangle?

$$1 = 1$$
$$4 = 1 + 3$$
$$13 = 1 + 3 + 3^2$$
$$\underline{} = 1 + 3 + 3^2 + 3^3$$
$$\underline{} = 1 + 3 + 3^2 + 3^3 + 3^4$$
$$\underline{} = 1 + 3 + 3^2 + 3^3 + 3^4 + 3^5$$

9 a Find the numbers in the fifth level of the tree diagram.

b Find the sum of the numbers at each level.

c How are the sums in part **b** related to the Sierpinski triangle?

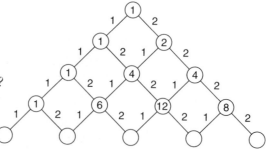

10 On graph paper begin at $(0, 0)$ and make a path in the following manner: Move 16 units up, turn right, move 27 units right, turn right, move 8 units down, turn right, move 9 units left, turn right, move 4 units up, turn right, and move 3 units right. Continue in this pattern. What unique point does this pattern spiral toward?

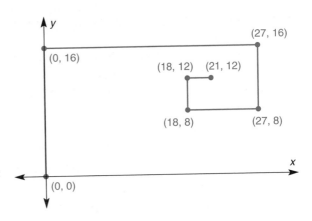

11 Start with an 8-inch-by-8-inch square. Divide it into four squares as shown, coloring the upper left square red and the lower right square blue. Iterate in the same manner on the remaining two uncolored squares.

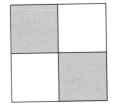

  a Copy and complete the following table.

Iteration	0	1	2	3	4
Blue area shaded on this iteration	0 in.²	16 in.²			
Total blue area shaded so far	0 in.²	16 in.²			
Red area shaded on this iteration	0 in.²	16 in.²			
Total red area shaded so far	0 in.²	16 in.²			

  b What does the total blue area converge to? The total red area? What happens to the picture as the blue and red areas converge?

12 If the largest equilateral triangle in the diagram is 1 inch on each side and if the "spiral" shown is continued indefinitely, what will be the total length of the spiral?

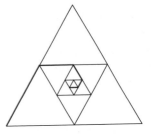

Investigation

Technology Talk to someone who knows how to program computers. See if you can come up with a program that can be used to generate the Sierpinski triangle, and demonstrate the program to the class.

CHAPTER 12

Summary

CONCEPTS AND PROCEDURES

After studying this chapter, you should be able to

- Recognize iterative processes (12.1)
- Interpret and construct iteration diagrams (12.1)
- Recognize situations in which an iterative calculation involves the number of preceding iterations (12.2)
- Express an iterative process in function notation (12.2)
- Perform iterative procedures on geometric figures (12.3)
- Recognize convergent iterations (12.4)
- Identify the limiting value of a convergent iteration (12.4)
- Identify the characteristics of a fractal (12.5)

VOCABULARY

convergent (12.4)
fractal (12.5)
iteration (12.1)
iteration diagram (12.1)
limiting value (12.4)
self-similarity (12.5)

Review

1 a Use the iteration diagram to make a table of values for the indicated number of iterations.

b Change the initial input to +25 and repeat part **a**.

c What changes when you switch from a negative initial input to a positive initial input? Why?

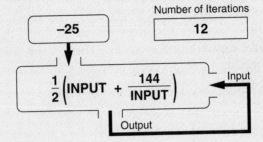

Number of Iterations

2 At the beginning of the quarter, Mr. Tuff Teacher lets his students choose how much homework they will be assigned. "You have two options," he says. "I will give you 45 minutes of homework daily, or I will give you 1 second of homework tonight, 2 seconds of homework tomorrow, 4 seconds the next day, and so forth." If Mr. Teacher's class meets 35 times per quarter, how many hours of homework would his students have under each option?

3 A new automobile decreases in value each year by about 13% of its value the previous year. Assume that a new Mitsundai car costs $17,500.

a Make an iteration diagram to describe this situation.

b Make a table to show the value of a Mitsundai each year for ten years.

c When will a Mitsundai be worth only 50% of its original value?

4 The following function can be used to calculate the amount of a loan that remains to be repaid.

$$f(0) = 5000$$
$$f(n) = f(n-1) + \frac{0.0875}{12} \cdot f(n-1) - 257$$

a What is the amount of the loan?

b What is the yearly interest rate?

c What is the monthly payment?

d How many payments are required to entirely pay off the loan?

5 For this iteration diagram, make a table showing the relationship between the counter number and the output.

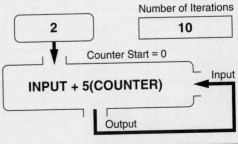

6 Each time a ball bounces, it rebounds to 75% of its height on the previous rebound. The ball was initially dropped from the top of a building 35 feet high.

  a Make a table of bounce number versus rebound height for this problem. When does the ball bounce less than 1 foot high?

  b Make a table to describe the total distance that the ball has traveled for a given number of bounces. (Hint: A spreadsheet might be useful here. Remember that on each bounce, the ball goes both up and down.)

7 Study the following pattern of toothpick figures.

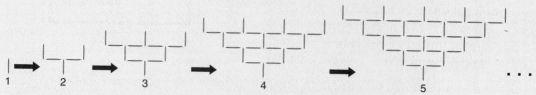

1   2   3   4   5

  a Make a table showing the relationship between the number of the figure and the number of toothpicks required to make the figure.

  b How many toothpicks would be required for the fifteenth figure?

  c Write an iterative function to describe the number of toothpicks necessary to make each figure.

8

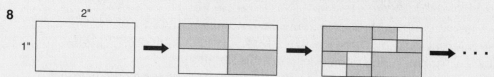

  a Iterate the figure for two more iterations.

  b Does this process satisfy the three conditions necessary for a fractal iteration? Explain your answer.

  c If the iteration is continued indefinitely, what will be the sum of the areas of the shaded sections?

9 Consider the iterations shown. Each horizontal segment is exactly one half as long as the preceding horizontal segment. Each vertical segment is exactly one third as long as the preceding vertical segment.

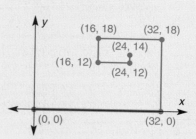

  a List the coordinates of the next three vertices of the figure.

  b How long will the tenth horizontal segment be? The tenth vertical segment?

  c What does the sum of the lengths of the horizontal segments converge to? What does the sum of the lengths of the vertical segments converge to? If the iterations continued forever, what would be the total length of all the segments in the diagram?

  d To what point does the diagram converge?

10 a Copy the following table, using the iteration diagram to complete it.

Iteration	Output
0	
1	
2	
3	
4	
5	
6	
7	

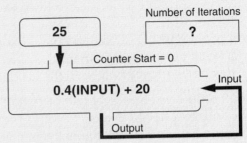

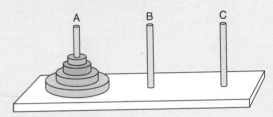

b To what number do the iterations converge if continued forever?

11 In the game Tower of Hanoi, the disks on peg A must be moved from that peg to peg C, using peg B to help. The only rules are (1) you may move only one disk at a time and (2) no disk may be placed on top of a smaller disk.

The number of moves needed to complete a game of Tower of Hanoi depends on the number of disks initially placed on peg A. For one disk, it takes only one move, so $f(1) = 1$. For n disks, we must move $n - 1$ disks from peg A to peg B, then the lowest disk from peg A to peg C, and then the $n - 1$ disks from peg B to peg C—that is, $f(n) = 2 \cdot f(n - 1) + 1$.

a Copy the following table, using the iterative function described above to complete it.

Number of disks	1	2	3	4	5	6	7
Total number of moves	1	3					

b Write the iterative function as an iteration diagram.

12 There are 60,000 people in Algebraville and 42,000 people in Geometry Town. Each year, 20% of the population of Algebraville moves to Geometry Town, and 16% of the population of Geometry Town moves to Algebraville. Assume that the rest of the people do not move at all.

a Copy and complete the table.
b Write iterative functions for both Algebraville and Geometry Town.
c At what population does each town converge?

Year	Population of Algebraville	Population of Geometry Town
0	60,000	42,000
1		
2		
3		
4		
5		

Test

1 Paul puts $1000 into a bank account that pays 5.5% interest per year.
  a Make an iteration diagram for this situation.
  b How much money will be in the account after eight years?

2 A ball is dropped from a height of 16 feet. Each time it bounces, it rebounds to a height that is 75% of its previous height.
  a After what bounce will the ball first fail to reach a height of 2 feet?
  b What is the total distance the ball will travel before coming to rest?

3 Peggy was offered a job for which she would be paid $0.01 the first day, $0.03 the second day, $0.09 the third day, and so forth. On which day would she first be paid more than $20.00?

4

   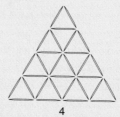

1   2   3   4

It takes 3 toothpicks to make the first figure, 9 to make the second, 18 to make the third, and 30 to make the fourth. How many toothpicks are needed to make the eighth figure?

5 Stephen puts $700 in a bank account that pays 5.5% interest per year. At the start of each year thereafter, he adds $500 to the account.
  a Write an iterative function to describe this situation.
  b How much money will be in the account at the start of the seventh year?

6 If $f(0) = 3$ and $f(n) = f(n-1) + n^2 + 2$, what is $f(8)$?

7 Draw a square, ABCD. Then connect midpoints of adjacent sides to form another square. Iterate on the innermost square two more times. If ABCD has a side length of 20 cm, what is the area of the innermost square after the three iterations?

8 If $f(1) = 5$ and $f(n) = \dfrac{f(n-1)}{n}$, do the outputs of the function converge? If they do, what is the limiting value?

9 Start at the origin of a coordinate system. For the first iteration, draw a segment 1 unit long along the negative y-axis, then turn right. For each subsequent iteration, draw a segment 2 units longer than the preceding iteration's, then turn right. Continue iterating for a while. How long will the segment drawn on the fifteenth iteration be? At what point will that segment end?

A kind of word puzzle you may not be familiar with is called the **cryptic crossword clue.** In this kind of clue, a word is both defined and given a wordplay clue. The number in parentheses is the number of letters in the word.

Examples

Clues: **a** To desire half a loaf is no good (4)

b Weird tone is live on video receiver (10)

c Sounds like buckets turn ashen (5)

Answers: **a** LONG ("To desire" is a definition of "long." The wordplay part is "half a loaf" or *lo* followed by *ng* for "no good.")

b TELEVISION ("Weird" implies an anagram of "tone is live" and a video receiver is a definition of television.)

c PALES (Buckets are pails. "Sounds like" implies a homonym. "Turn ashen" means pales.)

See if you can figure out these cryptic clues:

1 Mixed-up life wears down fingernails (4)

2 Auto weighing 2000 pounds in a package (6)

3 Silly lab gear in a mathematical discipline (7)

4 Chief school person is basic, I hear (9)

5 Live outdoors first half of run for office (4)

6 Proper speech and weird beam of light give meaning (10)

7 Sounds like totals includes minute measures occasionally (9)

8 Book of maps holds up the world (5)

Try to make up some cryptic clues of your own.

1: PLACE VALUE

The value that a digit represents depends on where the digit appears. For example, the 7 in 375 represents 70, and the 3 represents 300. In expanded notation, we can write

$$375 = 3(100) + 7(10) + 5.$$

We can also write decimals in expanded notation.

$$38.64 = 3(10) + 8 + 6(0.1) + 4(0.01)$$

Refer to the following place-value chart as you study examples 1–3. The chart shows the place value for each digit in the number 1,369,028.457.

Place-Value Chart

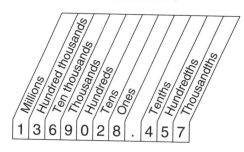

Example 1 Find the place value of the 4 in the number 14,982.

Solution The 4 is in the thousands place. Its value is 4,000.

Example 2 Find the place value of the 3 in the number 25.73.

Solution The 3 is in the hundredths place. Its value is 0.03.

Example 3 Use expanded notation to write 12,674.8.

Solution 12,674.8 = 1(10,000) + 2(1,000) + 6(100) + 7(10) + 4 + 8(0.1)

2: ROUNDING

The *Morning Herald* newspaper said that the city's education budget was $76 million. The exact amount of the school budget was $76,329,104. The paper had rounded the figure to the nearest million.

To round to a certain place value, look at the digit to the right of that place. If the digit is 5 or greater, round the number up by increasing the digit in the rounding place by 1 and changing all numbers to the right of it to 0. If the digit is less than 5, round down; that is, leave the digit in the rounding place unchanged and include zeros to the right of the rounding place as needed.

Example 1   Round 47,508 to the nearest thousand.

Solution   The digit in the thousands place is 7.
The digit to the right of the thousands place is 5.
5 fits the rule for rounding up. It is 5 or greater.
Answer: 47,508 rounded to the nearest thousand is 48,000.

Example 2   Round 8.123 to the nearest tenth.

Solution   The digit in the tenths place is 1.
The digit to the right of the tenths place is 2.
Since 2 is less than 5, round down.
Answer: 8.123 rounded to the nearest tenth is 8.1.

3: SIMPLIFYING FRACTIONS AND MIXED NUMBERS

Equivalent Fractions

A fraction shows a part of something. If the numerator and denominator of a fraction have a common factor, then the fraction can be reduced to an equivalent fraction that has a smaller denominator. When the numerator and denominator have no common factors other than 1, the fraction is in lowest terms, or simplest form.

Example 1   The total floor area of a school is 16,000 square feet. The library has a floor area of 2,000 square feet. In lowest terms, what fractional part of the school's floor space does the library take up?

Solution $\dfrac{\text{Library area}}{\text{Total area}} = \dfrac{2{,}000}{16{,}000} = \dfrac{2000(1)}{2000(8)} = \dfrac{1}{8}$

Example 2 Reduce $\frac{75}{45}$ to lowest terms.

Solution 15 is a common factor of 75 and 45.

Dividing by the common factor: $\frac{75}{45} = \frac{75 \div 15}{45 \div 15} = \frac{5}{3}$

The fraction $\frac{5}{3}$ is in lowest terms.

Converting mixed numbers and improper fractions

A mixed number is a number that includes both a whole number and a fraction, such as $2\frac{3}{5}$. An improper fraction is a fraction, such as $\frac{13}{5}$, in which the numerator is larger than the denominator. Mixed numbers can be converted to improper fractions, and improper fractions can be converted to mixed numbers.

Example 3 Alicia is preparing quarter-pound packages of cheese in the food market. She uses $3\frac{1}{4}$ pounds of cheese to prepare 13 quarter-pound packages. Show that these two amounts are equal.

Solution Converting from improper fraction to mixed number:

13 quarters is $\frac{13}{4}$.

Convert by dividing. $\frac{13}{4} = 3\frac{1}{4}$

Converting from mixed number to improper fraction:

There are 4 quarters in each pound.

So $3\frac{1}{4} = \frac{(3 \times 4 + 1)}{4} = \frac{13}{4}$.

4: ADDING AND SUBTRACTING FRACTIONS AND MIXED NUMBERS WITH COMMON DENOMINATORS

When you add fractions with common denominators, the denominator remains the same for the sum. Add the numerators, then simplify the resulting fraction if possible.

To add mixed numbers, add the whole number parts and the fraction parts separately and then simplify the resulting mixed number.

Example 1   The first part of a triathlon is a swim of $1\frac{3}{10}$ miles. The second part is a run of $3\frac{5}{10}$ miles. The third part is a bike ride of $20\frac{7}{10}$ miles. What is the total distance of the race?

Solution   We add to find the answer.

$$1\frac{3}{10}$$
$$3\frac{5}{10}$$
$$+\ 20\frac{7}{10}$$
$$24\frac{15}{10} = 24 + 1\frac{5}{10} = 25\frac{5}{10} = 25\frac{1}{2} \text{ miles}$$

To subtract fractions with common denominators, you keep the same denominator and subtract the numerators. Then, if possible, simplify the resulting fraction. With a mixed number, if you cannot subtract the fraction part, then you must rename the number. To rename, you take 1 from the whole number, convert 1 to a fraction and add it to the fraction part of the mixed number. In the following example, $\frac{5}{8}$ is less than $\frac{7}{8}$, so we rename $13\frac{5}{8}$ as $12\frac{13}{8}$ so we can subtract.

Example 2   Beth was framing a picture. She had a piece of glass $13\frac{5}{8}$ inches wide. She cut off a piece that was $2\frac{7}{8}$ inches wide. How wide was the remaining piece?

Solution   You must subtract fraction from fraction and whole number from whole number:

$$13\frac{5}{8} \rightarrow 12\frac{13}{8} \qquad \text{Rename. } 1 = \frac{8}{8} \text{ and } \frac{8}{8} + \frac{5}{8} = \frac{13}{8}$$
$$-2\frac{7}{8} \rightarrow -2\frac{7}{8} \qquad \text{Subtract whole numbers and fractions.}$$
$$10\frac{6}{8} = 10\frac{3}{4} \text{ inches, the width of the remaining piece.}$$

5: ADDING AND SUBTRACTING FRACTIONS AND MIXED NUMBERS WITH DIFFERENT DENOMINATORS

To add or subtract fractions with different denominators, one or more of the fractions must be converted so that the fractions have a common denominator.

The least common denominator (LCD) of a set of fractions is the smallest number that is a multiple of all of the denominators. The LCD of two fractions can be found by writing the multiples of the larger denominator and finding the smallest multiple that is divisible by the smaller denominator.

Example 1   Find the least common denominator and add the two fractions. Simplify the answer.

$$\frac{1}{2} + \frac{3}{5} = ?$$ The LCD for 2 and 5 is 10.

Solution $\frac{1}{2} \rightarrow \frac{5}{10}$ $\frac{1}{2} \cdot \frac{5}{5} = \frac{5}{10}$

$+\frac{3}{5} \rightarrow +\frac{6}{10}$ $\frac{3}{5} \cdot \frac{2}{2} = \frac{6}{10}$

$\frac{11}{10} = 1\frac{1}{10}$

Example 2   On Monday Carlos swims $\frac{5}{8}$ of a mile and on Tuesday he swims $\frac{3}{4}$ of a mile. What is the total distance he swims during the two days?

Solution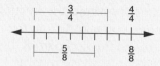

The LCD is 8. So convert $\frac{3}{4}$ to eighths: $\frac{3}{4} = \frac{3 \cdot 2}{4 \cdot 2} = \frac{6}{8}$.

$\frac{3}{4} + \frac{5}{8} = \frac{6}{8} + \frac{5}{8} = \frac{11}{8}$ or $1\frac{3}{8}$ miles

Example 3   Find the least common denominator and add the two fractions. Simplify the answer.

$$2\frac{5}{12} + 5\frac{7}{8} = ?$$ The LCD for 12 and 8 is 24.

Solution $2\frac{5}{12} \rightarrow 2\frac{10}{24}$ $\frac{5}{12} \cdot \frac{2}{2} = \frac{10}{24}$

$+5\frac{7}{8} \rightarrow +5\frac{21}{24}$ $\frac{7}{8} \cdot \frac{3}{3} = \frac{21}{24}$

$7\frac{31}{24} = 8\frac{7}{24}$

You can check addition of fractions by using a calculator to evaluate both sides of the equation. For Example 3, $\left(2 + \frac{5}{12}\right) + \left(5 + \frac{7}{8}\right) = 8.2916\overline{6}$, and $8 + \frac{7}{24} = 8.291\overline{6}$.

When subtracting either fractions or mixed numbers with different denominators, you should find the least common denominator, convert the fractions to equivalent fractions with the LCD, then do the subtraction.

Example 4 Subtract $2\frac{5}{6}$ from $7\frac{2}{5}$.

Solution The least common denominator of 6 and 5 is 30. Each fraction must be converted to an equivalent fraction with denominator 30.

$$7\frac{2}{5} \rightarrow 7\frac{12}{30} \rightarrow 7\frac{12}{30} = 6 + \frac{30}{30} + \frac{12}{30} = 6\frac{42}{30}$$
$$-2\frac{5}{6} \rightarrow -2\frac{25}{30} \rightarrow \qquad\qquad\qquad -2\frac{25}{30}$$
$$\qquad\qquad\qquad\qquad\qquad\qquad\qquad\qquad 4\frac{17}{30}$$

You can check this answer by doing the subtraction on a scientific calculator, then evaluating the answer as a decimal to see that the result is the same.

$$\left(7 + \frac{2}{5}\right) - \left(2 + \frac{5}{6}\right) = 4.5\overline{6}$$
$$4 + \frac{17}{30} = 4.5\overline{6}$$

6: MULTIPLYING FRACTIONS AND MIXED NUMBERS

To multiply fractions, multiply numerator by numerator and denominator by denominator.

Example 1 Of the land in Fairfax County, $\frac{5}{8}$ is used for farming. Of the farmland, $\frac{3}{4}$ is used for dairy farms. What fractional part of the county is used for dairy farming?

Solution $\frac{5}{8} \times \frac{3}{4} = \frac{15}{32}$

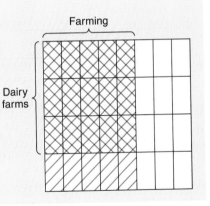

If there are common factors in the numerators and denominators, you can either multiply the fractions, then simplify, or divide out common factors, then multiply.

Example 2 Multiply $\frac{9}{2} \times \frac{4}{15}$.

Solution **Method 1** $\overset{3}{\underset{1}{\cancel{\frac{9}{2}}}} \times \overset{2}{\underset{5}{\cancel{\frac{4}{15}}}} = \frac{6}{5} = 1\frac{1}{5}$

Method 2 $\frac{9}{2} \times \frac{4}{15} = \frac{36}{30} = \frac{6}{5} = 1\frac{1}{5}$

To multiply mixed numbers, convert to improper fractions, then multiply.

Example 3 Multiply $5\frac{3}{4} \times 2\frac{1}{3}$.

Solution $5\frac{3}{4} \times 2\frac{1}{3} = \frac{23}{4} \times \frac{7}{3} = \frac{161}{12} = 13\frac{5}{12}$

The results of multiplication can be checked using a calculator.

$$\left(5 + \frac{3}{4}\right) \times \left(2 + \frac{1}{3}\right) = 13.41\overline{6}$$

$$13\frac{5}{12} = 13.41\overline{6}$$

7: DIVIDING FRACTIONS AND MIXED NUMBERS

Dividing by a number is the same as multiplying by the reciprocal of the number. The reciprocal of a number is the number that, when multiplied by the original number, will equal 1. The reciprocal of $\frac{4}{5}$ is $\frac{5}{4}$, so dividing by $\frac{4}{5}$ is the same as multiplying by $\frac{5}{4}$.

You can see this if you consider the following equations and expressions.

$$80 \div 2 = 40 \qquad 80 \times \frac{1}{2} = 40$$

$$50 \div \frac{1}{3} \text{ is equivalent to } 50 \times 3.$$

To divide one fraction by another, multiply by the reciprocal of the divisor.

Example 1 The eighth-grade class is dividing 15 pounds of candy into $\frac{3}{4}$-pound packages. How many packages will the class have?

Solution Divide 15 by $\frac{3}{4}$.

$15 \div \frac{3}{4} = 15 \times \frac{4}{3}$ Multiply by the reciprocal.

$\qquad = 20$

The class will have 20 packages.

8: RATIO AND PROPORTION

A ratio is a comparison of two numbers that uses division. A ratio may be written in different ways. The ratio of 2 to 3 may be written 2:3 or $\frac{2}{3}$.

Example 1 Write the ratio 42 to 56 as a fraction in lowest terms.

Solution $\frac{42}{56} = \frac{3}{4}$

A proportion shows the equality of two ratios. For example, $\frac{3}{4} = \frac{6}{8}$. Notice that if $\frac{a}{b} = \frac{c}{d}$, then $ad = bc$. This is called cross-multiplying. When you cross-multiply with the proportion $\frac{3}{4} = \frac{6}{8}$, you get $6 \times 4 = 8 \times 3 = 24$.

When three out of four terms in a proportion are known, you can find the fourth term by solving the equation.

Example 2 Solve the proportion $\frac{5}{12} = \frac{x}{18}$.

Solution

$$5 \cdot 18 = 12x \quad \text{Cross multiply.}$$
$$90 = 12x \quad \text{Solve.}$$
$$x = 7.5$$

Example 3 A recipe calls for $3\frac{1}{2}$ cups of flour to make 20 muffins. How much flour is needed to make 50 muffins?

Solution We use a proportion that relates cups of flour to muffins.

$$\frac{3.5}{20} = \frac{x}{50}$$

$$3.5 \cdot 50 = 20x$$

$$20x = 175$$

$$x = 8.75 \quad \text{To make 50 muffins you will need } 8\frac{3}{4} \text{ cups of flour.}$$

9: CONVERTING FRACTIONS, DECIMALS, AND PERCENTS

Any rational number can be written as a fraction, a decimal, or a percent.

For example:

$$\frac{1}{2} = 0.5 = 50\%$$

$$\frac{5}{8} = 0.625 = 62.5\%$$

$$2 = \frac{2}{1} = 2.0 = 200\%$$

Converting a fraction to a decimal and to a percent

To convert a fraction to a decimal, divide the numerator by the denominator and round to the desired place value.

Example 1 Convert to decimals, then to percents.
(a) $\frac{3}{4}$ (b) $\frac{2}{3}$

Solution (a) $\frac{3}{4}$ means $3 \div 4$.

Thus, $\frac{3}{4} = 0.75 = 75\%$.

(b) $\frac{2}{3} = 0.66 \ldots = 66.66 \ldots \%$

The answer can be written as $66.\overline{6}\%$, where the bar means that the 6 repeats. Or you can round the answer to 66.67%, 66.7%, or 67% depending on the amount of precision you want.

A mixed number can be converted to a decimal by separating the whole number from the fraction, converting the fraction to a decimal, then combining the whole number and the decimal. Since *percent* means "parts out of 100," a decimal is converted to a percent by multiplying by 100. An easy way to do this is to move the decimal point two places to the right. This procedure creates a number that is 100 times larger than the decimal number.

Example 2   Convert $1\frac{3}{7}$ to a decimal rounded to the nearest thousandth, and convert the decimal to a percent.

Solution $1\frac{3}{7} = 1 + \frac{3}{7} = 1 + 0.4286 = 1.429$

$1.429 = 142.9\%$ Multiply the decimal by 100.

Converting a percent to a decimal and a fraction

Percent means "parts out of 100," so 8% means 8 out of 100. This percent can be written as a decimal, 0.08. You can convert any percent to a decimal by removing the percent sign and dividing by 100.

Example 3   Convert to decimals, then to fractions.
  (a) 25%   **(b)** 7.5%   **(c)** 300%

Solution   **(a)** 25% $\rightarrow$ $0.25 = \frac{25}{100} = \frac{1}{4}$

  (b) 7.5% $\rightarrow$ $0.075 = \frac{75}{1000} = \frac{3}{40}$

  (c) 300% $\rightarrow$ $\frac{300}{100} = 3$

Equivalent fractions, decimals, and percents

The table shows some equivalent fractions, decimals, and percents. Working with percents will be much easier for you if you are familiar with most of these basic conversions.

Fraction	Decimal	Percent
$\frac{1}{100}$	0.01	1%
$\frac{1}{10}$	0.1	10%
$\frac{1}{8}$	0.125	12.5%
$\frac{1}{5}$	0.2	20%
$\frac{1}{4}$	0.25	25%
$\frac{1}{3}$	$0.\overline{3}$	$33\frac{1}{3}\%$
$\frac{1}{2}$	0.5	50%

10: USING PERCENT

Finding a percent of a number

To find a percent of a number, change the percent to a decimal and multiply the decimal by the number. A method that works for all percent problems is to use the linear equation $pN = A$. In this equation, p is the percent rate, N is the base number, and A is the percent amount. If p is a percent rate less than 100%, then A will be less than N.

Example 1   Find the amount of sales tax on an item selling for $30 if the sales tax rate is 7.5%.

Solution   The percent rate, p, is 7.5%. The base number, N, is 30. Find A.

$$p \times N = A$$
$$0.075 \times 30 = 2.25 \quad \text{The sales tax is \$2.25.}$$

Example 2   Find 110% of 400.

Solution   The percent rate, p, is 110%. The base number, N, is 400. Find A.

$$p \times N = A$$
$$1.1 \times 400 = 440$$

Finding what percent one number is of another

You have seen how the percent equation can be used to find the percent amount. The same equation can be used to find the percent rate when the base number and the percent amount are known. The solution will be in decimal form. You then convert this decimal to a percent.

Example 3   Ian had 56 items correct on a test with 80 items. What percent of the items did he have correct?

Solution   The percent amount is 56. The base number is 80. Find p.

$$p \times N = A$$
$$p \times 80 = 56$$
$$p = \frac{56}{80} = 0.7 \rightarrow 70\%$$

56 is 70% of 80.   Ian had 70% of the items correct.

Example 4 What percent of 78 is 120?

Solution
$$p \times N = A$$
$$p \times 78 = 120$$
$$p = \frac{120}{78} = 1.54 \rightarrow 154\%$$

Finding the number when a percent amount is known

The same equation used to find the percent and percent amount can be used to find the base number. You substitute values for p and A, and then you solve the equation.

Example 5 94.5 is 125% of what number?

Solution   The percent rate is 125%. The percent amount is 94.5. Find N.
$$p \times N = A$$
$$1.25 \times N = 94.5$$
$$N = 94.5 \div 1.25 = 75.6$$

11: SQUARE ROOTS

Because $6 \times 6 = 36$, we say that 6 is the *square root* of 36. Square roots are always positive numbers.

To find a square root on some scientific calculators, you press the square-root key after pressing the number. On other scientific calculators, you press the square-root key and then the number. When you are taking the square root of a sum or difference, it is important to use calculator grouping symbols so that you will find the correct square root.

Example 1 Find $\sqrt{78}$.

Solution   Using a calculator, you will find that $\sqrt{78} \approx 8.83$ or 8.8.

Example 2 Find the value of $\sqrt{26^2 + 30^2}$.

Solution   Use the appropriate grouping symbols.
$$\sqrt{26^2 + 30^2} = \sqrt{(26^2 + 30^2)} \approx 39.7$$

12: EXPONENTS

In the expression 3^4, we call 3 the base and 4 the exponent.

Example 1 Write each expression using exponents.
(a) $2 \cdot 2 \cdot 2 \cdot 2 \cdot 2$ **(b)** $a \cdot a \cdot a$

Solution **(a)** $2 \cdot 2 \cdot 2 \cdot 2 \cdot 2 = 2^5$ **(b)** $a \cdot a \cdot a = a^3$

Example 2 Write each expression without using exponents.
(a) t^5 **(b)** $3s^4$ **(c)** $(3s)^4$

Solution **(a)** $t^5 = t \cdot t \cdot t \cdot t \cdot t$ **(b)** $3s^4 = 3 \cdot s \cdot s \cdot s \cdot s$
(c) $(3s)^4 = (3s)(3s)(3s)(3s) = 81 \cdot s \cdot s \cdot s \cdot s$

Notice that the exponent in Example 2**(b)** applies only to the variable, s.

A quick way to remember powers of 10 is that the exponent shows the number of zeros that will follow the 1. Therefore, $10^2 = 100$, $10^4 = 10,000$, and so on.

Scientific notation is a shorthand method of using exponents to write large numbers. In scientific notation a decimal number between 1 and 10 is multiplied by a power of 10. For example, $6.75 \times 10^{11} = 6.75 \times 100,000,000,000 = 675,000,000,000$.

Example 3 Write the number 9.125×10^8 in standard notation.

Solution 9.125×10^8 means $9.125 \times 100,000,000$.
Moving the decimal point eight places gives $912,500,000$.

Example 4 Write $49,000,000,000$ in scientific notation.

Solution There are 10 places after the 4, therefore $49,000,000,000 = 4.9 \times 10^{10}$

Note that 4.9 is a number between 1 and 10.

Your scientific calculator uses scientific notation when a number is very large. Usually the calculator shows a number between 1 and 10 with a decimal part followed by E and an integer. The E stands for *exponent* and the integer represents a power of 10. For example, $9.3 \times 10^7 = 9.3$ E7 = 93,000,000.

The calculator shows a negative exponent for very small numbers. For example, 3.24 E–4 means 3.24×10^{-4}.

Example 5 a Write 3.24E–4 in standard form.
b Write 0.000082 in scientific notation.

Solution a 3.24 E–4 $= 3.24 \times 10^{-4} = 0.000324$
b $0.000082 = 8.2 \times 10^{-5}$

13: ORDER OF OPERATIONS

The rules for evaluating arithmetic expressions include performing mathematical operations in the following order:

1. Work within grouping symbols, starting from the innermost symbols.
2. Evaluate powers and roots.
3. Do multiplication and division from left to right.
4. Do addition and subtraction from left to right.

Example 1 Evaluate.
(a) $2(3 + 4)$ (b) $2(3 + 5) + 3(5 - 1)$

Solution (a) $2(3 + 4)$ (b) $2(3 + 5) + 3(5 - 1)$
$= 2 \times 7 = 14$ $= 2 \times 8 + 3 \times 4$
$= 16 + 12 = 28$

Example 2 Evaluate $5[6 + 4(4 - 7) - 8 \div (9 - 5)]$.

Solution $5[6 + 4(4 - 7) - 8 \div (9 - 5)]$
$= 5[6 + 4(-3) - 8 \div 4]$
$= 5[6 - 12 - 2]$
$= 5(-8) = -40$

Example 3 Evaluate $1 + n^2$ if $n = 7$.

Solution $1 + n^2 = 1 + 7^2 = 1 + 49 = 50$

TABLES AND CHARTS

Table of Measurements

English Units

Length

1 mile = 5280 feet
1 yard =   3 feet
1 foot =   12 inches

Mass and Weight

1 ton   = 2000 pounds
1 pound =   16 ounces

Capacity (Liquid Measures)

1 gallon = 231 cubic inches
1 gallon =   4 quarts
1 quart =   2 pints
1 pint   =   16 fluidounces

Area

1 square mile = 640 acres
1 acre   = 4840 square yards
1 square yard =   9 square feet
1 square foot = 144 square inches

Volume

1 cubic yard =   27 cubic feet
1 cubic foot = 1728 cubic inches

Metric Units

Length

1 kilometer = 1000 meters
1 hectometer = 100 meters
1 dekameter =   10 meters
1 decimeter = 0.1 meter
1 centimeter = 0.01 meter
1 millimeter = 0.001 meter

Mass and Weight

1 kilogram = 1000 grams
1 hectogram = 100 grams
1 dekagram =   10 grams
1 decigram = 0.1 gram
1 centigram = 0.01 gram
1 milligram = 0.001 gram

Capacity (Liquid Measures)

1 kiloliter = 1000 liters
1 hectoliter = 100 liters
1 dekaliter =   10 liters
1 deciliter = 0.1 liter
1 centiliter = 0.01 liter
1 milliliter = 0.001 liter

Area

1 square kilometer = 1,000,000 square meters
1 square meter   =   10,000 square centimeters
1 square centimeter =   100 square millimeters

Volume

1 cubic meter   = 1,000,000 cubic centimeters
1 cubic centimeter =   1,000 cubic millimeters

English-Metric Conversions

Length

1 mile ≈ 1.61 kilometers
1 yard ≈ 0.914 meter
1 foot = 30.48 centimeters
1 inch = 2.54 centimeters

Mass and Weight

1 pound ≈ 0.453 kilogram
1 ounce ≈ 28.35 grams

Capacity

1 gallon   ≈ 3.785 liters
1 fluidounce ≈ 29.57 milliliters

Area

$1 \ mi^2 \approx 2.58 \ km^2$
$1 \ yd^2 \approx 0.836 \ m^2$
$1 \ ft^2 \approx 0.093 \ m^2$
$1 \ in.^2 \approx 6.45 \ cm^2$

Volume

$1 \ yd^3 \approx 0.765 \ m^3$
$1 \ ft^3 \approx 0.028 \ m^3$
$1 \ in.^3 \approx 16.39 \ cm^3$

Densities of Selected Substances

Substance	Density g/cm³	Density lb/ft³
Air	0.0012	0.075
Aluminum	2.7	168.5
Copper	8.89	555
Gasoline	0.66	41.2
Glass	2.6	162
Gold	19.3	1204
Helium	0.00018	0.01123
Ice	0.922	57.5
Lead	11.3	705
Milk	1.03	64.27
Silver	10.5	655
Steel	7.8	486.7
Water	1.0	62.4
Wood (balsa)	0.13	8.11
Wood (oak)	0.72	44.9
Wood (pine)	0.56	34.9

The First 100 Prime Numbers

2	3	5	7	11	13	17	19	23	29
31	37	41	43	47	53	59	61	67	71
73	79	83	89	97	101	103	107	109	113
127	131	137	139	149	151	157	163	167	173
179	181	191	193	197	199	211	223	227	229
233	239	241	251	257	263	269	271	277	281
283	293	307	311	313	317	331	337	347	349
353	359	367	373	379	383	389	397	401	409
419	421	431	433	439	443	449	457	461	463
467	479	487	491	499	503	509	521	523	541

Table of Geometric Formulas

Perimeter Formulas

The perimeter of any polygon is the sum of the lengths of the sides of the polygon.

Rectangle

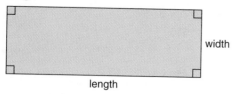

Perimeter = 2 · (length) + 2 · (width)

Circle

The perimeter of a circle is called the circle's **circumference**.

Circumference = π · (diameter)   Circumference = π · 2 · (radius)

Area Formulas

Rectangle

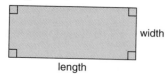

Area = (length) · (width)

Square

Area = (side) · (side)

Triangle

Area = $\frac{1}{2}$ (base) · (height)

Parallelogram

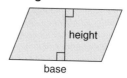

Area = (base) · (height)

Trapezoid

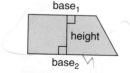

Area = $\frac{1}{2}$ · height · (base$_1$ + base$_2$)

Circle

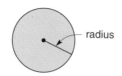

Area = π · (radius)^2

Surface Area

Prism

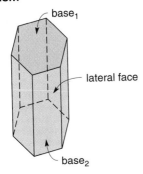

Total surface area =
(area of base$_1$) + (area of base$_2$) +
(sum of the areas of the lateral faces)

Pyramid

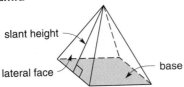

Total surface area = (area of base) + (sum of the areas of the lateral faces)

Cylinder

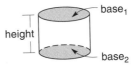

Total surface area =
(area of base$_1$) + (area of base$_2$) +
(circumference of either base · height)

Cone

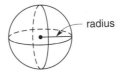

Total surface area =
(area of base) + (π · radius · slant height)

Sphere

Total surface area = 4 · π · (radius^2)

Volume

Prism

Volume = (area of base) · (height)

Pyramid

Volume = $\frac{1}{3}$ · (area of base) · (height)

Cylinder

Volume = (area of base) · (height)

Cone

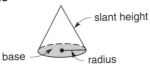

Volume = $\frac{1}{3}$ · (area of base) · (height)

Sphere

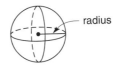

Volume = $\frac{4}{3}$ · π · (radius^3)

Symbols Used in Mathematics

Symbol	Meaning
Geometry	
$\overleftrightarrow{AB}$	line AB
$\overrightarrow{AB}$	ray AB
$\overline{AB}$	segment AB
AB	length of $\overline{AB}$
$\angle$	angle
$m\angle A$	measure of angle A
⌐	right angle
$\triangle$	triangle
⊙	circle
~	is similar to
≅	is congruent to
⊥	is perpendicular to
∥	is parallel to
⇉	parallel lines

Symbol	Meaning
Sets	
{ }	set
∩	intersection
∪	union
⊂	is a subset of

Symbol	Meaning
Computer Operations	
*	multiplication
/	division
^	power

Symbol	Meaning
Algebra	
+	addition
−	subtraction
× ·	multiplication
÷ —	division
$\sqrt{}$	root
$|x|$	absolute value of x
$n!$	n factorial
=	is equal to
≈	is approximately equal to
≠	is not equal to
<	is less than
≤	is less than or equal to
>	is greater than
≥	is greater than or equal to

Symbol	Meaning
Other Symbols	
°	degrees
′	feet
″	inches
π	pi
%	percent

Table of Squares and Square Roots

n	n^2	$\sqrt{n}$	n	n^2	$\sqrt{n}$	n	n^2	$\sqrt{n}$
1	1	1.000	51	2,601	7.141	101	10,201	10.050
2	4	1.414	52	2,704	7.211	102	10,404	10.100
3	9	1.732	53	2,809	7.280	103	10,609	10.149
4	16	2.000	54	2,916	7.348	104	10,816	10.198
5	25	2.236	55	3,025	7.416	105	11,025	10.247
6	36	2.449	56	3,136	7.483	106	11,236	10.296
7	49	2.646	57	3,249	7.550	107	11,449	10.344
8	64	2.828	58	3,364	7.616	108	11,664	10.392
9	81	3.000	59	3,481	7.681	109	11,881	10.440
10	100	3.162	60	3,600	7.746	110	12,100	10.488
11	121	3.317	61	3,721	7.810	111	12,321	10.536
12	144	3.464	62	3,844	7.874	112	12,544	10.583
13	169	3.606	63	3,969	7.937	113	12,769	10.630
14	196	3.742	64	4,096	8.000	114	12,996	10.677
15	225	3.873	65	4,225	8.062	115	13,225	10.724
16	256	4.000	66	4,356	8.124	116	13,456	10.770
17	289	4.123	67	4,489	8.185	117	13,689	10.817
18	324	4.243	68	4,624	8.246	118	13,924	10.863
19	361	4.359	69	4,761	8.307	119	14,161	10.909
20	400	4.472	70	4,900	8.367	120	14,400	10.954
21	441	4.583	71	5,041	8.426	121	14,641	11.000
22	484	4.690	72	5,184	8.485	122	14,884	11.045
23	529	4.796	73	5,329	8.544	123	15,129	11.091
24	576	4.899	74	5,476	8.602	124	15,376	11.136
25	625	5.000	75	5,625	8.660	125	15,625	11.180
26	676	5.099	76	5,776	8.718	126	15,876	11.225
27	729	5.196	77	5,929	8.775	127	16,129	11.269
28	784	5.292	78	6,084	8.832	128	16,384	11.314
29	841	5.385	79	6,241	8.888	129	16,641	11.358
30	900	5.477	80	6,400	8.944	130	16,900	11.402
31	961	5.568	81	6,561	9.000	131	17,161	11.446
32	1,024	5.657	82	6,724	9.055	132	17,424	11.489
33	1,089	5.745	83	6,889	9.110	133	17,689	11.533
34	1,156	5.831	84	7,056	9.165	134	17,956	11.576
35	1,225	5.916	85	7,225	9.220	135	18,225	11.619
36	1,296	6.000	86	7,396	9.274	136	18,496	11.662
37	1,369	6.083	87	7,569	9.327	137	18,769	11.705
38	1,444	6.164	88	7,744	9.381	138	19,044	11.747
39	1,521	6.245	89	7,921	9.434	139	19,321	11.790
40	1,600	6.325	90	8,100	9.487	140	19,600	11.832
41	1,681	6.403	91	8,281	9.539	141	19,881	11.874
42	1,764	6.481	92	8,464	9.592	142	20,164	11.916
43	1,849	6.557	93	8,649	9.644	143	20,449	11.958
44	1,936	6.633	94	8,836	9.695	144	20,736	12.000
45	2,025	6.708	95	9,025	9.747	145	21,025	12.042
46	2,116	6.782	96	9,216	9.798	146	21,316	12.083
47	2,209	6.856	97	9,409	9.849	147	21,609	12.124
48	2,304	6.928	98	9,604	9.899	148	21,904	12.166
49	2,401	7.000	99	9,801	9.950	149	22,201	12.207
50	2,500	7.071	100	10,000	10.000	150	22,500	12.247

GLOSSARY

A

absolute value (6.7) The distance of a number on the number line from zero. For example, |3| = 3, and |−3| = 3.

abundant number (10.5) A number whose *r* ratio is greater than two.

acute angle (3.3) An angle with a measure between 0 and 90.

adjacent angles (7.1) Angles that have the same vertex, have a side in common, and do not overlap.

adjacent sides (7.2) Sides of a polygon that have a common endpoint.

angle (3.5) A representation of a rotation using two rays meeting at a vertex.

area (2.3, 4.1) The size of a surface, usually expressed in square units.

artistic graph (5.3) A graph that displays information pictorially.

Associative Properties of Addition and Multiplication (9.5) Grouping does not affect the sum or product of three numbers. For numbers *a*, *b*, and *c*:
$(a + b) + c = a + (b + c)$, and $(ab)c = a(bc)$.

attribute (4.1) A characteristic that distinguishes an object from other objects.

average (5.4) A value that tells something about the center of a set of data. See *mean*; *median*; *mode*.

axes (6.8) In the rectangular coordinate system, the two number lines that intersect to form right angles.

B

bar graph (5.2) A graph that displays data as vertical or horizontal parallel bars.

base (2.2) The number that is raised to a power. In the expression 5^2, 5 is the base.

base of a triangle (2.3) The side to which the line segment for the height of the triangle is drawn.

base unit (4.2) An expression of rate as a fraction with a denominator of 1.

bases of a trapezoid (2.3) The two parallel sides of a trapezoid.

bisect (7.5) To divide into two congruent parts.

box-and-whisker plot (5.5) A graph used to identify the middle 50% of a set of data.

C

capacity (4.1) The amount (volume) that containers can hold.

cell (1.5) A spreadsheet "box," identified by its column letter and row number.

center of rotation (7.4) A point about which a figure is rotated.

center of symmetry (7.3) A point about which a figure is rotated until it fits on its original position exactly.

centi- (4.1) A prefix that indicates 0.01 unit.

centimeter (4.1) A unit of measurement equal to 0.01 meter.

circle graph (5.1) A graph in which pie-shaped parts of a circle represent data. Also called *pie chart*.

circumference (2.3, 9.4) The distance around a circle, equal to π times the diameter.

coefficient (8.1) The number multiplying the variable. In the term $2x$, 2 is the coefficient.

common factor (10.5) A number that is a factor of two or more numbers. The number 5 is a common factor of 15 and 20.

Commutative Properties of Addition and Multiplication (9.5) The order in which numbers are added or multiplied does not change the sum or product. For any numbers *a* and *b*: $a + b = b + a$ and $ab = ba$.

complement (3.5, 9.2) (1) One of two angles that have measures with a sum of 90. Each angle is the complement of the other. (2) The complement of set A is the set of all elements that are not in A.

complementary angles (3.5) Two angles with measures that add up to 90.

composite number (10.2) A natural number greater than 1 that has more than two factors.

cone (11.6) A three-dimensional figure with a circular base and a vertex.

congruent (3.1) Having exactly the same size and shape.

convergent (12.4) Approaching a value.

conversion factors (4.4) Ratios used to change units of measure.

convex polygon (3.7) A polygon in which any two interior points can be connected by a segment that is entirely within the polygon.

coordinate (6.1) The number associated with a point on a number line. Two coordinates identify a point in the coordinate plane.

counting numbers (9.3, 10.1) The set of natural numbers, {1, 2, 3, … }.

cross multiplying (4.5) A method used to solve proportions by multiplying the numerator of each ratio by the denominator of the other.

cylinder (11.6) A three-dimensional figure with two parallel congruent circular bases.

D

data analysis (5.1) A process for collecting, organizing, displaying, and interpreting data.

deficient number (10.5) A number with an r ratio less than 2.

degree (3.5) A unit of measure for an angle.

density (4.3) The ratio of the mass of a substance to its volume.

diagonal (3.1) A segment that joins two nonconsecutive vertices of a polygon.

diameter (2.3) A line segment that passes through the center of a circle and has endpoints on the circumference of the circle.

dimensional analysis (4.4) A technique that is used to convert a measurement from one type of unit to another.

dimensions of a matrix (5.6) The number of rows and columns; a 3 × 4 matrix has 3 rows and 4 columns.

disjoint (5.1) Able to be separated into categories that do not overlap.

disjoint sets (9.3) Two sets that have an intersection that is empty.

distance formula (9.6) The distance between X(a, b) and Y(c, d) is given by $XY = \sqrt{(c - a)^2 + (d - b)^2}$.

Distributive Property (8.1) For numbers a, b, and x, $ax + bx = (a + b)x$ and $ax - bx = (a - b)x$.

E

edge (11.5) In a polyhedron, the line of intersection of two faces.

encasement (7.6) A procedure used to find the area of a triangle.

equal matrices (5.6) Matrices with corresponding entries that are equal.

equation (1.6) A sentence stating that the values before and after an equal sign are equal.

equiangular (3.7) Figures in which all angles are congruent.

equilateral triangle (3.7) A triangle with all sides congruent.

equivalent expressions (8.1) Two expressions that produce the same value.

equivalent fractions (10.2) Two or more fractions that represent the same number.

estimate (3.3) To find the approximate value.

evaluate (2.1) To find the value of an expression.

exponent (2.2) A number used to indicate the repeated multiplication of a number. In the expression 10^4, 4 is the exponent.

extremes (5.5) The least and greatest value for a given set of data.

F

faces (11.5) The flat surfaces (polygons) of polyhedral solids.

factor (10.2) A number that divides into another number and leaves a remainder of zero.

Fibonacci sequence (8.1) A pattern in which the first and second numbers are both 1 and each following number is the sum of the two numbers that precede it (1, 1, 2, 3, 5, 8, 13, 21, …).

figurate numbers (10.7) Special numbers associated with geometric figures.

final ray (3.5) A ray that represents the final position in a rotation.

fractal (12.5) A figure resulting from iterations, in which each new part is similar to the previous figure.

function (8.7) A relationship in which one value depends on the other values. (See *input*; *output*.)

G

gram (4.1) The basic metric unit of mass.

greatest common factor (GCF) (10.5) The greatest number that is a factor of two or more numbers.

grouping symbols (2.1) Symbols that show which operation is to be done first.

H

height of a triangle (2.3) A perpendicular segment from a triangle's vertex to the opposite side.

heptagon (3.1) A polygon with seven sides.

hexagon (3.1) A polygon with six sides.

histogram (5.3) A graph that shows the number of times a value or range of values occurs in a set of data.

hypotenuse (2.3) In a right triangle, the side opposite the right angle.

I

image (7.4) A figure obtained through the transformation of an original figure (preimage).

inequality (6.2) A statement that two quantities are not equal.

initial ray (3.5) A ray that represents the initial direction of a rotation.

input (8.7) For a function, the value substituted for the variable. For example, let $f(x) = x + 1$. If $x = 5$ is the input, then 6 is the output.

integers (6.1, 9.3) The set I = { ... , –3, –2, –1, 0, 1, 2, 3, ... }.

intersection (9.2) The set that contains all common elements of two given sets.

inverse operations (3.4) Operations that reverse the effect of each other. For example, addition and subtraction are inverse operations.

irrational numbers (9.3) Real numbers that cannot be written as the ratio of two integers and cannot be written as terminating or repeating decimals.

isosceles trapezoid (7.5) A trapezoid in which the nonparallel sides are congruent.

isosceles triangle (7.5) A triangle with two congruent sides.

iteration (12.1) A process used to do repetitive calculations. Each calculation uses the results of the previous calculation as its starting value.

iteration diagram (12.1) A diagram used to model iterations.

K

kilo- (4.1) A prefix that indicates 1000 units.

kilogram (4.1) A unit of mass equal to 1000 grams.

kilometer (4.1) A unit of distance equal to 1000 meters.

kite (7.5) A quadrilateral that has two pairs of congruent adjacent sides.

L

lateral area (11.5) The area of the surfaces, other than bases, of a prism, pyramid, cylinder, or cone.

lateral faces (11.5) The faces of a prism or pyramid that are not bases.

least common denominator (10.2) The least common multiple of the denominators of the fractions being compared.

least common multiple (LCM) (10.2) The smallest number other than zero that is a multiple of two or more numbers.

legs (2.3) In a right triangle, the sides that form the right angle.

like terms (8.1) Terms that have the same variable raised to the same power.

limiting value (12.4) A number to which an iteration converges.

line A straight path of points that extend infinitely in opposite directions.

linear equation (9.7) An equation for which the graph is a line.

linear measurement (3.1) A measure of length or distance.

line graph (5.2) A graph that displays data as points that are connected by segments.

line of symmetry (7.3) A line that divides a figure into two halves that are mirror images of each other.

line plot (5.3) A histogram that has data graphed on a number line.

line segment Two points on a line, plus all the points in between. The two points are the endpoints of the segment.

liter (4.1) The basic metric unit of capacity.

lower quartile (5.5) The middle term of the lower half of a set of data.

M

magic square (6.6) A matrix in which the numbers in each row, column, and diagonal have the same sum.

matrix (5.6) A two-dimensional table of rows and columns.

mean (5.4) A type of average. It is the sum of data items divided by the number of data items.

measures of central tendency (5.4) The term given to various averages, such as mean, median, and mode, because they each measure the center of a set of data.

median (5.4) The middle term for a set of data that is arranged in order from least to greatest.

meter (4.1) The basic unit of length in the metric system. A meter is equal to 100 centimeters.

midpoint (6.8) A point that is halfway between two given points.

midpoint formula (9.6) If (a, b) and (c, d) are any two points, then M, the point midway between these two points, has coordinates given by $M = \left(\frac{a+c}{2}, \frac{b+d}{2} \right)$.

midquartile range (5.5) The difference between the upper and lower quartile. The middle 50% of a set of data.

milli- (4.1) A prefix that indicates 0.001 unit.

milligram (4.1) A unit of measurement equal to 0.001 gram.

milliliter (4.1) A unit of measurement equal to 0.001 liter.

millimeter (4.1) A unit of measurement equal to 0.001 meter.

mode (5.4) The value that occurs most often in a given set of data.

multiple (10.2) The product of a number and any whole number. The multiples of 3 are 0, 3, 6, 9, …

N

natural numbers (10.1) The set of counting numbers, {1, 2, 3, … }.

natural-number multiples (10.2) A set that contains the result of multiplying a number by each of the natural numbers. For example, the natural-number multiples of 5 are 5, 10, 15, 20, …

negative numbers (6.1) Numbers that are to the left of zero on a number line.

nonagon (3.1) A polygon with nine sides.

number line (6.1) A line used to represent the set of real numbers.

numerical term (8.1) In an equation or expression, the terms without the variable.

O

obtuse angle (3.3) An angle with a measure between 90 and 180.

octagon (3.1) A polygon with eight sides.

opposites (6.1) Numbers that are the same distance from zero on a number line.

opposite sides (7.2) The sides of a quadrilateral that do not have a common endpoint.

opposite vertices (7.2) The vertices of a quadrilateral that are not consecutive.

ordered pair (6.8) A pair of numbers, with specified order, that can be used to designate a point in the coordinate plane.

order of operations (2.1, 2.2) The order in which mathematical operations are performed.

origin (6.1) On a number line, zero; in the coordinate plane, the point (0, 0).

outliers (5.5) Data that are above the upper quartile or below the lower quartile by more than 1.5 times the midquartile range.

output (8.7) For a function, the result after evaluating for given input. For example, let $f(x) = x + 1$. If $x = 5$ is the input, then 6 is the output.

P

parallel (7.1) Two lines that are everywhere the same distance apart and never intersect.

parallelogram (7.2) A quadrilateral in which both pairs of opposite sides are parallel.

pattern (1.1) Any set (numbers, letters, figures, etc.) that seems to be in a certain order, from which you could predict the next element in the set.

pentagon (3.1) A polygon with five sides.

percent (2.4) Means "in each 100."

perfect number (10.5) A number whose factors, except itself, add up to the number.

perimeter of a polygon (2.1) The sum of the lengths of the sides.

perpendicular (7.1) Intersecting at right angles.

pi (π) (2.3, 9.4) The ratio of the circumference to the diameter of a circle. Pi is approximately 3.1416.

pictograph (5.3) A graph that uses symbols to represent data.

pie chart (5.1) See *circle graph*.

polygon (3.1) A closed figure made up of line segments that intersect only at their endpoints.

polyhedron (11.5) A three-dimensional figure in which each face is a polygon.

positive numbers (6.1) Numbers that are to the right of zero on a number line.

power (2.2) A number indicating repeated multiplication. The number 1000 is a power of 10 because $10^3 = 1000$.

preimage (7.4) The original figure in a transformation.

prime-factorization form (10.4) A number expressed as a unique product of prime factors usually multiplied in order from least to greatest.

prime number (10.2) A natural number greater than 1 and with only two factors, 1 and itself.

prism (11.5) A polyhedron with two congruent parallel bases.

probability (1.4) The ratio of the number of favorable outcomes to the number of possible outcomes.

proportion (4.5) An equation stating that two ratios are equal.

protractor (3.5) An instrument used to measure angles.

pyramid (11.5) A polyhedron with one base that is a polygon, several lateral faces that are triangles, and a vertex.

Pythagorean Theorem (2.3) States that in any right triangle,
$$(\text{leg}_1)^2 + (\text{leg}_2)^2 = (\text{hypotenuse})^2.$$

Pythagorean triple (10.7) Three natural numbers, such as 3, 4, and 5, that satisfy the equation $a^2 + b^2 = c^2$

Q

quadrants (6.8) The four regions in a rectangular coordinate system.

quadrilateral (7.2) A polygon with four sides.

quotient (6.4) The answer to a division problem.

R

radicand (2.2) The quantity inside a root symbol.

radius of a circle (2.3) A line segment with one endpoint at the center of a circle and the other endpoint on the circumference.

range (5.5) The difference between the greatest value and the least value for a given set of data.

rate (4.2) A ratio that compares the measurements of two different attributes, for example, miles per hour.

ratio (4.2) A way of comparing two values. The ratio of 3 to 5 can be written as 3:5 or as $\frac{3}{5}$.

rational number (9.3) A number that can be written in the form a/b where a and b are integers and $b \neq 0$.

ray (3.5) A straight path of points that start from one endpoint and extend indefinitely.

real numbers (9.3) The union of the sets of rational and irrational numbers; the numbers on a number line.

reciprocal (8.2) For any nonzero number $\frac{a}{b}$, the reciprocal is the number $\frac{b}{a}$. Zero has no reciprocal.

rectangle (7.2) A quadrilateral with four right angles and opposite sides that are congruent.

rectangular coordinate system (6.8) Two perpendicular number lines intersecting at their zero points, producing a plane in which each point can be identified by an ordered pair.

reflection (7.4) A kind of transformation that makes the new figure a mirror image of the original figure.

reflection symmetry (7.3) A type of symmetry in which a line can be drawn that divides the figure into two halves that are mirror images of each other.

regular polygon (3.1) A polygon in which all sides are congruent and all angles have the same measure.

relatively prime (10.6) Two numbers that have a GCF of 1. The numbers 20 and 27 are relatively prime.

rhombus (7.2) A quadrilateral with four congruent sides and opposite sides that are parallel.

right angle (3.3) An angle with a measure of 90.

Right angle property (9.4) If $\overline{AC}$ is a diameter of a circle and B is any point on the circumference of the circle other than A or C, then $\angle ABC$ is always a right angle.

right triangle (2.3) A triangle with one right angle.

root (2.2) The base that corresponds to a given power. For example, the third root of 8 is 2, because $2^3 = 8$.

root index (2.2) The number used to indicate what root to find.

rotation (7.4) A transformation that rotates a shape a certain number of degrees about a point.

rotation symmetry (7.3) Symmetry in which a figure can be rotated 180° or less in order to lie atop its original position exactly.

rounding (3.3) Using an approximate value, according to certain rules. If 297 is rounded to the nearest hundred, it becomes 300.

S

scalar (6.4) The number used to multiply each element in a matrix.

scalar multiplication (6.4) The multiplication of each element of a matrix by the same number.

scale (4.3) The ratio of distances on a model or map to real-world distances.

scale factor (4.6) The ratio that corresponds to the amount of enlargement or reduction of objects.

scattergram (5.3) Data plotted as points in a plane with vertical and horizontal axes. The data cannot be connected by a line.

scientific notation (3.2) A number expressed as the product of a number between 1 and 10 and a power of 10.

self-similarity (12.5) A property in which part of the figure that is added each time an iteration is completed is similar to the previous part.

set (9.1) A collection of objects.

side (3.1, 3.5) (1) A segment of a polygon. (2) A ray of an angle.

similar (4.6) Having the same shape but possibly a different size.

slant height (11.5) The height of one of the lateral faces of a pyramid or the distance from the vertex of a cone to the circumference of the cone's base.

slide (7.4) See *translation*.

solution (3.4) The value(s) of the variable(s) for which an equation or inequality is a true statment.

sphere (11.6) A round three-dimensional figure in which each point on the surface is the same distance from the center.

spreadsheet (1.5) A powerful data-analysis tool that creates tables and manipulates data in them.

square (7.2) A quadrilateral with four congruent sides and four right angles.

square root (2.2) One of two equal factors of a number.

stem-and-leaf plot (5.5) A numerical diagram used to organize data.

subset (9.1) Set A is a subset of set B if every element in A is also in B. This can be written as A ⊂ B.

supplement (3.5) One of two angles that have a sum of 180. Each angle is the supplement of the other.

supplementary angles (3.5) Two angles with measures that add up to 180.

surface area (11.5) The total area of the surface(s) of a solid figure.

symmetric prime numbers (10.7) A pair of prime numbers that are the same distance away from a given number on the number line.

symmetry (7.3) See *reflection symmetry; rotation symmetry*.

T

table (1.5) A chart that displays data.

tessellation (1.1) A design that repeats without leaving gaps and without overlapping.

transformation (7.4) A way a figure is moved so that the position of the figure changes, but its size and shape do not. See *reflection; rotation; translation*.

translation (7.4) A transformation that slides a figure from one position to another. Also called a *slide*.

translation numbers (7.4) Numbers used to find the image in a translation.

trapezoid (7.2) A quadrilateral with only one pair of parallel sides.

tree diagram (10.1) A diagram used to show all possible combinations in order to solve a problem.

U

union (9.2) Given sets A and B, the set of all elements that are in set A or in set B (or both).

unit cost (4.2) The cost of one unit of a product.

upper quartile (5.5) The middle term of the upper half of a set of data.

V

variable (3.4) A symbol that represents numbers.

Venn diagram (9.2) A diagram that shows relationships among sets.

vertex (3.1, 3.5, 11.5) (1) A point where two sides of a polygon intersect. (2) The center of rotation. (3) In a polyhedron, the intersection of two edges.

vertex matrix (7.6) A matrix that organizes coordinates of the vertices of a polygon.

vertical angles (7.1) Two nonadjacent angles formed when two lines intersect.

vinculum (2.1) A horizontal bar used as a grouping symbol.

volume (4.1) The amount of space an object takes up, usually expressed in cubic units.

W

whole numbers (9.3) The set of natural numbers and the number zero, $\{0, 1, 2, 3, \dots \}$.

X

x-axis (6.8) The horizontal axis in a rectangular coordinate system.

x-coordinate (6.8) The first number of an ordered pair. It indicates how far the point is to the right or the left of the y-axis.

x-intercept (9.7) A point at which a graph crosses the x-axis.

Y

y-axis (6.8) The vertical axis in a rectangular coordinate system.

y-coordinate (6.8) The second number of an ordered pair. It indicates how far the point is above or below the x-axis.

y-intercept (9.7) A point at which a graph crosses the y-axis.

Z

Zero Product Property (9.5) For numbers a and b, if $a \times b = 0$, then either $a = 0$ or $b = 0$.

Chapter 1: Patterns

1.1 A Tiling Problem   pages 5–9

1 36 **3a**

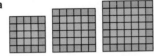

b 4, 8, 12, 16, 20 **c** 0, 1, 4, 9, 16 **5** 100
7a $\frac{3}{4}$ **b** $\frac{7}{8}$ **c** $\frac{15}{16}$ **d** $\frac{31}{32}$ **e** $\frac{63}{64}$ **9** 51
11a

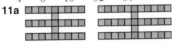

b Red: 15, 15, 21, 21; Blue: 14, 20, 20, 26
13a Layers: 4, 8, 16; Length of each layer: 3", 1.5",
0.75" **b** Direction of folds different in each case.
15a 12, 14, 36, 2, 144, 48, 72 **b** 0, 2, 0, 0, 0, 12, 0
17 Angles 1 and 4 **19a** $222.75 **b** $74.25

1.2 Number and Letter Patterns   pages 11–15

1 21, 28, 36, 45 **3** 6, 10 **5** −1, −2 **7** JC, RR, GB
9   **11** Any seven-sided figure

13 65, 129, 257, 513 **15**

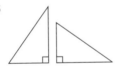

17 27 **19** 2.5
21

23a Count the smallest squares and multiply by 4.
b 64 **25a** 15, 60, 135, 240, 375, 540, 735
b 1,058,400
27

1	2	3	4	5	6
3	5	8	12	17	23
5	10	18	30	47	70
7	17	35	65	112	182
9	26	61	126	238	420
11	37	98	224	462	882
13	50	148	372	834	1716
15	65	213	585	1419	3135

29a $\frac{3}{7}$ **b** $\frac{5}{7}$

31 Not possible **33a** 56 **b** 93

1.3 Practical Patterns   pages 18–22

1 13 **3a** False **b** True **c** True **5** 6: $8.00, 7: $6.86,
8: $6.00; $6.86 **7a** $500 **b** $625 **c** $750
9   **11** 10 units **13**

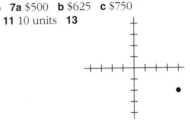

15 32, 64, 128, 256 **17** 72, 63, 56, 51 **19** A vehicle
that sometimes accelerates, slows down, travels at a
constant speed, and is at rest. **21a** 1, 3, 6, 10
b 15; 21 **23** XVI **25** (6, 36), (7, 49), (8, 64)
27a

#	3	4	6	7	8
3	3	12	6	21	24
4	12	4	12	28	8
6	6	12	6	42	24
7	21	28	42	7	56
8	24	8	24	56	8

b Least common multiple **29** 343 **31** 8 **33** $\frac{160}{100}$
35 6 **37** $11.52 **39** $1\frac{1}{3}$ gal

1.4 Probability   pages 24–28

1 $\frac{1}{2}$ **3** Always **5** A fraction, a quotient, etc.
7 Notes in a song; answers to a multiple-choice test
9 28; 12; 245; 80 **11** $\frac{4}{13}$ **13a** $\frac{1}{4}$, $\frac{1}{4}$ **b** $\frac{1}{6}$, $\frac{2}{3}$
15   **17a** $\frac{9}{10}$ **b** $\frac{7}{10}$ **c** $\frac{1}{2}$

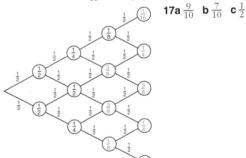

19a $\frac{1}{27}$ **b** $\frac{2}{9}$ **c** $\frac{4}{9}$ **d** $\frac{8}{27}$ **e** 0 **21** 9 **23** 3
25 0.3, 33%, $\frac{1}{3}$ **27** 6; 35

1a B2, B3, B4, C4, D4 **b** 20, 23, 71 **c** A2+3, A3+3, A4+3 **3a** 169 **b** 7 **5** **7** $1.90

	A	B	C	D
1	1	12	3	2
2	2	15	4	4
3	3	18	6	8
4	4	21	9	16
5	5	24	13	32
6	6	27	18	64

9 35 **11** **13a** 9 **b** 27 **c** 81 **d** 243 **e** 729

Miles	Amount (dollars)
10	2.80
20	5.60
30	8.40
40	11.20
50	14.00
60	16.80
70	19.60
80	22.40
90	25.20
100	28.00
110	30.80
120	33.60
130	36.40
140	39.20
150	42.00
160	44.80
170	47.60
180	50.40
190	53.20
200	56.00

15a 1980 **b** 1919 **c** Any reasonable answer accepted. **17** 124 ft
19 Possible answers:

	A	B	C	D
1	1	2	2	2
2	2	3	3	3
3	A2 + 1	A2 + B2	C1 + C2	D1 + D2
4	A3 + 1	A3 + B3	C2 + C3	D3 + D3
5	A4 + 1	A4 + B4	C3 + C4	D4 + D4
6	A5 + 1	A5 + B5	C4 + C5	D5 + D5

21a $\frac{1}{9}, \frac{1}{36}, \frac{1}{12}, \frac{1}{72}$ **b** $\frac{55}{72}$ **23a** 49 sq units **b** 343 cu units
25 25
27

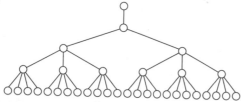

29a 11, 12, 33, 42, 45 **b** Two digits are the same or differ by less than 3.

1.6 Communicating Mathematics
pages 38–41

1 The center is the point of intersection of the diagonals. **3a** 13 **b** 2×A2+5; 2×A3+5; 2×A4+5; 31; 67; 139 **5** 56.23 **7** $\frac{3}{2}$ is greater than 1 **9a** 32°F or 0°C **b** 212°F or 100°C **11a** 64 sq units **b** 512 cu units **13** 2.828427125; nearly 8 **15** Add the second number to twice the first. **17** Multiply the area of a face by the length of an edge.

19 A1→5, A2→A1+2, etc. **21** Enter the numbers 1-7 in cells A1-A7. Enter 1 in cell B1, A2×B1 in cell B2, then copy the formula in cell B2 to cells B3-B7.
23a 180 **b** $\frac{1}{100}$ **c** $\frac{5}{9}$ **d** A1→0, A2→A1+1, etc; B1→32, B2→B1+9÷5, etc. **25** 5 × 8, or 8 × 5
27a 1320 **b** 906 **c** 23
29a

Square	1	2	3	4	5	6
Side length	1 cm	1 cm	2 cm	3 cm	5 cm	8 cm
Perimeter	4 cm	4 cm	8 cm	12 cm	20 cm	32 cm
Area	1 cm²	1 cm²	4 cm²	9 cm²	25 cm²	64 cm²

b 55 cm, 220 cm, 3025 cm² **31** $\frac{1}{4}$

Chapter 1 Review pages 43–45

1a 46.21 **b** 157.675 **c** 38.79 **d** ≈11.46 **3a** $17.50 **b** $8.75 **c** $5.85 **d** $4.40 **5** A sequence of items in which each item is generated by a rule from the preceding item **7** Any reasonable answer is accepted. **9** $\frac{3}{4}$ **11** $\frac{22}{25}$ **13a** True **b** True **c** False **d** True **e** False **f** False **15**

	A	B	C	D
1	1	1	2	3
2	2	3	5	5
3	3	6	11	16
4	5	11	22	38
5	8	19	41	79

17a $\frac{1}{4}$ **b** $\frac{1}{13}$ **c** $\frac{1}{52}$ **d** $\frac{4}{13}$ **19a** $19.25 **b** $28.00 **c** $18.25 **21** d, E, F
23

Length	Width	Perimeter	Area
6	6	24	36
9	4	26	36
3	12	30	36
18	2	40	36
36	1	74	36

25 G, K, L

Chapter 2: Formulas and Percent

2.1 Operations on Numbers pages 53–56

1 Possible answer: So that everyone will assign the same value to the expression **3** The operations were not performed from left to right. **5** The numbers 3 and 5 were added. However, 3 and (12-7) should be multiplied first. **7a** True **b** True **9a** 29 **b** 69 **c** 37 **d** 117 **11a** $\frac{1}{2}$ **b** $5\frac{5}{14}$ **c** $2\frac{4}{7}$ **13** 6 **15** 0 **17** 1 **19** Possible answer: two five-dollar bills and six one-dollar bills **21** 6 **23** 0 **25** 16 **27** 18.84 **29** 36 **31** $\frac{16}{15}$; ≈ 1.0667 **33a** Tom: 75.3, Serena: 92, Jamie: 74, Ivan 85.3, Mary 75.3 **33b** E2: (B2 + C2 + D2)/3 etc **c** 80.4 **d** (E2 + E3 + E4 + E5 + E6) ÷ 5 **35** Possible answer: $209.85 **37a** 16,807 **b** 117,649 **c** 279,936 **d** 6561 **39** False **41** True **43** Always **45a** 49 **b** 125 **c** 81 **47** Greek letter, symbol stands for ratio of a circle's circumference to its diameter.

2.2 Powers and Roots pages 60–63

1a If s is the length of the side of a square, s^2 is its area. **b** If e is the length of the edge of a cube, e^3 is its volume. **3a** True **b** True **c** False **d** False

5a Sometimes **b** Sometimes **7** 1135.87 ft/sec
9a 4 **b** ≈ 3.3556 **c** 5 **11** ≈ 2.236 **13** ≈ 29.275
15a 36 **b** 180 **17a** True **b** False **c** False **d** True
19 320 in.² **21** True **23a** 729; 2187; 6561 **b** 3^A7;
3^A8, 3^A9 **23c** 3 × B6; 3 × B7; 3 × B8 **25** 0
27 Willie **29** 25.92 sq units **b** 12.96 sq units **31** False
33 True **35** ≈2.320 **37a** 3 + 5 · (6 + 7) = 68
b (3 + 5) · 6 + 7 = 55 **c** (3 + 5) · (6 + 7) = 104
39a True **b** False **41** 13 lbs **43** 0.6 **45** $4.\overline{3}$ **47** Yes

2.3 Geometric Formulas   pages 67–70

1a 16 ft **b** 16 ft² **c** The units differ **3a** 28 **b** 21
c 112 **d** 60 **5a** Sometimes **b** Always **7** 6 **9** $\sqrt{12}$,
or ≈ 3.46 **11** 75 **13** 50 **15** $a = 10$, $b = 9$, c ≈11.18,
d ≈ 8.66, e ≈5.29 **17** $x = \sqrt{2}$, or ≈1.41; $y = \sqrt{3}$, or
≈1.73 **19a** 5(4 + 6); 5(4) + 5(6) **b** 50 **21a** $5^2\pi - 3^2\pi$
b ≈50.265 cm² **23a** $\sqrt{10}$ cm, or ≈3.16 cm
b $2\sqrt{20} + 2\sqrt{10}$ cm, or ≈15.27 cm **25** 7 **27** $\frac{7}{10}$
29 131 **31** 13 **33** $448 **35** $\frac{250}{100}$ **37a** $2775
b $21,275

2.4 Percent   pages 74–77

1a 45 **b** 200 **c** 46.98 **d** 9.4356 **e** 25% **f** 2 **g** 750
3a False **b** True **c** True **5a** $33.60 **b** 52%
7 37.5% **9** $33\frac{1}{3}$% **11** 0.6, 66%, $\frac{2}{3}$ **13** $\frac{153}{1000}$; 0.153
15 $\frac{3}{5}$; 0.6 **17** d **19** $788.40 **21** 52 g **23** Bob: $336
a week; Carol: $336 a week; Ted $350 a week
25a $151.80 or more **b** Answers will vary.
27a $\sqrt{125}$, or ≈11.18; $\sqrt{5}$, or ≈2.24 **b** $\frac{5}{1}$
29 D5: +(A5+B5+C5)/3, D6: +(A6+B6+C6)/3; ≈15.6̄,
≈42.6̄ **31** 0.1, 0.01 **33a** $\frac{4}{3}$ **b** $\frac{4}{3}$ **c** 5 **d** 7

2.5 More About Spreadsheets   pages 81–85

1

A	B	A + B	Percent
15	20	0.75	75%
3	15	0.2	20%
130	200	0.65	65%
4	25	0.16	16%
18	12	1.5	150%
6	30	0.2	20%

3 Values become smaller, toward 1.73205 or $\sqrt{3}$.
5 8 **7** True **9** 1490
11

	A	B	C
1	Prices	20% Discount	25% Discount
2	$ 3.00	$ 2.40	$ 2.25
3	$ 5.00	$ 4.00	$ 3.75
4	$ 7.00	$ 5.60	$ 5.25
5	$ 9.00	$ 7.20	$ 6.75
6	$11.00	$ 8.80	$ 8.25
7	$13.00	$10.40	$ 9.75
8	$15.00	$12.00	$11.25
9	$17.00	$13.60	$12.75
10	$19.00	$15.20	$14.25
11	$21.00	$16.80	$15.75

13 Always **15a** $\frac{5}{8}$ **b** $\frac{3}{5}$ **c** Cardinals **17** 9 hours tells
time, not distance **19** 36 in., or 3 ft **21** 56 mm,
or 5.6 cm **23** $\sqrt{\frac{13}{2}}$, $\sqrt{4 + 9}$, $\sqrt{4} + \sqrt{9}$ **25** Always
27 100% **29a** +A3·10 **b** +A3/2.54 **c** +C3/12

Chapter 2 Review   pages 87–89

1a 118 **b** 200 **c** 528 **d** 118 **e** 83 **f** $5.\overline{5}$ **3** A = 5.22;
P = 11.4 **5** ≈23% **7** 12 **9** 33.75 **11** 75% **13** 100%
15a 8 × 185 + 30 **b** $1510 **17a** 1728 **b** 756 **c** 1728
19 38.5°C **21**

	A	B	C	D
1	Width	Length	Perimeter	Area
2	1	2	6	2
3	2	4	12	8
4	3	6	18	18
5	4	8	24	32
6	5	10	30	50
7	6	12	36	72

23 60 **25** (4 + 4) · (4 + 4) · 4 = 256
27 (8 − 3) · (4 + 5) = 45 **29a** ≈497.18 **b** ≈79.04
c 6.29 **31** For any (x, y), find x% of y. **33** Values
become smaller, toward 1.41421 or $\sqrt{2}$

Chapter 3: Measurement and Estimation

3.1 Linear Measurements   pages 96–100

1 $2\frac{3}{4}$ in. **3** 24 posts **5** Always **7** Always **9** Always
11a About $2\frac{1}{8}$ in. **b** About 54 mm, or 5.4 cm
13a True **b** False **c** True **d** False **15** 2 ft
17 15 mm **19** 23,401 **21** Measure drawings
23 Yes **25a** $\frac{1}{6}$ **b** $\frac{1}{6}$ **c** $\frac{1}{6}$ **d** 0 **27a** 86 **b** 216
29 10% of 1 m **31** 1 m **33** $\frac{9}{16}$ **35a** $1\frac{5}{8}$ in. **b** 180 in.,
or 15 ft **37a** 31.4159265 **b** 314.159265
c 3141.159265 **d** 0.314159265 **e** 0.0314159265
f 0.00314159265 **39a** 4 **b** 1 **c** 0.25 **d** 0.0625; The
results get smaller as the exponents decrease in
value. **41** 2^6, greater by 28 **43a** ≈224% **b** ≈112%
45a ≈240 mi **b** Possible answer: ≈780 mi
47a In each cell, the cell named in the formula
changes to the cell above. **47b** Place 1 in A1. Enter
+A1*2 in A2 and copy down.

3.2 Scientific Notation   pages 103–106

1 For a shorter way to record numbers, etc.
3a −2 **b** 10^{-2} **c** 1.2×10^6 **5** True **7** 4.3×10^4
9a 10,100,000 **b** 1,000,000,000,000 **c** 100 **d** $\frac{1}{100}$
e −9,900,000 **f** 9,900,000 **11** 3.8512×10^2
13 5.647×10^3 **15** BC̄ **17** 5.2×10^5 **19** 0.234
21 87.643 **23** ≈1.539×10^{-6} **25a** 25% **b** 10% **c** 1%
27 $2.310679612 \times 10^{32}$ **29** 3.18253×10^{-4}
31a 1.7×10^{27} **b** 6×10^{53} **c** 4×10^{27} **33** 3
35 Measure drawings. **37** $\sqrt{0.1296}$ **39** Between 9
and 10 **41** About 6.9 **43** About 2 **45** No. He will
need to increase his body fat from 6.5%. **47** 1000,
125, 27, 8, 8, 1, 1, 1, 1 **49** 10 in. **51a** 36 **b** 32 **c** 4
d 2 **53a** $\frac{3}{8}$ **b** $\frac{2}{3}$ **55a** 4 + 12 + (7 × 9) **b** 4 × (12 − 7) + 9
c (4 + 12) ÷ (7 + 9) **d** 4 ÷ 12 × 7 × 9

3.3 Estimation and Rounding   pages 109–113

1 (Answers will vary.) **3** (Answers will vary.)
5 2 **7** 18 **9** Possible answer: To make measurement look as if it was not an estimate **11** 4.2600
13a 7 packages **b** 10 boxes **c** 3 bags
d 11 newspapers **15** Possible answer: The sale is designed to move goods. If the buyer does not meet the terms of the sale, he does not benefit.
17 475.39 **19** 132.62 **21** 263.11 **23** c **25** 4
27 52,500 to 53,499 **29** 49 movies **31a** ≈0.8 sec
b 72 beats per min **33a** 7 hr **-b** 13.6 gal **c** $17.95
35a Possible answer: A: line 34; B: line 32 **b** The numbers are so small that they are rounded to zero.
37 The greatest depth between the sea bottom and the sea surface is 3363 ft. **39** East **41** $\frac{3}{7}$ **43a** 44, 22, 11 **b** If the length and width are both divided in half, so is the perimeter. **c** +B3/2 **45a** 42,200
b ≈7.1154 **c** 31,800 **d** 1.924×10^8 **47** 52.3
49 5,230,000 **51** False **53** True **55** True

3.4 Understanding Equations   pages 117–120

1 7 **3** (0, 10), (1, 9), (5, 5) **5** 45 **7** 4.75 **9** 1.8
11 23 **13** 5184 **15** 113.6 **17** 9.4 **19** ≈6.3
21 Possible answers: $x = -1, y = -6$; $x = 12, y = \frac{1}{2}$
23 32.47 in. **25** −2 and 5 **27** 10 **29a** 7.5 cm
b Check drawing. **c** $\frac{2}{3}$ **31** 2.96 **33a** 2 **b** $\frac{1}{4}$ **c** 75
35a 2 **b** 6 **c** No such value. **37** 0 **39a** 4.2 cm, ≈6.1 cm, ≈6.1 cm **b** Check drawing. **c** ≈20.6 cm
41 25 **43** Greater than 6.6 cm

3.5 Angle Measurement   pages 125–128

1 West **3** Possible answer: S is the vertex of each angle. **5** Initial ray EF, final ray ED, or initial ray ED, final ray EF **7** 50° to the left **9** m∠DEF = 110, obtuse **11** m∠XYZ = 30, acute **13** 90, right
15 130, obtuse **17** Check drawing. **19** Check drawing. **21** ∠ADB, ∠BDC, ∠ADC **23a** 116
b 26 **25** Check drawing. **27** Check drawing.
29 Check drawing. **31** 63 **33a** B **b** About $45,000,000 **35** 30 **37a** 85.8 **b** 15.3 **c** 97.8
d 550.8 **39** 60 **41** 3.92×10^{-2} **43** 3.156×10^3
45 13 **47** 899 **49** 8.397

3.6 Constructions with Ruler and Protractor
pages 132–135

1 Both have four sides. Only one pair of opposite sides of a trapezoid is parallel. **3a** Angles are supplementary. **b** Angles are supplementary.
5a A Geometric theorem says if two lines are cut by a transversal and the corresponding angles are congruent, the lines are parallel. **5b** Use congruent alternate interior angles, congruent alternate exterior angles, or perpendicular lines. **7** Check drawing. **9** Check drawing. **11** Check drawing.
13a True **b** True **15a** 1:1 **b** Square **17** $\frac{2}{11}$
19a 5 **b** 7 **21a** $\frac{3}{8}$ **b** 37.5% **c** $\frac{3}{8}$ **23a** 2; 2 **b** 1.6; 2.4

c

	A	B	C
1	Percent of	Gallons of	Gallons of
2	antifreeze	water	antifreeze
3	40	2.4	1.6
4	50	2	2
5	60	1.6	2.4
6	70	1.2	2.8
7	80	0.8	3.2
8	90	0.4	3.6
9	100	0	4

25 About 12.7

27 About 3.5 **29** $\frac{1}{2}$ **31a** Always **b** Never **c** Never
d Always **e** Always **33a** $\frac{3}{4}$ **b** $\frac{5}{4}$ **c** $\frac{9}{10}$

3.7 Geometric Properties   pages 138–141

1a 45 **b** 85 **c** 33 **d** 37 **3** 360 **5** 1080 **7** Always
9 Always **11** Never **13a** $\overline{AC}$ **b** $\overline{BC}$ **15a** True
b False **c** False **d** True **e** False **17** ∠1:77;
∠2:68, ∠3:33 **19** m∠CBA = 100; m∠CBD = 80;
m∠ABE = 80; m∠DBE = 100; m∠FEB = 100;
m∠BEH = 80; m∠FEG = 80; m∠HEG = 100
21 Parallelogram **23a** $\frac{3}{41}$ **b** 7 **25** Areas are equal.
27a $\frac{2}{3}$ **b** $\frac{2}{3}$ **29a** $\frac{3}{2}$ **b** $\frac{3}{5}$ **c** 150% **d** 60% **31** 15 **33** $\frac{1}{3}$

Chapter 3 Review   pages 143–145

1a 40.5 **b** 3.25 **c** 76.5 **d** 1053 **3** 4.1758×10^{-3}
5 15 **7** 644,000 **9** Opposite sides are congruent. Opposite angles are congruent. Consecutive angles are supplementary. Opposite sides are parallel.
11 300 **13** ≈12 **15** ≈50 **17** 9.3×10^8 cm³ **19** 22
21 10^5 **23** 0.111 **25** $30 **27** The census, next year's enrollment, population of earth, etc. **29** ≈3.9 **31** 15
33 The measure of the other pair of opposite angles is 120. **35a** $\frac{1}{2}$ **b** $\frac{1}{2}$ **37a** 45 **b** 22.5 **c** 135 **39** 138
41a ≈153.9384 **b** 33.59 **c** 6.998217242

Chapter 4: Ratio and Proportion

4.1 A Closer Look at Measurement
pages 153–157

1 cm **3** mm **5** qt **7** g **9a** 10^2 **b** 10^{-1} **c** 10^{-3} **d** 10^3
e 10^{-2} **f** 10^1 **11a** Tape measure **b** Meterstick, ruler, or tape measure **c** Tape measure **d** Odometer
e Ruler **f** Meterstick or ruler **13** A league is about 3 mi so title refers to a 60,000-mi undersea journey in a submarine **15** $\frac{4}{1}$ **17** $\frac{2}{3}$ **19a** 15 ft 3 in. **b** $15\frac{3}{12}$ or $15\frac{1}{4}$
21a $\frac{1}{3}$ **b** $\frac{1}{9}$ **c** $\frac{1}{27}$ **23** $\frac{3}{2}$ **25** $\frac{2}{3}$ **27** 46 ft, or $15\frac{1}{3}$ yd
29 300 in.³ **31** 3 yd, or 9 ft **33a** $\frac{2}{3}$ **b** Distance covered in 2 hr 40 min at 42 mi/hr **35a** $\frac{9}{10}$ **b** $\frac{28}{27}$
37a The diagonal measurement **b** The amount of pull the line has consistently borne without breaking.
39 Enter +A3+1 in cell A4, and copy B3 to B4. Then copy A 4–B 4 to A102–B102. **41a** 427.2 **b** 1495.2
c 1.8 **d** 513,280.8 **e** −427.2 **f** −1495.2
43a $\frac{2}{7}$ **b** $\frac{a}{d}$ **45** 1979 **47a** 3 **b** 3 **c** x **d** x

4.2 Ratios of Measurements pages 161–164

1a 40 mi/hr **b** $15/book **c** 24 mi/gal **3a** False
b False **c** True **d** True **5** Shreds; Ingredients,
quality, brand loyalty **7** $\frac{5}{9}, \frac{4}{7}, \frac{3}{5}, \frac{2}{3}$ **9a** $0.45 **b** $11.25
11 About 720 bricks **13** 1512.5 mi **15** About
22,200 bushels **17** About 6.15 hr, or 6 hr 9 min
19 4:5 **21** 2 min. **23** Mayflower **25** $\frac{309}{173}$ **27** 30%
29a 1 **b** 13 **c** 0 **d** −4 **31** About 32%
33 About $11 **35** $\frac{2}{3}$

4.3 More Applications of Ratios pages 167–171

1 About 200 mi **3a** 1:240 **b** ≈2.9m × ≈4.8 m;
≈3.6 m × ≈4.6m **5** About 264.5 persons/sq mi
7 ≈0.14 lb/in.^{3} **9** 10 ft 8 in. **11** 1:10,000,000
13 About 2.5 kg **15a** ≈360 mi **b** ≈165 mi **17** The
map with scale 1:3,500,000. **19a** Oil floats on water.
b 2400g or 2.4kg; 2190g or 2.19kg **21** 40 in.
23 2150.4 kg **25** Aluminum, oak, and glass balls
27a About 11 persons/sq mi; about 675 persons/sq mi
b About 74,200,000 **c** About 7 persons/sq mi; about
755 persons/sq mi **29** Sandy **31** 290:375 or 58:75
33 8 P.M. **35** $x = \frac{5}{3}$ **37** $x = 3$

4.4 Working with Units pages 174–177

1 a, c, and **d** **3a** 3600 sec **b** 360 in. **5a** 180 sec;
$\frac{1}{15}$ mi/sec **b** 30 min; $1\frac{2}{15}$ mi/min **7a** $\frac{7}{3}$ **b** $\frac{7}{3}$ **c** $\frac{7}{3}$
d $\frac{7}{3}$ **9** About 310.6 lengths **11a** 20 qt **b** 48 pt
c 40 oz **13** 3 in./sec **15** ≈551.8 ft^3 **17** 16 pitchers
19a 112 mi **b** About 17 days 7 hr **21** About 306 km
23 5.4 hr, or 5 hr 24 min **25** $2\frac{2}{3}$ in. **27a** 3:21:36 P.M.
b About 4:2:7 **29** 1 **31** $x = 3$ **33** 10 ft 5 in.
35 $x = 51$, $y = 64$, $z = 19$ **37a** 655,360 bytes
b $1024 = 2^{10}$, near 1,000.

4.5 Proportions pages 181–184

1 $\frac{3}{4}, \frac{4}{3}$, or 12 **3** 10 in. **5** 27 in., or $2\frac{1}{4}$ ft **7** $x = 16$
9 $x = 10$ **11** $x = 60$ **13a** 25 **b** 8:25 **15** About 9 gal
17 $x = 7\frac{1}{5}$ **19** $z = 12$ **21a** 10 **b** 9 **c** 10% **23** 189 in.^{2}
25 About 17.14 **27** Fall short; 500 units **29a** $y = 6$
b $y = 6$ **c** $y = 8$ **d** $y = 6.71$ **31** 5:1 **33** $1\frac{1}{2}$ hr
35 The angle formed by the two segments is a right
angle and the sum of the measures of the other two
angles is 90. **37a** $1.\overline{6}$
b 13 **c** $17.\overline{3}$

4.6 Similarity pages 187–191

1 Possible answer: Check that corresponding
angles are congruent or that the ratios of the
lengths of corresponding sides are equal. **3** 12, 15
5 2 ft 1 in. **7a** Yes **b** No **c** No **9a** 1:3 **b** 1:3
c 1:3 **d** 9 **11a** 4:3 **b** 16:9 **c** 4:3 **13a** 6 in.
b About 16.67 in. **15a** 12 in. **b** 16 in. **c** 12 ft, 16 ft
17a About 3.43 **b** About 11.67 **19** 70 sq units **21** 15

23

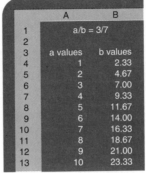

25 Slugger

27 $w ≈ 3.17$ **29** $w ≈ 7.74$ **31** Electric: about 271.9
milion barrels; residential and commercial: about
512.2 million barrels; industrial: about 1561.9 million
barrels; transportation: about 3977.5 million barrels.

Chapter 4 Review pages 193–195

1a Yards **b** Teaspoons **c** Quarts **d** Fluidounces
3b Daisies are 25¢ each in each case. **5** $x = 9.6$
7 $x = 9.6$ **9** 210 in., or 17 ft 6 in. **11** $6.\overline{6}$ **13** $\frac{1}{8760}$,
about $1.14 × 10^{-4}$ **15a** 38 m^2 **b** About 408.6 ft^2
17 Height, texture, weight, color, volume, girth;
height, weight, volume, girth **19** About 200 mi
21 About 35.76 mi/hr **23a** 60 ft^3 **b** 3450 lb
25 $810 **27** 34.5 **29** The two rectangles are not
similar. **31a** About 2.35 acres **b** $0.011 /yd^2
33 60; 135

Chapter 5: Data Analysis

5.1 Circle Graphs pages 203–206

1 An entire quantity divided into groups. **3** 360
5 So that the percents add up to 100%. **7** Answers
may vary. Discuss $\frac{42}{177} ≈ 24\%$ versus $\frac{42}{154} ≈ 27\%$
9 No **11** The "rock" pie segment is much larger
than the corresponding segment in problem 9. The
"country" pie segment is much smaller than the
corresponding segment in problem 9. **13** A: ≈155;
B: ≈65; C: ≈80; D: ≈60 **15** About 3,983,868,000
barrels **17** The answer cannot be determined.
Even though the percent went down, the total
amount consumed in 1970 is not known.
19b 139,500,000 **c** Less than 1 year: 5.6%; 1–5 years:
34.1%; 5–10 yrs: 30.6%; 10–15 yrs: 19.9%; 15 yrs or
older: 9.8% **d** Less than 1 year: 20°; 1–5 yrs: 123°;
5–10 yrs: 110°; 10–15 yrs: 72°; 15 yrs or older: 35°
e

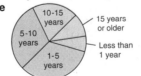

21 Possible answer:
Each number is 9
more than the
preceding number.

23 5 yds **25** ≈162° **27** About 74% **29** 4

5.2 Bar Graphs and Line Graphs   pages 209–212

1 The Richter-Scale readings would appear along the vertical axis, and the countries would appear along the horizontal axis.   **3** It appears that in the year 2000, the women's high jump record will reach 7 ft.   **5a** Data for which we know both the total and the breakdown of the total   **b** Data that are used to compare different conditions

7a

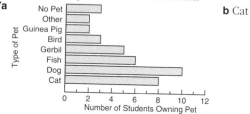

b Cat

9a Price per share in U.S. dollars   **b** Increased $\frac{7}{8}$ dollar or about $.88   **c** $37\frac{1}{8}$ to $33\frac{1}{2}$ **d** Tuesday

e

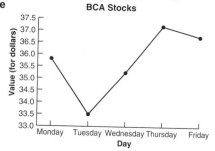

11a 0.85%   **b** 1.06%   **c** 1%   **d** Cannot determine. The answer would depend on the population in that year.   **e** 3.86; 3.72; 2.08; 2.04; 2.02
13 Possible answer: Plane takes off, circles the airport, lands, takes off again

15

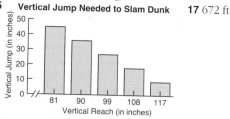

17 672 ft

19 7.5 gal   **21a** 0.059 kg

5.3 Other Data Displays   pages 216–220

1 In a histogram, a mark is made for each individual piece of data.   **3** Possible answer: Use a scattergram if data is given in pairs of numbers and you want to determine a relationship. Use a bar graph if you know the number of items in each category and you want to determine a trend.
5 It is easier to compare information on a bar graph.
7 About 3.2 years   **9** 15:41, or $\frac{15}{41}$
11 Possible answer: Long goods are more fun to eat.

13

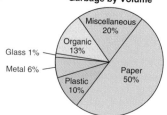

Legend: ✳ = 10 inches of snowfall

15 About 1.36×10^{10} gal; About 1.72×10^{10} gal
17 1970 to 1980   **19**

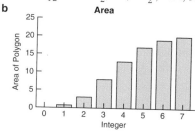

21 Answer depends on graph drawn in problem **20.**
23 0   **25** $\frac{1}{12}$ **27a** 1: $\frac{1}{2}$; 2:3; 3: $\frac{15}{2}$; 4:14; 5:17; 6:20; 7:21
b

29a The perimeter of rectangle 2 is half the perimeter of rectangle 1.   **b** The area of rectangle 2 is one fourth the area of rectangle 1.   **31a** Less than 1 year: ≈2.5 million; Between 1 and 5 years: ≈23.8 million; Between 5 and 10 years: ≈17.2 million; Between 10 and 15 years: ≈6 million; more than 15 years: ≈1 million.   **b** Less than 7; between 7 and 35; between 35 and 70; between 70 and 105; more than 105.   **33a** $\frac{61}{100}$ **b** $\frac{21}{50}$

5.4 Averages   pages 224–227

1 35; 48; $48\frac{1}{3}$ **3** Since each of the three averages may yield a different number, it is important to identify the average so that the data are not incorrectly interpreted.   **5a** 136.2; 130   **b** ≈148.8; 133   **c** Change in mean is about 12.6; Change in median is 3.   **7a** 72.46   **b** 65   **c** 95; No   **d** Possible answer: No, the data items vary in value.
9a 74   **b** 0   **11a** 8   **b** 15   **c** 11   **13** Since you don't know the number of women or the number of pieces in the "5 or more" category, the mean and median can't be found. The mode is zero.
15a ≈$9.23   **b** 0   **c** 0   **17a** 71
b,c

```
10              71              130
|---------------|----------------|
```

19a $\approx$30.7; 21.5
b

6	21.5 30.7		120

21a 233 **b** $\approx$21 **c** Health-care costs; Skill levels and aging work force **23** –56; $(-7)(8) = -56$
25a The larger the waist size, the larger the neck size **b** About 25 cm **c** A scale beginning at zero would not be a feasible set of numbers. **27a** No
b Possible answer: Other teams in Oakland's division may be weak. **c** Cincinnati won the World Series in 1975, 1976, and 1990. Los Angeles won the World Series in 1981 and 1988.

5.5 Organizing Data pages 230–233

1a
```
 6 | 3 9
 7 | 9
 8 | 2 8
 9 | 0 1 3 4 5 7
10 | 6
 : :
35 | 3    where 6|3 means 6.3
```
b 35.3 for Mt. Washington; 35.3 is more than 1.5 times the midquartile range above the upper quartile.

3 25% **5** Percentiles divide the data into 100 parts, and quartiles divide data into four parts.
7a 83 **b** 69 **c** 68 **d** 60 **e** 84
f

9a
```
2 | 3 3
3 | 3 3
4 | 2 4 8
5 | 1 5
6 |
7 | 4    where 2|3 means 2.3
```
b 4.3; 3.3; 5.1; 2.3 and 7.4; 5.1
c
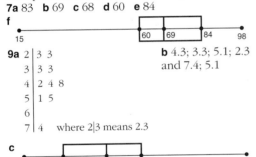

d No; none of the data are 1.5 times the midquartile range from the upper or the lower quartile.
11a 6, 9, 11, 16, 17, 21, 24, 38, 56, 80, 96, 106, 113, 126, 149, 157, 174, 191, 287, 336, 496, 651, 1356, 2639 **b** 109.5; 22.5; 239; 6 and 2639 **c** Most of the data are closer in value to median than mean.
d
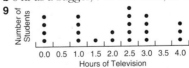

e 651, 1356, 2639 **f** Answers will vary. Fish are a main source of food in Alaska; Alaska has the longest coastline. **13** $\approx$4.7 cm **15a** False **b** True **c** False **d** True **e** False

5.6 Matrices pages 236–241

1 A matrix is a two dimensional table of rows and columns. **3** 2×3 **5** $\begin{bmatrix} 12 & 18 \\ 15 & 20 \end{bmatrix}$ **7** $\begin{bmatrix} 2 & 3 & 4 & 5 \\ 3 & 4 & 5 & 6 \\ 4 & 5 & 6 & 7 \\ 5 & 6 & 7 & 8 \end{bmatrix}$

9a $e_{1,2}, e_{2,1}, e_{2,3}$ **b** $e_{1,2}, e_{1,3}, e_{2,3}$
11

Perimeter	Area
6	2
12	8
18	18
24	32
30	50
36	72

13 $w = 6$; $x = 9$; $y = 6$; $z = -1$; $t = 2$

15 Possible answer: $\begin{bmatrix} 1 & 2 & 3 \\ 2 & 4 & 6 \\ 3 & 6 & 9 \end{bmatrix}$ **17** Job A: Arti; Job B: Tria; Job C: Rita

19

	A	B	C	D
A	0	3	1	1
B	1	0	1	1
C	3	3	0	1
D	2	3	2	0

21

Years Experience	Bagger	Stockboy	Cashier
1	4.80	5.07	7.84
2	5.23	5.60	8.54
3	5.71	6.24	9.28
4	6.08	6.56	10.14
5	6.67	7.20	11.15

23a

4	6	8 9	11

b 8 **c** $\frac{2}{5}$ or 0.4 **d** about 120 **25** 1 **27** 3 **29** 7
31a Kix: $182.00; Trox: $93.50; Soggies: $259.25
b Store A: $173.75; Store B: $93.25, Store C: $101.75; Store D: $166 **c** Store A **33** $\approx$0.11 **35** LCM
```
40
30
 6
42
10
24
```

37 8 **39** 8

Chapter 5 Review pages 243–246

1a $\approx$4.2 **b** $\approx$7.5 **c** 2:1 **d** Possible answer: Students do better in school if their attendance is better. **3** $\begin{bmatrix} 5 & 7 \\ 9 & 11 \end{bmatrix}$ **5** Answers will vary.

7a Bill: $188.75; Sue: $219; Harry: $246.25
b 6 hr as a bagger, 7 hr as a clerk, or 4 hr as a cashier
9

Number of Students

•			•		•	•		•
•			•		•	•		•
•		•	•	•	•	•		•
•	•	•	•	•	•	•		•

0.0 0.5 1.0 1.5 2.0 2.5 3.0 3.5 4.0
Hours of Television

11a East: Boston; West: Oakland **b** East: Toronto; West: Oakland **c** Texas **d** Oakland
13 Answers will vary. **15a** North Dakota and Texas **b** $\frac{1}{20}$ **c** Colorado and New Mexico

6.1 The Number Line   pages 256–259

1 0   **3** Possible answer: The integers consist of the natural numbers, their opposites, and zero.   **5** 45 sec **7a** 3.6   **b** –102   **c** 0   **9a** A: –2 or 8; B:11 or 19   **b** 13 units (–2 to 11); 21 units (–2 to 19); 3 units (8 to 11); 11 units (8 to 19)   **11** 16°   **13a** –11   **b** –7   **15a** –14 **b** –π   **c** $\sqrt{2}$ **d** 0   **e** 1   **f** $\frac{3}{4}$ **17a** 2   **b** –9   **c** –8   **d** –4 **e** –3.5   **f** –4$\frac{2}{3}$ **19a** 2   **b** 1   **c** 0   **d** –1   **e** –2   **f** –3   **g** –4

21

23a

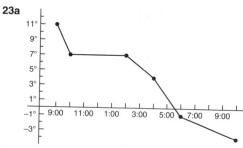

b –4°C   **25a** –2   **b** –2   **27a** 26   **b** 10   **c** –2   **d** 2 **29a** 6   **b** 3   **c** 0   **d** –3   **e** –6   **f** –9   **31** 0   **33** $206.25 **35a** 16   **b** 16 is the midpoint of the segment connecting x to y.   **37** In parentheses

6.2 Inequalities   pages 263–266

1a 3   **b** 5   **c** 1   **d** 4   **e** 2   **3** A shaded endpoint indicates that the endpoint is included in the set. **5** An arrowhead represents the continuation of the set in that direction.   **7** Possible answer: An *and* inequality represents a graph that is shaded between two numbers; an *or* inequality represents a graph that has two or more separate sections. **9a** –4   **b** Less than   **11** Yes   **13a** 6 and 7   **b** –7 and –6 **15a**

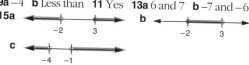

17a This inequality implies that $3 < –3$. **b** Number $< –3$ or number > 3 **19** $0 < L + W < 25$ **21a** Possible answer: $–2 < x \le 3$ **b** Possible answer: $y \ge –1$ **c** Possible answer: $z < 1$ **23** The graph of $x < –2$ or $x > –1$ is shaded to the left of –2 and to the right of –1. The graph of $x < –2$ and $x > –1$ has no shading because no numbers satisfy both conditions.   **25a** Yes, but it is customary to put the negatives to the left of zero and the positives to the right.   **b** No, because the distance from 0 to 1 establishes the scale, and this scale must be maintained along the number line.

27

29a 13   **b** 7   **c** 6

31 12, 6, 0, –6, –12, –18

33a

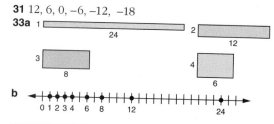

b

6.3 Adding Signed Numbers   pages 269–274

1 No, the dimensions of the matrices must be the same.   **3** $\frac{19}{24}$ **5** Possible answer: The sum of two positive numbers is positive; the sum of two negative numbers is negative.   **7a** 8   **b** 3   **c** –7   **d** –2 **9** –3 + 8 + (–2) = 3   **11** Yes   **13a** Never   **b** Always **c** Sometimes   **15** $\begin{bmatrix} -11 & -10 & 5 \\ -39 & 21 & 13 \end{bmatrix}$ **17** 1.54

19a $\frac{1}{4}$ **b** $\frac{1}{2}$ **c** $\frac{1}{4}$ **21a** 15   **b** 15   **c** 6.3   **d** 6.3   Possible answer: Adding the opposite of a number gives the same answer as subtracting that number.   **23** $\frac{1}{2}$ **25a** $\frac{57}{21}$, or ≈2.7   **b** $\frac{17}{12}$, or ≈1.4   **c** $\frac{-119}{24}$, or ≈–4.96

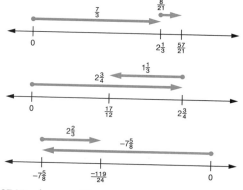

27 No change   **29a** Balance

$65.53
33.00
8.82
–7.60
–13.09
–32.34

b

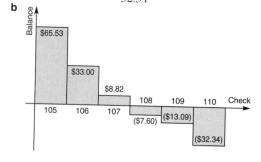

31 11.5 and −5.3 **33** $\begin{bmatrix} -4 & 0 \\ -10 & 0 \\ -18 & 0 \end{bmatrix}$

35 No; the negative numbers should *increase* from left to right. **37a** 20 **b** ≈9.22 **c** ≈4.47
39a −28 **b** −24 **c** 20 **d** −28 **e** −24 **f** 20
41a

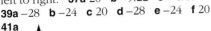

b Some athletes may have participated in more than one sport. A circle graph may be used only when each item belongs to exactly one category.

6.4 Multiplying and Dividing Signed Numbers
pages 278−281

1a −18 **b** −18 **c** −18 **d** −18 **3a** Possible answer: A scalar is a number by which a matrix is multiplied.
b Possible answer: Because a scalar changes the "scale" of a matrix by increasing or decreasing each element by the same factor **5a** 4 **b** −4 **c** Because the square of −2 is the opposite of the opposite of the square of 2 **d** −8 **e** 8 **f** Because the cube of −2 and the opposite of the cube of 2 are both negative **7** Possible answer: Division by a number is equivalent to multiplication by the number's reciprocal.
9a −20 **b** −15 **c** −10 **d** −5 **e** 0 **f** 5 **g** 10 **h** 15 **i** 20

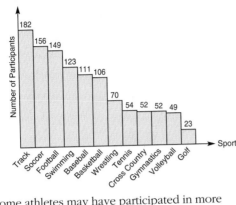

Possible answer: The products increase in increments of 5. **11a** −8 **b** 8 **c** 8 **d** −8 **13a** −29 **b** 9
15a Possible answer: $1.07 \begin{bmatrix} 4.95 \\ 5.65 \\ 4.85 \\ 5.75 \end{bmatrix}$ **b** Raul: $5.30; Pablo: $6.05; Sue: $5.19; Melissa: $6.15

17 −4 **19a** $\begin{bmatrix} 6 & -8 \\ 18 & -36 \\ -12 & 4 \end{bmatrix}$ **b** $\begin{bmatrix} 4.2 & 21 \\ -11.9 & 31.5 \\ -38.85 & 0 \end{bmatrix}$

21a $0.86 \begin{bmatrix} 175{,}000 \\ 98{,}000 \\ 112{,}000 \\ 145{,}000 \\ 205{,}000 \end{bmatrix}$ **b** $\begin{bmatrix} 150{,}500 \\ 84{,}280 \\ 96{,}320 \\ 124{,}700 \\ 176{,}300 \end{bmatrix}$

23a

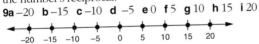

25 $\frac{2}{3}$ **27a** 80 posts **b** 56 posts **c** 66 posts

6.5 Matrix Multiplication pages 285−289

1a $\begin{bmatrix} -7 & 11 \\ -8 & 14 \end{bmatrix}$ **b** $\begin{bmatrix} 0 & -10 \\ -1 & 7 \end{bmatrix}$ **c** Possible answer: The order in which matrices are multiplied affects the answer.

3 Possible answer: 2 × 3 and 3 × 4 **5** 4 × 3 **7a** [22]
b $\begin{bmatrix} -6 & -8 \\ 21 & 28 \end{bmatrix}$ **9a** $\begin{bmatrix} 65 \\ 62 \end{bmatrix}$ **b** $\begin{bmatrix} 25 \\ -46 \end{bmatrix}$ **11** $\begin{bmatrix} 2 & 2 \\ 1 & 4 \end{bmatrix} \cdot \begin{bmatrix} 5 & -3 \\ -2 & -3 \end{bmatrix}$

13 Sometimes **15a** $\begin{bmatrix} 24 & 26 \\ 38 & 40 \end{bmatrix}$ **b** $\begin{bmatrix} 24 & -26 \\ -38 & 40 \end{bmatrix}$

17 Clyde: $70.80; Chloe: $71.20 **19a** Booth 1: $45,475; Booth 2: $47,766.10; Booth 3: $40,608.80
b $133,849.90 **c** Possible answer: Because they are responsible for more wear on the roadway
21a −156 **b** 156 **23** −1.468 × 10²⁹ **25** 36π, or ≈113.1
27a −19 **b** −75 **c** 30 **29** 10 **31a** −24 **b** −24 **c** −42

6.6 Subtracting Signed Numbers
pages 292−295

1 Possible answer: By multiplying the number by −1
3a The opposite of negative 100 **b** 100 **5a** 3 **b** 1
c 4 **d** 2 **7** $\begin{bmatrix} -6 & 1 & 7 \\ 6 & -2 & -2 \end{bmatrix}$ **9a** −3 **b** −13 **c** 13 **d** 3

11

x	−8	−6	−4	−2	0	2	4	6	8
y	12	10	8	6	4	2	0	−2	−4

13a 4 **b** −6 **c** 37 **d** −4.5 **e** −12.56 **f** 23.89 **15a** 11
b −2 **c** −12 **17a** 12 **b** 20 **c** 201 **d** 101
19

$\begin{matrix} 36 & -84 & 126 & -126 & 84 & -36 \\ & 120 & -210 & 252 & -210 & 120 \\ & & 330 & -462 & 462 & -330 \\ & & & 792 & -924 & 792 \\ & & & & 1716 & -1716 \\ & & & & & 3432 \end{matrix}$

21a −28 **b** −16 **c** −19 **d** 50

23 40 units **25a** 35 **b** 35 **c** 12 **d** 12

27a

Ted	12
Bill	12
Laura	10
Kim	19

b

Ted	3.0
Bill	2.0
Laura	2.0
Kim	≈3.2

29 1, −18; 2, −9; 3, −6; 6, −3; 9, −2; 18, −1

31a True **b** True **c** True **d** True

6.7 Absolute Value pages 298–301

1a 5 **b** 0 **c** 6.23 **d** $3\frac{2}{3}$ **3a** 10, –10 **b** 1.3, –1.3
c 0 **5a** 4 **b** 20 **7** Both expressions stand for the distance between the points whose coordinates are x and y. This distance is unique, so the expressions must be equal. **9a** 4 **b** –8
11 $|x-3|=2$ 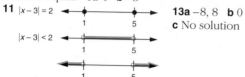 **13a** –8, 8 **b** 0
$|x-3|<2$ **c** No solution

15 $|-7|-|18|, |18+(-7)| = |-18+7| = |7-18| =$
$|-7-(-18)|, |-7-18|$ **17a** –5 or 5 **b** –5 or 5
c 4 or 14 **19a** 12 **b** 12 **c** 18 **d** 18 **21** –4, –2, 0
23a Possible answers: $|3+2| = |3|+|2|; |-3+(-2)| =$
$|-3|+|-2|; |3+0| = |3|+|0|$ **b** Possible answers:
$|3+(-2)| < |3|+|-2|; |-3+2| < |-3|+|2|; |-1+1| <$
$|-1|+|1|$ **c** The statement is never true.
25 –7 and 15 **27** 0.1 **29a** 9 **b** 21; 21 **c** $|x-9| = 2$
31a $|x-3| = 12$ **b** $|x+5| = 8$ **33** Mean: $\approx$–5.58;
median: –2; mode: –12 **35**

–65	40	–40
–105	80	
–185		

37

–32
38

39a –4 **b** –10 **c** –12 **41**

*	–3	–7	+4	–2
+2	–6	–14	8	–4
–5	15	35	–20	10
–6	18	42	–24	12

6.8 Two-Dimensional Graphs pages 305–309

1 (2, 4); (0, 1); (–2, 2); (–3, 0); (–3, –4); (3, –1)
3 Possible answer: Quadrant I ordered pairs have the form (+, +); Quadrant II ordered pairs, (–, +); Quadrant III ordered pairs, (–, –); and Quadrant IV ordered pairs, (+, –). **5** (2.5, 1)
7

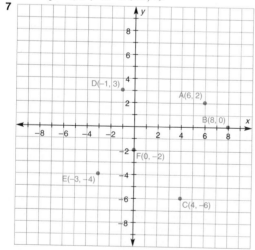

A: Quadrant I; B: No quadrant; C: Quadrant IV;
D: Quadrant II; E: Quadrant III; F: No quadrant
9 (–5, 1); (–3, 2); (1, 1); (0, –3); (–4, –2)

11 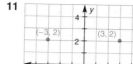 Possible answer: The points are the vertices of a rectangle.

13 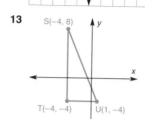 ST = 12; TU = 5; SU = 13

15a R(–6, 5); E(2, 5); C(2, –1); T(–6,–1) **b** 48 **c** 10
17a Possible answers: With the bottom side and the left side lying on the x- and y-axes; with the bottom side lying on the x-axis and the origin at its midpoint; with the origin at the figure's center
b Possible answer: With the bottom side and the left side lying on the x- and y-axes
c

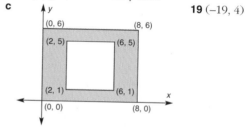

19 (–19, 4)

21 (5, –2); (8, –2); (8, –6) **23a** 88 **b** $\approx$13.6%
25 88 ft/sec **27**

29 (–1, 3); (–5, –1); (–2, –2) **31** –5394 **33** 36.7
35 2 or –2 **37** 4 or –2 **39** Possible answer: $|x| < 9$

Chapter 6 Review pages 311–313

1a –153 **b** –786 **c** 58 **d** 6 **e** 4956 **f** –8 **3a** 8 units
b $3\frac{1}{2}$ units **c** 7 units **d** 5.34 units **5a** $x \geq -4$
b $-5 \leq x < 1$ **7** 18 ft **9a** –10 **b** –6 **c** 16 **d** 4 **e** –4
f –12 **g** 4096 **h** –2 **11** $w = -80; x = 100; y = -9;$
$z = 9$ **13a** –27 **b** –64 **c** –125 **d** 81 **e** 256 **f** 625
15 $u = -13; v = 8; x = -3; y = 6; z = -20$
17a $-6(5+2) = -42$ **b** $-9(5) + (-9)(2) = -63$
c $-3[4+(-9)] = 15$ **19a** 45 **b** A′(–3, 1), B′(–3, 11),
C′(6, 6) **21** –42 **23a** False; $-2 \cdot -3 = 6$ **b** False;
$-2 + -3 = -5$ **25a** –64 **b** –64 **c** 64 **d** 64 **27a** 14
b –8 **c** 16 **29a** 13, –3 **b** –13, 3 **c** $-3 \leq w \leq 13$

Chapter 7: Exploring Geometry

7.1 Line and Angle Relationships
pages 320–324

1 Possible answers: Top edge and bottom edge of desk are parallel; top and side of chalkboard are perpendicular.   **3a** 33 **b** 147 **c** 147   **5** Not adjacent; the angles do not have a common vertex.
7 Adjacent **9a** 51 **b** 129 **c** 51
11 Possible answer:

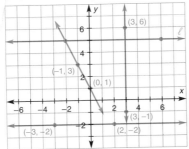

13 No **15** $\overline{QR} \parallel \overline{SE}$; $\overline{QS} \parallel \overline{RE}$; $\overline{QR} \perp \overline{RE}$; $\overline{RE} \perp \overline{ES}$; $\overline{ES} \perp \overline{SQ}$; $\overline{SQ} \perp \overline{QR}$ **17a** 90 **b** ≈101 **c** ≈27 **d** ≈63
19a m∠1 = 60; m∠2 = 150; m∠3 = 120; m∠4 = 60; m∠5 = 30; m∠6 = 150; m∠7 = 120; m∠8 = 60
b ∠1, ∠4, ∠8 are congruent. ∠2, ∠6 are congruent. ∠3, ∠7 are congruent. **c** ∠1 and ∠5, ∠4 and ∠5, ∠8 and ∠5 **d** ∠1 and ∠3, ∠1 and ∠7, ∠3 and ∠4, ∠7 and ∠4, ∠8 and ∠3, ∠7 and ∠8, ∠5 and ∠2, ∠5 and ∠6 **21a** 6 units **b** 6 **c** 20 units **d** 20
23 5; 5; 5; 5 **25**

Figure	Number of Rays	Number of Angles
A	3	3
B	4	6
C	5	10
D	6	15
E	12	66

27 5 and 6 **29** −3 and −2

7.2 Quadrilaterals
pages 328–331

1 Always **3** Never **5** Sometimes **7** A square is a rectangle because adjacent sides are perpendicular. A square is a rhombus because all four sides are congruent. A square is a parallelogram because opposite sides are parallel. A square is not a trapezoid because it has two pairs of parallel sides.
9a Square **b** Possible answer: They could be moved the same distance to the left. **c** Possible answer: They could be moved the same distance upward.
11

	Quadrilateral	Trapezoid	Parallelogram	Rhombus	Rectangle
a	✓				
b	✓		✓		✓
c	✓		✓	✓	
d	✓	✓			

13a Adjacent **b** Adjacent **c** Opposite **d** Adjacent
15   **17**

19a Square **b** Possible answer: They could be moved the same distance to the right or left.
c Possible answer: They could be moved the same distance up or down. **d** Possible answer: D could be moved to the left, and U could be moved the same distance to the right. **21** (−3, 4) **23** m∠F = 50, m∠R = 130, m∠E = 50, m∠D = 130; possible answer: opposite angles are congruent and consecutive angles are supplementary. **25** Possible answer: Wyoming and Colorado appear to be shaped like rectangles. **27** 3 parallelograms **29a** −8 **b** 200%
c 25% **31** | $x-2$ | < 4 **33b** = −28 **35** 90; 56

7.3 Symmetry pages 335–338

1 Both **3** Rotation **5a** Sometimes **b** Always
c Always **7**   **9**

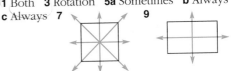

11a True; an equilateral triangle is one example.
b False for all finite figures
13   **15** 180° rotation symmetry about the midpoint of $\overline{PL}$

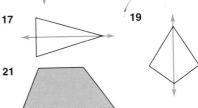

17   **19**

21

23 Impossible **25** Impossible **27** Impossible
29a Possible answer: An open-ended wrench can be slipped onto it from 6 directions instead of just 4.
b Possible answer: They are too "round," so that a wrench might slip on them, or wear away the corners. **c** Possible answer: Opposite sides are not parallel, and an open-ended wrench could not be used on them. **d** Pentagonal bolt heads are found on fire hydrants so unauthorized persons may not turn on the water. **31a** (−1, 1); (−4, 0); (−1, −1); (0, −4); (1, −1) **b** Yes; (0, 0); 90°
33 Possible answer: Many kinds of flowers have radial (rotation) symmetry; some other kinds, as well as many kinds of leaves, have bilateral (reflection) symmetry. The arrangement of leaves on plant stems is often bilaterally symmetric. Some lower animals (starfish, coral polyps) have radial symmetry, whereas most higher animals (including human beings) are bilaterally symmetric.
35 56 **37** −6 **39** The triangles are congruent right triangles. **41** The triangles are congruent isosceles triangles. **43** 2.45 m **45** ≈3.05 m

7.4 Rigid Transformations pages 343–346

1 At 6, 8, and 9, respectively

3a
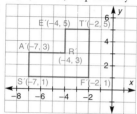

b
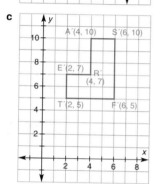

c
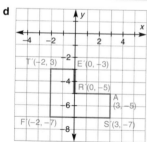

d
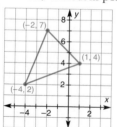

5 Possible answer: A figure is symmetric if it can undergo a transformation (reflection or rotation of 180° or less) without its position changing.

7a
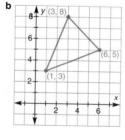

9
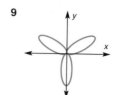

11 R′(4, 2), E′(4, −3), C′(−3, −3), T′(−3, 2)

13 130 **15** Parallelogram

17a
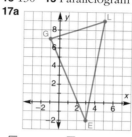

b
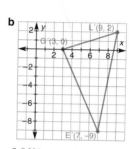

c $\begin{bmatrix} 4 & 4 & 4 \\ -7 & -7 & -7 \end{bmatrix}$ **19a** 0% **b** ≈2.96%

21 True **23** True **25** True **27a** $\frac{2}{5}$ **b** $\frac{3}{4}$

7.5 Discovering Properties pages 349–353

1 Possible answer: All four sides are congruent, so ABCD is a rhombus. **3a** Reflect △NST over $\overline{TN}$, forming △T′S′N′, △TSS′ will be equilateral.
b SN = $\frac{TS}{2}$ **5** Possible answers: One diagonal ($\overline{KT}$) bisects the other ($\overline{EI}$). The diagonals are perpendicular. One diagonal ($\overline{KT}$) bisects a pair of opposite angles. A pair of opposite angles (∠E and ∠I) are congruent.
7 74 **9** (5, 7); (11, 2) **11** 9
13
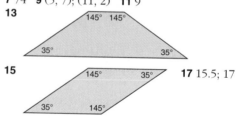

15 **17** 15.5; 17

19 68; 68 **21** 50 **23** 34; 24; 21.2; 20 **25** (10, 0); (0, 8)
27 Square and rectangle

29

	A	B	C
1	k	$2k$	AB
2	1	2	2.236
3	2	4	4.472
4	3	6	6.708
5	4	8	8.944
6	5	10	11.180
7	6	12	13.416
8	7	14	15.652
9	8	16	17.889
10	9	18	20.125
11	10	20	22.361
12	11	22	24.597
13	12	24	26.833
14	13	26	29.069
15	14	28	31.305
16	15	30	33.541
17	16	32	35.777
18	17	34	38.013
19	18	36	40.249
20	19	38	42.485
21	20	40	44.721
22	21	42	46.957
23	22	44	49.193
24	23	46	51.430
25	24	48	53.666

31 32° F **33** −25.6° F **35a** 20 mm **b** 100 mm²
c No. The answer to **a** is a linear measure in mm,
while the answer to **b** is a measure of area in mm².

7.6 Transformations and Matrices
pages 357–361

1 c **3a** $\begin{bmatrix} 0 & 10 & 14 \\ 6 & 16 & 4 \end{bmatrix}$ **b** 80 **c** 1:4

5 Possible answer: $\begin{array}{ccc} \mathbf{P} & \mathbf{Q} & \mathbf{I} \\ \begin{bmatrix} -3 & 4 & -4 \\ 3 & -1 & -2 \end{bmatrix} \end{array}$ **7** A′(0, −7),
B′(4, −5), C′(6, 5)

9a The x-coordinates change to their opposites; the
y-coordinates remain the same. **b** $\begin{bmatrix} 6 & -5 & 8 \\ 4 & 3 & 2 \end{bmatrix}$
11a $\begin{array}{ccc} \mathbf{Y}′ & \mathbf{E}′ & \mathbf{S}′ \\ \begin{bmatrix} 6 & -4 & -10 \\ 10 & 8 & 10 \end{bmatrix} \end{array}$

b

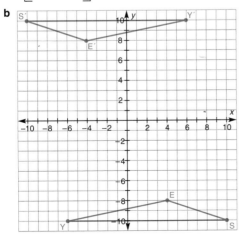

A rotation of 180° about the origin

13a $\begin{bmatrix} 4 & 2 & 7 \\ 9 & 6 & 5 \end{bmatrix}$ **b** $p = -3$; $q = -11$; S′ (1, −2);
A′ (−1, −5)

15 H′(−1, 6), A′(2, 4), T′(−5, 3) **17** H′(−1, 2), A′(1, 5),
T′(2, −2) **19a** $\begin{array}{ccc} \mathbf{R} & \mathbf{E} & \mathbf{V} \\ \begin{bmatrix} 0 & 0 & 3 \\ 4 & 0 & 0 \end{bmatrix} \end{array}$

b $\begin{array}{ccc} \mathbf{R}′ & \mathbf{E}′ & \mathbf{V}′ \\ \begin{bmatrix} 0 & 0 & -3 \\ 4 & 0 & 0 \end{bmatrix} \end{array}$

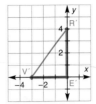

c $\begin{bmatrix} 0 & 0 & -3 \\ -4 & 0 & 0 \end{bmatrix}$

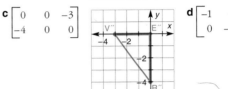

d $\begin{bmatrix} -1 & 0 \\ 0 & -1 \end{bmatrix}$

e $\begin{bmatrix} 0 & 0 & -3 \\ -4 & 0 & 0 \end{bmatrix}$; possible answer: Rotating a figure
180° is the same as reflecting it over
the y-axis, then reflecting the image
over the x-axis.

21 $\begin{bmatrix} 2 & -1 & 1 \\ 3 & -4 & 6 \end{bmatrix}$ The product is identical to the
multiplicand.

23a 18 **b** 18 **25** −3.585 **27** 398.068 **29** P′(−2, −3);
P″(2, −1); P‴(6, 1); P⁗(10, 3); P‴″(14, 5)

Chapter 7 Review   pages 363–365

1 Each is 55. **3** D′(−2, 5), E′(3, 1), F′(1, 0), G′(0, −5)
5 Both

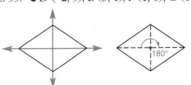

7 Both

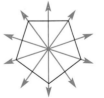

9a Rectangle **b** Move 4 units left. **c** Move 4 units up.
d Move 4 units down.

11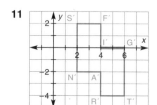

13a Move A to (8, 0). **b** Move A to (8, 0), or move H to (−3, 0), or move E to (3, 5).

15 **17**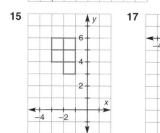

19a Similarities: 4 congruent sides, diagonals are perpendicular bisectors of each other. Differences: The angles of a rhombus need not be right angles; the diagonals of a rhombus need not be congruent. **b** Similarities: Opposite sides are congruent and parallel; opposite angles are congruent; consecutive angles are supplementary; diagonals bisect each other. Differences: The angles of a parallelogram need not be right angles; the diagonals of a parallelogram need not be congruent. **21** 100 **23a** K′(−1, −5), I′(1, −7), T′(3, −5), E′(1, 0) **b** K′(1, 5), I′(−1, 7), T′(−3, 5), E′(−1, 0)

Chapter 8: The Language of Algebra

8.1 Simplifying Expressions   pages 374–377

1 No **3** $8x + x = (8 + 1)x = 9x$ **5** Susie; Like terms have the same variable and the same power.
7a 135 = 135 **b** Right **c** 540 = 540 **d** Left **e** When it is easier to add first; when it is easier to multiply first
9 $3x + 4x = 7x$ is true for every value of x, but $x + 5 = 8$ is true only when $x = 3$. **11a** $14x$ **b** 0
c $11x + 7y$ **d** $-6x - 3$ **e** $-4x^2 - 5x$ **f** $46x - 9y$
13 $4xy + 9xy − 5xy = 8xy$ **15a** False **b** True **c** True
d False **17a** $-\frac{1}{4}$ **b** $-\frac{1}{4}x$ **c** Cannot be simplified.
19a $4x + 4$ **b** $3y + 1$ **c** $x = 3, y = 5$ **d** AB = 28, CD = 28 **21** $0x = 0$, so 0 is the simpler form.
23a $13x + 3$ **b** 4.3

25a $11x − 2$
b

	A	B	C	D	E
1	x	Side TR	Side RI	Side TI	Sum of Sides
2	1	1	5	3	9
3	2	5	7	8	20
4	3	9	9	13	31
5	4	13	11	18	42
6	5	17	13	23	53
7	6	21	15	28	64
8	7	25	17	33	75
9	8	29	19	38	86
10	9	33	21	43	97
11	10	37	23	48	108
12	11	41	25	53	119
13	12	45	27	58	130
14	13	49	29	63	141
15	14	53	31	68	152
16	15	57	33	73	163
17	16	61	35	78	174
18	17	65	37	83	185
19	18	69	39	88	196
20	19	73	41	93	207

27 $x = 6 − y$; $y = 6 − x$ **29a** True **b** False **31a** −17 **b** 2
33a 99; −11 **b** −495; 55 **c** −297; 33 **35a** > **b** = **c** <

8.2 Using Variables   pages 381–384

1a $8 + (−8)$; 0 **b** $\frac{2}{3} \cdot \frac{3}{2}$; 1 **c** $x + (−x)$; 0 **d** $y\left(\frac{1}{y}\right)$; 1

3 The sentence is true when you substitute any value for x. **5a** $31.20 **b** $3b + (0.12)d$ **7** $(2x + 1) + (8x − 3) + (15x + 2)$, or $25x$ **9a** $n − 6$ **b** Half of a number **c** $2(n + 3)$ **d** A number subtracted from 5
11 $C = P + 0.06P$ or $C = 1.06P$ **13a** $4(6) + 0.09($850)$, or $100.50 **b** $4(H) + 0.09(D)$ **15** Possible answers: $M = 14 + Y$, $Y = 3C$, $63 = C + (3C) + (14 + 3C)$
17a $a^2 = b^2 + c^2$ **b** $(t + 7)^2 = (k − 2)^2 + (m + 3)^2$
19 $4x + 17 = 2x + 21$ **21a** $33,000 − 400(1)$
b $33,000 − 400(2)$ **c** $33,000 − 400(3)$ **d** $33,000 − 400(4)$
e $33,000 − 400(m)$ **23a** Yes; $2x + 4y = 6x + 3$
b No; not unless the trapezoid is isosceles **25a** $−2x − 5$
b $11x + 11y$ **27** 55 **29a** < **b** < **c** < **d** < **e** > **f** >
31a Substitute 4 for x. Multiply 4 by 3, then add 7.
b Subtract 5 from 35 to get 30. Divide 30 by 2 to get 15.

8.3 Solving Equations   pages 388–391

1 Possible answer: Raising the shade, then opening the window, then closing the window and lowering the shade **3a** *ii* **b** *i* **c** *iv* **d** *iii*; Each is an inverse operation. **5a** $7 = n + 3$ **b** $n + 7$ or $7 + n$ **c** $3n + 7$
d $3n + 7 = 12$ **e** $3 + 7 = n$ **7a** $x = 5.5$ **b** $x = 5.25$
c $x = −8$ **9a** $3x + 7$ **b** $x = −1$ **c** $x = 3$ **d** $−17 − 7x$
11a $x = 4.5$ **b** $x = −193$ **c** $4a − 3b$ **d** $y = 146.51$
e $t = 27$ **f** $k = 19.3$ **g** $k = −13$ **h** $2m − 392$
i $5x − 10x^2$ **j** $d = 321$ **k** $t = 27$ **l** $15 − 3x$ **13** 135
15a $57 = 36 + 7x$ **b** $x = 3$ **17a** $23x + 19 = 180$
b $x = 7$ **c** m∠A = 89, m∠B = 78, m∠C = 13
19a $a + 4 = 15$ **b** $a = 11$ **c** 5; 5 **d** 6 **21a** $\frac{x^2}{36} = .4$
b $x ≈ 3.8$ **23a** 3 **b** 3 **c** 3 **d** −3 **25a** 4 **b** 33

27a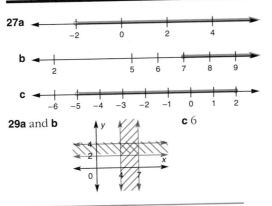

b

c

29a and **b**   **c** 6

8.4 Some Special Equations   pages 395–398

1a $x = 17$ or $x = -17$ **b** $x = 17$ or $x = -25$ **c** $x = -4$
d No solution   **e** Part a is absolute value of x,
Part b is absolute value of a sum.   **f** 4 has only
one additive inverse, -4.   **3** Kwamie; the first step
is to simplify each side of the equation.
5a Sometimes   **b** Sometimes   **c** Always   **d** Never
7a 1; 256   **b** 2; 4 and -4 **c** 2; 1 or 0   **d** All values
9a $x = 81$ **b** No solution   **c** $x = 3$ or $x = -3$
11a $x = 5.5$ ft   **b** Possible answer: Divide 162 by 12
and subtract 8   **13** $x = 2$ **15a** $C = 5(x^2) + 8(4)x^2$
b $259   **17** $a = 7$ or $a = -7$ **19** $x - 10$, x, $x + 5$,
$x + 75$, $x + 100$ **b** 195   **21** $x = 3$ **23a** $-3 \le x \le 7$
b $-5 < x \le 5$ **25** The values of $|x|$ and $\sqrt{x^2}$ are the
same.   **27a** True   **b** True   **c** True   **d** True   **e** False
f False   **29a** 40   **b** $C' = (11, 2)$, $D' = (3, 2)$ **c** 16
31a $x = 2$ **b** $x = 5$ **33** $A' = (-1, 5)$; $B' = (2, -2)$;
$C' = (10, 2)$

8.5 Solving Inequalities   pages 402–405

1 Parts **d** and **h** are the only operations that reverse
order.   **3** Both decrease the value by 5.   **5a** $x > -0.75$
b $13 + 4(7 - 2x) < 47$ means the length 13 plus the
length $4(7 - 2x)$ is shorter than 47 units.   **7a** False
b True   **c** False   **d** True   **9** $3 \ge 5$ **11a** 10   **b** -13 **c** -15
13 $x > -13$ **b** $x \ge 14$ **c** $x < -50$ **d** $x < 3$
15a $3(x - 2) + 8 < 39$ or $3x + 2 < 39$ **b** $x < \frac{37}{3}$ or $x < 12.\overline{3}$
c   **17** $x \ge 8.75$

19a $k > 4$ **b** $k < -6$ **c** $k > 8$ **21** $x \ge 6$
23   **25** She sold more than 18.

27a True   **b** True   **c** False   **d** False   **e** False   **f** False
g True   **h** True   **29** She always added the same
amount to each side.   **31** $\begin{bmatrix} -5 & 1 \\ -30 & 46 \end{bmatrix}$

33a $B = 6$ or $B = -10$ **b** $A = -4$ or $A = 4$, $B = -4$ or
$B = 4$ **35a** $\overline{AB} \parallel \overline{CD}$, $\overline{AD} \parallel \overline{BC}$ **b** $\overline{AB} \perp \overline{BC}$ and $\overline{AD}$,
$\overline{DC} \perp \overline{DA}$ and $\overline{CB}$, $\overline{AC} \perp \overline{DB}$

8.6 Substitution   pages 409–412

1a $x = 6$ **b** $NUM = 6$ **c** $a + b = 6$ **d** $5x - 9 = 6$ **e** $x = 3$
3a Possible answer: A store substitutes one brand
product for another; substitutes a generic prescription
drug for a brand-name prescription drug.
b A nonmathematical substitute can take the place
of something and not be equivalent. In mathematics,
the substituted value must be equivalent to the value it
replaces.   **5** Possible answer: The calculator stored at
least one more decimal place than it showed.   **7** $x = 3$
9 $a = 20$ **11** $x = -0.5$ **13** $5(2x - 7)$a $10x - 35$
15 b, d, f, g, h   **17** 60, 90, 90, 120   **19** Edna substituted
1 for $\frac{6}{6}$, then multiplied.   **21a** $x = -4$ **b** $11x + 66$
c $x \ge -4$ **d** 0   **e** All values of x **23** 36   **25** P = 1
27 $24,000, $24,000, and $30,000   **29a** $x \ge -12$
b $x > -3$ **c** $x \le -397.21$ **d** $x \le 5.5$ **31a** $2x + 7$
b $y = 1.5$ **c** $3z - 7$ **d** $a < 1.5$ **e** $110q$ **f** $q \approx 0.91$
33 85   **35a** $18x$ **b** $13x + 12$ **c** $18x = 13x + 12$; Tom
caught up with Bill.   **d** $x = 2.4$; Tom will catch up
with Bill in 2 hr 24 min   **37a** 0; 1; 3; 6   **b** 10

8.7 Functions   pages 416–419

1 A function uses a formula to assign an output value
to an input value.   **3a** The parentheses indicate
multiplication.   **b** The parentheses enclose the input
of a function.   **c** The parentheses indicate the order
of operation—addition before multiplication.   **5** 16
7a 1   **b** 1   **c** 7   **d** 11   **9a** 19   **b** 30   **c** 19   **d** 15   **e** 3.75   **f** 5
g 0   **h** 4   **11** $360   **13a** $P(s) = 4s$ **b** $P(l, w) = 2l + 2w$
c $P(b, s) = 2b + 2s$ **d** $P(s_1, s_2) = 2s_1 + 2s_2$ **e** $P(b_1, b_2, s) = b_1 + b_2 + 2s$ **15** $V(l, w, h) = lwh$ **17a** $A(s) = s^2$
b $A(b, h) = \frac{1}{2}bh$ **c** $A(b, h) = bh$ **d** $A(d_1, d_2) = \frac{1}{2}d_1 d_2$
e $A(b_1, b_2, h) = \frac{1}{2}h(b_1 + b_2)$ **19a** 48; 144   **b** $\frac{1}{3}$; 1
c 12; 36   **d** 0   **21** $f(x, y) = 2x + y$ **23a** $y = 20$ **b** $y > 5$
25a 72   **b** 8   **c** ≈ 51.8 **d** ≈ 139.2 **27** $b = 28$ **29** $x = 12$,
$x = 9$ **31** The points on $\overline{BE}$ **33** 10.5, 21, 28, 31.5
35a $\frac{15}{88}$ **b** $-\frac{1}{10}$ **c** $-\frac{2}{5}$ **d** $-\frac{17}{12}$ or $-1\frac{5}{12}$ **37** 15

Chapter 8 Review   pages 421–423

1a 137   **b** 137   **c** 110   **d** $\frac{49}{3}$ **3** $\begin{bmatrix} 5x & 5y & 5z \\ 5x & 5y & 5z \\ 5x & 5y & 4z \end{bmatrix}$

5 b, c, and d   **7a** $5x + 8$ **b** $3x^2 + x + 3$ **9a** 9 more
than 3 times a number   **b** 3 times the sum of a
number and 9   **c** 5 divided by a number is $\frac{2}{3}$
11 $P = 6x + 18y + 20$ **13a** $80   **b** $30 + 20h$ **15** 86
17 60, 80, 100, 120   **19** $P(AB, AC, BC) = 13x + 11$
21a $x = 5$ or $x = -5$ **b** $x = 5$ or $x = -11$ **c** No solution
d $x = -5$ or $x = -11$ **23** $x = 6$ or $x = -6$ **25a** $<$ **b** $>$
c $=$ **d** $<$ **27a** $2x + 33 > 99$ **b** $x > 33$ **29** Treat $(2x + 4)$
as a unit and combine like terms, or multiply to
remove parentheses, then combine like terms.
31a 5   **b** -17 **c** 16   **d** 16   **e** 9   **f** $\frac{1}{9}$ **g** 0   **h** -33
33 a is decreased by 6

Chapter 9: Real Numbers

9.1 Sets pages 431–434

1 The set of all points on the number line between -8 and 2 inclusive; $\{x:-8 \leq x \leq 2\}$; because there are infinitely many elements. **3a** True **b** False **c** True **d** True **5** No, since the set contains all real numbers greater than 4 (including, for example, 4.1)
7a The set of even integers between -4 and 16, inclusive
b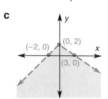
c $\{x:-4 \leq x \leq 16$ and x is an even integer$\}$ **d** Possible answer: Graphing **9** Possible answer: $\{(0, 0), (4, 0)\}$; the set of points consisting of the origin and $(4, 0)$
11 $\{5, 10, a\}$ **13** False **15** True **17** $\{\angle CAN, \angle CAP,$ $\angle CAT, \angle PAT, \angle PAN, \angle TAN\}$ **19** 100 **21** 1 **23** 0
25 $\{-1, 0, 1, 2, 3\}$ **27** 2 **29** 9 **31** Yes **33** $\{x:-5 < x < 15$ and x is an integer$\}$ **35** $\{9, 10, 11, 12\}$ **37a** $\{1, 2, 4,$ $8, 16, 32, 64\}$ **b** $\{2, 4, 8, 16, 32, 64\}$ **39a** 6
b $\{3, 6, 9, 12, 15\}$, $\{3, 6, 9, 12, 15, 18\}$, $\{3, 6, 9, 12, 18\}$, $\{3, 6, 9, 12\}$ **41** 4 **43** 13 from math club, 4 from science club **45** 40 **47a** $Z \subset X$ **b** $\{$Multiples of 12$\}$

9.2 Intersection and Union pages 438–441

1 It might refer to the members of the band and the members of the orchestra, or it might refer only to those who are members of both the band and the orchestra. **3** Intersection **5** The intersection is a region common to both roads. **7a** $\{1, 2, 3\}$ **b** $\{4, 5, 6, 7\}$
c $\{1, 2, 3, 4, 5\}$ **d** $\{3\}$ **e** $\{6.7\}$ **9** $B \cap C$ **11a** $\{3, 6, 9,$ $12, 15, 18, 21, 24, 27, 30, 33, 36, 39\}$ **b** $\{4, 8, 12, 16,$ $20, 24, 28, 32, 36, 40\}$ **c** $\{12, 24, 36\}$ **d** Possible answer: $\{x:x = 12n$, where $n = 1, 2, 3\}$ **13a** B **b** A
15a 27 **b** 141 **17a** Interior of rectangle BCFG
b Interior of rectangle ADEH **19a** $\{x:-4 \leq x \leq 4\}$
b $\{x:-6 \leq x \leq 6\}$

21a 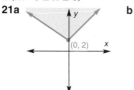 **b**

c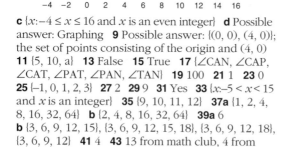

23a $\{$Rectangles measuring 2 cm by 3 cm$\}$ **b** $\{$Rectangles measuring 1 cm by 6 cm, 2 cm by 3 cm, and 1 cm by 4 cm$\}$

25a $\{4\}$ **b** $\{1, 3, 4, 5\}$ **c** $\{1, 3, 4, 5, 7, 10\}$ **d** $\{4\}$ **e** $\{\}$
f $\{1, 2, 3, 4, 5, 6, 7, 10\}$ **g** $\{1, 3, 4, 5\}$ **h** $\{4\}$ **27a** $\frac{3}{10}$
b $\frac{1}{3}$ **c** $\frac{3}{20}$ **d** $\frac{46}{5}$ **29a** $\{x:x < 7\}$ **b** $\{x:x \geq -1\}$ **31a** $\{-6, 6\}$
b $\{1296\}$ **c** $\{\}$ **d** $\{x:x \geq 0\}$ **33a** Possible answer: $\frac{1}{2}$, $1, \sqrt{30}$ **b** $\{x:0 < x < 3\}$

9.3 Important Sets of Numbers pages 444–447

1a True **b** False **c** True **d** False **3 a, b, d,** and **e**
5 a, b, c, and **d** **7** No **9** Possible answer: Because
$1 = \frac{1}{3} + \frac{2}{3} = 0.\overline{3} + 0.\overline{6} = 0.\overline{9}$ **11a** $\frac{7}{20}$ **b** $\frac{1}{3}$ **c** $\frac{5}{9}$ **d** $\frac{2}{3}$
13 a, b, and **c** **15** $\frac{100}{99}, \frac{11}{10}, 1.111\ldots, \sqrt{5} \div 2$ **17** $(1, 9),$ $(2, 8), (3, 7), (4, 6), (5, 5), (6, 4), (7, 3), (8, 2), (9, 1)$
19a True **b** False **c** False **d** True

21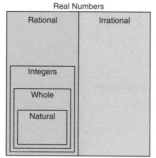
Real Numbers
Rational | Irrational
Integers
Whole
Natural

23 a, b, and **d**

25a $\sqrt{13}$ **b** 4 **27** $\begin{bmatrix} -18 & 32 \\ 20 & -34 \\ -33 & 61 \end{bmatrix}$ **29a** The set of positive multiples of 12 **b** $\{12\}$

31 $\{3, 6, 12, 15, 30, 60\}$

9.4 Pi and the Circle pages 451–454

1 Yes; for example, $\frac{\pi}{\pi} = 1$ **3** Rational

5a Rectangle, because it has four right angles and opposite sides congruent **b** Possible answer: Inscribe a rectangle in the circle and draw the rectangle's diagonals. Their intersection is the center of the circle. **7a** False **b** False **c** True **9** $\frac{1}{16}$
11a 49π, or ≈ 153.9 **b** 16π, or ≈ 50.3 **c** 9π, or ≈ 28.3
d 25π, or ≈ 78.5 **13** 20 ft **15** $56 + 8\pi$, or ≈ 81 **17** $(12,6), (12,-6)$ **19a** 5 **b** AB **21** 3π, or ≈ 9.4ft
23 $24 + 6\pi$, or ≈ 42.8 **25a** The rear-wheel gear
b $\frac{24}{7}$, or ≈ 3.4, revolutions **27** 4

29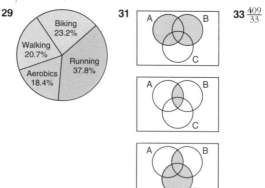
Biking 23.2%
Walking 20.7%
Running 37.8%
Aerobics 18.4%

31

33 $\frac{409}{33}$

9.5 Properties of Real Numbers pages 458–461

1 It doesn't matter—the expressions are equivalent (by the Associative Property of Multiplication).
3a $=$ **b** $<$ **c** $<$ **d** $=$ **5a** Yes **b** Yes **c** Yes **d** Yes

7 Yes   **9a** Commutative Property of Multiplication
b Associative Property of Addition   **c** Zero Product Property   **d** Distributive Property of Multiplication over Addition   **e** Commutative Property of Addition
11a =   **b** =   **c** >   **d** <   **13** {−2, −1, 0}, {−1, 0, 1} or {0, 1, 2}
15a Yes   **b** No   **c** Yes   **d** No   **17** According to the Associative Property of Multiplication, $(\frac{1}{2} \cdot 6) \cdot 11 = \frac{1}{2} \cdot (6 \cdot 11)$ **19a** No   **b** Yes   **21a** $\begin{bmatrix} 0 & 0 \\ 0 & 0 \end{bmatrix}$ **b** No

23a $A(x) = (6 - x)(x - 2)$ **b** $x = 6$ and $x = 2$
c $\{x : 2 < x < 6\}$ **25a** 5   **b** 70   **c** 9   **d** $-\frac{1}{2}$ **27a** 1; 8
b
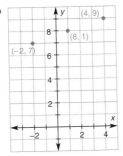
c (1, 8) is the midpoint of the segment joining (4, 9) and (−2, 7)

29 24, 60, 96   **31a** 4   **b** ≈8.06   **c** ≈25.32   **33a** 2   **b** 2
c 6   **d** 6   **e** 24   **f** 24   **g** 120   **h** 120   **35** $x = 11, y = -2$

9.6 Two Coordinate Formulas   pages 465–468

1 No, because $(x_2 - x_1)^2$ and $(y_2 - y_1)^2$ have the same value no matter in which order the coordinates are substituted.   **3** The coordinates of the midpoint are the average of the x-coordinates and the average of the y-coordinates.   **5a** (8, −3)   **b** Possible answer: Since the right triangles are congruent, AM = MB.
7a ≈9.90   **b** ≈9.90   **c** ≈9.90   **d** No matter what the values of a and b, the difference between a and $a + 7$ and between b and $b + 7$ is always 7.   **9a** (12, −7)
b (4, 7.5)   **c** (1.9, −0.1)   **d** (−0.4, 2)   **11a** 5   **b** 5   **c** 5
d 5   **13a** 3000 ft   **b** 4243 ft   **c** 4123 ft   **d** 5000 ft
15 AB = $\sqrt{32}$; BC = $\sqrt{80}$; AC = $\sqrt{80}$; isosceles
17a (0,4)   **b** (0,0.5)
19
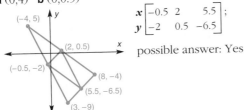
$x \begin{bmatrix} -0.5 & 2 & 5.5 \end{bmatrix}$;
$y \begin{bmatrix} -2 & 0.5 & -6.5 \end{bmatrix}$;
possible answer: Yes

21a Parallelogram   **b** (0, 2)   **c** (0, 2)   **d** $\sqrt{73}$, or ≈8.5
e $\sqrt{125}$, or ≈11.2   **23a** (5, 2.5)   **b** (5, 2.5)
c The midpoints are the same.   **25** $19.22
27a 13   **b** −7   **c** 6   **d** 2   **29** 4

31a Commutative Property of Addition
b Associative Property of Multiplication
c Commutative Property of Addition
d Distributive Property of Multiplication over Addition
e Commutative Property of Multiplication
f Commutative Property of Multiplication and Association Property of Addition

9.7 Graphs of Equations   pages 473–476

1 a and c   **3** Possible answer: 3 points to be safe
5 Each value of x is multiplied by 5.   **7a** $625   **b** $4
c

Mugs sold	0	1	2	3	4	5	6
Profit (dollars)	−625	−621	−617	−613	−609	−605	−601

d $p = 4m - 625$ **e** 257
9

x	−5	−4	−3	−2	−1	0	1	2	3	4
y	−13	−9	−5	−1	3	7	11	15	19	23

11a
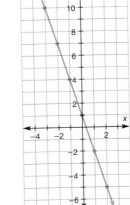
b
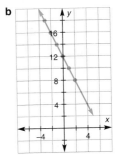

13a 0.5   **b** −0.5   **c** $y = 0.5x - 0.5$ **15a** $y = 3x + 6$
b $y = -3x - 2$
17a, b
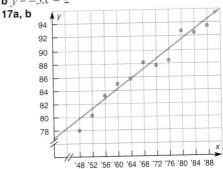
c Possible answer: About 96 or 97 in.
19a

x	−3	−2	−1	0	1	2	3
y	−15	−10	−5	0	5	10	15

b

x	−3	−2	−1	0	1	2	3
y	9	9	9	9	9	9	9

21a $y = x-1$ **b** $y = 2x + 3$

23

x	−4	−3	−2	−1	0	1	2	3	4	5	6
y	−2	−1.25	−0.5	0.25	1	1.75	2.5	3.25	4	4.75	5.5

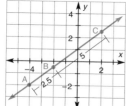

25a ≈ 5.31 **b** It is half of AC. **27** 32 **29** −15

31

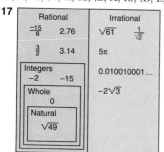

33a A′(2, −4); A″(7, −12)
b (2, −4)

Chapter 9 Review pages 478–481

1a $\{x:x < 5\}$ **b** $\{x:x < 0.2\}$ **c** $\{x:x \le 1\}$ **3a** {1} **b** $\sqrt{26}$
5 Possible answers: **a** $12 - (7 - 2) \ne (12 - 7) - 2$
b $36 \div (6 \div 2) \ne (36 \div 6) \div 2$ **c** $7 - 4 \ne 4 - 7$
d $81 \div 3 \ne 3 \div 81$ **7a**

x	−3	−2	−1	0	1	2
y	4	6	8	10	12	14

b

x	−3	−2	−1	0	1	2
y	5	2	−1	−4	−7	−10

9 {1, 3, 5, 7} **11** $\frac{36}{25\pi}$, or $\approx .46$ **13a** 13 **b** 6.5 **c** ≈ 132.7
d ≈ 40.8 **15a** { }, {□}, {@}, {□, @} **b** { }, {B}, {E}, {A},
{R}, {B, E}, {B, A}, {B, R}, {E, A}, {E, R}, {A, R}, {B, E, A},
{B, E, R}, {B, A, R}, {E, A, R}, {B, E, A, R}

17

Rational		Irrational	
$\frac{-15}{6}$	2.76	$\sqrt{61}$	$\frac{1}{\sqrt{2}}$
$\frac{3}{2}$	3.14	5π	
Integers		0.010010001…	
−2	−15	$-2\sqrt{3}$	
Whole			
0			
Natural			
$\sqrt{49}$			

19 $\left\{0, 4, \frac{3}{2}, \frac{-7}{3}\right\}$

21

x	−4	−3	−2	−1	0
y	$\frac{8}{3}$	3	$\frac{10}{3}$	$\frac{11}{3}$	4

23a {Positive integer divisors of 6} **b** 6

25 $\approx .611$ **27** 13π **29a** 11 **b** Infinitely many
31 About 2:1 **33a**

x	−3	−2	−1	0	1	2	3
y	4	6	8	10	12	14	16

$y = 2x + 10$
b

x	−3	−2	−1	0	1	2	3
y	5	3.5	2	0.5	−1	−2.5	−4

$y = -1.5x + 0.5$

Chapter 10: Topics of Number Theory

10.1 Techniques of Counting pages 489–493

1 8 **3** If one event can happen in m ways and another event can happen in n ways, then the number of ways both events can happen is $m \cdot n$.
5a 37.5% **b** 37.5% **7a** 12 **b** 9 **c** Possible answer: Neither the numbers in column C nor those in column D are relatively prime.
9

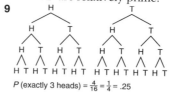

P (exactly 3 heads) $= \frac{4}{16} = \frac{1}{4} = .25$

11

13 12 **15** 24 **17** 900

19 15 **21** 16.8% **23** 32 **25** Possible answer: How many choices does Jane have for lunch if she can choose milk or juice and either a sandwich, a pizza, or a salad? **27** 15 **29a** $\frac{1}{6}$ **b** $\frac{1}{2}$ **c** $\frac{1}{12}$ **d** $\frac{1}{12}$ **e** $\frac{1}{6}$ **f** $\frac{8}{9}$
31 $576.00
33a Column 1, Minutes: 1, 2, 3, … 60
  Column 2, Machine A: 8, 16, 24, 32, … 480
  Column 3, Machine B: 12, 24, 36, 48, … 720
b 24, 48, 72, 96, 120, 144, 168, 192, 216, 240, 264, 288, 312, 336, 360, 384, 408, 432, 456, 480
c They are the common multiples of 8 and 12.
35 18, 24, 42

10.2 Primes, Composites, and Multiples
  pages 497–500

1 2, 3, 5, 7, 11 **3** 10 **5** All prime natural numbers; also 1 **7** 4, 6, 8, 9, 10, 14 **9a** 10 × 1, 5 × 2 **b** 11 × 1
c 9 × 1, 3 × 3 **11a** 16, 32, 48 **b** 24, 48, 72 **c** 48
13 30, 60, 90, 120, 150 **15a** Prime **b** Composite
c Composite **d** Prime **17a** 35 **b** 6 **c** 143 **19a** 35
b 12 **c** 24 **21a** 24 **b** 60 **23** 1, 2, 3, 4, 6, 12
25 20 × 1; 10 × 2 **27a** 7, 14, 21, 28,…
b 0, 7, 14, 21, 28,… **c** …, −14, −7, 0, 7, 14, 21,…
29a 24 **b** 24 **31a** 36 **b** $\frac{4}{36}, \frac{3}{36}$ **c** $\frac{1}{36}$
33a 144 **b** $\frac{136}{144} - \left(\frac{40}{144} + \frac{33}{144}\right)$ **c** $\frac{7}{16}$ **35** About 2:25 P.M.
37a 20 **b** 36 **39** $2\frac{2}{5}$ hr **41** 1680 **43** 375 min, or 6 hr 15 min

10.3 Divisibility Tests pages 503–506

1 Yes **3** Possible answer: Divide the larger number by the smaller number; If the answer is a whole number, the numbers are divisible. **5** Possible answer: A number is divisible by 27 if the sum of the digits is divisible by 27; No **7a** False **b** False
c True **d** True **9a** Yes **b** Yes **c** No **d** Yes
11a Yes **b** Yes **c** Yes **d** No **e** Yes **f** No **g** Yes
h No **i** No **j** Yes **13** Only c **15** Only e **17a** No
b Yes **c** No **d** No **e** No

19 Possible answer: According to the distributive property, $ax + bx = (a + b)x$, so the sum of two multiples of any number x will always have a factor of x. **21** Only a **23** $n = 2$, $n = 5$, or $n = 8$ **25** Yes **27** $n = 4$ **29** Possible answer: $51 = 1 \cdot 2 \cdot 3 \cdot 4 \cdot 5$, so it is a multiple of 2, 3, and 5, and therefore a multiple of $(2 \cdot 3 \cdot 5)$.
31a Possible answer: 6, 10, 14, 18, 22 **b** $4n + 2 = 2(2n + 1)$. $2n + 1$ is odd since $2n$ is even, and 1 is added to an even number.
33 Possible answer: A number is divisible by 9 if the sum of the digits is divisible by 9. In a palindromic pair the digits are the same; therefore, if the digits of one add up to a number divisible by 9, so will the digits of the other. **35** $\{x : -4 \leq x \leq 7\}$ **37** $y = 2x - 1$
39a 2 **b** 23 **41a** $-\frac{1}{4}$ **b** $2\frac{7}{20}$ **c** $\frac{11}{24}$ **43** About 643 breaths/hour; about 15,430 breaths/day

---

10.4 Prime Factorization   pages 510–512

1a 2.5 **b** 2^4 **c** 1.23 **d** 3^3 **3** Possible answer: Yes; if a number is not divisible by 3, it is not divisible by any multiple of 3. **5a** n **b** Because when you test numbers greater than $\sqrt{317}$, you find the same pairs of factors you've already found **7** $2^3 \cdot 3^3$
9 25 is not prime. **11** 1, 2, 3, 5, 6, 10, 15, 30
13 360 **15** $3 \cdot 7 \cdot 13 \cdot 31$ **17a** From right to left: 21, 105, 210 **b** From right to left: 15, 45, 90, and 4,360 **c** Multiply $5 \cdot 3 \cdot 7 \cdot 2$ and $2 \cdot 2 \cdot 2 \cdot 3 \cdot 3 \cdot 5$.
19a $225 = 3^2 \cdot 5^2$; $150 = 2 \cdot 3 \cdot 5^2$ **b** 75 **c** 75 **21** $\frac{2}{5}$
23 $a = 5$; $b = 3$ **25a** 3 **b** 6 **c** 35 **d** 18
27 $2^4 \cdot 3^2 \cdot 5 \cdot 7$ **29** 7, 11, 13 **31** 40 **33a** $\sqrt{53}$, or ≈ 7.28 **b** $\sqrt{442}$, or ≈ 21.02 **35** 6,760,000

10.5 Factors and Common Factors
pages 516–520

1a 2, 3, 5, 7 **b** Prime numbers **3a** Yes **b** No
5 Possible answer: List all the common factors, and pick the largest of them. **7** Yes
9

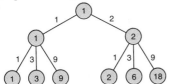

11a 4; 160 **b** 180; 54,000 **13** 5183; 1
17a 4 **b** 360
15

LCM	12	15	24
6	12	30	24
8	24	120	24
10	60	30	120

19 1, 2, 4, 7, 8, 14, 28, 56; 25% **21a** 160 **b** 8
23 1, 2, 3, 6, 9, 18, 27, 54 **25a** Yes **b** Yes **c** Yes **d** No **27a** 3 **b** 3 **c** The last nonzero number in column A is always the GCF of the two numbers.
29a 8 **b** 120 **c** 40 **d** 9

31a Possible answer: Each whole number in column B and the corresponding number in column A form a pair of factors of the number in C2. **b i** 1, 2, 4, 5, 7, 10, 14, 20, 28, 35, 70, 140 **ii** 1, 5, 25, 29, 145, 725 **iii** 1, 2, 4, 5, 7, 8, 10, 14, 20, 25, 28, 35, 40, 49, 50, 56, 70, 98, 100, 125, 140, 175, 196, 200, 245, 250, 280, 343, 350, 392, 490, 500, 686, 700, 875, 980, 1000, 1225, 1372, 1400, 1715, 1750, 1960, 2450, 2744, 3430, 3500, 4900, 6125, 6860, 7000, 8575, 9800, 12,250, 13,720, 17,150, 24,500, 34,300, 42,875, 49,000, 68,600, 85,750, 171,500, 343,000
33 Possible answer: original pile $= x$;
Tom $= \frac{1}{3}(x - 1)$; Bill $= \frac{1}{3}\left(\frac{2}{3}x - \frac{5}{3}\right)$; Sue $= \frac{1}{3}\left(\frac{4}{9}x - \frac{19}{9}\right)$; Juanita $= \frac{1}{3}\left(\frac{8}{27}x - \frac{65}{27}\right)$; Ralph $= \frac{2}{3}\left(\frac{8}{27}x - \frac{65}{27}\right)$
35a 11 **b** 17 **c** 7 **37** 390 **39a** {2, 3, 7}
b {2, 2, 2, 3, 3, 7, 7, 11} **c** 504 and 6468 **d** 84
e 38,808 **41** 2.5 min **43a** 6, −7, −3, or 0
b 6, 5, 4, 3, … **c** $1\frac{1}{6}$

10.6 LCM and GCF Revisited   pages 523–527

1a 4 **b** 24 **3** Yes **5** Yes; no **7a** Always **b** Never **c** Never **d** Sometimes **e** Sometimes **f** Never **g** Sometimes **9** LCM = 600; GCF = 15
11 About 89 days **13** LCM = 3060; GCF = 1
15a

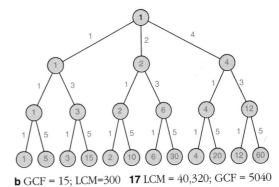

b GCF = 15; LCM=300 **17** LCM = 40,320; GCF = 5040
19a You need to find a common denominator.
b $\frac{111}{180} = \frac{37}{60}$ **c** 3; 1 **21** 2020 **23** 1987
25a 3,535,488,000,000 ft/hr **b** 2.5 hr **27** 80
29 16 and 12; 4 and 48 **31** About 64%
33 0, 5, 100, 225, 400 **35** 66% **37a** 2; 24 **b** 4; 48 **c** 6; 72 **39** 12" × 12"

10.7 Number-Theory Explorations
pages 532–535

1 14 **3** 3 + 3 **5** 3 + 11; 7 + 7 **7** Possible answer: A number that corresponds to the number of dots in a triangular array. **9 a** and **c** **11** Possible answer: 11 + 13 + 113, 17 + 17 + 103, 17 + 59 + 61 **13** 29, 31; 23, 37; 19, 41; 17, 43; 13, 47; 7, 53 **15** 5 = 4 + 1; 12 = 9 + 3; 22 = 16 + 6; 35 = 25 + 10 **17** Possible answers: 3, 4, 5; 6, 8, 10 **19** Possible answer: A different method of scoring would be necessary. **21** 3375 **23** The operations eventually result in the repeated results 1, 2, 1, 2, 1, ... **25a** 60 **b** 32 **27a** $12x$ **b** 28.8 **29** 8 **31** 18 min **33a** 5 **b** 9 **c** 45 **35** −1 **37** 289 **39**

Chapter 10 Review   pages 537–539

1a 3^3 **b** 2^4 **c** $2^4 \cdot 3^3$ **d** $2^3 \cdot 3^2 \cdot 5$ **e** $2^4 \cdot 3^2 \cdot 5$ **3** 120 **5a** .24 **b** .58 **c** .18 **7** One 8-ft board, four 10-ft boards, three 6-ft boards **9** To cell B49 **11** $n = 5$ or $n = 6$ **13** $1000; $500; $250; $200; $125; $100, $50 **15a** 24 **b** $-\frac{17}{24}$ **17a** Perfect **b** Deficient **c** Abundant **19** 28% **21a** 0 **b** $1\frac{1}{3}$ **c** $\frac{3}{4}$ **23** At noon **25a** 1, 2, 4, 373, 746, 1492 **b** 1, 2, 3, 4, 6, 8, 12, 16, 24, 37, 48, 74, 111, 148, 222, 296, 444, 592, 888, 1776 **c** 1, 3, 647, 1941 **27a** 5 **b** 4 **c** 20 **29** 1, 4, 9, 25, 36, 100, 225, 900 **31a** $\frac{13}{20}$ **b** $1\frac{14}{15}$ **c** $2\frac{1}{6}$

Chapter 11: Solving Problems with Algebra

11.1 Presenting Solutions to Problems
pages 549–552

1 No **3** 10 P.M.; Possible answers: Use a number line or set up an equation. **5** There is no downhill speed that will make the average 20 mph. **7** Portnos multiplied the wrong numbers. He needs to multiply the 5 racks times the number of suits per rack. Just because a number appears in a problem does not mean it will be used. **9** 10 **11a** $\frac{4}{100}$ **b** $\frac{1}{100}$ **c** $\frac{1}{100}$ **d** 1.75% **13a** 30 sec later **b** Every 15 sec **15** 1 hr 12 min **17** 1 **19** 14 **21a** (0, 10), (1, 7), (2, 4), (3, 1) **b** (1, 7), (2, 4), (3, 1) **23a** $x = -5$ **b** $x = -5$ **25a** $9x + 36 = 5x$ **b** $9x = 5x - 36$ **c** $4x + 6 = -30$ **d** $6 = -4x - 30$ **27** 120 **29** $n = 5$

11.2 Equations with Variables on Both Sides
pages 556–558

1 $x = \frac{14}{3}$ **3** $x = -5$ **5a** $x =$ any number **b** No solution **7** $x = -8$ **9** $x = 5.4$ **11** ≈ 4.66 **13** It is cheaper to hire Rob for any job over 1 hour. **15** AB = 10 **17** 70 **19** $1000 **21** $n = 4$ **23a** 1 **b** 1 **c** 1 **25** $x =$ any number **b** No real solution **27** 5 **29** 72°

11.3 More Word Problems   pages 561–565

1 Yes, if the number is negative **3** $x > 15$ **5** $3.01 **7a** 10 cm **b** 40 cm **9a** 13 hr; 10 hr **b** 10,400 **11** Possible answer: 50 coins **13** ≈156.26 ft **15** 8 hr **17** $195,652.17 **19** 20 **21** 12 **23** $A(b_1, b_2, h) = \frac{1}{2}h(b_1 + b_2)$ **25** 1296 **27a** ≈2.66 ft **b** ≈1.39 ft **c** ≈58.25 ft **29** $1500 **31** 15 **33a** 14 **b** 0 **c** 17 **d** 5

11.4 Equations with Several Variables
pages 569–572

1 a, b, c **3a** 27 **b** 29 **c** Only if $a = b$ **5a** 36 **b** 15 **c** −6 **d** −55 **7** 1 or 7 **9a** $x + y = 26$
b

x	1	2	3	4	5	6	7	8	9	10	11
y	25	24	23	22	21	20	19	18	17	16	15

12	13	14	15	16	17	18	19	20	21	22
14	13	12	11	10	9	8	7	6	5	4

23	24	25
3	2	1

11a A **b** A: 60 Kg; B: 45 Kg **13** 130.5 **15** For $\frac{18}{x + 2y}$ to be a natural number, $x + 2y$ must be a factor of 18 in order that the quotient is a natural number. **17** $18\frac{2}{3}$ in. **19a** Possible answer: $2(x + 3) + 2(4) = 3(2x)$ **b** 3.5 **c** 6.5 **d** 7 **21** (1, 6), (4, 4), (7, 2), (10, 0) **23** $\sqrt{\frac{8}{\pi}} \le r$ **25a** When $x = 2$, outputs 1-10 are 8, 26, 80, 242, 728, 2186, 6560, 19682, 59048 and 177146. **b** When $x = 1$, outputs 1-10 are 5, 17, 53, 161, 485, 1457, 4373, 13121, 39365, 118097. **27** $1\frac{1}{5}$ hrs, or 1 hr 12 min **29a** $-2x^2 - \frac{5}{12}x$ **b** $x = -\frac{35}{27}$ **c** $x = 2.5$ **d** $-5x + \frac{5}{2}$ **31a** 376 in.^{2} **b** 480 in.^{3} **33** $5175

11.5 Polyhedra   pages 576–580

1 Yes **3** Edges of the polyhedron that would not be visible from the given point of view. **5** The height of the pyramid is a segment from the vertex and perpendicular to the plane containing the base. The slant height is on the surface of the pyramid, extending from the vertex perpendicular to the base edge. **7** Figure I is an open box. Figure II is a rectangular prism. **9a** 24 **b** 90, 120, 150 **c** 360 **d** 408 **e** 360 **11** Possible answer: A quadrilateral with both diagonals drawn; a top view of a quadrilateral-based pyramid. **13a** 256 **b** 544 **c** 800 **d** 1280 **15** All have the same volume. **17a** 288 **b** 450 **19** Surface area: 216 in.^{2}; Volume: 216 in.^{3}; The surface area and volume are not equal because the units in.^{2} and in.^{3} measure different attributes of the polyhedron. **21** ≈40.5 lb **23a** $\frac{1}{96}$ **b** $\frac{1}{16}$ **c** $\frac{1}{32}$ **25** 1,860,480 **27** (1, 1), (4, 1), (13, 1), (8, 2), (3, 3)

11.6 Solids with Circular Cross Sections
pages 585–588

1 The circumference, since it is π × (diameter of ball) whereas the height is about 3 × (diameter of ball) and $\pi > 3$. **3** Possible answer: Immerse the egg in water and find the volume of the water displaced. **5a** ≈ 204.2 cm^2 **b** ≈ 78.5 cm^2 **c** ≈ 282.7 cm^2 **d** ≈ 314.2 cm^3 **7a** 6 in. **b** $\frac{1}{27}$ **9** Yes **11a** $\frac{1}{3}$ **b** $\frac{1}{3}$ **c** $\frac{1}{27}$ **13** $\approx 18,000$ people **15** Possible answer: The cube has more surface area so it will cool the drink faster. **17** Yes **19a** ≈ 5067 ft^3 **b** 188.5 ft^2 **21** 1, 2, 6, 17 **23** 5 hr **25a** $x = 1$ **b** $x = -5$ **27a** 7 **b** 11 **c** 15 **d** 19 **e** 23

11.7 Reading Information from Graphs
pages 592–595

1 $(\approx -0.77, \approx 0.59)$, $(2, 4)$, $(4, 16)$ **3a** $C = 7B + 4G$

b

Box seats	0	4	8	12
Grand stand	25	18	11	4

5

x	1	2	3	4	5	6	7	8	9
A	99	96	91	84	75	64	51	36	19

$A(x) = (10 - x)(10 + x)$

7

r	1	2	3	4	5
A	≈ 3.1	≈ 12.6	≈ 28.3	≈ 50.3	≈ 78.5

9 Possible answer: Let $y = 10x$. Draw the graph. **11a** $x = 4$ or $x \approx -1.2$ **b** $2^4 - 3 = 13$; $3 \cdot 4 + 1 = 13$; $2^{-1.2} - 3 \approx 2.6$; $3(-1.2) + 1 = -2.6$ **13a** $V = 8t + 5p$
b $8t + 5p = 34$;

t	0	1	2	3	4
p	6.8	5.2	3.6	2	0.4

c $(3, 2)$

15a $\ell = w + 20$; $80 = 2\ell + 2w$ **b** $w = 10$; $\ell = 30$

17

F	32	41	50	59	68	77	86	95	104
C	0	5	10	15	20	25	30	35	40

Converts temperature in degrees Fahrenheit to degrees Centigrade. **19a** 12 **b** 65π or ≈ 204.2 **c** 100π or ≈ 314.2 **21** B **23a** 10 **b** -15 **25** 432π cm^2 or ≈ 1357 cm^2 **27** $(3,2)$ **29a** 30 **b** 204 **c** 650

Chapter 11 Review pages 597–599

1 Possible answer: A cone is $\frac{1}{3}$ of a cylinder whose volume is $\pi r^2 h$. **3** 22m **5** 7 **7a** -5 **b** $-40 - 8x$ **c** $3x - 1$ **d** $x = 9$ **9a** $19.02 **b** $158.50 **c** $14.41 **11** $x = 13\frac{1}{3}$ **13** $20 **15** 30 **17a** 60 **b** 96 **c** 48 **19a** $V = 904.8$ Total Surface Area $= 144\pi \approx 452.4$ **b** $V = 108\pi \approx 339.3$ TSA $= 90\pi \approx 282.7$ **c** $V = 320\pi \approx 1005.3$ TSA $= 200\pi$, or ≈ 628.3 **21** $(-2, 3)$ **23a** Possible answers: Make a table; guess and check; solve an equation. **b** 13 dimes, 12 quarters

Chapter 12: Looking Ahead: Iterations and Fractals

12.1 Iterations pages 608–611

1a

Term	0	1	2	3	4	5	6	7	8	9	10
Output	8	11	14	17	20	23	26	29	32	35	38

c $y = 3x + 8$

3a Initial input: 1; Iteration rule: 2(INPUT); Number of Iterations: 63 **b** 2^{63} or $\approx 9.22 \times 10^{18}$ **c** Possible answer: checkerboard square could not hold this many grains of wheat **5a** Initial input: $750,000; Iteration rule: $\frac{\text{INPUT}}{2}$; Number of Iterations: 8 **c** Year 2030

b

Year	Amount
1960	$750,000
1965	$375,000
1970	$187,500
1975	$ 93,750
1980	$ 46,875
1985	$ 23,476
1990	$ 11,719
1995	$ 5,859
2000	$ 2,920

7a Initial input: 23; Iteration rule: INPUT + 4; Number of Iterations: 19 **b** 99 seats **9a** $1.526 \times 10^{-5} = \frac{1}{256} \cdot \frac{1}{256}$ **b** $85.\overline{3}$

11a

Seconds	0	1	2	3	4	5	6	7	8	9	10
Distance from wall	12	6	3	1.5	.75	.375	.188	.094	.047	.023	.012

b In 6 seconds **c** In theory, no, but in reality, the distances get too small to be meaningful **d** speed is decreasing **13a** $\approx 0.79\%$ **b** The first month's interest is charged on $9000, then $350 is subtracted from this total **c** Initial input: 9000; Iteration rule: INPUT $+ \frac{0.095}{12}$(INPUT) $- 350$ **d** 29 months **15** 15.5

12.2 More About Iterations pages 616–619

1 The value of $b(n)$ is constant.

3a

Length of side	0	1	2	3	4	5	6
Number of toothpicks	0	3	9	18	30	45	63

b $f(0) = 0$; $f(n) = f(n-1) + 3n$ **c** 360 **5** $f(1) = 11$; $f(2) = 17$; $f(3) = 29$; $f(4) = 53$ **7a** $8750 **b** 8.6% **c** $250 **d** $f(0) = 8750$; $f(n) = f(n-1) + f(n-1) \cdot \left(\frac{0.086}{12}\right) - 250$ **e** 41 months **9** $f(1) = 1$; $f(n) = f(n-1) + (2n-1)$ **11a** 20; 28; 36 **b** $f(1) = 12$; $f(n) = f(n-1) + 8$ **c** 100 **13** $f(1) = 0$; $f(n) = f(n-1) + (n-1)$

15

Counter	1	2	3	4	5	6	7	8	9	10	11	12
Output	1	4	9	16	25	36	49	64	81	100	121	144

The answer is the square of the counter. **17** The value of $b(n)$ decreases. **19** At age 38

12.3 Geometric Iterations pages 623–624

1 No; no (for a finite number of iterations); no **3** One possible answer is given. Others exist.

5a Rhombus **b** Alternates between a rhombus and a rectangle

7

9

(0, 1)

11 lattice points hit: (1, 1), (1, 2), (3, 1), (3, 2), (3, 3), (3, 4) lattice points missed: (1, 3), (2, 1) (2, 2), (2, 3) From the origin, go right one unit, turn left 90°, go up one unit, and turn left 90°. Each iteration consists of two line segments and two left turns. Increase the lengths of the segments by one unit each iteration.

12.4 Convergent Iterations pages 630–633

1a $2.8\overline{3}$, 2.828431, 2.828427; Following values remain constant at 2.828427 **b** Outputs converge to same result as part **a.** **c** Outputs converge to 8. **d** Answers will vary. **e** It computes $\sqrt{a}$, where $\frac{1}{2}\left(\text{INPUT} + \frac{a}{\text{INPUT}}\right)$ is the iteration rule. **3a** 100 **b** yes

5b

x	8	7	7	6.5	6.5	6.25	6.25	6.125	6.125	6.0625
y	7	7	6.5	6.5	6.25	6.25	6.125	6.125	6.0625	6.0625

7a 2.55 ppm, 2.17 ppm, 1.84 ppm, 1.57 ppm, 1.33 ppm **b** 0.3 ppm **9a** ≈0.79% **b** $5826.69; $4510.82; $3194.96; $1879.09; $563.23 **c** About $320 **d** Actual payment is $321.40 **11** Yes; 1.618033989 **13** 1250 mg **15** Let (x, y) represent the dimensions of ABCD (x the horizontal component, y the vertical). Let $f(x, y)$ represent the exit point of a ball shot diagonally from point A. The following properties hold:

x	y	f(x, y)
odd	even	B
even	odd	D
odd	odd	C
even	even	not A

17 9.3% annually **19** 2.293166287
21a

n	f(n)	g(n)
1	47000	64000
2	47200	63800
3	47330	63670
4	47414	63586
5	47469	63531
6	47505	63495
7	47528	63472
8	47543	63457
9	47553	63447
10	47559	63441
11	47563	63437
12	47566	63434
13	47568	63432
14	47569	63431
15	47570	63430

b ≈47,571 and ≈63,429

12.5 Introduction to Fractals pages 637–639

1 In each case, the length is 8.
3a,b   **c** No **5**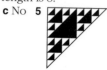

7

9a 1, 8, 24, 32, 16 **b** 1, 3, 9, 27, 81 **c** They are the numbers of shaded triangles for the iterations of the Sierpinski triangle.

11a

Iteration	0	1	2	3	4
Blue area shaded on this iteration	0 in.²	16 in.²	8 in.²	4 in.²	2 in.²
Total blue area shaded so far	0 in.²	16 in.²	24 in.²	28 in.²	30 in.²
Red area shaded on this iteration	0 in.²	16 in.²	8 in.²	4 in.²	2 in.²
Total red area shaded so far	0 in.²	16 in.²	24 in.²	28 in.²	30 in.²

b 32 in.²; 32 in.²; It looks like a square with a red half and a blue half and no white space.

Chapter 12 Review pages 641–643

1a,b

iteration	output	output
0	−25	25
1	−15.38	15.38
2	−12.3714	12.37140
3	−12.0055	12.00557
4	−12.0000	12.00000
5	−12	12
6	−12	12
7	−12	12
8	−12	12
9	−12	12
10	−12	12
11	−12	12
12	−12	12

c It converges on the opposite of −12. The results are the same; the signs of the numbers are just different.

3a Initial input: 17,500; Iteration rule: INPUT − INPUT(0.13)
b

year	value
0	$17,500
1	$15,225
2	$13,246
3	$11,524
4	$10,026
5	$ 8,722
6	$ 7,588
7	$ 6,602
8	$ 5,744
9	$ 4,997
10	$ 4,347

c In about 5 years

5

Counter	0	1	2	3	4	5	6	7	8	9	10
Output	2	7	17	32	52	77	107	142	182	227	277

7a

Figure number	1	2	3	4	5	6	7	8
Number of toothpicks	1	5	12	22	35	51	70	92

b 330 toothpicks **c** $f(1) = 1$; $f(n) = f(n-1) + (3n-2)$
9a $(20, 14)$ $\left(20, 13\frac{1}{3}\right)\left(22, 13\frac{1}{3}\right)$ **b** $\frac{1}{16}$, $\frac{2}{2187}$ **c** 64; 27; 91 **d** $\left(21\frac{1}{3}, 13\frac{1}{2}\right)$

11a

Number of disks	1	2	3	4	5	6	7
Total number of moves	1	3	7	15	31	63	127

b Initial input: 0; Iteration rule: 2(INPUT) + 1

INDEX

X

Y

Z

Credits

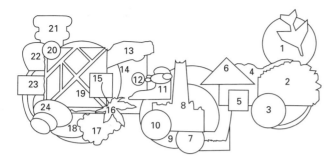

Cover

Collage by Carol Tornatore

1 The Earth as seen from space. © Telegraph Colour Library/FPG International; **2** Ferris Wheel. © SUPERSTOCK; **3** French Crown paperweight (blue cane with pink and green and blue and red ribbon twists) glass, diam.: 8.2 cm. The Art Institute of Chicago. Bequest of Arthur Rubloff, 1988.541.265; **4** Death Valley Sand Dunes. © Richard Pharaoh /International Stock Photography; **5** Quilt. Debora J. Bass; **6** Glass Pyramid at the Louvre, Paris, by I.M. Pei. © Telegraph Colour Library/FPG International; **7** Compact Disc. © Pete Saloutos/The Stock Market; **8** Golden Gate Bridge, San Francisco. © 1989 Luis Castañeda/The Image Bank. **9** Fiber Optics Bundle. © TSW; **10** French, Paperweight (green, red, and white swirls), Clichy, glass, diam.: 6.6 cm. The Art Institute of Chicago. Gift of Arthur Rubloff, 1977.825. Photograph by Christopher Gallagher; **11** Rippling water. © Comstock, Inc.; **12** Contemporary Marble. © David Young Wolff/PhotoEdit; **13** Silver Porsche 959. © 1989 Ron Kimball Photography; **14** *Fall.* 1988. Hand printed paper. Margaret Ahrens Sahlstrand; **15** *Rainbow Stars* pieced quilt. Jean Ray Laury. Photograph by Stan Bitters; **16** Orange Leaf. © Telegraph Colour Library/FPG International; **17** Mola, from Cuna Indians of Panama © Carmine Fantasia; **18** Epcot Center. © Carmine Fantasia; **19** Honey Bees. © Hans Pfletschinger/Peter Arnold, Inc.; **20** Antique Marble. Courtesy, Paul C. Baumann, Author, *Collecting Antique Marbles;* **21** Ionic Column, New Orleans. © W. Cody/Westlight; **22** Chambered Nautilus Shell Cross Section. © Louise K. Broman/Photo Researchers; **23** Circuit Board. © John Michael/International Stock Photography; **24** Solar Energy Collectors, Australia. © 1987 Otto Rogge/The Stock Market.

Fine Art and Photographs

ix Rippling Water. © Comstock, Inc.; **vi** (above) *Rainbow Stars* pieced quilt. Jean Ray Laury. Photograph by Stan Bitters; **vi** (below) Zodiac. Venice, Italy. © SUPERSTOCK; **vii** Glass Pyramid at the Louvre, Paris, designed by I.M. Pei. © Telegraph Colour Photography/FPG International; **viii** Space shuttle astronaut during space walk. NASA; **x** (above) The Earth as seen from space. NASA; **x** (below) Circuit Board. © John Michael/International Stock Photography; **xi** Taj Mahal, Agra, India. © Telegraph Colour Library/FPG International; **xii** (above) Death Valley Sand Dunes. © Richard Pharaoh/International Stock Photography; **xii** (below) Circuits printed on Computer Chip (200% enlargement). © Phil Degginger/TSW; **xiii** Fiber Optics. © TSW; **xiv** Compact Disc. © Robert George Young /Masterfile; **xv** Solar Energy Collectors, Australia. © Otto Rogge/The Stock Market; **xvi** St. Louis Arch. © Tom Till/ International Stock Photography; **2–3** *Rainbow Stars* pieced quilt. Jean Ray Laury. Photograph by Stan Bitters; **3** (inset, right) Space shuttle astronaut during space walk. NASA; **3** (inset, left) Space shuttle astronaut in pilot's station. NASA; **4** Tile mosaics in a mosque, Casablanca, Morocco. © Lisl Dennis/The Image Bank; **9** Rice Packets. © Guido Alberto Rossi/The Image Bank; **10** *Numbers in Color,* (detail) 1958–59, Jasper Johns. Albright-Knox Art Gallery, Buffalo, New York. Gift of Seymour H. Knox; **16** Bees on Honeycomb. © TSW; **21** Ancient Ruins at the Forum, Rome. © SUPERSTOCK; **23** from *Treatise on the Game of Chess* (Persian Manuscript 211). Royal Asiatic Society; **28** Aztec Calendar cartoon. © 1992 Nick Downes; **29** Stamp Mosaic. © Adrienne McGrath; **36** Crazy Quilt. © Adrienne McGrath; **41** Spider Web. © 1990 Tom Bean/The Stock Market. **48–49** Computer-aided-design workstation. Courtesy, Gerber Garment Technology; **49** (inset, left) Computer-aided-design program. © Art Montes de Oca; **49** (inset, right) Pattern cutting in clothing factory. © Bill Bachmann/Uniphoto; **50** Foreign currency. © Viesti Associates, Inc./The International Exchange Photo Library; **57** Wind generators, Altamont Pass, California. © Kevin Schafer/Peter Arnold, Inc.; **64** Pythagorean Theorem. © Adrienne McGrath; **66** Aerial photo of the Orange Bowl, Miami. © Walter Iooss, Jr./The Image Bank; **71** Varieties of apples. © Michel Viard/Peter Arnold, Inc.; **77** Sale sign. © Peter Southwick/Stock Boston Inc.; **78** Compact discs. © Ted Horowitz/The Stock Market; **84** Jim Abbott. © M. Grecco/Stock Boston Inc.; **92–93** Houston, Texas cityscape. © Superstock International Inc.; **93** (inset) *View of an Ideal City,* late 15th century, artist unknown. Central Italian School. The Walters Art Gallery, Baltimore; **94** Roger Bannister. © AP/Wide World Photos; **101** The Pleiades. © Hale Observatories/ Photo Researchers; **107** Fiesta, San Antonio, Texas. © Bob Daemmrich/Stock Boston Inc.; **114** Man with yoke on path beside rice paddies. © Margaret Gowan/TSW; **121** Hang gliding, Aspen, Colorado. © D. Brownell/The Image Bank; **129** *Cube and Four Panels*, 1975, Ron Davis. Albright-Knox Art Gallery, Buffalo, New York. By exchange, National Endowment for the Arts Purchase Grant and Matching Funds, 1976; **135** Photographed from Oliver Byrne's *The Elements of Euclid,*

10

published by William Pickering, 1847; **136** Kite. © Bill Ross/Westlight; **141** Cotton harvest, Arizona. © Jim Sanderson/The Stock Market; **148–149** United States Air Force Thunderbirds F-16 Fighting Falcons flying in formation. © 1991 Jordan Coonrad; **149** (inset, left) Boeing 737 jetliners, Boeing assembly plant, Renton, Washington. © 1982 David Barney/The Stock Market; **149** (inset, right) Electronic fuel control for aircraft. © 1982 Gabe Palmer/The Stock Market; **150** Attribute tiles; **158** *Out of This World* video game board. Courtesy, Brian Fargo, Interplay Productions; **165** Map of Nigeria and surrounding countries; **172** Beakers, flasks, and graduated cylinders. © 1988 Blair Seitz/Photo Researchers; **177** Sears Tower, Chicago. © Frank Cezus/FPG International; **178** Mural. Courtesy, Mexican Fine Arts Center Museum, Chicago; **179** Mac art of Mural. Joe Terrasi; **185** Russian nesting dolls. © Carmine Fantasia; **198–199** Democratic National Convention, Atlanta. © 1988 Christopher Morris/Black Star; **199** (inset, left) Harry Truman holding erroneous Dewey victory newspaper. The Bettmann Archive; **199** (inset, right) Exit polling. © Bob Daemmrich/Stock Boston Inc.; **200** Pizza segments. © Lois Ellen Frank/Westlight; **207** Earthquake photos. © Bill Ross/Westlight; **213** Aerial shot of cars in parking lot. © Ronn Maratea/International Stock Photography; **215** Map: *Rain Forest Priorities,* Dave Herring. Courtesy, *World Monitor: The Christian Science Monitor Monthly* © 1991; **218** Trash illustration by Pierre Mion. © 1991 National Geographic Society; **221** Group of blue men, one white. © Bruce Rowell/Masterfile; **228** Boxes of fish, Farmer's Market, Seattle. © Morton Beebe/The Image Bank; **233** © 1989 by Sidney Harris from *Einstein Simplified,* Rutgers University Press; **234** Attribute blocks; **250–251** Earth wind-speed patterns from space. © Telegraph Colour Library/FPG International; **251** (inset, left) Multi-colored world map with time zones. © TSW; **251** (inset, right) Man plotting data on a sonar-produced ocean map. © Franz Edson/TSW; **252** Roller coaster. © M. Timothy O'Keefe/Tom Stack & Associates; **260** *Blue Package with Ostrich Eggs,* 1971, Claudio Bravo. Courtesy, Staepfli Gallery, New York; **267** *Collection of Southern Signs,* 1924, Paul Klee. Washington University Gallery of Art, St. Louis; **275** Electronic stock ticker board. © C.P. George/H. Armstrong Roberts; **282** Double cheeseburger. © Karen McCunnell/Leo de Wys, Inc.; **289** Electronic brain for fuel injection. © Brownie Harris/The Stock Market; **290** Soo Canal locks, Sault Ste. Marie, Michigan. © 1992 Adrienne S. McGrath; **296** Weather instrument. Measures rainfall, temperature, wind direction, and wind speed. © Barry L. Runk/Grant Heilman Photography, Inc.; **302** Blue subway car reflection. © Joe Marvullo; **316–317** Multiple exposure bicycle photograph. © 1989 Globus Brothers/The Stock Market; **317** (inset) Wheelchair racing. © David Young Wolff/PhotoEdit; **318** Building based on crystal shapes, Poitiers, France. © Tony Craddock/TSW; **325** Lumber. © 1989 Albert Normandin/The Image Bank; **332** Abstract computer graphic. © Larry Keenan Assoc./The Image Bank; **339** Skyline with reflections. © Mark Stephenson/Westlight; **347** *Composition 8,* 1923, Vassily Kandinsky. Solomon R. Guggenheim Museum, New York. Gift, Solomon R. Guggenheim, 1937. © The Solomon R. Guggenheim Foundation, New York; **354** Origami. Kimi Igarashi; **368–369** Electric car dealership sign. © Comstock, Inc.; **369** Car engineer working on computer-aided designs. © Andrew Sacks/TSW; **369** Anecoic test chamber, Japan. © Ken Straiton/The Stock Market; **370** Tomb paintings, Valley of the Kings, Deir EL Bahari, Egypt. © Superstock International Inc.; **378** Basketball game with scoreboard. © D. Logan/H. Armstrong Roberts; **385** *Far Side* cartoon by Gary Larson. Reprinted by permission of Chronicle Features, San Francisco; **391** Matrix; **392** *Screwarch Bridge (State II),* 1980, Claes Oldenburg. The Museum of Modern Art, New York. Etching and aquatint 203 11/16 x 50 3/4 in. Gift of Klaus G. Perls and Heinz Berggruen in memory of Frank Perls, art dealer (by exchange). Photograph © 1992 The Museum of Modern Art, New York; **399** Pyramids, Egypt. © Camerique; **406** Triazzle. Courtesy Dan Gilbert and DaMert Company © 1991; **413** Oyster pearl beds, Japan. © Comstock, Inc.; **426–427** Prism. © Ted Mahieu/The Stock Market; **427** (inset, top left) Ophthalmoscope. © 1991 Larry Gatz/The Image Bank; **427** (inset, bottom right) Bar code. © David Young Wolff/PhotoEdit; **428** Sand buckets. © David Young Wolff/PhotoEdit; **435** *Several Circles* (detail), 1926, Vassily Kandinsky. Solomon R. Guggenheim Museum, New York. Gift, Solomon R. Guggenheim, 1941. © The Solomon R. Guggenheim Foundation, New York. Photograph by David Heald; **442** Tape measure. © Murray Alcosser/The Image Bank; **448** *The Red Sun Gnaws at the Spider,* 1948, Joan Miró. Private collection, Japan; **455** Commuters at rush hour, New York. © J. Ramey/The Image Bank; **462** The Isometric Map of Midtown Manhattan. © 1989 The Manhattan Map Co. All Rights Reserved; **469** The Romerberg facade, Frankfurt, Germany © Terry Williams/ The Image Bank; **484–485** Aerial view of wheat harvest. © Andy Sacks/TSW; **485** (inset) Produce market, Bali, Indonesia. © Steve Satushek/The Image Bank; **486** Pond study at outdoor education camp, Texas. © Bob Daemmrich/ Stock Boston Inc.; **494** Tiles; **501** Pastry slices. © Nino Mascardi/The Image Bank; **507** © 1977 by Sidney Harris from *What's So Funny About Science?* William Kaufmann, Inc.; **513** *School of Athens* (detail), Raphael. Vatican Rooms, Scala/Art Resource, New York; **521** Watch gears. © Bernard Van Berg/The Image Bank; **528** Mayan Glyphs, Chiapas, Mexico, A.D. 600–900. © Robert Frerck/Odyssey, Chicago; **542–543** Glen Canyon Dam, Arizona. © L. Jacobs/H. Armstrong Roberts; **543** (inset, lower left) Aerial view, sewage treatment plant. © Steve Proehl/The Image Bank; **543** (inset, upper right) Engineer testing water at sewage treatment plant. © 1982 Chris Jones/The Stock Market; **546** Fence painting contest. Courtesy Hannibal, Missouri, Visitor's Bureau; **553** Llama. © Kahl/Bruce Coleman, Inc.; **559** Cherry chocolate turtles and almond bark. © Skip Dean/The Image Bank; **566** Postage stamps from various countries. ©1989 Ed Bohon/The Stock Market; **573** Glass pyramid at the Louvre, Paris by I.M. Pei. © Walter Iooss, Jr./The Image Bank; **581** Cultivated flowers against geometric skyline. © Pete Turner/The Image Bank; **589** Golf balls. © The Harold E. Edgerton 1992 Trust. Courtesy of Palm Press, Inc.; **602–603** Recording studio sound-mixing console. © Ted Horowitz/The Stock Market; **603** (inset, left) Pythagoras' discovery of arithmetic ratios in stringed instruments, 1492. Woodcut. The Granger Collection; **603** (inset, right) Recording studio. © E. Masterson/H. Armstrong Roberts; **604** Ahu Akivi statues, Easter Island. © Harald Sund/The Image Bank; **612** *Government House Fort and Dalhousie Barracks,* Calcutta. The Granger Collection; **620** *Cubic Space Division* (detail), 1952 by M.C. Escher. Cornelius Van S. Roosevelt Collection. © 1992 National Gallery of Art, Washington, D.C.; **625** *Michigan Avenue with View of the Art Institute,* 1984, Richard Estes, American, b. 1937, oil on canvas 91.4 x 121.9 cm, Gift of the Capital Campaign Fund, 1984.177. © 1991 The Art Institute of Chicago. All Rights Reserved; **634** Fractal. © Homer W. Smith/Peter Arnold, Inc.

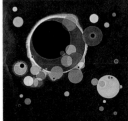

435